Settlers

of

Colonial

St. Mary's County

Maryland

Compiled by

Elise Greenup Jourdan

HERITAGE BOOKS
2019

HERITAGE BOOKS

AN IMPRINT OF HERITAGE BOOKS, INC.

Books, CDs, and more—Worldwide

For our listing of thousands of titles see our website
at
www.HeritageBooks.com

Published 2019 by
HERITAGE BOOKS, INC.
Publishing Division
5810 Ruatan Street
Berwyn Heights, Md. 20740

International Standard Book Number
Paperbound: 978-1-68034-926-9

Contents

iv

General Abbreviations

ac.	acres	g-mother	grandmother
acct.	account	gs/o	grandson of
assgn.	assigned or assignment	g-son	grandson
b.	born	g-sons	grandsons
bapt.	baptised	inv.	inventory
b-i-l	brother-in-law	m.	married
cert.	certificate	m-i-l	mother-in-law
cert./pat.	certificate, patent or warrant	neph.	nephew
		nok	next of kin
child.	children	pat.	patent or patented
ch/o	children of	poss.	possessed
d.	died	pur.	purchase
d/o	daughter of	resur.	resurvey or resurveyed
dau.	daughter	s/o	son of
esch.	escheat or escheated	sic	that's what it says
f/o	father of	s-i-l	son-in-law
g/s-i-l	grandson-in-law	sis.-i-l	sister-in-law
g-child.	grandchildren	sons-i-l	sons-in-law
g-dau.	granddaughter	sur.	survey
g-daus.	granddaughters	w/o	wife of
g-father	grandfather		

Maryland Counties

AA	Anne Arundel County	KE	Kent County
BA	Baltimore County	PG	Prince George's County
CA	Calvert County	QA	Queen Anne County
CE	Cecil County	SM	St. Mary's County
CH	Charles County	SO	Somerset County
DO	Dorchester County	TA	Talbot County
FR	Frederick County		

References and Explanations

The following sources were researched for vital statistics, relationships and land ownership in St. Mary's County during the colonial period.

A   Abstracts of the Administration Accounts of the Prerogative Court of Maryland, 1718-1777; V. L. Skinner, Jr.; 11 Volumes; Family Line Publications and Willow Bend Books
Reference: Liber and folio of original document

AFP   All Faith's Parish; Marriages and Birth; copied 1907 by Miss L. H. Harrison; filmed at Maryland Historical Society, Baltimore
Reference: Page number of microfilm

AM   Archives of Maryland on-line
Reference: Volume and page number of original document

BB   Abstracts of the Balance Books of the Prerogative Court of Maryland 1751-1777; 4 volumes; Liber 1, Debby Moxley; Libers 2-7, V. L. Skinner, Jr.; Family Line Publications
Reference: Liber and folio of original document

BRU   Maryland Records, Gaius Marcus Brumbaugh; Volume 2
Reference: Page number of book

CCR   Abstracts of Chancery Court Records of Maryland, 1669-1782, Debbie Hopper; Family Line Publications
Reference: Page number of book

CMN   Colonial Maryland Naturalizations, Jeffrey A. & Florence L. Wyand; Genealogical Publishing Company
Reference: Identifying number of record

COL   Settlers of Maryland, 1679-1783, Peter Wilson Coldham; 5 volumes; Genealogical Publishing Company
Reference: May refer to certificate, patent or warrant; page # not given

CSFM   Catholic Families of Southern Maryland, Timothy J. O'Rourke; Genealogical Publishing Company
Reference: Not given

CSM   Chronicles of St. Mary's, Volumes 5-7, 1957-1959, St. Mary's County Historical Society
Reference: Not given

HGM   Historic Graves of Maryland and The District of Columbia, Helen W. Ridgely; The Grafton Press
Reference: Not given

I Abstracts of the Inventories and Accounts of the Prerogative Court of Maryland, 1718-1777, V. L. Skinner, Jr.; 17 Volumes; Family Line Publications
Reference: Liber and folio of original document

I&A Abstracts of the Inventories and Accounts of the Prerogative Court of Maryland, 1674-1718, V. L. Skinner, Jr.; 11 Volumes; Family Line Publications
Reference: Liber and folio of original document

JM The Jesuit Missions of St. Mary's County, Maryland, Edwin Warfield Beitzell, Sponsored by St. Mary's Bicentennial Commission

MCW The Maryland Calendar of Wills, 1685-1777; 1st 8 volumes by Jane Baldwin Cotton, 2nd 8 volumes by F. Edward Wright; Family Line Publications
Reference: Volume and page number of book

MD Maryland Deponents, 1634-1799, Henry C. Peden, Jr.; Volume 1; Family Line Publications
Reference: Not given

MM Maryland Marriages, 1634-1777, Robert Barnes; Genealogical Publishing Company
Reference: Not given

PRPC Probate Records of the Provincial Court; unpublished manuscript by F. Edward Wright

RR 1704 Rent Rolls, Chronicles of St. Mary's, Vol. 21, No. 5
1707 Rent Rolls, Wilson Miles Cary Collection, Maryland Historical Society Library, 400 W. Monument St., Baltimore
Reference: Page number of rent roll
Verbatim memo at end of the Cary manuscript: The ½ of Choptico Hundred as the same was formerly is not in Charles County and the Hundred of Harvey and the Resurrection formerly were part of Calvert County are now in this county

SA St. Andrew's Parish; Births, Marriages and Deaths 1736-1886, Copied 1907 by Miss L. H. Harrison; filed at the Maryland Historical Society, Baltimore, MD
Reference: Page number of microfilm

SK The Early Settlers of Maryland, Gust Skordas; Genealogical Publishing Company
Reference: Liber and folio number of records of Land Patents, 1633-1680

SMH Sidelights of Maryland History, Hester Dorsey Richardson; Williams and Wilkins Company
Reference: Not given

TLC   St. Mary's County, Maryland, Rent Rolls, 1639-1771, TLC Genealogy, Miami Beach, FL
Reference: Page number of rent roll

SMAA St. Mary's County, Maryland Administrative Accounts, 1674-1720; T.L.C. Genealogy, Miami Beach, FL
Reference: Page number of original document

SMW St. Mary's County, Maryland, Registrar of Wills, Leslie & Neil Keddie; The Family Tree Bookshop
Reference: Liber and folio of original document
Information included in this type bracket [ ] was found in SMW and not in MCW.

ABELL

Abell, Samuel; <u>will</u>; St. Mary's Creek; 8 Jan 1697; 11 Apr 1698; [carpenter];
  sons John, Samuel; wife Ann; tract *My Lord's Manor* [*His Lordship's Manor*]
  (MCW 2.152) [SMW PC1.100]; <u>inv.</u>; 12 Apr 1698 (I&A 16.187); <u>acct.</u>; 25 Jul 1698;
  widow, 6 child.; extx. Anne Abell (I&A 16.183); <u>acct.</u>; 17 Jul 1699 (I&A 19½b.119)
Abell, John; *Squabble*; 75 ac.; sur. 20 Mar 1713 (TLC p. 69); 2 Dec 1714 cert./pat.
  (COL)
Abell, William; <u>inv.</u>; 24 May 1733; 8 Aug 1733; admx./extx. Ann Abell (I
  17.328); <u>acct.</u>; 9 Jun 1735; mentions John, William & Richard Abell (A 13.136)
Abell, Cuthbert; son Caleb [b. 10 Apr 1742] (SA p. 8)
Abell, John [Sr.]; <u>will</u>; yeoman; 25 Sep 1746; 8 Nov 1746; child. Enoch,
  Cudburd; wife's son John Howell; d-i-l Cactran Huchings; tract *Saturdans
  Conclusion* [*Southers ___ Condition*] (MCW 9.93) [SMW TA1.203]; <u>inv.</u>; 8 Apr
  1747; [Sr.]; nok John & Samuel Abell; admx./extx. Frances Abell (I 35.89)
Abell, Enoch; *Hobson's Choice*; 23 ac.; 13 May 1752 cert./pat. (COL)
  Slipe; 24 ac.; 10 Aug 1753 cert./pat. (COL)
  Abell's Content; 113 ac.; 28 Oct 1756 cert./pat. (COL)
Abell, John; s/o John; *Ripe*; 100 ac.; 10 Dec 1754 cert./pat. (COL)
  Abell's Addition; 9 ac.; 22 Sep 1760 cert./pat. (COL)
  Four Square; 22 ac.; 2 Mar 1761 cert./pat. (COL)
  Abell's Enclosure; 128 ac.; 2 Mar 1761 cert./pat. (COL)
  Harm Watch Harm Catch; 84 ac.; 2 Mar 1761 cert./pat. (COL)
  Abell's Purchase; 218 ac.; 27 Mar 1762 cert./pat. (COL)
  Foxes' Range; 70 ac.; 30 Apr 1762 cert./pat. (COL)
  Handkerchief; 21 ac.; 1 May 1762 cert./pat. (COL)
  John's Chance; 32 ac.; 12 Nov 1762 cert./pat. (COL)
  Oversight; 79 ac. ; 29 Sep 1763 cert./pat. (COL)
  Abell's Fancy; 98 ac.; 29 Sep 1763 cert./pat. (COL)
  Friends by Chance; 339 ac.; 29 Sep 1763 cert./pat. (COL)
  Last Shift; 55 ac.; 29 Sep 1764 cert./pat. (COL)
  Found by Chance; 50 ac.; 29 Sep 1764 cert./pat. (COL)
  Abell's Range; 92 ac.; 21 Apr 1766 cert./pat. (COL)
  John's Dread; 20 ac.; 29 Sep 1766 cert./pat. (COL)
  Abell's Angle; 30 ac.; 29 Sep 1767 cert./pat. (COL)
  Shrubby Thicket; 23 ac.; 17 Nov 1767 cert./pat. (COL)
  All That's Left; 42 ac.; 27 Jun 1768 cert./pat. (COL)
Abell, Samuel and Elinor; sons Samuel [b. 13 Jan 1755], Robert [b. 8 May
  1757]; Abner [b. 29 Jul 1759] (SA p. 38, 39)
Abell, Samuel, Jr.; *Abell's Chance*; 110 ac.; 25 Mar 1756 cert./pat. (COL)
Abell [Able], John; *John's Guess*; 170 ac.; 25 Mar 1756 cert./pat. (COL)
  Abell's Lot; 247 ac.; 25 Jun 1760 cert./pat. (COL)
Abell, John and Jane; dau. Elizabeth [b. 3 Dec 1759] (SA p. 16, 51)
Abell, Cuthbert; *Abell's Chance*; 124 ac.; 23 Apr 1760 cert./pat. (COL)

Mill; 5 ac.; 29 Sep 1762 cert./pat. (COL)

Abell, Edward and Susanna; child. Jane [b. 6 Nov 1760], Benjamin [b. 7 Apr 1764], Catharine [b. 22 Apr 1766], Samuel [b. 23 Jan 1768]; John [b. 23 Dec 1769], Mary [b. 3 Nov 1771] (SA p. 16, 30, 31, 51)

Abell, Samuel; inv.; 12 Nov 1762; 6 Feb 1763; nok John Abell (ss), James Wimsatt; admx. Frances Wimsatt (I 80.144); acct.; 2 Feb 1764; adm. Samuel Abell (A 50.364) (BB 4.28)

Abell, Caleb; m. 29 Dec 1763 Mary Williams (SA p. 57); child. Jeremiah Williams [b. 2 Apr 1766], Elizabeth [b. 12 Nov 1767], Mary [b. 20 Oct 1769], Rachel [b. 29 Sep 1772] (SA p. 8, 22, 42, 190)

Abell, George and Elizabeth; child. Elizabeth [b. 24 Jan 1766], George [b. 27 Jul 1768], Francis [b. 20 Jun 1774], Pollard [b. 20 Sep 1777] (SA p. 17, 28, 29, 42, 51)

Abell, John (younger) and Ann; sons James [b. 26 Jun 1766], John Standfill [b. 16 Jan 1768] (SA p. 52)

Abell, Peter and wife Lucy; dau. Sarah [b. 25 Oct 1769] (SA p. 1)

Abell, John, *Spring*; 7 ac.; 10 Nov 1769 cert./pat. (COL)

Abell, John, Sr.; *Aim At*; 69 ac.; 1 Jun 1772 cert./pat. (COL)

 Tit for Tat; 109 ac.; 14 Sep 1773 cert./pat. (COL)

Abell, Zacharia; m. 15 Oct 1772 Mary Strong (MM)

Abel, Phillip; wife Ann Dresden; son Philip, bapt. 18 May 1772 (CFSM)

Abel (Abell), Phillip; inv.; 2 Nov 1772; 1 Jul 1773; nok Samuel Abell, Jr. & the youngest; admx. Ann Dradon Abell (I 112.398)

Abell, Edward, Jr.; *By the Mill*; 34 ac.; 15 Sep 1773 cert./pat. (COL)

Abel, Ignatius; m. 8 Nov 1773 Mary Able (MM); son Elisha [bapt. 28 Jul 1776], dau. Ann [bapt. 19 Oct 1777]; St. Francis Xavier (CFSM)

Abell [Abel], Caleb [Cabbel]; inv.; 10 Nov 1773; nok Caleb Abell, John Abell Younger; admx. Mary Abell (I 114.31); acct.; 15 Aug 1776; admx. Mary Abell (A 74.10) (BB 7.68)

Abell, John; *Small Strife*; 18 ac.; 19 Nov 1774 cert./pat. (COL)

Abell, Edward and Statia Taylor; m. 7 Nov 1778; child. Barbara [b. 10 Jul 1777], Pharmel [b. 8 Jun 1780], Eleanor [b. 10 Mar 1782] (SA p. 31, 57)

Abell, Robert; m. 3 Nov 1777 Margarita Miles (MM)

Abell, Clarke and Catharine Hutchins; m. 3 Jun 1779 (SA p. 57)

Abell, John and Elizabeth Abell; m. 4 Jun 1780 (SA p. 58); child. Jean [bapt. 23 Sep 1781], Jonathan [bapt. 4 May 1783] (SA p. 30)

Abell, Edmund and Elizabeth; dau. Janet [bapt. 4 May 1783] (SA p. 30)

Abell, Arthur and Henrietta Raily (by license); m. 12 Jan 1784 (SA p. 61)

Abell, Cuthbert and Mary Simmons (by license); m. 1 Feb 1785 (SA p. 63)

Abell, Samuel and Sarah; dau. Elizabeth [b. 29 Nov 1799]; bapt. 3 Aug 1800] (SA p. 31)

ABINGTON

Abingdon, John; gent.; age ca 24 in 1659 (MD p. 1)

Abington, Andrew; *Netherbury*; 200 ac.; sur. 27 Nov 1680; listed 1704; no poss. in 1707; St. Mary's Hundred (RR p. 8); 30 Nov 1676 cert./pat. (COL)

Abbington, Andrew; immigrated by 1678 (SK WC2.258)

Abbington, Andrew; Deputy Surveyor of part of St. Mary's Co., 1680 (SK 21.207)

ADAMS

Adams, Thomas; inv.; 19 Apr 1714; 16 Dec 1714; approvers James Sesell & wife Rachel (I&A 36b.19); acct.; 21 Jul 1715 (I&A 36c.130) (SMAA p. 285)

Adams, William; inv.; 5 Apr 1743; nok John & Benhamin Redmon; adms./exs. Patrick Lurty & wife Mary (I 28.517); acct.; 16 Jul 1744; orphans Benjamin, Stephen, Kesia (A 20.423)

Adams, Thomas; inv.; 2 Aug 1749; 5 Sep 1749; nok James & Hoppatt Adames; admx./extx, Johannah Adams (I 40.355); acct.; 5 Sep 1749; child. Rachel [age 10], Ann [age 6], Solomon [age 2] (A 27.104)

Adams, Benjamin; inv.; 30 May 1757; 4 Apr 1757; nok James Adams, Thomas Redman (I 63.142); acct.; 12 Jun 1758 (A 41.491)

Adams, Abraham and Ann; child. Enoch [b. 18 Sep 1757], Austin [b. 3 Apr 1759], Elizabeth [b. 13 Jan 1762], Abraham [b. 13 Oct 1764] (SA p. 7, 8)

Adams, Daniel; inv.; 27 Sep 1758; 5 Apr 1759; nok John & James Adams; admx./extx, Jennitt Adams (I 67.97)

Adams, Thomas; inv.; 4 Jun 1765; 20 Oct 1765 (I 87.315)

Adams, James and Mary; son Hatton George [b. 11 Apr 1775] (SA p. 26)

Adams, James; will; 6 Jan 1775; 20 Apr 1777; sister Jean Beverly, cousin James Brinum, bro. Abraham; wife Mary; son George (MCW 16.174)

Adams, Abraham and Sabra Silance (by license); m. 14 Sep 1784 (SA p. 62)

ADDERTON

Adderton, Jeremiah; wife Mary, d/o James Heath; [filed with 1709] (CCR p. 17)

Adderton, Jeremiah; Gent.; will; 11 Apr 1713; 19 May 1713; wife Mary; son James; unborn child (MCW 4.201) [SMW PC1.188]; inv.; 22 Sep 1713; 26 Sep 1713 (I&A 35a.133); acct.; 9 Apr 1715; extx. Mary, w/o Joseph Vansweringen (I&A 36b.348) (SMAA p. 275); acct.;3 Jul 1716 (I&A 38b.3); acct.;13 Jul 1716 (SMAA p. 300); acct.;18 Apr 1718 (I&A 39c.158) (SMAA p. 342); acct.;12 Jul 1718 (A 1.34) (SMAA p. 330); acct.;13 May 1730; extx Mary, w/o William Deacon, Esq. (A 10.249); acct.; 24 Nov 1736 (A 15.233); acct.; 28 Jun 1755 (A 38.19)

ADDISON

Adison, John; immigrated by 1680 (SKWC2.309)

Addison, John; *Long Neck*; 100 ac.; sur. 10 Jun 1681; 1707 poss. Wm. Cecill; mentions 7 May 1709 William & Elizabeth Cole; New Town Hundred (RR p. 38) (TLC p. 37); 10 Jul 1681 cert./pat. (COL)

Swan's Harbour; 345 ac.; 1 Jun 1687 cert./pat. (COL)

Small Hope; 56 ac.; 56 ac.; sur. 5 May 1687; poss. Tho. Hebb; on 1704 RR not on 1707 RR; St. Georges Hundred (TLC p. 19); 5 Mar 1688 cert./pat. (COL)

AINSWORTH

Aynsworthy (Answorthy, Answorth, Ainsworth), George & wife Susanna to
Christopher Rousby of CA Co.; *Halfeheads Folly*; 1675; purchased from John
Halfehead & wife Elizabeth (AM LXVI.77)

Ainsworth, George; will; 9 May 1677; 20 Mar 1677/8; wife Susanna; [planter]
(MCW 1.201) [SMW PC1.28]; inv.; 23 Mar 1677 (I&A 5.1)

AISQUITH

Asquith (Aisquith), William; *Asquith Folly*; 100 ac.; sur. 28 Jan 1681; assgn.
Henry & David Lewis; 1707 poss. Margaret Jackson in New England; St.
Mary's Hundred (RR p. 9)

Stainmore; 100 ac.; sur. 10 Feb 1681; 1707 poss. Sm. Asquith; St. Mary's
Hundred (RR p. 9); 20 Feb 1682 cert./pat. (COL)

Hiccory Hills; 100 ac.; sur. 7 Apr 1682; assgn. Wm. Hartrap; 1707 poss. Wm.
Asquith; St. Mary's Hundred (RR p. 9) *Hickory Hills*; 7 Apr 1682 cert./pat. (COL)

Birch Spring; 125 ac.; sur. 23 Apr 1683; 1707 poss. Edw'd King; St. Georges
Hundred (RR p. 19)

Beaverdam; 118 ac.; sur. 6 Apr 1698; 1707 poss. same Asquith; St. Mary's
Hundred (RR p. 10); 5 May 1698 cert./pat. (COL)

Wellclose; 182 ac.; sur. 22 Apr 1698; 1707 poss. Wm. Golthorp; St. Mary's
Hundred (RR p. 10) (TLC p. 10); [1698] cert./pat. (COL)

White Marsh; 93 ac.; sur. 27 Nov 1705; (TLC p. 64) ; 10 Oct 1707 cert./pat. (COL)

Aisquith, William, Col.; inv.; 18 Jun 1719; nok Thomas & George Aisquith;
extx. Elisabeth Aisquith (I 2.161); acct.; 12 Sep 1720 (A 3.221) (SMAA p. 425)

Aisquith, William; will; 22 Jul 1740; 3 Apr 1741; sons William, Thomas; daus.
Mary, Susan; wife unnamed; tract *White Marsh, Mannor Land, T. B.* (MCW
8.123) [SMW TA1.110]; inv.; 4 Jul 1741; nok George & Thomas Aisquith;
admx./extx. Sausannah Aisquith (I 26.545); acct.; 14 Aug 1744; extx. Susanna,
w/o George Daffen (A 20.431); acct.; 31 Oct 1758; mentions William, Mary
Piercy [at age], Ann & Susannah [at age], Thomas [age 18] (A 42.156)

Aisquith, George; *Inclosure*; 33 ac.; sur. 13 Sep 1742; pat. 20 Jul 1745 (TLC p.
101); *Enclosure*; 14 Jul 1743 cert./pat. (COL)

Aisquith, George & Thomas; *Thomas & George in Company*; 4½ ac.; sur. 13
Sep 1742; pat. 5 Oct 1743 (TLC p. 101); 4 ac.; 5 Oct 1743 cert./pat. (COL)

Aesquith, Elizabeth; will; 10 Sep 1749 (sic); 22 Feb 1744; son George; dau. Ann;
[Aisquith] (MCW 9.16) [SMW TA1.183]

Asquith (Aisquith), Thomas, Col.; *Addition*; 31 ac.; 29 Sep 1757 cert./pat. (COL)
Hunting Neck Addn.; 48 ac.; 4 Jan 1759 cert./pat. (COL)

Asquith, Thomas; will; 18 Dec 1760; 5 Mar 1761; sons John, George; unborn
child; wife Elinor; nephew Thomas Asquith, Jr.; tracts *St. Richard Manner,
Addition to Hunting Neck, The Addition to Hamsted, Hicory Hills* (MCW 12.35)
[SMW TA1.405]; inv.; 5 Aug 1761; [Col.]; nok George & Ann Aisquith; ex.
Elener Aisquith (I 74.227,237); acct.; 21 Apr 1767; mentions Thomas, Jr.; exs.
Robert Watts & wife Eleanor (A 57.72)

Aisquith, George, Capt.; <u>inv.</u>; 23 May 1770; 1 Oct 1770; nok Ann Aisquith,
  Joseph Hopewell; admx. Elisabeth Aisquith (I 107.193, 197); <u>acct.</u>; 21 Mar 1771
  (A 66.162)
Aisquith, John and Mary Chesley; m. 3 Jun 1779 (SA p. 57)
Aisquith, George and Elizabeth Gruder (by license); m. 3 Mar 1784 (SA p. 62)

ALBERT
Alburt, William; <u>will</u>; 13 Feb 1738/90; 7 Mar 1738/9; wife Elizabeth Halbert
  (sic) (MCW 8.21) [SMW TA1.63]
Albert (Alburt), Elizabeth; <u>will</u>; 16 Apr 1739; 27 Apr 1739 (MCW 8.22) [SMW
  TA1.86]; <u>acct.</u>; 24 Oct 1743; estates of William & Elisabeth Albert (A 20.1)

ALLEN
Allen, Thomas; found shot at *Point Look Out*, St. Michael's Manor; 8 Aug 1648;
  sons Thomas, William, Robert (AM IV.403; XLI.122)
Allen, Philip; *Old Branford*; 350 ac.; 27 Jan 1687 cert./pat. (COL)
Allen, William; <u>inv.</u>; 4 Jan 1711(I&A 34.173); <u>acct.</u>; 16 Jun 1714; adms. John
  Crutlhet & wife Thomason (I&A 36a.175) (SMAA p. 264)
Allen, Thomas; <u>inv.</u>; 27 Mar 1733; 9 Apr 1733 (I 17.97); <u>acct.</u>; 13 Aug 1733 (A
  12.40)
Allen, Henry; <u>inv.</u>; 14 Mar 1742; 1743; nok Mary Allen, minors (I 28.195)

ALLISON
Allison, Penelope; immigrated by 1677 (SK 15.397)
Allison, Henry; m. 25 May 1779 Margaret Dillman (SA p. 57)
Allison, John; <u>will</u>; 12 Jun 1754; 12 Apr 1755; g-child. John, Ann and Mary
  Cole of dau. Margit Cole; wife Sarah; 9 (sic) child. (no commas in document)
  Thomas, Joseph, Jacob, John, James, Henry, Self (?), Mary, Elizabeth, George
  (MCW 11.83) [SMW TA1.332]; <u>inv.</u>; 28 Apr 1755; 3 Jul 1755; nok Thomas &
  Joseph Allison; admx./extx. Sarah Allison (I 59.6); <u>acct.</u>; 29 Mar 1757 (A
  40.296); <u>dist.</u> 28 Mar 1757; child. Thomas, Jacob, Joseph, John, James, Henry,
  Mary, Elisabeth, George (BB 2.49)
Allison, John; <u>inv.</u>; 16 Feb 1762; 8 Jun 1763 (I 81.235)
Allison, Henry; wife Mary; dau. Ann [b. 31 Jan 1768] (CFSM, p. 4)

ALVEY
Alvey, Pope; cooper; struck servant Alice Sandford; she d. 29 Feb 1663 (AM
  XLIX.230); Newtown Hundred; cooper; 19 Dec 1665 stole and killed a cow at
  Britton's Bay (AM XLIX.309)
Alvey, Pope; wife Ann, widow of John Hammond; vs. Thomas Wynne who m.
  relict of Richard Willan; 1664 (AM XLIX.300, 452)
Alvey, Joseph; and Elizabeth his wife; service by 1667 (SK11.103)
Alvey, Joseph; *Knotting*; 100 ac.; sur. 28 Mar 1668; 1707 poss. Edw'd Field; St.
  Clements Hundred (RR p. 45)
Alvey, Pope; immigrated by 1670 (SK12.550)

Alvey, Joseph; *Rome*; 100 ac.; sur. 24 Jun 1670; 1707 poss. Joseph Alvey; New
 Town Hundred (RR p. 35)

Alvey, Joseph; will; 26 Mar 1679; 21 May 1679; wife Elizabeth; sons Arthur
 and Joseph; bro. Pope Alvey (MCW 1.212) [SMW PC1.35]; inv.; 4 Jun 1679 (I&A
 6.211); acct.; 20 Jul 1680; extx. Elisabeth Alvey (widow) (I&A 7a.137)

Alvey, Pope; inv.; 22 Dec 1679; 26 Feb 1679; "widow" Alvey (I&A 6.678); acct.;
 [filed with 1681]; admx. Ann Alvey, w/o Thomas Alvey (I&A 7b.40 or 43a)

Alvery, Arthur; inv.; 3 Feb 1700 (I&A 20.217); acct.; [filed with 1701-2] (I&A
 21.382)

Alvery, Joseph; *Rooms Conveniencey*; sur. 10 Aug 1720 (TLC p. 80); *Roan's
 Conveniency*; 26 ac.; 25 Mar 1724 cert./pat. (COL)

Alvey, Joseph; will; probate 25 Jul 1729; sons Leonard, Joseph, Arthur; daus.
 Elinor, Margaret; tracts *Greens Inheritance, Noting* (MCW 6.126) [SMW PC1.331];
 inv.; 20 Jul 1729; 3 Nov 1729; nok Leonard & Elioner Alvey; admx. Margret
 Alvey (I 15.143)

Alvey, (Alney), John; will; 1 Mar 1742/3; 21 Apr 1743/4; sons John, Jeste; cous.
 Joseph; daus. unnamed; tracts *Batter's [Catler's (?)] Rest, Room, Nothing*
 (MCW 8.206) [SMW TA1.144]; inv.; 11 May 1743; 7 Jun 1743; nok Leonard &
 Elisabeth Alvey; admx./extx. Mary Alvey (I 28.2); acct.; 14 Dec 1744;
 mentions Mary, Winifred, Elinor & Elisabeth Alvey w/o James Walker; extx.
 Mary, w/o William Field (A 21.142)

Alvey, Margaret; will; 16 May 1736; 3 Jun 1746; child. Leonard, Joseph,
 Arthur, Mary, Margaret Graves, Elender [Eleanor] (MCW 9.75) [SMW TA1.206];
 inv.; 1 Jul 1746; 2 Sep 1746; nok Arthur & Elinor Alvey; adm./ex. Joseph
 Alvey (I 33.319); acct.; 3 May 1748 (A 24.291)

ANCTILL

Anketill, Francis; inv.; [filed with 1686-7] (I&A 9.329)

Anctill (Anctell), Barnaby; will; 21 Feb 1732; 12 Apr 1733; cousin Jean
 Thompson; wife Elizabeth (MCW 7.11) [SMW PC1.363]; inv.; 6 Jun 1733; nok
 Lewis & Hannah Griffith; admx./extx. Elisabeth Anctell (I 17.320, 322); acct.;
 20 Aug 1734 (A 12.526)

Anktell (Anctell), Elizabeth; will; 4 Apr 1737; 4 Jun 1739; cousins Margaret
 Cavenough, Margrett Trippe, Francis Brian, Barniby Angell, Margrett Brian
 (MCW 8.39) [SMW TA1.70]; inv.; 19 Jun 1739; 26 Aug 1739; nok William
 Cavenough, Edward Horn; adm./ex. Barnaby Angle (I 24.182); acct.; Sep 1740;
 ex. Barnaby Angell (A 18.57)

ANDERSON

Anderson, William; *Cornelius*; 78 ac.; sur. 5 May 1722 (TLC p. 82); *Carnelowe's*;
 20 May 1725 cert./pat. (COL)
 Pearth; 62 ac.; sur. 16 Jun 1724 (TLC p. 92); 23 Sep 1736 (COL)

Anderson, Gilbert; inv.; 20 Mar 1727; 15 Mar 1728 (I 13.92); acct.; 4 Nov 1728
 (A 9.109)

Anderson, William; planter; <u>will</u>; 27 Feb 1738/9; 19 Mar 1738/9; sons James, John, Benjamin, William; daus. Margrit, Jane; wife unnamed; tracts *Cornelius [Caruolour], Fortune, Fortune's Outlet; Pearth* (MCW 8.21) [SMW TA1.83]; <u>inv.</u>; 2 Apr 1739; nok Margaret Welch, James Anderson; admx./extx. Mary Anderson (I 24.137); <u>acct.</u>; 29 Sep 1740 (A 18.65)

Anderson, James; <u>inv.</u>; 3 Jan 1758; 14 Feb 1758; nok Ann Tanner, Mary Oliver; admx./extx. Catharine Anderson (I 64.430)

Anderson, John Baptist and Tabitha; sons James [b. 6 Jan 1758], John [b. 16 Jun 1761] (SA p. 39)

Anderson, Thomas and Henrietta; child. Ann [b. 15 Apr 1764], Mary [b. 2 Jan 1766] (SA p. 1)

Anderson, Aloysisus; s/o William, dec'd; *Fortune's Outlet*; 16 ac.; 11 Dec 1766 cert./pat. (COL)

Anderson, Thomas and Chloe; son John [b. 18 Sep 1768] (SA p. 1)

Anderson, William and Elizabeth; dau. Margaret [b. 27 Apr 1775] (SA p. 26)

ANDREWS
Andrews, Anthony; service by 1669; and Helen his wife (SK 12.372)

Andrews, Susanna; w/o Anthony; service by 1673 (SK17575)

Andrews, Anthony; <u>inv.</u>; 24 May 1697 (I&A 15.165)

ANGELL
Angell, John; service by 1673 (SK 15.171; 17.79)

Aingell (Angell), John; <u>inv.</u>; 10 Feb 1724; 19 Mar 1724; nok James Angell, Ann Carmichell; admx. Jane Angell (I 10.300); <u>acct.</u>; 14 Mar 1725; admx. Jane, w/o Joseph George Thompson (A 7.304)

Angel (Angell), James; <u>will</u>; 4 Apr 1736; 10 May 1736; son John; daus. Mary, Ann, Winifred; tracts *Mary's Hope, Cross Manner, Courtney's Fancy* (MCW 7.170) [SMW TA1.54]; <u>inv.</u>; 29 Oct 1736; nok Mary Clerke, Ann Angell; adm./ex. John Angel (I 22.78); <u>acct.</u>; 27 Jan 1740 (A 18.122)

Angell, Barneby (Barnaby); <u>inv.</u>; 25 Mar 1763; 9 Jun 1763; nok John & James Angell (I 81.233); <u>acct.</u>; 19 Oct 1764 (A 52.30)

ARMSTRONG
Armstrong, James; <u>inv.</u>; 23 Jun 1736; 27 Sep 1736 (I 21.250); <u>acct.</u>; 27 Sep 1736 (A 15.193)

Armstrong, James; doctor; <u>will</u>; 6 Nov 1762; 5 Sep 1764; daus. Catherine Crane, Christian Crabb, Hellen; sons Robert, John, George, James, [and William]; wife Dinah (MCW 13.43) [SMW TA1.481]; <u>inv.</u>; 3 Dec 1764; nok Robert & Helen Armstrong; extx. Diannah Armstrong (I 86.63); <u>acct.</u>; 25 Mar 1767 (A 56.70); <u>dist.</u>; 25 Mar 1767; child. Catherine Crane, Christian Crabb, Robert, John, George, James, Helen (BB 5.17)

ARMSWORTHY

Armsworthy (Annsworthy) [Ariswordy], John; [planter]; will; 1 Apr 1707; 23 Apr 1707; wife Mary; sons John, Thomas (MCW 3.86) [SMW PC1.150]; inv.; 24 Apr 1707 (I&A 27.147); acct.; 22 May 1709 (I&A 29.295) (SMAA p. 186)

Armsworthy, George and Rebecca; child. Thomas [b. 17 Aug 1756], Mack [b. 3 Apr 1758], Bennet [b. 5 Apr 1760], Sarah [b. 15 Feb 1762], Daniel [b. 17 Jun 1764] (SA p. 6)

Armsworthy, John and Frances; dau. Katey [b. 10 Nov 1757] (SA p. 38)

Armsworthy, Jonathan & Ann; dau. Henrietta [b. 15 Jun 1758] (SA p. 7)

Armsworthy, William and Mary; child. Aaron [b. 3 Sep 1765], Eleanor [b. 2 Sep 1767], Mary [b. 12 Feb 1777] (SA p. 19, 29, 54)

Armsworthy, James and Susanna; child. Ann [b. 5 Aug 1765], Barton [b. 2 Sep 1767] (SA p. 3)

Armsworthy, Abraham and Eleanor; sons Bennet [b. 26 Dec 1771], John [b. 4 Nov 1769] (SA p. 1, 21, 55)

Armsworthy, John; m. 16 Jan 1780 Mary Armsworthy (SA p. 58)

ARTHUR

Arthur, Grace; will; 11 Jun 1703; child., William, Richard, Grace and Mary Brewer; sister Mary, w/o Thomas Davis; tract *Bachellor's Rest* [SMW PC1.132]

Arthurs, William; will; 3 Jun 1733; 8 Aug 1733; wife Ann (MCW 7.31) [SMW TA1.7]; inv.; 15 Sep 1733; Nov 1733; nok John Goddard, Mary Pain; admx./exrtx. Ann Arthurs (I 17.537); acct.; 18 Sep 1734; extx. Ann, w/o Joseph Haden (A 12.546)

Arthor, John; inv.; 4 Mar 1754; 11 Nov 1754; nok Thomas Martin, Jennet Arthrea (I 58.326); acct.; 22 Sep 1755; orphans James [age 4], Henrietta [age 1] (A 38.173); dist.; 29 Jan 1756; widow and orphans James & Henrietta (BB 2.7)

Arthur, John; inv.; 12 Feb 1765 (I 87.16)

ASBESTON

Osbeston, Wm.; *Osbestons Oak*; 50 ac.; sur. 9 Mar 1658; 1707 poss. John White; St. Michael's Hundred (RR p. 14)

Asbeston, William; St. Michael's Hundred; age ca 43; 18 Feb 1668 (MD p. 4)

Albestone, William; will; 12 Dec 1680; 11 Feb 1681; son William; daus. Winifridge, Isabelle, Rebecca and Mary (MCW 1.102); inv.; [filed with 1681-2] (I&A 7c.45); acct.; 21 Aug 1682; child. Winnifreed, Mary, Isabella, Rebecca, William (I&A 7c.230); acct.; 11 Sep 1686 (I&A 9.88)

Asbriton, William; age ca 51; 11 May 1720; tract *St. Mary's Hill* (CCR p. 46)

Asbestone (Ashuston, Albestone), William; planter; will; 8 Feb 1736/7; 7 May 1737; daus. Rachel, w/o William Thomas, Elizabeth; g-dau. Mary Thomas; wife Mary; tract *Asbestone Oak* (MCW 7.214) [SMW TA1.65]; inv.; 25 Jul 1737; 24 Sep 1737; nok Charles Smith, Rachel Thomas; admx.extx. Mary Ashustone (I 22.409); acct.; 28 Mar 1738; extx. Mary Asbeston (A 16.88); acct.; 3 Feb 1741; exs. Robert Jackson & wife Mary (A 18.533)

ASHCOM

Ashcomb, John; *West Ashcomb*; 650 ac.; sur. 17 Jul 1652; 1707 poss. John
   Dansey who m. relict of Charles Ashcomb; resur. *No Name* 22 Feb 1705;
   Resurrection Hundred (RR p. 58) (TLC p. 55)
   Ashcombs Marsh; 32 ac.; sur. 14 Aug 1682; 1707 poss. John Dansey who m.
   widow Ashcomb; Resurrection Hundred (RR p. 62) (TLC p. 60)
Ascomb, Charles; will; 14 Oct 1702; 16 Nov 1702; sons Samuel, Charles, John;
   daus. Martha, Winifrede; wife Martha; tracts *The Marshy Neck, The Tongue
   Neck, My Quarter, Point Patience* (MCW 2.250); inv.; 19 May 1703; 20 Sep
   1703; approver Walter Ascomb (I&A 24.140); acct.; 23 Mar 1712; 4 child.;
   admx. Martha, w/o John Dansey, Esq. (I&A34.156) (SMAA p. 234)
Ashcombe, Charles & John; unnamed; 1,131 ac.; resur. for John Dansy & wife
   Martha for Charles & John, orphans of Charles Ashcum; formerly 650 ac.;
   pat. 15 Jun 1715; formerly *West Ashcomb* (TLC p. 67); 15 Jun 1713 cert./pat.
   (COL)
Ashcombe, Charles; gent.; *Ashcom's Greenfields*; 100 ac.; sur. 20 Feb 1714 (TLC
   p. 73); 10 Sep 1716 cert./pat. (COL)
Ashcom, Winifred; spinster; will; 21 Oct 1717; 27 Mar 1718; mother Martha
   Dansey, widow; nieces Mary Ashcom Greenfield, Elizabeth Greenfield &
   Martha Ashcom, d/o bro. Charles (MCW 4.127) [SMW PC1.235]; inv.; 29
   May1718; nok Charles & John Ashcome (I 1.309)
Ashcom (Ashcombe), John; inv.; 8 Dec 1721; 8 Mar 1721; nok Martha Dansey;
   adm. Charles Ashcombe (I 7.69); acct.; 16 Sep 1724 (A 6.128)
Ashcom, Charles; Gent.; will; 20 Nov 1725; 23 Mar 1726/7; wife Judith; daus.
   Martha, Susannah, Elizabeth; son Samuel; bro. John; g-mother Mrs. Martha
   Dansey; tracts *Ashcom's Mary Greenfield, Point Patience, March Neck, Town
   Neck* (MCW 6.20) [SMW PC1.311]; inv.; 5 Sep 1727; nok Elisabeth Greenfield,
   Elisabeth Jenifer; extx. Mrs. Judith Brook (I 12.257); 29 May 1728 (I 13.102);
   acct.; 29 May 1728; extx. Judith w/o Thomas Brooke (A 9.195); 21 Nov 1732;
   (A 11.525)
Ashcome, Samuel, Mr.; inv.; 17 Dec 1754; nok Anne & Thomas Brome;
   adms./exs. Abraham Neverson & wife Sarah (I 58.320); acct.; 16 Aug 1755;
   orphans Ann [age 14], John [age 1], Sarah [age 10], Charles [age 9], Samuel
   [age 5], Nathaniel [age 3] (A 38.185); dist.; 1756; same orphans named (BB 2.8)
Ashcomb, John; inv.; Jun 1761; 8 Dec 1761; nok Thomas & Mary Brome; adms.
   Ann Ashcomb (I 76.316)
Ashcom (Askom), Charles; inv.; 14 May 1772; admx. Margaret Ashcom
   (Ashcomb) (I 109.350); inv.; 9 Apr 1772; 14 May 1772; nok Samuel &
   Nathaniel Ashcom (I 110.91); acct.; 11 Apr 1774; adms. John Cartwright &
   wife Margaret (A 69.368)

ASKINS

Askins, John; inv.; 22 Jul 1680; admx. Rebecca Askins (I&A 7a.174)

Askin(s), William; *Askins' Choice*; 53 ac.; sur. 7 Jul 1686; 1704 poss. William
    Askins; land not found; St. Georges Hundred; on 1704 RR, not on 1707 RR
    (TLC p. 20); 53 ac.; 7 Jul 1686 cert./pat. (COL)
Askins, John; <u>will</u>; 26 Feb 1697; 4 Mar 1697; bro. George; mentions Bryan, s/o
    Bryan Daly; Mary, widow of John Rottle; Samuel, s/o William Asberstone,
    John Priest & his bro. Charles (MCW 2.132) [SMW PC1.99]; <u>inv.</u>; 4 Mar 1698 (I&A
    17.103)
Askins, William; <u>inv.</u>; 29 Oct 1705 (I&A 25.173)
Askins, Sarah; <u>inv.</u>; 30 Oct 1706 (I&A 26.155); <u>acct.</u>; 7 Apr 1708; adm. William
    Askin (I&A 28.223) (SMAA p. 166)
Askins, William; <u>inv.</u>; 12 Sep 1720; 10 Jan 1720; nok Elisabeth & Rebecca
    Askins; admx. Mary Askins (I 4.195); <u>acct.</u>; 30 Oct 1721 (A 4.42)

ASSITER

Assiter, William; tailor of New Towne; age ca 31 in 1647 (AM IV.354); 38 in 1651
    (MD p. 5)
Assiter, Wm.; *Hopewell*; 350 ac.; sur. 31 Jan 1666; poss. John Bullock, Robert
    Assiter; not in 1704 or 1707 RR; New Town Hundred (TLC p. 41)
Assetter, William; <u>inv.</u>; [filed with 1677] (I&A 4.170)
Assiter, Henry [Ann]; <u>will</u>; 4 Nov 1693; 20 Mar 1693/4; ch/o Henry Paine
    [Payne] & dau. Mary: Henry, Thomas, Charles, Francis (f), [Ann], Ezchiel &
    Mary Paine (MCW 2.54) [SMW PC1.82]

ATCHESON

Acheson (Atchinson), Vincent; records cattle for dau. Mary; 14 Nov 1668 (AM
    LVII.351)
Atcheson, Vincent; service by 1671; and Hannah his wife (SK16.359)
Acheson, Robert; s/o Vincent and Hannah Acheson, dec'd; 3 Jul 1679 (CCR p. 6)

ATTAWAY

Attaway, Thomas, Capt.; <u>inv.</u>; 23 Dec 1707 (I&A 28.59); 2 May 1709; <u>acct.</u>; 2
    May 1709; admx. Elisabeth Attaway (I&A 29.301) (SMAA p. 172)
Attaway, Elizabeth; <u>will</u>; 20 Jul 1709; 9 Mar 1709/10; sons Samuel, John,
    Thomas; dau. Elizabeth Reeder; g-dau. [dau.] Susannah Attaway and d-i-l
    Susannah Attaway (MCW 3.171) [SMW PC1.164]; <u>inv.</u>; 28 May 1710; nok Thomas
    Attoway (I&A 31.188); <u>acct.</u>; 23 Feb 1710; ex. John (SMAA p. 193) (I&A 32c.66)
Attaway, Samuel; <u>will</u>; 23 Nov 1716; 6 Mar 1722/3; bro. John (MCW 5.137) [SMW
    PC1.275]
Attoway (Attaway), Thomas; carpenter; <u>will</u>; 17 Feb 1715; 6 Jun 1716; wife
    Ann; bro. John Attoway (MCW 4.70) [SMW PC1.206]; <u>inv.</u>; 12 Jun 1716; 30 Nov
    1716; nok John Attaway, Elisabeth Reeder (I&A 37a.187); <u>acct.</u>; 20 May 1718;
    extx. Elisabeth Davisse (A 1.48) (SMAA p. 330)
Attaway, John, Mr.; *Rich Neck*; 500 ac.; resur. 13 May 1713 (TLC p. 76); 500 ac.;
    [1718] cert./pat. (COL)

Attaway, John; <u>will</u>; 23 Oct 1732; 8 Nov 1732; daus. Elizabeth, w/o John Bond; Susanna Clark, Judith, Mary & Sarah Attaway; tracts *Molsly, Attaway's Purchase* (MCW 7.9) [SMW PC1.353]; <u>inv.</u>; 18 Apr 1733; 3 Jul 1733; [Capt.]; nok George Clarke, James Swann (I 17.172); <u>acct.</u>; 19 Aug 1734 (A 12.465)

ATTWICK

Atwize, Humphrey; age ca 29; 24 Nov 1652 (AM X.195)
Attwick, James; age ca 65 in 1661 (AM XLI.500)
Attwicks, Humphrey; age ca 40; 12 Aug 1661; mentions d-i-l Anne Hungerford, widow (AM XLI.470)
Adwicke, James; <u>will</u>; 7 Dec 1665; 20 May 1666; eld. son William; youngest son John; wife Grace (MCW 1.34)

ATTWOOD

Atwood, Johanna; service by 1658; of St. Mary's 1675 (SK 18.378)
Attwood, Richard; <u>inv.</u>; 7 Jun 1703 (I&A 1.695); <u>acct.</u>; 13 Sep 1705; 3 orphans; admx. Elinor Harwood (relict) (I&A 25.51) (SMAA p. 130)
Attwood, Peter; <u>will</u>; 29 Nov 1733; 30 Dec 1734 (MCW 7.120) [SMW PC1.31]
Atwood, Peter; priest; 25 Dec 1734; age 52 (HGM)
Atwood, Charles; <u>will</u>; 22 Sep 1773; 16 Apr 1774; child. Ann, Charles, Elizabeth, George, James; wife Tereza (MCW 15.130) [SMW TA1.705]; <u>inv.</u>; 18 Apr 1776; 15 Nov 1776; nok Ann Jarboe, Charles Atwood; adm. James Atwood (I 125.263); <u>acct.</u>; 1 Jun 1777 (A 74.32)

AUSTIN

Austin, John; planter; <u>will</u>; 21 Mar 1732/3; 16 Jul 1733; g-s-i-l William Harrison; wife Ellinor; sons-i-l William Harrison & John Smoote; d-i-l Elizabeth Trigg; wife Ellinor (MCW 7.30) [SMW TA1.6]; <u>acct.</u>; 9 Dec 1734; ex. Elanor Austin (A 12.737)
Austin, Edward; <u>acct.</u>; 3 Sep 1754 (A 36.403) (BB 1.114)
Austin, George and Eleanor; daus. Elizabeth [b. 24 Feb 1774], Priscilla [b. 11 Sep 1775] (SA p. 27)

BACON

Bacon, Henry; <u>will</u>; [planter]; 4 Oct 1747; 20 Feb 1747; g-dau. Ann Bacon Smith; g-son Henry Bacon Smith; daus. Frances and Ann Bacon, Christian Smith (MCW 9.133) [SMW TA1.202]; <u>inv.</u>; 25 Jul 1748; 5 Sep 1748; nok John Medley; adm./ex. James Pike & wife Ann (I 37.98); <u>acct.</u>; 29 Jun 1749 (A 27.24)

BAGGLEY

Baggley [Bagley], Ralph; planter; <u>will</u>; 27 Mar 1729; 7 May 1729; son Samuel; bro. William Willson (MCW 6.105) [SMW PC1.339]; <u>inv.</u>; 23 Jul 1729; 5 Aug 1729; nok Joseph Allen, Sarah Guibertt (I 14.281); <u>acct.</u>; 6 Jul 1730 (A 10.413)

Baggley, Samuel; <u>will</u>; 10 Jun 1744; 5 Mar 1745; wife Drayden; bro. Benjamin
Reada [Reader]; wife's bro. Thomas Bond; mentions Thomas, s/o Thomas
Reada (MCW 9.16) [SMW TA1.164]; <u>inv.</u>; 23 Mar 1744; 4 Jun 1745; nok Thomas
& Benjamin Reeder; adm./ex. Drayden Baggley (I 31.155); <u>acct.</u>; 2 Sep 1746;
extx. Drayden w/o Thomas Allstone (A 23.7)

BAILEY
Balley, John; immigrated by 1662 (SK17.615)
Bayly, John; *Febne [Fibne]*; 100 ac.; sur. 29 Apr 1667; 1707 poss. Peter Smith;
New Town Hundred (RR p. 34) (TLC p. 33)
Bayly, John; s/o John Bayly; d.1669 AA Co. (SK 12.395)
Bayly, John; *Small Hopes*; 100 ac.; sur. 17 Oct 1675; 1707 poss. Jos. Waters;
New Town Hundred (RR p. 37) (TLC 36)
   The Bottom; 100 ac.; sur. 10 Aug 1685; 1707 poss. John Bayly; mentions
Mark Burley & sisters; New Town Hundred (RR p. 41) (TLC p. 41); 15 Aug 1685
cert./pat. (COL)
   Baylys Rest; 350 ac.; sur. 24 Aug 1694; 1707 poss. John Bayly; St. Clements
Hundred (RR p. 48) (TLC p. 46); 24 Aug 1694 cert./pat. (COL)
Bayley, John; <u>acct.</u>; [filed with 1679] (I&A 6.230)
Bayly (Bailye), Robert; <u>will</u>; 6 Jul 1697; 31 Mar 1698; child. James, Robert,
Thomas, Margaret; wife Margaret; tracts *Bayly's Purchase, Small Hopes*
(MCW 2.133) [SMW PC1.97]; <u>inv.</u>; 8 Apr 1698 (I&A 16.31); <u>acct.</u>; 16 Feb 1698
(SMAA p. 104)
Bayle, John; <u>inv.</u>; 11 Dec 1698 (I&A 16.191)
Bayley, Henry; <u>acct.</u>; 26 May 1711 (I&A 32c.16); <u>acct.</u>; adm. Elisabeth (SMAA p.
225)
Bailye (Baly), John; St. Clements Bay; <u>will</u>; 5 Jan 1712; 16 Feb 1712; dau.
Charity Thompson & her child. Mary, Arthur, Charity & Monica Thompson;
son William & his child. John and Eliza.; son John; dau. Mary Shanks & her
dau. Mary Shanks; g-dau. Mary Bailye; son James; g-dau. Susannah Shanks;
tract *The Bottom* (MCW 3.250) [SMW PC1.191]; <u>inv.</u>; 3 Feb 1712; planter; nok
William & John Bailey (I&A 33b.146); <u>acct.</u>; 13 Sep 1713; ex. James (SMAA p.
249); 25 Apr 1716 (I&A 37c.159) (SMAA p. 306)
Bayly, William; age ca 32 in 1715 (MD p. 10)
Bayley, James; *Barren Doe*; sur. 13 Feb 1719 (TLC p. 81); 1720 cert./pat. (COL)
Baley, Patrick; <u>inv.</u>; 11 Aug 1733; 1 Oct 1733; nok minors; admx./extx. Ann
Baley (I 17.535)
Bailey (Baley, Bayley), John; *Little Yielding*; 218 ac.; resur. 23 Sep 1725 (TLC p.
94); 27 Jun 1737 cert./pat. (COL)
Bailey (Baly), John, Mr.; <u>inv.</u>; 8 Jun 1737; 4 Aug 1737; nok Mark Baily;
admx./extx. Ann Bailey (I 22.403); <u>acct.</u>; 7 Nov 1740 (A 18.91)

Baily (Baley), Luke; <u>will</u>; 28 Sep 1741; 17 Dec 1741; aunt Ann Baily; mentions Jane, d/o Robert Hendley (MCW 8.155) [SMW TA1.128]; <u>inv.</u>; 10 May 1742; 4 Jun 1742; nok John Batson, Samuel Baton (I 26.581); <u>acct.</u>; 24 Oct 1743 (A 19.542)

Bailey, James; *Bailey's Fortune*; 213 ac.; sur. 2 Apr 1742 (TLC p. 99); 28 Oct 1742 cert./pat. (COL)

Baley, John; <u>acct.</u>; 6 May 1748; widow; orphans John, Henry, Benedick, Elinor, Ann; admx. Mary w/o Lazarus Ross (A 25.67)

Baley, Thomas; <u>inv.</u>; 11 Aug 1750; 8 Nov 1750; nok John Medley, Margarett Ford; adms./exs. John Fear & wife Mary (I 44.234); <u>acct.</u>; 31 Aug 1752; orphans Thomas [age 7], Mary [age 5], Elisabeth [age 3]; admx. Mary, w/o John Tear (A 33.208); <u>dist.</u>; 31 Aug 1752 (BB 1.60)

Bailye (Bailey), John; <u>will</u>; 20 Jul 1751; 3 Mar 1752; sons John Ignatius, James, John Baptis; daus. Mary and Henrita Bailye & Elinor Howard; wife Elinor (MCW 10.200) [SMW TA1.284]; <u>inv.</u>; 7 Apr 1752; 4 Aug 1752; nok Ignatius & James Bailye; admx./extx. Eliner Baily (I 49.102); <u>acct.</u>; 4 Dec 1753; child. John Ignatius, Elisabeth & Mary [all of age]; James [age 16], John Baptist [age 12], Henneretta [age 10]; (A 36.27); <u>dist.</u>; 4 Dec 1753 (BB 1-89)

Bailey, Henry; <u>acct.</u>; 6 May 1755; extx. Margaret, w/o Nicholass Mills (A 37.167)

Bailey, Eleanor; <u>inv.</u>; 29 Aug 1763; nok Ignatius & James Bailye; adm. John Bailey (I 81.231)

Baley (Bailey), James; <u>inv.</u>; 15 Dec 1763; 2 Feb 1764; admx. Anastacia Bailey (I 83.86)

Baley (Bailey), Elisabeth; <u>inv.</u>; 22 Apr 1767; nok Clement & William Gardiner (I 91.342); <u>acct.</u>; 14 Nov 1767 (A 57.334)

Bailey, Ignatius; <u>inv.</u>; 14 Mar 1774; nok Elender & Elisabeth Bailey; adm. William Hambleton (Hamilton) (I 118.222)

Bailey, Basil and Dorothy Hutchins (by license); m. 28 Dec 1780 (SA p. 58)

BAKER

Baker, Caleb; immigrated by 1668 (SK 17.40; 11.344)

Baker, William; immigrated from VA by 1675 (SK15.313)

Baker, William; <u>inv.</u>; 28 Dec 1675; 22 Jan 1675 (I&A 1.497); <u>acct.</u>; 31 Jul 1679 (I&A 6.248)

Baker, John; innholder; *Governor's Friendship*; 1 ac.; 12 Jun 1681 cert./pat. (COL)

Baker, Hugh; <u>inv.</u>; 1 Dec 1684 (I&A 8.313); <u>acct.</u>; 23 Feb [1685-6]; admx. Elizabeth, w/o Robt. Davis (SMAA p. 83)

Baker, John; elected sheriff in 1685 (MD p. 7)

Baker, John; <u>inv.</u>; 20 Jun 1687 (I&A 10.111)

Baker, James; <u>will</u>; 12 Jul 1701; 22 Jul 1703; wife Ann; son James; daus. Ann and Jane (MCW 3.10) [SMW PC1.128]

Baker, James; <u>acct.</u>; 1 Apr 1709; widow dec'd; adm. Francis Hopewell (I&A 29.182) (SMAA p. 179)

Baker, Eliza.; widow; <u>will</u>; 2 Feb 1712; 21 Aug 1712; g-son John , s/o son John; tracts *Bliston Neck, Cross Neck* (MCW 3.231) [SMW PC1.172]

Baker, John; <u>acct.</u>; 20 Mar 1713; admx. Ann Baker (I&A 35a.317) (SMAA p.237)

Baker, John; <u>inv.</u>; 2 May 1714 (I&A 35a.229)

Baker, James & Priscilla, widow of William Hebb; *Gardiner's Purchase*; 58 ac.; 13 Jun 1719 cert./pat. (COL)

Baker, John; s/o Elizabeth Baker (d. ca 1713); 11 May 1720; tract *St. Mary's Hill* (CCR p. 46)

Baker, John, Capt.; *Baker's Fancy*; 203 ac.; sur. 28 Nov 1722 (TLC p. 83); 20 May 1725 cert./pat. (COL)
Thirds; 424 ac.; 425 ac.; sur. for John Baker & Wm. Jenkins 7 Jun 1720; pat. Baker & Jenkins 13 Jul 1726 (TLC p. 86); 11 Jul 1725 cert./pat. (COL)
Baker's New Fancy; 25½ ac.; sur. 11 Sep 1723 (TLC p. 85); 25 ac.; 15 Jul 1726 cert./pat. (COL)

Baker, John, Col.; <u>inv.</u>; 22 Apr 1730; 5 Mar 1730; nok John Baker, Vachel Denton; admx./extx. Mrs. Ann Baker (I 16.189); <u>acct.</u>; 24 Jan 1731; 1 son (A 11.326); <u>acct.</u>; 1 May 1735; admx. Ann w/o William Thompson (A 13.122)

Baker, James, Mr.; <u>inv.</u> 2 Feb 1739; 28 Apr 1739; nok Sarah Lee, John Baker; admx./extx. Precilla Buckler (I 24.53)

Baker, Priscilla; widow; <u>will</u>; 29 Oct 1739; 12 Feb 1739; father John Miller; sons Thomas, John, James Baker; son William Hebb; [son Matthew Hebb]; tracts *Chelsey, Snow Hill* (MCW 8.66) [SMW TA1.91]; <u>inv.</u>; 2 Aug 1740; 29 Aug 1740; adm./ex. Thomas Backer (I 25.196); <u>acct.</u>; 1 Aug 1741; mentions William & Matthew, orphans of William Hebb (A 18.281)

Baker, John; <u>will</u>; 9 Feb 1754; 4 Mar 1754; dau. Mary; g-son Charles Calvert Egerton; wife Elizabeth (MCW 11.38) [SMW TA1.308]; <u>inv.</u>; 2 Dec 1754; admx./extx. Elisabeth Baker (I 58.307); <u>acct.</u>; 3 Nov 1755 (A 38.291)

Baker, William and Jane Davis (by license); m. 1 Jan 1782 (SA p. 59)

BANKS

Banks, Rich'd & Will'm Wright; *Poplar Hill*; 200 ac.; sur. 24 Jan 1641; poss. 1707 Geor. Cox, Enoc Combs; Poplar Hill Hundred (RR, p. 21) (TLC p. 20)

Banks, Richard; *Dunbar*; 100 ac.; sur. 14 Mar 1648; poss. Widow Mason; Poplar Hill Hundred; on 1704 RR, not on 1707 RR (TLC p. 21)
Banks; 100 ac.; sur. 13 Mar 1648; 1707 poss. Enoc Combs; Poplar Hill Hundred (RR p. 22)
North Banks; 100 ac.; sur. 7 Apr 1654; 1707 no poss.; Poplar Hill Hundred (RR p. 23); [poss. Enoc Combs] (TLC p. 22)

Bankes, Thomas, Mr.; <u>inv.</u>; 2 Apr 1688 (I&A 9.475); <u>acct.</u>; 3 Apr 1688; mentions child. of George Beckwith, dec'd: Charles and Margaret, w/o Michael Taney; extx. Ann Dennis (relict) (I&A 9.475)

Banks, Thos.; *The Ripe*; 872 ac.; sur. undated; 1707 poss. Thomas Smith who m. relict of Andrew Abington; Harvey Hundred (RR p. 56) (TLC p. 54)

BANNISTER

Banister, Henry; St. George's River; will; 18 Feb 1674; 13 Mar 1674; kinsman John Paty (MCW 1.87); inv.; 15 Mar 1674 (I&A 1.206)

Bannister, William; *Colebrook's Levels*; 129 ac. (TLC p. 89); sur. 23 May 1720 cert./pat. (COL)

Well Close; 200 ac.; sur. 19 Feb 1713 (TLC p. 71); 10 Dec 1714 cert./pat. (COL)

Banister, William, Jr.; inv. 4 Nov 1724; nok Thomas Banister, Hugh Williams; admn. William Banister, Sr. (I 10.164); acct.; 18 Jun 1725 (A 6.437); 8 Dec 1726 (A 8.148)

BARBER

Barbier, Luke; wife Elizabeth; 1663 (AM XLIX.57)

Barber, Luke, Esq.; 1,000 ac./300 ac.; sur. 1662; *Mitcham Hills*; no. poss. 1707; Choptico Hundred (RR, p. 50) (TLC p. 48)

Mitcham Meadows; 300 ac.; sur. 29 Nov 1663; 1707 poss. Rob't Phillips; Poplar Hill Hundred (RR p. 23) (TLC p. 22)

Eastham; 400 ac.; sur. 12 Nov 1665; 1707 poss. Jno. Gardiner; Choptico Hundred (RR p. 50) (TLC p. 48)

Westham; 1,200 ac.; sur. 12 Nov 1665; 1707 poss. Luke Barber; Choptico Hundred (RR p. 50); poss. Luke Gardiner (TLC p. 48)

Barber (Barbier), Luke; will; 31 Jul 1664; 4 Jan 1674; wife Eliza:; sons Luke, Edward, Thomas; daus. Eliza: and Mary; tracts *Michan Hall, Lukeland, Michan Hills* (MCW 1.72-73); inv.; Dr.; [filed with 1674] (I&A 1.5); acct.; 9 Mar 1674; John Blomfield m. unnamed relict (I&A1.191)

Barber (Barbier), Edward; will; 2 Mar 1693; 21 May 1694; wife Cibbil; dau. Mary; bro. Thomas; cous. Thomas Nicholls; mentions Mary & Martha, daus. of Sam'l Williamson; sis. Elizabeth Guibert & Mary Nichols (MCW 2.70); acct.; 26 Mar 1695; mentions James, s/o Jacob Morris; Mary and Martha, daus. of Samuel Williamson; ex. unnamed relict, w/o William Holms (Houlms) (I&A 13a.252)

Barber, Thomas; gent.; age ca 53 or 60 in 1714 (MD p. 8)

Barber, Luke; wife Elizabeth; 20 Dec 1714; tract *Revill* (CCR p. 33)

Barber, Thomas; inv.; 19 Sep 1718; nok Matthew Guibert, Thomas Clarke (I 1.411); acct.; 2 Dec 1719; mentions dec'd child; adms. Mary Barber, alias Jeamston & William Jeamston (A 2.410) (SMAA p. 368); acct.; 6 Jun 1720; admx. Mary, w/o William Jamstone (Jamestone) (A 2.504) (SMAA p. 449); acct.; 30 Jul 1722 (A 4.244)

Barber, Samuel; inv.; 16 Mar 1733; 27 Jul 1734; nok William Smith, Thomas Gerard; admx./extx. Rebeccah Barber (I 18.346); acct.; 15 Dec 1735; admx. Barbary, w/o Thomas Bright (A 14.173)

Barber, Luke; will; 29 Apr 1739; 27 Dec 1743; bro. Edward; sons Baptist, Cornelius, Edward; dau. Dorothy Greenfield; tracts *Westham, Luckland* (MCW 8.242) [SMW TA1.140]

Barber, Thomas; inv.; 25 Mar 1743; nok Elias & John Barber; adm./ex. Baptist
Barbert (I 28.4); acct.; 29 Feb 1743; mentions Elias Barber, dec'd (A 20.64)

Barber, Elias; will; 24 Dec 1743; 27 Dec 1743; bro. John; cousins Baptist,
Cornelius, Edward (s/o Luke and Rebecca) and Abram Branson; sisters
Elizabeth Power [Boon], Eleanor Sanders, Margaret Taylor (MCW 8.260) [SMW
TA1.133]

Barber, Baptist; will; 15 Aug 1752; 8 Nov 1752; son Archibald Donaldson
Barber; dau. Rebecka; wife unnamed; tracts *Westham, Luckland, Stansbury
Plains* (MCW 10.237) [SMW TA1.291]; inv.; 29 Nov 1752; 5 Nov 1753; nok
Cornelius & Edward Barber; admx./extx. Elisabeth Barber (I 57.37); acct.; 15
Jan 1754; orphans Rebecca [age 5], Archbold Donalsson [age 3], Baptis [age
1] (A 36.162); dist.; 15 Jan 1754 child. Rebecca [age 6 next 28 May], Archibald
Donallson [age 4 next 9 Feb], Baptist [age 2 next 25 Dec] (BB 1.96)

Barber, Edward; will; 11 Apr 1764; 26 Jun 1764; daus. Elizabeth, Sarah,
Rebecca; wife Sarah; sons Edward, Luke, John Missett (Miphett?), Thomas;
g-dau. Rebecca; tracts *Westham, Swans Forrest, Luck [Luck Land]* (MCW 13.42)
[SMW TA1.458]; inv.; 18 Sep 1764; [Sr.]; nok Luke & Sary Barber; exs. John
Mivert & Elisabeth Barber (I 84.305); acct.; 24 Jun 1765; admx. John Mivert
(Mevert) Barber, Edward Barber (A 53.89); dist.; 25 Jun 1765; legatees widow,
Elisabeth, daus. Mary & Sarah, g/d Rebecca; ch/o Sarah (widow): Edward &
John Miphert & Elisabeth & Sarah (BB 4.133)

Barber, Luke; *Westham's Support*; 37 ac.; 8 Oct 1767 cert./pat. (COL)

Barber, Edward; will; 9 Jun 1769; 2 Feb 1770; sons Barnet [Bennet], Luke; dau.
Price Barber; bro. Cornelius; tracts *Luckland, Westham* (MCW 14.132) [SMW
TA1.607]; inv.; 1 Aug 1770; 11 Sep 1770; mentions Cornelius Barber; ex.
Barnett Barber (I 104.152); dist.; 11 May 1772; child. Bennet, Price & Luke
Barber (BB 6.198)

Barber, Thomas; inv.; 17 Sep 1775; 12 Mar 1776; nok John Myvert & Luke
Barber; admx. Rebecca Barber (I 123.307); dist.; 6 May 1776 (BB 7.51)

Barber, Elias; m. 14 Dec 1777 Elizabeth Wainwright (MM)

BARNES

Barnes, John; service by 1670 (SK12.554); acct.; 21 Mar 1723 (A 5.392)

Barnes, Elisabeth; inv.; 25 Apr 1726; 5 Jul 1726 (I 11.377); acct.; Feb 1726 (A
8.156)

Barnes, John; Clemens Bay; will; 17 Jan 1738; 3 Jul 1739; child. Katherine,
Edward, John, Henry, Elizabeth, William; wife Elizabeth (MCW 8.43) [SMW
TA1.80]; inv.; 4 Aug 1740; merchant; ex. William Barnes (I 25.189); acct.; 7 Aug
1740 (A 18.52)

Barnes, William, Mr.; gent.; inv.; 1 Sep __; 6 Jun 1744; nok Samuel Perrie,
Henry Barnes (I 29.2280); acct.; 3 Dec 1744 (A 21.139)

Barnes, Abraham, Col.; *America Felix Secundus*; 1,096 ac.; sur. 2 Mar 1744;
   incl. *Friends Goodwill*, part of *St. Lawrances* alias *Barton Obert & Dominick*,
   part of *Ranglefield & Long Lane* (TLC p. 108); 2 Mar 1745 cert./pat. (COL)
   Fox Grape Barron; 106 ac.; pat. 31 Mar 1746; orig. *Harvy Forrist* (TLC p. 110);
   31 Mar 1746 cert./pat. (COL)
   Horsey's Forest (petition only); 400 ac.; [15 Aug 1746] cert./pat. (COL)
   Addition; 86 ac.; 29 Jun 1758 cert./pat. (COL)
   Westberry Manor Addn.; 361 ac.; 16 Nov 1774 cert./pat. (COL)
Barnes, James; m. 18 Jan 1784 Anne Grimes (BRU 2.535)

BARNHOUSE
Barnhouse, Timothy; inv.; 6 Jun 1764; nok Richard & B. Barnhouse; admx.
   Elisabeth Barnhouse (I 84.281); acct.; 31 Oct 1765; mentions Rodolph
   Barnhouse (A 53.250); dist.; 31 Oct 1765 (BB 4.143)
Barnhouse, Richard; will; 13 Dec 1770; 11 Jun 1771; wife Jeane; child.
   Rodolph, Richard, Caleb, John, Ann, Jeane, William, Timothy; g-dau. Ann
   Rogers; [son Raphael]; g-child. Ann, Jane & William Barnhouse] (MCW 14.181)
   [SMW TA1.623]; inv.; 1 Jul 1771; 27 Aug 1771; nok Ann & Elisabeth
   Barnhouse; ex. James Barnhouse (I 110.97); inv.; 26 Mar 1772; admx./extx.
   Jean Barnhouse (I 109.365)

BARRATT
Barratt, Edward; 26 Aug 1719; 1 Sep 1719; relation John Barratt; sons John,
   Peter (MCW 4.216) [SMW PC1.251]
Barrett, William and Margaret Malley (by license); m. 23 Feb 1783 (SA p. 61)

BARRON
Barron, John; inv. 8 Sep 1701 (I&A 21.159); acct.; 11 Sep 1702 (I&A 23.90)
Barrons, Thomas, Sr.; will; 28 Nov 1716; 4 Feb 1716; sons Richard, Thomas;
   daus. Alloner, Margaret, Ann; tracts *Cochells Hall, Doggwood Springs* (MCW
   4.72) [SMW PC1.220]; inv.; [filed with 1716]; nok Thomas & Ellinor Barrom
   (I&A 38a.3)
Barron, Robert, Mr.; inv.; 6 Oct 1717 (I&A 39c.197); acct.; 15 Mar 1717; extx.
   Mary Barron (I&A 39a.20); Rev. (SMAA p. 315)
Baron (Barron), Robert; clerk; will; 10 Aug 1717; 1 Oct 1717; child. Benjamin,
   Martha, Bridget; wife Mary (MCW 4.109) [SMW PC1.219]
Barron, Mary; widow; will; 21 Mar 1733/4; 2 Apr 1734; bro. James Mills; late
   husband Richard Barron; dau. Eleanor (MCW 7.69) [SMW TA1.27]; inv.; 23 Mar
   1734; 7 Aug 1734; nok Thomas Barron, Margarett Higton (I 19.48); acct.; 5 Jun
   1735; 1 child dec'd; widow & orphans Thomas, Elves, Richard, James & Mary
   Barron (A 13.164)
Barron, James; inv.; 23 Oct 1762; 1 Nov 1762; nok Bennet Bencraft, Thomas
   Barron; admx. John Barron (I 79.251)

BATEMAN

Bateman, Edward; carpenter; estate admn. 4 Feb 1638 (AM IV.54, 73)

Bateman, John, Esq.; *Thorp;* 400 ac.; sur. 26 May 1663; pat. 26 May 1663; poss. atty. of Capt. Perry in England; 234½ ac. in *Resurvey of Hazard*; Resurrection Hundred (RR p. 59); *Throne* (TLC p. 56)

Bateman, Mary; *The Farm;* 500 ac.; sur. 28 Aug 1666; 1707 poss. Geo. Plowden (RR p. 57); 1707 poss. Geo. Akeeth; Resurrection Hundred (TLC p. 57)

Batman (Bateman), Lawrance; inv.; Oct 1734; 19 Apr 1738; nok John & Thomas Beattman (I 23.80); acct.; 3 Aug 1743; mentions Richard, s/o George Bateman (A 19.535)

BATES

Bates, Lowry and Susanna; child. John [b. 10 Nov 1758], Ann [b. 3 Dec 1764] (SA p. 7)

Bate(s), James, Dr.; *Bates' Prospect;* 64 ac.; 9 Sep 1767 cert./pat. (COL)

BATSON

Bateson, Thomas; service by 1677 (SK 15.402)

Batson, Tho.; *Poplar Point;* 100 ac.; sur. 9 Nov 1680; 1707 poss. Tho. Batson; St. Mary's Hundred (RR p. 8) (TLC p. 9); 29 Nov 1680 cert./pat. (COL)

Battson, John; *Fortune;* 50 ac.; sur. 8 Jun 1705; (TLC p. 64); 1 Aug 1706 cert./pat. (COL)
Batson; 50 ac.; sur. Aug 1695; 1707 poss. same Batson; St. Mary's Hundred (RR p. 10) (TLC p. 11)

Batson, Tho.; *Strife;* 100 ac.; sur. 7 Sep 1695; 1707 poss. same Batson; 1714 from John Batson & Ann 50 ac. to Thomas Batson; St. Mary's Hundred (RR p. 10) (TLC p. 11)

Batson, Thomas; inv.; [filed with 1708] (I&A 29.173); acct.; 18 Sep 1710 (I&A 31.369) (SMAA p. 203)

Batson, Thomas; inv.; 10 Jun 1735; 14 Jul 1735; nok Ann & Jane Batson; admx. Mary Battson (I 21.30); acct.; 21 Feb 1736; orphans Ann, Jane & Mary Batson; admx. Mary, w/o John Thompson (A 15.267)

Batson, John; inv.; 4 Jan 1741; 15 Mar 1741; nok John & Samuel Batson; admx./extx. Ann Batson (I 26.487); acct.; 4 Mar 1744 (A 21.184)

Batson, John; inv.; 2 Oct 1750; 30 Oct 1750; nok Thomas & Richard Battson; adms./exs. Joseph Miller [& wife Ann] (I 44.41); acct.; 20 May 1751 (A 30.96)

BATTIN

Battin, William; will; written 29 May 1662; wife Margery; dau. Ledia Newman & her child. George, William and Margaret Newman; son George Newman; sister Jone Smute & her son William; b-i-l Thos. Smute (MCW 1.22)

Battin, Margery; admx. of husband William Battin; 25 Mar 1663 (AM XLIX.1)

BAXTER

Baxter, John; inv.; 20 Feb 1637 (AM IV.76, 103)

Baxter, Edward; inv.; 12 Feb 1694 (I&A 13a.232); acct. May 1697; wife and child. unnamed; adms. Samuell Lee and wife Susanna (I&A 14.148)

Baxter, William; inv.; 13 Feb 1716; nok Richard & Edward Baxter (I&A 38b.181)

Baxter, Richard; inv.; 1 Dec 1720; nok Edward Baxter; admx. Ellenor Baxter (I 4.196); acct.; 15 Sep 1721; admx. Ellinor, w/o William Langley (A 4.22)

Baxter, Edward; acct.; 1 Mar 1730; admx. Eleanor, w/o William Langley (A 10.640)

Baxter, John; will; oral; 30 Dec 1737; bro. William; cousin Sus__ Baxter [SMW TA1.67]; inv.; 24 Feb 1737; 21 Aug 1738; nok Ales & George Jenkins; adm./ex. William Baxter (I 23.353); acct.; 4 Dec 1740 (A 18.111)

Baxter, Edward; will; 2 Jan 1747; 30 Mar 1748; wife Katharine (MCW 9.143) [SMW TA1.215]

Baxter, Richard, Mr.; inv.; 29 Mar 1755; 14 Jul 1755; nok Catern & George Baxter; admx./extx. Ann Baxter (I 59.3); acct.; 12 Sep 1757; orphans Cuthbert [age 7], Elianor [age 3]; admx. Ann, w/o Moses White (A 41.226); dist.; 12 Sep 1757 (BB 2.68)

Baxter, Katharine; will; 19 Jun 1758; 5 Mar 1760; sons Thomas, Edward, George; daus. Pennelephe, Susanna Cox; mentions Cuthbert and Elenor (ch/o Richard Baxter) (MCW 11.261) [SMW TA1.391]; inv.; 5 Feb 1760; 15 Apr 1760; nok Penelope Baxter, Susannah Cox; adm./ex. Thomas Baxter (I 68.249); acct.; 8 Jan 1762 (A 47.381); dist.; 8 Jan 1762 (BB 3.116)

Baxter, John; inv.; 20 Jun 1772; 10 Aug 1772; mentions George & Anthony Baxter; admx. Elisabeth Baxter (I 109.364); acct.; 3 Mar 1774 (A 69.373)

Baxter, Francis and Margaret; son Francis [b. 20 Jan 1773] (SA p. 25)

BEACH

Beach, Anne; now w/o Ellis [Elias] Beach; contracted in Nov 1642 to be taken to Elizabeth River in VA; 1644 (AM IV.269.174)

Beach, Elias; s/o Elias; recorded cattle mark; 29 Sep 1649 (AM IV.507)

Beach, Anna; widow of Elias; will; written 22 Jan 1663; daus. Mary [age 10 yrs., 7 wks.], Rebecca [age 3 yrs., 6 mos.], son Thomas [age 1 yr., 7 wks.] (MCW I.23)

Beach, Elias; inv.; 17 Feb 1697 (I&A 16.34); acct.; 1 Feb 1698; 2 child. (I&A 18.128) (SMAA p. 101)

BEALE

Beale, Thomas; service by 1672 (SK17.57)

Beal, Ninian; *Edenburgh*; 380 ac.; sur. 19 Apr 1672; 1707 poss. Thomas Hutchison's orphan (f); lies in CH Co.; Choptico Hundred (RR p. 52) (TLC p. 50)

Baill (Beale), John; 15 Nov 1677; extx. Rebecca Davis (relict) (I&A 4.537)

Beale, Daniel; inv.; [filed with 1703] (I&A 9b.8)

Beale, Thomas; <u>will</u>; 17 Mar 1712/3; 25 May 1713; son John; dau. Eliza. (MCW 3.238) [SMW PC1.191]

Beale, Jane; <u>inv.</u>; 1733; 20 Aug 1733; nok Ann Balay, Will. Morgin (I 17.337); <u>acct.</u>; 26 Aug 1734 (A 12.472)

Bealy, John, Sr.; <u>acct.</u> 5 Jun 1745; Mary, w/o Thomas Greenwell (A 21.361)

Beall, Moses; <u>inv.</u>; 2 & 3 Feb 1775; 2 Aug 1775; nok Basil & Nathaniel Beall; <u>inv.</u>; adm. Roger Beall (I 123.175, 182, 184, 187)

Beal, Josias and Mary Hellen (by license); m. 14 Dec 1780 (SA p. 58)

BEAN

Bean, Rob. [?Ralph]; *Pyney Point*; 1,500 ac.; sur. & pat. 20 Aug 1649; 1707 poss. Hannah Harpam & Tho. Palmer who m. widow Waughop; St. Georges Hundred (RR p. 18) (TLC p. 18)

Bean, John; *Friends in Conjunction*; 250 ac.; sur. 2 Jan 1737 for John Sykes & John Beane (TLC p. 94); 7 Sep 1738 cert./pat. (COL)
Bean's Thoroughfare; 13½ ac.; sur. 14 Sep 1742 (TLC p. 94); 13 ac.; 4 Aug 1743 cert./pat. (COL)

Beenes (Beans), Alexander; <u>inv.</u>; 13 Jun 1742; 6 Jul 1742; nok Thomas & Edward Hilliard Hebb; adm./ex. John Beenes (I 26.58); <u>acct.</u>; 5 Dec 1743; orphans Thomas, John, Robert, Alexander, Frances; admx. Jane, w/o Thomas Jenkins (A 20.57)

Bean, John [Sr.]; <u>will</u>; 26 Mar 1745; 20 May 1745; child. John, Benjamin, Joshua [Jeseaway (?)], Robert, Philip, Elizabeth, Faith; wife Mary; tracts *Friends Congoneon, Beans Thurofare* (MCW 9.28) [SMW TA1.174]; <u>inv.</u>; 20 Aug 1745; 21 Aug 1745; nok Robert & Benjamin Bean; adms./exs. Mary & John Bean (I 31.278, 280); <u>acct.</u>; 29 Aug 1746; mentions child. of William Askens: William and a dau. who m. Joseph Anderson (A 23.5)

Bean, Robert and Margaret; son Bennet [b. 5 Aug 1771] (SA p. 20, 55)

Bean, George and Anne Dillion; m. 14 Oct 1778; son Barton, bapt. 7 May 1780 (SA p. 57, 30)

Bean, John and Ann Henning (by license); m. 26 Jun 1781 (SA p. 59)

BEARD

Beard, Robert; *Beards Choice*; 100 ac.; sur. 23 Sep 1667; 1707 poss. Wm. Meekin [by marrying d/o Beard]; Choptico Hundred (RR p. 38) (TLC p. 37)
Beard's Choice; 50 ac.; sur. 8 Oct 1680; 1707 poss. John Cecill; New Town Hundred (RR p. 37) (TLC p. 49); 8 Dec 1680 cert./pat. (COL)
St. Margaret's Field; 100 ac.; sur. 20 Sep 1667; 1707 poss. Wm. Mitchell; New Town Hundred (RR p. 35) (TLC p. 34)
St. Margaret's Forrest; 100 ac.; sur. 29 Apr 1682; 1707 poss. Wm. Mitchell New Town Hundred (RR p. 39) (TLC p. 38); 29 Apr 1682 cert./pat. (COL)

Beard, Robert; <u>will</u>; 18 Mar 1683; 7 Aug 1685; g-sons William and Robert Meakin; daus. [g-daus.] Margaret & Elizabeth Meakin; bro. Christopher; s-i-l

William Meakin (MCW 1.162) [SMW PC1.54]; <u>inv.</u>; 18 Jul 1685 (I&A 8.312); <u>acct.</u>; 9 Aug 1686 (I&A 9.135) (SMAA p. 88)

Beard, Robert; <u>acct.</u>; 6 Jun 1711; admx. Muriall Beard (I&A 33a.45)

Beard, John; <u>inv.</u>; 4 May 1771; 1 Jun 1771 (I 107.90); <u>dist.</u>; 10 Jan 1773 (BB 6.198)

BEAVIN

Beavin, Hugh; 16 Oct 1661; 23 Nov 1661 (MCW 1.21)

Bevine, William; <u>inv.</u>; 19 Mar 1693 (I&A 12.93)

BELL

Bell, Daniel; *Hopewell*; 200 ac.; sur. 6 May 1686; sold by Bell to Timo. Keen, both dec'd; 1707 no poss.; Poplar Hill Hundred (RR p. 25) (TLC p. 24); 6 May 1686 cert./pat. (COL)

St. Williams; 114 ac.; 10 Nov 1695 cert./pat. (COL)

Bell, Daniel; 11 Jan 1702; 22 Jul 1703; wife Ellinor; child. John & Jane (MCW 3.28) [SMW PC1.131]

Bell [Beall], Adam; <u>will</u>; 21 Nov 1718; 30 Dec 1718; wife Ann; sister Margaret Hackney; cousins Margaret Hunter, Thomas Hunter, John Critchett; nephew Richard (s/o Richard Hopewell, Sr.); tracts *Paradise, St. Richard's Mannor, Hampstead, Scotch-Mans Wonder, Shirley's Point* (MCW 4.209) [SMW PC1.247]; <u>inv.</u>; 26 Jul 1719; 6 Sep 1719; extx. Mrs. Ann Bell (I 3.57); <u>acct.</u>; 19 Mar 1720 (A 2.426); <u>acct.</u>; 19 Mar 1720 (SMAA p. 460); <u>acct.</u>; 17 Sep 1724; extx. Anne, w/o Thomas Aisquith (A 6.133)

Beell [Beall], Jane; <u>will</u>; 20 Apr 1733; 21 May 1733; dau. Mary & sons John, Thomas, William [Bell] (MCW 7.16) [SMW TA1.4]

BELLWOOD

Bellwood, Samuel; *Bellwood's Grove*; 128 ac.; sur. 29 Sep 1742 (TLC p. 108); 27 Mar 1744 cert./pat. (COL)

Bellwood, Samuel, Mr.; <u>inv.</u>; 3 Apr 1751; 27 Apr 1752; nok minors; admx.extx. Frances Bellwood (I 48.447); <u>acct.</u>; 10 Apr 1753; child. see dist. (A 34.162); <u>dist.</u>; 10 Apr 1753; admx. Francis w/o Henry Greenwell; child. Ann [age 12 next 21 Feb], Samuel[age 9 next 28 Apr], William [age 6 next 15 Jun], Henry [age 3 next 25 Apr] (BB 1.79)

BENDIN

Bending (Bendin), Gilbert; <u>will</u>; 4 Sep 1749; 11 Nov 1749; son John; dau. Elizabeth; wife Jane (MCW 10.66) [SMW TA1.222]; <u>inv.</u>; 7 Apr 1750; 23 Apr 1750; admx./extx. Jean Binding (I 42.206); <u>acct.</u>; 29 Oct 1750 (A 29.50)

Benden, John and Monica; dau. Elizabeth [b. 8 Jan 1762] (SA p. 10.44)

BENHAM

Benham, Martin; inv.; 6 Feb 1733; 6 Mar 1733; nok George & Martin Benham; admx./extx. Mary Benham (I 17.648); inv.; 27 Feb 1734; 9 Jun 1735; nok James Morgin, Thomas Banham; adm./ex. Martin Benham (I 20.479)

Benham, Martin; inv.; 24 Mar 1749; 30 Apr 1750; nok minors; admx./extx. Ann Bennam (I 42.207)

BENNETT

Bennett, Thomas; s/o Elizabeth; under age 21; gift of calf; Jan/Feb 1648; [Richard Bennett, husband of Elizabeth] (AM IV.537)

Bennett, Richard; *Poplar Hill*; mother Sarah Taylor, w/o John; dau. Sarah; son Richard; 16 Jan 1651 (AM X.84)

Bennet, Rich'd; *Bennet (Tunnel)*; 200 ac.; sur. 27 May 1651; 1707 poss. Wm. & Rob't Tunnel; resur. into *Bleak Creek*; Poplar Hill Hundred (RR p. 22) (TLC p. 21)

Bennett, Richard; younger; s/o Richard the elder; *Poplar Neck*; mentions sister Mary; 27 Dec 1655 (AM X.447)

Bennett, Richard; age ca 44; 4 Jan 1657 (AM XLI.86)

Bennitt, Thomas; age ca 18; wife Margaret; 1661 (AM XLI.552)

Bennett, Richard W.; d. 4 May 1821; age 50 yrs., 6 mos. (HGM)

BENTON

Benton, Richard; will; probate 27 Dec 1696; wife Sarah; tracts *Wignall's [Wiggwall's] Rest, Dayly's Desire* (MCW 2.132) [SMW PC1.96]; inv.; 15 Jan 1697 (I&A 15.332)

Benton, Sarah; acct.; 16 May 1709 (I&A 29.304) (SMAA p. 189)

BEVERLY

Beverly, George; inv.; 30 Jun 1750; 16 Jul 1750; nok George Beverly, Mary Nowlen; admx./extx. Ann Beverly (I 43.292); acct.; 29 Jul 1754; orphans see dist; omits Eve (A 36.400); dist.; 29 Jul 1754; admx. Ann; child. George, Margaret King, Jane Bohanan, Hannah Prescoat, Mary Nowland, Margery Beverly & Ann Beverly [of full age], William Highett [age 7 next 29 Jul], Rose [age 15 next 25 Jan], Eve [age 15 next 25 Jan], Judith [age 11 next 13 Nov], Adam [age 8 next 18 Jun] (BB 1.114)

Beverley, George and Mary; child. Annastatia [b. 2 Feb 1756], William [b. 14 Feb 1757], Jemima [b. 2 Sep 1763] (SA p. 37, 49, 14)

BIGGS

Biggs, Henry; inv.; 17 Feb 1700 (I&A 20.216)

Biggs, John; will; 4 Jun 1747; 7 Jul 1747; wife Ann (MCW 9.112) [SMW TA1.200]

Biggs, Ann; will; 26 Jul 1754; 7 Aug 1754; g-s John Cole; daus. Sarah Fowler, Elizabeth Goldsmith; son John Biggs (MCW 11.47) [SMW TA1.323]

Biggs, Sarah; inv.; 1 Dec 1758; 3 Apr 1759; nok James Jones, Virlinder Johnson; adm./ex. Jeremiah Biggs (I 66.314)

Biggs, John; inv.; 5 Jun 1769; 20 Jun 1769; mentions Ann Biggs (I 102.185); acct.; 3 Sep 1770; admx. Ann Biggs (A 64.237); dist.; 3 Sep 1770 (BB 5.387)

BILLINGSLY

Billingly, Bowles; inv.; 4 Jun 1744; 5 Jun 1744; nok Samuel & William Billingsley; admx./extx. Rachel Billingsly (I 29.223); acct.; 2 Sep 1746; orphans John, James, Clement, Zachariah, Rachel (A 23.1)

Billingsly, William; will; 11 Aug 1745; 16 Dec 1745; child. Mary Wood, Ann Hardesty, William, James, Margaret, Clare, Francis, Elizabeth [& Si___] (MCW 9.60) [SMW TA1.180]; inv. 28 Apr 1746; 4 Jun 1746; nok Samuel & Mary Billingsle; ex. son William Billingsley (I 33.47); acct.; 6 Oct 1747; mentions Mary & Rachel Billingsly; ex. William Sumner Billingley (A 24.237)

Billingsley, Samuel; inv.; 13 Mar 1749; 4 Sep 1750; nok minors; adm./ex. William Billingsley (I 43.393); acct.; 3 Mar 1752; child. Martha [age 11], Basil [age 9], Walter [age 7] Mary [age 5], Elisabeth Wilmouth; adm. William Billingsley (A 32.104); dist.; 3 Mar 1752 (BB 1.29)

Billingsley, William; inv.; 4 May 1768; 4 Jul 1768; nok Allen Billingsley; admx. Jane Billingsly (I 97.283); acct.; 9 Nov 1768; admx. Jane Billingsley (A 60.189); dist.; 1769 (BB 5.245)

BISCOE

Bisco, John; age ca 49; 1658 (AM XLI.181)

Bisco, John; dec'd; Thomas Doxey (Dorsey) m. relict; 1667/8 (AM LVII.253)

Biscoe, John; acct.; admx. Elenor, w/o Richard Baxter; [filed with 1710/1] (SMAA p. 190, 193); inv.; 27 Sep 1716; nok James Biscoe (I&A 37a.155); 19 Nov 1718 (I 1.464); acct.; [filed with 1718] (A 1.200)

Biscoe, John; acct.; 16 Mar 1720; extx. Ann, w/o Owen Smithson (A 2.433) (SMAA p. 455)

Bissco, Thomas; will; 4 Jun 1733; 6 Aug 1733; sons John, Thomas, Joshua; daus. Sarah, Ann, Annah, Martha; wife Catherine (MCW 7.30) [SMW TA1.43]; inv.; 5 Jul 1733; 19 Nov 1733; nok John & James Bissco; admx./extx. Catherine Bissco (I 17.541); acct.; 13 Sep 1735; extx. Catherine, w/o Joseph Kirke (A 13.318)

Bisco, Joseph; inv.; 29 Oct 1735; 24 Nov 1735; nok James, Sr. & Jonathon Bissco; admx./extx. Catherine Bissco (I 21.206); acct.; 5 Jul 1736; orphans James, Joseph & Sarah Bissco (A 15.87)

Bisco, James; oral; will; probate 22 Nov 1736; son Jonathan (MCW 7.200) [SMW TA1.51]; inv.; 14 Mar 1736; nok Sarah Mackey, Sarah Alason; adm./ex. Jonathon Bissco (I 22.202)

Biscoe, Thomas; *Barren Woods*; 46 ac.; sur. 20 Dec 1732 for Thomas Briscoe (TLC p. 93); 18 Nov 1737 cert./pat. (COL)

Biscoe (Briscoe), John; planter; age ca 44; 21 Apr 1737 (CCR p. 81)

Bisco, Jonathon; acct.; 5 Feb 1738; orphans John, Jonathon, Sarah, Ann, Hannah & Margaret Bisco; admx. Margrett, w/o Isaac Pavett (A 17.68)

Biscoe, John & James; *Titch Combs Freehold*; 344 ac.; resur. 16 Jun 1741 for Wm. & Mary Parish church (TLC p. 104); *Itchcomb's Freehold*, 10 Sep 1744 cert./pat. (COL)

Biscoe, John; *Williams' Fortune*; 182 ac.; 18 Mar 1747 cert./pat. (COL)

Besco (Bessco), Thomas; inv.; 1 Aug 1752; 24 Aug 1752; nok James Keech, John Biscoe; admx./extx. Mary Thomas (I 49.109)

Biscoe, James; inv.; 1 Dec 1768; 17 Jul 1769; nok John, Jr. & Thomas Biscoe (I 102.245)

Biscoe, Ann; will; 21 Nov 1774; 17 Jan 1775; child. Samuel, Littleton, John and Mary Biscoe; sister Mary Biscoe; d-i-l Nancy Biscoe; mentions Bennett Biscoe (MCW 16.90) [SMW TA1.733]; inv.; 21 Mar 1775; 14 Feb 1770 (sic); nok Stephen & Ignatius Biscoe; adm./ex. Barnet Biscoe (I 121.397)

Biscoe, Bazil; inv.; 21 Sep 1761; 25 Mar 1762; mentions James & Bennett Biscoe; admx. Mary Ann Biscoe (I 77.76, 78); acct.; 17 Aug 1763; son [infant] (A 49.531)

Biscoe, Margaret; b. 14 Apr 1764; d. 20 Jul 1835 (HGM)

Biscoe, Thomas; acct.; 1 Sept 1770; admx. Mary, w/o William Langley (A 64.241)

Biscoe, George; will; 20 Jan 1774; 20 Mar 1774; sons Ignatius, George, James, Basil, Bennet, Jonathan, William; daus. Mary, Susannah; tract *Arbestons Oak, Pleasant Springs* [QA Co.] (MCW 15.148) [SMW TA1.698]; inv.; 12 Apr 1774; 3 Aug 1774; nok Jonathon & George Biscoe; ex. Ignatius Biscoe (I 119.127)

Biscoe, John; acct.; 5 Mar 1774; 16 Apr 1774; sons Ignatius, Samuel Coldwell, Littleton, John; daus. Ann, Mary; wife Ann (MCW 15.129); inv.; 21 Jul 1774; 10 Jul 1774; nok Thomas & Stephen Biscoe; extx. Ann Biscoe (I 119.178)

Biscoe, John; inv.; 21 Mar 1775; 16 Feb 1775; adm.ex. Barnett Biscoe (I 121.418)

Biscoe, Jonathon; St. Inigoes Hundred; will; probate 10 Aug 1775; wife Mary; dau. Alanda; mentions Biscoe s/o John Biscoe Smith, Margaret w/o John Smith (MCW 16.110) [SMW TA1.721]; inv.; 30 May 1775; 3 Nov 1775; nok John Smith (I 122.188)

Biscoe, Thomas and Margaret Bennet (by license); m. 27 Nov 1782 (SA p. 60)

Biscoe, Basil and Mary Standworth (by license); m. 9 May 1784 (SA p. 62)

Biscoe, Mary; d. 15 Aug 1800; age 31 (HGM)

Biscoe, Elisabeth; d. 9 Mar 1804; age 71 (HGM)

BLACK

Black, William; 18 Nov 1668; 11 Feb 1668; wife Ann (MCW 1.46)

Black, Albert; service by 1673 (SK 17.535)

Black, James (sic), Dr.; inv.; 5 Feb 1754 (I 58.62)

Black, Samuel (sic), Dr.; <u>acct.</u>; 19 Apr 1754 (A 36.313)

Black, John; <u>will</u>; 31 Dec 1774; 10 Jan 1775; wife unnamed; bro. William; sister Frances; nephew William Black; nieces Frances Taylor [Black], Ann Dent Black (MCW 16.92) [SMW TA1.716]; <u>inv.</u>; 15 Apr 1775; 10 Aug 1775; extx. Susannah Black (I 122.147)

BLACKISTONE

Blackiston, Nehemiah; m. 6 May 1669 Elizabeth, d/o Thomas Gerard, dec'd (AM LXVIII.121)

Blackstone, John; immigrated by 1670 with Sarah, George, Barbary, Robert, Hannah and Justice (SK 16.70)

Blackiston, Nehemiah; wife Elizabeth; 300 a. called *Langworth Pointe* and *Thomas Donnes Neck* on 6 Jun 1672 to John Shanks (AM LXV.180, 490)

Blackiston, William; service by 1674 (SK 18.150)

Blackiston, Nehemiah; immigrated by 1674 (SK 18.126)

Blakistone, Nehemiah, Col., Esq.; <u>acct.</u>; 18 May 1696; admx. Elisabeth Blakistone (I&A 13b.62) (I&A 15.35); <u>acct.</u>; 14 Oct 1696 (I&A 15.37); <u>acct.</u>; 21 Mar 1698 (I&A 18.81); <u>inv.</u>; 11 May 1699 (I&A 18.152, 153, 164, 254); <u>acct.</u>; 20 Jun 1699; admx. Elisabeth, w/o Ralph Rymer (I&A 19.159)

Blackiston, John, Mr.; <u>inv.</u>; 18 Jan 1724; 5 Feb 1724; nok Roswell Neale, Robert Mason; extx. Ann Blackiston (I 10.292); <u>acct.</u>; 3 Aug 1726 (A 7.510); <u>acct.</u>; 2 Aug 1727 (A 8.292)

Blackistone, Thomas; <u>will</u>; 10 Nov 1742; 8 Dec 1742; bro. John; bro. Robert Mason & his 3 child. Mate [Matt], Nehemiah, Rodolph; mentions Dorcus Mason; bro. Roswell Neal & his sons James, Bennett, Raphael; sister Elizabeth Neale (MCW 8.195) [SMW TA1.121]; <u>inv.</u>; 8 Jun 1743; nok Roswell Neale, Robert Mason; adm./ex. John Blackiston (I 28.6); <u>acct.</u>; 20 Apr 1744 (A 20.233)

Blackiston, John; memorandum; <u>will</u>; probate 18 Jan 1756; wife Elener; sons John, Nehemiah Harbert, George; sister Susannah Mason (MCW 11.123) [SMW TA1.352]; <u>inv.</u>; 18 Mar 1756; 3 Jun 1756; nok John & Matthew Mason; admx.extx. Eleanor Blakiston (I 61.318); <u>acct.</u>; 4 Jul 1758; orphans Nicholas Herbert [age 8], George [age 6], John [age 3] (A 41.486); <u>dist.</u>; 4 Jul 1758; mentions Nehemiah Herbert, George, Joseph, John (BB 2.108)

Blackiston, Nehemiah Hubert, s/o John and Eleanor Blackiston, m. Mary Cheseldine, d/o Kenelm and Chloe Cheseldine on 30 Jan 1772 (AFP 2.349)

Blackiston, Nehemiah and Mary; child.: Thomas [b. 10 Apr 1773], Kenelm [b. 24 Dec 1776], Mary [b. 6 Dec 1778], George [b. 6 Dec 1778] (AFP 2.349)

Blackstone [Blackiston], George; <u>will</u>; 13 Jan 1774; 30 Apr 1774; mother unnamed [Bayard]; bros. John, Herbert (MCW 15.151) [SMW TA1.695]

BLACKMAN
Blackman, William; will; written 31 Mar 1712; wife Cisly [Sisely] (MCW 3.227) [SMW PC1.182]; inv.; 9 Jun 1712 (I&A 33b.14, 209); extx. Cecila; 3 Jun 1713 (SMAA p. 252); acct.; 3 Jun 1713 (I&A 34.172)
Blackman, Cecill (Caecily, Cecilly); inv.; 30 Nov 1715 (I&A 36c.215); acct.; 3 Jul 1716 (I&A 37c.155) (SMAA p. 305)
Blackman, Thomas; inv.; 23 Jan 1738; 8 Mar 1738; nok minors; admx.,/extx. Ann Blackman (I (I 24.51); acct.; 14 Jun 1740; orphans Thomas, William & Mary Blackman; admx. Ann Blackman (A 17.528)
Blackman, Thomas; inv.; 1 Dec 1747; 22 Feb 1747; nok Ann Blackman, John Brewer; admx./extx. Elisabeth Blackman (I 35.465)

BLOOMFIELD
Blomfield, John; immigrated by 1669 (SK 12.308)
Blomfield, John; m. Elizabeth Barbier, admx. of Luke Barbier; 1669 (AM LI.334)
Blomfield, John; acct.; 28 Jul 1694 (I&A 13a.192)
Bloomfeild, Jafield; acct.; 9 Feb 1729; admx. Ann, w/o Robert Hagar (A 10.183)
Bloomfield, James; *Crooked Billet*; 38 ac.; sur. 27 Oct 1725 (TLC p. 91); 8 May 1736 cert./pat. (COL)
Bloomfield, James and Mary; both age ca 60 in 1738 (MD p. 15)
Blumfield, James; will; 15 Jan 1744; 5 Mar 1744/5; s-i-l Matthew Daft; tract *Crucked Billt* (MCW 9.16) [SMW TA1.184]

BOAGE
Boage, John; *Gradon*; 200 ac.; sur. 21 Jun 1657; assgn. & pat. John Sewall & Andew Robinson; 1707 poss. John Hall & Wm. Stone (RR p. 58) (TLC p. 55)
Fawkskirk; 500 ac.; sur. 16 May 1663; pat. 16 May 1663; 1707 poss. by Vestry of All Faith Parish & Raphael Haywood; Resurrection Hundred (RR p. 59) (TLC p. 56)
Parting Path; 300 ac.; sur. 1 Sep 1665; 1707 poss. Robert Strutton; Resurrection Hundred (RR p. 59) (TLC p. 57)

BOARMAN
Boreman, William; age ca 20; 28 May 1650 (AM X.12); age ca 22 in 1650 (MD p. 17)
Boarman, Wm.; *Hunting Quarter*; 150 ac.; sur. 5 Mar 1664 (RR p. 4); 1707 poss. Rich. Richardson; St. Mary's Hundred; sur. for Thos. Courtney (TLC p. 5)
Boarman, William, Maj.; *Boarman's Reserve*; 588 ac.; 2 Nov 1685 cert./pat. (COL)
Wardle; 780 ac.; 5 Jul 1686 cert./pat. (COL)
Hard Shift; 115 ac.; 10 Mar 1696 cert./pat. (COL)
St. Dorothy's; 263 ac.; resur. 25 Jun 1714 for William Borman, Jr. & wife Monica (TLC p. 70); 10 Apr 1715 cert./pat. (COL)

Boarman, Francis and Batris; child. John [b. 8 Oct 1758], Francis Ignatius [b. 14 Mar 1762], Sarah [b. 1 Mar 1764] (SA p. 9, 43)

Boarman, Francis; will; 12 May 1773; 1 Jul 1773; child. John, Francis Ignatius, Sarah (MCW 15.71) [SMW TA1.674]; inv.; 10 Jun 1773; 10 Jun 1774; nok Timothy Bowes, Bennet Riley, Richard Boarman (I 119.106)

BODKIN

Bodkin, James; gent.; *Charlesborough Swamp*; 326 ac.; 2 Jul 1683 cert./pat. (COL) *Wardner's Desire*; 50 ac.; [29 Mar 1683]

Bodkin, James; gent.; age ca 20 in 1684 (MD p. 15)

Bodkin, James; the younger; acct.; 7 Mar 1686; admx. w/o Robert Carvele (I&A 9.219)

BOND

Bond, Zachary (Zachariah); inv.; 3 Nov 1716; nok Thomas Sikes, Thomas Bond, Elisabeth Tennison (I&A 38b.120); acct.; 28 Jun 1718; admx. Ann, w/o George Hoskins (A 1.40) (SMAA p. 336)

Bond, Thomas; inv.; 15 Jun 1740; 18 Aug 1740; nok John & Zachariah Bond; admx./extx. Catherine Bond (I 25.195); acct.; 23 Jul 1741; orphans Zachary, Jeremiah, Thomas, Ann, Mary, Dryden (A 18.278)

Bond, William; acct.; 15 Jul 1745; extx. Elisabeth, w/o William Daft (A 21.369)

Bond, Thomas; *Strife*; 7 ac.; 17 May 1758 cert./pat. (COL)

Bond, Peregrine; inv.; 8 Mar 1759; 28 Aug 1759; nok John, Jr. & Gerrard Bond; adm./ex. Capt. John Bond (I 67.332)

Bond, John; will; 13 Jan 1760; 27 Feb 1760; wife Elizabeth; sons John, Thomas, Gerrard, Samuel, William, Richard; daus. Elizabeth, Susanna, Mary; bro. Zachariah; tracts *Moseley, Attoway's Purchase, Burlington, St. Johns, Maidens Bower, Hopton Park, Coods Island, Gardners Purchase, Denbish* (MCW 11.260) [SMW TA1.387]; inv.; [Capt.]; 6 Aug 1760; nok William & Zachariah Bond; adm./ex. Thomas & Zachariah Bond (I 70.58, 65); acct.; 17 Aug 1763 (A 49.532)

Bond, William; inv.; 2 Jun 1765; nok Zachariah & Thomas Bond; adms. Zachariah & Zephaniah Bond (I 84.275)

Bond, Zachariah; *Bond's Rest*; 1,011 ac.; 18 Apr 1768 cert./pat. (COL)

Bond, Thomas; *Cambridge*; 96 ac.; 24 May 1776 cert./pat. (COL)
Flower of the Forest; 39 ac.; 24 May 1776 cert./pat. (COL)

Bond, Richard, s/o John & Elizabeth Bond, m. 18 Jul 1773 Susanna Gardiner Key, d/o Dr. John and Cecilia Key (AFP 2.349)

Bond, Richard and Susanna; child. John Key [b. 14 May 1774], Ann [b. 13 May 1775], Cecilia Brown [b. 17 Mar 1778], Elizabeth Allaway [b. 17 Jun 1779], Susanna Key [b. 2 Mar 1781] (AFP 2.349, 350)

Bond, Zechariah; will; 14 Mar 1775; 1 Feb 1775; s-i-l Henry Greenfield
  Sothoron; wife Margaret; g-daus. Mary Sothoron, Clarissa Bond, Harriet
  Claggett, Rebecca Jowles Sothoron; neph. Thomas Bond, his son Thomas &
  his son Jeremiah; Matthew and Absalom Tennison, sons of my sister; William
  Bond, s/o Zachariah; John Hesletin, s/o Charles; tracts *Middle Quarter,
  Chaptico, Upper Mills, Calverts Manor, Indian Town, Bonds Rest, Saint
  John's, Manor Land, Tillency* [*Tilloney*] (MCW 16.139) [SMW TA1.741]
Bond, Thomas; *Wee Bit*; 7 ac.; 24 May 1776 cert./pat. (COL)
Bond, William; m. 28 Feb 1777 Mary Nevison (MM)
Bond, Richard and Susanna G.; child.: Matilda [b. 7 Jul 1784], Samuel [b. 16
  Oct 1778], Clarissa [b. 2 Jun 1790], William [b. 2 Oct 1792] (AFP 2.350)

BOOTH
Booth, John; transported by 1671; service by 1671 (SK16.135)
Booth, John; acct; 14 Nov 1677 (I&A 4.531)
Booth, Isack (Isaac); inv.; [filed with 1722]; nok Abraham & Isaac Booth (I
  8.102); acct.; 5 Jan 1723; admx. Frances, w/o Robert Hutchins (A 5.342)
Booth, John; will; 18 Feb 1729; 5 Mar 1729/30; son Basil; wife Mary (MCW
  6.147) [SMW PC1.325]; inv.; 19 May 1730; 16 Sep 1730; nok Thomas Atterbury,
  Elisabeth Brome; admx./extx. Mary Booth (I 15.660); acct.; 14 Aug 1731;
  mentions orphan Basell Booth (A 11.222)
Booth (Bouth), Jacob.; will; 7 Feb 1731/2; 2 Mar 1731; bro. Abraham; sister
  Ann (MCW 6.210) [SMW PC1.350]; inv.; 10 Mar 1731; 3 Jun 1732; nok Abram
  Buth, Isaac Boouth; admx./extx. Ann Booth (I 16.442); acct.; 29 Jan 1732 (A
  11.581)
Booth, Bazil (Basil); will; 16 Nov 1750; 5 Dec 1750; nephews John and James
  Keachen; niece Mary Henwood [Kewood] (MCW 10.124) [SMW TA1.243]; inv.; 5
  Dec 1750; 6 Feb 1753; nok James Keech, Stephen Cawood (I 52.84); acct.; 6
  Feb 1753 (A 33.316); dist.; 6 Feb 1753 (BB 1.61)
Booth, Thomas and Mary; child. Ignatius [b. 4 Nov 1754], Rebecca [b. 4 Jun
  1756], Leonard [b. 5 Mar 1758], Mary [b. 7 Sep 1760], Eleanor [b. 17 Jun
  1761], Sarah [b. 20 Jun 1763], George [b. 11 Jul 1765], Justinian [b. 12 Nov
  1767] (SA p. 12, 46)
Booth, Elizabeth; will; 3 Jan 1756; 3 Feb 1756; daus. Elizabeth Wooten, Mary
  Booth, Monica Boalds (MCW 11.122) [SMW TA1.351]

Booth, John and Mary; child. Elizabeth [b. 14 Mar 1762], Jane [b. 14 Aug
    1763], Rodolph [b. 30 Nov 1765], John Baptist [b. 10 Mar 1768], Ann [b. 10
    Feb 1770] (SA p. 15, 50, 192)
Booth, George, Sr.; will; 22 Oct 1762; 14 Sep 1767; dau. Elizabeth, w/o William
    Bradburne; sons George, John, Thomas, Richard, James, Basil; wife Monica
    (MCW 14.19) [SMW TA1.504]; inv.; 7 Oct 1767; 1 Nov 1767; extx. Monica Booth
    (I 94.199); acct.; 25 Oct 1768 (A 60.196); dist.; 25 Oct 1768; child. George, John,
    Thomas, Richard, James, Basil, dau. unnamed (BB 5.177)
Booth, John; *Long Level*; 34 ac.; 18 Apr 1768 cert./pat. (COL)

BOROUGH
Borough (Boroughs), Joseph; inv.; 14 Mar 1763, 6 Feb 1764; nok John &
    Stourton Edwards; admx. Elisabeth Boroughs (I 83.88)
Borough, Ann; transported by 1674 by Joseph (SK 18.89)

BOULD
Bould (Bald), John, Mr.; inv.; 3 Mar 1735; nok William & Elisabeth Bould;
    admx./extx. Elenor Bould (I 21.237); acct.; 11 Jul 1737; orphans John, James,
    Elisabeth, Mary, Winifred, Elenor & Mary Ann Bould; admx. Elinor, w/o
    John Medley Thompson (A 14.301)
Bold, William; planter; will; 28 Sep 1743; 3 Nov 1743; sons John, James; wife
    Elizabeth; tracts *Curry Glass, Rocky Part, Swamp* (MCW 8.241) [SMW TA1.137]
Bould, John and Monica; child. William [b. 7 Jan 1752], Susanna [b. 1 Oct
    1753], Jane [b. 25 Mar 1757], Henrietta [b. 15 Sep 1760], John Baptist [b. 15
    Nov 1762], Mary [b. 30 Jun 1767], Catharine [b. 20 Oct 1769] (SA p. 193, 194)
Bould, John; will; probate 9 Nov 1752; sons Ignatius, William, John; wife
    Susanna (MCW 10.237) [SMW TA1.290]; inv.; 9 Nov 1752; 8 Mar 1753; nok Mary
    & Elisabeth Cissell; admx./extx. Susannah Bould (I 53.42); acct.; 5 Dec 1753 (A
    36.24); acct.; 2 Dec 1754; extx. Susannah, w/o William Madcalf (A 36.514)
Bould, William and Mary; daus. Elizabeth [b. 9 Mar 1776], Mary Ann [b. 1 Jun
    1778] (SA p. 27, 29)

BOULT
Boult, Thomas [planter]; will; 13 Jun 1745; 8 Aug 1745; wife Elizabeth; child.
    John, Thomas, Anne, Kenelin, Susanna Hobb [Hebb], Ann; g-child. Joshua
    Watts, Kenelen Boult Watts, Elizabeth [d/o Thomas Boult] (MCW 9.44) [SMW
    TA1.167]; inv.; 24 Sep 1745; 27 Jan 1745; nok John & Thomas Boult;
    adms./exs. Kenelm & Ann Boult (I 32.2); acct.; 22 Dec 1746 (A 23.132)
Boult, Elisabeth; inv.; 29 Dec 1761; 3 Mar 1762; nok Zechariah & Jeremiah
    Bond (I 77.78)
Boult, Kenolm (Kenelm); oral; will; 7 Nov 1757; child. Thomas, Susanah,
    Mary, Sarah [& Elizabeth]; wife Ann (MCW 11.191) [SMW TA1.362]; inv.; 20 Feb
    1758; 14 May 1758; nok Edward Hillard Hebb, Thomas Watts; admx./extx.

Ann Boult (I 65.419); <u>acct.</u>; 28 Jul 1759; orphans Elisabeth [age 15], Susannah [age 10], Mary [age 8], Thomas [age 6], Sarah [age 4]; extx. Ann, w/o John Tarlton (Tarltow) (A 43.272); <u>dist.</u>; 1 Sep 1761; unnamed child. (BB 3.77)

Boult, Susannah, Miss; <u>inv.</u>; 6 Aug 1768; 12 Aug 1768; nok Stephen Tarlton, Mary Morris; adms. Mary Boult, John, s/o James Tarlton (I 97.285), <u>acct.</u>; 16 Oct 1768 (A 62.19), <u>dist.</u>; 16 Sep 1769; admx. Mrs. Mary Boult, John, s/o James Parlton (BB 5.237)

BOWLES

Bowles, James, Esq.; *Abington's Square*; 300 ac.; 18 Jun 1702 cert./pat. (COL)
　　Charles's Bounty; 1,000 ac.; 10 Apr 1706 cert./pat. (COL)
　　Double Gore; 37 ac.; 3 Mar 1713 cert./pat. (COL)
　　Bowles Preservation; 890 ac.; resur. 29 Dec 1716 (TLC p. 73)
　　Bowles' Separation; 890 ac.; 18 Jan 1717 cert./pat. (COL)

Bowles, John; *Venture*; 50 ac.; sur. 5 Apr 1711 (TLC p. 67); 2 Sep 1713 cert./pat. (COL)

Bowles, James; merchant; <u>will</u>; 13 Jun 1727; 3 Jan 1727; daus. Elimor, Mary, Jane [Jean]; wife Rebecca; uncle George; tracts *Half Pone, Hogg Neck, Mason's* (MCW 6.48) [SMW PC1.314]; <u>inv.</u>; 8 Feb 1727; 4 Apr 1728; nok George Bowles; extx. Madam Rebecka Bowles (I 13.79); <u>acct.</u>; 31 Oct 1734; extx. Rebecca, w/o George Plater, Esq. (A 12.518)

Bowles, James; s/o Tobias; 18 Aug 1730 (CCR p. 67)

Bowles, James, Esq.; <u>acct.</u>; 6 Jul 1730; relations in England; extx. Thomas Truman Greenfield & wife Ann (A 10.320)

Bowles, John; <u>will</u>; 27 Mar 1750; 4 Jun 1752; s/o Valentine Bowles, Town of Deal, KE Co., Gent.; bro. George; tracts *John Long's, Quakers Lately* in KE Co. (MCW 10.224) [SMW TA1.298]

Bowles, George; <u>will</u>; 29 Feb 1760; 6 May 1761; wife Lillian (MCW 12.76) [SMW TA1.416]

Bowls (Bowld), Lillias (Lilias); <u>will</u>; 15 Jul 1772; 11 Jan 1773; bro. & 3 sisters in Scotland: John, Jane, Grace & Elizabeth Watson (MCW 15.31) [SMW TA1.666]; <u>acct.</u>; 1775 (A 73.236); <u>dist.</u>; 1775; [Silas] (BB 7.44)

Bowles, John; m. 11 Jan 1776 Elizabeth Payn (MM)

Bowles, Ignatius; m. 21 Jan 1777 Catherine Gough (MM)

BOWLING

Bowling, James; *Bowlings Reserve*; 100 ac.; sur. 22 Sep 1668; 1707 poss. Thos. Clark; Choptico Hundred (RR p. 51) (TLC p. 49)

Bowling, James; <u>will</u>; 7 May 1692; 10 Oct 1693; bro. Thomas; cous. Bowling Speake; wife Mary; f-i-l Henry Darnall; nephews John & Roger, sons of bro. Thomas Bowling; cous. Millicent Higden; tracts *Keet's Rest, Miller's Choice, Chesam, Charles, Bowling's Plains, Calvert's Hope* (MCW 2.68) [SMW PC1.84]; <u>inv.</u>; [Capt.]; 26 Jul 1694 (I&A 13a.176)

Bowling, John; <u>will</u>; 30 Apr 1711; 9 Jun 1711; sons William, John, Thomas; wife Mary; dau. Mary; tracts *High Park, Charley, Charley's Addition, Chessam, The Widow's Mite* (MCW 3.208)

Bowling, John; <u>inv.</u>; 20 Dec 1723; 3 Jul 1723 (I 8.314)

Bowling, Edmond; <u>will</u>; 1 Mar 1756; 22 Apr 1756; unnamed wife [Luce]; child. John, William, Elizabeth, w/o Matthew Gibson; tract *Collinwood* (MCW 11.128) [SMW TA1.340]; <u>inv.</u>; 3 May 1756; 4 Aug 1756; nok Matthew Gibson, William Tippett; adm./ex. John Bowling (I 61.331); <u>acct.</u>; 5 Apr 1757; orphans Elisabeth Gibson, John, Susannah Tippett [all of age], William [age 12] (A 41.29); <u>dist.</u>; 5 Apr 1757; widow Elisabeth Gibson, John & William Bowling, Susannah Tippett (BB 2.58)

Bowling, John; planter; <u>will</u>; probate 7 Jun 1758; wife Susannah; mother unnamed; son Edmond [Edward]; father Edmond ,dec'd; mentions unnamed child. and dau. Mary (MCW 11.207) [SMW TA1.366]; <u>inv.</u>; 24 Jun 1758; 6 Feb 1759; nok William Tippeth, Mathew Gibson (I 66.222)

Bawling, John; <u>acct.</u>; 20 Mar 1759; extx Susannah, w/o Notley Maddox (A 43.104)

Bowling, John; <u>acct.</u>; 3 May 1763; exs. John Cartwright & wife Susanna; Notley Maddox & wife Susanna (A 49.620)

BOYD

Boyd, Adam; planter; age ca 45; 3 Jan 1723 (CCR p. 57)

Boyd, James; *Boyds Chance*; 81 ac.; sur. 24 Aug 1726; assign. Robert Elliott (TLC p. 89)

Boyd, George; <u>inv.</u>; 3 Dec 1745; 4 Mar 1745; nok Philip Boyd; adm./ex Margaret Boyd (I 32.89); <u>acct.</u>; 6 Oct 1746 (A 23.11)

BRADBURN

Bradburn, William; <u>will</u>; 31 Oct 1745; 7 Nov 1745; child. John, Henrietta, Priscilla, Appolonia, Monica Redman, wife Anne; s-i-l Francis Spinke; [g-sons Mark, John, William and Bennet Bradburn; s-i-l William Yates and wife Mary; tract *Hattfield Hills*] (MCW 9.53) [SMW TA1.175]; <u>inv.</u>; 6 Nov 1745; 4 Mar 1745; nok John Bradburn, Henrita Wimsett (I 32.78); <u>acct.</u>; 22 Jun 1747 (A 23.317)

Bradburn, Mark and Susanna; child. John Baptist [b. 27 Sep 1757]; Elizabeth [b. 27 Oct 1759] (SA p. 15, 50)

Bradburn, Benjamin and wife Ann; child. Mary [b. 4 Jun 1765], Matthew [b. 10 Feb 1767], Anastatia [b. 16 Oct 1768], Sarah [b. 25 May 1772] (SA p. 2, 21)

Bradburn, Notley and Eleanor; dau. Catherine [b. 14 Mar 1772] (SA p. 21)

Bradburn, James and Margaret; dau. Mary Ann [b. 15 May 1772] (SA p. 21)

BRADY

Bradey, William; service by 1678 (SK 15.523)

Breadey (Bredey), Owen; <u>will</u>; probate 19 Jan 1716; [wife Elizabeth]; sons Owen, Pott, Charles; dau. Liza. Malohan [Elizabeth W__ham]; mentions William Malohan (MCW 4.84) [SMW PC1.201]; <u>inv.</u>; 27 Jan 1716; nok sons Charles & Owen Brady (I&A 38b.176); <u>acct.</u>; 18 Jun 1718 (A 1.31) (SMAA p. 337); 3 Jun 1719; extx. Elisabeth Bradey (A 2.217) (SMAA p. 308)

Brady (Bradey), Elizabeth; <u>will</u>; 17 Mar 1720; 7 Jun 1721; sons Patrick, Charles, Owen; dau. Elizabeth Mulahone (MCW 5.56) [SMAA PC#1.252]; <u>inv.</u>; 21 Aug 1721; nok Charles & Patrick Bradey; ex. Owen Brady (I 6.127); <u>acct.</u>; 2 May 1722 (A 4.161)

Brady, John; 25 ac.; *Brady's Lot*; 25 ac.; sur. 9 May 1744 (TLC p. 106); 11 Jun 1744 cert./pat. (COL)

Braydy (Brady), John; <u>inv.</u>; 21 Apr 1757; 9 Jun 1757; nok John Herbert, Jr.; George Wearring; admx./extx. Rebecca Brady (I 63.395); <u>acct.</u>; 7 Jun 1758; orphans Mary [of age], Ann [age 15], Elinor [age 10], Sarah [age 7], Lydia [age 4], Rebecca [age 2]; admx. Rebecca Brady (A 41.493); <u>dist.</u>; 7 Jun 1758; mentions Mary, Elianor, Susannah, Sarah, Lydia & Rebecca Brady; admx. Rebecca Brady (BB 2.90)

Brawdy, John; m. 8 Apr 1778 Elizab. Davis (BRU 2.535)

BRANSON

Branson, Thomas; <u>acct.</u>; 8 Jul 1686; admx./extx. Amy, w/o Joseph Peetrs (I&A 9.52)

Branson, Benjamin; *Branson's Meadow*; 133 ac.; 2 Aug 1759 cert./pat. (COL)

Branson, John, Sr.; <u>will</u>; 11 Jan 1770; 18 Feb 1770; child. Michl., Luke, Leonard, Elizabeth Wood, Abraham, John, Benjamin, Vincent, James (MCW 14.132) [SMW TA1.604]

Branson, John; <u>will</u>; 18 Jul 1769; 21 Sep 1775; daus. Elizabeth Scrogin [Jurefin (?)], Jane; sons Jonathan, Leonard, [& John]; tract *Bransons Fitgur* (MCW 16.110) [SMW TA1.721]

BREEDEN

Breeding, Edward; <u>inv.</u>; 22 May 1727; 24 Jul 1727; nok minors; admx. Mary Breeding (I 12.141); <u>acct.</u>; 30 Apr 1728; admx. Mary, w/o Thomas Watt (A 9.166)

Breaton (Breeton, Breden, Breeden), Thomas; <u>inv.</u>; 31 Mar 1757; 20 Jun 1757; nok James & Mathew Breedon; adms./exs. Elisabeth Breedon, Joseph Breaton (I 63.399, 403); <u>acct.</u>; 20 Nov 1758; orphans Joseph, Enoch, Matthias [all at age] (A 42.214); <u>dist.</u>; 20 Nov 1758 (BB 2.100)

Breeden, Enoch and Elizabeth; child. Robert Hammett [b. 12 Nov 1762], Sarah [b. 4 Mar 1765], Elizabeth [b. 9 Mar 1768] (SA p. 14, 41, 49)

Breeden, James and Sarah; son Aaron [b. 12 Oct 1766] (SA p. 6)

Breeden, James; <u>will</u>; 30 Sep 1766; 31 Oct 1766; wife Sary; unborn child (MCW 13.136) [SMW TA1.489]; <u>inv.</u>; 27 Dec 1766; extx. Sarah Breeden (I 91.328)

Breedin, Mark and Darkas Baker (by license); m. 15 Sep 1784 (SA p. 62)

Breedin, Robert Hammett and Ann Nuthall (by license); m. 29 Sep 1782 (SA p. 60)

BRENT

Brent, Giles; *The White House*; sur. 9 Oct 1639 for 63 ac.; poss. 1704 & 1707 by William Guyther; St. Mary's Hundred (RR p. 1) (TLC p. 1)

Brent, Margaret & Mary; *The Sisters Freehold)*; 70½ ac.; sur. 7 Oct 1639; sold 26 Nov 1681 to Daniel Clocker; resur. 50 ac. called *St. Andrew's Freehold;* 1707 poss. Daniel Clocker; St. Mary's Hundred (RR p. 1) (TLC p. 1)

Brent, Margaret; age ca 60; 8 Apr 1661 (AM XLI.454)

Brent, Henry; wife Ann (extx. of Baker Brooke); 168! (AM LXX.113, 156)

Brent, Henry, Mr.; acct.; 31 Oct 1709; admx. Ann, w/o Mr. Richard Marsham (I&A 30.221); acct.; 31 Oct 1709; admx. Ann, w/o Richard Marsham (SMAA p. 172)

BRETTON

Bretton, William; wife Mary Nabbs; d/o Thomas Nabbs and wife; arrived in MD 12 Jan 1637 with 4 year old William, s/o William and Mary; dau. Mary b. MD; m/2 1651 Mrs. Temperance Jay (JM p. 37)

Bretton, Wm.; *Little Brittain*; 750 ac.; sur. 29 Jun 1646; 1707 poss. Mr. William Hunter; New Town Hundred (RR p. 26) (TLC p. 24))

Bretton, William; wife Temperance; Newtown; gave land for a Catholic Church 10 Nov 1661 (JM p.34)

BREWER

Brewer, William; inv.; 29 Mar 1701 (I&A 20.120); acct.; 8 Dec [filed with 1701-2] (I&A 23.164)

Brewer, ____; 8 Dec 1701 (SMAA p. 106)

Brewer, Geo.; *Prattlewell*; 100 ac.; sur. 22 May 1667; 1707 poss. Geo. Brewer, Jr.; Choptico Hundred (RR p. 51) (TLC p. 49)

Brewer, William; sold *Batchelor's Rest* to Richard Kewellirin by 29 Jun 1730 (CCR p. 64)

Brewer, George; inv.; 5 Feb 1733; 6 Jun 1734; nok Thomas Blackman, John Brewer; admx./extx. Christian Brewer (I 18.327)

Brewer, Richard; planter; will; 16 Feb 1752; 5 Mar 1752; child. Mark, Susanna, Richard, William, Mary, Mary Ann, Thomas, John Baptist, Margrett (MCW 10.201) [SMW TA1.285]; inv.; 7 Jul 1752; nok John Mattingly; Richard Lake; admx./extx. Susannah Brewer (I 49.99); acct.; 19 Apr 1754 (A 36.320)

Brewer, Thomas; m. 27 Sep 1773 Minta Dawsey (MM)

BRIAN

Brian, John; acct.; 22 Aug 1722 (A 4.254)

34   *Colonial Settlers of St. Mary's County, Maryland*

Brian, Willliam; will; 21 Sep 1734; 7 Aug 1739; sons Henry, William, Ignatius,
   John; daus. Henerita, Elener, Mary, Elizabeth; tracts *Williams Indeavor,*
   Locust Thicket, Black Oke Levill (MCW 8.43) [SMW TA1.80]

BRIGHT
Bright, John; service by 1678 (SK 15.524)
Bright, John, Sr.; will; 22 Jan 1705/6; 27 Jul 1710; sons William, James, John,
   Benjamin; wife Isabella; [tract *Beaver Dam Manor*] (MCW 3.177) [SMW PC1.168];
   acct.; 25 Oct 1711 (I&A 33a.45); exs. John and Benjamin (SMAA p. 223)
Bright, William; inv.; 27 Mar 1712; nok Benjamin & James Bright (I&A 33b.12,
   212); acct.; 5 Aug 1713; admx. Mary [w/o Thomas Cooper] (I&A 35b.95) (SMAA
   p. 241)

BRIMMER
Brimar, James; *Weems*; 424 ac.; 16 Sep 1687 cert./pat. (COL)
Brimmer, Elisabeth; inv.; d/o James Brimmer; 6 Jun 1698 (I&A 16.190)
Brimmer, James; inv.; 27 Oct 1688 (I&A 10.144)

BRISCOE
Brisco, John; St. Michael's Hundred; will; 9 May 1718; 11 Nov 1718; sons
   Thomas, John, James; daus. Mary, Anna; wife Ann; tract *Underwood's*
   Choice (MCW 4.188) [SMW PC1.241]
Briscoe, Philip, Maj.; age ca 72; 2 Dec 1719; tract *Luckland* (CCR p. 40)
Briscoe, George; inv.; 9 Mar 1720; 6 Jun 1721; nok Phill & Susannah Briscoe;
   admx. Mary Briscoe (I 5.70); acct.; 5 Jul 1726; admx. Mary, w/o William
   Tippolls of CA Co. (A 7.406)
Brisco, Jonathon; inv.; 12 Mar 1737; 19 Jun 1738; nok Sarah Mackey, Sarah
   Ellson; admx./extx. Margaret Brisco (I 23.205)
Briscoe, Philip, Mr.; inv.; Nov 1743; 6 Feb 1743; nok Richard Wanright, Philip
   Briscoe; admx.extx. Elisabeth Briscoe (I 28.518); acct.; [filed with 1745];
   orphans John, Philip, Edward, James, Walter, George Cole, Elisabeth & Sarah
   Briscoe (A 21.446)
Briscoe, Philip; *Briscoe's Purchase*; 265 ac.; 20 May 1768 cert./pat. (COL)
   Briscoe's Range; 711 ac.; 19 Apr 1768 cert./pat. (COL)
   Harrow Hills; 1,043 ac.;14 Dec 1768 cert./pat. (COL)
Briscoe, Thomas; dist.; 10 Sep 1770; admx. Mary, w/o Mr. William Langley (BB
   5.387)

BROME
Broom, William; inv.; 4 Feb 1684 (I&A 8.227)
Brome (Broom, Broome), Thomas; will; 4 Jan 1761; 5 Jun 1761; wife Dorcas;
   child., Sarah, Mary, Elizabeth, Thomas, John Hooper, Nancy; sons-i-l John
   Hooper, Mathew Travers; tracts *Young's Alliant, Hope Range, Hop at a*

Venture, all in CA Co.; son John Hodges (?) Brome? (MCW 12.75); inv.; 10 Sep 1761; 2 Nov 176_; nok Mary & John Hooper Brome; extx. Dorcas Brome (I 76.312); dist.; 3 Feb 1764; child. Sarah, Mary, Elisabeth, Thomas, Hooper, Nancy; extx. Dorcas Broome (BB 4.28)

Broome [Brown], Thomas; will; 11 Jan 1772; 8 May 1772; bro. John Hooper Brome; mother Dorcas (MCW 14.237) [SMW TA1.637]

Broom, John Hooper; *Adam's Disturbance*; 33 ac.; 9 Aug 1775 cert./pat. (COL)

BROOKBANK

Brookbank (Brookesbank), Abraham; inv.; [filed with 1717-8] (I 1.311); acct.; 18 Nov 1718; admx. Ann Brookbank (A 1.318) (SMAA p. 326); acct.; 5 Aug 1719 (A 2.306) (SMAA p. 382)

Brookbank, Abraham; inv.; 18 Dec 1749; 1 May 1750; nok Juday Brookbank, Joseph Elles; admx./extx. Jean Brookbank (I 42.217); acct.; 3 Sep 1751; James [age 13], John [age 9], Thomas [age 7], Cloe [age 4]; adms. John Weaklin & wife Jean (A 31.63); dist.; 3 Sep 1751 (BB 1.4)

Brookbank, James; *Ward's Defence*; 212 ac.; 5 Aug 1771 cert./pat. (COL)

BROOKE

Brooks, Fran.; *Boulton's (Boltons) Freehold*; 200 ac.; sur. 15 Apr 1651; 1707 resur. as *Drapers Neck*; St. Mary's Hundred (RR p. 2) (TLC p. 3)
    Brooke; 150 ac.; sur. 29 Jan 1655; 1707 poss. Wm. Morgan; St. Inigoes Hundred (RR p. 15) (TLC p. 15)

Brooks, Anne; w/o Francis Brooks; will; 19 Oct 1653; 15 Feb 1653; son Francis (MCW 1.8)

Brooke, Ignatius, b. ca 1660/1; d. 10 Mar 1751 St. Omer in Flander; priest; s/o Thomas Brooke and Eleanor Hatton (JM p. 314)

Brooke, Tho.; *Kietch and Price*; 600 ac.; sur. 11 Feb 1662; pat. Feb 1662; 1707 poss. 200 ac. James Keetch & 400 ac. Jone Price; Resurrection Hundred (RR p. 59) (TLC p. 56)
    Asburnham alias *Hardshift*; 200 ac.; sur. 25 Sep 1662; 1707 poss. Leonard Brooke; Resurrection Hundred (RR p. 59) (TLC p. 56)

Brooke, Robert, b. 24 Oct 1663; d. *Newtown* 18 Apr 1714; s/o Thomas Brooke and Eleanor Hatton; priest (JM p. 315)

Brooks, Thomas; under age 16; s/o Mary; St. Michael's Hundred; 8 Jun 1663 (AM XLIX.302)

Brooke, Baker; *The Wedge*; 250 ac.; sur. 13 Mar 1667; incl. *Resurvey of Delabrook Manor*; 1707 no poss.; Resurrection Hundred (RR p. 60) (TLC p. 57)
    Longfield; 100 ac.; sur. 16 Mar 1667; in *Delabrook Mann'r*; 1707 no poss.; Resurrection Hundred (RR p. 60) (TLC p. 58)

Broock (Brookes), John; acct.; 13 Apr 1674 (I&A 1.27); acct.; 18 Apr 1674 (SMAA p. 39)

Brooke, Baker, Esq.; *Summer Seat*; 95 ac.; 1 Jun 1685 cert./pat. (COL)

Brooke, Charles; *Brook Chance*; 81 ac.; sur. 1 Apr 1694; 1707 poss. John
Langley; Resurrection Hundred (RR p. 64) (TLC p. 62)

Brooke, Baker; <u>will</u>; 5 Feb 1697/8; 27 May 1698; wife Catherine; sons Baker,
Leonard, Richard; dau. Ann; bro. Charles; f-i-l William Marshall [Marsham];
tracts *De-La-Brooke* [*Cela Brooke*], *Black Walnut Thicket, Brooke Wood,
Brooke Forest, Sumersett, Westfield* (MCW 2.142) [SMW PC1.114]

Brook, Charles; <u>will</u>; 13 Feb 1697; 15 Aug 1698; bro. Leonard (MCW 2.153) [SMW
PC1.110]; <u>inv.</u>; 5 Oct 1698 (I&A 18.29)

Brook, John; wife Sarah; 8 Aug 1698 (SMAA p. 97)

Brooke, Matthew; b. 1672; d. 1705 *St. Thomas Manor*; priest; s/o Thomas
Brooke and Eleanor Hatton (JM p. 315)

Brooke, Rob't; *Dela Brooke Mannour*; 2,000 ac.; 1707 poss. Leonard Brooke;
Resurrection Hundred (RR p. 58) (TLC p. 55)

Brooke, Robert; priest; d. 18 Jul 1714; age 51 (HGM)

Brooke, Leonard, Gent.; <u>will</u>; 1 Nov 1716; 2 Apr 1718; daus. Elinor, Jane, Ann;
son Charles; cousins Richard and Leonard Brooks; b-i-l Raphael Neale; tracts
Hardshift, Haphazard (MCW 4.131) [SMW PC1.232]; <u>acct.</u>; 24 Mar 1718 (A 1.368)
(SMAA p. 323); <u>inv.</u>; 2 Apr 1718 (I 1.53); <u>acct.</u>; 14 Oct 1719 (A 2.276) (SMAA p. 375)

Brook, Richard; <u>acct.</u>; 27 Jul 1720; ex. Leonard Brooke (A 3.88) (SMAA p. 431);
<u>acct.</u>; 9 Sep 1724 (A 6.91); <u>acct.</u>; 19 Nov 1726; widow Clear Brooke; ex. Mr.
Leonard Brooke (A 8.74)

Brooks, Richard & Baker; *Two Brothers*; sur. 11 Aug 1719 (TLC p. 70); 225 ac.;
10 Sep 1723 cert./pat. (COL)

Brooke, Leonard, b. 14 Jan 1750; d. 7 Jul 1813 Lulworth Castle, Dorset; priest;
s/o Baker Brooke and ?Anne (JM p. 315)

Brook, Alford; <u>inv.</u>; Sep 1753; 11 Jul 1754; nok Mary Crak (?), John Tenn (?);
adms./exs. Jeremiah Daffin & wife Elinor (I 58.184); <u>acct.</u>; 1 Mar 1756; orphan
Susannah [age 4] (A 39.77); <u>dist.</u>; 28 May 1756 (BB 2.23)

Brooke, Richard, Mr.; <u>inv.</u>; 16 Feb 1754; 4 Dec 1754; nok Baker Brooke,
Richard Boarman; admx./extx. Monnica Brooke (I 58.311); <u>acct.</u>; 2 Sep 1755 (A
38.183)

Brooke, Baker; <u>will</u>; 13 Feb 1756; 3 Mar 1756; wife Mary; bro. Richard;
nephew Richard Shierburn; dau. Elinor Thompson (MCW 11.123) [SMW TA1.353];
<u>inv.</u>; 18 Mar 1756; nok Richard Boarman, Nicholas Shierburn; extx. Mary
Brook (I 61.315); <u>acct.</u>; 20 Jun 1757 (A 41.87)

Brooke, Roger; m. 3 Dec 1770 Maria Brooke; parties were 3rd cousins (MM)

BROUGH

Brough, Will'm; *Poplar Neck*; 200 ac.; sur. 25 Nov 1642; 1707 poss. Wm.,
James, Thomas Cecill & Mary Dant; New Town Hundred (RR p. 26) (TLC p. 24)
Brough; 300 ac.; sur. 27 May 1651; 1707 poss. Thomas Cook; lies in *Wolseley
Manor*; Poplar Hill Hundred (RR p. 22) (TLC p. 21)

Brough, William; <u>will</u>; 4 Dec 1651; 5 Dec 1651; wife Sarah (MCW 1.6)

BROUGHTON

Broughton, Richard; acct.; admx. Arbella; 19 Jan 1711 (SMAA p. 219)

Broughton, Daniel; acct.; 16 Feb 1737; admx. Sarah Broughton (A 16.35)

BROWNE

Brown, John; dec'd 22 Aug 1655; Letters of Administration granted (SK ABH.429)

Broune [Browne], William; will; 27 Feb 1665; 26 Jul 1666; son John, dau. Mary (MCW 1.35) [SMW PC1.4]

Brown, John; immigrated from VA by 1671 (SK 13.127)

Brown, Robert; will; 16 Jul 1683; 16 Aug 1683; sons Gerrard, Walter; wife Eliza.; daus. Mary, Rebecca and Susanna; tract *Browne's* (MCW 1.126) [SMW PC1.47]

Browne, James, Dr.; oral; will; 7 Nov 1684; 11 Nov 1684 [SMW PC1.50]

Browne, James; will; 7 Sep 1698; 7 Nov 1698; dau. Mary; wife unnamed (MCW 2.160) [SMW PC1.115]

Browne, John, Sr.; inv. 28 Feb 1701 (I&A 21.307)

Browne, Richard; inv.; 22 Feb 1702; 16 Mar 1702 (I&A 1.645); acct.; 1 Feb 1703; adm. Derrick Browne (I&A 3.43) (SMAA p. 115)

Browne, John; inv.; 17 Sep 1705 (I&A 25.40); acct.; 1 Oct 1707 (I&A 27.135) (SMAA p. 139)

Brown, Michaell; acct.; 1 Aug 1707; admx. Anne, w/o Anthony Sim (I&A27.148)

Brown, John; *Doe Park*; 146 ac.; 2 Sep 1713 cert./pat. (COL)

Brown, John; inv.; 19 Feb 1716; nok Elisabeth Scriben, William Chester (I&A 38b.173); inv.; 7 Nov 1717 (I&A 39c.11); acct.; 1 Nov 1718 (A 1.315) (SMAA p. 324)

Browne, Derrick; planter; age ca 70 in 1721 (MD p. 23)

Brown, Abraham; will; 21 Apr 1724; 13 Jun 1724; bro. Anthony Simmes; sister Ellen (MCW 5.171) [SMW PC1.289]

Browne, Michael; acct.; 2 Aug 1726 (A 7.508)

Brown, Peter; *White Acre*; 222 ac.; 17 Oct 1753 cert./pat. (COL)

Browne, Anthony and Mary; child. Dorothy [b. 27 Mar 1755], Benedict [b. 7 Jun 1758], Susanna [b. 12 Sep 1761], Frances [b. 6 Mar 1764], Anthony [b. 7 Apr 1768], Monica [b. 22 May 1771] (SA p. 13, 48, 20)

Brown, Wm.; *Brown Woodhouse*; 50 ac.; sur. 5 Mar 1657; 1707 poss. Rob. Thomas; New Town Hundred (RR p. 31) (TLC p. 30)

Brown, James [?of QA Co.]; dist.; 9 Jun 1757; widow & 10 child. Sarah, Elizabeth, John, James, Joel, William, Samuel, Ann & Rebecca Brown & Esther Hall; extx. Sarah Brown (BB 2.71)

Brown, Peter, Sr.; will; probate 3 Oct 1758; sons James, Peter; tracts *Clarks Rest, White Acre* (MCW 11.217) [SMW TA1.364]; inv.; 16 Oct 1758; 6 Dec 1758; nok Nicholas & James Brown; adm.ex. Peter Brown (I 66.23)

Brown, Christopher; will; 2 Mar 1759; 23 Mar 1759; cousins Anthony and Peter Brown (MCW 11.231) [SMW TA1.383]; inv.; 2 Apr 1759; 8 Aug 1759; nok Nicholas & Anthony Brown (I 67.330)

Brown, Leonard and Ann; child. Dryden [b. 25 May 1760], Chloe [b. 20 Feb 1762], Leander [b. 27 May 1765], Allusia [b. 13 Aug 1769], Lucy [b. 11 Apr 1775] (SA p. 28)

Brown, Raphael, s/o John Baptist Brown and Heneretta; child. Raphael [b. 4 Oct 1761], Rebecca [b. 4 Apr 1767], Winifred [b. 16 Sep 1772] (SA p. 28)

Brown, Thomas; 3 Feb 1764; extx. Dorcas Brown (A 50.361)

Browne, Peter and Frances; child. Jereboam [b.16 Nov 1764], Anna [b. 9 Apr 1768], Eleanor [b. 4 Jul 1774] (SA p. 14, 15, 25, 49)

Brown, Nicholas; will; 19 Feb 1767; 12 Sep 1770; child. Ignatius, Nicholas, Mary, Monica, Elizabeth, Appalonia, Peter; g-s Richard Brown; unnamed g-child.; cousin Peter Brown; g-dau. Ann Brown (MCW 14.142) [SMW TA1.589]

Brown, Richard; will; 26 Jan 1767; 17 Feb 1767; wife Annastasa; son Richard; dau. Ann; unborn child (MCW 13.150) [SMW TA1.529]; inv.; 11 May 1767; nok Nicholas & Peter Brown; extx. Annastatia Brown (I 93.290); acct.; 10 Oct 1768 (A 60.195); dist.; 10 Oct 1768 (BB 5.178)

Brown, James; will; 24 Oct 1768; 10 Oct 1771; wife unnamed; sons John Baptis, Leonard [his wife Ann], Basil; daus. Susanna, Eloner, Ann Cloatilda, Mary Ann (MCW 14.188) [SMW TA1.617]; inv.; 22 Oct 1771; 10 Aug 1772; nok Leonard & John Baptist Brown; ex. Bazil Brown (I 109.393); acct.; 23 Apr 1774 (A 70.139)

Brown, Peter and Frances; child. Mary [b. 30 Sep 1770], Martin [b. 16 Nov 1775], Peter [b. 25 Sep 1779] (SA p. 27, 29, 190)

Brown, Anthony and Mary; dau. Monica [b. 22 May 1771] (SA p. 55)

Brown, Anton; m. 31 Jan 1774 Ann Brewer (MM)

Brown, Nicholas and Eleanor; son John Barton [b. 6 Mar 1775] (SA p. 28)

Brown, Basil; m. 20 Jun 1777 Ann Mattingly (MM)

Brown, Thomas; m. 29 Jun 1777 Sarah Taylor (MM)

Brown, Robert; m. 26 Dec 1777 Mary Ireland (MM)

BRYAN

Bryan, Mathias; *Bryan*; 100 ac.; sur. 30 May 1651; 1707 no poss.; land not found; New Town Hundred (RR p. 41) (TLC p. 41)

O'Bryan (Obrayon), Bryan; inv.; [filed with 1688] (I&A 10.140); acct.; 25 Jul 1689; admx. relict, w/o Richard Winsett (I&A 13a.186)

Bryan, James; inv.; 9 Jan 1729; 4 Mar 1729; admx./extx. Susannah Bryan (I 15.420); acct.; 4 Nov 1732; mentions William & James Bryan; admx. Susanna, w/o Robert Lewas of CH Co. (A 11.516)

Brion (Bryan), William; inv.; 8 Aug 1739; 27 Sep 1739; nok Richard & Henry Winstt; adm./ex. Henry Bryane (I 24.265); acct.; 18 Aug 1740; ex. Henry Bryan (A 18.55)

Bryan, Henry; will; 17 Jul 1761; 3 Feb 1763; wife Monica; dau. Eleanor Bryan; bros. Ignatius and John; s-i-l Thomas Shircliff; d-i-l Monica Shircliff; tract *Green's Plot, Beaver Dam Mannor* (MCW 12.176) [SMW TA1.438]; inv.; 3 Feb

1763; 11 Apr 1763; nok Ignatius & John Bryan; admx. Eleanor Bryan (I
80.135); acct.; 24 Jun 1765 (A 53.87); acct.; 4 Apr 1767 (A 56.72) (BB 5.21½)
Bryan, John; inv.; 7 Mar 1774; 20 May 1774; nok Ignatius Bryan, Elenor Able;
adm. Philip Bryan (I 117.338)
Bryan, Thomas; m. 1 Dec 1777 Maria Mattingly (MM)

BUCHANAN

Buchannan, George and Margaret; son Aaron [b. 6 Apr 1764] (SA p. 40)
Buchanan, George and Elizabeth; child. George [b. 22 Sep 1769], Rebecca [b.
15 Jun 1772] (SA p. 23, 190)
Buchanan, John; will; 23 Nov 1770; 1 Feb 1771; child. George, John, Jane
(MCW 14.181) [SMW TA1.625]
Buchanan, Moses and Eleanor ____ (by publication); m. 15 Oct 1780 (SA p. 58); son
William Thompson Buchanan; bapt. 24 Dec 1780 (SA p. 30)
Buchanan, Aron and Joanna Wells (by publication); m. 21 Feb 1785 (SA p. 63)

BUCKLER

Bucklar, Benjamin; inv.; 3 Apr 1714; nok John & William Goldsbery (I&A
36a.101); acct.; 20 Jan 1714 (I&A 36b.266) (SMAA p. 258)
Buckler, Robert; m. 10 Jan 1778 Anna Bullock (BRU 2.535)

BULLOCK

Bullock, John; [planter]; will; 27 Nov 1700; 23 Apr 1705; sons John, William;
daus. Mary Adkey w/o John Adkee, Elizabeth Allvoy & Margaret, [also
Francis]; s-i-l John Adkee; tract *Hopewell* (MCW 3.59) [SMW PC1.136]; inv.; 8
Jun 1705 (I&A 26.222); acct.; 3 Oct 1707; ex. John Bullocke (I&A 27.105) (SMAA
p. 139)
Bullock, Richard; inv.; 30 Jul 1734; 7 Aug 1734; nok John Jr. & William
Bullock (I 19.51); acct.; 4 Nov 1736 (A 15.227)
Bullock, John; will; 15 Oct 1736; 16 Nov 1736; sons John, George, James,
William and Richard; dau. Margret Griffin; wife Catherine (MCW 7.200) [SMW
TA1.49]; inv.; 9 Apr 1737; 8 Jun 1737; nok John Bullock, Margaret Bullock;
admx./extx. Katherine Bullock (I 22.322); acct.; 20 Apr 1739; extx. Catherine
[w/o Thomas Chamberlain] (A 17.105)
Bullock, William; inv.; 25 Mar 1737; 9 Jun 1737; nok John Bullock, John Alvey
(I 22.323); acct.; 28 Nov 1739 (A 17.351)
Bullock, John; planter; will; 17 Sep 1773; 10 Apr 1774; sons James, John,
Richard, Jesse; dau. Mary; sons-in-law Owen Allen, John Carpenter (MCW
15.151) [SMW TA1.708]

BURCH

Burch [Birch], John; 5 Jul 1710; 24 Jul 1710; d-i-l Elizabeth Phillips; sons John
and Benjamin (MCW 3.174) [SMW PC1.168]

Burch (Birch), Benjamin; <u>inv.</u>; 30 Jun 1721; 8 Mar 1721; nok Richard Breawer; admx. Sarah Birch (I 7.52)

Burch, Benjamin; <u>inv.</u>; 11 Mar 1744; 4 Jun 1745; nok Jonathon & Rebecca Burch; admx./extx. Winifred Burch (I 31.157); <u>acct.</u>; 6 May 1747; orphans Jonathon, Elisabeth, Barbary, Winefred, Sarah, Susanna; admx. Winifred Burch (A 22.250)

Burch, John; *Burch's Forest*; 90 ac.; sur. 11 Sep 1727 (TLC p. 90); 4 Jan 1757 cert./pat. (COL)

BURCHMORE
Birchmore, William and Margaret; dau. Rebekah [b. 8 Dec 1746] (SA p. 37)

Burchmore, William; [planter]; <u>will</u>; 17 Nov 1760; 4 Mar 1761; wife Margaret; daus. Rebecca and Ann (MCW 12.36) [SMW TA1.420]; <u>inv.</u>; 18 Apr 1761; 5 Aug 1761; nok Thomas & Ann Edwards; extx. Margaret Burchmore (I 74.282)

BURGESS
Burgesse, George; service by 1673 (SK 17.609)

Burgis (Burges), William; <u>inv.</u>; 11 Mar 1675 (I&A 2.8); <u>acct.</u>; 22 Mar 1676; admx. Anne Fisher (relict) (I&A3.124)

Burgus, Samuell; planter; <u>inv.</u>; 6 Feb 1684 (I&A 8.312)

Burges, William; St. Mary's Hundred; <u>will</u>; 5 Apr 1702; 20 Jun 1706; wife Constance (MCW 3.73) [SMW PC1.129]

Burgess [Burgiss], Constance; <u>will</u>; 4 Dec 1712; 5 Jan 1712; tract *Courtney's Neck* (MCW 3.237) [SMW PC1.184]

BURNE
Burn, Richard; perriwig maker; <u>inv.</u>; 17 Jun 1730; 6 Nov 1730 (I 16.44)

Burne (Burn), Patrick; planter; <u>will</u>; 13 Dec 1737; 16 Jan 1737/8; sons Dennis, James, Michael, Patrick, Mathias; g-sons Denis & John Burne and James, s/o s-i-l Solomon Joans [Jones]; tract *Hurry James* (MCW 7.241) [SMW TA1.62]; <u>inv.</u>; 6 May 1738; 17 Jul 1738; nok Patrick & Matt. Burne; adm./ex. Dennis Burne (I 23.194); <u>acct.</u>; 17 Aug 1740 (A 18.56)

Burns, Michael; oral; <u>will</u>; 29 Apr 1745; 1 May 1745; dau. Mary Burns (MCW 9.44) [SMW TA1.170]; <u>inv.</u>; 19 Aug 1745; 26 Nov 1745; nok ___ & James Burn; admx./extx. Pricilla Burn (I 31.426); <u>acct.</u>; 13 Feb 1746; orphans Michael, Mary (A 23.189)

Burne, Denis; <u>will</u>; 29 Oct 1750; 17 Dec 1750; wife Martha; their sons Nicholas, Ignatious, Patrick, Bennit, Denis; bros. Michael & his son Michael, James [John], Matthias & his dau. Ann; tracts *Becquith's Lodge, Jones Chance* (MCW 10.125) [SMW TA1.245]; <u>inv.</u>; 5 Feb 1750; 25 Mar 1750; nok Martha & Dennis Burne; Catharine Waughop; admm./ex. James Burne (I 45.82); <u>acct.</u>; 28 Dec 1751; mentions William Holton and his orphans: Catherine & Elisabeth Mekins; exs. James Burne, Robert Holton (A 32.69); <u>dist.</u>; 21 Dec 1751; ex.

James Burne (BB 1.27); <u>inv.</u>; 10 Nov 1752; 1 Nov 1753; nok Dennis Byrn, Martha Burne (I 57.60); <u>acct.</u>; 1 Nov 1753 (A 36.18)

Burns, Dennis; <u>inv.</u>; 13 Mar 1777; extx. Mary Byrn (I 125.279)

BURNET

Burnet, Stephen and Anastatia Jones (by license); m. 12 Mar 1783 (SA p. 61)

Burnit, Henry and Eleanor Dougan (by publication); m. 3 Aug 1784 (SA p. 62)

BURRELL

Burrell, Elizabeth; <u>will</u>; 1 Mar 1720/1; 21 Apr 1721; son Charles Kirkley; dau. Rebecca Kirkley; g-son George Kirkley; g-dau. Henrietta Walker; son Charles Curby; tracts *Edenborough, Denyard's [Dowyards], St. James, Cole Park, Raley* (MCW 5.47) [SMW PC1.261]; <u>inv.</u>; 13 May 1721; 5 Sep 1721; nok Charles & Rebecah Kirkley (I 6.128); <u>acct.</u>; 2 Oct 1722 (A 4.239); <u>acct.</u>; 5 Jun 1724 (A 6.32)

Burrell, Provis (Provest); <u>inv.</u>; 24 Jul 1711 (I&A 32c.90); <u>acct.</u>; 5 Jun 1713; admx. Elisabeth Burrell (I&A 35b.64) (SMAA p. 242)

BURROUGHS

Burroughs, John; *Hogg Hunters Hall*; 300 ac.; sur. 7 Oct 1671; 1707 poss. James Hulse; Choptico Hundred (RR p. 52) (TLC p. 50)
Horse Ranger; 200 ac.; sur. 1 Feb 1672; 1707 poss. John Dent, Sr.; Resurrection Hundred (RR p. 61)
Hold Fast; 76 ac.; [John Burras]; 10 Jul 1705 cert./pat. (COL)

Burroughs, John; age ca 68; 30 Dec 1712 (CCR p. 22, 23, 29, 35); age 70 in 1714/6 (MD p. 26)

Burroughs, John; planter; <u>will</u>; 13 Mar 1715/6; 5 Dec 1717; wife Mary; sons John, Richard; daus. Margaret Cartwright and Sarah Carter; mentions John Cartwright (MCW 4.170) [SMW PC1.226]; <u>inv.</u>; 20 Dec 1717 (I&A 39c.176); <u>acct.</u>; 12 Mar 1719; adm. John Burroughs (A 2.417) (SMAA p. 390); <u>acct.</u>; 11 Nov 1719 (SMAA p. 377) (A 2.320)

Burroughs, John; *Mere Chance*; 113 ac.; *Meer Chance* sur. for John Burras (TLC p. 82); 20 May 1725 cert./pat. (COL)

Burroughs, John; <u>will</u>; 28 Mar 1735; 2 Nov 1736; sons John, Benjamin, George; daus. Ann, Margaret, Barbara; wife Ann; tracts *Trent Forte [Troutforts* (?)], *Long Lookt for Come at Last* (MCW 7.199) [SMW TA1.47]

Burrows, Mary; d/o Thomas Keech, dec'd; *Charles's Lot*; 332 ac.; 15 Dec 1741 cert./pat. (COL)

Burroughs, Richard; *Burroughs' Lot*; 33 ac.; 25 Mar 1758 cert./pat. (COL)

Burroughs, Benjamin; <u>inv.</u>; 24 Jan 1765; 7 Mar 1765; nok John & George Burroughs; admn. James Burroughs (I 87.21); <u>inv.</u>; 22 Sep 1768 (I 98.109); <u>acct.</u>; 22 Sep 1768 (A 60.199); <u>dist.</u>; 22 Sep 1768 (BB 5.141)

Burroughs, Joseph; acct.; 30 Oct 1765; admx. Elisabeth Burroughs (A 53.238); dist.; 3 Oct 1763 (sic) (BB 4.141)

Burroughs, Richard; will; 8 Nov 1768; 3 May 1769; sons John, Mathew, Samuel, Richard, Jonathan, Hezekiah, Harry Edwards, Benjamin Burroughs, & his son Ignatius; dau. Lydia Woodbine [Woodburn] & [Mary Edwards]; g-son Joseph Burrows (MCW 14.91) [SMW TA1.570]; inv.; 13 Jun 1769; 11 May 1770; nok Jonathon & Richard Burroughs; ex. Hezekiah Burroughs (I 103.238); acct.; 3 Sep 1771; ex. Hezekiah Burroughs (A 66.174); dist.; 3 Sep 1771; child. Mathew, Samuel, Hezekiah, John, Richard, Jonathon, Henry, Lydia, Benjamin; g-son Joseph Burroughs (BB 6.91)

Burroughes, Elisabeth; inv.; 22 Feb 1770; 9 Mar 1770; nok John, s/o John, & Elisabeth Edwards (I 103.225); acct.; 28 Feb 1771 (A 66.171); dist.; 28 Feb 1771 (BB 6.92)

Burroughs, Wm. m. 9 Feb 1783 Susanna Dent (BRU 2.535)

Burroughs, Richard; m. 9 Nov 1783 Barbara Wilson (BRU 2.535)

BUSHELL

Bushell, Thomas; *Blunt Point*; 100 ac.; sur. 24 Jan 1642; 1707 poss. Daniel Smith; New Town Hundred (RR p. 26) (TLC p. 25)
Bushells Rest; 150 ac.; sur. 7 Jun 1647; 1707 poss. Will'm Watts; Poplar Hill Hundred (RR p. 20)

Bushell, Thomas; will; _ Mar 1653; 12 Feb 1661; wife and child. unnamed; bro. William Bushell (MCW 1.21)

Bushell, William; will; 8 Mar 1663; 1 Aug 1663 (MCW 1.29)

BUTLER

Butler, George; gent.; *Hebdon's Hole*; 700 ac.; 16 Jan 1693 cert./pat. (COL)

Buttler, John; inv.; 27 Apr 1701 (I&A 20.213); inv.; 3 Apr 1703 (I&A 24.84); acct.; 17 Jun 1703; 2 orphans; relict Francis (runaway), w/o William Hanitt (I&A 24.32)

Butler, Cecill; *Radnor*; 331 ac.; resur. 21 Jul 1703; assgn. John Dansey; 1707 poss. Jno, Dansey (RR p. 41) (TLC p. 40)

Butler, Cecilus; inv.; 7 Mar 1712 (I&A 34.123); admx. Margaret Butler; 1 Apr 1714 (SMAA p. 265); acct.; 14 Apr 1714 (I&A 35a.110); acct.; 10 May 1716 (I&A 36c.281) (SMAA p. 303)

Buttler, Margret; widow; will; 14 Aug 1721; 4 Sep 1721; son Cisill; daus. Frances, Mary; mentions Joseph Kelly and his sister Margaret; tract *St. John's* (MCW 5.66) [SMW PC1.265]; inv.; 9 Oct 1721; 10 Jan 1721; nok Thomas, Jr. & Francis Jameson; ex. Mr. Cecile Butler (I 6.223); acct.; 10 Apr 1722; legatees Mary Butler and w/o Thomas Jameson (A 4.131)

Butler, John; acct.; 2 Jun 1726 admx. Johannah Butler (A 7.372)

BUTTERWORTH

Butterworth, Michael; *Rich Thicket*; 100 ac.; sur. 23 Apr 1705 St. Clement's
   Manor (TLC p. 64); 1 Aug 1706 cert./pat. (COL)
Butterworth (Butterwich), Michaell; will; 1 Feb 1717; 5 Feb 1717/8; wife Jane;
   mentions William and Mary Pritchard; Thomas, s/o Gerrard and Rebecca
   Jordan; [Jane Pritchard, d/o William and Mary] (MCW 4.131) [SMW PC1.238];
   inv.; 12 Mar 1717 (I 1.310); acct.; 6 Aug 1719; extx. widow Jane Butterworth (A
   2.283) (SMAA p. 373); acct.; 6 Aug 1720 (A 3.66); acct.; 5 Aug 1720 (SMAA p. 435)
Butterworth, Jane; inv.; 17 Nov 1724; 1 Dec 1724; nok William Prichett, Gerard
   Jordan (I 10.215); acct.; 1 Dec 1724 (A 6.204)
Butterworth, James; acct.; 6 Oct 1725 (A 7.101)

CAGER

Cadger, Thomas; immigrated by 1649 (SK3.1)
Cager, Robert; will; 10 Aug 1667; 5 Sep 1667; child. Robert Cager, Jr. and
   Dorothy, wife of George Monroe [Moures] (MCW 1.41) [SMW PC1.4]
Cager [Cagoe], Robert; St. George's Hundred; will; 24 Jan 1675; 4 Feb 1675
   (MCW 1.115) [SMW PC1.16]; inv.; 2 Mar 1675; 9 May 1676 (I&A 2.136); acct.; 11
   May 1678 (I&A 5.92); acct.; 26 Nov 1679 (I&A 6.529)
Cager, Thomas; inv.; [filed with 1676] (I&A 2.246)

CAINE

Cain (Cane, Kaine), William; will; 25 Jan 1675; 5 Feb 1675; son William;
   mentions Jean [Jane], d/o Joseph and Jean Edloe (MCW 1.115) [SMW PC1.19];
   acct.;[filed with 1674-6] (SMAA p. 44); acct.; 4 Jul 1676 (I&A 2.165); acct.; 16
   Oct 1677; mentions Jeane Edloe, d/o Joseph of CA Co. (I&A 4.420)
Cane, William; wife Ann; to William Burgis; 50 a. called *Keenes Rest*; 1675
   (AM LXVI.126)
Okaine, Martha, w/o Rickart Okaine; 1677 (CCR, p. 4)
Okane, Richard; planter; inv.; 13 Feb 1677 (I&A 5.78)
Ocaine, John; acct.; 27 May 1707; admx. Elisabeth (relict), w/o William Willis
   (I&A 27.67) (SMAA p. 157)
Okane (Ocane, Ocaine) [Chance], John; planter; will; 12 Mar 1726/7; 27 Apr
   1727; wife Elizabeth; mother Elizabeth Willis; sister Nappler Mills; f-i-l
   Thomas Scott (MCW 6.25) [SMW PC1.322]; inv.; 6 Jun 1727; 7 Jun 1727 (I 12.11);
   acct.; 7 Jun 1727 (A 8.229)

CALVERT

Calvert, Leonard; *The Governours Field*; 100 ac.; sur. 13 Apr 1641; 1707 poss.
   George Parker (RR p. 13) (TLC p. 13)
   Trinity Mann'r; 600 ac.; sur. 13 Apr 1641; 1707 poss. George Parker; St.
   Michael's Hundred (RR p. 13) (TLC p. 13)

St. Michaels Mannour; 1,500 ac.; sur. 13 Aug 1641; 1707 poss. George Parker of CA Co. by right of his child. by d/o Gabriel Parrot; St. Michael's Hundred (RR p. 13) (TLC p. 13)

St. Gabriels Mannour; 900 ac.; sur. 13 Aug 1641; 1707 poss. George Parker; St. Michael's Hundred (RR p. 13) (TLC p. 13)

Calvert, Leonard; will; probate 14 Jun 1644 (MCW 1.2); inv.; acct.; 19 Jun 1647; Margaret Brent, admx. (AM IV.314, 320, 388)

Calvert, Phillip; *Wolselly Mannour*; 1,900 ac.; sur. 18 Aug 1664; 1707 poss. His Lordship; St. Georges Hundred (RR p. 18) (TLC p. 18)

St Peters; 150 ac.; pat. 7 Oct 1664; 1707 poss. by His Lordship; St. Mary's Hundred (RR p. 3) (TLC p. 3)

Whitewell; 100 ac.; sur. 10 Oct 1664; 1707 poss. His Lordship; St. Mary's Hundred (RR p. 3) (TLC p. 4)

Calvert, John; demands land for having served his time to the Hon. Philip Calvert, 24 Apr 1669 (SK 20.531-2)

Calvert, George [b. 15 Dec 1672]; s/o William Calvert and Elizabeth Stone (JM p. 315)

Calvert, Charles, Lord Baltimore; unnamed; 2,400 ac.; 30 Apr 1675 cert./pat. (COL)

Fresh Pond Neck; 500 ac.; St. Michaels Hundred to cousin Col. William Calvert, 1676 (SK 19.294)

Calvert, Leonard; *St. Leonards*; 2,400 ac.; sur. 30 Apr 1675; 1707 poss. His Lordship; later called *Mill Manor*; St. Georges Hundred (RR p. 19) (TLC p. 20)

Calvert, Philip; *Intack*; 57 ac.; sur. 5 Oct 1677; 1707 poss. by His Lordship; St. Mary's Hundred (RR p. 7) (TLC p. 8)

Calvert, Benedict Leonard; unnamed; 2,400 ac.; 21 Apr 1682 cert./pat. (COL)

Calvert, William; acct.; 30 Apr 1686; admx. Elisabeth Calvert (widow) (I&A 8.479); acct.; 17 Aug 1694 (SMAA p. 88)

Calvert, William; sons Charles & Richard; [filed with 1709-10] (CCR p. 17)

Calvert, Charles, gent.; age ca 57; 11 May 1720 (CCR p. 46); s/o William; age ca 59; 8 Oct 1721 (CCR p. 50)

Calvert, Charles; will; 25 Oct 1733; 31 Dec 1733; daus. Sarah Howser [Housen], Ann; wife Barbary; mentions Barbary, d/o Martin Keirk [Kirby] (MCW 7.53) [SMW TA1.14]; inv.; 7 Mar 1733; 25 Mar 1734; nok John Hicks, Mary Deacon, Charles Egerton; admx./extx. Barbary Calvert (I 17.718); acct.; 14 Oct 1736; extx. Barbary, w/o Andrew Foy (A 15.194)

CAMBELL

Cambell, John; *Fox Hill*; 30 ac.; sur. 14 Oct 1662; 1707 poss. Thos. Cambell; 1 Dec 1736 from Stephen Martin & wife 30 ac. to George Clarke; Poplar Hill Hundred (RR p. 22) (TLC p. 22)

Gravelly Hill; 50 ac.; sur. 14 Oct 1662; 1707 poss. Thos. Cambell; Poplar Hill Hundred (RR p. 22) (TLC p. 24)

Outlett; 100 ac.; sur. 14 Oct 1662; 1707 poss. Rob't Tunnell; 7 Sep 1716 from Andrew Delavee & wife Ann; Poplar Hill Hundred (RR p. 23) (TLC p. 24)

Oyster Shell Neck; 50 ac.; sur. 10 Apr 1666; 1707 poss. Tho. Cambell; Poplar Hill Hundred (RR p. 22) (TLC p. 24)

Forrest of Dean; 100 ac.; sur. 3 Jun 1685; 1707 poss. John Miller; Poplar Hill Hundred (RR p. 24) (TLC p. 24); 100 ac.; 6 Nov 1685 cert./pat. (COL)

Joining; 50 ac.; 18 Jan 1687 cert./pat. (COL)

Cambell, John; *Poplar Hill*; will; 6 Dec 1694; 4 Nov 1695; wife Catherine; sons Richard, James, Thomas; daus. Faith w/o Henry Taylor, Rachel w/o John Russell, Dorothy; tracts *Cambell's Farm, The Forrester Deane* (MCW 2.109) [SMW PC1.90]; inv.; 20 Feb 1696; 18 Apr 1696;[Maj.] (I&A 13b.28); acct.; [filed with 1697]; child. unnamed; ex. son Thomas Cambell (I&A 15.325); acct.; [1695-8] (SMAA p. 93)

Campbell, John; *Vineyard*; 100 ac.; 10 Jan 1706 cert./pat. (COL)

Campbell, William; planter; will; 15 May 1707; 16 Jun 1708 (MCW 3.111) [SMW PC1.156]

Campbell, John; will; 27Oct 1710; 20 Jan 1710/1; son John; wife Mary; tract *Beaver Dam Manor* (MCW 3.208) [SMW PC1.34]acct.; [filed with 1711-2]; admx. Mary Cambell (I&A 33b.138); undated [1718] (SMAA p. 335)

Campbell, Thomas; will; 19 Jan 1723/4; 28 Jan 1723/4; wife Jean; sons John, James, Richard, Joshua; dau. Jeane (MCW 5.155) [SMW PC1.284]; inv.; 8 Feb 1723; 2 Jun 1724; extx. Jane Martens (I 9.450); acct.; 1 Mar 1724; extx. Jane, w/o Stephen Martin (A 6.288); acct.; 3 Aug 1725 (A 7.94)

Campbell, Jean; inv.; 20 Apr 1775; nok Edward & Enoch Cambwell; adm./ex. Ignatius Camel (I 121.406)

CANADAY

Kennedy, Cornelius; unnamed; 300 ac.; sur. 8 Mar 1652; in *Fenwick Mannor*; 1707 no poss.; Resurrection Hundred (RR p. 58) (TLC p. 56)

Canaday, William; will; 18 Dec 1732; 4 May 1733; son John; g-child. Richard, Catherine and William Canady Forest; b-i-l John Waughop; tracts *Smoots Hollow, Hunting Quarter* (MCW 7.16) [SMW PC1.362]; inv.; 25 May 1733; 14 Sep 1733; nok Francis Hebb, John Cannaday (I 17.341); acct.; 10 Jan 1734 (A 12.745)

Kannady, William; *Forrest*; will; 26 Feb 1745/6; 26 Mar 1748; bro. Richard; sister Catharine Hebb; b-i-l William Hebb (MCW 9.143)

Canada, Mathew; inv.; 5 Aug 1754; 3 Sep 1754; nok sons Palmer & Mathew Canada; admx./extx. Ann Cannaday (I 57.333); acct.; 1 Jul 1755; orphans James [age 16], Mathew [age 14], Margaret [age 11], Ann [age 4], Monica [age 1]; admx. Ann Canaday (A 38.37); dist.; 19 Sep 1755; admx. Ann; child. James [age 17], Mathew [age 14], Margaret [age 11], Ann [age 4], Minica [age 1] (BB 2.1)

Canady, Ann; inv.; 18 Apr 1758; 10 Oct 1758; nok Margaret & Monica Cannady (I 65.418); acct.; 6 Sep 1759 (A 43.303)

CARBERRY

Carberry, John Baptist; *Carberry's Discovery*; sur. 10 Mar 1715 (TLC p. 74); 190 ac. 25 Apr 1717 cert./pat. (COL)

Carberry, John Baptist, Mr.; inv.; 19 Nov 1728; 6 Jun 1729; nok Nicholas Mills, Eleanor Carbery; admx. Mrs. Elisabeth & John Batpis Carberry (I 14.182); acct.; 6 Mar 1729; admx. Elisabeth & John Baptist Carberry (A 10.208); acct.; 31 Aug 1731; John Bapt. & Eleanor Carbery, Ann Rishwith (A 11.230)

Carbery, John Baptis, Jr.; inv.; 23 Jul 1771; 1 Aug 1771; nok John Baptis & Joseph Carbery; adm. Peter Carbery (I 107.96)

Carbery, Thomas; m. 29 May 1772 Monica Reily (MM)

CARMICHAEL

Carmichael, John; inv.; 25 Aug 1733; nok Philip & Antony Evans; admx./extx. Mary Carmichael (I 17.338); acct.; 18 Nov 1734; mentions John, Joseph, Mary, Elisabeth & Ann Carmichael (A 12.733)

Cromichel, John; will; 12 Jan 1744; 11 Mar 1744/5; child. Mary, Elizabeth, Ann; bros. Philip and Luke Merrill; wife Priscilla (MCW 9.28) [SMW TA1.153]

Carmical, Ann; will; 5 Oct 1749; 7 Mar 1764; mentions Jonathan Jeru (?) and Mildred, ch/o John Pirce and wife Mary; Augustine and Monica Warring, ch/o b-i-l Thomas Warring and wife Mary (MCW 13.6) [SMW TA1.456]; inv.; 30 Apr 1764; 7 May 1764; nok Joyllin Hildredhager, Mary Worren (I 84.286)

CARNALL

Carnall, Christop.; unnamed; 100 ac. sur. 14 Jul 1647; unnamed; not claimed; eschild. Rev'd Lawrence Debuts into *Towel Kill* or *Tower Kill*; Poplar Hill Hundred (RR p. 21) (TLC 20, 110)

Carnell, Christopher; will; 25 Nov 1661; 17 Jun 1662; dau. Eliza. Carnell (MCW 1.20)

CARPENTER

Carpenter, Charles; immigrated by 1673 with wife and 3 child.; wife Rebecca; child. Charles, Rebecca and Elizabeth (SK 17.477)

Carpinder (Carpender, Carpenter), John; planter; will; 4 Feb 1723/4; 17 Mar 1723; tracts *Finchle, The Wemes* (MCW 5.162) [SMW PC1.288]

Carpenter, John; inv.; 3 Mar 1752; nok James Weeden, William Carpenter; admx./extx. Elisabeth Carpenter (I 48.284)

Carpenter, George and Elizabeth; son William [b. 21 Mar 1757] (SA p. 37)

Carpenter, George; m. 14 Jul 1777 Catharine Maddox (MM)

CARR

Carre [Cane], Wm.; *Carres Rest* [*Canes Rest*]; 50 ac.; 24 Mar 1670; 1707 poss. Constance Burges; St. Mary's Hundred (RR p. 5) (TLC p. 7)

Carr, John; inv.; 9 Nov 1756; 14 Dec 1756; nok Elisabeth Carr, Mary Ann Payne; adm./ex. William Carr (I 62.198); acct.; 2 Nov 1757; adm. William Carr (A 41.252)

CARROLL

Carroll, Charles; surgeon of Annapolis; *Chancellor's Point*; 224 ac.; resur. 21 Nov 1705 (TLC p. 66); 13 May 1711 cert./pat. (COL)

Carroll, James; priest; 12 Nov 1756; age 39 (HGM)

Carroll, Henry; age ca 40 in 1767 (MD p. 29)

Carroll, Ignatius; m. 5 Aug 1771 Winifred Contsidur (MM)

Carroll, Henry; will; 16 Sep 1775; 16 Apr 1776; daus. Julian, Margaret, Hariot; wife unnamed (MCW 16.117); inv.; 19 Apr 1776; 14 Aug 1776; nok Juliana & Charles Carroll of *Carrollton*; extx. Arament, w/o George Biscoe (I 125.256)

CARTER

Carty (Cartey, Carter), Darby; will; 16 Feb 1723/4; 7 Mar 1723; dau. Mary; son Richard; wife Elizabeth (MCW 5.160) [SMW PC1.278]; inv.; 16 May 1724; 2 Jun 1724; nok Richard Moye, Grace, Taylar; admx. Elisabeth Carter (I 10.7); acct.; 7 Jun 1724; admx. Elisabeth [w/o William Holmes] (A 6.434)

Carter, Sarah; widow; will; 21 Nov 1733; 3 Aug 1757; child. Mary & Matthew [Cartwright] and Elizabeth Cartwright [Edwards]; granddau. Elizabeth Herbut (?Hubert); s-i-l John Edwards; sister Elizabeth Burraughes; tract *Mere Chance* (MCW 11.176) [SMW TA1.361]; inv.; 25 Aug 1757; 3 Aug 1758; nok Margaret Cartwright, Richard Burroughes; adms./exs. Edward Wilks & wife Mary (I 64.432)

Carter, Henry and Elizabeth Hogan; m. 7 Feb 1779 (SA p. 57)

CARTWRIGHT

Cartwright, Math'w; *Westons Addition*; 200 ac.; sur. May 1678; 1707 poss. John Wilson; St. Clements Hundred (RR p. 46) (TLC p. 45)

Cartwright, Matthew; will; 21 Feb 1688/9; 18 Mar 1688/9; sons John, Matthew, Thomas, Peter; dau. Joanna; wife Sarah; [tracts called *Weston, Weston Addition*] (MCW 2.41) [SMW PC1.77]; inv.; 15 May 1689 (I&A 10.236)

Cartwright, John; acct.; 20 Jul 1710; admx. Sarah Cartwright (I&A 31.367) (SMAA p. 202)

Cartwright, Thomas; inv.; 15 Mar 1711 (I&A 33a.242)

Cartwright, Johanah; inv. 19 Jan 1714 (I&A 36c.56)

Cartwright, Mathew; will; 6 May 1714; 15 May 1714; son John; dau. Mary; wife Susannah; bro. Peter (MCW 4.21) [SMW PC1.196]; inv.; 20 Jul 1714 (I&A 36a.184)

Cartwright, John; gent.; *Cartwright's Pasture*; 20 ac.; sur. 9 Jun 1739 (TLC p. 96); 3 Oct 1739 cert./pat. (COL)

Cartwright, Matthew; <u>inv.</u>; 28 Mar 1751; 5 Jun 1751; nok Sarah Carter, Elisabeth Edwards; admx./extx. Elisabeth Cartwright (I 47.114); <u>acct.</u>; 7 Nov 1751; admx. Elisabeth, w/o John Horrill (Harrill) (A 31.227)

Cartwright, William; <u>inv.</u>; 13 Jan 1755; 24 Mar 1755; nok Elisabeth & Sarah Hammett; admx./extx. Dorothy Cartwright (I 60.222); <u>acct.</u>; 1 May 1756; admx. Dorothy, w/o Robert Hammitt, Jr. (A 40.21)

Cartwright, John; <u>inv.</u>; 22 Apr 1755; 3 Jun 1758 (sic); nok Judith & Catharine Cartwright; admx./extx. Elisabeth Cartwright (I 60.313, 316); <u>acct.</u>; 1 May 1756; admx. Elisabeth, w/o John Hommitt (A 40.20); <u>dist.</u>; 28 May 1756; orphans Elisabreth, Catherine, Margaret, William (BB 2.24)

Cartwright, John; *Cartwright's Pasture*; 34 ac.; 29 Sep 1758 cert./pat. (COL)

Cartwright, Matthew; 19 Apr 1761; b. Middlebourgh, Province of Zealand; naturalized (CMN N5)

Cartwright, William; <u>acct.</u>; 26 May 1763; child. Mary, John, Dorothy, Margaret, Sarah; admx. Dorothy, w/o Robert Hammett (A 49.605)

Cartwright, Dorothy; <u>will</u>; 10 Feb 1769; 6 Jun 1770; bro. John; sister Sarah (MCW 14.133) [SMW TA1.603]

Cartwright, Mathew; <u>inv.</u>; 26 May 1772; 10 Aug 1772; nok John Cartwright; admx. Teresia Cartwright (I 109.395)

CARVILE

Carvill, Robert; immigrated by 1669 (SK 12.321)

Carvile, Robert; City of St. Mary's; gent. age ca 38 in 1674 (MD p. 29)

Carvile, Robert; gent.; unnamed; 1 ac.; 9 Jun 1678 cert./pat. (COL)

Carvile, Thomas; *Salter's Load*; 800 ac.; 12 Jan 1683 cert./pat. (COL)

Carvile, Robert; age ca 48 in 1684; age 64 (sic) [?46] (MD p. 30)

Carvile, Robert; gent.; *Inclosure*; 170 ac.; 27 Oct 1686 cert./pat. (COL)

CARWARDINE

Carwardine, Peter; immigrated by 1670 (SK 16.12)

Carwardine, Peter; *Rissington Barn*; 50 ac.; sur. 10 Dec 1670; within bounds of *Mitcham Meadows*; 1707 no poss.; Poplar Hill Hundred (RR p. 25) (TLC p. 23)

Carwardyne, Peter; Poplar Hill Hundred; age ca 45; 1679/80 (AM LXIX.121)

Carwarde (Carwardine), Peter; Poplar Hill Hundred; <u>will</u>; 28 Jun 1698; 16 Sep 1701; sons Peter, Thomas, John (MCW 2.218); <u>inv.</u>; 2 Jul 1701 (I&A 21.32)

Carwarden, John; <u>acct.</u>; 15 Jul 1702; ex. son John (I&A 22.49); <u>acct.</u>; 15 Jul 1702 (SMAA p.112)

CAVENAUGH

Cavenaugh, William; *Good Friendship*; 14 ac.; 14 Jul 1770 cert./pat. (COL)

Cavenough, William, Jr.; *Tryal*; 96 ac.; 10 Oct 1772 cert./pat. (COL)

CAWOOD

Cawood, Steven; *Cawood's Expense*; 157 ac.; resur. 13 Apr 1749 Stephen Cawood and wife Eleanor (TLC p. 115); 16 Apr 1751 cert./pat. (COL)

Cawood, Stephen; will; 4 Jan 1767; 23 Apr 1767; wife unnamed; sons Stephen, Thomas, Benjamin; daus. Anne, Dorothy, Esther, Elizabeth, Martha, Elianor; tracts *Westham, Cawood's Experience, [Mount] Paradise, Cawood's Expence* (MCW 13.177) [SMW TA1.536]; inv.; 4 Jul 1767; 5 Mar 1768; nok Dorothy & Martha Cawood; exs. Eleanor & Stephen Cawood (I 97.100, 268); acct.; 11 Jul 1768 (A 58.248)

Caywood, Thomas; will; 6 Apr 1769; 10 Apr 1777; bro. Benjamin (MCW 16.216)

Caywood (Cawood), Stephen; *Caywood's Discovery*; 19 ac.; 1 Apr 1774 cert./pat. (COL)

Cawood, Elinor; will; 13 Jan 1775; 16 Feb 1775; son Thomas; daus. Elinor Wingate, Dorothy Garner, Ann, Elizabeth, Martha; grandson Benjamin Davis; mentions Stephen and Benjamin Cawood (MCW 16.93) [SMW TA1.716]

Caywood (Cawood), Stephen, *Caywood's Inheritance*; 21 ac.; 19 May 1783 cert./pat. (COL)

CHAMBERLIN

Chamberlain, Thomas; age ca 37; 26 Jun 1719; tract *Bodle ats Knight* (CCR p. 41); age ca 43; 31 Jan 1723 (CCR p. 57)

Chamberlin, Charles; Brunswick Co., Colony of Virginia; 2 Jan 1750; 7 May 1751; wife Ann (MCW 10.154) [SMW TA1.271]

Chamberlin, Thomas, Mr.; inv.; 13 Sep 1740; nok Thomas & John Chamberlin; admx./extx. Elisabeth Chamberlin (I 25.431); acct.; 27 Apr 1744; admx. Elisabeth Chamberlin (A 20.144)

CHAMBERS

Chambers, Robert; inv.; 24 Nov 1713 (I&A 35a.229)

Chambers, George; acct.; 9 Nov [filed with 1714] (I&A 36b.39); acct.; 9 Nov 1714 (SMAA p. 271)

Chambers, Thomas; will; 4 Feb 1733/4; 28 Feb 1733/4; mentions Ann Branson and Judith Swan, daus. of James Compton; [Judith d/o James Swann] (MCW 7.59) [SMW TA1.19]; inv.; 8 Apr 1734; 17 Apr 1734; nok one minor (I 18.122); acct.; 5 Jun 1735 (A 13.159)

Chambers (Chamlers), George; inv.; 10 Jul 1738; nok Margaret Taylor, Timothy Paden, Jr. (I 23.196); acct.; 18 Dec 1739 (A 17.403)

CHARLESWORTH

Charlesworth, George; service by 1672 (SK 17.60); son John transported by 1666 (SK 10.1, 2; 11.236)

Charlesworth, George; acct.; 27 Jan 1677 (I&A 4. 585) (SMAA p. 77)

CHESELDINE

Cheseldyn, Kenelem; immigrated by 1669 (SK 12.346; 14.477)

Cheseldyn, Kenelm; *Dryden*; 334 ac.; resur. 483 ac.; 12 May 1676; 1707 poss.
   same Cheseldyn; St. Georges Hundred (RR p. 19) (TLC p. 19); 483 ac.; 1 Apr
   1700 cert./pat. (COL)

Cheseldine, Kenelinn; d. ca 1708; wife Mary; mentions son Kenelinn [age ca 4
   in 1708]; sisters Mary who m. George Forbes, Susanna the 1st w/o Thomas
   Truman Greenfield and Dryden who m/1 Henry Peregrine Jowles & m/2 John
   Forbes, dec'd; 14 Dec 1740 (CCR p. 94)

Cheseldyne, Kenelm; Gent.; will; 6 Dec 1708; 18 Dec 1708; son Kenelm; daus.
   Mary Hay (Hey) the w/o James [William] Hay, Susannah Greenfield, Dryden
   Cheseldyne; granddau. Mary Hay; tracts *Matapany, White Neck, St.
   Katherynes Island, Broad Neck, Westwood Lodge* of CH Co., *Drydenn* (MCW
   3.115) [SMW PC1.151]; acct.; 10 Oct 1710; ex. Kenelm Cheseldyne, gent. (I&A
   32a.38) (SMAA p. 195)

Cheseldine, Kenelinn; d. ca 1717; George Gordon questions marriage to Mary
   Phippard, mother of son Kenelinn; daus. Mary Hayes, Susanna Greenfield,
   Dryden; son Kenelinn; 23 May 1743 (CCR p. 94)

Chiseldyne [Cheseldine], Kenelm; will; 4 Jan 1717/8; 29 Jan 1717; 29 May
   1719; 5 Jun 1719; wife Mary; son Cyrenius; bros.-i-l T. Truman Greenfield,
   Hen. Paregrine Jowles (MCW 4.212) [SMW PC1.221]; inv.; 15 Jun 1719; 11 Sep
   1719; extx. Mrs. Mary Cheseldine (I 3.46); acct.; 20 Jul 1722 (A 4.185); acct.; 6
   Aug 1724; extx. Mary w/o Hugh Collins (A 6.39)

Chiseldine, Kenelm; will; 4 Jan 1717; 9 Sep 1737; youngest son Cyrus; b-i-l
   Thomas Trueman Greenfield; niece Mary Hay; tract *Crouch* [SMW TA1.63];
   Note: This appears to be a 2nd filing of the will found in SMW PC1.221.

Cheseldine, Cyrenius; inv.; 4 Feb 1762; 6 Oct 1762; nok Kenelm Chesldine, Sr.,
   John Haskins, Sr.; admx. Kenelm Cheseldine (I 79.252); acct.; 10 Feb 1764 (A
   51.1); dist.; 10 Feb 1764; ex. Bennett Fenwick (BB 4.29)

Cheseldine, Kenelm; inv.; 18 Mar 1765; 26 May 1765; nok Kenelm Cheseldine,
   Sr., Ursular Haskins; admx. Chloe Cheseldine (I 88.66); inv.; 1 Aug 1768 (I
   97.267, 269, 270); acct.; 1 Aug 1768 (A 58.263)

Cheseldine (Chesheldine), Ruban (Reuben); inv.; 14 Sep 1765; 24 Sep 1765;
   nok Kenelm Cheseldine, Jr., Ursular Haskins; adm. Kenellum Chesheldine (I
   87.316); acct.; 15 Sep 1767; adm. Kenelm Cheseldine, Sr. (A 57.358)

Cheseldine, Knelm; acct.; 27 Mar 1772 (A 66.281)

Cheseldine, Kenelm; inv.; 20 Aug 1773; 7 May 1775; nok Mary Blackiston,
   Elisabeth Fulton; admx./extx. Mary Neale (I 121.399)

Cheseldine, Seneca and Elizabeth Biscoe; m. 4 Nov 1779 (SA p. 57)

CHESHER

Cheshier, William; acct.; 23 Mar 1702; adm. Stephen Cheshire (I&A 23.27) (SMAA
   p. 112)

Chesher (Chesshire, Cheshier), Steven (Stephen); inv.; 20 Apr 1707 (I&A 27.54); acct.; 9 Aug 1708; admx. Elizabeth, w/o Thomas Barremand (Barron, Barrow) (I&A 28.293) (SMAA p. 160); acct.; 21 Oct 1710 (I&A 32c.24) (SMAA p. 206)

Chesher [Cheshire], William; will; 12 Mar 1732/3; 27 Mar 1733; son William; cousin Absalom Tennison, Sr.; bro. John; tract *Pheabuses Fort [Cheshire's Fort]* (MCW 7.11) [SMW TA1.17]; acct.; 28 Oct 1734; orphans William, John, James, Justinian, Elisabeth & Ann Chesshur (A 15.549)

Chesire, John; will; 19 Jan 1746; 6 Mar 1746; wife Priscilla; child. Jonathan, John, Tenesan, Philemon, Mary Noble (MCW 9.100) [SMW TA1.187]; inv.; 6 Mar 1746; 19 May 1747; nok Philomon Chesher, Edward Pratt; admx./extx. Precilla Chesher (I 35.101); acct.; 30 Aug 1748; mentions William, John, Matthew, Thomas, Philemon, Teneson, Jonathon, Elisabeth, Mary; admx. Prissilla Chesher (Cheser) (A 25.180)

Chesher (Cheshire), William; inv.; 30 Jul 1752; 7 Aug 1752; nok Jameson & Priscilla Cheshire; admx./extx. Mary Chesher (I 49.103); acct.; 5 Dec 1754; orphan Dorothy [age 3]; admx. Mary Chesher (A 36.522); dist.; 5 Dec 1754; admx. Mary; 1 child Dorothy [age 4 next 10 Feb] (BB 1.123)

Chesher, Tennison; *Rogers' Venture*; 50 ac.; 16 Apr 1772 cert./pat. (COL)

CHESLEY

Chesley, John; *Good Luck*; 275 ac.; resur. 30 Jul 1734 (TLC p. 93); 20 Nov 1737 cert./pat. (COL)
   Cragbourne's Island; 13 ac.; sur. 30 Jul 1745 for John Clesley (TLC p. 108); 13 Dec 1745 cert./pat. (COL)
   Cragbourn's Marsh; 17½ ac.; sur. 11 Mar 1745 (TLC p. 108); 17 ac.; 11 Mar 1746 cert./pat. (COL)
   Craigbourn's Swamp; 17 ac.; 14 Apr 1753 cert./pat. (COL)

Chesley, Thomas; inv.; 17 Apr 1761; 5 Aug 1761; nok John Chesley; adm. Robert Chesley (I 74.292)

Chesley, John; will; 24 Jan 1765; 24 Dec 1767; son [Benjamin] Chesley; wife Elizabeth; sons John, James, Alexander; daus. Elizabeth Pile, Mary, Rebecca; tracts *Crockburne, Crockburns Marsh, Crockburns Swanp, Crockburns Island, Hard Fortune, Indian Creek with Addition, Canoe Neck [Cause Neck]* (MCW 14.33) [SMW TA1.506]; inv.; 4 Dec 1767 (sic); 3 Dec 1768; [Esq.]; extx. Elisabeth Chesley (I 98.125, 126); inv.; 9 May 1768; 3 Dec 1768; nok Richard Bile (I 98.144); acct.; 3 Dec 1768 (A 60.191)

Chesley, Robert; gent.; will; 4 Nov 1767; 11 Mar 1768; sons Robert, John Langford; daus. Susanna, Anne, Mary, Elisabeth; tracts *The Vineyard, Langford's Quarter* [SMW TA1.567]; inv.; 15 Jun 1768; 8 Mar 1769; mentions dau.; ex. Ann Chesley (I 100.129); acct.; 27 Mar 1771 (A 66.161)

CHESUM

Cheasum, James; <u>will</u>; 11 Feb 1698; 8 Mar 1698; wife Ann; sons James,
William; dau. Mary (MCW 2.176) [SMW PC1.124]; <u>inv.</u>; 22 Apr 1699 (I&A
19½b.118)

Chesum, William; <u>inv.</u>; 4 Jun 1698 (I&A 16.30); <u>acct.</u>; 10 Mar 1700; admx.
unnamed relict, w/o William Morgan (I&A 21.115)

Chesam, William; <u>inv.</u>; 31 Aug 1731; nok James & Mary Chesam; admx./extx.
Mary Chesam (I 16.293)

CHEVERELL

Cheverill, Clement; planter; service by 1679 (SK 15.17)

Cheverell, John; <u>will</u>; 5 Apr 1702; 4 Jun 1702; wife Jeane; sons John and
Clement; dau. Jeane [Jane] (MCW 2.239) [SMW PC1.129]

Cheveral (Cheverall, Chevrell), Jane; <u>inv.</u>; 10 Dec 1710; nok John Cheverall
(I&A 32b.69); <u>acct.</u>; 29 Nov 1712; adm. Clement Cheverall (I&A 33b.172) (SMAA p.
233)

Cheveral, John; <u>inv.</u>; 20 Jul 1717 (I&A 37b.100)

Cheverell (Chiverall), Clement; planter; <u>will</u>; 14 Jan 1744; 29 Apr 1745; son
Clement; dau. Hannah; grandson William Oare; mentions John and Mary
Oare; wife Jane (MCW 9.28) [SMW TA1.172]; <u>inv.</u>; 5 May 1745; 15 Jul 1745; nok
Jane Oer, Joanna Chiverell; admx./extx. Jane Chiverell (I 31.159); <u>acct.</u>; 12 Jun
1746 (A 22.257)

Cheverill, John; <u>inv.</u>; 25 May 1743; 29 Jun 1743 (I 28.13)

CHILMAN

Chilman, Richard; immigrated by 1674 (SK 18.151 & 301)

Chilman, Richd.; *Galloways* or *Betty's Folly*; 50 ac.; sur. 6 May 1675; assgn.
Jno. Hall; 1707 poss. Cecill Buttler by marrying d/o Rob. Carville; St. Mary's
Hundred (RR p. 6) (TLC p. 7)

Chillman (Chilman), Richard; innholder; <u>will</u>; 5 Nov 1678; 14 Nov 1678; cous.
Thomas Locker; bro. Thomas Griffin (MCW 1.207) [SMW PC1.33]; <u>acct.</u>; 22 Apr
1680 (I&A 7a.38)

CHILTON

Chilton, Stephen; <u>will</u>; 16 Sep 1770; 10 Jul 1773; sons Stephen, Charles,
George, William, John, Thomas; dau. Ann Leigh, Elizabeth; g-dau. Elizabeth
Lynch; wife unnamed [Ann] (MCW 15.72) [SMW TA1.652]; <u>inv.</u>; 3 Nov 1773; nok
Stephen & George Chilton; extx. Ann Chilton (I 114.38); <u>inv.</u>; 18 Apr 1774 (I
118.113); <u>inv.</u>; 6 Nov 1775 (I 124.16)

Chilton, Stephen; <u>will</u>; 25 Nov 1776; 14 Feb 1776; mother Ann; bros. William,
Thomas, John; tract *Woodward's Frolick* (MCW 16.174)

CHISUM
Chisum, William; [planter]; written 21 Oct 1697; <u>will</u>; daus. Jane, Mary, Ann; wife Ann (MCW 2.134); planter [SMW PC1.98]

Chissam, William; <u>acct.</u>; 31 Aug 1731; mentions James, Mary & Ann Chassam; admx. Mary Chissam (A 11.226)

CHUNN
Chuner, Catharine; <u>inv.</u>; 30 Jan 1775; 14 Jan 1775; adm./ex. Edward Gardiner (I 121.416); <u>acct.</u>; 1775; [Chunn] (A 73.243); <u>dist.</u>; 1775 (BB 7.33)

Chunn, Joseph, Mr.; <u>inv.</u>; 7 May 1765; 4 Jun 1765; nok Rebecca Barber, Mary Morris; adm. Catharine Chunn (I 88.84); <u>dist.</u>; 2 Jul 1765 (BB 4.130)

CISSELL
Cissell (Sissell, Sessill), John; <u>will</u>; 28 Apr 1698; 6 Jun 1698; sons John, William, Thomas, Richard, Robert, Edward, James; wife Mary; tracts *White Acre, Long Neck* (MCW 2.138) [SMW PC1.104]; <u>inv.</u>; 26 Jul 1698 (I&A16.200)

Sissell (Cissell), Thomas; <u>will</u>; 18 Oct 1700; 28 Mar 1701; wife Mary; d-i-l Betty, s-i-l George ____, s-i-l James Thompson (MCW 2.215); <u>inv.</u>; 16 Apr 1701 (I&A 20.109); <u>acct.</u>; 21 May 1702; extx. Mrs. Mary Cecill (relict) (I&A 21.367) (SMAA p. 106)

Cecill, William & wife Catherine & John Cecill, Jr.; *Scotland*; 100 ac.; 10 Sep 1716; resur. 10 Dec 1714 for Wm. Caecil (TLC p. 72)

Cissell (Chissell, Sissell), James; <u>will</u>; 30 Mar 1717; 22 Apr 1717; son James; daus. Mary, Ruth; tracts *Poplar Neck, Boardneck* (MCW 4.98) [SMW PC1.217]; <u>inv.</u>; 8 Jul 1717 (I&A 37b.231); <u>acct.</u>; 9 Jun 1718 (A 1.53) (SMAA p. 358); <u>acct.</u>; 19 Sep 1719 (SMAA p. 374); <u>acct.</u>; 26 Oct 1719 (A 2.279)

Cissell (Cisell, Cecill), John, Sr., Mr.; <u>inv.</u>; 2 Oct 1722; 16 Nov 1722; nok Thomas Cisell (I 9.14); <u>acct.</u>; 9 Aug 1723 (A 5.205)

Cissell, Thomas; planter; <u>will</u>; 30 Apr 1724; 24 Aug 1724; son John; bro. James; tract *White Acres* (MCW 5.174) [SMW PC1.289]; <u>inv.</u>; 16 Nov 1724; 23 Nov 1724; nok William & Mathew Sissell; ex. John Cissell (I 10.254); <u>acct.</u>; 1 Nov 1725 (A 7.183)

Cissell (Cissel), Francis, Mrs.; widow; <u>inv.</u>; 16 Mar 1732; 10 Aug 1733; nok Elender Thomas (I 17.335); <u>acct.</u>; 15 Dec 1735 (A 145.174)

Cecill (Cissell), Arthur; <u>will</u>; 5 Nov 1737; (filed with 1750); sons John, James; father William, dec'd; wife Mary; tract *Scotland* (MCW 10.103) [SMW TA1.253]; <u>inv.</u>; 30 Oct 1750; 8 Nov 1750; nok John & James Cissell; admx./extx. Mary Cessell (I 44.231); <u>acct.</u>; 2 Jul 1751; orphans John, Elinor, Margret, Ann & Monica [all of age], James [age 16] (A 30.200)

Cissell, William; planter; <u>will</u>; 22 Jun 1742; 28 Nov 1744; child. Arthur, Luke, Margaret Thompson, Ann Edwards, Mathew, Elizabeth w/o Charles Payne [Charles Neale], Clare Barton; g-child. William s/o son John Cissell and

Elizabeth Neal, William s/o son William and Clara Cissell [Clare Batson],
Eliner d/o son Arthur; tracts *Scotland, White Acre, Cissells Improvements*
(MCW 9.13) [SMW TA1.159]

Sissel (Cissell), John; inv.; 31 May 1743; 6 Jul 1743; nok Thomas Vanreshwick,
John Baptist Reshwick; admx./ex. Sarah Sissel (I 28.15); acct.; 28 Nov 1744;
orphans Thomas, John, Mary Ann; admx. Sarah Cissell (A 21.133)

Cissell, John and Henrietta; child. Anastatia [b. 11 Feb 1745], Mary [b. 4 Jan
1750], James [b. 24 Jan 1753], John [b. 15 Oct 1757], Delbert [b. 30 Jul 1763]
(SA p. 8, 9, 36)

Cissell, Luke, Mr.; inv.; 10 Aug 1747; 4 Mar 1747; nok Susannah Mitchell,
William Cissell (I 35.521)

Cessill, James; *Cissells Venture*; 88 ac.; sur. 22 Jan 1744 (TLC p. 113); 18 Mar
1747 cert./pat. (COL)

Sissel (Ciswell, Cissell), Mathew; inv.; 30 May 1748; 5 Jul 1748; nok Arthur &
James Cissell; admx.extx. Mary Cessell (I 36.110); acct.; 2 Aug 1749; child.
Thomas, Mary, Alexander [all of age], Margaret [age 15], James [age 5] (A
27.102)

Cessill, Thomas; *White Acre Addition*; 43 ac.; sur. 25 Aug 1746 for Matthew
Cissell; part of *Crackbournes Purchase* (TLC p. 113); 14 Feb 1749 cert./pat. (COL)

Cissell, John and Margaret; child. Shedrick [b. 18 Nov 1754], Dorothy [b. 17
Apr 1756] (SA p.11, 12, 46)

Cassell, Thomas; inv.; 3 Apr 1756; 4 Aug 1756; nok Margret Sissell, James
Sissell; admx./extx. Ann Cissell (I 61.339); acct.; 4 Aug 1756; orphan Staple
[age 4] (A 39.214); acct.; 3 Apr 1756; 4 Aug 1756; (A 39.214); dist.; 25 Oct 1756
(BB 2.33)

Cissell, John and Ann; sons John [b. 18 Oct 1757], Delbert [b. 30 Jul 1763] (SA
p. 43)

Cissell, James and Elizabeth; child. Bernard [b. 12 Feb 1759], Susanna [b. 28
Jan 1760], Peter [b. 29 Jun 1764] (SA p. 10, 39, 45)

Cissell, Ignatius and Elizabeth; child. Edmund Barton [b. 25 Jun 1760], James
Rodolph [b. 8 Apr 1762], Ignatius [b. 12 Mar 1764], Joseph [b. 28 Jun 1766],
James [b. 22 May 1768], Mary [b. 10 Mar 1770], Wilford [b. 10 Jul 1772] (SA
p. 10, 22, 39, 44, 45)

Cissell, John Baptist and Rebekah; son Thomas [b. 14 Apr 1762], Jeremiah [b.
26 Sep 1773], Ann [b. 2 Feb 1766], William [b. 10 Aug 1767] (p. 10, 21, 24, 44)

Cissell, John and Mary; son Joseph [b. 27 Dec 1772] (SA p. 26)

Cissell (Siscell, Sissell), James; will; 30 Sep 1774; 27 Oct 1774; bro. John & his
dau. Mary; sisters Margaret Thompson & her son Thomas, Ann Thompson,
Monaca Payn & her child. Ann, Mary; tract *Scotland* (MCW 16.21) [SMW
TA1.680]; inv.; 16 Nov 1774; 20 Aug 1775; father Abraham; nok Mary &
Thomas Thompson; ex. John Sissell (I 122.168); acct.; 17 Aug 1776 (A 74.14)

Cissell, John Baptist and Ann; son Matthew [b. 20 Feb 1775] (SA p. 26, 27)

Sissill, John; m. 26 Aug 1777 Eleanor Combs (MM)

Sissel, William and Sarah Adams (by license); m. 27 Apr 1784 (SA p. 62)

CLARK

Clark, Robert; assgn. Philip West; *St. Laurances*; 50 ac.; sur. Jul 1641; 1707 no poss.; St. Georges Hundred (RR p. 33) (TLC p. 16)
   Clarks Freehold; 50 ac.; sur. 2 Jul 1641; 1707 poss. Daniel Clocker; St. Mary's Hundred (RR p. 4) (TLC p. 6)

Clarke, Robert; age ca 71 [b. 5 Nov 1651]; 8 Oct 1721; tract *Crop Manor* (CCR p. 49)

Clarke, Rob't; *St. Laurances Freehold*; 1,000 ac.; sur. 25 Mar 1652; 1707 no poss.; New Town Hundred (RR p. 29) (TLC p. 28)

Clark, Edward; transported by 1665; m. Ann, d/o John Shirclif prior to 1667 (SK 8. 502)

Clark, Edward; *Dowhham [Dounham]*; 100 ac.; sur. 29 Apr 1667; 1707 poss. Rob. Ford; New Town Hundred (RR p. 34) (TLC p. 33)
   Turvey; 350 ac.; sur. 5 Sep 1673; 1707 poss. Edward Clark, Martin Yates; New Town Hundred (RR p. 36) (TLC p. 35)
   Clarks Rest; 300 ac.; sur. 21 Aug 1674; 1707 poss. Rich'd Brown; New Town Hundred (RR p. 36) (TLC p. 35)

Clarke, Edward; will; 22 Feb 1675;12 Mar 1676; wife Anne; son Edward; bros. John and William Shercliffe; tracts; *Clarke's Rest, Turvey* (MCW 1.185) [SMW PC1.25]

Clarke, Gilbert; age 27 in 1684 (MD p. 34)

Clark, John; will; 28 Nov 1685; 6 Mar 1686; wife Ann; child. John, Robert [Francis], Benjamin, Franklin and Ann [& dau. Rowenen (?Clarke)] (MCW 2.1) [SMW PC1.60]

Clark, Rob.; *Addition*; 100 ac.; sur. 9 Nov 1694; 1707 poss. same Clark; Resurrection Hundred (RR p. 64) (TLC p. 62)

Clarke, Philip; will; 30 May 1699; 11 Aug 1699; sons George, Roger, Philip; 2 daus. & wife unnamed; tracts *Piney Point, Harpers* (MCW 2.180) [SMW PC1.123]

Clark (Clarke), Benjamin; inv.; 16 Aug 1709 (I&A 30.296); acct.; 4 Aug 1710 admx. Judith, w/o Robert Parker (I&A 31.356) (SMAA p. 196)

Clark, Thomas; will; 4 Jun 1711; 4 Dec 1711; sons Thomas, John, Adam, William, Benjamin, Luke; wife Julian; [dau. Mary]; tracts *Calverton, Mardike, Bowling's Reserve* (MCW 3.221) [SMW PC1.177]; inv.; Apr 1712; nok Fran. & John Clark (I&A 33a.192); acct.; 2 Jun 1714; extx. Julian (SMAA p. 259); acct.; 29 Jun 1715; planter; ex. Julian Clarke (I&A 36c.75)

Clarke, Richard; inv.; 17 Feb 1710 (I&A 32c.61); acct.; 16 Nov 1711; admx. Kathrine Clarke (I&A 33a.46) (SMAA p. 222)

Clarke (Clark), Edward; will; 30 Apr 1713; 24 Jun 1714; sons John, Edward, Clement; daus. Mary, Henrietta; wife Mary; tracts *Turvey, Houndslow's [Homule's] Addition* (MCW 4.22) [SMW PC1.198]; inv.; 15 Jul 1714; nok Thomas Walker, Martin, Yates (I&A 36a.229); acct.; 15 Mar 1715; extx. Mary Clarke (I&A 36c.279) (SMAA p. 281)

Clark, George; age ca 25; 2 Aug 1717 (CCR p. 39)

Clark, Thomas; <u>will</u>; 6 Nov 1719; 10 Nov 1719; wife Mary; bro. John (MCW 4.221); <u>inv.</u>; 22 Dec 1719; 12 Feb 1720; mentions John Clark, Jr.; admx. Marry Clark (I 3.221); <u>acct.</u>; 26 Aug 1720 (A 3.227) (SMAA p. 441)

Clark (Clarke), George; *Clarks Range*; 392 ac.; resur. 14 Mar 1720; 7 tracts *Stanhopes Neglect, Stamps Neglect, Ambersly, The Ponds,* part of *Governours Gift, Masons Purchases* (TLC p. 78); 5 Aug 1721 cert./pat. (COL)

Clarke, Robert; age 71 in 1721 (MD p. 34)

Clarke, Robert; <u>will</u>; 19 Aug 1721; 31 Jan 1725; sons Thomas, Robert, Benjamin, s/o wife Elizabeth; daus. Sarah Grinwell, Anne Hall, Jeny Gough [Jove], and Elinor, w/o Henry Grinwell [Greenwell]; tract *Addition* (MCW 5.210) [SMW PC1.302]; <u>inv.</u>; 19 Apr 1726; 28 Jun 1726; extx. Elisabeth Clark (I 11.337); <u>acct.</u>; 17 Jul 1727 (A 8.282)

Clarke, John; planter; <u>will</u>; 20 Jan 1727/8; 9 Feb 1727/8; sister Mary Compton; bros. Adam, Benjamin; mentions Thomas, s/o Luke Clarke, dec'd, and Electious, s/o Adam Clarke; tract *Chaptico Manor* (MCW 6.51) [SMW PC1.346]; <u>inv.</u>; 12 Feb 1727; 27 Feb 1727; nok Leonard Clark; ex. Adam Clarke (I 13.5); <u>acct.</u>; 16 Apr 1729 (A 9.339)

Clark, Francis; <u>inv.</u>; 10 May 1728; 4 Jun 1728; nok John & Leonard Clark; admx. Mary Clark (I 13.103); <u>acct.</u>; 3 Nov 1729; admx. Mary Clarke (A 9.494); <u>acct.</u>; 16 Sep 1730; 9 child. (A 10.466)

Clarke, Elisabeth; <u>inv.</u>; 7 Jun 1732; 7 Nov 1732; nok Mary Olnewy, Robert Clarke; adm./ex. James Clarke (I 16.653); <u>acct.</u>; 6 Mar 1734; mentions Robert, James, John, Mary, Winifred & Henaretta Clarke; adm. James Clarke (A 13.7)

Clarke, Adam; <u>will</u>; 1 Jun 1733; 8 Aug 1733; sons Electious, Joseph, Anthony; dau. Eliza; wife Mary; tract *Gravely Hill* (MCW 7.31) [SMW TA1.8]; <u>inv.</u> 5 Nov 1733; 11 Dec 1733; nok Elias & Thomas Barber; admx./extx. Mary Clarke (I 17.545); <u>acct.</u>; 2 Dec 1734 (A 12.736)

Clarke, Benjamin; <u>inv.</u>; 6 Aug 1733; 8 Aug 1733; nok James & Ann Clarke (I 17.329)

Clark, Harmon; <u>will</u>; 16 Nov 1733; 16 Nov 1733; bros. Lenard, Francis, William, Benjamin, John; sisters Susan [Leann], Mary, Joan, Ann (MCW 8.122) [SMW TA1.115]

Clark, Thomas; <u>inv.</u>; 24 Dec 1733; 14 Jan 1733; nok Abraham & Thomas Clark; admx./extx. Grace Clark (I 17.646); <u>acct.</u>; 15 Jan 1734; orphans Abraham, Thomas, James, John, Robert, Cutbert, Philip, William, Pricilla, Mary, Eleanor & Jane Clarke; admx. Grace Clark (A 12.747)

Clark, Robert; clerk; <u>acct.</u>; 22 May 1734; niece Susannah Murray (A 12.264)

Clark, James; *Clark's East Discovery*; 99 ac.; 10 Jun 1734 cert./pat. (COL) *Clark's West Discovery*; 212 ac.; 8 Nov 1735 cert./pat. (COL)

Clarke, George, Capt.; <u>acct.</u>; 16 Sep 1734; extx. Susannah Clarke (A 36.405)

Clark, Elisabeth, Mrs.; <u>inv.</u>; 25 Feb 1735; 12 Apr 1736; nok William Road, Ellinor Clarke (I 21.296); <u>acct.</u>; 13 Aug [filed with 1740]; mentions Joseph, Anthony, Eleanor, Mary Clark and Anne Reed (A 1854)

Clark, Robert; <u>inv.</u>; 3 Mar 1735; 6 Jul 1736; nok James & Benjamin Clarke; admx./extx. Mary Clarke (I 21.513); <u>acct.</u>; 12 Feb 1738; orphans William, Matthew, Robert, Richard & Thomas Clark; admx. Mary Clark (A 17.72)

Clarke, Mary; <u>will</u>; 24 Mar 1738/9; 19 Apr 1739; son Frances, William, Benjamin, John, Leonard (MCW 8.39) [SMW TA1.76]; <u>inv.</u>; 27 Jul 1739; 19 Sep 1739; nok Mary Morris, Leonard Clarke; admx./extx. Frances Clark (I 24.264); <u>acct.</u>; 10 Feb 1742; child. of Francis Clarke: William, Benjamin, John , 3 daus., wives of John Sotheron, Thomas Morris,Williamson Hay (A 19.369)

Clark, Benjamin; <u>acct.</u>; 5 Jul 1739; mentions Luke Clark, Mary Clark (A 17.192)

Clark, Robert; <u>inv.</u>; 21 Aug 1740; 4 Aug 1741; nok James & John Clark; admx./extx. Elizabeth Clark (I 26.327); <u>acct.</u>; 28 Nov 1744; orphans Bennitt, Susanna (A 21.135)

Clark, James; oral; <u>will</u>; 15 Feb 1742/3; sons Joseph, James; dau. Mary Ann & 3 unnamed younger daus.; wife unnamed (MCW 8.206) [SMW TA1.145]; <u>inv.</u>; 23 Apr 1743; 7 Jun 1743; nok John Clark, Mary Alroy; admx./extx. Henrietta Clark (I 28.1); <u>acct.</u>; 14 Nov 1744; orphans Joseph, James, Mary Ann, Elisabeth, Winerferd, Heneritta, Susanna; admx. Henneritta, w/o Joseph Howard (A 21.131)

Clark, George; *Itchcomb's Freehold*; 344 ac.; 10 Sep 1744 cert./pat. (COL)

Clarke, Mary [Mary Ann]; <u>will</u>; 28 Jan 1750; 15 Jul 1751; cousins Elizabeth Clarke, Elizabeth Read, Cary Read; bro. Anthony Clarke (MCW 10.164) [SMW TA1.272]

Clark, Leonard; <u>inv.</u>; 18 Jun 1750; 4 Sep 1750; nok Frances & Elisabeth Clark; admx./extx. Mary Clark (I 44.29); <u>acct.</u>; 4 Sep 1750 (A 28.280)

Clark, Ann; <u>inv.</u>; 4 Aug 1751; 9 Mar 1752; nok Joseph Clark, Eliar Reed; admx./ex. Anthony Clark (I 48.294)

Clarke, Robert and Ann; child. John [b. 15 Oct 1751], Mary [b. 29 Oct 1755], Robert [b. 17 Nov 1757], Ann [b. 17 Aug 1760], Eleanor [b. 22 May 1764] (SA p. 3)

Clarke, John and Eleanor; son Richard Langham [b. 19 Jan 1753] (SA p. 13, 48)

Clarke, George, Col.; <u>will</u>; oral; 29 Jun 1753; d. 23 Jun 1753; wife Susanna; daus. Ann, Sarah (MCW 10.278) [SMW TA1.351]; <u>inv.</u>; 5 Dec 1753; nok John Somervell, Thomas Aisquith; admx./extx. Susannah Clarke (I 57.49)

Clarke, George; <u>will</u>; 13 May 1753; 21 Jul 1753; son John Attaway Clarke; 1st wife Hannah; present wife Susanna; daus. Susanna Markall Smoote, Hannah Hey & Ellen, Susanna, Anne and Sarah Clarke; tracts *Piney Point, Clarkes Range;* mentions Jane, w/o Stephen Martin (MCW 10.278) [SMW TA1.304]

Clark, Cuthbert; *Clark's Lot*; 19 ac.; 10 Aug 1753 cert./pat. (COL)

Clark (Clarke), John; <u>will</u>; 1 Jan 1755; 31 Mar 1755; dau. Ann Wheatley, Elizabeth, Angelica; son Richard; wife Elizabeth; tract *Marys Hope* (MCW 11.81) [SMW TA1.328]; <u>inv.</u>; 23 Apr 1755; 22 Jul 1755; nok Joseph Wheatly, R. Barnhouse; adm./ex. Elisabeth Clarke (I 59.207)

Clark, Matthew; *Clark's Lot*; 52 ac.; 25 Mar 1756 cert./pat. (COL)

Clark, John; inv.; 14 Aug 1756; nok John Wiseman & John Baptist Greenwell; adms./exs. John Baptist Greenwell & wife Elinor (I 61.341); acct.; 1 Aug 1758; orphans Jane [age 15], Richard [age 8] l (A 42.93)

Clark, George, Col.; acct.; 31 Aug 1756; extx. Susannah, w/o John Black (A 39.211)

Clark, John; acct.; 29 Sep 1760; exs. Timothy Barnhouse & wife Elisabeth (A 46.13); dist. 29 Sep 1760; son Wheatly (BB 3.39)

Clark, James; inv.; 8 Jun 1761; nok Mark Gray, Philip Verim; admx. Mary Clark (I 74.288)

Clarke, James; will; 21 Nov 1762; 2 Mar 1763; sisters Henrietta Brown, Elizabeth, Susan; bro. Joseph Clarke; cousin Bennett Spalding; uncles John Clark, Thomas Spalding (MCW 12.175) [SMW TA1.444 (sic) ?434]; inv.; 30 Oct 1765; nok John & Suaney Clark; ex. Joseph Clark (I 87.317); acct.; 31 Oct 1765 (A 53.231)

Clark, John Attaway; *Brough*; 283 ac.; 28 Feb 1763 cert./pat. (COL)
   Blake's Creek; 384 ac. 29 Sep 1766 cert./pat. (COL)
   Clark's Victory; 142 ac.; [Capt.]; 28 Feb 1765 cert./pat. (COL)
   Clark's Discovery; 31 ac.; 21 Jun 1775 cert./pat. (COL)

Clarke [Clark], Phillip; will; 16 Feb 1766; 17 Nov 1766; sons Philip & his child.: John, Hannah, Catharine; George McCaul, Kenelon [Kenelm], Roger; g-daus. Rachel M. and Susanna McCaul Clark; wife Catharine; [tract *Bendex Neck*] (MCW 13.135) [SMW TA1.497]

Clarke, Thomas and Elizabeth; dau. Mary [b. 21 Jan 1771], Ann [b. 2 Mar 1773], Thomas [b. 3 Mar 1775] (SA p. 27)

Clark, Joshua; m. 16 Sep 1772 Mary Bowles (MM); dau. Eleanor [b. 12 Aug 1773], dau. Susanna [b. 19 Sep 1775] (SA p. 24, 27)

Clark, Cuthbert; m. 19 Jun 1774 Mary Ann Brown (MM)

Clarke, William and Monica Woodward (by license); m. 18 Oct 1781 (SA p. 59)

CLERK
Clerke, Edward; service by 1674 (SK 18.132)

Clerk, Thomas, Sr.; will; 20 Jan 1777; 15 Feb 1777; dau. Pressiller; son Ignatius (MCW 16.173)

CLOCKER
Clocker, Mary; wife of Daniel; 22 Mar 1651 (AM X.148, 171, 273)

Clocker, Daniell; *Clocker's Marsh*; 100 ac.; sur. 21 Apr 1651; 1707 poss. George Thompson; 14 Jul 1727 mentions Jane & John Thompson; St. Mary's Hundred (RR p. 2) (TLC p. 3)

Clocker, Mary; d/o Daniel Clocker; 1658 (AM XLI.210)

Clocker, Mary (alias Lane); age ca 45 in 1659 (MD p. 35)

Clocker, Mary; wife of Daniel; relict of James Courtney; her son Thomas
 Courtney [age 19 on 7 Jan 1660] (AM XLI.185, 210, 208, 212, 256, 391, 420)
Clocker, Daniel; cattle mark for child.: Elizabeth, Daniell, Mary, John and
 Catheryn; 7 Jan 1660 (AM XLI.392); Mary; wife of Daniel; 1666 (AM LVII.24)
Clocker, Daniel; will; 4 Feb 1675; 12 Feb 1675; son Daniel; dau. Rebecca; s-i-l
 Peter Watts; g-child. Peter and Mary Watts (MCW 1.116); acct.; 6 Feb 1676;
 sister Rebecca, w/o John Mekin; ex. Daniell Clocker (I&A 3.68)
Clocker, Daniel; *Lewis's Neck*; 30 ac.; 26 Nov 1681 cert./pat. (COL)
 St. Andrew's Freehold; 50 ac.; 26 Nov 1681 cert./pat. (COL)
Clocker, Daniell; inv.; 15 Sep 1683 (I&A 8.223)
Clocker, Daniell; acct.; 17 Apr 1689; admx. Patience (relict), w/o James Yore,
 (I&A 10.232); acct.; 17 Apr 1689 (SMAA p. 84)
Clocker, Daniel; age ca 40; wife Alice age ca 50; 11 May 1720 (CCR p. 46); age
 ca 40 in 1721 (MD p. 35)
Clocker, Daniel; sur. 18 Feb 1742 (TLC p. 108); *Clocker's Fancy*; 56 ac.; 5 Jun
 1745 cert./pat. (COL)
Clocker, Daniel, Sr.; will; 14 Apr 1747; 8 Jun 1747; dau. Elizabeth; son Daniel;
 tracts *Clocker's Fancy, Sisters Freehold* (MCW 9.112) [SMW TA1.199]
Clocker, Daniel; will; 26 Jan 1766; 9 Jun 1766; 6 child. Benjamin, Mary,
 Elizabeth, Daniel, William, Ann; wife Rebeccah; tracts *Clarkes Freehold,
 Luiss Neck* (MCW 13.109) [SMW TA1.495]; inv.; 9 Aug 1766; 14 Aug 1766; nok
 Ann Milburn; extx. Rebecca Clocker (I 91.89); acct.; 24 Dec 1769 (A 62.401);
 dist.; 24 Dec 1769 (BB 5.225)
Clocker, Benjamin and Lydia Baldwin (by license); m. 19 May 1784 (SA p. 62)

CLOUDS
Clouds, Richard, Mr.; inv.; 2 Feb 1701 (I&A 21.273); acct.; 6 Sep 1709 (SMAA p.
 211); 12 Sep 1710 (SMAA p. 209)
Cloud, Nicholas; will; 12 Jun 1714; 11 Aug 1714; bro. Benjamin; cous.
 Justinian Jordan (MCW 4.18) [SMW PC1.195]; acct.; 26 Jul 1716 (I&A 38b.9) (SMAA
 p. 307)
Clouds, Nicholas; age ca 63 in 1714 (MD p. 36)

COLE
Cole (Coale), William; *St. Williams* or *Coles Purchase*; 200 ac.; sur. 17 Oct
 1667; resur. 13 Jun 1683 for 210 ac. for Robert Cole; 1707 poss. Edward
 Cole; Choptico Hundred (RR p. 51) (TLC p. 49)
Coale, William; *St. Jerome's*; will; 25 Mar 1659; 17 Jul 1669; dau. Sara, w/o
 Elias Beach; wife Sarah; child. Richard, William, John, Nicholas and dau.
 Mary Coale (MCW 1.47); William Cole, planter of St. Georges [SMW PC1.8]
Cole, Robert; St. Clement's Bay; will; 2 Apr 1662; 8 Sep 1663; 3 sons Robert,
 William, Edward; s-i-l Francis Knott; daus. Mary and Eliza; sister Anne
 Harinton; mother Mrs. Jane Cole; cous. Henry Hankes (MCW 1.25)

Cole, Robert (Ensign); wife Elizabeth; both dec'd 1663; child. Robert, Mary, William Maria, Edward, Elizabeth (MD p. 21)

Cole, Robert; *St. Roberts*; 200 ac.; sur. 17 Oct 1667; let fall; 1707 no poss.; Choptico Hundred (RR p. 51) (TLC p. 49)

Cole, Edw'd; *St Edward*; 115 ac.; sur. 17 Oct 1667; 7 Mar 1710 from Edward Cole 115 ac. to Cornelius Wildman; 1707 poss. Edw'd Cole; Resurrection Hundred (RR p. 61) (TLC p. 58)

Cole, William & Edward; acct.; 24 Mar 1674 (I&A 1.61)

Cole, Robert; acct.; mentions son Robert, dau. Mary, w/o Ignatius Warren; undated [1677-9] (SMAA p. 49)

Cole, Richard; inv.; [filed with 1677] (I&A 4.108)

Cole, William; wife Margaret, extx. of Michael Rochford; 1679 (AM LXIX.26)

Cole, Wm.; *Manly*; 50 ac.; sur. 19 Jan 1680; 1707 poss. John Cole; New Town Hundred (RR p. 38) (TLC p. 37); 19 Jan 1681 cert./pat. (COL)

Cole, Edward; *Coles Adventure*; 150 ac.; sur. 1 Jun 1682; 1707 poss. Edward Cole; St. Clements Hundred (RR p. 47) (TLC p. 46]; 1 Jun 1682 cert./pat. (COL)

Cole, Robert; *Cole's Addition*; 50 ac.; 1707 poss. James Blomefield; New Town Hundred (RR p. 41) (TLC p. 40); 10 Jun 1686 cert./pat. (COL)

Cole, William; acct.; 9 Aug 1686; admx. Margarett (relict), w/o Richard Vowles (I&A 9.143) (SMAA p. 87)

Cole, John; will; 3 Jan 1687; 3 Mar 1687; son William; wife Ann (MCW 2.21) [SMW PC1.62]; inv.; 6 Mar 1687 (I&A 9.471)

Cole, Nicholas; will; 4 Feb 1687/8; 15 Mar 1687/8; William Cole, s/o John and Ann Cole; sister Mary Guyther and Mary, d/o William Guyther (MCW 2.22); inv.; 17 Mar 1687 (I&A 9.470)

Cole, Edward; *Cole's Purchase*; 210 ac.; 13 Jun 1689 cert./pat. (COL)

Cole, Robert; acct.; 30 Apr 1695; extx. Rebecca Cole (relict), w/o Thomas Warren (I&A 13a.292)

Cole, Thomas; inv.; [filed with 1698] (I&A18.133); acct.; 8 May 1698 (I&A 18.133)

Cole, Thomas; inv.; 25 Oct 1705 (I&A 25.44); acct.; 1 Mar 1706; admx. Hannah Cole (I&A 26.156) (SMAA p. 135)

Cole, Jonah; inv.; 21 Jan 1709 (I&A 29.436)

Cole, Johannah; acct.; 30 Jul 1709; admx. of Thomas Cole; Valentine Cole, admn. of Johannah (SMAA p. 173)

Coale, William; inv.; 15 Jul 1715; 31 Aug 1715; nok b-i-l Gerrard Hopkins; bro. Phil. Coale (I&A 36c.69)

Cole, Francis; inv.; 29 Mar 1716; nok bro. Lentine Cole (I&A 37a.163); acct.; 10 Apr 1717; admx. Mary Cole (I&A 39b.62) (SMAA p. 322)

Cole, Valentine (Volintine); planter; 26 May 1716; 17 Sep 1716; son John (MCW 4.70) [SMW PC1.208]; inv.; 1 Oct 1716 (I&A 38b.78); acct.; ex. John Cole; 14 Sep 1717 (I&A 39a.18) (SMAA p. 338)

Cole, Mary; widow of Francis; inv.; 14 Jun 1716 (I&A 37a.163)

Cole, Edward; <u>will</u>; 16 Apr 1717; 20 Dec 1717; wife Elizabeth; child. Edward, Elizabeth Heard, Robert, Honour Spalding, Ruth Mattingly, Susanna Jenkins and Mary Jenkins; tract *Maiden Bower* (MCW 4.171) [SMW PC1.225]; <u>inv.</u>; 3 Mar 1717; nok Edward Cole, William Head (I&A 39a.22); <u>acct.</u>; 24 Mar 1718; mentions orphans; admx./extx. Mrs. Elisabeth & Robert Cole (A 1.367) (SMAA p. 346); 16 Aug 1720 (A 3.57) (SMAA p. 417); <u>acct.</u>; 12 Feb 1720 (A 2.441) (SMAA p. 450); <u>inv.</u>; 20 Apr 1720; 18 Jun 1720; nok Edward & Robert Cole, Jr.; extx. Elisabeth Cole (I 4.56)

Cole, Robert; <u>will</u>; 3 Mar 1719/20; _ Apr 1720; sons John, Robert; dau. Mary; wife Elizabeth; bro. Edward; tracts *Cole's Purchase, Pearewales* (MCW 5.2); tract called *Poor Wales* [SMW PC1.255]; <u>acct.</u>; 9 Jun 1721; extx. Mrs. Elisabeth Cole (A 3.373); <u>acct.</u>; 1 Apr 1723; extx. Elisabeth, w/o James Thompson (A 5.107); <u>acct.</u>; 6 Jun 1724 (A 6.38)

Cole, Elizabeth, Mrs.; age ca 53; sister of Gerrard Slye; 25 Jun 1722 (CCR p. 50); age ca 57; 12 Apr 1725 (CCR p. 59)

Cole, Edward; wife Anne Neale; sons Joseph [b. 9 Apr 1727; d. 10 Dec 1863 Rome], Robert [b. 23 Dec 1732; d. 28 Apr 1812 Bury St. Edmund's in Suffolk] (JM p. 315)

Cole, Elizabeth, b. 1729; d. 8 Mar 1816 Hartpury Court, Gloucester; d/o Edward Cole and Anne Neale; widow of James Brooke of Calvert Co.; Dominican Nun (JM p. 315)

Cole (Coll), William; <u>will</u>; 7 Feb 1732; 31 Mar 1733; wife Elizabeth; mentions Susanah, d/o John Langley (MCW 7.11) [SMW PC1.17]; <u>inv.</u> 8 Jun 1733; nok Thomas Griffin, Luke Lee; admx./extx. Elisabeth Cole (I 17.156); <u>acct.</u>; 29 Jul 1734 (A 12.457)

Cole, Elisabeth, Mrs.; <u>inv.</u>; 1 Mar 1734; 18 Jun 1734; nok Luke Gardiner, Mary King (I 18.335); <u>acct.</u>; 30 Jun 1735 (A 13.232); 3 Mar 1736 (A 15.296)

Cole, Mary; <u>inv.</u>; 20 Jul 1738; 8 Aug 1738; nok Peter & Ann Thompson; adm./ex. Francis Cole (I 23.353); <u>acct.</u>; 13 Aug 1739 (A 17.241)

Cole, John; *Jones's Woods Addn.*; 59½ ac.; sur. 6 Oct 1737 (TLC p. 95); 59 ac.; 5 Oct 1738 cert./pat. (COL)

Cole, James; mariner; <u>will</u>; 8 Jun 1747; 20 Sep 1749; father Edward (MCW 10.48) [SMW TA1.236]

Cole, Elizabeth; widow; <u>will</u>; 1 Nov 1750; 19 Jan 1750; cousin Joshua; sister Anna; John, Joshua & Josiah, sons of John Langley; John, s/o John Langley, Sr.; Hugh, s/o Hugh Hopewell; Anna, d/o cousin Hugh Hopewell; Thomas, s/o Thomas Griffin; tract *Halley's Grant* (MCW 10.142) [SMW TA1.281]

Cole, John; <u>will</u>; 8 Mar 1752; 4 Apr 1752; son John; daus. Elener Daffin, Mary Hebb [Hobbs], Hannah Lynch, Ann, Pasaince, Elizabeth, Rebeckah; tract *Addition to Jonesis Woods* (MCW 10.201) [SMW TA1.287]; <u>inv.</u>; 30 May 1752; 6 Nov 1752; nok John Lynch, Joseph Webb; adm./ex. John Cole (I 51.61); <u>acct.</u>; 21 May 1755 (A 38.22)

Cole, Francis and Ann; child. Susanna [b. 27 Feb 1757], Mary Ann [b. 2 Feb 1760], Winifred [b. 3 Sep 1766] (SA p. 4, 37, 191)

Cole, Francis; inv.; 4 Mar 1760; mentions Francis & John Cole; admx./extx. Susanna Cole (I 71.145)

Cole, Edward; will; 26 Mar 1761; 21 Dec 1762; wife Ann; g-child. Ignatius Fenwick, Francis Brooke s/o James, James Cole, James & Jane Smith, Joseph & Robert Cole; son Joseph, Robert, Henry; daus. Mary Fenwick, Elizabeth Brooke; tracts *Delabrooke Mannor, Partnership* in CH Co. (MCW 12.177) [SMW TA1.553]; inv.; 31 Aug 1763; nok Robert Cole, John Smith; extx. Ann Cole (I 81.248; 82.205); acct.; 11 Sep 1765 (A 53.91); dist.; 14 Sep 1765; legatees g-child. John & Jane Smith, Francis Brooke, sons Joseph & Robert, daus. Mary Fenwick & Elisabeth Brooke; mentions child. of dau. Mary: Ignatius & Edward Fenwick (BB 4.134)

Cole, Susanna; acct.; 29 Jun 1763; child. Judith, Fran., Elisabeth, John, Ann, Jeremiah, Barnaby, Eleanor; admx. Susanna Cole (A 49.602)

Cole, Ann; widow; will; 11 Jun 1768; 6 Dec 1768; son Robert Cole; daus. Mary Fenwick, Elizabeth Brooke; g-child. Francis Brook, Jane & John Smith; niece Mildred Neale; [dau. Constantia Swann] (MCW 14.68) [SMW TA1.560]; inv.; 7 Dec 1768; 18 Jul 1769; nok John Smith, Ignatius Chamberlin (I 101.325); acct.; 25 Aug 1770 (A 64.226); 10 Oct 1774 (A 71.319); dist.; 10 Feb 1774; child. Mary Fenwick, Robert Cole, Elisabeth Brooke; grandchild. Francis Brooke, John & Jane Smith, Constantia Swan; niece Mary Neale; mentions Ann Lowe (BB 7.20)

Cole, John; inv.; 7 Apr 1770; nok Robert Cole (I 103.236); acct.; 17 Dec 1770 (A 66.69)

Cole, Robert; will; 26 Nov 1771; 2 Dec 1771; wife Sarah alias Elizabeth; child. Eleanor, Elizabeth, Mary, Henritta w/o Basil Haden, Jane dec'd w/o Robert Mattingly, Margaret Melton dec'd w/o Richard Melton; granddau. Catharine Mattingly (MCW 14.188) [SMW TA1.629]; inv.; 24 Aug 1772 (I 110.105)

Cole, Elisabeth; inv.; 16 Nov 1774; 17 May 1775; nok Basil Hayden, Cuthbert Fenwick (I 121.418); acct.; 20 Aug 1776 (A 74.9); dist.; 20 Aug 1776 (BB 7.68)

COMBS

Comes, Abraham; immigrated by 1679 with dau. Sarah (SK WC2.47)

Combe, Abraham; will; 26 Dec 1684; 30 Jan 1684; wife Margaret; dau. Sarah Clarke (MCW 1.142) [SMW PC1.51]

Combes (Combs, Croombes), Simmond (Simon); Mr.; inv.; 6 Mar 1716; nok Mary Combes (I&A 37b.130); acct.; 1 Sep 1719; admx. Mary, w/o Henry Celby (A 2.209) (SMAA p. 387)

Combs, William; age ca 50; 8 Oct 1721 (CCR p. 50)

Coombs (Coombes, Comeses), Thomas; inv.; 26 Oct 1721; nok Chistopher & Mary Combes; admx. Mary Combes (I 6.131); acct.; 29 Jan 1721; admx. Mary Coombs (A 4.78); 3 Oct 1722 (A 4.241); acct.; 2 Jun 1724; adms. William Morgaine & wife Mary (A 6.34)

Combs, William; inv.; 5 Jan 1742; 18 Mar 1742; nok Enoch Combs; admx./exs. Joseph Inking (Jenkins) & wife Mary (I 27.372); acct.; 23 May 1744 (A 20.237)

Combs, William; Gent.; will; 13 Oct 1742; 20 Dec 1742; child. Mary Waughop, Elianor Medley, Enoch, Thomas Hatton, Susannah, William, Jr., James, Philip; wife Mary (MCW 8.191) [SMW TA1.116]

Combs, Enock (Enoch); will; 18 Apr 1756; 6 Jul 1756; sons Enock, William, Bennet, Ignatious; wife Mary (MCW 11.137) [SMW TA1.344]; acct.; 2 Nov 1757; orphans Enoch & William [of age], Ignatious [age 18], Bennet [age 10]; exs. Mary & Enoch Combs (A 41.258); dist.; 2 Nov 1757 (BB 2.73)

Combs, Enock (Enoch); inv.; 11 Mar 1761; 2 Jun 1761; nok Ignatius & William Combs; admx. Catharine Combs (I 74.258); acct.; 18 Feb 1762 (A 47.379); dist.; 10 Feb 1762 (BB 3.116)

Combes, William and Eleanor; child. Raphael [b. 6 Oct 1760], Eleanor [b. 29 Aug 1762], Margaret [b. 13 Apr 1764], William [b. 12 Apr 1766], Mary Ann [b. 18 Dec 1768] (SA p. 192)

Combes, Bennet and Elizabeth; daus. Mary [b. 28 Jun 1765], Barbara [b. 9 Feb 1767] (SA p. 193)

Combs, Thomas Hatten (Hatton); will; 1 Apr 1766; 17 Jun 1766; sons William, George Craghell, Thomas Hatten; wife Mary (MCW 13.110) [SMW TA1.494]; inv.; 25 Jul 1766; 24 Aug 1766; nok William Contanceanwaughot (William Coutanceau Waughop), William Combs; extx. Mary Coombs (I 91.91); inv.; 10 Oct 1767; extx. (I 95.25); acct.; 12 Nov 1767 (A 57.335); acct.; 22 Sep 1772 (A 67.143); dist.; 22 Sep 1772; widow; 5 daus. (BB 6.187)

Combs, Mary; will; 8 Nov 1768; 12 Apr 1769; sons Bennett, William, Ignatius; granddaus. Mary Walbred Combs and Elizabeth Combs (MCW 14.93) [SMW TA1.568]

Combs, James; will; 20 Aug 1772; 22 Sep 1772; bros. William, Philip; sister Susannah Cooper (MCW 14.237) [SMW TA1.637]

Combs (Combes), Elizabeth; will; 29 Nov 1772; 10 Feb 1773; sisters Mary, Eleanor, Tabethey; bro. Thomas Hatton Combs (MCW 15.31) [SMW TA1.666]

Combs, William; will; 22 Jan 1774; 4 Apr 1774; sons Raphael, William; wife Mary; unnamed child.; bro. Ignatius; tract *Wilderspoole, Forest of Dean* (MCW 15.149) [SMW TA1.711]; inv.; 3 Aug 1774; nok Ignatius & Bennet Combs; extx. Mary Eleanor Combs (I 119.131)

COMPTON

Compton, Fairfax; will; 1760; 13 Oct 1760; child. James, Mary & Ann or Mary Ann, [Mary Ann] Knott, Ignatius, Joseph, John Baptist; wife Sarah (MCW 12.2) [SMW TA1.400]; unclear re names Mary, Ann or Mary Ann; inv.; nok John Baptis & James Compton; admx./extx. Sarah Compton (I 71.159); acct.; 10 May 1761; extx. Sarah Compton (A 47.220); dist.; 10 May 1761; child. James, Mary, Ann, Knott, Ignatius, Joseph, John; (BB 3.110)

Compton, Matthew; <u>will</u>; Feb 1770; 3 Sep 1770; wife Rachel; child. Barton &
Alexander [or Barton Alexander], Edmund Howard, Stephen, Matthew, John
and Susannah Compton; tract *Worncoat* (MCW 14.142) [SMW TA1.592]; <u>inv.</u>; 24
Oct 1770; 10 Oct 1771; nok William & Matthew Compton; extx. Rachel
Compton (I 107.184)

Compton, Stephen; m. 1 Apr 1784 Abigail French Moore (BRU 2.535)

CONNARY

Connery, Tho.; unnamed; 200 ac.; sur. 8 Mar 1652; in *Fenwick Mannor*;
Resurrection Hundred (RR p. 58) (TLC p. 56)

Conary (Connary), Edward; <u>acct.</u>; 31 Oct 1677; extx. Mary Heyley (relict) (I&A
4.522); <u>acct.</u>; 19 Oct 1680 (I&A 7a.280)

CONNELL

Connell, Daniel; age ca 52 1702 (MD p. 39)

Connel, James, Sr.; <u>inv.</u>; 20 Jan 1739; 22 Mar 1741; nok Thomas & Dinis
Connell; adm./ex. James Connell (I 25.439)

CONNELLY

Connally, Charles; <u>inv.</u>; 6 Oct 1709 (I&A 30.294); <u>acct.</u>; 8 Jan 1711; admx.
Honnor Connelly (I&A 33a.162) (SMAA p. 221)

Connelly, Daniel; <u>inv.</u>; 6 Nov 1719 (I 3.53); <u>acct.</u>; 6 Nov 1719; admx. Elisabeth
Hennington of CH Co. (A 2.321) (SMAA p. 377)

Connoly, Phillip; <u>inv.</u>; 28 Mar 1734; 1 Jul 1734; adm./ex. John Conoley (I
18.338); <u>acct.</u>; 21 Apr 1735 (A 13.121)

Connelly, Rhodolph and Ann Chloe; son Rhodolph [b. 29 Mar 1767] (SA p. 193)

Conely, Michael; <u>inv.</u>; 4 Dec 1773; 3 Mar 1774 (I 116.199)

CONNER

Conner, Humphrey; immigrated by 1667 (SK 18.12)

Conner, Richard; age ca 51 in 1718 (MD p. 39)

Conner, Elisabeth; <u>inv.</u>; 20 May 1757; 6 Dec 1757; nok Fran. Pilbrow, Elisabeth
Brown; adm./ex. Thomas Pilbrox (I 65.10)

COODE

Coode, John; wife Susanna, late w/o Robert Slye; mother and guardian of
Elizabeth and Frances Slye, daus. of Robert; 1679/80 (AM LXIX.136, 179, 313;
LXV.395, 418, 506)

Coade, John; age ca 56 in 1705 (MD p. 36)

Coode, John; <u>will</u>; 27 Feb 1708; 28 Mar 1709; sons John, William, Richard;
daus. Mary, Ann, Winifred; wife Elizabeth; tracts *Pendreine, Pissimore Point,
Second Thought, Bluff Point* (MCW 3.121) [SMW PC1.152]

Cood, John; d. ca 1709; child. Richard, Mary, Ann, Winifred; wife Elizabeth; she m/2 William Hook; Mary m. Justinian Jordan; Ann m. William Scot; 9 May 1723 (CCR p. 56)

Cood, John, Col.; <u>acct.</u>; 6 Jun 1715; exs. William Hooke and wife Elisabeth (I&A 36c.66); <u>acct.</u>; 6 Jun 1715 (SMAA p. 282)

Coode, John; <u>will</u>; 20 Apr 1718; 29 Apr 1718; sons Thomas, John, William; daus. Jane, Susannah, Ann; wife Ann; tracts *Crosshall, Dinard's Point, Frogg Hall* (MCW 4.171) [SMW PC1.229]; <u>inv.</u>; 21 May 1718; nok John Blackiston, William Coode (I 1.315); <u>acct.</u>; 11 May 1719; extx. Anne Coode (A 1.419); <u>acct.</u>; 5 Jun 1719 (A 2.313) (SMAA p. 380, 397); <u>acct.</u>; 2 Aug 1720 (A 3.78)

Coade, Richard, Mrs.; <u>inv.</u>; 28 Jun 1736; 23 Aug 1736; nok Winifred Burch, N. Scot; admx./extx. Judith Coode (I 21.517)

Coode, William; <u>inv.</u>; 11 Dec 1741; 6 Apr 1742; nok John Coode, William Mills; adm./ex. Thomas Coode (I 26.488); <u>acct.</u>; 19 Oct 1743 (A 19.541)

Coad, James; <u>inv.</u>; 26 Jun 1766; 29 Jul 1766; nok George Pembrook, Joseph Coud; admx. Isabell Coad (I 91.97); <u>acct.</u>; 27 Nov 1766 (A 55.322)

Coode, Thomas; <u>inv.</u>; 21 Nov 1766; 25 Jun 1767; nok Daniel Rawlings, Richard King; adms. Ann Rawlings, Charles King & wife Susannah (I 93.117); <u>acct.</u>; 25 Jun 1771 (A 66.168); <u>dist.</u>; 25 Jun 1771 (BB 6.93)

Coode, John; <u>inv.</u>; 16 Jan 1767; 17 Mar 1767; nok John & William Coode; admx. Susanna Coode (I 91.322); <u>inv.</u>; 26 Apr 1768 (I 97.96); <u>acct.</u>; 30 Jun 1768 (A 58.246); <u>acct.</u>; 18 Feb 1770 (A 64.98)

COOKE

Cooke, William; <u>inv.</u>; 17 Sep 1685 (I&A 9.63)

Cooke, Thomas; planter; <u>will</u>; 3 Jun 1715; 3 May 1716; sons Thomas, John, Henry, William; daus. Margaret, Bethe, Elinor, Mary; wife Elizabeth (MCW 4.71) [SMW PC1.203]; <u>inv.</u>; 7 May 1716; nok Thomas, Jr. and Elisabeth Cook, Jr. (I&A 37a.159)<u>acct.</u>; 15 Apr 1717; extx. Elisabeth Cooke (I&A 39b.63) (SMAA p. 320)

Cooke, Thomas; *Borough*; 220 ac.; 6 Jun 1719 cert./pat. (COL) *Brough*; 212 ac.; resur. 23 Feb 1714; pat. 10 Sep 1716; St. Clements Manor (TLC p. 72)

Cook, Thomas; <u>inv.</u>; 31 Mar 1720; 20 Jul 1730; nok Thomas & Henry Cook; admx./extx. Johannah Cooke (I 15.605)

Cooke, Robert; <u>inv.</u>; 14 Jan 1729; 3 Mar 1729; nok minors; admx./extx. Sarah Cooke (I 15.372)

Cooke, Thomas; <u>will</u>; oral; 13 Nov 1729; dau. Dianna; wife Johannah; mentions Catherine, w/o Walter Sykes of Poplar Hill (MCW 6.142); <u>acct.</u>; 22 Feb 1730; 2 child.; admx. Johanna, w/o John Wharet (A 10.634)

Cooke, Eleanor; <u>inv.</u>; 22 May 1731; 16 Aug 1731; nok Thomas & William Cook; adm./ex. Henry Cook (I 16.292); <u>acct.</u>; 16 Aug 1731 (A 11.225)

Cooke, Richard [?Robert]; <u>acct.</u>; 4 Aug 1731; mentions John & Alexander Cooke; admx. Sarah, w/o Richard Melton (A 11.220)

Cooke (Cook), Mary; inv.; 13 __ 1754; 4 Dec 1754; nok Mary Campbell, John Hammond (I 58.314); acct.; 4 Dec 1754; orphans Mary Campbell & Rachel [both of age]; adm. Joshua Campbell (A 36.518)

Cooke, Thomas and Jane; child. Susannah [b. 19 Sep 1755], Thomas [b. 13 Jan 1757], Benjamin [b. 6 Oct 1759], Jane [b. 27 Sep 1763], Joanna [b. 2 Nov 1765], Catharine [b. 18 Mar 1768] (SA p. 4)

Cooke, John; dist.; 18 Feb 1770; admx. Mrs. Susanna Coode (BB 5.384)

Cook, Robert; m. 7 Jan 1778 Susannah Watson (BRU 2.535)

COOPER

Cooper, Thomas; St. Michaels Hundred; carpenter; d. by 15 Jun 1640 (AM IV.64)

Cooper (Coop), Robert; 28 Apr 1641; 12 Jan 1641; wife Eliza, extx. (MCW 1.1)

Cooper, Anne; widow of Walter Cooper; will; 10 Sep 1651; 21 Sep 1651; child.: Katharine, Eliza:, Dorothy and Susan Cooper; Henry Hastings who m. dau. of Walter Cooper; bro. John Depotter and cous. Richard Bridgman, both of Holland; exs. bros. William and Thomas Daynes (MCW 1.4)

Cooper, Samuel; [s/o Sampson (alderman of Rippon, Yorke, England)] whose will 11 Aug 1659 mentions sons Samuel & Jonathan and wife Bridgett] (AM XLI.456; XLIX.94, 221, 222, 242; LVII.169, 236)

Cooper, Robert; inv.; 28 Sep 1699 (I&A 19½a.26)

Cooper, Thomas; freeholder; 1 Feb 1714; 17 Mar 1714/5; sons Thomas and Richard (MCW 4.73) [SMW PC1.199]

Cooper, Nathaniel; age ca 42; Jun 1715; tract *Fenwick Manor* (CCR p. 33)

Cooper, Christina Barbara; widow; St. Mary's City; will; 5 Oct 1717; 23 Oct 1717; son Nicholas Guyther; g-child. Richard Beard, Mary Leigh; daus. Dorothy Leigh, Ann Beckwith; s-i-l John Leigh (MCW 4.172) [SMW PC1.179]; acct.; 8 Mar 1717 (SMAA p. 341)

Cooper, Richard; *Cooper's Addition*; 94 ac.; 12 Oct 1721 cert./pat. (COL) *Frightful*; 180 ac.; 21 Sep 1730 cert./pat. (COL)

Cooper, Thomas; will; 13 Mar 1722; 1 Apr 1723; daus.-i-l Elizabeth and Frances Bright; cousins Thomas, Mary and Teresa Cooper; bro. Richard; dau. Katherine; wife Teresa; tract *Crackbourn's Purchase* (MCW 5.137) [SMW PC1.277]; inv.; 11 Apr 1722; 14 Jun 1723; nok Elisabeth Bright, Elisabeth Heally; adm./ex. Richard Cooper (I 8.229); acct.; 3 Aug 1724; mentions Mary, d/o David Everson (A 6.125); acct.; 7 Oct 1728 (A 9.105)

Cooper, Nathaniel, Jr.; *Part of Scotland*; 151 ac.; sur. 8 Jun 1725; sur. formerly *Scotland* for Nath'l Cooper & Tho. William (TLC p. 83); 150 ac.; 26 Mar 1726 cert./pat. (COL)

Cooper, Nathaniel; planter; will; 1 Apr 1729; 3 Jun 1729; son Henry; wife Heneritta; tract *Part of Scotland* (MCW 6.119) [SMW PC1.343]; inv.; 22 Jul 1729; 17 Sep 1729; Jr.; nok Nathan Cooper, William Spalding; admx./extx. Henrietta Cooper (I 15.107); acct.; 5 Aug 1730; mentions Clement & Lucretia, orphans of Henry Speake; extx. Henrietta, w/o Joseph Woodward (A 10.421)

Cooper, Teresa; age 25; 17 Jul 1730; widow of Thomas Cooper, innkeeper; m. Richard Winsett (CCR p. 64)

Cooper (Cowper), Nathaniel; <u>will</u>; _ __ 1730; 22 Jan 1732; wife Mary; sons Nathan, Mark, Basil; g-son Henry [age ca 10], s/o Nathan; daus. Mary, Ann, Elizabeth; tract *St. Helling's [Holling's] Swamp* (MCW 7.10) [SMW PC1.363]; <u>inv.</u>; 1 May 1733; 28 Jun 1733; nok Mary & Anne Cooper; admx./extx. Mary Cooper (I 17.172); <u>acct.</u>; 8 Jul 1734 (A 12.449)

Cooper, Nathan; <u>inv.</u>; 24 Sep 1733; 12 Nov 1733; nok Ann & Mark Cooper; admx./extx. Mary Cooper (I 17.540); <u>acct.</u>; 8 Jul 1734 (A 12.354)

Cooper, Mary; widow; <u>will</u>; 30 Apr 1735; 19 May 1735; daus. Ann, Elizabeth; sons Mark, Basil (MCW 7.147) [SMW PC1.40]; <u>inv.</u>; 22 Oct 1735; 15 Dec 1735; nok Mary & Elisabeth Cooper; admx./extx. Ann Cooper (I 21.205); <u>acct.</u>; 11 Feb 1737; admx. Ann, dec'd, w/o John Dorsey (A 16.3); <u>acct.</u>; 1 Jan 1738 (A 17.36)

Cooper, Basil; <u>will</u>; 24 Apr 1748; 2 May 1748; bro. Mark; Levin s/o John Dorsey; Mary Ann, d/o James [John] Egerton; Henrietta White, Matthew, Ann & [John], ch/o Mark Cooper; Nathan s/o Nathaniel Cooper (MCW 9.144) [SMW TA1.213]; <u>inv.</u>; 10 May 1748; 12 Sep 1748; nok Henerita Lukile, Martha Cooper; adm./ex. William Looker (I 37.195); <u>acct.</u>; 8 Sep 1749 (A 27.110); <u>acct.</u>; 1 Jul 1751 (A 30.197)

Cooper, Henry and Susanna; child. Mary [b. 30 Oct 1749], William [b. 5 Nov 1751], Henrietta [b. 10 Jan 1754] (SA p. 36)

Cooper, Richard; <u>will</u>; 29 Jan 1758; 3 Aug 1758; daus. Mary Hopewell [?dec'd], Treascia Spink, Monica Finwick, Susannah Noble, Elizabeth, Elinor, Henrietta, Catherine; sons Thomas, Richard, Clement; bro. Thomas; wife Elizabeth; tracts *Coopers Addition, Hopewell, Frightfull* (MCW 11.212) [SMW TA1.367]; <u>inv.</u>; 17 Dec 1758; nok Catharine & Mary Ann Spalding; adms./exs. Elisabeth & Thomas Cooper (I 66.18, 22); <u>acct.</u>; 8 Jun 1759 (A 43.172)

Cooper, Richard; <u>will</u>; 27 Nov 1766; 17 Dec 1766; sister Catharine Raper; cousins Mark, Francis, Sary, Elizabeth and Eliner Noble, Elizabeth and Robert Fenwick; bros. Thomas, Clement; sisters Eleanor, Henriette; mentions John s/o James Sissells; mother unnamed; tract *Crackburn's Purchase* (MCW 13.150) [SMW TA1.533]; <u>inv.</u>; 4 Mar 1767; nok Susanna Nobel, Clement Cooper; ex. Thomas Cooper (I 91.327); <u>acct.</u>; 22 Aug 1768; ex. Thomas Cooper (A 58.261)

Cupper, Clement; <u>will</u>; 14 Feb 1774; 14 Apr 1774; bro. Thomas; mother Elizabeth; sisters Eleanor, Heneritta (MCW 15.129) [SMW TA1.703]

CORBIN

Colbin (Corbin), William; <u>inv.</u>; 13 Aug 1764; 5 Nov 1764; adm. Henry Corbin (I 86.57); <u>acct.</u>; 16 Oct 1765 (A 53.230)

Corbin, Henry; <u>inv.</u>; 18 Jan 1768; nok Sary Corbin (I 97.178); <u>acct.</u>; 30 Oct 1769; adm. George Corbin (A 62.14)

CORDEA

Cordea, Marke; 19 Apr 1761; naturalized; b. Normandy (CMN N5)

Cordea, Hester; 6 Jun 1674; b. Deepe, Normandy; naturalized (CMN N8)

Cordea, Mark; gent.; *Hog Quarter*; 250 ac.; 24 Sep 1680 cert./pat. (COL)
  Hog Ridge; 150 ac.; 25 Sep 1680 cert./pat. (COL)
  Cordea's Hope; 1 ac.; [1684] cert./pat. (COL)

Cordea, Mark (Marke); will; 27 Mar 1685; 7 Nov 1685; wife Hester; sons-i-l
  Henry Fox, Anthony Lecompte [Lecount], James Cullen; mentions Mary, d/o
  Col. Jarboe & Elizabeth, d/o Garret Van Sweringen, Samuel s/o Samuel
  Brockwist; tracts *Cross Manor, Elizabeth Manor, Hoggs Ridge & Hoggs Neck*
  in DO Co., *Screton* and [*Rumbley Marsh* in SO Co.] (MCW 1.159) [SMW PC1.53];
  inv.; 15 Dec 1685 (I&A 8.515); acct.; [filed with 1696-7] (I&A 15.40)

CORNWALLIS

Cornwalyes, Thomas, Esq.; came to MD on the *Ark* in 1634 with partner, John
  Saunders, who d. during the voyage, and 12 servants (SK ABH.244)

Cornwallis, Tho.; *Cornwallis Cross*; 2,000 ac.; sur. 9 Sep 1639; 1707 poss.
  William Herbert; St. Inigoes Hundred (RR p. 15) (TLC p. 15)
  St. Elizabeths; 2,000 ac.; sur. 9 Sep 1639; 1707 poss. Mary Vansweringen &
  Wm. Bladen; St. Inigoes Hundred (RR p. 15) (TLC p. 15)
  West St. Marys Mannour; 2,000 ac.; sur. 20 Sep 1640; 1707 poss. His
  Lordship; St. Georges Hundred (RR p. 16) (TLC p. 16)
  Resurrection Mannour; 4,000 ac.; sur. 24 Mar 1650; 1707 poss. George
  Plowden; Resurrection Hundred (RR p. 58) (TLC p. 55)
  Nutthall; 200 ac.; sur. 28 Jul 1654; within lines of *St. Mary Hill Freehold*;
  1704 called *Town Land, Cross Town Land, Cross Neck*; 1707 poss. by Eliza.
  Baker; St. Mary's Hundred (RR p. 2) (TLC p. 2)

Cornewalleys, Thomas and wife Penelope; 9 Aug 1661 conveyed 2000 ac. on
  St. Inegoes Creek to John Nutthall of Northampton Co., VA (AM XLIX.3)

CORUM

Corom, Henry; acct.; 5 Sep 1740; orphan James Corom; admx. Elisabeth, w/o
  John Letherland (A 18.62)

Corum, James; inv.; 12 May 1774; 29 Nov 1774 (I 118.223); 10 Aug 1775 (I
  124.16)

Corum, Isaac and Barbara; son John Rollins [b. 20 Nov 1799; bapt. 3 Aug 1800]
  (SA p. 31)

COURTNEY

Courtney, Thomas; wife Sarah, now or late of CA Co.; 1664 (AM XLIX.281, 425)

Courtney, Thomas; *Come Away*; 100 ac.; sur. 26 May 1664; 1707 poss. Mary
  Courtney, widow; St. Mary's Hundred; [land not located] (RR p. 3) (TLC p. 4)

Courtneys Neck; 150 ac.; sur. 17 Jul 1664; 1707 poss. Edwd. Horn &
Constance Burgess; St. Mary's Hundred (RR p. 4) (TLC p. 4)
Cow Ridge; 50 ac.; sur. 17 Jul 1664; 1707 poss. Tho. Hopkins; St. Mary's
Hundred (RR p. 4) (TLC p. 4)
Halfes; [with Henry Darnall] 400 ac.; sur. 30 Apr 1675; 1707 poss. widow
Mary Courtney; St. Mary's Hundred (RR p. 6) (TLC p. 7)
Courtneys Fancy; 100 ac.; sur. 3 May 1675; 1707 poss. widow Mary
Courtney; St. Mary's Hundred (RR p. 6) (TLC p. 7)
Fishing Creek Neck; 44 ac.; sur. 20 Feb 1676; 1707 poss. Wm. Goldsmith; St.
Mary's Hundred (RR p. 7) (TLC p. 8)
Croydon; 100 ac.; sur. 18 Jun 1681; 1707 poss. widow Mary Courtney; St.
Mary's Hundred (RR p. 8) (TLC p. 9); *Creydon*; 15 Jun 1681 cert./pat. (COL)
St. Thomas; 300 ac.; sur. 28 Apr 1682; 1707 poss. widow Mary Courtney; St.
Mary's Hundred (RR p. 9) (TLC p. 10); 300 ac.; 28 Apr 1682 cert./pat. (COL)
Drapers Neck; 500 ac.; resur. 28 Mar 1683; 1707 poss. widow Mary
Courtney; St. Mary's Hundred (RR p. 11) (TLC p. 12); 28 Mar 1683 cert./pat. (COL)
Addition; 103 ac.; sur. 26 Aug 1701; 1707 poss. widow Mary Courtney; St.
Mary's Hundred (RR p. 10) (TLC p. 11); 2 Dec 1702 cert./pat. (COL)
Courtney, Thomas; will; 18 Jan 1705; 26 Jun 1706; son Thomas; dau. Ann, w/o
John Baker; dau. Mary; d-i-l Ann Strong; kinsman Daniell Clocker and cous.
Peter Watts; tracts *Courtney's Fancy; Crayden [Graydon]* (MCW 3.79); [SMW
PC1.141]; inv. 13 Nov 1706; 8 Jan 1706; Capt. (I&A 26.161); acct. 25 May 1708;
admx. Mary w/o Robert Hagar (I&A 28.218) (SMAA p. 162)
Courtney, Thomas; inv.; 23 Mar 1716; nok John Baker, Mary Courtney (I&A
37b.12); acct.; 14 Oct 1717; sister Mary Courtney; w/o adm. Owen Smithson
(I&A 37b.113) (SMAA p. 317, 322)

COX

Cocks, John; *Leith*; 100 ac.; sur. 4 Apr 1673; 1707 poss. Tho. Reeves; Choptico
Hundred (RR p. 53) (TLC p. 51)
Cox, Henry; m. by 22 Apr 1652 the widow of Robert Ward (MM)
Cox, Thomas; service by 1667 (SK 11,313; 17.30)
Cox, William; service by 1678 (SK 15.522)
Cox, Thomas; immigrated by 1680 (SK WC2.281)
Cox, Charles; acct.; 2 Jan 1693; admx. Elisabeth Talbot (I&A 12.62)
Coks (Cocks), Nicholas; inv.; 22 Aug 1710 (I&A 32b.197); acct.; 9 Aug 1711 (I&A
32c.94); acct.; admx. Jane, w/o Edward Millam; 9 Aug 1711 (SMAA p. 190)
Cox, George; planter; will; 17 Sep 1710; 11 Nov 1710; son William; dau. Mary,
w/o Lawrence Dillon (MCW 3.183) [SMW PC1.167]; acct.; 29 Nov 1712 (I&A
33b.170) (SMAA p. 235)
Cox, Phillip; Harris (sic) Hundred; will; 11 Apr 1714; 20 Mar 1718/9; daus.
Jeane Manghoin [Manahan], Elizabeth; wife Mary (MCW 4.196) [SMW PC1.258];

inv.; 6 Apr 1719; 12 Jun 1719 (I 2.103); acct.; 12 Nov 1719; extx. widow Mary
    Cox, alias Dean & John Dean (A 2.411) (SMAA p. 367)

Cox, James; inv.; 27 Oct 1726; 29 Dec 1726; nok John Horn, Elisabeth Holmes;
    admx. Alce Cox (I 11.719); acct.; 19 Dec 1726; admx. Alice Cox (A 8.151)

Cox, Elisabeth; inv.; 24 May 1727; 5 Jun 1727 (I 12.2); inv.; 5 Aug 1728 (I
    13.174); acct.; 14 Apr 1729 (A 9.338)

Cox, Alice; acct.; 8 Apr 1729 (A 9.336)

Cox, Jeremiah; inv.; 28 Jul 1729; 8 Sep 1729; nok Samuel & Ann Cox;
    admx./extx. Ann Cox (I 15.103); acct.; 28 May 1736; mentions Samuell,
    Summer, Ann, Elisabeth, Mary & Susanah Cox; admx. Ann Cox (A 15.78)

Cox, John and Anne Shermintine (by license); m. 2 Sep 1782 (SA p. 60)

CRACKSON

Crackson, James; *Crackson's Rest*; 50 ac.; sur. 27 Mar 1723 (TLC p. 86); 6 Feb
    1729 cert./pat. (COL)

Crackson (Cracson), James; inv.; 2 May 1744; 7 Jun 1744; nok James Adams,
    Mary Crackson (I 29.240); acct.; 14 Aug 1745; mentions widow, James &
    Elisabeth Crackson (A 21.444)

CRAGHILL

Creighill, George; *Fish Pond*; 243 ac.; sur. 10 Mar 1730 (TLC p. 87); 13 Dec 1732
    cert./pat. (COL)

Craghill, George; will; probate 22 May 1749; bros. Thomas, Joshua; tract
    Hamstead, The Fish Pond (MCW 10.35) [SMW TA1.227]

Craghill, George; will; probate 22 May 1749; sons George, Thomas, Joshua;
    daus. Mary Comly [Combs], Ann, Grace; wife Mary; tracts *Hamstead, The
    Fish Pond* (MCW 10.36) [SMW TA1.226]; inv.; 26 Jun 1749; 11 Jun 1750; nok
    Mary & Thomas Hatton Combs; admx./exs. James Smith & wife Mary (I
    44.24); acct.; 19 Dec 1752 (A 33.323); dist.; 19 Dec 1752 (BB 1.72)

Craghill, Thomas; inv.; 30 Oct 1775; 12 Aug 1776; admx. Mary Craghill (I
    125.266)

CRAIG

Cragg, Peter; inv.; 16 May 1727; 7 Jun 1727; one child; admx. Elisabeth Crage
    (I 12.8); acct.; 6 Nov 1728; admx. Elisabeth Cragg (A 9.112)

Craigg, Jesse and Sarah; child. Elizabeth [b. 7 Jul 1747], Peter [b. 6 Sep 1749],
    Eleanor [b. 17 Jan 1752], Rachel [b. 17 Feb 1754], Reuben [b. 25 Apr 1756]
    (SA p. 38, 39)

Craig (Cragg), Jessee (Jesse); inv.; 2 Mar 1756; nok John Billock, Any Bullock;
    admx./extx. Sarah Craig (I 62.250); acct.; 3 Oct 1758; orphans Elisabeth [age
    11], Peter [age 9], Eleanor [age 6], Richard [age 4], Rubin [age 2]; admx.

Sarah Craig (A 42.160); dist.; 3 Oct 1758; orphans Elisabeth, Peter, Eleanor, Rachael, Ruben (BB 2.99)

CRANE

Crane, William; *Cuckolds Haven*; 88 ac.; sur. 5 Dec 1676; 1707 poss. Matt'w Carter & Thos. Melton; St. Clements Hundred (RR p. 46) (TLC p. 45)

Crane (Craine), Robert, Jr.; inv.; 30 Dec 1701 (I&A 21.200); acct.; 7 Sep 1704; admx. widow, w/o Mr. Ginder (I&A 3.420)

Crane, Robert; inv.; [filed with 1705-6] (I&A 26.1)

Crane, Robert; St. George's Hundred; will; 20 Oct 1705; 12 Aug 1708; g-son Robert; granddau. Jane [Jeanne], d/o Edward Morgan (MCW 3.72) [SMW PC1.156]

Craine Robert; 4 Nov 1707; ex. Marshall Lowe & widow Mary (SMAA p. 138)

Crane, John; age ca 49 in 1723 (MD p. 43)

Crean (Crane), Robert; inv.; 13 Feb 1732; 18 Jun 1733; nok William & Thomas Guyther; admx./extx. Sarah Crean (I 17.164); acct.; 28 Aug 1734; mentions William, Thomas, Robert and Mary Ann Crane; admx. Sarah Crane,w/o John Smoot (A 12.473)

Crain (Crane), William; inv.; 13 May __; 19 Aug 1751; nok Robert Crane, Thomas Guyther; adm./ex. Thomas Crane (I 47.279); acct.; 10 Mar 1752 (A 32.118); dist.; 10 Mar 1752 (BB 1.30); acct.; 24 Aug 1752; brothers Thomas & Robert Crane [both at age]; John Smoot [age 15], George Smoot [age 10], Cuthbert Smoot [age 8], Caleb Smoot [age 5] (A 32.417); dist.; 24 Aug 1752 (BB 1.71)

CRAWLEY

Crowley, Bryan (Bryon); will; 16 Dec 1687; 21 Apr 1688; wife Ann; daus. Mary, Ann, Elizabeth, Ellinor; s-i-l John Wilson (MCW 2.26) [SMW PC1.76]; inv. 23 Apr 1688 (I&A 10.99)

Crawley, Thomas; will; 12 Mar 1774; 4 Mar 1775; sons Thomas, Basil, James; dau. Judith; bros. James, Thomas, Basil; tracts *St. Jeroms, Hawley's Manner* (MCW 16.91) [SMW TA1.735]

CRAYCROFT

Craycoft, Ignatius; unnamed; 500 ac.; 1705 cert./pat. (COL)

Craycroft (Crecraft), Ignatius, Mr.; inv.; 5 Dec 1752; 21 Dec 1752; nok Thomas, s/o Thomas Spaulding; admx./extx. Elisabeth Craycroft (I 52.92); acct.; 1 Nov 1753 (A 36.22)

Creycroft [Craycroft], Elizabeth; will; 27 Oct 1769; 1 Mar 1770; daus. Eleanor, Jean [Jane], Susana, Henrieta; son Level; mentions Ignatius, s/o Enoch Fenwick (MCW 14.133) [SMW TA1.602]

Craycroft, Susanna; will; 22 Nov 1771; 26 Aug 1772; sisters Elinor, Jane, Heneritta; bro. Levin (MCW 14.237) [SMW TA1.648]

CRESSEY

Cressey, Samuel; <u>will</u>; 2 Feb 1675; 4 Feb 1675; daus. Mary and Susanna (MCW 1.116)

Cressey, Susanna & Mary, orphans of Samuel of CH Co.; *Proprietor's Gift*; 150 ac.; 12 Apr 1683 cert./pat. (COL)

CRITCHET

Crichet, Frances; alias Watkins; <u>will</u>; 31 Mar 1718; 7 Apr 1718; husband William Critchett; tract *The Ripe*; mentions James, s/o Henry Horn and Ann d/o John Woodward (MCW 4.133) [SMW PC1.232]

Cretchett (Croatchett, Creattchet, Creatcheatt), William; <u>inv.</u>; 1 Jun 1719; 17 Aug 1719; nok Charles King, Joseph Hopewell (I 2.194); <u>acct.</u>; 23 Aug 1720 (A 3.229) (SMAA p. 439); <u>acct.</u>; 30 Mar 1722 (A 4.154)

Critchell, William; <u>inv.</u>; 14 Jan 1743; nok Henry Traverse; adm./ex. John Critchet (I 28.362)

Critchard, John; *Crichatt's Trial*; resur. 13 Apr 1742; part of *Abbingtons Mannor* (TLC p. 107); 50 ac.; 27 Oct 1743 cert./pat. (COL)

CROOKE

Crooke, John; <u>acct.</u>; 8 Aug 1698; 3 orphans; admx./extx. widow Sarah Crooke (I&A 16.185); <u>acct.</u>; 13 Jul 1699 admx. Sarah, w/o Samuell Warren (I&A 19.159)

Cruck, George; <u>inv.</u>; 15 Mar 1717 (I 1.307)

Crook (Crooke), James; <u>will</u>; 24 Jan 1725; 30 Mar 1726; sons John, James, Joseph; dau. Margaret; wife Mildred (MCW 5.218) [SMW PC1.306]; <u>inv.</u>; 4 Jul 1726; nok Philip & Sarah Singer; extx. Mildred Crook (widow) (I 11.489); <u>acct.</u>; 26 Apr 1727; extx. Muriel Crook (A 8.188)

CUFFNEY

Cufny (Cuffny), John; <u>inv.</u>; 12 Feb 1712 (I&A 34.135); <u>acct.</u>; 21 May 1714; admx. Anne, w/o John Authors (I&A 36b.81) (SMAA p. 266)

Cuffney, John; of CA Co.; <u>will</u>; 1 Mar 1748/9; 8 Aug 1750; wife Mary; William, s/o James Chizzam; tract *Baker's Fancy* (MCW 10.103) [SMW TA1.254]; <u>inv.</u>; 13 Aug 1750; 31 Dec 1750; adms./exs. Henry Raley,& wife Mary (I 44.249); <u>acct.</u>; 19 Nov 1751 (A 31.228); <u>dist.</u>; 19 Nov 1751 (BB 1.16)

CULLISON

Cullison, James; <u>inv.</u>; 3 Jan 1742; 25 Jul 1743; nok Joseph Collason Jr. & Sr.; admx./extx. Mary Cullason (I 28.18); <u>acct.</u>; 22 Apr 1751 (A 30.83)

Colloson, Joseph; <u>inv.</u>; 1 Dec 1750; nok William & Josulton Cullison (I 44.241)

CUMMING

Cumming, William, Esq.; of Annapolis; *Hollyday*; 142 ac.; sur. 24 Jul 1730 (TLC p. 87); 3 Nov 1733 cert./pat. (COL)

The Ripe; 592 ac.; escheat land; resur. 10 Sep 1731; incl. in resur. of *Spring Blossom* (TLC p. 88); 597 ac.; 10 Jun 1734 cert./pat. (COL)
Spring Blossom; 221ac.; sur. 21 Aug 1741; tract called *The Ripe* (TLC p. 99); 6 Dec 1742 cert./pat. (COL)

CURREY
Currey, Alexander; will; 12 Nov 1694; 13 Nov 1694 (MCW 2.84) [SMW PC1.87]; acct.; 6 Sep 1699 (I&A 14.8)
Currey, John; will; 6 Dec 1696; 21 Jan 1696; child. John [now age 8] and Edward [now age 4] (MCW 2.122); inv.; 1 Mar 1696 (I&A 15.84)

CURTIS
Curtis, Robert; inv.; 3 Feb 1684 (I&A 8.32); acct.; 18 Mar 1685 (I&A 8.456)
Curtis, Michael; gent.; 19 Oct 1695; naturalized (CMN N24)
Curtis (Curtice), Michael; will; 13 Jul 1716; 19 Jul 1716; mentions Sarah, w/o John Turner; Priscilla, w/o Robert Saintclaire; Sarah, wife of Roderick Loyd; Mary, w/o Thomas Reaves, Sr.; Frances, w/o Thomas Jordan; Elizabeth, w/o Thomas Jordain, Sr. (MCW 4.51) [SMW PC1.211]; inv.; 19 Aug 1716 (I&A 37a.156); acct.; 8 Apr 1718 (I&A 39b.80) (SMAA p. 339)

CUSACK
Cusack, Michael; will; 8 Apr 1703; 27 May 1703; bro. George; sons-i-l Richard Smith and John Smith (MCW 3.14) [SMW PC1.132]; inv.; 17 Jun 1703 (I&A 3.346); acct.; 24 Jul 1704; ex. George Cusack (I&A 3.416) (SMAA p. 127)
Cusack (Cussick), George; will; 15 Jan 1717; 5 Mar 1717/8; son Michael; dau. Mary (MCW 4.184) [SMW PC1.228]; acct.; 5 Nov 1719 (A 2.318) (SMAA p. 378)
Cusack, Ben; m. 22 Jul 1771 Ann Jones (MM)

DABRIDGECOAT
Dabridgecourt, John; inv.; 24 Aug 1680 (I&A 7a.224)
Daybridgecoat (Dabridgecoate), John; inv.; 20 Feb 1709 (I&A 31.21); acct.; 19 May 1711 (I&A 32b.201) (SMAA p. 225)

DAFFIN
Dafferne, George; *Maid's Delight*; 78 ac.; sur. 2 Feb 1714; where Sanly Ferguson dwells (TLC p. 78); 5 Aug 1721 cert./pat. (COL)
Daffern, George; wife Susanna, d/o Charles King; *T. B.*; 119 ac.; sur. 30 Jan 1718 for Charles King (TLC p. 111); 20 Jun 1747 cert./pat. (COL)
Daffine (Daffin), George; inv.; 6 Jun 1729; 27 Aug 1729; nok Katherine Baxter, Mary Mackey; admx./extx. Penelope Daffin (I 15.101); acct.; 11 May 1730; 2 sons & 2 daus. (A 10.349)
Daffin, Penelope; inv.; 6 Dec 1732; 26 Feb 1732; nok Cathrin Baxter, Marshall Daffan; adm./ex. John Daffin (I 17.19); acct.; 30 Dec 1734 (A 12.743)

Daffin, John; will; 24 Dec 1751; 29 Jan 1753;wife Faith (MCW 10.245) [SMW TA1.746]

Daffin, Joseph; inv.; 18 Jun 1768; nok James Daffin, Benjamin Bean; admx. Eleanor Daffin (I 95.249); inv.; 10 May 1769 (I 101.29); acct.; 10 May 1769 (A 61.107)

Daffin, Robert and Elizabeth Simmonds (by license); m. 16 Jan 1781 (SA p. 59)

DAFT

Daft, William; inv.; 4 Feb 1712 (I&A 36b.18)

Daft (Dalft, Dafft), Charles; planter; will; 26 Mar 1721; 22 Apr 1721; sons Charles, Mathew; wife Elizabeth; daus. Anne Blumfield, Mary (MCW 5.47) [SMW PC1.267]; inv.; 4 May 1721; 6 Jun 1721; nok children; extx. Elisabeth Dafft (I 5.48); acct.; 8 Jan 1721 (A 4.51); acct.; 27 Jun 1723; extx. Elisabeth, w/o Henry Winsett (A 4.288)

Daft, Charles; inv.; 13 Aug 1730; 16 Sep 1730; nok Mathew & Elections Daft; admx./extx. Elisabeth Daft (I 15.663); acct.; 4 Aug 1731; mentions Charles, Susanna & Monaca Daft; admx. Isaac Booth & wife Elisabeth (A 11.220)

Dafft, Elizabeth; will; 26 Mar 1743; 3 Aug 1743; sons-i-l William and John (Dafft); father James Bloomfield; husband Matthew (MCW 8.228) [SMW TA1.134]

Dast, Matthew; *Huckleberry Lane*; sur. 18 Sep 1745 for Matthew Daft (TLC p. 111); 10 ac.; 18 Nov 1747 cert./pat. (COL)

Daft, Matthew; inv.; 25 Jun 1750; 25 Jun 1750; nok William Daftt, Mary Pane; admx./extx. Elionor Daft (I 43.283); acct.; 17 May 1751; mentions John Daft [age 15]; admx. Elenor, w/o James Roach (A 30.180)

Daft, Charles; inv.; 3 Mar 1754; 25 Jun 1757; nok Monica Bauld, William Daft (I 63.406); acct.; 29 Aug 1757; sisters m. Thomas Wootten, John Bowles, Joseph Wootten (A 41.188); dist.; 13 Jun 1757 (BB 2.63)

Daft, William and Elizabeth; son John Baptist, b. 15 Mar 1760; dau. Mar, b. 6 Apr 1762 (SA p. 13, 39, 47)

DALEY

Dayly, Bryan; *St. Patricks*; 100 ac.; sur. 23 Jun 1674 for Constant Daniell; pat.; 1707 poss. John Symons; St. Michael's Hundred (RR p. 14) (TLC p. 14)

O'Daly (Daly) [Dally], Bryan [Broine]; will; 10 May 1675; 13 Dec 1675; son Bryan; sisters Eliza: Daly [& her child] and Margaret in Ireland; mentions Thomas Keiting and his sister Nell; [son Broine Dally to be 23 this Aug.; dau. Adree, 10 years old Oct 9th; Catherine St. George & poss. child; bro. Avollna Dally in Ireland; Thomas Heyton and sister Nell] (MCW 1.113) [SMW PC1.22]; acct.; 16 Oct 1677; 2 unnamed orphans (I&A 4.407)

Daly (Dely), Bryant; will; probate 15 Jul 1684; wife Rebecca; bro. Thomas Keelon & his children Nicholas and Ellen Keelon (MCW 1.134); inv.; 19 Aug 1684 (I&A 8.209)

Daley?, Daniel and _____; dau. Susanna [b. 29 Jul 1752], Charles [b. 25 Sep 1746], Eleanor [b. 16 Oct 1748] (SA p. 36)

DAMMER
Damer, Thomas; service by 1673 (SK 17.578)
Dammer, Thomas; inv.; 24 Apr 1695 (I&A 13a.271); acct.; 10 Jun 1696; admx. Thomasine Dammer (relict) (I&A 14.5); acct.; 2 Jun 1718 (A 1.56) (SMAA p. 359)

DANIELL
Daniell, John; assign. John Chun; *Chuns Purchase*; 50 ac.; sur. 23 Apr 1673; 1707 poss. John Contee of CH Co.; lies in CH Co.; Choptico Hundred (RR) *Daniells Dream*; 150 ac.; sur. 23 Apr 1678; 1707 poss. John Wilson; St. Clements Hundred (RR p. 53) (TLC p. 51)
Daniell, Constant; acct.; 1 Aug [filed with 1679] (I&A 6.256)
Daniell, Thomas; *Daniell's Security*; 100 ac.; 27 Apr 1682 cert./pat. (COL)
Daniell's Helicon; 150 ac.; 28 Apr 1682 cert./pat. (COL)
Daniell's Elizium; 200 ac.; 12 May 1682 cert./pat. (COL)

DANSEY
Danzey, Martha; age ca 44; widow of Charles Ashcome; 17 Mar 1713; tract *Trent Neck* (CCR p. 23)
Dansey, John; *Radnor*; 404 ac.; resur. of 4 tracts (TLC p. 67); 15 Jun 1713 cert./pat. (COL)
Dansey, John; collector of Patuxent District; will; 18 Sep 1716; 27 Sep 1716; bro. Robert Dansey; ante-nuptial agreement with Martha Dansey; tract *Radner* (MCW 4.51) [SMW PC1.210]; inv.; 21 Dec 1716 (I&A 38b.161); acct.; 23 May 1718; bros. Charles & John (A 1.131); acct.; 23 May 1718; ex. Robert Dansey; 23 May 1718 (SMAA p. 359)
Dansey, Robert; inv.; 29 May 1723; mentions Johannah Dansey (I 8.256); acct.; 17 Oct 1722 (A 4.252)
Dansey [Dausey], Johnanna (Johana); widow; will; 7 Feb 1723/4; 16 Mar 1723; daus. Mary Delleny [Dausey], age 11 next Oct, and Elizabeth, b. 2 Mar 1720/1 (MCW 5.161) [SMW PC1.287]; inv.; 17 Mar 1723; 6 May 1724 (I 9.379); acct.; 15 Mar 1724 (A 6.289); acct.; 2 May 1726 (A 7.332)
Dansey [Dausey], Martha; widow; will; 19 Feb 1723; 22 Apr 1724; g-ch. Mary Ashcom Greenfield, Elizabeth Greenfield; g-ch. Samuel, Martha and Susannah Ashcom (ch/o son Charles Ashcom); d-i-l Judith Ashcom; son John Ashcom; Winifred Ashcom; mentions Elizabeth, w/o William Shelly (MCW 5.165) [SMW PC1.281]; acct.; 8 Sep 1726 (A 7.517)

DANT
Dant, Thomas; service by 1674 (SK 18.131); service by 1680 (SK WC2.159)

Dant (Dantt), William; planter; will; 31 Jan 1714; 16 May 1715; cousins John
Dant, William Mills [Dant], Elinor Nevet; bro. [cous.] Peter Mills [Jr.]; tract
Poplar Neck, Annstroder (MCW 4.68) [SMW PC1.199]; inv.; 28 May 1715 (I&A
36c.68); acct.; 28 Oct 1717 (I&A 39c.24) (SMAA p. 309)

Dant, John; will; 3 Oct 1763; 1 Nov 1763; daus. Ann Spalding, Mary Ann Dant,
Mary Mills; s-i-l Edward Spalding; sons John Baptist, Charles and Joseph
Frans. Excel. Dant; wife Eleanor; tract *Hopewell, Westfield* (MCW 12.217); inv.;
1 Dec 1763; 16 Oct 1764; nok Justn. Mills, Edward Spalding; ex. John Baptist
Dant (I 86.59)

DARNALL

Darnall, John; inv.; 10 Jul 1679; 8 Sep 1679 (I&A 6.389)

Darnall, John, Esq.; acct.; May 1697; admx. Susanna Maria (relict), w/o Mr.
Henry Lowe (I&A 14.117)

Darnall, Henry, Esq.; age ca 53; s/o Col. Henry, d. ca 1711; dau. m. Daniel
Carroll ca 1721-2 (CCR p. 76)

DART

Dart, Thomas; inv.; 29 Mar 1729; 17 Sep 1729; nok Sary Headen, John Dart;
admx./extx. Esabell Dart (I 15.108)

Dart (Bartt), John; inv.; 7 Mar 1733; 6 Jun 1734; nok Richard & Sarah Harden (I
18.325); acct.; 4 Jun 1735; orphans Ann & Mary Dart (A 13.162)

DASH

Dash, John; acct.; 30 Jan 1707; adm. Oswell Dash (I&A 28.75); acct.; admn. John;
30 Jan 1707 (SMAA p. 167)

Dash, Oswald; age ca 43; s/o John; 3 Jan 1723 (CCR p. 57)

Dash (Deish), Oswald; will; 14 Oct 1734; 19 Nov 1734; cousins John
Pilborough, John Spragg; wife Elizabeth (MCW 7.120) [SMW TA1.31]; inv.; 27
Feb 1734; 5 Jun 1735; nok Richard & Mary Brewer (I 20.470); acct.; 5 Jul 1736
(A 15.84)

DAVIDSON

Davidson, Robert; of VA; immigrated by 1667 (SK 11.198)

Davison, Christopher, Mr.; inv.; 30 May 1716 (I&A 37a.160); acct.; 13 May 1717;
admx. Mary Davidson (I&A 39b.58) (SMAA p. 321)

DAVIE

Davie [Davis], John; will; 21 Dec 1733; 6 Mar 1733/4; wife Ann; daus. Martha,
Elizabeth, Ann, Elinor w/o John Murphey and their son Thomas Truman
Murphey, Violetta, Arabela, Rebecca and Sarah [Elliott]; son Adlard;
grandson John Elliott; sons-i-l William Elliott, Thomas Notley Goldsmith
(MCW 7.62) [SMW TA1.23]; inv.; 24 May 1734; 7 Jun 1734; nok sons-i-l Elisas

Smith, Joseph Kine; admx./extx. Ann Davie (I 18.329); acct.; 17 Sep 1735 (A 13.326)

Davie, John; inv.; 15 Nov 1742; 8 Jun 1743 (I 28.10); acct.; 9 May 1744; admx. Ann Davie, dec'd; her adm. Thomas Wilson (A 20.167)

DAVIS

Davis, John; *Davis's Rest*; 100 ac.; sur. 17 Nov 1664; 1707 poss. Mr. Nicho. Gulick; New Town Hundred (RR p. 33) (TLC p. 32)

Davies, John; will; 24 Jan 1666; 26 Apr 1667; eld. son John; wife Mary; bro. John Harrinton [Houvretton] (MCW 1.38) [SMW PC1.1]; acct.; 15 Aug 1676; extx. Mary Jones (relict) wife of Morgan Jones (I&A2.175)

Davis, Thomas; immigrated by 1675 (SK 15.331, 412)

Davis, John; CH Co.; 19 Sep 1688; 7 Mar 1697; also filed in SM Co.; wife Mary; daus. Rachel, Mary; son John; cous. Mary Babcock [Badcocke] (MCW 2.133) [SMW PC1.76]

Davis, John; planter; 2 Feb 1690; 24 Jul 1698; wife Mary; tract *Dahere's Forest* [SMW PC1.117]; inv.; 14 Apr 1698 (I&A16.20); acct.; 28 Jun 1698;mentions dec'd dau. Mary; unnamed orphan; extx. Mary, w/o Peter Harris (I&A 16.64) (SMAA p. 98)

Davis, Edward; *Davis's Hazard*; 200 ac.; 24 Jul 1694 cert./pat. (COL)

Davis, John; will; probate 29 Mar 1699; sons Thomas Stockett, George, John Yate; daus. Frances w/o Marein Duvall, Eliza.,wife of Thomas Plummer; tracts *The Range; Vale of Benjamin* (MCW 2.168)

Davies, Thomas; inv.; 9 Apr 1712; nok. Samuell Abell, Mary Peacoke (I&A 33b.12)

Davis, Thomas; will; 19 Jan 1711; 31 Jul 1718; son Samuel; wife Mary (MCW 4.180) [SMW PC1.235]; inv.; 30 Jul 1718; nok James French (I 1.407); acct.; 31 Jul 1719; wife dec'd (A 2.120) (SMAA p. 396)

Davis, John; will; 23 Dec 1716; 29 Mar 1717; sons George, John, Briscoe; dau. Mary [& Priscilla]; wife Ann (MCW 4.72) [SMW PC1.213]; inv.; 26 Apr 1717 (I&A 37b.125); acct.; 3 Jun 1718; extx. Ann, w/o Samuell Wood (A 1.54) (SMAA p. 356)

Davis, George; will; 17 Apr 1740; 23 Jun 1740; f-i-l Samuel Wood; bros. John, Briscoe; mother unnamed (MCW 8.90) [SMW TA1.97]

Davis, Joseph; inv.; 3 Apr 1750; 3 Jul 1750; nok Ignatius Chamberlin, Walter Davis; admx./extx. Elisabeth Davis (I 43.288); acct.; 28 May 1751; orphans Rebecca [age 4], Mary [age 3], Joseph [age 1]; admx. Elisabeth Davis (A 30.97)

Davis, Walter; will; 15 Jul 1754; 17 Apr 1755; wife Sarah; sons Walter, Anthony, Rosanna, Anne, Mary, Elizabeth, Sarah, Peter, Stephen and John Barton Davis; mentions children by former wife (MCW 11.94) [SMW TA1.326]; acct.; 29 Nov 1756; extx. Sarah Davis (A 40.237); dist.; 19 Dec 1757; children Ann, Anthony, Rosannah, Mary, Elisabeth, Sarah, Peter, Stephen; extx. Sarah, w/o Peter Howard (BB 2.74)

Davis, Briscoe; <u>inv.</u>; 2 Dec 1757; 8 Mar 1758; nok George Carpenter; James Mardaw; admx,.extx. Mary Davis (I 65.146); <u>acct.</u>; 25 Oct 1759; orphans Briscoe, Rachell & Mary Ann [all at age], Hezekiah [age 14], Philip [age 12], Sophur [age 9], Thorist [age 5]; admx. Mary Davis (A 43.355)

Davis, William; <u>acct.</u>; 19 Dec 1757; orphans William, Ignatious, Luke, James, Walter, Peter & Ann [all at age], Stephen [age 17], Mary [age 15], Elisabeth [age 13], John Barton [age 11], Sarah [age 9], Rose Anna [age 5], Anthony [age 3]; extx. Sarah, w/o Peter Howard (A 41.328]

Davis, Jonathon; <u>inv.</u>; 4 Jun 1765; nok Barak & Walter Davis; admx. Ann Davis (I 88.71)

Davis, John Briscoe; <u>inv.</u>; 21 Feb 1774; 20 Apr 1774; mentions Mary & Rachel Wood Davis; adm. Lawson Davis (I 116.206)

Davis, Moses and Anne Evans; m. 18 May 1779 (SA p. 57)

DAY

Day, Geo.; *Burwastcott*; 50 ac.; sur. 5 May 1665; assgn. Dan. Jenifer; 1707 poss. Cosmus Parsons; St. Mary's Hundred (RR p. 4) (TLC p. 5)

Day, Henry; *Pimlico*; 9 Oct 1672; 50 ac.; sur. 9 Oct 1672; 1707 poss. John Bayly; St. Clements Hundred (RR p.45) (TLC p. 44)

Day, Rich'd; *Dayes Fortune*; 100 ac.; sur. 7 Apr 1682; 1707 poss. orphan Rich'd Day; Harvey Hundred (RR p. 57) (TLC p. 54)

DEAGAN

Deagan, John; <u>will</u>; 20 Dec 1718; 5 Mar 1718; dau. Mary; sons William, John, James [SMW PC1.242]

Degan, Thomas; <u>will</u>; 23 Dec 1760; 7 Mar 1770; son Jeremiah; wife Monica; her son James McLaine [SMW TA1. 607]

DEAN

Dean, John; <u>acct.</u>; 11 Jan 1721; admx. Mary, w/o William Able (A 4.48); <u>acct.</u>; 23 Mar 1722 (A 5.110); <u>acct.</u>; 2 Jun 1724 (A 6.35)

Dean, Jos.; m. 4 Dec 1770 Joan Stone (MM)

Dean, John; m. 12 Sep 1774 Mary More (MM)

DEAVOUR

Deavour, Richard, Mr.; <u>inv.</u>; 4 May 1747; nok William & John Dever; admx./extx. Assilla Dever (I 35.94); <u>acct.</u>; 28 Aug 1749; planter; mentions Thomas, s/o Thomas Little (A 27.43)

Devor [Dever], Assilla; <u>will</u>; 9 Jun 1750; 8 Oct 1750; sister Elinor Ivey [Fecy]; sons Peter Dever, Thomas Little; niece Ann Woodward (MCW 10.111) [SMW TA1.250]; <u>inv.</u>; 3 Aug 1751; nok John & Ann Woodward (I 47.135)

Devour [Deavour], Richard; will; 25 Jul 1746; 7 Nov 1746; children Richard, Elizabeth, Sarah, Peter; wife Appella [Asilla] (MCW 9.93) [SMW TA1.205]; acct.; 27 May 1751 (A 30.183)

DEBUTTS
Debutts, Lawrence, Rev.; *Itchcomb's Freehold*; 344 ac.; 10 Sep 1744 cert./pat. (COL)
   Tower Hill; 25 ac.; resur. 29 Mar 1738 (TLC p. 110); 6 Jun 1746 cert./pat. (COL)
   Addition; 20 ac.; sur. 23 Nov 1747 (TLC p. 112); 23 Nov 1747 cert./pat. (COL)
Debutts, Robert, Capt.; *Sun is Down*; 500 ac.; 2 Jan 1752 cert./pat. (COL)
Debutts, Lawrence, Rev.; inv.; 11 Jun 1753; nok James Smith Blide, Elisabeth Smith; admx./extx. Elisabeth DuButts (I 54.54); acct.; 23 Sep 1756 (A 40.178)
Debutts, Elisabeth, Mrs.; inv.; 2 May 1754; nok John & Hannah Clarke (I 58.193); acct.; 23 Sep 1756 (A 40.184)
De Butts, Samuel; will; 11 Aug 1754; 5 Sep 1754; wife Mary; wife's niece Catharine Benson; tracts *Clocker's Marsh, Dunbarr, Strife, The Brook, His Lordships Favour* (MCW 11.47); inv.; Apr 1755; 7 Nov 1755; nok James Smith, minors (I 61.121); acct.; 9 Mar 1756 (A 39.56); acct.; 18 Nov 1758 (A 42.147)
DeButts, Mary; widow of Samuel; will; 2 Sep 1754; 20 Nov 1754 (MCW 11.60) [SMW TA1.316]

DECOSTA
De Costa, Mathias; 20 Oct 1671; Portuguese; naturalized (CMN N6)
Decosta, Franck; acct.; 26 Mar 1695; admx. Elisabeth w/o Thomas Williams (I&A 13a.249)

DEERY
Deery, John; d. 2 Dec 1677, innholder of St. Mary's City; sister Ellinor Deery; bro. Owen Quigley; mentions cous. John Quigley of VA (CCR p. 9)
Deery, John; inv.; 16 Apr 1678 (I&A 5.229)

DELAHAY
Delahay, Charles, s/o Arthur; transported by 1637 (SK 7.462)
Delahay, Arthur; immig. from VA by 1670; transported wife Mary (SK 12.550)
Dela Hay, Arthur; *Hopewell*; 75 ac.; sur. 9 Jun 1670; 1707 poss. Wm. Johnson; New Town Hundred (RR p. 35) (TLC p. 34)
Dillihay, John and Winifred; children Stephen [b. 19 Nov 1766], Joseph [b. 22 Feb 1768] (SA p. 195)

DELAROCHE
Delaroach, Peter; transp. by 1664 by Charles (SK 17.574; 15.330)
de la Rock, Cha.; *Paris*; 150 ac.; sur. 17 Sep 1675; 1707 poss. Cecill Butler [by m. d/o Robt. Carvile; St. Mary's Hundred (RR p. 7) (TLC p. 9)

Dela Roche(de la Roche), Charles; <u>will</u>; 16 Dec 1675; 22 Jan 1675; wife Eliza; brother Peter; mentions Mary, w/o Dr. Burt; tracts *Galloway, Paris* (MCW 1.114) [SMW PC1.14]; <u>inv.</u>; Jan 1675; 14 Feb 1675; innholder (I&A 1.515)

Delaroch, Elizabeth; widow; extx. of Charles Delaroch; City of St. Mary's; innholder; 1677 (AM LXVII.91)

DENT

Dent, Thomas, gent.; immigrated by 1662; transported John by 1662/3 (SK 5.245)

Dent, Thomas; <u>will</u>; 28 Mar 1676; 21 Apr 1676; sons William, Thomas, Peter, George; dau. Margaret; wife Rebecca; tracts *Westbury Manor, Ginsbrough, Brothers' Joint Interest* (all in CH Co.) (MCW 1.169) [SMW PC1.25]; <u>inv.</u>; 22 Apr 1676; 19 May 1676 (I&A 2.191); <u>acct.</u>; 21 May 1677l extx. Rebecca Addison, relict (SMAA p. 45)

Dent, Thomas; *Peterborough*; 100 ac.; sur. 23 Jul 1680; pat. surrendered; 1707 no poss.; New Town Hundred (RR p. 38) (TLC p. 37)

Dent, John; <u>will</u>; 25 Sep 1711; 5 May 1712; sons John, George, Christian, Peter; daus. Mary, Lydia, Anna, Abigail; tracts *Cumberson, Barnaby, Reading, Evan's Addition, Providence, Pearly Progress, Harrison's Adventure, Haphazard, Freestone Point, Ashman's [Askous] Freehold, St. Anne, St. Stephen, Coldman, Evan's Reserve, Love's Adventure, Coldwell's, Horserange*; wife unnamed (MCW 3.229) [SMW PC1.181]; <u>inv.</u>; 5 May 1712; nok George Dent, Sarah Turner (I&A 33b.14)

Dent, Mary, Mrs.; 22 Nov 1712; age ca 65; d/o John & Ann Schertilife; niece of Henry Spinck (CCR p. 22)

Dent, George, Sr.; <u>will</u>; 5 Apr 1746; 7 Jun 1750; sons John, Peter, Thomas, William; daus. Lidia, Charity; wife Mary; son George & dau. Mary Ann Strong (MCW 10.110) [SMW TA1.251]

Dent, Hatch, Rev.; s/o Hatch Dent; gs/o John Dent; b. May 1757; d. 30 Dec 1799 (HGM)

Dent, Thomas; <u>inv.</u>; 4 Mar 1774; 10 Jun 1774; nok John & Chloe Dent; admx. Mary Ann Dent (I 119.135); <u>inv.</u>; 10 Oct 1775; admx. Ann Dent (I 122.189, 190); <u>acct.</u>; 1775 (A 73.247)

DENTON

Denton, Henry; gent.; *Hackett's Choice*; 500 ac.; 2 Apr 1684 cert./pat. (COL)

Denton, Henry; *Warnell*; 100 ac.; sur. 7 Jul 1687; 1707 poss. Anne Chisam; St. Michael's Hundred (RR p. ?14) (TLC p. 15)

DERMOTT

Dermott, Edmond; age ca 26 in 1678; John Deery [d. 2 Dec 1677] (MD p. 51)

Dermott [Demmatt], Edmond; [merchant]; <u>will</u>; 2 May 1683; 29 May 1683 (MCW 1.124) [SMW PC1.44]

DICKSON

Dickeson, Samuel; service by 1668 (SK 11.293)

Dickeson, Samuel; acct.; 20 Jun 1678 (I&A 5.183)

Dickson, James; will; 24 Oct 1748; 5 Mar 1752; brethren George, Hugh, William & Andrew Dickson; sister Elizabeth McConnall (MCW 10.213) [SMW TA1.299]

DIGGES

Digges, William, Col.; *Baltimore's Gift*; 650 ac.; 3 Aug 1682 cert./pat. (COL)
Baltimore's Gift Addition; 115 ac.; 9 Nov 1682 cert./pat. (COL)
St. Peter's; 10 ac.; 8 Mar 1687 cert./pat. (COL)

Digges, Mary (dau.); b. 1687; d. 10 Feb 1757 Liege; 1st native of MD to become a nun; son John Dudley, b. 1689; d. May 1771 Ingatestone, Essex; ch/o William Digges and Elizabeth Sewell (JM p. 315, 316)

Digges, John Dudley; s/o William Digges and Elizabeth Sewell (JM p. 315)

Digges, John; b. 23 Oct 1746; d. bef. 1806; s/o Edward Digges and Mary Neale (JM p. 316)

Digges, Edward; will; 10 Jun 1769; 18 Dec 1769; bros. William, Henry; daus. Elizabeth, Elianor, Mary, Ann; sons John, Edward; sons-i-l Charles and Jesse Whorton; bros.-i-l Raphael Neale and George Sly; wife Elizabeth, she m/2 Wilfred Neale; tracts *Dillinger's, Hampton Iron Works, [Resurvey on Brother's Agreement]* (MCW 14.113) [SMW TA1.570]; inv.; 10 Mar 1770; 17 Mar 1770; nok John & H. Diggs; exs. Wilfred Neale, & wife Elisabeth, Eleanor Diggs (I 103.230); 28 Nov 1771; exs. Wilfred Neale & wife Elisabeth, Eleanor & Raphael Diggs (A 66.67); 11 Jul 1774 (A 73.1); acct.;1 Aug 1775 (A 73.249)

Digges, Jos.; m. 30 Sep 1777 Anne (Digges?) (MM)

DILLION

Dillon (Dellion), Thomas; *Strife*; 200 ac.; 2 Sep 1714 cert./pat. (COL)
The Chance; 50 ac.; sur. 20 Feb 1715 (TLC p. 75); 25 Apr 1717 cert./pat. (COL)

Dillon, Lawrence; inv.; 16 Mar 1718; 21 Mar 1718 (I 1.523); acct.; 11 Dec 1720 (A 3.175) (SMAA p. 409)

Dillon, Charles; *Charles' Chance*; sur. 73½ ac.; 11 Oct 1717 (TLC p. 76); 73 ac.; 6 Aug 1719 cert./pat. (COL)

Dillion, Thomas; inv.; 13 Mar 1720; 8 Jun 1721; admx. Rose Dillion (I 5.54)

Dillon, Rose; *Rose Land*; 50 ac.; sur. 22 Sep 1721; resur. into *Roseland with Addition* (TLC p. 80); 10 Sep 1723 cert./pat. (COL)

Dillon, Lawrence (Larrance); inv.; 14 May 1743; 25 Jul 1743; nok Charles & Charles Dillon (sic); admx./extx. Rebecca Dillon (I 28.18); acct.; 11 Aug 1744; orphan Thomas (A 20.429)

Dillion, James; acct.; 4 Dec 1752 (A 33.325)

Dellians (Dilon) [Dillian], John; will; (filed with 1763); son Lawrence; daus. Ellianor, Elizabeth; unborn child; wife Ann; ex. Thomas Matthews and my wife; tract *Inclosure* (MCW 12.175) [SMW TA1.432]

Dillon, Charles, Mr.; inv.; 30 Apr 1768; nok Ann Mathews, Thomas Dihione; admx. Ann Dillon (I 96.170); acct.; 12 Apr 1769 (A 60.361)

DIXON

Dison, Thomas; *Dison's Chance*; 60 ac.; 24 Jul 1694 cert./pat. (COL)
     St. John's; 115 ac.; 10 Dec 1694 cert./pat. (COL)

Dixon, Joshua, Capt.; inv.; 10 Dec 1748; 15 Sep 1749 (I 40.356, 358)

Dixon (Dickson), James; *Dixon's Adventure*; 111 ac.; 16 Sep 1752 cert./pat. (COL)

Dixon, George, Jr.; inv.; 5 May 1774; 31 Oct 1775; nok Jonathon & Absolom Dixon; admx. Sarah Dixon (I 122.144); acct.; 1775 (A 73.248); dist.; 1775 (BB 7.40)

Dixon, George; inv.; 10 Sep 1785; admx./ex. Sarah Dixon (I 122.188)

DOGAN

Doagan (Doagance, Doagaines), John; will; 11 Dec 1718; 5 Mar 1718/9; dau. Mary; sons William, John, Thomas (MCW 4.199); acct.; 5 Nov 1720 (A 3.234) (SMAA p. 428)

Dogan, John and Ann; children Eleanor [b. 13 Apr 1761], William [b. 10 May 1763], James [b. 5 Nov 1765], John [b. 15 Apr 1768] (SA p. 8)

Dogan, Thomas and Monica; son Jeremiah [b. 2 Feb 1763] (SA p. 6)

Dogan [Degan], Thomas; will; 23 Dec 1769; 7 Mar 1770; son Jeremiah; wife Monica; James McClain, s/o wife Monica (MCW 14.132) [SMW TA1.607]

DONALDSON

Donaldson, John; Presbitor; will; 20 Dec 1747; 6 Apr 1748; wife Elizabeth; daus. Mary Magdalene Cook, Sabina Stoddart & her heirs Elizabeth, Mary Magdalene and Anne Stoddart (MCW 9.143) [SMW TA1.216]

Donaldson, Elizabeth; will; 14 Dec 1753; [20 Oct 1756]; g-s John Donaldson Debuts; daus. Elizabeth Barber, Magdalin Cook; g-daus: Sarah, Elizabeth, daus. of Thomas and Jennet Stodard; Elizabeth, d/o Benjamin and Sabina Stodart; g-son Richard Donaldson Cook (MCW 11.145) [SMW TA1.344]; inv.; 10 Oct 1756; 21 Aug 1757; nok Mary Magdelen & Richard Donaldson Cooke (I 63.542); acct.; 21 Aug 1757 (A 41.183); dist.; 21 Aug 1757 (BB 2.63, 72, 75)

DONNAVAN

Donnavin [Dunnavan], Derby [Darby]; will; 25 Apr 1683; 7 May 1683; mentions John, s/o Thomas Milton; Lawrence, s/o Thomas Dillon of CH Co.; Anne, w/o Thomas Edwards, and her dau. Martha Murly; Ellinor, d/o Dennis Hurley; tract *Morrises Mount* (MCW 1.123-4) [SMW PC1.43]; acct.; 4 Apr 1684;

mentions Lawrence, s/o Thomas Dillon; son dec'd (I&A 8.248); acct.; 5 Aug 1684 (I&A 8.211)

DORSEY
Dorsey, Edward; wife Sarah; 14 Oct 1679 (CCR p. 10)

Dorsey, John; widow and admx. Rose; called Rose Doxey in text; 8 Jul 1703 (SMAA p. 114)

Dorsey, Bartholomew; inv.; 19 Aug 1732; nok Margret & Mary Dorsey; admx./extx. Mary Dorsey (I 16.574); acct.; 24 Sep 1733; mentions John, Margaret, Mary, Elisabeth, Sarah, Bridget, Hannah, Eleanor & Ann Dorsey; admx. Mary, w/o John Binks (Binkes) (A 12.135)

Dossey, Mary; inv.; 25 Sep 1747; 14 Dec 1747; nok John Dossey, Mark Load (I 35.469); acct.; 16 Apr 1750; mentions Hannah Dossey (A 28.118)

Dorsey, Hannah; inv.; 24 Apr 1756; 3 May 1756; nok Mark Roads, minors; adm./ex. John Dorsey (I 60.578); acct.; 3 May 1756 (A 30.18)

DOWNIE
Downie (Downe), John; inv.; 1 Apr 1734; 22 Apr 1734; nok Robert & Mary Taylor; admx./extx. Elisabeth Downie (I 18.124, 126); acct.; 22 Sep 1735; orphans David & John Downe; admx. Elisabeth , w/o John Griffeth (A 13.327)

Downie, David; *Town's Support*; 81 ac.; 11 Aug 1753 cert./pat. (COL)

Downes, Joseph and wife Ann; children Ignatius [b. 18 Nov 1759], John [b. 25 May 1762], Mary [b. 26 May 1764], Elizabeth [b. 23 Jun 1766], Ann [b. 24 Oct 1768] (SA p. 2)

Downey [Downie], David; will; 7 Apr 1764; 7 Mary 1764; wife Elizabeth; bro. John; tract *Dryden* (MCW 13.42) [SMW TA1.485]; inv.; 28 Jul 1764; 7 Aug 1764; nok John Downes, Elisabeth Mooris; ex. Elisabeth Downie (I 84.288)

Dowine (Downey) [Downie], John; will; 3 Jan 1773; 2 Apr 1774; mentions Henry, s/o John and Mary Shanks; Ann, d/o John and Elizabeth King (MCW 15.148) [SMW TA1.698]; inv.; 20 Sep 1774; nok Elisabeth King, Rebecca Flint Watts (I 119.145); acct.; 17 Jan 1777 (A 74.17)

DOXEY
Doxey, Thomas; m/2 prior to 1669, Ann, widow of Robert Hooper; he and his m/1 had performed their terms of service (SK 12.267)

Doxey [Dossey, Dosey, Dossy], Thomas; [St. Michael's Hundred]; will; 6 Aug 1685; 11 Sep 1685; niece Elizabeth, d/o bro. John; mentions John Doxey, Jr., Mary and Sarah Doxey; wife Anne; daus. Mary Haddock, Eliza: Lees and Tomasin; [dau. Elisabeth Huse]; tract *John Briscoe's Plantation* (MCW 1.152) [SMW PC1.55]; inv.; 24 Sep 1685; 28 Nov 1685 (I&A 8.496)

Doxsey, John; inv.; 30 May 1702 (I&A 22.24); acct.; 8 Jul 1703; admx. widow Rose Doxsey (I&A 3.407); acct.; 12 Oct 1710; widow Rose, w/o Thomas Ward (I&A 32b.10) (SMAA p. 207)

Doxey, John; <u>inv.</u>; 27 Aug 1714 (I&A 36b.18)

Doxey (Doxoey), Thomas; 2 Jun 1720; admx. Susanah, w/o John Guyther (A 2.514) (SMAA p. 442)

Doxey (Doxcey), John; <u>acct.</u>; 2 Jun 1718 admx. Sarah, w/o George Griggs (A 1.34) (SMAA p. 334)

Doxey, James; <u>inv.</u>; 10 Oct 1720; mentions William Doxcey (I 4.227)

Doxey (Doxsey). John; <u>inv.</u>; 27 Aug 1753; nok Thomas & William Doxey; admx./extx. Catharine Doxey (I 55.24); <u>acct.</u>; 19 Aug 1754; orphans Ann [age 9], John [age 6]; admx. Catherine, w/o John Whitherinton (A 36.409); <u>dist.</u>; 19 Aug 1754; admx. Catherine, w/o John Witherinton; children Ann [age 10 next Jun], John [age 7 next Jun] (BB 1.114)

Doxsey [Doxey], Thomas; <u>will</u>; 26 May 1766; 24 Nov 1766; daus. Sapphira [Sopphia], Susanna; sons Jeremiah, Austin (MCW 13.137) [SMW TA1.496]; <u>inv.</u>; 20 Feb 1767; 2 Mar 1767; nok William & Joseph Doxey; adm. Austin Doxey (I 91.110); <u>acct.</u>; 6 Apr 1767 (A 56.73)

Doxey, William; <u>will</u>; 20 Dec 1770; 13 Jun 1772; wife Mary; daus. Ann Daues, Mary Handle; son James; mentions Ann, Mary & Roger Handel; g-sons John & Joseph, sons of James Doxey; Aaron & John, sons of John Daues (MCW 14.237); g-son Aaron Doxey [SMW TA1.636]; <u>inv.</u>; 14 Aug 1772; 22 Jun 1773; nok Ann & Aaron Davis; adm./ex. James Doxey (I 112.406); <u>acct.</u>; 26 Oct 1773 (A 69.206); <u>dist.</u>; 26 Oct 1773 (BB 6.278)

DOYNE

Doyne, Joshua; immigrated by 1680; transported wife Barbera (SK WC2..302-3)

Doyne, Robert; <u>inv.</u>; 1695 (I&A 16.243)

Doyne, Joshua; <u>will</u>; 10 Mar 1697; 16 Aug 1698; wife Jane, sons Jesse, William, Ethelbert, Joshua, Ignatius, Edward Aloysius; dau. Mary, w/o Ignatius Mathews; dau. Jane; g-ch. Jane & Thomas Mathews; testator's 1st wife Barbara; tracts *Bachelor's Hope, Derby's Plantation, Notley's Addition, Jimma [Timma] Sarah* in DO Co., *Range* in DO Co., *St. Bernard's, Beverly's Week* (MCW 2.159) [SMW PC1.118]; <u>inv.</u>; 16 Aug 1698; 12 Nov 1698; [Capt.] (I&A 17.97)

Doyne, Joshua; gent.; age ca 52; 1-8 May 1721 (CCR p. 51)

Doyne, Ethelbert, Mr.; <u>inv.</u>; 21 Jul 1725; 15 Oct 1725; nok Jesse & Edward Aloysius Doyne; admx. Jane Doyne (I 11.130); <u>inv.</u>; 17 Nov 1725; 14 Nov 1725; nok Jesse & Edward Aloysius Doyne; admx. Jane Doyne, d. bef. 17 Nov 1725 (I 11.163); <u>acct.</u>; 21 Sep 1726 (A 7.534); <u>acct.</u>; 9 Nov 1727 (A 8.448)

Doyne, Jane; <u>will</u>; 17 Oct 1738; 5 Mar 1738; husband Joshua Doyne, dec'd; "his son Dennis"; Joseph, 2nd s/o Jese Doyne, dec'd, heir to Denis Doyne afsd.; son Joshua, wife Ann; their children Robert, Jane; g-dau. Hennerita Wharton; dau. Jane Wharton; sons Igantius and Edward [Aloysious]; mentions Mary & Jane, daus. of Ethelbert Doyne, dec'd; mention Madam Elizabeth Calvert & son John (MCW 8.38) [SMW TA1.108]

Doyne, Joshua, Mr.; inv.; Aug 1743; 4 Oct 1743; nok Isaac & Edward Aloysius Doyne; admx./extx. Ann Doyne (I 28.201); acct.; 6 Jun 1744 (A 20.288)

Doyne, Edward Aloysius; will; 6 Jul 1748; 3 Aug 1748; bro. Ignatius; sister Mary Jameson [Tenneson] (MCW 9.170) [SMW TA1.218]

DRURY

Drury, Robert; *Dry Dockings*; 200 ac.; sur. 20 Aug 1672; 1707 poss. James Tant; New Town Hundred (RR p. 36) (TLC p. 35)

Dry Docking Addition; 100 ac.; sur. 20 Oct 1683; 1707 poss. John Cecill; New Town Hundred (RR p. 41) (TLC p. 40); 20 Oct 1683 cert./pat. (COL)

Drury, John; acct.; 4 May 1726; admx. Mary Drury (A 7.333)

Drury, Ignatius; m. 11 Dec 1769 Anastasia French (MM)

Drury, Philip; m. 4 Sep 1770 Ann Newton (MM)

Drury, Michael; m. 3 Nov 1770 Ann Yets/Yates (MM)

Drury, Peter; will; 12 Mar 1770; 1 Apr 1771; son Michael; *Drury's Venture* (MCW 14.180) [SMW TA1.633]; inv.; 10 Apr 1771; nok Robert & Peter Drury; ex. Michael Drury (I 106.380); acct.; 14 Mar 1772 (A 66.280); dist.; 14 Mar 1772 (BB 6.109)

DUCKWORTH

Duckworth, John; inv.; 29 Mar 1699 (I&A 19.17)

Duckworth, Anne; *His Lordship's Flavour*; 100 ac.; sur. 19 Oct 1713; part of *Mill Manor* (TLC p. 68); 10 Dec 1714 cert./pat. (COL)

Duckworth, Ann, Mrs.; age ca 70; 25 Jun 1722 (CCR p. 50)

Duckworth, Ann; widow; will; 9 May 1731; 27 Nov 1732; sons Richard and Joseph Hopewell; daus. Ann Aisquith and Susannah King; g-ch. Hugh, John, Ann, Elizabeth, William, Richard and Thomas Francis Hopewell (MCW 6.240) [SMW PC1.355]; inv.; 11 Dec 1732; 28 Feb 1732; nok. Richard Hopewell, Charles King, Jr. (I 17.22)

DUFF

Duff, James; inv.; 17 Jun 1750; 20 Aug 1750; nok Francis Herbert, Phillip Merritt; admx./extx. Mary Duff (I 43.374); acct.; 13 May 1751; orphans Ann [of age], James [age 11]; admx. Mary, w/o Thomas Drury (A 30.94)

Duff, William; acct.; 12 Aug 1715; admx. Ann, w/o John Carmichaell (I&A 36c.61) (SMAA p. 285)

DUNBAR

Dunbar, John; will; 22 Mar 1708/9; 30 Apr 1709; son William; daus. Mary and Sara; 3 daus.; 2 sons; [also son John & wife Anne] (MCW 3.132) [SMW PC1.161]; acct.; 27 Aug 1710; extx. Ann, w/o Thomas Underwood (I&A 31.363) (SMAA p. 200)

Dunbar, John; gent.; *Chance*; 145 ac.; 14 Feb 1734 cert./pat. (COL)

Dunbar, James; 1 Jul 1750; 24 Sep 1750; father John; niece Hennritta Guibert [Dunbarr]; father John; John, s/o John Coods; tract *Timber Neck* (MCW 10.111) [SMW TA1.249]; acct.; 19 Nov 1751; ex. John Dunbar (A 31.230); dist.; 19 Nov 1751 (BB 1.17)

Dunbarr (Dunbar), James, Mr.; inv.; 12 Oct 1750; 2 Apr 1751; nok John & James Coode; adm./ex. John Dunbar (I 45.86)

Dunbar, William; 15 May 1754; 24 Jun 1754; children Joseph, William, Mary Bragg, Anastatia Reader; wife Elizabeth; "remainder to Mary Ann Bisco, w/o Joseph & Jeane and John Dunbar"; [ch. Jane, John & James Dunbar and Mary Ann Brisco] (MCW 11.38) [SMW TA1.309]; inv.; 23 Jul 1754; 9 Sep 1754; nok Jonathon & Joseph Dunbar; admx./extx. Elisabeth Dunbar (I 57.335); acct.; 17 Nov 1755; extx. Elisabeth, w/o John Stevens (A 38.291); dist.; 29 Jan 1756 (BB 2.7)

Dunbarr (Dunbar), John, Mr.; inv.; 8 Apr 1763; 21 Jun 1763; nok Joseph Dunbar; admx. Elisabeth Dunbar (I 81.244); acct.; 3 Aug 1763; admx. Elisabeth, w/o James Woodward (A 49.599)

DUNN

Dunn, Obadiah; *The Plaines*; 150 ac.; sur. 5 Dec 1676; 1707 poss. Ethelbert Doyne in Choptico Hundred; St. Clements Hundred (RR p. 46) (TLC p. 45)

Dunn (Dun), Patrick; inv.; 3 Mar 1713 (I&A 35a.328); acct.; Oct 1714; admx. Elisabeth Guibert (I&A 36b.39); acct.; 22 Oct 1714 (SMAA p. 268)

EATON

Eaton, Henry; service by 1680 (SK WC2.342)

Eaton, John; acct.; 4 Jun 1728 (A 9.194)

Eaton, Andrew; inv.; 22 Aug 1751; 9 Dec 1751 (I 48.236); acct.; 3 Aug 1752 (A 32.414); acct.; 16 Apr 1753 (A 34.177)

EDELEN

Edelen, Richard; Deputy Surveyor of SM Co.; immig. by 1664 (SK WC2.300-301; 7.508)

Edlen [Edeling], Richard; will; 5 Mar 1694; 31 Jul 1694; sons Richard, Edward, Christopher, Thomas; dau. Catharine; tracts *St. Christophers, Dublin* in CH Co. (MCW 2.90) [SMW PC1.93]

Edelen, Richard, Jr.; will; probate 15 Aug 1738; wife Margaret; bro. Philip; father Richard Edelin, Sr. (MCW 7.256) [SMW TA1.61]; inv.; 15 Aug 1738; 6 Mar 1738; nok William Neale, Richard Edelen; adms./exs. Margarett & Phillip Edelen (I 24.49); acct.; 3 May 1741; children Joseph, Richard & Mary Anne; exs. Zachary Bond & wife Margritt (A 18.198)

EDEN

Eden, John; <u>will</u>; 3 Feb 1775; 22 Jul 1775; wife Betty; sons James, John, Townshend, Thomas; g-daus. Mary, Jane, Margarete, Ann and Naples Llewellin; [2 g-daus. Mary & Jane Margaret Ann Napler Llewellin]; children's grandparents Mills; tracts *Bashford Manor, Neales Lot Resurveyed, Darts Hills, Barron Doe, The Weems, Partnership, Chaptico Forest* (MCW 16.89) [SMW TA1.714]

Eden, James; <u>will</u>; probate 2 Jan 1777; bros. Thomas, Toun'd, John; cousins Margret Lwellin, Elizabeth Briscoe (MCW 16.173)

EDLOE

Edloe, Joseph; *Edloe*; 300 ac.; sur. 2 Mar 1648; 1707 poss. Edw'd Edloe & 200 ac. resur. into *Susquehannough Point*; Harvey Hundred (RR p. 55) (TLC p. 53)

Edlowe, Barnaby; s/o Joseph; 12 Apr 1651 (AM X.87)

Edloe, Barnaby; d. age 25-26; s/o Joseph, dec'd; 18 Feb 1668 (MD p. 58)

Edloe, Joseph and Jane his wife; service by 1671 (SK 16.282)

Edloe, Joseph; *Edloes Addition*; 37 ac.; 13 Jan 1680; 1707 poss. Edw'd Edloe; Resurrection Hundred (RR p. 65) (TLC p. 63)

   Forest of Harvey; 400 ac.; sur. 2 Dec 1680; 1707 John Noble who m. d/o Jos. Edloe; 21 Mar 1712 mentions John Noble & wife Jane; Harvey Hundred (RR p. 57) (TLC p. 54)

   Park; 300 ac.; sur. 17 Feb 1681; 1707 poss. Edw'd Edloe; Harvey Hundred (RR p. 57) (TLC p. 54)

Edloe, Joseph; <u>inv.</u>; 23 May 1700 (I&A 20.35)

Edloe, Edward; <u>inv.</u>; 19 Jun [filed with 1711] (I&A 33a.46); <u>acct.</u>; 2 Jun 1712 (I&A 33a.224) (SMAA p. 231); <u>acct.</u>; Nov 1714 (I&A 36b.121) (SMAA p. 269); <u>acct.</u>; 1 Mar 1716 (I&A 38b.69); <u>acct.</u> (SMAA p. 309)

EDWARDS

Edwards, Isaac; *Edwards Freehold*; 50 ac.; sur. 4 Dec 1640; poss. William Whivret under Col. Addison; 1707 esch. & no poss.; St. Georges Hundred (RR p. 17) (TLC p. 17)

Edwards, John; service by 1680 (SK WC2.340-341)

Edwards, Joseph; *Plaines of Jericho*; 93 ac.; sur. 29 Mar 1704; 1707 poss. same Edwards; Resurrection Hundred (RR p. 65) (TLC p. 63)

Edwards, John; <u>acct.</u>; 28 Feb 1709 (I&A 31.38) (SMAA p. 175)

Edwards, John; <u>will</u>; 1 Jan 1710/1; 15 Jan 1710/1; mentions John [or Thomas], s/o John Stoakes; *Wastwood* in BA Co. (MCW 3.209) [SMW PC1.175]; <u>inv.</u>; 20 Sep 1711 (I&A 33a.43)

Edwards, Joseph; <u>inv.</u>; 21 Apr 1718 (I 1.306)

Edwards, Joseph; *Edwards' Back Land*; 52 ac.; sur. 20 Feb 1728 (TLC p. 88); 10 Jun 1734 cert./pat. (COL)

Edward, John; *Edwards' Discovery*; 269 ac.; sur. 3 Oct 1737 (TLC p. 94); 19 May 1738 cert./pat. (COL)

Edward, John; inv. 18 Feb 1743; nok Barbery Edwards, William Hazle; adm./ex. Houston Edwards (I 28.355); inv.; [filed with 1743]; adm. Stourton Edwards (I 28.367); acct.; 11 Apr 1744 (A 20.108); acct.; 14 Sep 1744 (A 20.392); acct.; 10 Sep 1746 (A 22.346)

Edwards, Stourton; *Doe Park*; 69 ac.; sur. 18 Mar 1743 (TLC p. 101); 60 ac.; 13 Aug 1743 cert./pat. (COL)

Edwards, Joseph; *Taunton Dean*; sur. 19 Mar 1744 (TLC p. 108); 164 ac.; 1 Apr 1746 cert./pat. (COL)

Edwards, Joseph; will; 3 May 1746; 3 Jun 1746; children Joseph, Benjamin, Stourton, John, Josias; wife Mary; tracts *Dimonds Venture, Edwards Back Land, Taunton Deen* (MCW 9.75) [SMW TA1.207]

Edwards, Benjamin; *Good Yielding*; 86 ac.; sur. 20 Apr 1744 (TLC p. 100); 18 Mar 1747 cert./pat. (COL)

Edward, John; *Buck Park*; sur. 12 Nov 1732 (TLC p. 93); 100 ac.; 18 Nov 1747 cert./pat. (COL)
John Edwards' Discovery; 241 ac.; 10 Aug 1753 cert./pat. (COL)
Lot; 22 ac.; 10 Aug 1753 cert./pat. (COL)

Edwards, Joseph; *Plains of Jericho Addition*; 241 ac.; 10 Aug 1753 cert./pat. (COL)

Edwards, Jane; son John [b. 17 Feb 1758] (SA p. 195)

Edwards, Benjamin; inv.; 28 Feb 1761; 9 May 1761; nok Stourton & Robert Edwards; adm. Benjamin Edwards (I 74.257, 258); acct.; 6 Sep 1763; adm. Benjamin Edwards, Jr. (A 49.638)

Edwards, John; inv.; 8 Apr 1761; 15 Jul 1761; nok Stourton Edwards; admx./extx. Elisabeth Edwards (I 74.279); acct.; 6 Feb 1764 (A 50.356); dist.; 6 Feb 1764 (BB 4.28)

Edwards, John and Henrietta; daus. Elizabeth [b. 23 Feb 1762], Ann Chloe [b. 4 May 1763] (SA p. 14, 49)

Edwards, John; inv.; 14 Apr 1763; 23 Apr 1763; nok Jeremiah & Jane Edwards; admx. Henerita Edwards (I 81.229); acct.; 28 Oct 1763 (A 50.180)

Edwards, Stourton; approx. 1765; age 40 [SMW TA1.539.556]

Edwards, John; s/o Joseph; *Edward's Back Land*; 162 ac.; 29 Oct 1765 cert./pat. (COL)

Edwards, Stourton; will; 11 Sep 1766; 2 Oct 1766; wife Barbara; s-i-l Zachariah Forrest, wife Ann; John, s/o Jane Edwards (MCW 13.137) [SMW TA1.488]; inv.; 14 Apr 1767; nok John Edwards, Jr., Elisabeth Lock; ex. Jeremiah Edwards (I 91.334, 336); acct.; 23 Aug 1768 (A 58.239, 241, 244, 245)

Edwards, Jonathan; *Long Reach*; 31 ac.; 22 Jul 1768 cert./pat. (COL)

Edwards, Richard Swan; will; 24 Feb 1769; 18 Oct 1769; wife Martha; children Sarah, John; d-i-l Nancy Caldwell; tract *Narrows* (MCW 14.108) [SMW TA1.578]

Edwards, John; s/o John; *Bite the Fox*; 75 ac.; 22 Nov 1769 cert./pat. (COL)

Edwards, Robert; <u>inv.</u>; 19 May 1770; 23 Mar 1771; mentions John & Jesse Edwards; admx. Mary Edwards (I 106.366)

Edwards, Richard Swan; <u>inv.</u>; 1 Oct 1770; nok orphans; ex. Martha Edwards (I 103.326); <u>acct.</u>; 24 Mar 1772; exs. Robert Armstrong & wife Martha (A 66.279); <u>inv.</u>; 18 Apr 1774 (I 117.413); <u>acct.</u>; 18 Apr 1774 (A 70.143)

Edwards, Barbara; widow; 23 Apr 1774; 3 Aug 1774; daus. Jane Edwards & her son John, Eleanor Hayes (widow) (MCW 16.21) [SMW TA1.683]

Edwards, Josias; <u>will</u>; 15 Sep 1774; 10 Nov 1774; bro. John; cousin Thomas, s/o Joseph [or Thomas] Edwards; tract *Taurlon Dean* (MCW 16.1) [SMW TA1.691]

Edwards, Stourton; <u>acct.</u>; 10 May 1775; mentions Barbara, Jeremiah, Jane & John Edwards (A 72.157)

Edwards, John and Mary Morgan (by license); m. 8 Aug 1784 (SA p. 62)

EGERTON

Egerton, Thomas; Gent.; <u>inv.</u>; 22 Aug 1642 (AM IV.89, 106)

Egerton; Charles; exs. Jeremiah Adderton and wife Mary; [filed with 1674] (SMAA p. 38)

Egerton, Charles Sr.; <u>will</u>; 11 Mar 1689; 11 Apr 1699; wife Ann; sons George, Charles, John, Thomas, Randolph, James; dau. Mary; tracts *Pountney [Pamunkey's] Marsh, Piney Neck*; mentions *"Pascotowagh"* (MCW 2.174) [SMW PC1.123]; <u>inv.</u>; 29 May 1699 (I&A 19.51); <u>acct.</u>; 12 Mar 1700 (I&A 20.162)

Egerton, Charles; <u>inv.</u>; 5 Apr 1706 (I&A 26.255); <u>acct.</u>; 17 May 1708; admx./extx. Mary, w/o Jeremiah Adderton (I&A 28.221) (SMAA p. 164); <u>acct.</u>; 30 Dec 1710 (I&A 32b.11) (SMAA p. 205)

Edgerton, Charles; m. Mary, d/o James Neale & Elizabeth Calvert; 18 Jul 1721 (CCR p. 53)

Egerton, Charles; <u>inv.</u>; 21 Apr 1738; 19 Jun 1738; nok John Hicks, Mary Deacon; admn./ex. James Egerton (I 23.207, 208); <u>acct.</u>; 11 Jun 1739 (A 17.190)

Edgerton (Egerton), James; <u>inv.</u>; 12 Mar 1742; nok Mary Underwood, Ann Gough; adm./ex. William Egerton (I 27.370)

Egerton, James; <u>will</u>; 16 Jan 1765; 26 Jul 1768; son Charles Calvart Egerton; dau. Mary Ann, w/o Michael Jenifer; g-son Parker Jenifer; g-dau. Darkey Jenifer; tracts *Piney Neck, Blewstone Neck* (MCW 14.52) [SMW TA1.559]; <u>inv.</u> 17 Aug 1768; nok James Aderton, William Egerton; ex. Charles Calvert Egerton (I 98.117); <u>acct.</u>; 10 Sep 1770 (A 64.240)

ELLERY

Ellery, Henry; m. widow of William Stephenson; 23 Apr 1659; wife Elizabeth; 7 Dec 1659 (AM XLI.283; LXV.674)

Ellery, Henry; <u>will</u>; 15 Apr 1668; 16 May 1668; wife Elizabeth; mentions Elizabeth, d/o Patrick Forrest (MCW 1.44) [SMW PC1.6]

ELLIOTT

Elliott, Henry; service by 1673 (SK 17.557)

Elliott, Henry; m. Jane, widow of John Halfhead who d. 6 Jan 1678; 10 Mar 1678 (CCR p. 5)

Elliot, Henry; will; 13 Sep 1679; 18 Oct 1679; wife Jane (MCW 1.218) [SMW PC1.33]; inv.; 13 Nov 1680 (I&A 7a.229)

Elliot, Robert; age ca 31 in 1728 (MD p. 59)

Elliot, Robert; Deputy Surveyor for SM Co.; *Friendship*; sur. 24 Aug 1725 for Robert Elliot & Leo. Kilpack; poss. Robt. Elliot (TLC p. 84); 81 ac.; 2 Nov 1730 cert./pat. (COL)

Elliott, Robert, Mr.; inv.; 16 Nov 1737; 20 Nov 1738; nok Henry & Mark Jarboe; adms./exs. John Newton & wife Monica (I 23.500); acct.; Sep 1740 (A 18.60)

Elliot, William; will; 24 Jun 1755; 4 Apr 1758; wife Elizabeth (MCW 11.198) [SMW TA1.369]; inv.; 16 May 1758; 4 Jul 1758; nok Richard Whitely, Ann Scott; admx./extx. Elisabeth Elliott (I 65.267); acct.; 4 Jul 1758 (A 41.495); dist.; 8 Jul 1758 (BB 2.108)

ELLIS

Ellis, John; 1665; lived at *Kitts Martins Point* (MD p. 59)

Ellys, Robert; *Oxford*; 209 ac.; sur. 3 May 1675; 1707 poss. Charles Carroll; St. Mary's Hundred (RR p. 6) (TLC p. 7)
Addition; 41 ac.; sur. 7 May 1675; 1707 poss. Charles Carroll; St. Mary's Hundred (RR p. 7) (TLC p. 7)

Ellis, Joseph; inv.; 29 Nov 1752; nok Philip & John Elliss (I 52.88); acct.; 2 Dec 1756; mentions William Ellis (A 40.231)

ELTONHEAD

Eltonhead, Wm.; *Rich Neck*; 2,000 ac.; sur. 8 Mar 1648; Harvey Hundred (RR p. 55) (TLC p. 52)

Eltonhead, Jane; will; probate 28 Feb 1659; eld. son Thomas Taylor of *Cedar Point*; dau. Sarah and g-son Roger Anderton; mentions Edward Eltonhead (MCW 1.12)

ENNIS

Ennes, Thomas; inv.; 14 Dec 1698 (I&A 15.311); acct.; 15 Mar 1698; admx. Ann Ennis (I&A 18.124) (SMAA p. 93)

Ennis, William; will; 20 Sep 1773; 2 Nov 1773; children William, Ann, Henyritte, Zekel, James, Barton and Elizabeth Curry Ennis; wife Mary; mentions John Ennis (MCW 15.90) [SMW TA1.663]; inv.; 20 Jan 1774; 2 Mar 1774; nok Henry & William Ennis; ex. Mary Ennis (I 116.204); acct.; 31 Jan 1775; exs. Mary & William Ennis (A 73.246); dist.; 31 Jan 1775 (BB 7.44)

ERVANE

Irvine, John; will; 13 Oct 1718; 20 Nov 1718; mother Margaret Thompson [SMW PC1.241]

Ervain, George; inv.; [filed with 1718] (I 1.477); acct.; 7 Mar 1720; [George Ervine] (A 3.406); acct.; 26 Feb 1720; [George Irvane] (A 2.424)

EVANS

Evans, Wm. & John Jarbo; *Evans Quarter*; 100 ac.; sur. 15 Mar 1648; 1707 poss. Daniell Langhorn; 23 Mar 1680 resur. into *Hopton Park*; New Town Hundred (RR p. 27) (TLC p. 26)

    Evans Quarter; 100 ac.; 8 Nov 1652; incl. *Resurvey Hopton Park*; 1707 no poss.; New Town Hundred (RR p. 27) (TLC p. 28))

    Evans Freehold; 550; sur. 14 Aug 1665; 1707 no poss.; incl. in *Resurvey of Hopton Park*; New Town Hundred (RR p. 33) (TLC p. 32)

Evans, William, Lt. and wife; exs. of William Tompson of Newtowne Hundred [her late husband]; 1649/50 (AM X.23)

Evans, Sarah; age ca 26 on 20 Dec 1664 (AM XLIX.318)

Evans, William; will; written 10 Feb 1667; wife Eliza: (MCW 1.46)

Evans, Thomas; and Sarah his wife; service by 1668 (SK 18.150; 9.432; 17.67)

Evans, William; d. Mar 1669; wife Elizabeth; she m/2 Capt. John Jordain who d. ca 8 Sep 1678; m/3 28 Oct 1678 Cuthbert Scott (CCR p. 7)

Evans, Tho.; *Cole Brooke*; 180 ac.; sur. 12 Nov 1676; 1707 poss. Wm. Bannister; New Town Hundred (RR p. 37) (TLC p. 36)

Evans, Thomas; will; 17 Mar 1678; 12 Apr 1679; wife Ann; unnamed child. (MCW 1.212) [SMW PC1.33]; inv.; 9 May 1679; approver Anne Evans (I&A 6.181)

Evans, Edward; *Evans' Reserve*; 100 ac.; [16 Feb 1679] cert./pat. (COL) *Content*; 99 ac.; 8 Mar 1688 cert./pat. (COL)

Evans, Anth.; *Poplar Hill*; 63 ac.; sur. 8 Apr 1682; 1707 no poss.; St. Mary's Hundred (RR p. 8) poss. Caleb Williams (TLC p. 9) (TLC p. 9)

Evans, John; will; 5 Mar 1687/8; 25 May 1688; wife unnamed; minor dau. Mary; Matthew, s/o Robert Mason; John, s/o Robert Jones; Catherine, d/o Henry Lawrence; Eliza. Phyppes, widow; tracts *Hogg's Neck, Salleum* in CH Co. (MCW 2.25) [SMW PC1.68]; inv.; 21 Jun 1688 (I&A 10.69; 10lc.20); acct.; 15 Feb 1692; mentions Katherine, d/o Henry Lawrence (I&A 10.345); acct.; 7 Jul 1694; dau. m. Peter Watts (I&A 13a.190)

Evans, Charles; *Evans' Lot*; 26 ac.; 10 Aug 1687 cert./pat. (COL)

Evans, Anthony; inv.; 6 May 1699 (I&A 19½a.24)

Evans, John; will; written 18 Sep 1700; son Philip; bro. Anthony; wife and children unnamed (MCW 2.216); inv.; 26 Mar 1701 (I&A 20.166); acct.; 28 Jul 1703; extx. Mrs. Elisabeth Evans (I&A 24.34) (SMAA p. 119); acct.; 26 May 1704 (I&A 3.66); acct.; 6 Sep 1709; extx. Elisabeth Williams (I&A 31.83) (SMAA p. 209)

Evans, Anthony; acct.; 23 Jul 1703; adm. John Evans; Mrs. Elizabeth Evans, extx. of John Evans; mentions coffins for him and his wife (SMAA p. 115)

Evans, Edward; inv.; [filed with 1712] (I&A 34.120); acct.; 17 Mar 1713 (I&A 35a.317) (SMAA p. 237)

Evans, David; carpenter; grant 10 ac. on Nicholas Run; 2 Sep 1714 (CCR p. 33-4)

Evans, Susan; age ca 65; midwife; 3 Aug 1717 (CCR p. 39)

Evans, Philip; age ca 27; 11 May 1720 (CCR p. 47)

Evans, Owen; inv.; 30 May 1726; 30 Jul 1726; nok minors; admx. Willin Evans (I 11.496); acct.; 17 Jul 1727; adm. Willen Evans (A 8.284); acct.; 7 Oct 1728; ch/o William Thomas: John, Benjamin & Dorothy Thomas and dau. who m. William Cutter; adms. John Basset, and wife Willen (A 9.108)

Evans (Evins), Thomas; inv.; 11 Oct 1726; 2 Jan 1726; nok minors (I 11.720); acct.; 31 Jul 1727 (A 8.291)

Evans, David; will; 16 Jul 1734; 31 Mar 1735; g-dau. Isabella Hebb; g-sons David and Joseph Hebb; daus. Susannah, w/o Henry Tucker, d-i-l Eleanor, w/o David Evans (MCW 7.134) [SMW TA1.46]; inv.; 15 May 1735; 30 Jun 1735; nok Susanna Evins, Elisabeth Hebb (I 20.480); acct.; 21 Jan 1735; children Hugh, John, Susanah, Judith & Grace Evans; admx. Elinor, w/o Thomas Fish (A 14.179); acct.; 19 Jul 1736 (A 15.88)

Evans, Philip; planter; will; written 5 Feb 1738-9; sons John, William, Jeremiah, Philip; wife Patience; tracts *Broushey [Brouthey] Neck, Poplar Hill* (MCW 8.213) [SMW TA1.142]; inv.; 2 Jul ___; 16 Jul 1743; nok Anthony & John Evans admx./extx. Patience Evans (I 28.16); acct.; 1 Sep 1744; extx. Patience,w/o William Taylor (A 20.438)

Evans [Eavens], Anthony; will; 20 Jun 1744; 3 Sep 1744; cousin Elizabeth Carmitchell [Carmichael] tract *Brusey Neck* (MCW 8.278) [SMW TA1.155]; inv.; 8 Sep 1744; 4 Mar 1744; nok William Williams, Elisabeth Cirmichell; admx./extx. Winifred Treppe (I 30.297); acct.; 26 May 1746 (A 22.256)

Evans, William; acct.; 6 Aug 1754; extx. Judith Evans (A 36.401)

Evans, John; will; 2 Jul 1756; 30 Aug 1756; wife Mary; children Mary, Thomas, Richard, William, Philip, Elizabeth, Jonathan (MCW 11.145) [SMW TA1.346]; inv.; 20 Feb 1757; nok Thomas & Mary Evans; admx./extx. Mary Evans (I 62.248); acct.; 28 Nov 1757 (A 41.327)

Evans, Philip and Ann; daus. Mary [b. 10 Sep 1764], Elizabeth [b. 12 Jul 1767] (SA p. 192)

Evans, Evan; inv.; 9 Oct 1764; nok James & Sarah Brown; admx. Sarah Evans (I 86.55)

Evans, William; m. 16 Nov 1778 ____ Bull (BRU 2.535)

Evans, Richard and Jane; children Ann [b. 30 Oct 1798; bapt. 9 Sep 1799] Daniel [b. 15 Oct 1805; bapt. 28 Nov 1805] (SA p. 31, 32)

EWING

Ewing, John; *Scott's Close*; 100 ac.; 15 May 1706 cert./pat. (COL)

Ewing, Nathl.; m. 24 Feb 1784 Catharine Reeder (BRU 2.535)

EXON

Exon, Henry; *Temple Barr*; 100 ac.; sur. 18 Jul 1672; poss. Charles Carroll; not
found in 1707; St. Mary's Hundred (TLC p. 8)
Loughbourough; 150 ac.; sur. 1 Aug 1673; 1707 poss. Charles Carroll; St.
Mary's Hundred (RR p. 6) (TLC p. 6)
Exon, Henry; innholder; age ca 49 in 1684 (MD p. 62)
Exon, Henry; innholder; wife Elizabeth; conveyed *Temple Barr* to Robert Ellys;
1676 (AM LXVI.187)

FADERY

Fordery, John; inv.; [filed with 1699] (I&A 19½b.117)
Fadery (Fudery), John; will; 23 Feb 1724/5; 22 Mar 1724/5; daus. Anne,
Rachell; son John (MCW 5.185) [SMW PC1.294]; inv.; 31 Mar 1725; 2 Jun 1725;
nok Herbert & Luke Thomas (I 10.416, 417); acct.; 8 Jun 1726 (A 7.379); 3 Jul
1727 (A 8.274); 9 Nov 1728; legatee dau., w/o Robert Nugen (A 9.115)
Fawdrie, James; inv.; 3 Dec 1729; nok Nicholas & John Fawdrey (I 15.277)
Fardarie, John; inv.; 28 Dec 1742; nok Rachel & William Lucas; admx./extx.
Eliza Fardarie (I 27.229)
Fandery, Nicholas; inv., 13 Mar 1744; 5 Mar 1745; nok James & Ann Fandery (I
32.81); acct.; 3 Aug 1747; orphans Joseph, Nicholas, Vachel, Ann, Patience;
admx. Mary, w/o Luke Marrat [Marrall] (A 24.173)
Faudra, James; inv.; 5 Jul 1765; nok Thomas & Mary Smith (I 88.79)

FANNING

Fanning, Edmond; immigrated by 1669 (SK 12.348)
Fanning (Fleming), John; will; 1 Dec 1745; 4 Feb 1745; child. Josiah, John,
Elizabeth; wife Mary; mentions Elizabeth Wakefield (MCW 9.54) [SMW
TA1.165]; inv.; 5 May 1746; 6 May 1747; nok Hilton John Phelips, Elizabeth
Tegnum Wakefield; admx./extx. Mary Flanning (I 32.226); acct.; 19 May 1747;
extx. Mary, w/o Thomas Simpson (A 23.311)
Fermins (Fanning), John; inv.; 2 Jun 1761; nok Josias & Elisabeth Fanning;
adm. John Fanning (I 74.264); acct.; 10 Dec 1761; dau. Elisabeth; son Josias;
extx. Mary (widow) (A 47.221); acct.; 1 Mar 1763; adm. John Fanning (A 49.96);
dist.;12 Mar 1763 (BB 3.178)
Fanning, Josias; inv.; 20 Jul 1762; nok John Fanning, Elisabeth Frasor; admx.
Mary, w/o George Carpenter (I 79.244)
Fanning, John; inv.; 26 Oct 1771; nok John & Joshua Gibson; admx. Ann
Fanning (I 107.182); acct.; 5 Apr 1773; admx. Ann, w/o John Goldsmith (A
68.195)

FARR

Farr, Edmond; *Boston*; 50 ac.; 12 Oct 1721 cert./pat. (COL)

Farr, Edmund (Edman); will; 8 Dec 1730; 5 Jan 1730; son Clement; daus. Mary, Sarah (MCW 6.176) [SMW PC1.356]; inv.; 12 Jan 1730; 6 Apr 1731; nok Peter & Matthew Cartwright (I 16.186); acct.; 9 Dec 1731 (A 11.318, 406)

FARRELL
Forrell, Patrick; inv.; 13 Jun 1704 (I&A 3.311); acct.; 4 Dec 1706; admx. Honor, w/o Thomas Warren (I&A 27.63) (SMAA p. 132)

Farrell, James; acct.; 2 Jul 1742; child. Daniel, Sarah, Harrison; admx. Elisabeth, w/o James Aires (A 19.135)

FARTHING
Farthing, William Maria; *William's Endeavour*; 50 ac.; sur. 30 Apr 1714; (TLC p. 69); 2 Sep 1714 cert./pat. (COL)

St. Ignatius; 100 ac.; sur. 23 Sep 1715 (TLC p. 79)

Headen's Fear; 300 ac.; 2 Feb 1715 (TLC p. 74); 24 Apr 1717 cert./pat. (COL)

Chance Conclusion; 97 ac.; sur. 18 May 1714 (TLC p. 75); 25 Apr 1717 cert./pat. (COL)

Farthing's Adventure; 180 ac.; sur. 30 Apr 1716 (TLC p. 75); 25 Apr 1717 cert./pat. (COL)

Hannover; 1,525 ac.; resur. 18 May 1719; 1,125 ac.; escheat; mentions Alice & William Watts (TLC p. 78); 1 May 1719 cert./pat. (COL)

Farthing's Fortune; 50 ac.; 19 Jun 1719 cert./pat. (COL)

Farthing's Discovery; 520 ac.; 9 Sep 1719 cert./pat. (COL)

Truth & Trust; 773 ac.; sur. 15 Aug 1720 (TLC p. 85)

Frightfull; 180 ac.; sur. 16 Jan 1723 (TLC p. 84)

Wolf Holes; 262 ac.; resur. 5 Feb 1723; 7 Aug 1723 (TLC p. 84)

Cleever; 155 ac.; sur. 16 Feb 1723/4 (TLC p. 86)

Friends Good Will; 612 ac.; sur. 14 Nov 1723 (TLC p. 85)

James Addition; 158 ac.; sur. 5 Dec 1723 (TLC 86)

Farthing, James; planter; age ca 31; 9 Feb 1721 (CCR p. 44)

Farthing, John; bro. of William Maria Farthing; 9 Feb 1721 (CCR p. 44)

Farthing, William Maria; inv.; 22 Mar 1734; 16 Jun 1735; nok Richard & John Farthing; admx./extx. Ann Farthing (I 21.95); acct.; 5 Nov 1736; admx. Ann Farthing (A 15.231); 26 Mar 1738 (A 17.109)

Farthing, Richard; *Hanover Addition*; 366 ac.; escheat land originally called *St. Francis*; resur. 7 Jun 1720; (TLC p. 91); 4 Oct 1735 cert./pat. (COL)

Farthing, James; will; 26 Jan 1739/40; 27 Mar 1740; wife Mary; son James (MCW 8.78) [SMW TA1.93]; inv.; 25 Jun 1740; 15 Sep 1740; nok Richard & John Farthing; admx./extx. Mary Farthing (I 25.298); acct.; 30 Jul 1744; extx. Mary, w/o Thomas Tarlton (A 20.424)

Farthing, John; carpenter; age ca 60 in 1747 (MD p. 62)

FENWICK

Fenwick, Cuthbert; unnamed; 400 ac.; sur. 27 Jul 1641; divided by 1707:
   Chappell Freehold, 25 ac., 1707 poss. His Lordship (RR p. 2); poss. Robert
   Brook (TLC p. 2)]
   St. Inigoes Neck, 120 ac., poss. Mary Vanswearingen (RR p. 2) (TLC p. 2)
   St. Mary's Freehold; 255 ac., poss. 1707 Maj. Nicholas Sewall; St. Mary's
   Hundred (RR p. 2) (TLC p. 2))
   Fenwick Mannour; 2,000 ac.; sur. 24 Apr 1651; 1707 poss. Adam Head who
   m. John Sewall's relict; Resurrection Hundred (RR p. 58) (TLC p. 55)
Fenwick, Cuthbert; intent to marry Jane Moryson, widow of Robert Moryson of
   Kecoughtan Co., VA; 1 Aug 1649; will dated 21 Feb 1649 names wife Jane,
   child. Ignatius, Robert, Richard, John; bro. Eltonhead (AM XLI.261)
Fenwick, Cuthbert; cattle marks for sons Thomas, Cuthbert, Ignatius and dau.
   Teresa; 29 Sep 1649 (AM IV.509)
Fenwick, Cuthbert; age ca 40; 18 Apr 1654 (AM X.372)
Fenwick, Cuthbert; <u>will</u>; written 6 Mar 1654; wife Jane; child. Cuthbert,
   Ignatius, Robert, Richard, John and Teresa; bro. ____ Eltonhead (MCW 1.219)
Fenwick, Jane; *Little Fenwick*; 100 ac.; sur. Jun 1659; in *Delabrook Manor*;
   1707 poss. Rich'd Fenwick; Resurrection Hundred (RR p. 58) (TLC p. 56))
Fenwick, Cuthbert; *Manor of St. Cuthberts*; 1663/4; divided between Cuthbert,
   s/o Cuthbert, and his brothers (AM XLIX.131)
   Prevention; 200 ac.; sur. 22 Nov 1665; 1707 poss. Adam Head, m. relict of
   John Sewall; Resurrection Hundred (RR p. 59) (TLC p. 57)
Fenwicks, Ignatius; wife Ellen; Nov 1712 (CCR p. 23)
Fenwick, Richard; <u>will</u>; 1 Apr 1714; 26 Apr 1714; sons Richard, Cuthbert, John,
   Enoch, Ignatius; bro. John Fenwick (MCW 4.13) [SMW PC1.192]; <u>inv.</u>; 10 May
   1714 (I&A 36a.196); <u>acct.</u>; 21 May 1715; exs. Richard, Cudbert, John, Enoch
   and Ignatius Fenwick (SMAA p. 287) (I&A 36c.55)
Fenwick, John; <u>will</u>; 20 Mar 1720; 28 May 1720; cousins John, Cuthbert,
   Ignatius, Richard and Enoch Fenwick; tract *Beaver Dam Mannor* (MCW 4.229)
   [SMW PC1.256]; <u>inv.</u>; 23 May 1720; 3 Aug 1720; nok Ann Head, Catharine
   Sawell (I 4.43); <u>acct.</u>; 26 Oct 1720; exs. Richard, Cuthbert, John, Enoch &
   Ignatius Fenwick (A 3.138) (SMAA p. 417); <u>acct.</u>; 19 May 1721 (A 3.408)
Fenwick, Richard, Mr.; <u>inv.</u>; 20 Jul 1722; 8 Aug 1722; nok Cuthbert & Enoch
   Fenwick; admx./extx. Dorothy Fenwick (I 7.315); <u>acct.</u>; 8 Aug 1723 (A 5.204)
Fenwick, Dorothy; <u>will</u>; 1 Apr 1724; 19 Jun 1724; bro. Edmond Plowden (MCW
   5.171) [SMW PC1.285]; <u>inv.</u>; 11 Sep 1724; mentions Eruk Fenwick; nok Cuthbert
   & Cuthbert Fenwick, Jr. (I 10.117); <u>acct.</u>; 16 Jun 1725 (A 6.437)
Fenwick, Cuthburt; <u>will</u>; probate 23 Mar 1729; child. Elizabeth, Bennet,
   Cuthbert, Robert; g-ch. Robert and Mary Brooke (MCW 6.147) [SMW PC1.340];
   <u>inv.</u>; 20 May 1730; 11 Jul 1730; nok John & Cuthbert Fenwick; admx./extx.
   Mrs. Elisabeth Fenwick (I 15.603); <u>acct.</u>; 11 Jul 1730; 5 orphans (A 10.416)

Fenwick, Ignatius, Mr.; <u>inv.</u>; 6 Dec 1732; 8 Mar 1732; nok John & Enoch
  Fenwick; admx./extx. Ellenor Fenwick (I 17.23); <u>acct.</u>; 22 Jul 1734; orphans
  Ignatius, Philip, John, George, Richard & Eleanor Fenwick (A 12.454)
Fenwick, John, Mr.; <u>inv.</u>; 15 Mar 1733; 4 Jun 1734; nok Edmund Plowden,
  Cuthbert Fenwick; admx./extx. Winefred Fenwick (I 18.315); <u>acct.</u>; 22 Aug
  1735; orphans Jane, Doryty & Mary Fenwick (A 13.317)
Fenwick, Ellen; <u>will</u>; 7 Aug 1737; 1 Nov 1737; dau. Ellen; sons Philip, John,
  Ignatius, George, Richard (MCW 7.231) [SMW TA1.71]; <u>inv.</u>; 4 Jan 1737; 23 Jan
  1737; nok Philip Fenwick, George Clarke; adm./ex. Ignatius Fenwick (I 23.19);
  <u>acct.</u>; 6 Jul 1738 (A 16.223)
Fenwick, Cuthbert, Jr.; <u>inv.</u>; 29 Jan 1745; 4 Jun 1746; nok Robert Fenwick;
  adm./ex. Benjamin Fenwick (I 33.45); <u>acct.</u>; 21 Jul 1747 (A 24.20)
Fenwick, Philip; <u>will</u>; 13 Oct 1749; 15 Jan 1749; son Robert; daus. Eliner &2
  unnamed; wife Mary; [son Philip] (MCW 10.71) [SMW TA1.232]; <u>inv.</u>; 5 Apr
  1750; 1 May 1750; nok Ignatius & Richard Fenwick; admx./extx. Mary
  Fenwick (I 42.215); <u>acct.</u>; 31 Jan 1750; orphans Robert [age 7], Philip [age 3],
  Elinor [age 10], Jane [age 6], Barbary [age 1] (A 29.200)
Fenwick, Richard; *Fenwick's Gain*; 55 acres; 11 Mar 1754 cert./pat. (COL)
Fenwick, Cuthbert; 55 ac.; *Fenwick's Prevention*; 29 Apr 1756 cert./pat. (COL)
Finwick, Richard; <u>inv.</u>; 3 Apr 1758; 2 May 1758; nok George & Ignatius
  Fenwick; admx./extx. Ann Fenwick (I 65.239)
Fenwick, Enoch [Sr.]; <u>will</u>; 30 Jan 1758; 8 Nov 1758; sons Enoch, John,
  Ignatious; dau. [Elizabeth] Joseph (sic) (MCW 11.217) [SMW TA1.373]; <u>inv.</u>; 2 Feb
  1759; 8 Mar 1759; nok Joseph Fenwick, William Josephs; adm./ex. Ignatius
  Fenwick (I 66.234); <u>dist.</u>; 10 Dec 1759 (BB 3.8)
Fenwick, Joseph; <u>will</u>; probate 6 Dec 1758; mentions Cudbert, s/o Robert
  Fenwick of Harvey Town (MCW 11.226) [SMW TA1.363]; <u>inv.</u>; 26 Mar 1759; nok
  Elisabeth Spalding, Benjamin Fenwick (I 66.220); <u>acct.</u>; 29 Nov 1760; nok
  Robert & Benjamin Fenwick, John Fields, John Bopt Mattingley, Clem.
  Spaulding, Robert Brooke, John Taney; adm. Robert Fenwick (A 46.157); <u>dist.</u>;
  29 Nov 1760 (BB 4.14)
Fenwick, Joseph; <u>acct.</u>; 26 Jun 1764; adm. Robert Fenwick (A 51.146); <u>dist.</u>; 26
  Jun 1764 (BB 4.34)
Fenwick, John; b. ca 1759; d. 1815 *St. Thomas Manor*; s/o Ignatius Fenwick and
  Mary Cole of *Cherryfields* (JM p. 316)
Fenwick, Richard; <u>acct.</u>; 16 Mar 1759; orphans Elianor [age 8], Elisabeth [age
  6], John [age 2], James [age 9 mos.]; admx. Ann Fenwick (A 43.95); <u>dist.</u>; 1
  Mar 1759; mentions Eleanor [age 9 next Nov], Elisabeth [age 7 next Dec],
  John [age 3 next Apr], James [age 1 next Jul]; (BB 2.107); <u>acct.</u>; 3 Sep 1759;
  admx. Ann, w/o John Baptist Matingley (A 43.300)
Fenwock, Mary; <u>inv.</u>; 14 May 1759; 20 Aug 1759; mentions Samuel Abell, Jr.
  & Samuel, s/o John Abell; nok Benedict & George Fenwick; admx./extx.
  Eleanor Fenwick (I 67.324); <u>acct.</u>; 5 May 1760; orphans Eleanor [at age],

Robert [age 16], Jennett [age 14], Barbara [age 12], Philip [age 10]; admx.
Eleanor Fenwick (A 44.270); dist.; 5 May 1760 (BB 3.26)

Fenwick, Sarah; acct.; 11 Dec 1759; ex. Ignatius Fenwick (A 44.177)

Fenwick, Cuthbert, Sr.; will; 1 Sep 1762; 8 Sep 1762; cousins Benedict, s/o
George Fenwick, & Cuthbert, s/o Bennet Fenwick;mentions Rebecca, w/o
William King, Jr.; bro. Bennett; tract *Swamp Island* in *Beaver Dam Mannor*
(MCW 12.159) [SMW TA1.426]; inv.; 8 Sep 1762; 4 Mar 1763; ex. Bennett
Fenwick (I 80.167); acct.; 10 Feb 1764 (A 50.366); dist.; 10 Feb 1764 (BB 4.29)

Fenwick, Richard; inv.; 8 Jun 1764; 2 Oct 1764; nok Ignatius & Benjamin
Fenwick; adm. George Fenwick (I 86.60); acct.; 31 Oct 1765 (A 53.240); dist.; 31
Oct 1765 (BB 4.141)

Fenwick, Edward; b. 19 Aug 1768; d. 26 Sep 1832 Wooster, OH of cholera;
consecrated Bishop of Cincinnati 13 Jan 1822; s/o Ignatius Fenwick and Sarah
Taney of *Wallington* (JM p. 316)

Fenwick, Benedict; will; 2 Apr 1769; 2 May 1763 (sic); mother unnamed; bros.
William, George; sister Jean (MCW 14.91) [SMW TA1.583]; inv.; 25 Apr 1769; 10
Nov 1769; nok Ignatius, s/o Enoch & Jane Fenwick; ex. William Fenwick (I
102.183); acct.; 30 Aug 1770 (A 64.228); dist.; 30 Aug 1770; mentions William,
George & Jane Fenwick (BB 5.399)

Fenwick, George; inv.; 15 Jul 1769; cous. Enoch Fenwick; admx. Belinda
(widow), w/o Robert Fenwick (I 102.239); acct.; 18 Jul 1769 (A 62.156); dist.; 18
Jul 1769 (BB 5.220)

Fenwick, George; will; 15 Jul 1769; 27 Apr 1772; child. William, George, Jean;
wife Jane; tract *Chances Conclusion* (MCW 14.213) [SMW TA1.644]; inv.; 10 Aug
1772; nok Benjamin & Robert Fenwick; adm./ex. James Fenwick (I 110.99);
inv.; [filed with 1774]; extx. Jane Fenwick (I 118.228)

Fenwick, Bennett; will; 19 May 1770; 5 Feb 1771; child.Cuthburt, Francis,
Michael, Richard, Elizabeth, Mary, Dorety, Henryitea Maria, Priscella; bro.
Cuthburt (MCW 14.181) [SMW TA1.632]; inv.; 17 Apr 1771; 20 Apr 1771; nok
Mary Ann & Cuthbert Fenwick; ex. Richard Fenwick (I 107.97); inv.; 1 Jan
1773 (I 112.416, 419); acct.; 1 Jan 1773 (A 68.209); dist.; 1 Jan 1773; ch. Elisabeth,
Mary, Richard, Dorothea, Henrietta, Francis, Michel, Priscilla (BB 6.256)

Fenwick, Philip; m. 3 Sep 1770 Rebecca Greenwell (MM)

Fenwick, Elizabeth; will; 30 Aug 1771; 20 Jul 1771; nephew Francis Spalding;
niece Ann Spalding; sister Eleanor, w/o Bennet Spalding (MCW 15.70) [SMW
TA1.671]

Fenwick, John; m. 11 Nov 1772 Mary Thompson (MM)

Fenwick, Robert; will; 16 Feb 1774; 2 Oct 1774; sons Joseph, Edward; dau.
Elener; bro. Philip; sister Barbery (MCW 16.24) [SMW TA1.685]; inv.; 25 Oct
1774; 28 Jan 1775; nok Barbara & Ignatius Fenwick (of E.); adm./ex. Philip
Fenwick (of Philip) (I 121.402)

Fenwick, Thomas; m. 3 Jul 1774 Eliz. Thomas (MM)

Fenwick, Robert; inv.; 10 Jun 1775; 14 Jul 1776; nok Robert & Bennet
Fenwick; admx. Mary Fenwick (I 125.255)

Fenwick, Ignatius; will; 24 Jan 1776; 8 Oct 1776; sons Edward, James, Richard,
John, Joseph, Henry; daus. Helena, Elizabeth, Ann Clark, Mary (?Jenkins);
g-father Cole left legacies to each dau.; tracts *St. Mary's Hill, St. Peters,
Holdons Hole, Drapers Neck, Poiney Point, Millmans Adventure, Small Hope*
(MCW 16.175)

Fenwick, Jacob; m. 12 Jun 1776 Henrietta Howard (MM)

Fenwick, Richard; d. 10 Apr 1799; age 52 (HGM)

FERGUSON
Ferguison (Forginson), Alexander; will; 29 May 1727; 6 Jun 1727; son James;
wife Kathrine (MCW 6.25) [SMW PC1.323]; inv.; 7 Aug 1727; 4 Sep 1727; nok
Catherine Ferguison, John Green (I 12.254); acct.; 27 May 1728 (A 9.193)

Forguson [Ferguson], Alexander; will; 21 Apr 1755; 10 May 1755; wife
Rebecca (MCW 11.83) [SMW TA1.334]

Ferguson, Charles; inv.; 22 Jun 1775; 20 Aug 1776 (I 125.254)

FERRELL
Ferrell, James; inv.; 18 Sep 1741; 1 Feb 1741; nok Mary Mohoney, D. Suliven;
admx./extx. Catherine Ferrell (I 26.429)

Ferrill, James; inv.; 12 Jan 1755; 26 May 1755; nok Mary Mohoney, Abrahm
Ferrill (I 60.313); acct.; 26 May 1755; admx. w/o Daniel Sullivane (A 38.25)

FIELD
Field, Edward, Jr.; *Young Man's Venture*; 130 ac.; sur. 12 May 1706 (TLC p. 65);
10 Oct 1707 cert./pat. (COL)

Field, Edward, Sr.; age ca 64; Edward, Jr. age ca 25; 21 May 1716 (CCR p. 38);
age ca 74; 25 Jun 1722 (CCR p. 50)

Field, Edward; will; 6 Oct 1724; 4 Nov 1724; g-sons William, Edward; son
Edward; dau. Monica Mohany; sons John Spalding, Edward Field, Samll.
Mohany (MCW 5.178) [SMW PC1.292]; inv.; 13 Nov 1724; 17 Aug 1725; nok John
& Mary Spalding; ex. Edward Field (I 11.91); acct.; 22 Feb 1725 (A 7.254)

FIELDER
Fielder (Filder), William; 18 Dec 1718; 24 Jan 1718/9; son William; dau. Mary
Lee; wife Barbary (MCW 4.192) [SMW PC1.240]; inv.; 7 Feb 1718; 9 Apr 1719;
mentions William & Nicholas Fielder; extx. Barbary Fielder (I 2.82); acct.; 19
Jan 1719; extx. Barbara Feilder [alias Barbara Johnson] (A 2.439) (SMAA p. 388)

Feilder, Nicholas; inv.; 8 Jul 1732; 2 Oct 1732; nok Barbery Johnston, John
Feilder; admx./extx. Mary Felder (I 16.613); acct.; 17 Jan 1736; orphan William
Feilder; admx. Mary Miller (A 15.266)

Feilder, John; inv.; 27 Jul 1738; 2 Aug 1738; nok Reltte Stockin, Henry Feilder;
admx./extx. Susanna Feilder (I 23.251); acct.; 21 Apr 1740; orphans Samuel,
Barbara & Francis Fielder (A 17.467)

Fealder, William; <u>acct.</u>; 17 Jun 1754; admx. Jane Fealder (A 36.310); <u>dist.</u>; 17 Jun
1754; child. Jane, Rachel & Mary (BB 1.111)

Fielder, Nicholas and Anne Collosen; m. 16 Jan 1780 (SA p. 58)

FISH

Fish, Thomas; <u>acct.</u>; 31 May 1753; orphans Thomas [of age], Robert [age 15],
William [age 15], James [age 12], Joseph [age 9]; admx. Elenor Fish (A 34.170)
<u>dist.</u>; same (BB 1.79)

Fish, James and Elizabeth; child. Thomas [b. 14 Aug 1763], Bennet [b. 15 Dec
1765] (SA p. 5)

Fish, Robert and Priscilla; son Robert [b. 9 Mar 1765] (SA p. 41)

Fish, William and Jennet; child. William [b. 30 May 1765], Ann [b. 11 May
1768], Robert [b. 11 Oct 1771] (SA p. 19, 20, 54)

Fish, Robert and Janet; son Robert [b. 11 Oct 1771] (SA p. 55)

Fish, Jac.; m. 22 Aug 1777 Ann Wheatley (MM)

FISHER

Fisher, Edward; <u>inv.</u>; 13 Jan 1712 (I&A 33b.193); <u>acct.</u>; 13 May 1714; child's part
to wives of John Abell and Thomas Butson (I&A 36b.75) (SMAA p. 274)

Fisher, Ann; <u>inv.</u>; 26 Jun 1727; 14 Aug 1727; nok Alexander Fargeo, John
Noble (I 12.256); <u>acct.</u>; 14 Aug 1727 (A 8.357)

Fisher, Thomas, Mrs.; <u>inv.</u>; 20 Jun 1752; 31 May 1753; nok Hughe Evans,
Robert Fish; admx./extx. Elenor Fish (I 54.59); <u>inv.</u>; 1 Jan 1753 (I 52.91)

Fisher, Malcom; <u>inv.</u>; 18 Feb 1767; 4 Aug 1768; nok Mary & Sarah Hand; adm.
John Hand (I 97.314); <u>acct.</u>; 13 Jul 1768 (A 58.255)

FISHWICK

Fiswick, Edward; immigrated from VA by 1671 (SK 13.127)

Fishwick, Edward; immigrated from VA by 1680 (SK WC2.223-224)

Fishwick, Edward; <u>inv.</u>; 4 Oct 1683 (I&A 8.112); <u>acct.</u>; 8 Apr 1684; admx.
Margrett, w/o Abraham Combe (I&A 8.247)

FITZJEFFERYS

Fitz Jefferys, Joseph; age ca 29; 11 May 1720 (CCR p. 47)

Fitzjeffery, Joseph, Jr.; <u>will</u>; 26 Dec 1752; 9 Apr 1753; wife Winifred; son
Ezekiel, Aaron, Ezekiel; bro. Ezekiel (MCW 10.269) [SMW TA1.371]; <u>inv.</u>; 18 Apr
1753; 13 Aug 1753; nok Joseph & Ezekiel Fitzjefferys; admx,.extx. Winifred
Fitzjeffery (I 55.15); <u>acct.</u>; 23 Sep 1754; admx. Winifred, w/o Henry Welch (A
36.411); <u>acct.</u>; 13 Mar 1757; orphans Aaron [age 10], Elisabeth [age 7] (A
40.297); <u>dist.</u>; 14 Mar 1757 (BB 2.49)

Fitzjefferys, Ezekiell; <u>will</u>; 24 Feb 1765; 8 Jul 1766; sons Whitton, Charles,
Richard, Joseph, Michael, Ezekiell; wife Sarah (MCW 13.152) [SMW TA1.502]

inv.; 5 Aug 1766; 21 Nov 1766; nok Whiton Jefery, Charles Jeferis; extx.
Sarah Fitzjeffry (I 91.93)

FLETCHER
Fletcher, Curtis; immigrated by 1670 (SK 13.34)
Fletcher, William; will; 19 Apr 1769; 8 May 1769; s-i-l James Carter; d-i-l
Susannah Fletcher (MCW 14.93) [SMW TA1.669]

FLOWER
Flower, William; inv.; 20 Feb 1743; 16 Apr 1744; nok Thomas & Charles Holt
Flower; admx./extx. Elisabeth Flower (I 28.515); acct.; 8 Apr 1745; admx.
Elisabeth, w/o John Noble (A 21.263)
Flower, Charles and Mary Hutchins (by publication); m. 28 Oct 1780 (SA p. 58)
Flower, Thomas and Eleanor Bond (by license); m. 2 Dec 1781 (SA p. 60)
Flower, Joseph and Patty Wise (by license); m. 19 Jul 1785 (SA p. 63)

FLOYD
Floyd, Jesse; m. 5 Nov 1774 Eliz. Swailes (MM)
Floyd, Jess; m. 18 Mar 1777 Mary Carey Reed (MM)
Floyd, Jesse and Elizabeth Taylor (by license); m. 6 Feb 1785 (SA p. 63)

FORBES
Forbes, John; d. 26 Jan 1737; age 37 (HGM)
Forbes, George; age 52 in 1738 (MD p. 64)
Forbes, John; gent.; inv.; 15 May 1738; 7 Jun 1738; nok G. Forbes; admx./extx.
Mrs. Dreedon Forbes (I 23.210, 212); acct.; 31 May 1739; admx. Mrs. Dryden
Forbes (A 17.140); acct.; 3 Jul 1740 (A 17.497)
Forbes, George; will; 10 Oct 1739; 31 Oct 1739; g-dau. Mary Gordon; James,
s/o nephew John Forbes, dec'd; s-i-l George Gordon; bro. Thomas Forbes; son
George, dec'd; mentions Robert, Margert, Jane and Margory Forbes; tract
Simms Forest [CE Co.] (MCW 8.49) [SMW TA1.79]; inv.; 17 Nov 1739; 5 Dec
1739; [Mr.]; nok 2 child. age 7 & 8 (I 24.322); inv.; Nov 1739; 23 Nov 1741 (I
25.335); acct.; 18 Apr 1741 (A 18.156)
Forbes, John; b. 19 Mar 1757; d. 31 Dec 1804; age 45 (HGM)
Forbes, Dryden; will; 25 Jan 1759; Aug 1760; son James; g-son Charles Samuel
Forbes; dau. Rebecca Jowles (MCW 12.1) [SMW TA1.394]

FORD
Ford, Robert; *The Strand*; 100 ac.; sur. 28 May 1667; 1797 poss. Robert Ford;
New Town Hundred (RR p. 34); sur. 22 May 1667 (TLC p. 33)
May Pole; 96 ac.; sur. 16 Nov 1674; 1707 poss. Rob't Ford; New Town
Hundred (RR p. 36)

Long in Dispence; 75 ac.; sur. 9 Jun 1679; 1707 poss. Robert Ford; New
Town Hundred (RR p. 35) (TLC p. 35)

Ford, Robert; age ca 51 in 1715 (MD p. 64)

Ford, Robert; *Strand*; 182 ac.; resur. 25 May 1714 (TLC p. 77); 19 Jun 1719
cert./pat. (COL)
Revell Backside; 222 ac.; resur. 28 Nov 1725 for Robert Ford & John Cole
(TLC p. 31); 30 Sep 1737 cert./pat. (COL)
Revell; 302 ac.; orig. grant to Randall Revell for 300 ac.; resur. 4 Feb 1734 for
Ford (TLC p. 93); 28 Sep 1737 cert./pat. (COL)

Ford, Robert; of *Strand*; will; 27 Dec 1735; 15 Sep 1740; wife Margaret; child.
John, Robert, Peter, Monica Sherlly, Teresa Winstead [also dau. Winifred;
gives Ford as family name for all daus. but Annastasia] and Annastasia
Mattingly; tracts *Strand, May Pole Purchase, [Swipe His Land, Devonham]*
(MCW 8.100) [SMW TA1.104];inv.; 28 Nov 1740; 4 Mar 1741; nok Robert &
John Ford; adm./ex. Peter Ford (I 25.433); acct.; 13 Jul 1741 (A 18.375)

Ford, Robert; *Ford's Hopewell*; 100 ac.; VAC(?) 1742; sur. 10 Feb 1742 (TLC p.
102); 179 ac.; 5 Oct 1743 cert./pat. (COL)

Ford, Monica; will; 10 Oct 1751; 26 Nov 1751; dau. Mary Ford; bro. Ignatius
Ford; sisters Francis Wimsatt, Mary West, Anastatia Ford, Susan Fenwick and
Jane Greenwell (MCW 10.198) [SMW TA1.444]; inv.; 7 Nov 1752; 2 Jun 1752;
nok Athanathus & John Ford; adm./ex. Peter Ford (I 49.20); acct.; 14 Jul 1755;
ex. Peter Ford (A 38.39)

Ford, Robert; _ __ 1753; 31 Jan 1754; wife Teresia; g-sons Joseph and Robert
Fenwick; g-dau. Mary Fenwick; dau. Mary Fenwick, w/o John Fenwick;
mentions Susannah, d/o Margaret Dunn & Monica, w/o William Williams;
sister Teresia Wimsatt; bros. John and Peter Ford & his son Peter, Jr. (MCW
11.18) [SMW TA1.314]; inv.; 10 Apr 1754; 20 Apr 1754; nok John & Peter Ford (I
58.204, 213); acct.; 5 Dec 1754 (A 36.520); acct.; 24 Sep 1755; Finwick g-ch.
Robert [age 13], Margerit [age 12], Mary [age 10], Joseph [age 6], Ann &
Monica [both age 3]; ex. John Fenwick (A 38.178);dist.; 30 Jan 1756 (BB 2.9)

Ford, Amon T. Teresia; widow, relict of Robert Ford; will; 31 Dec 1753; Feb
1754; married twice; d. 1 Jan 1754; mentions James, s/o Henry Neale of *Cob
Neck*; Mary Neale, w/o John Lancaster; Teresia, w/o John Parke; Gerrard
Neale, bro. of James; Teresia, d/o Henry and Mary Neale; Susannah, w/o
Charles Craycroft; William, s/o Richard Gardiner; Mary, w/o Michael
Thompson; tract *Chancellors Point* (MCW 11.36) [SMW TA1.318]

Ford, John; *Ford's Enclosure*; 255 ac.; 2 Mar 1754 cert./pat. (COL)

Ford, Teresia, Mrs.; inv.; 30 Apr 1754; nok William & Benjamin Williams (I
58.310); acct.; 23 Oct 1755 (A 38.288)

Ford, John; s/o Peter; *Primus*; 11 ac.; 21 May 1755 cert./pat. (COL)

Ford, Peter and Anastatia; child. Ignatius [b. 26 Sep 1755], John Francis [b. 8
Mar 1758] (SA p. 191)

Ford, Bennett; inv.; 12 Mar 1762; 1 Jun 1762; nok Peter, Sr. & John Ford;
admx. Susanna Ford (I 78.90)

Ford, Athanasius; *Ford's Discovery*; 470 ac.; 16 Dec 1762 cert./pat. (COL)
  Strand Addition; 7 ac.; 16 Jul 1770 cert./pat. (COL)
  Ramble; 1,185 ac.; 10 Oct 1772 cert./pat. (COL)

Ford (Foord), John; will; 28 [Jul]1764; 22 Jan 1765; sons John, Jesse, Ignatius;
  tracts *Farlings [Farthings] Gift, Long in Dispence, Downham* (MCW 13.73)
  [SMW TA1.471]; inv. 8 Mar 1765; [Sr.]; nok John & Ignatius Ford; ex. Jesse
  Ford (I 87.1); acct.; 6 Apr 1767 (A 56.84); dist.; 6 Apr 1767 (BB 5.26)

Ford, Jesse; planter; will; 15 Nov 1767; 29 Dec 1767; nephew John Kennellum
  Madcalf; bro. Ignatius Ford; sister Sarah Madcalf; tracts *Downham, Long In
  Dispence* (MCW 14.32) [SMW TA1.508]; inv.; 5 Jan 1768; 6 Dec 1768; nok John
  Ford (weaver), Ignatius Ford; extx. Sarah, w/o Silvester Wheatley (I 98.119);
  acct.; 9 Jun 1770 (A 64.217); dist.; 9 Jun 1770; mentions John, s/o Peter Ford
  (BB 5.400)

Ford, John; will; 5 Apr 1760; 9 May 1770; wife Henrietta, m-i-l of John, Jr.;
  sons Philip, John, Robert, Joseph, Anne, Margaret, Eleanor; tracts *Ford's
  Inclosure, Birth Hanger* (MCW 14.134) [SMW TA1.605]; inv.; 28 Sep 1770; 5 Mar
  1771; [Sr.]; nok Athanathius & Philip Fenwick; extx. Hennitta Fenwick (I
  106.372); acct.; 10 May 1772; extx. Henrietta Ford (A 67.138); dist.; 10 May
  1772; widow; ?ch. John, Philip, Robert, Joseph, Anne, Margaret & Eleander
  Ford (BB 6.179)

Ford, Peter, Sr.; will; 10 Feb 1763; 4 Jun 1766; wife Mary; sons Richard, John,
  Peter, Bennett; wife Mary; dau. Persilla; g-sons Peter, John Jarrat [Jannat], s/o
  Bennet, dec'd; tracts *St. Giles, May Pole, Mount Pleasant* (MCW 13.108) [SMW
  TA1.402]; inv.; 9 Jun 1766; 15 Dec 1766; nok Richard & John Ford; admx.
  Mary Ford (I 91.87, 102); acct.; 30 Jun 1768 (A 58.252); acct.; 4 Apr 1769; (A
  60.367); dist.; 4 Apr 1769; widow Mary; ch. Richard, Peter, John, Priscilla; g-
  sons Peter & John Javett, sons of Bennett Ford (BB 5.174)

Ford, Peter, Jr.; acct.; 3 Mar 1767; admx. Mary Ford (A 55.315); dist.; 3 Mar 1767
  (BB 5.11)

Ford, Rob't; *The Strand*; 100 ac.; sur. 22 May 1667; 1707 poss. Robert Ford;
  New Town Hundred (RR p. 34) (TLC p. 33)

Ford, Ignatius; will; 17 Dec 1770; 12 Mar 1771; wife unnamed [Dorothy]; son
  Joseph (MCW 14.181) [SMW TA1.620]; inv.; 2 Apr 1771; 10 Apr 1771; nok John
  & Robert Ford; admx. Dorothy Ford (I 106.376); acct.; 20 Oct 1772; exs.
  Mathew Daft, & wife Dorothy (A 67.145)

Ford, Raphael; m. 20 Jan 1771 Anne Spalden (MM)

Ford, Philip and Eleanor; dau. Clare [b. 5 Jul 1771], son Charles [b. 2 Jan 1773]
  (SA p. 26, 27)

Ford, John; *Lampton's Pleasure*; 153 ac.; 27 Sep 1771 cert./pat. (COL)

Ford, George; m. 4 Jan 1773 Dominica Plowden (MM)

Ford, Philip; m. 30 Sep 1775 Elizabeth Spalden (MM)

FORREST

Forrest, Patrick; *Forrest Lodge*; 150 ac.; sur. 16 Dec 1665; 1707 poss. Rich'd Forrest; St. Georges Hundred (RR p.) (TLC p. 18)

Forrest, Patrick; St. George's Hundred; will; 31 Jan 1675; 14 Feb 1675; wife Ellinor; son Richard; daus. Ann, Margaret; son George Dundasse [Dundes] & Eliza: his wife; mentions Ellinor, d/o John Cheverill [Chevrall] (MCW 1.116-117) [SMW PC1.29]; inv.; 1 Mar 1675; 6 Mar 1675 (I&A 1.562)

Forrest, Helena; probate 24 Apr 1676; dau. Eliza: Dundasse [Durdaine], widow of George Dundasse (MCW 1.169) [SMW PC1.169]; inv.; 8 May 1676 (I&A 2.118)

Forrest, John; *The Forrest*; 225 ac.; 20 Jul 1679; 1707 poss. 112½ ea. Henry How & Thos. Price (RR p. 63) (TLC p. 61)

Forest, Richard; age ca 46; 2 Aug 1717 (CCR p. 39); age 40 in 1718 (MD p. 65); age ca 50; 27 Oct 1721; tract *Watt's Lodge* (CCR p. 45-6)

Forest (Forrest), Richard; inv.; 13 Feb 1723; 2 May 1724; nok Patrick & William Forest; admx. Christian Forest (I 9.382);acct.; 29 May 1725 (A 6.430)

Forest, Patrick; [innholder]; will; 31 Mar 1746; 25 May 1747; wife Frances; son Richard; daus. Sarah, Elizabeth, Bethelem; tracts *North East, Forest Lodge* (MCW 9.111) [SMW TA1.200]; inv.; 4 Apr 1749; 19 Jun 1749; nok Henratia Forrest, Will Hebb, Jr.; adm./ex. Richard Forrest (I 40.37); acct.; 27 Apr 1750; widow; children Richard & Catherine [at age], Hineritta [b. 8 Nov 1732], Sarah [b. 24 Sep 1736], Elisabeth [b. 18 Mar 1738] (A 28.119)

Forrest, Richard; will; 22 May 1760; 27 Oct 1760; wife unnamed; cousins Kennday, Richard, Ann and William Hebb; mentions Mary, w/o Richard Wise [SMW TA1.403]; inv.; 17 Nov 1760; 1 Mar 1761; nok McKelvie Hammet, G. Chilton (I 71.162); acct.; 17 Jun 1761 (A 47.214);inv.; 27 Jun 1761; 28 Jun 1761 (I 74.278)

Forrest, Richard; acct.; 21 Apr 1769 (A 61.116); dist.; 21 Apr 1769 (BB 5.138)

Forrest, Zachariah and Ann; son Richard [b. 15 Nov 1767] (SA p. 14, 49)

Forrest, Zachariah and Nancy; son Uriah, bapt. 14 May 1780 (SA p. 30)

FOSEY

Fossey (Fosse), John; *Shocks Park*; 100 ac.; sur. 15 Feb 1682; 1707 poss. John Fossey; New Town Hundred (RR p. 39) (TLC p. 39); 15 Feb 1683 cert./pat. (COL)

Fosey, John, Jr.; inv.; 14 Jun 1708 (I&A 28.307); acct.; 30 May 1709 extx. Mary, w/o William Sikes (I&A 29.296) (SMAA p. 187)

Fosieg, John,; age ca 73; 22 Nov 1712 (CCR p. 22)

Fossee, John; will; written 16 Nov 1713; daus. Ruth Thomas, Treacha Fossee; son Harbart Thomas; tracts *Kingston, Shocks Park, Nun's Oeck* (MCW 3.256) [SMW PC1.186]; inv.; 10 Dec 1713 (I&A 35a.327)

Fosey, John; acct.; 24 Jul 1718; mentions James of James Tubb (A 1.197) (SMAA p. 353)

FOSTER
Foster, Richard; acct.; 9 Oct 1677; mentions Lidia, widow of Benjamin Solley (I&A 4.345)

Foster, Robert; will; 1 Mar 1697; 10 Mar 1697; mentions Eliza., d/o Thos. Reeves (MCW 2.134); inv.; 26 Mar 1698 (I&A 18.23)

Foster, Ralph; *Pyana's Groves*; 17 ac.; sur. 24 Dec 1703 for Foster and Peter Johnson (TLC p. 63); 1 Aug 1706 cert./pat. (COL)

Foster, Ralph; inv.; 21 Apr 1714; nok Elizabeth Briscoe, James Foster (I&A 36a.201); acct. 6 Sep 1715 (I&A 36c.53) (SMAA p. 288); inv.; 22 Sep 1717 (I&A 37b.167) (SMAA p. 319)

Forster, James; acct.; 6 Mar 1738; orphans John, James, William, Elisabeth & Sarah Forster; admx. Elenor Forster (A 17.100)

Forster, James; inv.; 16 May 1738; 6 Jun 1738; nok John, Jr. & Elisabeth Briscoe; admx./extx. Elisabeth Foster (I 23.212)

Foster, George; inv.; 4 May 1774; 10 Sep 1774; nok Francis & James Hayden (I 119.185)

FOWLE
Fowle, William; service by 1680 (SK WC2.260)

Fowle, Roger; *Fowle's Discovery*; 100 ac.; 16 Oct 1680 cert./pat. (COL)

FOWLER
Fowler, William; service by 1672 (SK 17.351; 12.496)

Fowller, Joseph; will;15 Oct 1706; 8 Nov 1706; g-son Joseph Hopkins; s-i-l Joseph Hopkins; s-i-l Thomas Glover (MCW 3.85) [SMW PC1.174]; inv.; 19 Nov 1706 (I&A 26.154); acct.; 27 Dec 1707 (I&A 28.75)

Fowlar, John; inv.; 28 Mar 1750; 6 May 1750; nok Henry & Samuel Fowler; admx./extx. Elisabeth Fowler (I 42.225); acct.; 1 Dec 1750 (A 29.131)

Fowler, William; m. 19 Feb 1776 Mary Mattingly (MM)

Fowler, Sarah; dau. Margaret, bapt. 16 Jul 1780 (SA p. 30)

FRASIER
Frazer (Frasier), John; inv.; 10 Dec 1736; 26 Apr 1737; nok Elisabeth King, Fislliosity Waker; admx./extx. Jane Smith (I 22.316); acct.; 22 Aug 1738; orphans John & Elisabeth Frasier; adms. Matthew Wise & wife Elisabeth of PG Co. (A 16.297)

Frasier, William; inv.; 7 May 1772; 39 Aug 1772; nok Ann Simpson; admx. Elisabeth Frasier (I 110.108)

FRENCH
French, Martin; inv.; 5 Apr 1716; 26 Apr 1716; nok James French, Elisabeth Thompson (I&A 37a.164); acct.; 12 Mar 1716; admx. Mary French (I&A 39b.60) (SMAA p. 307)

French, James; age ca 72 on 25 Jun 1722; ca 74 on 12 Apr 1725 (CCR p. 50, 59)

French, James; planter; will;4 Mar 1733; 18 Mar 1733/4; g-son John; g-dau.
  Mary, w/o John Leek; tracts *Hopton Park, Mayland* (MCW 7.68) [SMW TA1.26];
  inv.; 18 Mar 1733; 5 Jun 1734; [Mr.]; nok Ignatius & Elisabeth French;
  adm./ex. John French (I 18.322); acct.; 11 Aug 1735 (A 12.313)

French, Anastatia, d/o John French, Jr., and Monica [b. 29 Jul 1750] (SA p. 38)

French, William and Rinah; child. Rodolph [b. 1 Aug 1755], Jeremiah [b. 13 Oct
  1761], Susanna [b. 14 Oct 1766] (SA p. 15, 50)

French, Ignatius and Susanna; child. Ignatius [b. 26 Mar 1757], Mary [b. 14 Jan
  1755] (SA p. 38)

French, John and Monica; child. Bennet [b. 27 Jun 1757], Ann [b. 16 Sep 1759],
  Bernadine [b. 20 Dec 1761], Elizabeth [b. 3 May 1764] (SA p. 11, 45, 46)

French, John, Sr.; will; 19 Feb 1767; 13 Jun 1770; sons John, Ignatius; daus.
  Susannah, Mary Yates, Elizabeth Medcalf, Monico Davis; g-sons Barnet,
  Bennet; tract *Hopton Park* (MCW 14.135) [SMW TA1.610]

French, Ignatius and Elizabeth; dau. Mary [b. 28 Oct 1769], Joseph [b. 27 Sep
  1771], Ignatius [b. 14 Oct 1773], Elizabeth [b. 27 Nov 1775] (SA p. 26, 27)

French, Ignatius, Sr.; will;18 Jul 1771; 20 Mar 1772; child. Ann Yates, Elinor,
  James, Martin, Raphel, Mary, Ignatius, Stephen (MCW 14.213) [SMW TA1.644];
  inv.; 22 May 1772; 21 Jul 1772; mentions John & Ignatius French; ex. James
  French (I 110.103); acct.; 29 Jun 1774 (A 71.364); dist.; 29 Jun 1774; 7 child.
  Eleanor, James, Martin, Ralph, Mary, Ignatius, Stephen (BB 7.18)

French, John; inv.; 9 Aug 1773; nok James & Martin French (I 112.415); acct.; 9
  Aug 1773; ex. Ignatius French (A 68.204); dist.; 17 Aug 1773; 6 child.; Mary,
  John, Elisabeth, Monica, Ignatius, Susannah (BB 6.257)

French, John and Jane; sons Philip [b. 27 Nov 1774], Peter [b. 12 May 1776] (SA
  p. 27)

FRISSELL

Frissell, Dennis; age ca 25 in 1659 (MD p. 66)

Frissell, Forker; will; 13 Dec 1661; 23 Apr 1662; mentions Denish Frissell;
  Mary, d/o James Halles; Rebeck, d/o Alexander Frissell; Joan, d/o George
  Mackahill (MCW 1.20)

Frizell, Alex'r; *Bennets Delight*; 250 ac.; sur. 10 Mar 1663; 1707 poss. Peter
  Watts; Poplar Hill Hundred (RR p. 23) (TLC p. 22)

Frissell, Alexander; Herring Creek; will; 30 Aug 1666; 27 Sep 1666; wife Sarah;
  dau. Rebecca Frissell (MCW 1.36)

FURGOE

Furgeo, Alexander; inv.; 30 Aug 1745; 23 Dec 1745; adm. Mazslen Fargeo (I
  31.432); acct.; 2 Feb 1746 (A 23.186); acct.; 27 Aug 1750; sons Mazotin [at age],
  James [age 8] (A 28.279)

Furgoe, Mazotin; acct.; 14 Aug 1758; mentions Alexander Furgoe; admx. Ann
  Furgoe (A 42.96)

GALLEY

Galle [Gallo], Lawrence; 13 Mar 1735/6; 6 Jul 1736; wife Grace (MCW 7.185) [SMW TA1.57]; inv.; 2 Mar 1736; nok Jonathan & Charles Greenwell; admx./extx. Grace Galle (I 22.212); acct.; 5 Jul 1737 (A 14.298)

Galley, Grace; widow; will; 31 Nov 1737; 5 Mar 1739; sons Charles, Henry, Justiman [Justinian], Thomas, Stephen and John Greenwell; d-i-l Mary, w/o Charles; daus. Grace, w/o Michael Rayley, Jr.; Jane, w/o Thomas Norris; Mary, w/o John Heard (MCW 8.77) [SMW TA1.89]; inv.; 6 Aug 1740; 6 Aug 1740; nok Charles & Henry Greenwell; admx./ex. Stephen Greenwell (I 25.193);acct.; 20 Jul 1741 (A 18.276)

GANYOTT

Ganiott, Charles; *Ganiott's Lot*; 50 ac.; sur. 19 Aug 1702 (TLC p. 63); 1 Aug 1706 cert./pat. (COL)

Ganyott, Charles; inv.; 10 Apr 1709; 20 Apr 1709 (I&A 29.294); acct.; admx. Mary Ganyott; 26 Jul 1710 (I&A 31.362) (SMAA p. 199); acct.; 15 Jan 1711 (SMAA p. 218); acct.; 1 Jun 1714 (I&A36b.36) (SMAA p. 267)

Ganyoss, Margaret; inv.; 4 Mar 1717; nok Richard Power, William Lucas, Jr. (I 2.190)

Ganyot, Marry (Mary); acct.; 28 May 1720 (A 3.10); acct.; 18 May 1720 (SMAA p. 421)

Ganyott, Charles; *Yoakly Chance*; sur. 6 Mar 1741 for Cornelius Ganyott (TLC p. 97) ; *Yoak by Chance*; 61 ac.; 10 Nov 1742 cert./pat. (COL)

Ganyott, Charles; will; 11 Nov 1744; 6 Mar 1744/5; child. Charles, Mary, Constantia, Margaret; wife Elizabeth; bros.-i-l John and Ignatius Fenwick; tracts *Zoak [Yoake] by Chance, Ganyott's Lott* (MCW 9.17) [SMW TA1.149]; inv.; Mar 1745; 22 Jul 1745; nok Mary Power, William Lucos, Jr.; admx./extx. Elisabeth Ganyott (I 31.161); acct.; 19 Apr 1749; orphans Mary [age 14], Margret [age 11], Charles (dec'd); extx. Elisabeth, w/o William Joseph (A 26.47)

GARDINER

Gardiner, Luke; *Gardiners Neck*; 200 ac.; sur. 19 Aug 1652; 1707 poss. Rich'd Hopewell; Harvey Hundred (RR p. 56) (TLC p. 53)

Gardiner, Luke; *St. Johns*; 300 ac. sur. 28 Jun 1653, 375 & 300 ac. sur. 9 Sep 1661and 1,480 ac. sur. 28 Aug 1668; resur. 2293 ac.; 1707 poss. Widow Gardiner & Wm. Joseph; Resurrection Hundred (RR p. 61) (TLC p. 58)

Gardner, Luke; wife Elizabeth; ack. 100 a. *Manor of St. Richards* to be right of Luke Barber; 23 Sep 1662 (AM XLIX.33)

Gardiner, Luke; *St. Johns Landing*; 300 ac.; sur. 10 Apr 1665; 1707 poss. Luke Gardiner; St. Clements Hundred (RR p. 44) (TLC p. 42)

Gardiner, Thomas; b. 15 Nov 1665; s/o Luke Gardiner and Elizabeth Hatton (JM p. 316)

Gardiner, Luke; *Hilly Lee*; 500 ac.; sur. 30 Dec 1665; 1707 poss. John Gardiner; St. Clements Hundred (RR p. 44) (TLC p. 43)

Gardiner, Luke, *Gardiners Landing*; 100 ac.; sur. 6 Oct 1667; 1707 poss. Ethelbert Doyne; Choptico Hundred (RR p. 51) (TLC p. 49)

Gardner, Luke; age ca 50 in 1672 (MD p. 68)

Gardner, Luke; will; 4 Dec 1673; 12 Aug 1674; wife Eliza; sons Richard, John, Luke, Thomas; bros.-i-l Zacharay Wade, Major Thomas Brooke; tracts *Barberton Manor, Grimditch* in CH Co., *St. John's, Hillilee, Gardner's Land* (MCW 1.82-83); inv.; [filed with 1674]; *St. Clement's Island, St. John's Quarter* (I&A 1.111, 148)

Gardiner, Richard; *The Garden Spot*; 80 ac.; sur. 11 Nov 1675; 1707 poss. Rob. Strutton; Resurrection Hundred (RR p. 62) (TLC p. 60) *Collewood*; 100 ac.; 1 Jun 1685 cert./pat. (COL)

Gardiner, Richard; s/o Luke, dec'd; *St. John's Landing*; 300 ac.; 1 Jun 1687 cert./pat. (COL)

Gardner, Richard; will; 19 Apr 1687; 3 Dec 1687; sons Luke, John; wife Eliza:; bro. Luke Gardner; f-i-l Clement Hill; niece Eliza: Gardner, d/o Luke Gardner; Monica, w/o Luke Gardner; uncle Col. Henry Darnall; tracts *Barbeton Manor* in CH Co., *St. John's* (MCW 2.20) [SMW PC1.63]; inv.; 25 Mar 1689; orphan Richard Hame, age 8 (I&A 10.201); acct.; 6 Jul 1696; bro. Thomas Gardiner (I&A 14.78)

Gardiner, Luke, Mr.; *Gardiner's 2nd Addn.*; 250 ac.; 10 Nov 1695 cert./pat. (COL) *Gardiner's 3rd Addn.*; 119 ac.; 5 Oct 1695 cert./pat. (COL) *Gardiner's 4th Addn.*; 400 ac.; 5 Oct 1695 cert./pat. (COL) *Fourth Addition*; 83 ac.; sur. 30 Jul 1695; 1707 poss. Widow Gardiner; New Town Hundred (RR p. 40) (TLC p. 39); 30 Jul 1695 cert./pat. (COL)

Gardiner, Luke, Sr.; will; 25 Apr 1703; 4 May 1705; sons Clement, Thomas, Luke; daus. Elizabeth Joseph & Monica, Mary, Susannah & Elinor Gardiner; nephews Luke & John Gardiner; wife Elizabeth; b-i-l Peter Miles; tracts *St. Johns, The Fourth Addition, Hillelee, Grimditch* (MCW 3.54) [SMW PC#1.145] inv.; 26 Jul 1705 (I&A 25.29); acct.; 13 May 1707; extx. Elisabeth Gardner (relict) (I&A 26.307) (SMAA p. 146); acct.; 11 May 1708 (I&A 28.220) (SMAA p. 163); acct.; 22 Sep 1710 (I&A 31.360) (SMAA p. 198)

Gardiner, Luke of PG Co.; Duputy Surveyor for SM Co.; *Gardiners Chance*; 155 ac.; sur. 8 May 1700; 1707 poss. LukeGardiner; Resurrection Hundred (RR p. 64) (TLC p. 62); Luke Gardiner of PG Co.; 1700 cert./pat. (COL) *Double Discovery*; 150 ac.; 10 Jan 1706 cert./pat. (COL) *Rich Hills*; 500 ac.; sur. 16 Apr 1705; 1707 poss. same Gardiner; Resurrection Hundred (RR p. 65) (TLC p. 63); sur. 1705; ? county (COL)

Gardiner, Clement, Mr.; *Hazard*; 257 ac.; sur. 20 Mar 1710/1; pat. 10 Aug 1713; (TLC p. 68); 26 Apr 1717 cert./pat. (COL)

Gardiner, John; Deputy Surveyor for SM Co.; *Rich Thicket*; 100 ac.; 1706 cert./pat. (COL)

    Gardiner's Gore; 42 ac.; sur. 20 Apr 1715 (TLC p. 74); 24 Apr 1717 cert./pat. (COL)

    Addition of Gardiners Grove; 82 ac.; sur. 20 May 1715 (TLC p. 72); *Addition*; 10 Sep 1723 cert./pat. (COL)

    Gardiner's Grove; 82 ac.; 10 Sep 1716 cert./pat. (COL)

Gardiner, John, Gent.; will; 13 Oct 1717; 9 Dec 1717; sons John, Clement, Richard, Willfraid; daus. Susannah, Elizabeth, Mary, Ann, Henrietta Maria; wife Mary; tract *Hillaley, Gardiner's Grove, Addition of Gardiner's Grove, Cannon Neck* (MCW 4.128) [SMW PC1.218]; acct.; 29 Nov 1718; extx. Mary, w/o Gerard Sly (A 1.311); acct.; 22 Oct 1720 (A 3.186); acct.; 9 Jan 1724 (A 6.229)

Gardiner, John; mariner; will; 9 Dec 1742; 4 Aug 1743; cousins John Key, Bartin Milo; bro. Phillip Key (MCW 8.228) [SMW TA1.136]; inv.; 7 Jun 1744; [Capt.]; nok John Miles, Richard Ward Key (I 29.241)

Gardiner, Henry; inv.; 4 Jun 1744; 7 Jun 1744; nok minors; admx./extx. Mary Gardiner (I 29.246)

Gardiner, Clement, Mr.; inv.; 18 Jun 1746; 21 Aug 1746; nok Luke Gardiner, Richard Brooke; admx./extx. Elinor Gardiner (I 33.314); acct.; 27 Jun 1748; mentions Ann, Elinor, Mary & Jean Gardiner (A 25.69)

Gardner, Luke; inv.; 17 Sep 1754; 2 Dec 1754; nok John & Joseph Thomas Gardner; admx./extx. Mary Gardner (I 58.304); acct.; 8 Sep 1755; (A 38.179); acct.; 4 Jul 1758; orphans John, Mary, Susannah, John & Jane [all of age], Luke [age 14], Elisabeth [age 13], Richard [age 11] (A 41.496); dist.; 4 Jul 1758; widow and orphans John, Mary, Susannah, Joseph, Jane, Luke, Elisabeth, Richard (BB 2.90)

Gardiner, John, Mr.; inv.; 26 Feb 1757; 9 Jun 1757; admx.extx. Jane Gardiner (I 63.395); acct.; 6 Mar 1758 (A 41.351)

Gardiner, Jane [Jeane]; d/o Eliner; will; 1 Jan 1760; 6 Jun 1760 (MCW 12.1) [SMW TA1.393]

Gardiner, Eliner; will; 28 Jan 1760; 16 Oct 1760; daus. Monica Queen, Ann Boarman, Mary Boarman (MCW 12.2) [SMW TA1.396]; inv.; 9 Jul 1762; nok Henry Queen, George Boarman (I 78.95); dist.; 6 Aug 1765; ex. Richard Borman (BB 4.130)

Gardiner, Thomas; m. 27 Sep 1777 Henrietta Goodrum (MM)

Gardner, Isaac and Ann Hollyday (by license); m. 23 Sep 1784 (SA p. 62)

GARNISH

Garnis, John; service by 1667 (SK 11.236)

Garnish, Catherine; service by 1670; wife of John (SK 12.571, 622)

Garnish, "her husband's estate"; inv.; 3 Jan 1679; admx./extx. Katherine
Garnish (I&A 6.598); inv.; 9 Oct 1679 (I&A 6.547); acct.; 1 Mar 1679; widow
Katherine (I&A 6.658) (SMAA p. 70)

GARRET
Garret, Rich'd; *St. Richards Mannour*; 1,000 ac.; sur. 6 Dec 1640; 1707 poss.
Thomas Smith [m. relict of Andrew Abington]; Harvey Hundred (RR p. 55)
(TLC p. 52)
Garrett, Nathaniel; immigrated by 1671 (SK 16.117)
Garret, Peter; will; 14 Feb 1750/1; 2 Apr 1751; wife Mary; tract *Garrets
Purchase* (MCW 10.144); acct.; name spelled Genet; tract *Genet's Purchase*
[SMW TA1.280]

GATES
Gates, Robert; [carpenter]; will; 5 Feb 1694; 6 Jun 1698; wife Dorothy; tracts
*Gate's Hope, Gate's Purchase, New Branford, Maidstone, St. Michael's, St.
Mary's, Gate's Swamp, Poppleton, Branford, Maidstone*; child. Catherine [b.
7 Jul 1676], Susanna [b. 12 Oct 1678], John [b. 19 Sep 1681], Robert [b. 13
Feb 1686], Ann [b. 23 Jul 1690], Joseph [b. 8 Dec 1693] (MCW 2.148) [SMW
PC1.89]
Gates, Daniell; acct.; 8 Jul 1703 (I&A 24.12)
Gates, Joseph; m. 31 Aug 1778 Elizab. Jones (BRU 2535)

GEE
Gee, John; age ca 27 in 1660; mentions Samuel Harris & wife Elizabeth (MD p.
69)
Gee, John; age ca 40; 12 Oct 1665 (AM XLIX.480)
Gee, John; inv.; 19 Feb 1686 (I&A 9.217)

GERRARD
Gerrard, Justinian; *St. Clement's Mann'r*; 11,400 ac.; sur. 2 Nov 1639 [950 ac.],
11 Dec 1641 [6,000 ac.]; + purchased parcels; 1707 Mich'l Curtis [by m. to
Widow Gerrard]; St. Clements Hundred (RR p. 47) (TLC p. 45)
Gerrard, Thomas; *Gerrards Freehold*; 243 ac.; sur. 21 Apr 1640; 1707 poss.
Thomas Taylor; St. Mary's Hundred (RR p. 1) (TLC p. 1)
Basford Mannour; 1,500 ac.; sur. 27 Mar 1651; res. 4,000 ac.; sold to Gov.
Notley; devised to His Lordship & 300 ac. *Batchelors Hope* granted Joshua
Doyne; 1707 poss. by widow Doyne; St. Clements Hundred (RR p. 43) (TOC p.
41)
St. Winefrides Freehold; 500 ac.; sur. 28 Mar 1651; 1707 poss. Roswell Neall;
St. Clements Hundred (RR p. 43) (TOC p. 41)

Gerard, Susan; w/o Thomas; Luke Gardiner stated in 1652 he purchased
Caonow Neck from Thomas (AM XLI.143)

Gerard (Gerrard), Susanna; w/o Thomas Gerard of *St. Clement's Manor*; sold
220 ac. on 26 Oct 1666 to Edward Conery (AM XLI.188; LVII.282)

Gerrard, Thomas; of Mathotick River; formerly of *St. Clement's Manor*; will; 5
Feb 1672; 15 Dec 1673; dau. Mary; sons Justinian, John, Gerrard (?); wife
Rose; dec'd wife Susannah; unnamed child.; g-child. Gerrard Paten, Gerrard
Tucker (MCW 1.76-77); Rose and John; exs. of Thomas Gerard; to answer to
Thomas, the younger, s/o Thomas Gerard; 1674/5 (AM LXV.486, 571)

Gerard, Thomas; s/o Thomas; dec'd; 14 Apr 1674 (CCR p. 9); Justinian; s/o
Thomas, dec'd; 17 Jun 1678 (CCR p. 9) (AM XLIX.451, 579)

Gerrard, Thomas; will; 17 Nov 1685; 20 Oct 1686; wife Anne (MCW 2.6) [SMW
PC1.58]; inv. 18 Jan 1686; [gent.] (I&A 9.413); inv.; [filed with 1688]; extx. Ann,
w/o John Bayne (I&A 10.177); acct.; 7 Oct 1696 (I&A 14.53)

Gerrard, Justinian; will; 4 Aug 1682; 22 Jan 1688; St. Clement's Manor; wife
Sarah; *Bramly Manor*; *New Hall* in England [SMW PC1.69]; acct.; 20 Mar 1693;
extx. Sarah, w/o Michaell Curtis (I&A 12/63); acct.; 7 Feb 1694 (I&A 13a.220);
acct.; 18 Aug 1703 (I&A 24.13) (SMAA p. 120)

Gerrard, Thomas; his sons Justinian, Thomas, John; all dec'd without issue; 25
Jun 1722 (CCR p. 50)

Gerrard, Thomas; child.: Elizabeth, m. Col. Nathaniel Blackistone; Susannah
m/1 Robert Slye; m/2 Col. John Coode; sons Justinian, Thomas, John; 12 Apr
1725 (CCR p. 59)

GIBBONS

Gibbens, John; inv.; 11 Jan 1741; 5 Apr 1742; nok John & Stephen Gibbens;
admx./extx. Martha Gibbens (I 26.542); acct.; 25 Jul 1743 (A 19.442)

Gibbons, Martha; inv.; 3 Jan 1744; 23 Feb 1744; nok Mary Hickman, Henry
Gibbens; adm./ex. John Gibbens (I 30.295); acct.; 2 Aug 1746; mentions John,
Stephen, Henry, Mager (Major, s/o John), Elenor & Precilla Gibbins; adm.
John Gibbins (A 23.3)

Gibbins, Major; inv.; 5 Mar 1765; mentions John Gibbins (I 87.1)

Gibbons, John; inv.; 28 Mar 1767; 4 Jun 1767 (I 93.109); acct.; 18 Oct 1769 (A
62.17)

Gibbons, Francis and Rebecca Eden; m. 20 Feb 1780 (SA p. 58)

GIBSON

Gibson, Henry; immigrated by 1674 (SK 18.142; 15.335)

Gibson, William; inv.; 26 Sep 1737; 1 Nov 1737; nok John Gibson, Ann
Henikin (I 22.536); acct.; 28 Mar 1739; John, William & Thomas Gibson (A
17.107)

Gibson, John; <u>will</u>; 8 Apr 1745; 6 Aug 1745; child.: Susanna, Elizabeth, Joshua, William, Mathew, Jeremiah, John; wife Alice [Alse] (MCW 9.44) [SMW TA1.170]; <u>inv.</u>; 9 Aug 1745; 9 Nov 1745; nok John & William Gibson; admx./extx. Alice Gibson (I 31.297); <u>acct.</u>; 6 Oct 1746 (A 23.13)

Gibson, Joshua; m. 10 Feb 1778 Mary Ann Anderson (BRU 2535)

GIFFORD
Gifford, Henry; service by 1674 (SK 18.136)
Gifford, William; probate 5 Nov 1675 (MCW 1.110)

GILBERT
Gilbert, Joshua; age ca 60 in 1705 (MD p. 70)
Gilbert, Rose; widow of Richard Gilbert; St. Mary's Hundred; recorded 3 Jan 1637 (AM IV.5)

GLOVER
Glover, William; age ca 28 in 1702 (MD p. 72)
Glover, John; <u>inv.</u>; 15 Feb 1730; nok Joseph & Rachel Glover; admx./extx, Sarah Glover (I 16.83); <u>acct.</u>; 26 Jun 1732; orphans Jos., Will, Rach. & Math. Glover; adms. Richard Griffin & wife Sarah (A 11.431)
Glover, Thomas; <u>will</u>; 2 Jun 1731; 3 Nov 1731; planter; sons Thomas, Richard; wife Weneford (MCW 6.199) [SMW PC1.358]; <u>inv.</u> 22 Jan 1731; 11 Apr 1732; Sr.; nok minors; admx./extx. Winefred Glover (I 16.440); <u>acct.</u>; 7 Dec 1733; extx. Winifred Glover (A 12.138)
Glover, Richard; <u>inv.</u>; 12 Mar 1749; 5 Jun 1750; nok John & Robert Long; admx./extx. Mary Glover (I 43.273)
Glover, William; m. 16 Dec 1783 Phebe Hutchinson (BRU 2.535)

GODDARD
Goddard, John; *Heart's Delight*; 200 ac.; 12 Feb 1686 cert./pat. (COL)
Gowdard (Gawdard), John; <u>will</u>; written 23 Nov 1700; son John; daus. Margaret and Eliza.; tract *Heart's Delight* (MCW 2.209); <u>inv.</u>; 20 Jan 1700 (I&A 20.65); <u>acct.</u>; 5 Jun 1713 extx. relict, w/o John Jones (I&A 34.175) (SMAA p. 250)
Goddard, John, Sr.; <u>will</u>; 25 Jul 1761; 12 Jan 1762; sons John Baptist, Ignatius; wife Mary; tract *Godard's Delight* (MCW 12.118) [SMW TA1.429]; <u>inv.</u>; 14 Jan 1762; 3 Jun 1762; nok John & Ignatius Godard; extx. Mary Godard (I 78.89)
Goddard, Ignatius; m. 23 Dec 1772 Ann Payn (MM)

GOLDSBERRY
Goldsberry [Goldsbury], John; <u>will</u>; probate 29 Mar 1718; sons Robert, William; g-son Edward Goldsberry and John ,s/o William Goldsberry; mentions Margaret Goldsberry (MCW 4.170); <u>inv.</u>; 7 May 1718 (I 1.313)

Goldsberrey, William; <u>inv.</u>; 8 Apr 1726; 7 Jun 1726; nok Robert & John
   Gouldsberey; admx. Sarah Goldbary (I 11.334); <u>acct.</u>; 20 Mar 1727 (A 9.163)
Gouldsberry, Robert; planter; <u>will</u>; 20 Mar 1756; 12 Oct 1756; wife Elizabeth;
   sons John Baptist, Ignatius, Henry, Jonathan; dau. Margaret Swailes; g-dau.
   Elizabeth Swailes; s-i-l Charles Joy [SMW TA1.349] [NOTE: The will in SMW 11.149
   is the will of Ann Watts, not Robert Gouldsberry]; <u>inv.</u>; 2 Nov 1756; 14 Feb 1757; nok
   John & William Goldsberry; admx./extx. Elisabeth Goldsberry (I 62.245); <u>acct.</u>;
   12 Sep 1757; orphans Henry & Jonathon [of age], Margaret Swailes [of age],
   Igna. [age 19], John Baptis [age 15] (A 41.233); <u>dist.</u>; 12 Sep 1757; mentions
   John, s/o Samuel Able; legatees John Baptist, Ignatius, Henry, Jonathon
   Goldsberry & Margaret Swailes (BB 2.69)
Goldsbury, Jonathan and Christian; son Charles [b. 4 Mar 1765] (SA p. 4)
Gouldsberry, Ignatius; <u>inv.</u>; 10 Jun 1766; nok Jonathon Goldsberry, Margaret
   Swails; admx. Jane Gouldsberry, admx. of Henry Gouldsberry] (I 93.119)
Goldsberry (Gouldsberry, Goldsborough), Henry; <u>inv.</u>; 6 Apr 1767; 18 Jun
   1767; nok Margaret Waits, Jonathon Greenwell (I 93.107); <u>acct.</u>; 24 Nov 1767;
   admx. Jane Goldsborough (A 57.348); <u>acct.</u>; 24 Dec 1769 (A 62.400); <u>dist.</u>; 24
   Dec 1769; admx. Jane, w/o Henry Raley (BB 5.227)
Goldsburry, James and Araminta Roberts (by license); m. 9 Jan 1783 (SA p. 60)

GOLDSMITH

Goldsmith, John; *Underwood*; 300 ac.; sur. 4 Nov.1671; 1707 poss. Tho. Notley
   Goldsmith; St. Clements Hundred (RR p. 45) (TLC p. 44)
   Hepworth; 100 ac.; sur. 13 Dec 1674; 1707 poss. Tho. Notley Goldsmith; St.
   Clements Hundred (RR p. 46); *Hopworth* (TLC p. 44)
Goldsmith, John; <u>will</u>; 17 Apr 1683; 31 Jul 1683; wife Judith; sons Thomas
   Notley, John Gerrard & William Goldsmith; daus. Priscilla, Margaret, Sarah
   & Nottley Goldsmith and Eliza: Jourdaine; sons-i-l Wm. Nefinge [Hilfinger],
   Thos. Jourdaine, Thomas Love; tract *Intirement* (MCW 1.124) [SMW PC1.44];
   <u>acct.</u>; 16 Jun 1696; Mrs. Clouds m. Maj. Boarman; legatees Nicholas Clouds
   & wife, Thomas Love, wife of William Nifinger; extx. Judith, w/o Richard
   Clouds; [dau. Nelly Goldsmith] (I&A 13b.112) (SMAA p. 96)
Goldsmith, William; <u>will</u>; 23 Feb 1708; 7 May 1709; sons Richard, John; wife
   Elizabeth (MCW 3.132) [SMW PC1.159]
Goldsmith, Thomas Notley; <u>will</u>; 14 Apr 1746; 3 Jun 1746; sons John, Michael,
   Notely, Benoni, William; daus. Truman (sic) Goldsmith, Mary Tayler, Judith
   Shanks, Susanna Roberts; tract *Nichols's Hope* (MCW 9.75) [SMW TA1.205]; <u>inv.</u>;
   9 May 1747; nok Benoney & Notley Goldsmith; adms./exs. John, William &
   Michel Goldsmith (I 35.97); <u>acct.</u>; 4 Nov 1747 (A 24.245)
Goldsmith, Notly; <u>will</u>; 21 Mar 1757; 21 Apr 1757; sister Sarah Truman
   Musgrove & her dau. Anney Musgrove; bro. Michael Goldsmith & his dau.
   Mary (MCW 11.164) [SMW TA1.360]; <u>inv.</u>; 4 May 1757; 5 Jul 1757; admx./extx.

Sarah Farmon Musgrove (I 63.407); acct.; 5 Dec 1758; admx. Sarah Truman Musgrove (A 43.14)

Goldsmith, John; will; 20 Jan 1765; 5 Aug 1773; sons John, Thomas, Notley; daus. Lidia, Ann, Elizabeth; wife Jane (MCW 15.150) [SMW TA1.683]; inv.; 31 Dec 1773; 7 Mar 1774; nok Ann & John Goldsmith (I 116.200); inv.; 10 Jan 1775 (I 121.419); acct.; 10 Jan 1775 (A 72.148); dist.; 10 Jan 1775; Notley, Lydia, Ann and Elisabeth Goldsmith (BB 7.50)

Goldsmith, J. and Ann; child.: William [b. 30 Dec 1776], William [b. 20 May 1778] (AFP 2.350)

GOSLING

Gosling, Thomas; gent.; *Gosling's Addition*; 30 ac.; sur. 20 Mar 1718 (TLC p. 86); 14 Oct 1726 cert./pat. (COL)

Golfling (Gosling), Thomas; 27 Apr 1740; 21 Feb 1744; wife Elizabeth (MCW 9.16); names testator Gosling [SMW TA1.153]; inv.; 26 Feb 1744; 6 Mar 1744; nok William Tiler (I 30.303); acct.; 10 Sep 1746 (A 22.348)

Gostin [Goslin], Elizabeth; widow; will; 30 Sep 1760; 10 Mar 1761; cousins William Tailor [Failor], William Tycor (?) [Tycey], Ann Robertson; mentions Martha and Betty, w/o and d/o Roger Copsey, Jr.; Bridget, ?w/o Enoch Jones (MCW 12.37) [SMW TA1.411]; inv.; 13 Aug 1761 (I 74.249)

GOUGH

Gough, Stephen; will; 22 Oct 1700; 2 Jan 1700; sons James, Benjamin; daus. Mary and Morrica; wife Clare; tracts *Vacooun Point, St. Barnard's, St. Margaret's, Beaver Dam Manor* (MCW 2.214); inv.; 22 Jan 1700 (I&A 20.85); acct.; 29 Apr 1703; ex. son James Gough (I&A 23.44) (SMAA p. 113); acct.; 13 Apr 1714; mentions Benjamin and Monica Gough and ___ Miles, siblings of James Gough (I&A 35a.143); acct.; 13 Apr 1714 (SMAA p. 266)

Gough, James; *Bacon Neck*; 200 ac.; sur. 27 Jan 1703; pat. 10 Dec 1713 (TLC p. 68)

Gough, Elizabeth; age ca 28; former w/o George Medcalf, dec'd; 28 Sep 1711 (CCR p. 20)

Gough, James; *Racoon Neck*; 200 ac.; 14 Apr 1714 cert./pat. (COL)
Gough's Level; 42 ac.; sur. 10 Oct 1715 (TLC p. 73); 24 Apr 1717 cert./pat. (COL)

Gough, James; will; 18 Dec 1725; 31 Jan 1725; sons James, Stephen, Peter, Baptista; daus. Elizabeth, Ann; wife Elizabeth; bro. Benjamin; tracts *Rachoon Point, St. Bernards, St. Margarett's, Ladyland, Jarboes, Gough's [George's] Levell* (MCW 5.209) [SMW PC1.301]; inv.; 21 Apr 1726; 11 Jul 1726; nok Benjamin Gough, Mary Mills; admx./extx. Mrs. Elisabeth Gough (I 11.493); acct.; 11 Jul 1726 (A 7.500)

Gough (Gaugh), Benjamin; will; 21 Mar 1735/6; 2 Jun 1736; sons Benjamin, James; daus. Mary, Perselea; wife Jane; [dau. Jane] (MCW 7.185) [SMW TA1.56]

inv.; 29 Jul 1736; 26 Aug 1736; nok Stephen & James Gough; admx./extx.
Jane Gough (I 21.518); acct.; 22 Jun 1737; orphans Benjamin, James, Mary,
Priscilla, Jane, Sarah, Elisabeth & Susannah Gough (A 14.296)

Gough (Gaugh), Stephen; planter; will; 30 Mar 1743; 21 Apr 1743; sons
Ignatius, Matthew; dau. Anastaticia; b-i-l John Norris; wife Mary; tract
Galigh's [Goughs] Level, Gough's Convenience (MCW 8.207) [SMW TA1.145];
inv.; 21 Apr 1743; 7 Jun 1743; nok James & John Baptist Gough; admx./extx.
Mary Gough (I 28.3)

Gough (Gaugh), Mary; widow; will; 31 Oct 1743; 30 Nov 1743; dau. Anastatia;
husband Stephen; son James; bro. John Norris [Neviss]; [son Ignatius] (MCW
8.242) [SMW TA1.140]; inv. 30 Nov 1743; 2 Mar 1743; nok Thomas & Clement
Norris (I 28.446); acct.; 27 May 1745; husband dec'd; dist. to Ignatious,
Annastatia Gough (A 21.353)

Gough, Charles; inv.; 28 Aug 1753; nok Joseph Price, Mary Brice; admx./extx.
Ann Gough (I 55.16); acct.; 27 Aug 1753; orphans George [age 13], Monica
[age 9]; Stephen [age 6], Elisabeth [age 3], Charles [age 1]; admx. Ann Gough
(A 35.119); dist.; 27 Aug 1753; child.: George [age 14 next 10 Nov], Monica
[age 10 next 12 Nov], Stephen [age 7 next 26 Nov], Elizabeth [age 4 next 4
Sep], Charles [age 2 next 4 May] (BB 1.89)

Gough, John Baptis; inv.; 11 Mar 1755; 17 Apr 1755; nok Peter Gough,
Elisabeth Daft (I 60.215); acct.; 6 Jul 1756; dist. to widow w/o accountant,
James [age 2], John Baptis [age 1] (A 39.217); dist.; 25 Oct 1756 (BB 2.33)

Gough, Benjamin and Susanna; child.: Charles [b. 25 May 1755], Mary [b. 24
Jun 1762], Rebecca [b. 5 Jun 1766], Britainnia [b. 19 Dec 1768] (SA p. 18, 53,
192)

Gough, James and Susanna; child.: Jane [b. 9 Oct 1755], Elizabeth [b. 18 May
1757], Anastatia [b. 9 Apr 1760], John Baptist [b. 18 Feb 1764], Matthew [b.
30 Jun 1766], Ann [b. 3 Feb 1768] (SA p. 14, 49, 192)

Gough, Benjamin; *Gough's Addition*; 67 ac.; 29 Sep 1760 cert./pat. (COL)

Gough, James, Sr.; will; 12 Jun 1764; 19 Jun 1764; sons Stephen, James,
Ignatius; daus. Eleanor Greenwell, Susanna, Mary, Elizabeth Jenkins; wife
Priscilla; tracts *Raccoon Neck, St. Leonards, Lady [Lady Land], Margarets
[St. Margaret's] , Gough's Mill* (MCW 13.42) [SMW TA1.478]; inv.; 18 Sep 1764;
nok Elisabeth Daft, Peter Gough; exs. Prissilla & Stephen Gough (I 84.284);
acct.; 7 Nov 1767; ex. Stephen Gough (A 57.357); dist.; 4 Nov 1769; child.:
Stephen, James, Ignatius, Eleanor Greenwell, Susannah, Mary, Elizabeth
Jenkins (BB 5.212)

Gough, Peter; will; 24 Sep 1766; 10 Feb 1767; sons Ignatious, Bennet; dau.
Elizabeth Martindall, Anne, Mary, Elinor, Keacia [Theresa (?)]; [other daus.
Sarah, Susanna, Katherine]; wife Eleanor (MCW 13.150) [SMW TA1.526]; acct.; 30
Jun 1768; extx. Eleanor, w/o Peter Howard (A 58.250)

Gough, Prisciller (Priscilla); <u>will</u>; 23 Jun 1767; 17 Nov 1767; sons Steaven, James, Ignatius; daus. Ellener Greenwell, Elizabeth Jenkins (MCW 14.18) [SMW TA1.515]; <u>inv.</u>; 27 Feb 1768; 29 Feb 1769; nok Luke & Mark Heard, Stephen Gough; ex. James Gough (I 101.21); <u>acct.</u>; 15 Aug 1770; mentions Stephen & Ignatius Gough (A 64.224); <u>dist.</u>; 15 Aug 1770; dau. Eleanor Greenwell; mentions Elisabeth Jenkins, Mary Roads, James & Ignatius Gough, Susanna Dante (BB 5.397)

Gough, James & Ignatius; *Lady Land*; 108 ac.; 29 Sep 1769 cert./pat. (COL)

Gough, James; <u>will</u>; written 19 Feb 1774; child.: John Baptist, Jane, Elizabeth, Annesary, Mathew, Ann, Mary; wife Susannah (MCW 15.130) [SMW TA1.687]; <u>inv.</u>; 5 Aug 1774; extx. Susannah Gough (I 119.165)

Gough, Benjamin; <u>will</u>; 20 Mar 1774; 1 Sep 1774; child.: Charles, Rebeckah, Mary, Britann, Jeremiah; wife Susanna; mentions John, s/o James Greenwell (MCW 16.37) [SMW TA1.693]

GOWNDRIL

Gowndril, George; came to Maryland in May 1770; m. Hannah Simpson d/o William Simpson of Yorkshire (SA p. 23)

Gowndril, George, Rev., and Hannah; child.: Katherine [b. 16 Nov 1770; bapt. 17 Nov 1770], George [b. 2 Jul 1772, bapt. 19 Jul 1772] (SA p. 23)

Goundril [Gowndrail], George; <u>will</u>; 3 Nov 1775; _ __ 1775; unnamed child. (MCW 16.93) [SMW TA1.730]

GRACE

Grace, John; *Basford Manor [Bafford Manor]*; <u>will</u>; 10 Jan 1675; 21 Mar 1675; wife Ann (MCW I.120) [SMW PC1.22]; <u>inv.</u>; 22 Mar 1676 (I&A 2.145)

Grace, Thomas; <u>inv.</u>; 30 Apr 1713 (I&A 34.122); <u>acct.</u>; 12 May 1716; admx. Dorothy Grace (I&A 38b.11) (SMAA p. 295); <u>acct.</u>; 31 Jun 1719; mentions Susanna Grace (A 2.195) (SMAA p. 394)

GRAHAM

Graham, Robert; immigrated by 1666 (SK 16.97)

Graham, Robert; wife Ann , extx. of George Macall; 1678 (AM LXVII.440)

Graham, George; <u>inv.</u>; 7 Nov 1764; 6 Mar 1765; nok Nelson Calvert, Thomas Hunt; adm. Alexander Graham (I 87.18); <u>acct.</u>; 29 Aug 1768 (A 60.197)

GRAVES

Graves, John; *Hard Shifts*; 196 ac.; 16 Sep 1720 cert./pat. (COL)
North Addn. to Doe Park; 147 ac.; sur. 16 Jun 1720 (TLC p. 82); *Doe Park Addition*; 10 Dec 1724 cert./pat. (COL)
Graves' Chance; 224 ac ; sur. 11 Feb 1719 (TLC p. 83); 10 Dec 1724 cert./pat. (COL)

Graves' Swamp; 108 ac. ; sur. 19 Feb 1719 (TLC p. 83); 10 Dec 1724 cert./pat. (COL)

Graves, Thomas; acct.; 9 Mar 1722; admx. Rosamon, w/o John Austin (A 5.106)

Greaves, John; planter; age ca 58; 12 Apr 1725 (CCR p. 59)

Graves, Thomas; *Joshua's Plain*; 16¾ ac.; sur. 7 Jul 1743 for Thomas Graves (TLC p. 110); 16 ac.; 7 Jul 1743 cert./pat. (COL)

Maiden's Lot; 236 ac.; sur. 10 Mar 1730 (TLC p. 103); 24 Mar 1744 cert./pat. (COL)

Baptist's Hope; 409½ ac.; resur. 11 Sep 1728; orig. called *Happstead* (TLC p. 104); 409 ac.; 23 May 1744 cert./pat. (COL)

Greaves (Graves), John, Mr.; inv.; 17 Oct 1745; 5 Mar 1745; nok John, Jr. & George Greaves; admx./extx. Margaret Graves (I 32.82); acct.; 16 Apr 1747 (A 23.305); acct.; 22 Aug 1749 (A 27.29); acct.; 13 Apr 1753; admx. Margaret Pane (A 33.443)

Greaves, John, Sr.; will; 27 Jan 1746; 5 Jul 1748; sons Thomas, George, John, Jr. (dec'd); daus. Eleanor, Ann, Elizabeth Nelson, Margaret Standidge; d-i-l Margaret Greaves; g-child. Thomas, Jr., Joshua, John, Henrietta Anderson (ch/o Thomas); Tabitha, John and Jesse (ch/o John, Jr.); Mary Ann, Seneca (m), Chloe Nelson (ch/o Elizabeth); tracts *Rockey Point, Hopewell, Greaves Chance, Greaves Lott, Greaves Swamp, Hardships [Hardshift's] Addition, Doepark, Doepark's Addition, North Addition of Doepark*; [mentions *Gardiner's Chance, Bachelor's Rest*] (MCW 9.157) [SMW TA1.190]; inv.; 7 Mar 1748; nok George Graves, Elisabeth Nelson; admxs./extxs. Elenor & Ann Greaves (I 38.61); acct.; 3 Oct 1749 (A27.99)

Greaves, Thomas and Ann; son Jeremiah Adkey [b. 15 Jan 1758] (SA p. 38)

Groves [Greves], Robert; 10 Nov 1758; 6 Dec 1758; son Robert; wife Johanna; tract *Piney Point* (MCW 11.232) [SMW TA1.365]; inv.; 14 May 1759; 7 Jun 1759; nok Thomas Guyther, Benjamin McKay; admx./extx. Johannah Graves (I 67.180)

Graves, Thomas; inv.; 5 Feb 1760; 1 Jul 1760; nok George Greaves, Alexander Anderson; admx./extx. Ann Graves (I 69.135)

Graves, Elinor; inv.; 26 Apr 1773; 23 Apr 1774; nok John Graves, Jr.; Sarah Tippett (I 116.214)

Graves, Tabitha; will; 23 Jul 1773; 1 Mar 1774; cousin Mary Craighill, bro. John; mentions Mary Ann Graves (MCW 15.151) [SMW TA1.697]

Graves, Jeremiah and Rachel Craig; m. 3 Oct 1780 (SA p. 58)

Greaves, Absolom and Alathia Smith (by license); m. 16 Jan 1781 (SA p. 59)

GRAY

Gray, Peter; inv.; 17 Apr 1701 (I&A20.120); acct.; 1 Jun 1702 (I&A 21.385) (SMAA p. 111)

Gray, John and Elizabeth Turner (by license); m. 27 Nov 1783 (SA p. 61)

GREENE

Green, Thomas, Gov.; location of house; 1639 (SK 12.560)

Green, Thomas; *St. Anns*; 55 ac.; sur. 15 Oct 1639; also called *Green's Freehold* 1704; 1707 poss. Mary Vansweringan; St. Mary's Hundred (RR p. 2) (TLC p. 1)

Green, Winifred; w/o Thomas Green; child.: Thomas, Leonard, Robert and Francis; 18 Nov 1650 (AM X.88)

Green, Thomas; Governor; will; 18 Nov 1650; wife Winifred; child.: Thomas, Leonard, Robert and Francis (MCW 5.235)

Green, Tho., Esq.; *Plumb Point* or *Greens Rest*; 500 ac.; 17 Apr 1651; 1707 poss. Thomas Green at Piscattaway; St. Georges Hundred (RR p. 18) (TLC p. 18)

Greene, Elizabeth; w/o William; age ca 34; 1660 (AM XLI.440); 1663, 1665/6, 1667/8 (AM XLIX.56; LVII.5, 250)

Green, Walter; service by 1669; carpenter; and wife (SK 12.348); father of Mary Green; recorded cattle mark; 27 Mar 1674 (AM LXV.232); Elizabeth; w/o Walter; destitute; 1674 (AM LXV.387)

Robert Green; 29 Jan 1676; age 29 [SMW PC1.24]

Green, Leonard; *Proprietor's Gift*; 50 ac.; 8 Feb 1682 cert./pat. (COL) *Green's Content*; 100 ac.; sur. 27 Oct 1682; 1707 poss. Thomas Green at Piscattaway; St. Georges Hundred (RR p. 19) (TLC p. 19); 27 Oct 1682 cert./pat. (COL)

Greene, James; acct.; 9 Aug 1686 (I&A 9.148) (SMAA p. 84)

Greene, Leonard; will; 10 Jan 1687; 4 Jul 1688; wife Ann; son Thomas; bros. Francis, Robert; daus. Wynyfred [Wynefred], Mary, Margaret; bro. Thomas Clarke; tracts *Greene's Rest, Greene's Inheritance* in CH Co. (MCW 2.27) [SMW PC1.72]; inv. 18 Sep 1688 (I&A 10.82)

Green, John; *Ease Guilt*; 200 ac.; sur. 23 Jun 1705; land not found; in 1704 not in 1707; poss. John Gunn; not found; Choptico Hundred (TLC p. 52); *Gase Gift*; 200 ac.; 10 Jan 1706 cert./pat. (COL) [NOTE: may be land called *Ease Gift*; see *Tanyard*, TLC p. 66)

Green, John; Chaptico Manor; will; 21 Sep 1706; 1 Feb 1706/7; sons John, James; wife Elizabeth; tracts *Brightwell Range* in PG Co., *Promution, East Gate* (MCW 3.83); calls tract *Pro Utiam (?)*; mentions dau. Ann Chesher [SMW PC1.174]; inv.; 5 Feb 1706 (I&A 28.196); inv.; 13 Mar 1708 (I&A 30.295); acct.; 4 Jun 1708 (I&A 28.215); acct.; 4 Jun 1708; extx. Elisabeth wife of Ralph Foster; son John Green (SMAA p. 168)

Greene, John; acct.; 31 May 1712; admx. Jane, w/o William Innis (I&A 33b.16; 34.55) (SMAA p. 229)

Green, John; inv.; 4 Sep 1713; approvers John & Christian Green (I&A35b.5)

Green (Greene), Mary; widow; will; written 12 May 1716; sons Thomas and James; dau. Sarah, w/o John Squires; g-son, Thomas Squires; tract *Guyther's Purchase* (MCW 4.71) [SMW PC1.205]; inv.; 7 Jul 1716; nok Thomas Greene,

John Squiers (I&A 37a.162); acct.; 4 Jul 1718; ex. James Greene (A 1.36) (SMAA p. 354)

Greene, John; acct.; 2 Aug 1718 (A 1.198) (SMAA p. 353)

Green, James; inv.; 10 Jun 1721; 30 Jan 1721; nok Thomas Camble, John Squires; admx. Agnus Green (I 5.148b); acct.; 30 Apr 1722; extx. Augnes (Agnes), w/o William Cutler (A 4.160); acct.; 5 Aug 1723 (A 5.200)

Green, John; inv.; 11 May 1730; 22 May 1730; nok William Shaw, John Clark; admx./extx. Catharine Green (I 15.493); acct.; 15 Jun 1730; 2 orphans (A 10.348)

Green, John; will; 11 May 1744; 22 Jul 1745; child.: Joseph, Thomas, Moses; wife unnamed; [tract *Underwood's Plantation*] (MCW 9.38) [SMW TA1.165]; inv.; 15 Sep 1745; 21 Oct 1745; nok Benjamin Green, Sarah Sutton; admx./extx. Rachel Green (I 31.300); acct.; 1 Nov 1746 (A 23.124)

Green, Thomas; will; 9 Jan 1749/50; 6 Feb 1749; wife Mildred Green (MCW 10.71) [SMW TA1.234]

Green, Mildred; will; probate 6 Feb 1749; g-sons Joseph Baley, Henry Sheirclif, Henry Miles [& Joseph Raley]; dau. Tecla (Ucla?) (MCW 10.71) [SMW TA1.235]

GREENFIELD

Greenfield; Thos. Trueman; *Trent Neck*; 2,354 ac.; resur. 10 Jul 1705; 6 tracts: *Trent Neck, Wedge, Refuse, Back Land, Trenton & Inclosure*; (TLC p. 73); pat. PG Co. 10 Sep 1716 cert./pat. (COL)

Callacome; 100 ac.; sur. 16 Apr 1707; (TLC p. 66); 10 Jun 1708 cert./pat. (COL)

Mount Olivet; 109 ac.; 10 Aug 1713 cert./pat. (COL)

Trumania; 184 ac.; sur. 4 Apr 1711; poss. Sam'l Queen (TLC p. 68); 10 Aug 1713 cert./pat. (COL)

Keech's Folly; 100 ac.; 10 Apr 1715 cert./pat. (COL)

Indian Creek etc.; 2,490 ac.; *Indian Creek with Addition, Truemans Chance, Chance, Truemans Hope & Seegsby*; resur. 10 Oct 1714 for Greenfield & Leonard Hollyday; poss. Capt. Peregreen Jowles (TLC p. 73); 10 Sep 1716 cert./pat. (COL)

Holbridge Town or *Hallbridge Town;* 260 ac.; sur. 7 Apr 1707 for Greenfield & Henry Peregrine Jowles (TLC p. 70); 260 ac.; 10 Dec 1714 cert./pat. (COL)

Lamly; 100 ac.; sur. 15 Feb 1714 (TLC p. 72); 10 Sep 1716 cert./pat. (COL)

Arcadia; 100 ac.; sur. 22 Aug 1713; lies in resur. of *Trent Neck* (TLC p. 75); 25 Apr 1717 cert./pat. (COL)

Greenfield's Discovery; 90 ac.; sur. 8 Jun 1715 (TLC p. 72); 10 Sep 1716 cert./pat. (COL)

America Felix; 152 ac.; sur. 14 Jun 1720 (TLC p. 81); 1720 cert./pat. (COL)

Penny Farthing; 206 ac.; 10 Sep 1723 cert./pat. (COL)

Greenfield, Thomas; age ca 64; 9 Apr 1713; tract *Trent Neck* (CCR p. 23)

Greenfield, Thomas, Col.; acct.; 22 Oct 1720; exs. James and Thomas Truman Greenfield (SMAA p. 429)

Greenfield, Truman, Maj.; inv.; 7 Oct 1726; 29 Nov 1726; nok bros. T. T. &
James Greenfield; admx. Mrs. Elisabeth Greenfield (I 11.714); acct.; 21 Jul
1728; adms. John Chesley & wife Elisabeth (A 9.37)

Greenfield, Thomas Truman; d. 10 Dec 1733; age 50 (HGM)

Greenfield, Thomas Truman; will; 3 Feb 1730; 11 Mar 1733/4; sons Thomas
Truman, Kenhelm Truman, Gerard Truman, Walter Truman, Nathaniel
Truman and James Truman Greenfield; daus. Marianne Truman Stoddert,
Sabrina Truman Greenfield; wife Anne; niece Rebecca Jowles; bro. James;
mentions uncle Thomas Truman; mentions mother unnamed; tracts *Trent
Neck, Stoke Bardolph, Arcadia, Greenfield's Discovery, The Wedge, Refuse,
Backland [Buckland], Snenton, The Inclosure, Trumans Hope, Scegby
[Seegby], St. Margaret's Island, Retaliation, Addition, The Barrens, Golden
Race, Truman's Chance, Fishing Place, The Forks, Farthing's Discovery,
Lamley, Keeche's Folly, Holbydge Town, Peny [Perry] Farthing, Truman's
Acquaintance, Wolf's Den, America Felix, Cross Gutt, Mount Olivet, Coock's
Hope* (MCW 7.60) [SMW TA1.32]; inv.; 5 Nov 1734; nok Sabina Truman &
Thomas Truman Greenfield; admx./extx. Ann Greenfield (I 20.83); acct.; 6 Jun
1735; legatee Sab. Greenfield (A 13.116); inv.; 4 May 1739 (I 24.175); inv.; 20
Apr 1745; 5 Jun 1745; nok G. T. & Sabina Truman Greenfield; adm./ex.
Kenelm Truman Greenfield (I 31.152); acct.; 24 Sep 1745; child.: Gerrard
Truman, Kenelm Truman, Thomas Truman, Sabina Truman & Walter Truman
Greenfield (dec'd); extx. Mrs. Ann Greenfield (A 21.447)

Greenfield, Walter Truman; d. 28 May 1739; age 13; s/o Col. Thomas Truman
Greenfield and wife Ann (HGM)

Greenfield, Henry; will; probate 6 Dec 1748; bros. Thomas, George; cousin
Catharine Cartwright; mentions Rebecca, d/o Elizabeth Barber; tract *Good
Luck*; [tract *Folley*] (MCW 10.4) [SMW TA1.221]; inv.; 30 Mar 1749; 6 Jun 1750;
nok John Cartwright, N. T. Greenfield; adm.ex. Thomas Greenfield (I 43.275)

Greenfield, George; inv.; 5 Dec 1750; nok Elisabeth Cartwright, Rebecca
Greenfield; adm./ex. Thomas Greenfield (I 44.242); acct.; 7 Nov 1751; bro.
Thomas; sisters Elisabeth Cartwright, Rebecca Greenfield, Elisabeth Pile; bro.
Benjamin Chesley, age 14; adm. Thomas Greenfield (A 31.225)

Greenfield, Ann; widow; will; 10 Aug 1757; 29 Oct 1759; dau. Susanna
Addison, sons James Truman and Nathaniel Trueman Greenfield, Francis
Wilkinson & his dau. Ann; sister Elinor Adison; tract *Bareneck* in BA Co.
(MCW 11.245) [SMW TA1.378]

Greenfield, Nathaniel Truman; will; 28 Nov 1762; 19 Feb 1763; wife Rebecca;
son Thomas Truman Greenfield; dau. Nancy; other child. (MCW 12.176) [SMW
TA1.438]; inv.; 17 Mar 1763; 1 May 1764; nok Thomas & R. T. Greenfield; ex.
Rebecah Greenfield (I 84.242); acct.; 30 Oct 1765 (A 53.243); acct.; 30 Jun 1768;
mentions Martha & Mary, orphans of Samuel Billingsly (A 58.257); dist.; 30

Oct 1765; legatees widow, son Thomas Truman Greenfield, dau. Nanny (BB 4.148)

Greenfield, Kenelm Truman; <u>inv.</u>; 20 Apr 1765; 24 Nov 1767; nok James Forbes, Thomas Greenfield; admx. Mrs. Margaret Greenfield (I 95.27); <u>acct.</u>; 24 Nov 1767 (A 57.344)

Greenfield, Thomas; approx. 1765; age 49 [SMW TA1.539-556]

Greenfield, Thomas; <u>will</u>; 25 Oct 1773; 15 Apr 1774; daus. Dorothy Tubman, Rebecca Broome [Brown]; sons Truman, Thomas; wife Dorothy (MCW 15.130) [SMW TA1.700]; <u>inv.</u>; 5 May 1774; 6 Apr 1775; nok Rebecca & Truman Greenfield; adm./ex. Thomas Greenfield (I 121.413)

Greenfield, Truman; <u>will</u>; 2 May 1775; 9 Jun 1775; wife Susannah; son Georrge Fepherd, Thomas; daus. Mary, Dorothy, Susanah, Elizabeth; tracts *Fosters Neck, Indian Ourk [Creek]* (MCW 16.92) [SMW TA1.717]; <u>inv.</u>; 18 Sep 1775; 15 Jul 1776; nok Thomas Greenfield, Dorothy Tubman; extx. Susannah Greenfield (I 125.276)

GREENOCK

Greennoch, Elizabeth; widow; <u>will</u>; 24 Nov 1742; 29 Nov 1742; bro. Richard Brewer [his son Richard]; b-i-l John Matting (MCW 8.193) [SMW TA1.117]; <u>inv.</u>; 22 Dec 1742; 5 Mar 1742; nok William & Richard Brewer (I 27.368)

Greenock, Richard; oral; <u>will</u>; died 1 Nov 1742 (MCW 8.193) [SMW TA1.118]

GREENWELL

Greenwell (Greenewell), John; New Towne; 27 Mar 1658; 3 Apr 1658; son James; wife Bridgett (MCW 7.262)

Greenwell, Stephen; *Hickory Hill*; 105 ac.; sur. 27 Mar 1711 (TLC p. 67); 2 Sep 1713 cert./pat. (COL)

Greenwell, James; <u>will</u>; 28 Nov 1709; 14 Aug 1714; wife Grace; sons John, Justinian, Ignatius, Stephen, Charles, Henry, Thomas William, James; daus. Mary Heard, Grace Clarke, Jane; tract *Pileswood Lane [Pile's Woodlane]* (MCW 4.17) [SMW PC1.194]; <u>inv.</u>; 26 Aug 1714; nok Ignatius & Charles Greenwell (I&A 36a.231); <u>acct.</u>; 11 Jun 1710; [recorded with 1716]; exs. Grace and John Greenwell (SMAA p. 299)

Greenwell, James; *Holly Tree*; 148 ac.; sur. 5 Jan 1713 (TLC p. 70); 10 Dec 1714 cert./pat. (COL)
Greenwell's Defence; 30 ac.; 26 Feb 1759 cert./pat. (COL)

Greenwell, Ignatius; *St. Ignatius' Dread*; 100 ac.; 23 Apr 1720 cert./pat. (COL)
Addition; 25½ ac.; sur. 15 Jan 1722 (TLC p. 82); 25 ac.; 10 Sep 1725 cert./pat. (COL)

Greenwell, James; <u>will</u>; 20 Mar 1723/4; 11 Apr 1724; sons James, Enoch; wife Sarah, bro. Ignatius (MCW 5.161) [SMW PC1.288]; <u>inv.</u>; 24 May 1724; 13 Jul

1724; nok Jo. & William Greenwell; extx. Sarah Greenwell (I 10.9); acct.; 27 Mar 1725 (A 6.304)

Greenwell, Ignatius; will; 22 Jun 1724; 1 Sep 1724; wife Mary; sons William, Ignatius; f-i-l William Davis; tract *Ignatius' Dread [Dead]* (MCW 5.174) [SMW PC1.290]; inv.; 1 Oct 1724; 4 Nov 1724; nok John & Stephen Greenwell; ex. Mary Greenwell (I 10.168); acct.; 8 Jun 1726 (A 7.378)

Greenwell, John; *This or None*; 50 ac.; sur. 15 Jan 1722 (TLC p. 82); 10 Sep 1724 cert./pat. (COL)

Greenwell, William; inv.; 4 Jul 1727; nok John & Stephen Greenwell; admx. Mary Greenwell (I 12.139); acct.; 13 Nov 1727; admx. Mary, w/o Robert Hammett (A 8.465)

Greenwell, James; minor s/o William, dec'd; *Wheatley's Content*; 150 ac.; 10 Jun 1734 cert./pat. (COL)

Greenwell, John; *Last Shift*; 100 ac.; sur. 14 Oct 1731; 19 Nov 1751 from John Greenwell 100 ac. to Enoch Fenwick, Jr. (TLC p. 93); 17 Nov 1737 cert./pat. (COL)

Greenwell, Stephen; *Saturday's Conclusion*; 55 ac.; sur. 29 Mar 1729 (TLC p. 93); 18 Nov 1737 cert./pat. (COL)

Greenwell, John; will; 22 Dec 1739; 15 Jul 1741; sons John Wiseman, John Basil, James, Joshua, John Baptist; wife Catherine; tracts *Pilese Woodland, Last Shift, Rochester* (MCW 8.138) [SMW TA1.131]; inv.; 21 Aug 1741; 1 Sep 1741; nok John & John Wiseman Greenwell; admx./extx. Catherine Greenwell (I 26.333)

Greenwell, Robert; *Greenwells March*; 68 ac.; sur. 26 Aug 1741 (TLC p. 97); *Greenwell's Neck*; 68 ac.; 1 Dec 1741 cert./pat. (COL)

Greenwell, Joshua; will; 24 Feb 1749/50; 3 Jul 1750; bros. Basil, John; sisters Susanna and Ann Lettice [Little] Greenwell; nephew James Manning; tract *Last Shift* (MCW 10.96) [SMW TA1.258]; inv.; 4 Sep 1750; 28 Dec 1750; nok John Baptist & John Basell Greenwell; adm./ex. John Wiseman Greenwell (I 44.248)

Greenwell, Thomas; will; 11 Mar 1749/50; 4 Sep 1750; sons Philip, George, Raphael; daus. Anne Cole, Anastasia, Monica, Mary, Winifret; child.-i-l Anne, Elizabeth and Bennet Riley; wife Mary (MCW 10.104) [SMW TA1.253]; inv.; 1 Sep 1750; Mar 1750; nok Philip & George Greenwell; adms. Mary Greenwell, Robert Cole (I 45.88); acct.; 20 Oct 1751; orphans Philip, Winifret, George & Ann [all of age], Anastacia [age 11], Monica [age 8], Mary [age 4], Rachael [age 2]; ex. Mary (A 31.223); dist.; 20 Oct 1751; ex. Mary Greenwell (BB 1.16)

Greenwell, Ignatius and Jane; sons William [b. 26 Nov 1752], Ignatius [b. 23 Dec 1754] (SA p. 19, 54)

Greenwell, Ann Lettcoher (Letticher); inv.; 28 Feb 1753; 5 Jun 1753; nok John Basil & John Baptis Greenwell (I 54.50); acct.; 30 Jul 1754; mentions Basill & Susannah Greenwell; admn. John Wiseman Greenwell (A 36.410)

Greenwell, Henry and Frances; child.: Emma Ransean Anna [b. 10 Jan 1754], Richard [b. 9 Jan 1760], Joseph [b. 17 Apr 1764] (SA p. 15, 16, 50)

Greenwell, Philip and Mary; son Thomas [b. 4 Sep 1754] (SA p. 19) [NOTE: SA p. 54 lists his mother as Winifred]

Greenwell, Philip and Winifred; child.: Mary [b. 17 Oct 1762], Ann [b. 6 Jun 1767], Elizabeth [b. 23 Feb 1769] (SA p. 19, 54,194)

Greenwell, George and Elizabeth; child.: Joseph [b. 2 Aug 1755], Justinian [b. 15 Oct 1757], Bennet [b. 7 Dec 1761], Austin [b. 14 Mar 1765] (SA p. 194, 195)

Greenwell, James and Hannah; child.: Bennett [b. 28 Aug 1755], William [b. 21 Jul 1757], Joseph [b. 3 Aug 1759], Elizabeth [b. 23 Jul 1763] (SA p. 18, 53)

Greenwell, John Basil and Eleanor; child.: Joshua Leonard [b. 5 Nov 1756], James [b. 15 Jan 1761] (SA p. 48)

Greenwell, Henry; will; probate 1 Mar 1757; codicil 28 Jan 1757; wife Eleanor; child.: Edmund, Henry, Ignatious, John, Sarahone [Sarah], Anne, Eleanor, Jeane (MCW 11.155) [SMW TA1.356]; inv.; 1 Mar 1757; 21 May 1757; nok Charles & Thomas Greenwell; adms./exs. Ignatius & John Greenwell (I 63.175); acct.; 20 Mar 1758 (A 41.408); dist.; 26 Mar 1758; legatees Sarah, Ann, Edmund, Ignatius, John, Elinor, Jane, Ann, Henry (BB 2.75)

Greenwell, Ignatius; will; 17 Jan 1757; 1 Mar 1757; wife Jean; child.: Rebecca, William, Ignatius, John; wife's bro. Athanatious Ford (MCW 11.155) [SMW TA1.355]; inv.; 27 Jul 1757; 3 Mar 1757; nok George Greenwell, Elenor Roach; admx./extx. Jane Greenwell (I 63.546, 603); acct.; 24 Oct 1757; orphans John [age 8], Rebeccah [age 6], William [age 4], Ignatious [age 2]; Francis [age 6 mos.]; extx. Jane Greenwell (A 41.260a); dist.; 26 Oct 1757; mentions Rebeccah, William, Ignatius, Francis (BB 2.74)

Greenwell, Stephen; will; 25 Mar 1757; 17 Jun 1757; child.: Rodulph [Rodolphus], William, John, Elizabeth, Henerita, William, Susanna w/o William Stone, Mary w/o Henry Jarboe, Leonard, Ignatius; wife Monica; tracts *Colebrook Levil, Spinks Rest, Beaverdams Manner* (MCW 11.170) [SMW TA1.357]; inv.; 1 Jul 1757; nok Charles & Thomas Greenwell; admx./extx. Monica Greenwell (I 65.237); acct.; 5 Dec 1758; mentions Rhode, Elisabeth & Heneritta Greenwell [all of age] (A 43.18)

Greenwell, Charles, Sr.; will; probate 24 Mar 1760; sons Charles, Thomas, James, Ignatius; g-child. Mary and Joseph David; tracts *Farthings Adventure, Locust Thicket* (MCW 11.260) [SMW TA1.386]; inv.; 24 Mar 1760; 23 Oct 1750; mentions Ignatius Greenwell; nok Charles Greenwell, Jean Norris; adm./ex. James Greenwell (I 70.53)

Greenwell, Charles and Eleanor; child.: John [b. 2 Oct 1760], Jane [b. 20 Mar 1763], Richard [b. 7 Oct 1765], Edward [30 Jan 1768] (SA p. 17, 18, 52)

Greenwell, Justinian and Mary; child.: Noah [b. 10 Nov 1760], Benedict [b. 3 Feb 1763], Elizabeth [b. 2 Sep 1765], Jeremiah [b. 17 Jul 1767] (SA p. 189)

Greenwell, Susannah; inv.; 1 Sep 1761; 1 Sep 1761; nok Basil Greenwell; admn.
John Wiseman Greenwell (I 76.322)

Greenwell, John Basil (Bazil); [planter]; will; 10 Sep 1761; 13 Oct 1761; sons
Joshua, James; wife Eleanor; sons-i-l Langhorn and Richard Clark; *Evans
Quarter, Piles Wood Lane* (MCW 12.99) [SMW TA1.407]; inv.; 5 Mar 1762; nok
John Wiseman & John Baptist Greenwell; extx. Aleanor, w/o James Wheatley
(I 77.64); dist.; 1 Aug 1764; sons Joshua, James; widow Eleanor, w/o James
Wheatly (BB 4.65)

Greenwell, John Baptist and Susanna; child.: John Basil [b. 17 Aug 1764], Mary
Ann [b. 17 Mar 1767] (SA p. 189)

Greenwell, Leonard; inv.; 16 Feb 1767; 10 Mar 1767; nok John & Ignatius
Greenwell (I 93.105); acct.; 1 Oct 1767 (A 57.350)

Greenwell, Monica; will; 14 Jan 1768; 1 Apr 1768; mentions Ellinor d/o Joseph
Medley & Mary d/o George Greenwell; aunts Monica Ford, Frances Williams,
Jane Manning; sister Anastacia Medley (MCW 14.32)

Greenwell, John Wiseman; *Greenwell's Park*; 117 ac.; 1 Mar 1768 cert./pat. (COL)

Greenwell, James; will; 27 Apr 1770; 24 Jul 1770; wife Hannah; sons John,
Clement, James, Joseph, Barnaby, Bennett, William; daus. Dorothy,
Elizabeth; tracts *Holly Tree, Greenwells Defence* (MCW 14.143) [SMW TA1.596];
inv.; 22 Jul 1770; 5 Mar 1771; nok Enoch & Cuthbert Greenwell; extx.
Hannah Greenwell (I 107.93); acct.; 20 Oct 1772 (A 67.140); dist.; 21 Oct 1772;
son John; mentions Clement and James Greenwell (BB 6.168)

Greenwell, Justinian; inv.; 11 Jun 1771; 10 Jan 1772; nok Christopher & Arnold
Greenwell; admx. Margaret Greenwell (I 109.1)

Greenwell, John Baptist; inv.; 15 Feb 1774; 29 Nov 1774; nok Archibald &
Elisabeth Greenwell; admx. Susannah Greenwell (I 118.221)

Greenwell, Philip; will; 4 Sep 1774; 1 Nov 1774; sons Thomas, Joseph; wife
Winefred; dau. Mary (MCW 16.2) [SMW TA1.690]; acct.; 1 Aug 1776; extx.
Weinford Grenwell (A 74.12); inv.; 25 Nov 1774; 1 Feb 1775; mentions
Thomas Greenwell; [NOTE: decedent named "David Greenwell"] (I 120.185)

Greenwell, Stephen and Henrietta Wise (by license); m. 18 Feb 1783 (SA p. 61)

GRIFFIN

Griffin, Thomas; St. Jerome's; will; 27 Nov 1687; 3 Dec 1688; child.: Richard,
John, Thomas, Mary; g-child Sarah Lee; tract *Beaver Dam* (MCW 21.37); inv.;
26 Feb 1688 (I&A 10.184); acct.; [filed with 1688-1693]; ex. Thomas Griffin
(I&A 10.328)

Griffen, Thomas, Sr.; inv.; 3 Dec 1726; 19 Dec 1726; nok Thomas Griffin, Ann
Cooper; admx. Elisabeth Griffin (I 11.717)

Griffin, Thomas, Jr.; acct.; 21 Jul 1727; admx. Elisabeth Griffin (A 8.285)

Griffen (Griffin, Griffing), William; <u>will</u>; 24 Mar 1729/30; 25 Apr 1730; son
William by 1ˢᵗ wife Mary, son Ezekiel by last wife Parthena; William Jaction
s/o other wife Mary; [or Catherine] (MCW 6.154) [SMW PC1.327]; <u>inv.</u>; 28 Apr
1730; 27 Jul 1730; nok minors; admx./extx. Parthenia Griffing (I 15.607); <u>acct.</u>;
14 Jun 1731; extx. Parthenia, w/o Theophilus Millard (A 11.136); <u>acct.</u>; 16 Jul
1733 (A 12.36)

Griffin, Richard; *Elizabeth*; 89 ac.; sur. 15 Aug 1727 (TLC p. 84); 16 Jun 1730
cert./pat. (COL)

Griffin, Thomas; <u>will</u>; 11 Oct 1736; 24 May 1742; sons Nicholas, Philip, James,
Thomas, Abraham; g-son John Griffin; daus. Ann Cooper, Mary, Susannah;
tract *Scotland* (MCW 8.171) [SMW TA1.123]; <u>inv.</u>; 17 Jul 1742; 23 Aug 1742; nok
Susannah & Richard Griffin (I 27.57)

Griffith, John; *Long Lane*; 110 ac.; sur. 1 May 1741; part of *Mill Land* (TLC p.
100); 1 Jul 1742 cert./pat. (COL)

Griffin (Griffen), Charles, Mr.; <u>inv.</u>; 9 Mar 1743; 8 Aug 1744; nok minors;
admx./extx. Mary, w/o Mathias Nottingham (I 29.415); <u>acct.</u>; 3 Jun 1745;
orphans Charles, Mary, Margarett, Elisabeth, Eleanor (A 21.355)

Griffen, Thomas; <u>acct.</u>; 24 Oct 1743; mentions John & Thomas, orphans of Jane
Beal; ex. Nicholas Griffen (A 19.543)

Griffin, Richard; <u>will</u>; 4 Mar 1744; 18 Aug 1744; wife Mary; dau. Willen
Bassett, Anne, Elizabeth, Parthenia Mitchell, Sarah Tell [Sarah Tole & her
son Parimeious], Elizabeth Thompson; son Parnemas; tract *Beaver Dam Neck*
(MCW 8.277) [SMW TA1.155]; <u>inv.</u>; 15 Oct 1744; 19 dec 1744; nok Pharmenas &
Elisabeth Thompson; admx./extx. Mary Griffin (I 30.217)

Griffen, Richard; <u>acct.</u>; 28 Apr 1746; mentions Martha & William, orphans of
John Glover; extx. Mary, w/o Thomas Beale (A 22.248)

Griffin, Nicholas; <u>inv.</u>; 25 Mar 1752; 25 May 1752; nok James Griffin, Susana
Payn; admx./extx. Elisabeth Griffin (I 48.452); <u>acct.</u>; 7 May 1753 (A 34.178);
<u>dist.</u>; 7 May 1753 (BB 1.79)

Griffin, Permanious (Parmenus, Perminus); <u>inv.</u>; 15 May 1752; 25 May 1752;
nok William Basset, Mary Morgan (I 48.450); <u>acct.</u>; 2 Jun 1753 (A 34.168); <u>acct.</u>;
26 Apr 1757 (A 41.37)

Griffen, Elisabeth; <u>inv.</u>; 29 Nov 1752; 3 Apr 1753; nok Samuel, Jr. & Ladia
Abell; adm./ex. Samuel Abell, Sr. (I 53.35)

Griffin, Elisabeth; <u>inv.</u>; 25 Jun 1755; 3 Nov 1755; nok Joshua, William Sledman
& Edward Morgan; mentions James Griffin (I 61.120); <u>acct.</u>; 20 Oct 1756 (A
40.232)

Griffin, Philip; <u>inv.</u>; 25 Sep 1766; 6 Nov 1766; nok James & Thomas Griffin;
admx. Margaret Griffin (I 91.94, 96); <u>acct.</u>; 17 Sep 1768 (A 60.181); <u>dist.</u> 17 Sep
1768 (BB 6.207)

Griffen, Nicholas; will; 14 Mar 1769; 3 Sep 1771; wife Ann; child. Margarh [Margaret], Henrieta, Philip (MCW 14.182) [SMW TA1.621]; inv.; 29 Oct 1771; 25 Mar 1772; nok Thomas & James Griffin; admx. Ann Griffin (I 109.15); acct.; 21 Sep 1773 (A 68.203); dist.; 21 Sep 1773;admx. Ann, w/o John Goldsmith (BB 6.223)

Griffin, Thomas and Elizabeth Jarboe (by license); m. 29 Jan 1784 (SA p. 61)

GRIGGS

Griggs, John; immig. by 1672; m. widow & extx. of Rich'd Keen 1676 (SK 16.592; 15.387)

Grigs, John; acct.; 24 Jun 1702; admx. Mrs. Margaret King; 8 Sep 1705 (I&A 25.47) (SMAA p. 107)

Greggs [Griggs], John; St. Inegoes Hundred; will; 19 Sep 1754; 9 Jun 1755; nephew John, s/o bro. William Griggs; g-dau. Elizabeth Lowrey; daus. Sarah Allison, Mary Beal, Margt. Jones, Susanah Sanner [Sermer (?)]; wife Elizabeth (MCW 11.93) [SMW TA1.325]; inv.; 1 Mar 1756; nok Mary Beale, Susannah Lanner; admx.extx. Elisabeth Griggs (I 60.373); acct.; 9 Aug 1756 (A 39.224)

GRINGOE

Gringoe, Grace; s/o William, blacksmith; 5 Jun 1668 (AM LVII.335)

Greengoe, William; inv.; 1 May 1695 (I&A13a.385)

Gringoe, Mary; age ca 76; w/o William Gringoe; 14 Jul 1714; tract *Jones Woods* (CCR p. 31)

GRISTY

Grisley, Benjamin; *Grisley's View*; 34 ac.; 13 Nov 1752 cert./pat. (COL)

Gristy, Benjamin; inv.; 21 Feb 1775; 1 Mar 1775; nok Clement & Elisabeth Gristy; adms./exs. Ann & Richard Ward Gristy (I 121.419)

GRUBB

Grubb, Mary; being with a bastard child; 1670 (AMLVII.615)

Grubb, John; will; written 14 Apr 1695; wife Ann (MCW 2.159) [SMW PC1.111]; inv.; 4 Mar 1697 (I&A 17.108)

GRUGAN

Grugan, Paul; inv.; 13 Feb 1750; 19 May 1750; nok minors (I 42.232); acct.; 22 Jun 1751 (A 30.195)

Grogan, Catharine; dau. Anastatia [b. 27 Apr 1766] (SA p. 196)

GRUNWIN

Grunwin, Thomas; *Bamfield Wood*; 150 ac.; sur. 2 Nov 1694; 1707 poss. Henry Low [ex. of Grunwin]; St. Michael's Hundred (RR p. 14) (TLC p. 15)

Grunwyn (Grunwin), Thomas; <u>will</u>; 20 Oct 1703; 13 Dec 1703; sisters Mary
    Chamberlain & Sarah; tracts *Banfield Woods; Barrow Keyton* (MCW 3.36); <u>inv.</u>;
    14 Jan 1703 (I&A 3.43); <u>acct.</u>; 25 Mar 1707 (I&A 28.76) (SMAA p. 161); <u>acct.</u>; 17
    Jun 1715 (I&A 36c.58) (SMAA p. 288)

GUIBERT

Guibert, Joshua; *Guibert's Chance*; 131 ac.; sur. 12 Jan 1703; 1707 poss. Joshua
    Guibert; St. Clements Hundred (RR p. 48) (TLC p. 47); 20 Jul 1704 cert./pat. (COL)
    Guibert's Chance Addition; 38 ac.; sur. 15 Aug 1705; St. Clements Hundred
    (RR p. 48); 10 Jan 1706 cert./pat. (COL)
Guybert, Joshua; Gent.; age ca 60; 12 Aug 1705 (CCR p. 15)
Guibert (Gwibert), Joshua; <u>will</u>; 26 Feb 1713; 16 May 1713; sons Thomas,
    Matthew, Joshua; dau. Mary, and daus. Eliza. Carberry [Carboy], formerly
    w/o Thos. Turner; Ann Blackston, w/o John Blackston; wife Elizabeth; tracts
    Guibert's Chance, Tower Hill (MCW 3.252) [SMW PC1.188]; <u>inv.</u>; 19 May 1713;
    24 Jul 1713; [Sr.]; nok Thomas & Joseph Guibert (I&A 35b.85); <u>acct.</u>; 29 Oct
    1714; exs. Elisabeth, Thomas and Mathew Guibert (I&A 36b.34) (SMAA p. 261)
Guibert, Luke, Mr.; <u>acct.</u>; 6 Mar 1714; extx. Elisabeth Guibert (I&A 36b.70)
    (SMAA p. 273)
Guibert (Guybert), Elizabeth; <u>will</u>; 19 Dec 1715; 17 Sep 1716; son John
    Blackiston; daus. Susannah Attoway, Rebecka Walters [Waters], Mary
    Mason, Ann Blackiston; g-dau. Elizabeth Blackiston; g-son Nehemiah
    Blackiston; tract *Langworth Point* (MCW 4.69); calls dau. Rebeckah Waters
    [SMW PC1.207]; <u>inv.</u>; 2 Oct 1716; 22 Dec 1716; nok John Attaway, Mathew
    Mason (I&A 38b.30); <u>acct.</u>; 23 Sep 1717; ex. John Blackiston (I&A 37b.111) (SMAA
    p. 318); <u>acct.</u>; 27 Sep 1717 (SMAA p. 319); <u>acct.</u>; 6 Jun 1718 (SMAA p. 357); <u>acct.</u>; 7
    Jun 1718 (A 1.55)
Guybert, Elizabeth or Ann; <u>inv.</u>; 8 Mar 1722; nok Matthew & John Guibert;
    adm./ex. Mr. Thomas Guibert (I 8.54); <u>acct.</u>; 24 Apr 1724 (A 5.408; 6.311)
Guibert, Thomas; <u>will</u>; 17 Mar 1728/9; 7 May 1729; daus. Elizabeth, Anne; wife
    Sarah; bro. Joshua (MCW 6.110) [SMW PC1.341]; <u>inv.</u>; 7 May 1729; 5 Aug 1729;
    nok Joseph & Matthew Guibert; admx./extx. Sarah Guibert (widow) (I 14.286)
Guibert (Guybert), Joshua; <u>will</u>; 10 Nov 1743; 1 Dec 1743; wife Jane; child.:
    Elizabeth, Anne, Joshua, Susannah Goode [Coade], Mary Woodward,
    Susannah Guibert, [Hannah Guibert]; g-child. Luke and Joseph Woodward,
    Joshua and John Sandys (MCW 8.254) [SMW TA1.744]; <u>inv.</u>; 9 Mar 1743; 15 May
    1744; nok Thomas Coade, James Dunbarr; admx./extx. Jane Guibert (I 29.136);
    <u>inv.</u>; 19 Dec 1744; 3 Sep 1745; nok John Woodward, John Coode (I 31.285);
    <u>acct.</u>; 1 Jul 1746; mentions Josua, Heneritta, Elisabeth, Ann, Susannah
    Guybert; extx. Jane Guybert (A 22.260)
Guibert, Matthew; <u>will</u>; 28 Jan 1749/50; 5 Jun 1750; wife Elizabeth; sons John,
    Gerard; daus. Rose, Rebecka; tract *Guibert's Chance* (MCW 10.96) [SMW

TA1.256]; <u>inv.</u>; 5 Jun 1750; 4 Sep 1750; nok John & Joshua Guibert;
admx./extx. Elisabeth Guibert (I 43.397); <u>acct.</u>; 7 May 1751 (A 30.179)
Guibert (Guybert), John; <u>inv.</u>; 26 Jun 1762; 11 Jan 1763; adms. Thomas Green
Martin & wife Dorothy Martin (I 80.156); <u>acct.</u>; 1 Aug 1764 (A 51.360); <u>dist.</u>; 1
Aug 1764 (BB 4.59)

GUYTHER
Guither, Nicholas; age 30; s/o William [b. ca 1647]; 11 May 1720 (CCR p. 46)
Gwyther, Nicholas; age ca 28; 11 Apr 1654 (AM X.42)
Goyther (Gwither), Nicholas, Capt.; dec'd; sons John and Nicholas; 1666 (AM
LVII.22)
Gwither, Nicholas; age ca 16; 1667 (AM LVII.184)
Guither, Nicholas; <u>inv.</u>; 3 May 1680; adm. William Guither (I&A 7a.59)
Gwyther (Gwither, Guither), William; *St. Barbaras*; 250 ac.; sur. 8 Apr 1682;
1707 poss. Wm. Taylard of AA Co.; St. Michael's Hundred (RR p. 14) (TLC p.
14); 8 Mar 1682 cert./pat. (COL)
Gwyther's Purchase; 100 ac.; sur. 2 Aug 1705; 7 Sep 1708 from Wm.
Gwyther & wife Barbara 100 ac. to Mary Green; incl. in other surveys (TLC p.
65); 10 Oct 1705 cert./pat. (COL)
Guither, William, Jr.; <u>will</u>; 16 Mar 1705; 14 Aug 1705; sons Nicholas, William,
Thomas; dau. Audrie Guither; [wife Mary]; tract *Pope's Hogpen* (MCW 3.80);
[SMW PC1.138]; <u>inv.</u>; [filed with 1706] (I&A 26.2)
Guyther, William; <u>acct.</u>; 4 Nov 1707; extx. Mary w/o Marshall Lowe (I&A 27.232)
Guyther, William; <u>inv.</u>; 15 Feb 1711; mentions Nicholas & George Guyther (I&A
33a.180); <u>acct.</u>; 3 Jun 1713 (I&A 35b.107); 13 Jun 1713 (SMAA p. 238)
Guyther, Owen; <u>inv.</u>; 24 Mar 1712; nok Nicholas & George Guyther (I&A 34.173)
Guyther, Mary; widow; <u>will</u>; 29 Oct 1716; 29 Nov 1716; son Owen; daus.
Sarah, Dorothy, Mary; cousin Elinor Keave [sister Elinour Keen]; tracts *The
Folly, Barron Neck* (MCW 4.90) [SMW PC1.202]; <u>inv.</u>; 30 Nov 1716 (I&A 38b.53);
<u>acct.</u>; 10 Mar 1720 (SMAA p. 454); <u>acct.</u>; 16 Mar 1720 (A 2.433)
Guyther, Nicholas, Mr.; <u>inv.</u>; 9 Feb 1724; 20 Apr 1725; nok Dorothy Leigh,
Owen Guyther; admx. Catherine Guyther (I 10.338); <u>acct.</u>; 2 May 1726 (A 7.329);
<u>acct.</u>; 23 Aug 1726 (A 7.516)
Gwyther (Guither), John; *Crafts*; 253 ac.; *The Crofts*; resur. 27 Nov 1722; resur.
into *Crofts Rectified* (TLC p. 84); 9 May 1727 cert./pat. (COL)
Saturday's Venture; 55 ac.; sur. 13 Nov 1731 (TLC p. 88); 8 May 1734 cert./pat.
(COL)
Saturday's Venture Addition; 24 ac.; sur. 5 Oct 1742 (TLC p. 101); 17 Aug 1743
cert./pat. (COL)
Fragments Addition; 34 ac.; sur. 15 Aug 1745; incl. *Resurvey of Crofts
Rectified* (TLC p. 105); 27 Aug 1745 cert./pat. (COL)

Crofts Rectified; 247 ac.; 2 tracts *The Crofts* and *Additional Fragments*; resur. 21 Jan 1745 (TLC p. 114); 1 Dec 1750 cert./pat. (COL)

Guyther (Gayther), Owen; inv.; 17 Nov 1729; 14 Jun 1729; nok Sarah & Mary Guyther; adm./ex. John Guyther (I 15.362); acct.; 14 Dec 1730 (A 10.631); acct.; 18 Dec 1732 (A 11.579)

Guither, (Gwyther), William; *Itchcomb's Freehold*; 344 ac.; 10 Sep 1744 cert./pat. (COL)

Guyther, Owen; inv.; 25 Jun 1750; 24 Sep 1750; nok Issab. Coolk, John Guyther; admx./extx. Mary Guyther (I 44.31); acct.; 9 Sep 1751; orphan John [age 4]; admx. Mary Guyther (A 31.70); dist.; 9 Sep 1752 (BB 1.5)

Guyther, John; will;16 Jul 1765; 1 May 1767; dau. Elizabeth, w/o John Fenwick; g-child. John Guyther and John, Ignatius, Susana, Mary, Elizabeth, Ann and Margaret Fenwick, Eleanor Taney; tracts *Old Crafts, Cornabes His Swamp, Rigg Land, Baret Neck* (MCW 13.177) [SMW TA1.536]; inv.; 7 May 1767; 2 Jun 1767; nok Raphael Janey, Josiah Langley (I 93.111, 114); inv.; 25 Oct 1768 (I 98.109); acct.; 25 Oct 1768 (A 60.178)

Guither, William; *Guither's Tarltons*; 34 ac.; 25 Oct 1769 cert./pat. (COL) *Guither's Addition*; 22 ac.; 26 Jul 1770 cert./pat. (COL)

Guyther, William, Mr.; inv.; 10 Nov 1772; adm. George Guyther (I 110.192)

Guyther, Jean [Jane]; will; 3 Jan 1774; 1 Mar 1774; dau. Elizabeth (MCW 15. 149) [SMW TA1.746]; inv.; 28 Feb 1774; 20 Jul 1774 (I 119.182); dist.; 1 Aug 1775 (BB 7.30)

Guyther, Elizabeth; will; 7 Aug 1775; 20 Aug 1775; son George (MCW 16.111) [SMW TA1.728]

Guyther, William; will; probate 3 Nov 1775; sons William, George; wife Elizbeth; g-dau. [dau.] Elizabeth; tract *Hickory Bottom* (MCW 16.110) [SMW TA1.719]; acct.; 26 Feb 1777; adms. William Taylor & wife (A 74.20)

HACKETT

Hackett, William; age ca 67 in 1714 (MD p. 79)

Hackett, Tobias; inv.; 1733; 18 Jun 1733; nok Mary Mackenzy, Elisabeth Hackett; admx./extx. Jane Hackett (I 17.164)

Hackett [Hackitt], Richard; planter; will; 15 Mar 1754; 4 Jun 1754; wife unnamed; her son Rodelphua Nevitt [Nert (?)]; dau. Rachel Hackett; bro. John Thompson (MCW 11.38) [SMW TA1.308]; inv.; 17 Aug 1754; 7 Nov 1754; nok John Thompson, Patrick Conely; adm./ex. Mary Hackett (I 58.317)

Hackett, Rhodolph and Mary; child. Henrietta [b. 14 Aug 1757], Ann [b. 7 Nov 1758], Joshua [b. 13 Nov 1763], Mary Magdalene [b. 10 Dec 1766] (SA p. 14, 18, 19, 48, 53)

Hackett, Rudolphus; *Hagstone & Wheatly's Hills*; 205 ac.; 9 Mar 1763 cert./pat. (COL)

Hackett, James; inv.; 22 Feb 1763 (I 80.162)

HAGAN

Hagan, Thomas; *Cadcock Measure*; 150 ac.; sur. 8 Aug 1672; 1707 poss. Tho.
Hagan; New Town Hundred (RR p. 36) (TLC p. 35)

Haggan, William; acct.; 7 Apr 1733 (A 11.682)

HAGAR

Hagar, Robert; inv.; 20 Aug 1709 (I&A 31.15); acct.; 4 Apr 1710; [Jr.]; adm.
Robert Hager (I&A 31.130) (SMAA p. 206)

Hager (Hagar), Robert; planter; will; 29 Aug 1712; 6 Oct 1712; sons James and
Robert; g-dau. Mary Hagar; wife Eliza. (MCW 3.237) [SMW PC1.171]; inv.; 16 Jan
1712 (I&A 34.126); acct.; 28 May 1715; extx. Elisabeth, w/o Henry Nowell (I&A
36c.63) (SMAA p. 284)

Hagar (Hagan), Robert, Sr.; will; 12 Sep 1761; 17 Oct 1761; daus. Milburn,
Mary Ann and Sarah Hilton Hagar, Ann Smith; wife Milburn; sons Robert,
Matthew, William Jenkins Hagar; tracts *The Addition, Wheatley's Neglect,
Beaver Dam, Truth and Trust* (MCW 12.97); inv.; 7 __ 1762; nok Susannah
Hagur, Henry Nowel; extx. Milburn Combs, w/o ___ Combs (I 79.259); acct.; 4
Feb 1763; exs. William Combs & wife Milburn (A 49.104]; dist.; 4 Feb 1763
(BB 3.178); acct.; 24 Nov 1767 (A 57.337)

Hagan (Hager), Robert; inv.; 4 Jun 1764; 6 Aug 1764; nok Mathew Hagur, Peter
Smith; admx. Mildred Hager (I 84.286); acct.; 20 May 1769; admx. Mildred,
w/o William Hilton (A 62.15); acct.; 8 Jul 1770 (A 64.219); dist.; 8 Jul 1770 (BB
5.386)

HALFEHEAD

Halfhead, Jno.; *Halfheads Folly*; 200 ac.; sur. 24 Jul 1664; 1707 poss. Edw.
Horn & Xtopher Rousby's heirs; St. Mary's Hundred (RR p. 5) (TLC p. 6)

Halfehead, John; acct.; 28 Jul 1679; admx. Jane Elliott, w/o Henry; she married
immediately after his death (I&A 6.222)

HALL

Hall, Walter; *Revells Back Side*; 100 ac.; sur. 30 Sep 1663; 1707 poss. Widow
Tant; New Town Hundred (RR p. 32) (TLC p. 31)

Hall, William; will; 28 Mar 1666; 31 May 1666; mentions Anne, wife of John
Cage (MCW 1.34)

Hall, Henry; immigrated by 1670 (SK 12.584)

Hall, John; immigrated by 1672 (SK 17.395)

Hall, John, inv.; 10 Jan 1675; 13 Mar 1675 (I&A 1.573); acct.; 15 Oct 1677 (I&A
4.386)

Hall, Walter; *Cross Manor*; will; 22 Nov 1678; 5 Dec 1678; s-i-l Henry Fox;
wife Margaret (MCW 1.206) [SMW PC1.30]; inv.; 17 Feb 1678 (I&A 5.419)

Hall, Thomas; inv.; [filed with 1699] (I&A 19½a.69)

Hall, John; age ca 50; Jun 1715 (CCR p. 33)

Hall, Edward; <u>will</u>; 13 Oct 1718; 5 Nov 1718; sister Mary; bro. Thomas; mentions Abraham, s/o Thomas Hall; James Hall [Hase (?)], s/o John; William and Mary, ch/o Thomas King; Susan, w/o Charles King; Anne, d/o Charles King (MCW 4.188) [SMW PC1.242]; <u>inv.</u>; 14 Nov 1718; 19 Mar 1718 (I 1.535); <u>acct.</u>; 11 Nov 1719; ex. Charles King (A 2.317); <u>acct.</u>; 11 Nov 1719 (SMAA p. 379)

Hall, Simon; planter; <u>will</u>; _ _ 1725; 22 Nov 1725; cousin Margarett Brown in county Durham (MCW 5.205) [SMW PC1.298]; <u>inv.</u>; 9 Sep 1725; 2 Mar 1725; nok Benedict & John Boarman (I 11.227)

Hall, John; <u>will</u>; 29 Nov 1727; 13 Feb 1727/8; sons John, William, Thomas; daus. Elizabeth, Mary; wife unnamed (MCW 6.48) [SMW PC1.315]; <u>inv.</u>; 21 Mar 1727; 29 Apr 1728; nok Elisabeth & William Hall; ex. John Hall (I 13.94); <u>acct.</u>; 7 Apr 1729 (A 9.379)

Hall, Thomas; <u>inv.</u>; <u>will</u>; 26 Apr 1729; 28 Jun 1729; nok John & William Hall; admx./extx. Mary Hall (I 14.185); <u>acct.</u>; 21 Mar 1729; admx. Mary, w/o James Watts (A 10.229)

Hall, Daniel; <u>will</u>; 30 Apr 1729; 26 May 1729; sons John, William, Daniel; dau. Ann; wife Margaret; tract *Coursey [Coveny (?)] Point* (MCW 6.111) [SMW PC1.342]; <u>inv.</u>; 9 Jun 1729; 4 Aug 1729; nok William & John Halle; admx./extx. Margaret Hall (I 14.279); <u>acct.</u>; 29 Sep 1730 (A 10.466)

Hall, Henry and Catherine; child. Ann Mary [b. 11 Jun 1754], George [b. 10 May 1756], John Basil [b. 21 Oct 1762], Frances [b. 11 Jul 1765] (SA p. 41, 51)

Hall, William; <u>inv.</u>; 17 Dec 1759; nok Anthony Underwood, Daniel Hall; admx./extx. Priscilla Hall (I 68.103)

Hall, Benjamin and Ann; child. Priscilla [b. 20 Aug 1761], Mary [b. 1 Dec 1763], Bennet [b. 25 Nov 1765], Elizabeth [b. 12 Dec 1768], Joseph [b. 12 Aug 1769] (SA p. 5)

Hall, Joseph and Mary; child. Dorothy [b. 18 Apr 1767], Thomas [b. 5 Sep 1769] (SA p. 1)

Hall, Aquilla; m. 22 Dec 1772 Mary Davis (MM)

Hall, Joseph and Mary McGill; m. 2 Jul 1780 (SA p. 58)

Hall, Arthur and Rebecca; dau. Catharine, bapt. 22 Jul 1781 (SA p. 30)

HALY

Haly, Clement; wife Mary, admx. of Edward Conery; 28 Apr 1677 (AM LXVII.218)

Haly, Clement; Chaptico; <u>will</u>; 4 Jan 1694; 23 Feb 1695; daus. Mary, Elizabeth; mentions Tracy, w/o Abraham Price; tracts *Chesup, Haly's Lot, Watson's Choice* (MCW 2.84) [SMW PC1.87]

HAMILTON

Hamilton, John; <u>inv.</u>; 28 Mar 1735; 4 Jun 1735; admx./extx. Jane Hamelton (I 20.468); <u>acct.</u>; 5 Nov 1735; adm. John Hamelton (A 14.102)

Hambleton (Hamilton), Arthur, Esq.; of Liverpool; inv.; 20 Nov 1737; 4 Jul
  1738 (I 23.199, 202); acct.; merchant in Liverpool; 4 Jul 1738 (A 17.217)
Hamilton, George; m. d/o George Gordon; mentions James Forbes, s/o Mrs.
  Dryden Forbes; 23 May 1743 (CCR p. 94)
Hamilton, Hugh; inv.; 16 Jun 1749; 27 Jul 1749; nok Ignatius Bailey, William
  Hamilton (I 40.44)
Hambleton, Jean; acct.; 8 Aug 1751; mentions William & John Hambleton;
  Ann, w/o Joseph Hopkins (A 31.58)
Hamilton, Jonathan and Margaret Abell; son Philemon [b. 8 Mar 1774] (SA p. 24)

HAMMERSLEY
Hamersly, William; *Gore*; 16 ac.; 10 Aug 1753 cert./pat. (COL)
Hammersley, Francis; *Francis's Discovery*; 25 ac.; 6 Sep 1768 cert./pat. (COL)

HAMMETT
Hammet, Robert; inv.; 31 Jul 1719; 15 Aug 1719; nok William & Joseph
  Lawrance; admx. Cathrine Hammett (I 2.196); acct.; 18 Mar 1720; admx.
  Kathrine, w/o John MackKellvie (A 2.434) (SMAA p. 453)
Hammett, Robert; *Hammett's Beginning*; 34 ac.; sur. 1 Apr 1731 (TLC p. 87); [5
  Oct 1731] cert./pat. (COL)
  Hemmetts Chance; 69 ac.; sur. 17 Dec 1741 for Robert Hemmetts (TLC p. 99);
  11 Jun 1742 cert./pat. (COL)
  Wild Cat Neck; 104 ac.; 104½ ac.; sur. 1 May 1744 (TLC p. 99); 1 May 1744
  cert./pat. (COL)
  Hickory Hall; 17 ac.; 4 Sep 1745 cert./pat. (COL)
Hammett, McKelvie and Henrietta; child. Richard [b. 12 Jan 1754], Henry [b.
  10 Feb 1757], Dolly [b. 12 Aug 1759], Mary [b. 5 Feb 1762], Frances [b. 25
  Nov 1764], Sarah [b. 1 Mar 1767] (SA p. 17, 52)
Hammett, Robert; will; 30 Nov 1758; 8 Sep 1760; wife Elizabeth; sons
  McKelves [McKelvie], Robert, John, William, Cartwright; daus. Mary, Ann,
  Elizabeth; tracts *Wldcat Neck, Hammett's Beginning, Lordship's Mill
  Manner, King's Purchase, The Birch Spring, Hammetts Chance, Hickery
  Flatt* (MCW 12.1) [SMW TA1.395]; inv.; 7 Apr 1761; nok John Hammett, Ann
  Norris; admx./extx. Elisabeth Hammet (I 71.168); acct.; 16 Jun 1761 (A 47.223);
  dist.; 16 Jun 1761; legatees Cartwright, William, Margaret, Ann, Elisabeth,
  McKelvie, Robert, John, Mary; extx. Elisabeth Hamett (BB 3.110)
Hammett, John, Jr.; *Hammett's Swamp*; 20 ac.; 16 Aug 1759 cert./pat. (COL)
Hammet, Robert and Rebecca; son Jeremiah [b. 1 Dec 1766] (SA p. 6)
Hammet, John and Margery; dau. Frances [b. 26 Feb 1771], James [b. 11 Apr
  1775], John [b. 7 Feb 1777] (SA p. 21, 28, 29)
Hammett, Cartwright and Elizabeth; dau. Margaret [b. 17 Oct 1771] (SA p. 20, 55)
Hammet, William and Ann; dau. Ann [b. 19 Nov 1771] (SA p. 21)

Hammet, John, Jr. and Margery; son Bennet [b. 6 Mar 1772] (SA p. 23)
Hammet, McKelvie and Ann; child. Frances [b. 24 Jan 1773], John [b. 16 May
    1775] (SA p. 22, 23, 26)
Hammett, Robert; *Hammett's Discovery*; 98 ac.; 15 Dec 1774 cert./pat. (COL)
Hamett, John, Jr.; dau. Catharine, bapt. 18 Mar 1781 (SA p. 30)

HAMMOND
Hammond, Daniel; age ca 17 in 1655; mentions f-i-l Pope Alvey (MD p. 82)
Hamond, Maudlin; *St. Bernards*; 100 ac.; sur. 29 Apr 1664; 1707 poss. James
    Joseph (TLC says James Gough); New Town Hundred (RR p. 33) (TLC p. 32)
Hamond, Daniel; age ca 17 in 1665 (MD p. 82)
Hammond, Anne; w/o John Hammond; [1670/1-1675] (AM LXV.671)
Hamon, Mordecay; will; 12 Jan 1671; 24 Jan 1671; wife Margaret; tract *St.
    Margaret's*; bro. Daniel Hamond; f-i-l Pope Aley and wife Ann; sis. Martha
    Tossey (MCW 1.65)
Hamond, Daniell; *Lewgers Plains*; 430 ac.; sur. 1 Jul 1682; 1707 poss. John
    Norris, John Hamond; New Town Hundred (RR p. 39) (TLC p. 38)
Hammond (Hamon), Daniell; inv.; 10 Nov 1684 (I&A 8.333); acct.; 30 Apr 1687
    (I&A 9.262); acct.; [filed with 1688] (I&A 9.503)
Hammond, John; inv.; 30 Jan 1727; 28 Feb 1727; nok Ann Teren, Rachel
    Hammond; admx. Barbary Hammond (widow) (I 13.7); acct.; 20 May 1731;
    mentions John, Sarah, Ann, Mary, Monneca, Elisabeth & Rachal Hammon (A
    11.69)
Hammond, Uel and Susanna; dau. Ann [b. 11 May 1768] (SA p. 194)

HAMPSTEAD
Hampstead, Wm.; *Hampstead*; 200 ac.; sur. 6 May 1665; 1707 poss. Adam Bell,
    & Geo. Thompson; St. Mary's Hundred (RR p. 4) (TLC p. 5)
Hampstead, William; acct.; 19 Jun 1676; unnamed child.; admx. Mary Reevely
    (relict) (I&A 4.143)

HARDIN
Harden (Harding), Joseph & wife; inv.; 18 Mar 1684 (I&A 8.292); acct.; 27 May
    1686 (I&A 9.12) (SMAA p. 81)
Hardin, Joseph; acct.; 28 May 1751; orphans Mary [age 15], Ann [age 12],
    Elisabeth [age 10], Monica [age 8], Annistaca [age 5]; admx. Ann Hardin (A
    30.98)

HARPER
Harper, Robert; service by 1673 (SK 18.335)
Harper, James and Mary; child. Elizabeth [b. 15 May 1760], Henrietta [b. 4 Mar
    1763], Mary Ann [b. 27 May 1766], Rebecca [b. 25 Jul 1769] (SA p. 195)

HARRIS

Harrys (Harris), John; *St. Peter's Key*; 50 ac.; sur. 15 Jul 1640; same tract as
Van Swearingen's Point 1704; poss. Wm. Goldsmith 1707; St. Mary's
Hundred (RR p. 2) (TLC p. 2)

Harris, Samuell; *Whitaker*; 150 ac.; sur. 12 Nov 1652; 1707 poss. John Cecill,
Wm. Cecill, Tho. Cecill; New Town Hundred (RR p. 31) (TLC p. 29))

Harris, Thomas; will; written 28 Mar 1654; wife Anne; son Thomas (MCW 1.9)

Harris, Elizabeth; now wife of Samuell; accused of killing her infant Easter
1657 at *St. Wynifrid*, St. Clements Hundred (AM XLI.430)

Harris, William; immigrated Nov 1669 (SK 17.578)

Harris, Morris; service 1673 (SK 17.573)

Harris, William; immigrated 1675; carpenter (SK 18.280)

Harris, Samuel; will; 3 Aug 1681; son William; wife Elizabeth; tract *The
Grapevine* [SMW PC1.38]; inv.; 27 May 1682 (I&A 7c.129)

Harriss, James; inv.; 16 Dec 1700 (I&A 20.87); acct.; 1 Oct 1701; admx. Elisabeth
Haris (I&A 21.110)

Harris, Samuel; inv.; 16 Jan 1711 (I&A 33a.180); acct.; 28 Mar 1713; admx.
Margrett Harris (I&A 34.115) (SMAA p. 253)

Harris, Peter; will; 25 May 1722; 14 Jan 1722; tracts *Fishing Place, Indian
Creek* (MCW 5.129) [SMW PC1.277]; inv.; 7 Feb 1722 (I 8.146); acct.; 22 Jan 1723
(A 5.348)

Harris, John; will; 24 Sep 1727; 3 Oct 1727 (MCW 6.41) [SMW PC1.325]; inv.; Oct
1727; 9 Nov 1727 (I 12.408); acct.; 12 Oct 1730 (A 10.468)

Harass [Harris], Danall [Darnall]; will; 17 Dec 1751; 2 Jun 1752; sister Mary,
w/o Richard Hackit [Hawkit], & her son Roaday Nevett; tracts *Whatty
[Whatley], Kiniston* (MCW 10.223) [SMW TA1.297]

Harris, William; acct.; 29 Apr 1754 (A 36.312)

Harris, Samuel and Elizabeth; sons Zachariah [b. 5 Nov 1763], Austin [b. 13 Oct
1766] (SA p. 17, 51)

HARRISON

Harrison, William; *Pineland*; 388 ac.; sur. 14 Nov 1728; 27 May 1734 cert./pat.
(COL)

Harrison, John; inv.; 1 Sep 1738; 20 Nov 1738; nok Robert & John Harrison;
adms./exs. Elisabeth & William Harrison (I 23.533); acct.; 31 Mar 1741;
orphans William, Robert, John, Elisabeth, Susanna, Margret (A 18.167)

Harrison, Robert, Jr.; inv.; 29 May 1759; 8 Nov 1759; nok William Harrison;
admx./extx. Mary Ann Harrison (I 68.105,107)

Harrason [Harrison], William; will; 26 Nov 1748; 14 Mar 1748/9 (MCW 10.4)
[SMW TA1.229); inv.; 29 Nov 1749; 1 Jan 1749; nok. Margritt King, William
Harrison (I 41.464)

Harrison, William; will; 1768; 15 Feb 1770; wife Elizabeth; bro. Robert; sons
John, Kenelm; daus. Ann, Elizabeth, Sarah, Eleanor, Susanna; wife Elizabeth;

tracts *Harrison's Hazard, St. Margaret's* (MCW 14.132) [SMW TA1.598]; <u>inv.</u>; 24 Feb 1770; 12 May 1770; nok Ann Edwards, Elisabeth Harrison (I 103.242);<u>acct.</u>; 1 Jun 1771; extx. Elisabeth Harrison (A 66.66)

Harrison, George; m. 16 Dec 1777 Sarah Dent (MM)

Harison, Robert; m. 17 Feb 1778 Elizab. Douglas (BRU 2.536)

HART

Hart, Peter; <u>inv.</u>; 20 Sep 1749; 21 Sep 1749; nok Margaret Reeder, John Hart; admx./extx. Elisabeth Hart (I 41.454)

Hart, Peter; <u>inv.</u>; 7 Jun 1755; 2 Sep 1755; nok Mary Molahorn; admx./extx. Mary Hart (I 59.202); <u>acct.</u>; 2 Jan 1756; sister Margaret Mahoney; admx. Mary Hart (A 39.220); <u>dist.</u>; Oct 1756 (BB 2.32)

Hart, Mary, Mrs.; <u>inv.</u>; 7 May 1773; nok Thomas Allston, Jr., Elisabeth Woodward (I 112.400); <u>inv.</u>; 10 Apr 1775 (I 121.407); <u>acct.</u>; 10 Feb 1775 (A 72.149)

HARTLEY

Hartley, Joseph; *White Horse* [?*Hope*]or *White Haven*; 164 ac.; sur. 12 May 1697; 1707 poss. Geo. Akeeth for Jos. Hartley, orphan; Resurrection Hundred (RR p. 64); same tract as *Whitehaven*; St. Clements Hundred (TLC p. 47); 20 May 1697 cert./pat. (COL)

Hartley, Joseph; <u>inv.</u>; 25 Apr 1698; widow Ann Hartley (I&A 17.104)

Hartley, Joseph, <u>will</u>; 14 May 1725; 2 Jun 1725; wife Ann; bro. Joshua; daus.-i-l Elizabeth, Ann, Frances Brookbank; s-i-l [b-i-l] Abraham Brookbank (MCW 5.193) [SMW PC1.296]

HARWOOD

Harwood, John; <u>will</u>; 11 Dec 1659; 19 Jan 1659; wife Alice (MCW 1.11)

Harwood, John; <u>inv.</u>; 24 Oct 1733; 7 Jan 1733; nok minors (I 17.598); <u>acct.</u>; 12 Aug 1734; mentions John Bapt. & Susannah Elisabeth Harwood (A 12.464)

HASELER

Haseler, Levin; age ca 65; Jun 1715 (CCR p. 33)

Haselor, William; <u>inv.</u>; 23 Jul 1719; nok Lewis & Richard Haselor (I 2.198)

Haseler, Richard; <u>inv.</u>; 9 Feb 1735; 3 Jun 1736; nok Peter Foord, John Edwards; admx./extx. Elisabeth Hazelor (I 21.417); <u>acct.</u>; 8 Mar 1738; orphans John, Richard, Phillip, Henry, Barbara, Ann, Mary & Elisabeth; admx. Elisabeth Haselier (Hasler) (A 17.102)

Hasler, William and Elizabeth; child. Henrietta [b. 9 Feb 1752], William [b. 19 May 1755], Richard [b. 5 Feb 1757] (SA p. 36)

HASKINS

Haskins, John; <u>will</u>; 12 Feb 1699; 12 Feb 1699; son John; dau. Sarah Doxee; wife Sarah; tract *Westberry* (MCW 2.199)

Haskins, John, Sr.; inv.; 22 Aug 1700 (I&A 20.29)

Hoskins, William; inv.; 28 Jan 1722; nok John & George Hoskins (I 8.114)

Haskins, George; planter; inv.; 23 Aug 1725; 1 Feb 1725; nok John Haskins, Katherine Bond; admx. Anne Haskins (I 11.191)

Haskins, Robert; inv.; 5 Jun 1765; nok Lucretia Jordan, Benjamin Haskins; admx. Mary Haskins (I 88.75); acct.; 4 Jun 1766 (A 54.99)

Haskins, Aaron; inv.; 1 May 1767; 2 Jun 1767; nok Thomas Noales, Bennet Slarey; admx. Priscilla Haskins (I 93.114); inv.; 31 Aug 1767 (I 95.23); acct.; 31 Aug 1767 (A 57.351)

HATTON

Hatton, Thomas; *Hunting Creek*; 250 ac.; sur. 15 Mar 1654; poss. 1707 James Attaway; St. Mary's Hundred (RR p. 2) (TLC p. 3)
Hunting Neck; 200 ac.; sur. 26 Aug 1655; 1707 poss. Wm. Asquith; St. Mary's Hundred (RR p. 4) (TLC p. 4)

Hatton, Margaret; St. Mary's City; will; 4 Feb 1656; 29 Aug 1657; son Thomas, others unnamed; bro. Richard Banks (MCW 1.10)

Hatton, Richard; m. Ann Price, d/o John who d. ca 1660 (CCR p. 9)

Hatton, William; wife Elizabeth; mentions 500 a. in TA Co. called *Haddon*; 12 Oct 1665 (AM XLIX.515)

Hatton, Grace; wife of John; 1668 (AM LVII.318)

Hatton, Thomas; will; 27 Jan 1675; 4 Feb 1675; wife Elizabeth; previous wife unnamed; son Thomas; f-i-l Randolph [Randall] Hanson and his child. James Johnson, Richard, Thomas, Timothy; sisters-i-l Barbara and Elizabeth Hanson; b-i-l Thomas Wahop and his sisters Margaret and Rebecca Wahop; mentions Robert, s/o John Cheverill and Margaret, d/o Patrick Forrest (MCW 1.114-5) [SMW PC1.15]; inv.; 23 Feb 1675 (I&A 2.85)

Hatton, Richard; Poplar Hill; will; 5 Feb 1675; 14 Feb 1675; wife Ann; son Richard; cous. Eliza: Henson [Souten]; bros. William Hatton and Randolph Hanson; mentions Isaac Booth, s/o widow Booth (MCW 1.119) [SMW PC1.20]; inv.; 1675; 18 Apr 1676 (I&A 2.215)

Hatton, Richard; acct.; 10 Aug 1686; mentions Thomas, orphan of William Whitle; adm./ex. William Hatton (I&A 9.137)

Hatton, Thomas; will; written 11 Aug 1701; b-i-l John Blackston; dau. Eliza; wife Susanna (MCW 2.223); inv.; 23 Sep 1701 (I&A 21.156); acct.; extx. Susanna, wife of John Attaway; 15 Sep 1705 (SMAA p. 131); acct.; 17 Sep 1714; relict and extx. Susanna, wife of John Attaway (SMAA p. 262)

HAWKINS

Hawkins, Richard; service 1681 (SK WC2.410)

Hawkins, Robert; inv.; 4 May 1734; 5 Aug 1734; nok minors (I 19.47)

Hawkins, Robert; age ca 21 in 1757 (MD p. 88)

HAWLEY

Hawley, Jerome, Esq.; will; 20 Oct 1633 England; inv. 9 Sep 1637; widow
Eleanor; 27 Aug 1638 (AM IV.40, 100)

Hawley, Wm., Capt.; *St. Jeroms*; 4,250 ac.; resur. 22 Sep 1653 for 5,700 ac.;
1707 poss. Wm. Coursey; St. Michael's Hundred (RR p. 13) (TLC p. 13)

HAYDEN

Heyden, Francis; will; 30 Apr 1697; 12 Jun 1697; wife Thomasin (MCW 2.152)
[SMW PC1.98]; inv.; 30 Jan 1697; admx. Thomasin Heyden, relict (I&A 15.339)

Hayden [Heydon], Thomasin; will; 19 Sep 1701; 27 Nov 1702; daus. Mary
Reeder, Penelope Allman; son William; tract *Small Hopes* (MCW 2.250) [SMW
PC1.125]; acct.; 12 Oct 1704; ex. William Hayden (I&A 3.371) (SMAA p. 131)

Hayden, George; age ca 60 in 1715 (MD p. 88)

Haydon, William; planter; age ca 49; 3 Jan 1723 (CCR p. 57)

Hayden, William; inv.; 30 Apr 1726; 3 Aug 1726; admx. Mary Walker (I 11.499);
acct.; 6 Jun 1727; admx. Thomas Walker & wife Mary (A 8.228)

Hayden, William, Sr.; planter; will; 14 Jul 1732; 6 Mar 1733-4; child. Charles,
William, Grace Herbert, Thomasen Cissell, Francis (m), Susanna, James,
George, John, Clement, Richard; wife Elizabeth; tract *Finchly* (MCW 7.63)
[SMW TA1.21]; inv.; 6 Mar 1733; 4 Jun 1733; nok Charles & William Hayden;
admx./extx. Elisabeth Hayden (I 18.319); acct.; 12 May 1735 (A 13.127)

Hayden, Francis, Mrs.; inv.; 26 Apr 1748; 5 Sep 1748; nok John Medley;
adm./ex. Elisabeth Hayden (I 37.97); acct.; 4 Apr 1749; orphans George [age
11], James [age 3], Ann [age 13], Elisabeth [age 8]; admx. Elisabeth, w/o
Sebaston Thompson (A 27.13)

Haiden (Hayden), Joseph; inv.; 20 Mar 1749; 3 Apr 1750; nok Margarett Myles,
John Wooten; admx.extx. Ann Haiden (I 42.11)

Hayden, Elizabeth; *Roach's Discovery*; 251 ac.; 7 Mar 1754 cert./pat. (COL)

Hadon, George, Mr.; inv.; 9 May 1754; 5 Jun 1754; nok Clement & James
Haydon; admx./extx. Charity Haydon (I 57.253); acct.; 7 Aug 1755; orphans
William [age 13], Basill [age 12], Charles [age 8], George [age 7], Mary [age
6], Francis [age 4]; admx. Charity, w/o William Morgan (A 38.188); dist.; 1756
(BB 2.8)

Hayden, Elizabeth; will; 30 Oct 1760; 4 Mar 1761; child. James, John, Richard
and Susanna Drury; g-son William Drury; son Clement Hayden; g-sons
George and James, sons of Francis Hayden & William and Bassett, sons of
George Hayden; mentions Joseph, s/o James Clark; tracts *Roaches Discovery,
Shanks Wrisgue, Hayden Riskue* (MCW 12.36) [SMW TA1.412]; inv.; 5 May 1761;
nok James & John Hayden; ex. Clement Hayden (I 74.275)

HAYES

Hayes, John; <u>will</u>; 8 Mar 1735/6; 2 Jun 1736; child. William [Williamson], James, John, Thomas, Samuel, Jake [Jesse], Leonard, Mary; wife unnamed; tracts *Gardiner's Grove, Gardiner's Addition* (MCW 7.184) [SMW TA1.56]; <u>inv.</u>; 22 Jun 1736; 23 Aug 1736; nok Williamson Hayes, minors; admx./extx. Ann Hayes (I 21.515); <u>acct.</u>; 3 Mar 1736 (A 15.295)

Hayes, James; <u>will</u>; 22 Feb 1741/2; 6 Apr 1742; mother Ann; bro. John; tracts *Gardner's Grove, Addition to Gardner's Grove* (MCW 8.161) [SMW TA1.127]

Hayes, John; <u>will</u>; 8 Sep 1748; 8 Mar 1748/9; bros. Samuell, Jesse, William; mother Ann; tracts *Gardners Grove, Gardners Addition* (MCW 10.4) [SMW TA1.227)

Hayes, Thomas; <u>will</u>; 20 Aug 1764; 1 Oct 1764; wife Ruth Hawkins Hayes; son John Hawkins Hayes; dus. Elizabeth Keech Hayes, Ann Hays (MCW 13.58) [SMW TA1.456]; <u>inv.</u>; 19 Dec 1764; 6 Mar 1765; nok Samuel & Ebenezar Hayes; extx. Ruth Hawkins Hayes (I 87.13)

HAYNES

Haynes, George; immigrated by 1672 (SK 17.364)

Hanes, John; <u>inv.</u>; 15 May 1718 (I 1.39)

Henis (Hains), John; <u>acct.</u>; 3 Aug 1720 admx. Joice Haines (A 3.70)

HAYWOOD

Haywood, Raphael; age ca 70 in 1710 (MD p. 88)

Haywood, Anne; <u>inv.</u>; 1 Dec 1714 (I&A 36b.58); <u>acct.</u>; 13 Jan 1714 (I&A 36c.51) (SMAA p. 272)

Haywood, Raphael; <u>acct.</u>; 16 Jun 1716 (I&A 38b.8) (SMAA p. 299)

Haywood, John; <u>inv.</u>; 4 Mar 1761; admx./extx. Jane Haywood (I 71.143); <u>acct.</u>; 4 Nov 1761; admx. Jane, w/o James Brinnum (A 47.230); <u>dist.</u>; 4 Nov 1761 (BB 3.109)

Haywood, Thomas and Mary Shermentine (by license); m. 16 Oct 1781 (SA p. 59)

HEAD

Head, Will'm; *Headly*; 100 ac.; sur. 7 May 1659; lies in *St. Clements Manor*; St. Clements Hundred (TLC p. 42)

Head, Andrew; age ca 40 in 1715 (MD p. 88)

Head, Anne; age ca 45; Jun 1715; niece of Richard Fenwick; tract *Fenwick Manor*; husband Adam Head, age ca 40 (CCR p. 33.)

Head, Ann; <u>will</u>; 22 May 1727; 7 Jun 1727; husband Adam; daus. Elizabeth Herbert, Prissilla Head; tract *Prevention* (MCW 6.31) [SMW PC1.324]

Head, Adam; <u>inv.</u>; 22 Jun 1739; nok Francis & Elisabeth Herbert, Presilea Head; admx./extx. Ann Head (I 24.377); <u>acct.</u>; 14 Mar 1742; orphans Cuthbert, Jane, Anne, Sarah (A 19.376)

Head, Ignatius; <u>inv.</u>; 21 May 1774; nok Cuthbert Head, David Johnson (I 118.130)

HEARD

Heard, John; *Offley*; 180 ac.; sur. 12 Nov 1676; 1707 widow Susanna Heard; land not found; New Town Hundred (RR p. 37) (TLC p. 36)

Heard, John; *Coventry*; 100 ac.; sur. 19 Oct 1680; 1707 poss. widow Susanna Heard; New Town Hundred (RR p. 38) (TLC p. 37); 19 Oct 1680 cert./pat. (COL) *Heards Choice*; 150 ac.; sur. 22 Oct 1681; 1707 poss. widow Susanna Heard; New Town Hundred (RR p. 38) (TLC p. 37); 22 Oct 1681 cert./pat. (COL)

Herd, John; Brittain's Bay; will; 29 Jul 1696; 31 Aug 1696; son John; wife Susanna; tracts *Coventry, Poole* (MCW 2.112); inv.; 21 Sep 1697 (I&A 15.163); acct.; 1698; admx./extx. Susan Heard (I&A 16.63) (SMAA p. 99)

Heard, William; 115 ac.; *William Heards Purchase*; 115 ac.; sur. 10 May 1696; 1707 poss. Widow Heard; New Town Hundred (RR p. 40) (TLC p. 39); *Heard's Purchase*; [12 May 1697] cert./pat. (COL)

Heard, Susanna; widow of John Heard; will; 13 May 1706; 9 Dec 1707; sons William, John; g-ch John, Luke, Mark & Elizabeth Norris; sons-i-l John Norris and Nicholas Mills; dau. Mary Tant; g-ch Matthew Tant, Monica Norris and Elizabeth Heard; dau. Susanna Norris; tracts *Poole, Heard's Choice, Ossly, Nevitts [Nevitts Beginning]* (MCW 3.98) [SMW PC1.147); inv.; 10 Dec 1707; nok John Heard, Susanna Norris, Elisabeth Mills (I&A 27.256); acct.; 16 May 1709; ex. William Heard (I&A 29.297) (SMAA p. 188)

Heard, John; planter; age ca 40 in 1721 (MD p. 89)

Heard, William; will; 18 Apr 1732; 3 Jan 1732; dau. Mary, w/o Francis Hopewell; g-dau. Susannah Hopewell; sons Marke, Mathew, Luke; daus. Susannah, Prisilla, Elioner, Elizabeth Wiseman, Mary Hopewell; wife Elizabeth; bro. Edward Cole; tract *Thirds, William Heard's Purchase* (MCW 6.250) [SMW PC1.360]; inv.; 3 Feb 1732; 18 Apr 1733; nok Mary & John Heard; admx./extx. Elisabeth Heard (I 17.98); acct.; 11 Jun 1734 (A 12.447)

Heard (Herd, Hurd), John; *Well Found*; 212 ac.; sur. 6 Sep 1732 (TLC p. 88); 1 Jun 1734 cert./pat. (COL) *Hardship [originally Coventry]*; 147 ac.; resur. 4 Sep 1736 (TLC p. 97); *Herd's Hardship*; 14 Oct 1741 cert./pat. (COL)

Heard, Elizabeth; will; 30 Apr 1745; 6 Mar 1750; daus. Eliza. Wiseman, Mary Greenwell, Prissilla Gause [Gough], Elinor Clark; sons Luke, Mark and Mathew Heard (MCW 10.142) [SMW TA1.281]

Heard, John; will; 23 Dec 1746; 20 Jan 1746/7; child. John, Jonah, William, James, John Basil, Susanna Norris, Mark Peake; [son Ignatius]; tracts *Well Found, Heard Hearship* (MCW 9.94) [SMW TA1.185]; inv.; 11 Apr 1747; 13 Apr 1747; [Sr.]; nok Ignatius & John Heard; adm./ex. James Heard (I 35.92); inv.; [filed with 1748]; (I 37.91); acct.; 15 Aug 1748 (A 25.175)

Heard, Matthew; *Heard's Security*; 476 ac.; orig. *St. Lawrences Freehold*; escheated and resur. 9 Sep 1748 (TLC p. 115); 9 Sep 1748 cert./pat. (COL)

Heard, James; *Two Friends*; 131 ac.; sur. 28 May 1747 (TLC p. 115); 28 Jul 1749 cert./pat. (COL)

Heard's Addition; 58 ac.; 10 Aug 1753 cert./pat. (COL)
Well Found Addition; 50 ac.; 25 Feb 1767 cert./pat. (COL)
Heard, Mark; *Thirds*; 530 ac.; 25 Apr 1760 cert./pat. (COL)
Heard, John and Ann; child. Mary [b. 9 Jul 1764], Ann [b. 5 Apr 1766], Hellen
[b. 29 Sep 1767] (SA p.18, 52, 53)
Heard, Matthew; will; 27 May 1766; bros. Luke and Mark Heard; sister Eleanor
Clark; cousins Francis Hopewell, Elizabeth d/o Abraham Clark; mentions
Matthew, s/o Mary [Mark] Heard; tracts *Heard's Choice, Heard's Security*
(MCW 13.151) [SMW TA1.503]; inv.; 22 Jul 1766; 12 Aug 1766; nok bro. Luke
Heard; Stephen Gough s/o sister; exs. Mark Heard, Abraham Clark (I 91.105);
acct.; 15 Mar 1769 (A 61.109)
Heard, John; will; 1 Aug 1766; 5 Nov 1766; sons Richard, John, Bennet; daus.
Dorothy, Rebecca, Eleanor; g-sons John Fenwick, Edward Neale and James
Heard; tracts *Mill Land, H. [St.] Laurence Freehold, Hanover* (MCW 13.136)
[SMW TA1.474]; inv.; 3 Jun 1767; 19 Nov 1767; nok Jeams & John Heard; exs.
Richard & Bennet Heard (I 94.202); acct.; 19 Nov 1767; mentions Bennett,
John, Rebeccah, Eleanor & Bennett Heard (A 57.353)
Heard, Richard, Mr.; inv.; 22 Sep 1768; nok James & Bennet Heard; adms. John
& Barbara Heard (I 98.120) ; inv.; 24 Jul 1769 (I 101.335); acct.; 1 Feb 1771 (A
66.165); acct.; 10 Jun 1771; adm./ex. John Heard (A 66.160)
Heard, James; will; 26 May 1769; 14 Aug 1769; wife Jane; child. Ann, Polley,
James, John Baptist, Ignatius, Jenny; tracts *Heard's Hardship, Nevits
Beginning, 2 Friends* (MCW 14.108) [SMW TA1.575]
Heard, James; inv.; 17 May 1770; 19 May 1770; nok Ignatius & Edmund Heard;
extx. Jane Heard (I 103.245); acct.; 16 Dec 1770; exs. Jane & James Heard (A
66.75)
Heard, Mark; will; 16 Jun 1771; 10 Sep 1771; wife Susannah; child. Matthew,
John, William, Richard, Ann, Elizabeth, Susannah; tracts *Thirds, Small
Addition* (MCW 14.181) [SMW TA1.624]; inv.; 10 Sep 1771; 10 Feb 1772; nok
Matthew & Luke Heard; adms./extx. Susannah & Mark Heard (I 109.17); acct.;
1 Sep 1774 (A 72.17); acct.; 28 Jan 1777 (A 72.423); dist.; 28 Jan 1777; legatees,
Mathew, John, William, Richard, Ann, Elisabeth, Susannah, widow (BB 7.15)
Heard, John, Jr.; *Heard's Discovery*; 14 ac.; 22 Dec 1773 cert./pat. (COL)
Heard, John; s/o John; *Hanover Addition*; 14 ac.; 10 Jul 1783 cert./pat. (COL)
Heard, John; s/o Mark, dec'd; *Heard's Addition*; 8 ac.; 21 Dec 1773 cert./pat.
(COL)
Heard, William; s/o Mark, dec'd; *Heard's Purchase*; 18 ac.; 22 Dec 1773
cert./pat. (COL)

HEBB
Hobb, Thomas; service by 1673 (SK17.547)
Hebb, Thomas; s-i-l of Emanuel Ratliffe, St. George's Hundred; 1679/80 (AM
LXIX.378)

Hebbs, Thomas, Jr.; *Little Recovery of the Birth Right*; 13 ac.; sur . 15 Mar 1713 (TLC p. 71); *Recovery of Birthright*; 10 Dec 1714 cert./pat. (COL)

Hebb [Hobb], William; will; 2 Oct 1718; 9 Jan 1718/9; sons William, Mathew; wife Priscilla; bro. Thomas; tract *Small Hogs [Hopes]* (MCW 4.191) [SMW PC1.239]; inv.; 23 Apr 1719; 4 May 1719 (I 2.87); inv.; 19 Mar 1720; extx. Pressillia, w/o James Baker (I 3.221); acct.; 19 Mar 1720; extx. Priscilla, w/o John Baker (A 2.419); acct.; 17 May 1722; extx. Prescilla, w/o James Baker (A 4.155)

Hebb, Joseph, Mr.; inv.; 11 May 1727; 22 May 1727; nok Thomas & George Hebb; admx. Alice Hebb (I 12.1); inv.; 19 Jun 1728; 4 Aug 1728; nok William Watts; adm. Thomas Hebb (I 13.188); acct.; 7 Oct 1728 (A 9.111); acct.; Nov 1729 (A 9.495)

Hebb, David; s/o Joseph; *Edward's Freehold*; 75 ac.; resur. 20 Jan 1715 (TLC p. 17); *The Freehold*; 17 Nov 1742 cert./pat. (COL)

Hebb, Thomas; will; 14 Jan 1744; 13 Mar 1744/5; sons Edward Hillard, William, John; daus. Jane Jenkins, Anne Baxter, Lucretia Hebb; g-son Francis Bean; sister Elizabeth Rule (MCW 9.17) [SMW TA1.162]; inv.; 14 Mar 1744; nok Thomas & William Watts; admx./exs. Elisabeth Rale, William & Edward Hilliard Hebb (I 31.147); acct.; 26 Sep 1757; exs. William & Edward Hilliard Hebb (A 41.228); dist.; 26 Sep 1757 (BB 2.68)

Hebb, William; *Itchcomb's Freehold*; 344 ac.; 10 Sep 1744 cert./pat. (COL) *Pasture Ground*; 18 ac.; 8 Oct 1756 cert./pat. (COL)

Hebb, Matthew; inv.; 17 Oct 1757; nok John & James Baker; adm./ex. John Hebb (I 64.1); acct.; 1 Jan 1758; adm. John Hebb (A 43.29)

Hebb, William; d. 23 May 1758; in his 46th year (tombstone, Porto Bello)

Hebb, William; will; 22 Dec 1757/5 (sic); Jun 1758; wife Hopewell; daus. Priscilla Hicks, Elizabeth, Grace, Ann; son Vernon; tracts *Cross Manner, Poplar [Pepper] Hill, Grainge, Hebdons [Hobson's] Hole, Hutton Calout [Calvert]* (MCW 11.202) [SMW TA1.448]; inv.; 7 May 1759; nok Hopewell & Elisabeth Hebb (I 67.67, 69); acct.; 11 Jun 1759 (A 43.174)

Hobbs [Hebb[, Sabins [Sabina]; will; 30 May 1764; 20 Feb 1765; sister Sarah and Ann (?); unnamed parents living (MCW 13.72) [SMW TA1.469]; inv.; 7 Mar 1765; 2 Jul 1765; nok Thomas & An Hebb; adm. Edward Hillard Hebb (I 88.74)

Hebb, Vernon; *Town Land*; 27 ac.; 27 Oct 1765 cert./pat. (COL)

Hebb, Joseph; inv.; 1 Jul 1767; nok ___ Watt, John Hebb (I 93.97); inv.; 2 May 1769; admx. Mary Hebb (I 100.123); acct.; 2 May 1769 (A 60.358)

Hebb, Hopewell; will; 14 Oct 1767; 4 Nov 1773; daus. Elizabeth Wilson, Gracy Guyther, Ann Hebb, Priscilla Hicks; son Vernon (MCW 15.91) [SMW TA1.661]

Hebb, Kennedy (Kennady); will; 20 Jul 1776; 12 Sep 1776; bros. Richard, Samuel; father William (MCW 16.174)

William Hebb, d. 24 Mar 1804, aged 45 years and Elizabeth C., his wife, d. 20 Apr 1823, aged 50 years (tombstone. St. George's, Valley Lee)

HEBDEN
Hebden, Tho.; unnamed; 1,000 ac.; sur. 4 Feb 1641; let fall; assgn. Tho. Weston; same as *Westbury Mannour*; St. Georges Hundred (RR p. 17) (TLC p. 17) *Hebdens Hole*; 700 ac.; sur. 4 Feb 1641; 1707 poss. Hannah Harpam; St. Georges Hundred (RR p. 17) (TLC p. 17)

Hebden, Thomas; will; 30 May 1647; 25 Oct 1649; wife Katharine, extx. (MCW 1.3)

HENDERSON
Henderson, Sarah; service by 1676 (SK 15.395)

Henderson, George; acct.; 9 Jul 1686 (I&A 9.46)

HENDLEY
Henley, Daniel; age ca 70 in 1722 (MD p. 90)

Henley, Daniel; planter; age ca 74; 12 Apr 1725 (CCR p. 59)

Hentley, Joseph; inv.; 3 Aug 1725; nok Joshua Hentley; extx. Ann Hentley (I 11.5)

Henley, Robert; *John's Content*; 93 ac.; 93½ ac. sur. 17 Jun 1738 (TLC p. 96); 26 May 1740 cert./pat. (COL)

Hendly, Roger; inv.; 24 Dec 1750; 10 Jan 1750; nok Robert & Jeremiah Hendley; admx./extx. Johannah Hendly (I 44.251); acct.; 21 Dec 1751; mentions John Waughop [age 5] & Mary Hendley [age 3] (A 32.67); dist.; 21 Dec 1751; child. Mary & John Waughope Hendley (BB 1.26)

Hendly (Hendley), Robart [Robert]; will; 9 Jun 1753; 23 Jul 1753; son John, Jeremiah, James; daus. Elizabeth Garber, Rebecca Adams, Mary Combs; g-daus. Elizabeth and Ann Horn; wife unnamed; tract *Hopsons Choyce* (MCW 10.277) [SMW TA1.306]; inv.; 22 Feb 1753; 4 Mar 1754; nok John & Jeremiah Hendley; admx./extx. Jane Hendley (I 58.64); acct.; 9 Sep 1754 (A 36.407); dist.; 9 Sep 1754 (BB 1.114)

Handley [Henley], Jean [Jane]; will; 10 Mar 1755; 19 May 1755; sons Jeremiah, James (MCW 11.94) [SMW TA1.327]

Henley, John; *Henley's Addition*; 23 ac.; 27 Sep 1756 cert./pat. (COL)

Hendley, Robert; oral; will; 28 Mar 1757; sons Jeremiah, James (MCW II.158) [SMW TA1.354]

Hendley, Jeremiah, Mr.; inv.; 15 Feb 175_; 9 Apr 1759; nok Ann Daffin, Elisabeth Jarboe; adm./ex. John Hendley (I 67.91)

Hendley, Jeremiah; acct.; 17 Dec 1759; mentions John Wanb & Mary, orphans of Roger Hendley; adm. John Hendley (A 44.175)

Hendley (Hendeley), John; [planter]; will; 16 Aug 1766; 10 Feb 1767; son William; wife Sarah (MCW 13.150) [SMW TA1.531]; inv.; 4 Mar 1767; 3 Jun 1767; nok James Hendley, Elisabeth Jarby; exs. Sarah & William Hendly (I 93.103)

Hendley, James; will; 18 Dec 1776; 12 Jan 1777; child. Robert, Jean, James, Elizabeth; widow unnamed (MCW 16.173)

HENNING

Henning, John; planter; <u>will</u>; 19 May 1775; 20 Aug 1775; sons Gilbert, Caleb, Nathan and Thomas Arnold Henning; dau. Mary Ann Sanner [Sammer]; wife Ann (MCW 16.109) [SMW TA1.724]

Henning, Jeremiah and Ann; dau. Sarah [b. 24 Dec 1776] (SA p. 29)

Henning, John and Mary Abell (by license); m. 5 Sep 1781 (SA p. 59)

Henning, Caleb and Susanna Kelly; m. 22 Jun 178_ (CSM)

HERBERT

Herbert, Michael; b. 29 Sep 1694; d. Jul 1720 Rome; s/o William Herbert and Elizabeth Pattison (JM p. 317)

Harbut, John; <u>inv.</u>; [filed with ca 1699] (I&A 11b.11)

Herbert, William, Mr.; <u>inv.</u>; 22 Jul 1718; nok William & Francis Herbert (I 1.302); <u>inv.</u>; 1719; 20 Feb 1720; admx. Ellinor, w/o William Tomson (I 3225); <u>acct.</u>; 29 Feb 1720 (A 2.427) (SMAA p. 457); <u>acct.</u>; 21 Sep 1720; mentions f-i-l James Pattison; Luke, Franciss & Marke Herbert (dec'd) (A 3.224) (SMAA p. 459); <u>acct.</u>; 22 Apr 1722 (A 4.154)

Herbert, William; <u>inv.</u>; 27 Jun 1720; 27 Jun 1720; nok Vitus & Francis Harbert (I 4.58); <u>inv.</u>; 2 Feb 1720; 12 Feb 1721; mentions Mark & Francis Herbert (I 4.269)

Herbert, Vitus; <u>will</u>; 20 Feb 1725; 14 Mar 1725/6; sons William, Vitus, Joseph; wife Winifred; tracts *Fresh Pond Neck, New Ground* (MCW 5.224) [SMW PC1.304]; <u>inv.</u>; 28 Jun 1726; 22 Oct 1726; nok Marke & Francis Harbert; extx. Winifred Harbert (I 11.600)

Herbert, John; *Herbert's Invention*; 109 ac.; sur. 23 Nov 1724 (TLC p. 84); 11 Jan 1727 cert./pat. (COL)

Herbert (Harbutt), Winifred; widow; <u>will</u>; 6 Jun 1733; 16 Nov 1733; son Vitus, William [dec'd], Joseph; sister Susannah Thompson; bro. Richard Thompson (MCW 7.47) [SMW TA1.10]; inv.; 11 Dec 1733; 3 Jul 1734; nok Margaret & Edward Pye (I 18.342)

Herbert, Winifred; <u>acct.</u>; 28 Jun 1735; admx. Susannah Thompson (A 13.231)

Herbert, Mark; *Herbert's Grief*; 147 ac.; 2 parcels resur. 14 Jun 1736 (TLC p. 94); 15 Aug 1737 cert./pat. (COL)

Herbert, Mark; <u>will</u>; 14 Feb 1738; 19 Sep 1739; bros. Francis, Matthew; wife Elizabeth; tracts *Herbert's Greef, Nun's Cake, Shocks Park* (MCW 8.49) [SMW TA1.78]; <u>inv.</u>; 3 Oct 1739; 7 Mar 1739; nok Matthew Herbert, Barnaby Angell; adms./exs. Elisabeth & Francis Herbert (I 24.536); <u>acct.</u>; 22 Dec 1740; exs. Mathew Daft & wife Elisabeth (A 18.112)

Herbert, Matthew; *Herbert's Swamp*; 21 ac.; sur. 23 Apr 1744 (TLC p. 107); 9 Oct 1745 cert./pat. (COL)

Harbert (Herbert), Mathew; <u>will</u>; 16 Oct 1746; 20 Jan 1746; child. William, Mathew, Francis; wife Grace; tract *Herberts Swamp, Harbert's Rest* (MCW

9.94) [SMW TA1.184]; inv.; 20 Jan __; 2 Jun 1747; nok William & Elender
Herbert; admx./extx. Grace Herbert (I 35.107)

Herbert (Harbut), Vitus; will; 28 Feb 1749/50; 38 May 1750; sons Michael,
Mathew, William, Bennet; wife Elizabeth (MCW 10.82) [SMW TA1.265]; inv.; 10
Jun 1750; 20 Aug 1750; nok Francis & Michael Herbert; admx./extx.
Elisabeth Harbert (I 43.376); acct.; 10 Jun 1751; orphans Michel [age 8],
Matthew [age 6], William [age 4], Bennitt [age 2] (A 30.190)

Harbert, William; will; 18 Aug 1749; 3 Apr 1750; bros. Mathew, Francis; sister
Elisabeth Herbert (MCW 10.81) [SMW TA1.263]; acct.; 14 Apr 1752 (A 32.234)

Herbert; William; inv.; 10 Mar 1750; 17 Apr 1752; nok William & Jane
Heayden; adm./ex. James Thompson (I 48.298)

Herbert (Harbert), John; *Good Yielding*; 153 ac.; 10 Aug 1753 cert./pat. (COL)

Herbert, Frances; will; probate 24 Dec 1754; wife Elizabeth; son Frances; 9
child. Michael, William, Priscilla, Mary [others unnamed] (MCW 11.66) [SMW
TA1.310]; inv.; 1 Apr 1755; 15 Apr 1755; nok Cuthbert & Michael Herbert;
admx./extx. Elisabeth Herbert (I 60.217); inv.; 14 Feb 1756 (I 60.359); acct.; 14
Feb 1756 (A 39.62); acct.; 21 Aug 1757; orphans Ann, John, Cuthb., Elisabeth
Spaulding, Michael, William, Priscilla & Margaret [all of age], Francis; extx.
Elisabeth Herbert [age 15] (A 41.185); dist.; 21 Aug 1757; dist. to Michael,
William, Priscilla & Mary Herbert; mentions Francis Herbert; widow (BB
2.2.68)

Herbert [Harbert], Elizabeth; widow; will; 20 Apr 1759; 7 May 1759; sons
Francis, Cuthbert, Michael, William; daus. Priscilla, Mary, Jane [Jean]
Fenwick, Elizabeth Spalding (MCW 11.237) [SMW TA1.381]; dist.; 8 Oct 1761;
Francis, Cuthbert, Jane Fenwick, Elisabeth Spalding, Priscilla, Mary, Michael,
William (BB 3.109)

Hubert [Harbert], William; will; 29 Oct 1759; 7 Dec 1759; sisters Priscilla,
Mary; bros. Michael and Francis (MCW 11.253); acct.; 8 Oct 1761; extxs.
Priscilla & Mary Herbert (A 47.229); dist.; 8 Oct 1761 (BB 3.111)

Herbert, John; inv.; 30 Jun 1761; 26 Aug 1762; nok William Herbert, Peter
Moran; admx. John Herbert (I 79.268)

Herbert, Sarah; will; 20 Dec 1763; 21 Jan 1764; dau. Mary; sons William and
Samuel Brackingbury; sister Notly Lloyd (MCW 13.6) [SMW TA1.457]

Harbert, Cuthbert; inv.; 1 Oct 1765; 31 Oct 1765; nok Michael, Sr. & Mathew
Herbert; admx. Sarah Harbert (I 87.317)

Herbert, Mathew; inv.; 21 Sep 1767; admx. Henrietta Herbert (I 95.26); acct.; 20
Sep 1767 (A 57.339)

Herbert, William; m. 10 Jan 1768 Anne Milbourne (MM)

Herbert, Michael; planter; will; 30 Jul 1774; 20 Oct 1774; wife Barbara; bros.
William, Bennet; tract *Cross Manor* (MCW 16.23) [SMW TA1.682]; inv.; 1 Feb
1775; 10 Aug 1775; nok William Herbert; extx. Barbara Herbert (I 11.181);
acct.; 27 Jun 1723 (A 4.289)

Herbert, James; m. 2 Jan 1778 Mary Marshall (BRU 2.536)

HICKS

Hicks, John; <u>will</u>; 30 May 1749; 20 Aug 1753; sons William, George; dau.
Mary, w/o William Henner of Cherry Point, VA; mentions William
Thompson, wife Ellinor, d/o James Pattinson & previously w/o Matthew
Harbert; wife unnamed; tracts *St. Johns, St. Barbarys, Church Hill* (MCW
10.277) [SMW TA1.445]; <u>inv.</u>; 21 Aug 1753; 24 Aug 1753; nok George Hicks,
minors; adm.ex. William Hicks (I 55.27); <u>inv.</u>; 31 Aug 1753; 3 Sep 1753; nok
George Hicks (I 57.59); <u>acct.</u>; 3 Sep 1753 (A 35.122)

HIGGS

Higgs, John; *Wednesday's Project*; 98 ac.; sur. 26 Feb 1728 for John Hickes
(TLC p. 90); 13 Jun 1734 cert./pat. (COL)
    Higgs Purchase; 49 ac.; sur. 15 Dec 1742 (TLC p. 105); 12 Oct 1744 cert./pat.
(COL)
Higgs, Samuel; <u>inv.</u>; 6 Dec 1758; nok John & Zacharias Higgs; admx./extx.
Elisabeth Higgs (I 66.4); <u>acct.</u>; 7 Aug 1759; orphans Susanna, Eleanor,
Elisabeth, Mary [all at age], Samuel [age 16], Sarah [age 13], Jonathon [age
12], Mary Ann [age 10], Cloe [age 7]; admx. Elisabeth (A 43.271)

HILL

Hill, Rich'd; unnamed; 50 ac.; sur. 14 Dec 1641; resur. into *Medley* or *Medleys
Neck*; New Town Hundred (RR p. 26)
Hill, Francis; 19 Sep 1696; 10 Jul 1697; dau. Eliza. Hopewell; her child. Hugh,
Eliza, Susannah (MCW 2.126)
Hill, Clement, Sr.; <u>will</u>; 17 Nov 1702; 26 Apr 1708; nephew Clement Hill;
mentions Luke, Jr. & John Gardiner, sons of Richard Gardiner; tracts *Hill's
Camp* in BA Co., *Friends's Hope* in PG Co. (MCW 3.107) [SMW PC1.155]; <u>inv.</u>;
17 Jul 1708 (I&A 28.254); <u>acct.</u> 1 Aug 1710 (I&A 31.365) (SMAA p. 201)
Hill, Giles; <u>inv.</u>; 3 Dec 1702 (I&A 1.649); <u>acct.</u>; 13 Oct 1703 (I&A 3.222) (SMAA p.
118)
Hill, Clem't & Wm. Heard; *Hazzard*; 257 ac.; sur. 20 Mar 1710; pat. 26 Apr
1717 (TLC p.74)
Hill, Simon; <u>acct.</u>; 14 Mar 1725 (A 7.278)
Hill, John; <u>will</u>; 1 Aug 1734; 23 Jan 1734; sons Clement, John, Bennitt, Leonard
and James Notlen Hill; dau. Susanna; wife Anne; tract *The Hope* (MCW 7.120)
[SMW PC1.43]; <u>inv.</u>; 11 Feb 1734; nok John Whill (sic), Clement Hill;
admx./extx. Ann Hill (I 20.465); <u>acct.</u>; 3 Nov 1736 (A 15.223)
Hill, Jane (Jean); <u>inv.</u>; 31 Mar 1761; 19 Feb 1763; nok James Neall, John
Oneall; extx. Elisabeth Hill (I 80.164); <u>acct.</u>; 15 Jun 1767; mentions Elisabeth
Hill (A 57.247); <u>dist.</u>; 15 Jun 1767 (BB 5.35)
Hill, Clement; <u>inv.</u>; 2 Dec 1771; 2 Jul 1772; nok Henry & Henry Hill, Jr.; admx.
Ann Hill (I 109.356); <u>acct.</u>; 26 Jul 1774; admx. Anne, w/o John Lucas (A 71.321);
<u>dist.</u>; 26 Jul 1774 (BB 6.344)

Hill, ___; m. 2 Sep 1778 Elizab. Miller (BRU 2.536)
Hill, Richard; m. 7 Jan 1783 Sarah King (BRU 2.536)

HILTON

Hilton, John; will; 26 Nov 1697; 21 Jan 1705; wife Jane; sons John and Francis (MCW 3.72) [SMW PC1.139]; inv.; 23 Jan 1705 (I&A 25.172); acct.; 4 Mar 1706; widow Jane Hilton (I&A 26.157); acct.; 5 Feb 1717 (I&A 39c.26) (SMAA p. 312)
Hilton, John; inv.; 25 Jul 1734; nok Abell Simons, Francis Hilton; admx./extx. Ann Hilton (I 18.344); acct.; 24 Jan 1735; orphans Frances, Mathew & Mary Hilton; admx. Anne, w/o Robert Alexander (A 14.181)
Hilton, Andrew; inv.; 16 Aug 1746; 5 Mar 1746; nok Andrew & Thomas Hilton; adm./ex. John Hilton (I 34.217); acct.; 21 Aug 1749; child. John, Susanna, Andrew & Thomas [all of age], James [age 18], William [age 18], Richard [age 15], Elisabeth [age 13], Jonathon [age 13], Juda [age 10], Leonard [age 7], Samuel [age 4]; adm. John Hillton (A 27.100)
Hilton, Francis; will; probate 1 Jan 1759; sons John, Francis, Stephen, William, Thomas; dau. Sarah; other unnamed child.; tracts *William and Joseph, Hittons Purchase, Carter Jane* (MCW 11.226) [SMW TA1.374]; inv.; 28 Mar 1759; 31 Mar 1759; nok John & Stephen Hilton; adms./exs. Sarah & William Hilton (I 67.94); acct.; 24 Nov 1760; orphans John, Francis, William, Stephen, Thomas, Mary Bruden, Ann Dillen, Elisabeth Bryan, Milburn, Hagar, Sarah (A 46.155)
Hilton, Stephen and Diana; son John [b. 11 Jan 1770] (SA p. 190)
Hilton, Thomas and Anne; dau. Elizabeth, bapt. 30 Sep 1781 (SA p. 30)

HINTON

Hinton, Alice; service by 1681; wife of Thomas (SK 12.393)
Hinton, Thomas; *Ambersly*; 65 ac.; sur. 11 Jun 1681; 1707 poss. Widow Mason; incl. in *Clarks Range*; Poplar Hill Hundred (RR p. 25) (TLC p. 24)

HODGKINS

Hodgkinson, Charles; *Draton*; 57 ac.; sur. 26 Aug 1710; (TLC p. 67); 10 Aug 1713 cert./pat. (COL)
Hodgkins, Charles; *Middle Ground*; 102 ac.; 1 Mar 1724 cert./pat. (COL)
Hodgkins, Charles; planter; will; 5 Feb 1729; 5 Nov 1730; sons Charles & Daniel; wife Jane; mentions John, s/o John Rigby; tract *Middle Ground* (MCW 6.171) [SMW PC1.327]; inv.; 27 Jan 1730; 16 Feb 1730; nok Daniel Hodgkin; exs. Jane & Charles Hodgkin (I 16.81)
Hodgekin [Hodgkin], Charles; planter; will; 29 Oct 1749; 9 Nov 1749; wife Mary (MCW 10.66) [SMW TA1.224]
Hodgkins, Bennett; m. 20 Apr 1771 Susan Gatten (MM)

HOGAN

Hogan, Thos. & Geo. Asqeeth; *Newcastle*; 100 ac.; sur. 9 Jun 1670; 1707 poss.
Edward Cole; New Town Hundred (RR p. 35) (TLC p. 34)

Hogan, William; inv.; 20 Apr 1732; 29 May 1732; nok John Price, Philip Evins
(I 16.441)

Hogan, Patrick; m. 9 Jul 1775 Eliz. Engleton (MM)

HOLDSWORTH

Holdsworth, Joshua; age ca 61; 13 Oct 1714; tract *Norwood* (CCR p. 29)

Holdsworth (Holsworth, Houldsworth), Joshua; inv.; 4 Mar 1716 (I&A 38b.83);
inv.; 7 Jul 1717 (I&A 37b.131); 19 Aug 1718 (I 1.301); acct.; 28 Apr 1719;
mentions Jeremiah Swann, bro. of Susanna Attaway (A 1.416) (SMAA p. 402)

HOLLAND

Holland, William; inv.; 30 Nov 1719; 9 Dec 1719; nok William Holland; adm.
Thomas Holland (I 3.183); acct.; 3 Aug 1720 (A 3.68)

Holland, William; inv.; 11 Jun 1733; nok John Holland, Mary Duffe;
admx./extx. Mary Horn (I 17.160); acct.; 17 Aug 1735; mentions William &
John Holland; admx. Mary, w/o William Mackgee (A 13.315)

Holland, Charles; inv.; 24 Apr 1750; 5 Jun 1750; nok Andrew & John
Williames; admx.extx. Ann Holland (I 43.267)

Holland, John; will; 28 Jul 1754; 9 Sep 1754; sons James, John Hendley,
William, Zachariah and Edward Kindriet Holland; dau. Mary (MCW 11.47)
[SMW TA1.324]; inv.; 3 Feb 1755; nok James & Joseph Holland (I 60.105); dist.;
25 Oct 1756; John, William, Mary, Zachariah & Edward Holland (BB 2.32);
acct.; 18 Sep 1758; orphans James [at age], John [age 20], William [age 15],
Mary [age 13], Zachild. [age 10] (A 42.105); dist.; 18 Sep 1758 (BB 2.108)

HOLLIDAY

Holliday, John; service by 1677 (SK 15.401)

Hollyday, Leonard; of PG Co.; *Indian Creek*; 2,490 ac.; 10 Sep 1716 cert./pat.
(COL)

HOLT

Holt, David; inv.; 28 Aug 1679; admx. Elisabeth Holt (I&A 6.383)

Holt, John, Mr.; inv.; 23 Dec 1751; 4 Mar 1752; nok John, Sr. & Aaron Haskins;
admx./extx. Lucretia Hoult (I 48.286)

HOLTON

Holton, William; inv.; 7 Jun 1769; nok Robert & William Holton; admx.
Elisabeth Holton (I 102.242); inv.; 11 Dec 1769; 6 Mar 1770; nok William &
Ellinor Holton, Dennis Byrn; adm. Robert Holton (I 103.228); acct.; 1 Oct 1771
(A 66.73); dist.; 1 Oct 1771 (BB 6.84)

Holton, Elisabeth; acct.; 1 Oct 1771; mentions William Holton; adm. Robert
    Holton (A 66.72); dist.; 1 Oct 1771; adm. Robert Holton (BB 6.84)
Holton, William and Elizabeth Craghill; m. 31 Dec 1779 (SA p. 58)

HOMAN
Homan, Harbert; service by 1671 (SK 16.123)
Homan, Herbert; acct.; [file with 1679] (I&A 6.237)
Homan, Dorothy; of Poplar Hill Hundred; will; 22 July 1683; 4 Mar 1683/4;
    mentions Anne, w/o Thomas Renalds and Elizabeth, w/o John Cambell [SMW
    PC1.47]; 1676 will of Herbert Homan of CH Co. names wife Dorothy (MCW
    1.185); acct.; 10 Aug 1686 (I&A 9.144)
Horman, Thomas; acct.; 5 Aug 1720 (A 3.67)

HOOKE
Hooke, William; age ca 47 1730 (MD p. 95)
Hooke, William; will; 20 Jan 1732/3; 2 Apr 1733; wife Susanna (MCW 7.11)
    [SMW PC1.361]; inv.; 4 May 1733; 8 Aug 1733; nok Margarett Kevellin;
    admx./extx. Susanna Hooke (I 17.332); acct.; 24 Aug 1734 (A 12.468)

HOOPER
Hooper, Henry, Dr.; St. Inigoes; will; 27 Jan 1649; 6 Feb 1649 (MCW 1.4)
Hooper, Robert; wife Ann; 1 Sep 1665 (AM LVII.437)
Hooper, Robertt; acct.; 28 May 1675; orphan Mary and ?others; admx. relict,
    w/o Thomas Doxey (I&A 1.335)
Hooper, Mary; age ca 60; 26 Aug 1723 (CCR p. 56)

HOPEWELL
Hopewell, Hugh; *Hoggpen Neck*; 150 ac.; sur. 6 Oct 1650; 1707 Wm. Jessop;
    Harvey Hundred (RR p. 55) (TLC p. 53)
    Persimmon Branch; 180 ac.; 11 Sep 1766 cert./pat. (COL)
Hopewell, Francis; *Hopewells Delight*; 200 ac.; sur. 3 Mar 1670; 1707 poss.
    Rich'd Shirly, m. widow of John Wiseman; Harvey Hundred (RR p. 56) (TLC p.
    54)
    Force Putt; 100 ac.; sur. 10 Jan 1681; 1707 poss. Rich'd Shirly; Harvey
    Hundred (RR p. 57) (TLC p. 54)
Hopewell, Hugh; acct.; 1 Apr 1709; adm. Francis Hopewell (I&A 29.175) (SMAA p.
    177)
Hopewell, Richard; s/o Richard Hopewell, Gent.; will; oral; 25 Nov 1732; bros.
    Joseph, John; sisters Ann, Elizabeth, Mary; ex. father (MCW 6.249) [SMW
    PC1.354]
Hopewell, Richard; gent.; *Aisquith's Defence*; 122 ac.; sur. 12 Nov 1730 (TLC p.
    87); 17 Mar 1733 cert./pat. (COL)

Hopewell's Chance; 170 ac.; sur. 11 Nov 1730 (TLC p. 87); 17 Mar 1733 cert./pat. (COL)

Hopewell, Joseph; will; 21 Sep 1737; 12 Oct 1737; cousins Hugh and John Hopewell; bro. Richard; mentions Ann, sister of Thomas Aisquith] (MCW 7.230) [SMW TA1.69]; inv.; 13 Jan 1738; 5 Feb 1738; nok Richard & Joseph Hopewell (I 23.535); acct.; 4 Sep 1740 (A 18.61)

Hopewell, Francis; will; 9 Apr 1739; 4 Jul 1739; dau. Susanna; tract *Lampton's [Sampton's] Pleasure* (MCW 8.40) [SMW TA1.77]; inv.; 3 Oct 1739; 8 Dec 1739; nok Samuel Leigh, Richard Hopewell; admx./extx. Mary Hopewell (I 24.416); acct.; 15 Apr 1741 (A 18.169)

Hopewell, Richard; will; 15 Nov 1741; 6 Jan 1745; child. Joseph, Hugh, John, Thomas Francis, Anna Mary [or Anne & Mary], Susanna, Elizabeth; [wife Elizabeth]; tracts *Bloomsbury* in TA Co., *Hogpen Neck, Joseph Hopewell's Defense, The Irish Discovery* TA Co., *Aisquith Defense, The Inclosures, Edloe's Lot* (MCW 9.53) [SMW TA1.177]; inv.; 2 Aug 1746; nok Joseph & Hugh Hopewell; [Col.]; admx./extx. Elisabeth Hopewell (I 33.55, 58)

Hopewell, Hugh; will; 14 Aug 1746; 13 Oct 1746; mother Elizabeth Hopewell; bros. Joseph & John; tracts *Hogpen Neck, Booomsberry* TA Co. (MCW 9.86) [SMW TA1.209]; inv.; Oct 1746; 3 Mar 1746; nok John & Ann Hopewell; adm./ex. Joseph Hopewell (I 34.216); acct.; 28 Aug 1758 (A 42.91)

Hopewell, Hugh, Jr.; *Hopewell's Adventure Addition*; 52 ac.; orignial *The Ripe*; part escheated resur. 30 Sep 1746 (TLC p. 111); 18 Mar 1747 cert./pat. (COL)

Hopewell, Thomas Francis; inv.; 11 Aug 1747; 14 Jan 1747; nok John & Ann Hopewell; adm./ex. Joseph Hopewell (I 35.464); acct.; 25 Aug 1748; mentions Joseph, Hugh, John, Elisabeth (Sr.), Ann, Elisabeth (Jr.), Mary, Susanna (A 25.178)

Hopewell, Elizabeth; will; [recorded with 1752]; widow; daus. Ann, Elizabeth; son Joseph (MCW 10.213) [SMW TA1.299]

Hopewell, Joseph and Dorcas; child. Richard [b. 26 Feb 1753], George [b. 28 Jan 1757], John [b. 3 Jun 1763] (SA p. 5)

Hopewell, Bennet and Teresia; son Richard [b. 23 May 1759] (SA p. 22)

Hopewell, John; will; 7 Aug 1761; 20 Oct 1761; wife Eleanor; Richard, George, Mary the ch/o Joseph Hopewell; Hannah d/o Phillip Clark, Jr.; Amey, d/o Clark Read; James, s/o Hugh Hopewell (MCW 12.99); inv.; 2 Feb 1762; nok Joseph Hopewell, Ann Clarke; extx. Eleanor Hopewell (I 77.67, 69); acct.; 18 May 1763 (A 49.613)

Hopewell, Richard and Eleanor; dau. Mary [b. 12 Jan 1763] (SA p. 192)

Hopewell, Bennet and Mary Ann; child. Jane [b. 22 Dec 1763], Joshua [b. 23 May 1765], Bennet [b. 4 Oct 1766], Francis [b. 20 Feb 1770], Mary Ann [b. 1 May 1772] (SA p. 22)

Hopewell, Hugh; of *Sackawst* in Patuxant; planter age ca 30 in 1765 (MD p. 96)

Hopewell, Ellen; will; 19 Feb 1774; 26 Apr 1774; son Samuel Jenifer; g-son Daniel of St. Thomas Jenifer; g-dau. Ellin (MCW 15.130) [SMW TA1.699]

HOPKINS

Hopkins, John; service by 1669 (SK 12.386)

Hopkins, John; *Fair Fountain Delight*; 100 ac.; sur. 3 Mar 1670 ; 1707 poss. Dan. Laurance; New Town Hundred (RR p. 35) (TLC p. 34)

Hopkins, Luke; inv.; 25 Jun 1746; 6 Aug 1746; nok William & Thomas Mollahon; admx./extx. Elisabeth Hopkins (I 33.309); acct.; 3 Mar 1746; admx. Elisabeth, w/o Notley Jordan (A 23.194)

Hopkins, Mark; inv.; 8 Jun 1754; 17 Jun 1754; nok William & Eleazabeth Steavens (I 58.202)

Hopkins, Peter; age ca 43 (AM LXIX.121)

Hopkins, Thomas; will; 22 Mar 1708/9; 18 Apr 1709; dau. Margaret; wife Ann; tracts *Cowridge, Wethertons* [*Netherton's Beginning*], *Clocker's Marsh* (MCW 3.138) [SMW PC1.158; typo says 188]; inv.; 24 Jun 1709; 14 Jul 1709 (I&A 30.1); acct.; 13 Jul 1710; extx. Anne, w/o Thomas Richardson (I&A 31.368) (SMAA p. 203)

HORN

Horn, Edward; *Cole Harbour*; 150 ac.; sur. 26 Sep 1664; 1707 poss. 50 ac. each Edwd., John and Hen. Horn; St. Mary's Hundred (RR p. 3) (TLC p. 4)

Horn, Winefride; *Maidens Lott*; 100 ac.; sur. 5 Apr 1682; 1707 poss. John Wheatly; St. Mary's Hundred (RR p. 9) (TLC p. 10); 5 Apr 1682; adj. Edward Horne cert./pat. (COL)

Horne, Edward; acct.; [filed with 1692-3]; legatee John Horne (I&A 10.330)

Horn (Horne), Hennry; inv.; 26 Jun 1720; 4 Aug 1720; nok John Horn, Elisabeth Aisquith; admx. Sarah Horne (I 3.344); acct.; 21 Jan 1720 (A 3.236) (SMAA p. 422)

Horn, Henry; will; 20 Mar 1731; 7 Apr 1732; sister Francis Forrest; wife Patients (MCW 6.219) [SMW PC1.350]; inv.; 23 May 1732; 16 Aug 1732; nok Sarah Lee; admx./extx. Patience Horn (I 16.560); acct.; 14 Oct 1734; extx. Patience (dec'd), w/o Stephen Chelton (A 12.547)

Horne (Horn), Francis (Franck); will; 14 Feb 1732; 31 Mar 1733; sisters Winnifred, Mary; "My Coo Hana Horne" [Johanna Horne] (MCW 7.11) [SMW TA1.18]; inv.; 23 Aug __ ; 11 Jun 1733; nok John & Mary Horn; admx./extx. Winnifret Horn (I 17.158); acct.; 5 Aug 1734 (A 12.459)

Horne, Edward; will; 12 Jul 1746; 13 Nov 1749; son Edward, daus. Frances Griffen, Ann, Elizabeth; wife Mary; tract *Harford Folly* (MCW 10.66) [SMW TA1.223]; inv.; 15 Nov 1749; 9 May 1750; nok Edward Horn; George Slacum; admx./extx. Mary Horn (I 42.227); acct.; 11 Feb 1750; mentions Anne [dec'd] (A 29.201)

Horn, John; inv.; 15 Oct 1747; 9 Dec 1747; nok John Williams, Charles Jarboe; adm./ex. John Horn (I 35.374); acct.; 29 Aug 1748 (A 25.179)

Horn (Horne), John; inv.; 30 Aug 1750; 6 Dec 1750; nok Susannah Clake; Pissillar Horn; admx./extx. Ann Horn (I 44.243); acct.; 4 Mar 1752; orphans

Elisabeth [age 5], Ann [age 2]; admx. Ann, w/o James Daffin (A 32.107); <u>dist.</u>; 4
Mar 1752; child. Eliz'a & Ann Horne (BB 1.29)

Horn, Mary; widow; <u>will</u>; 3 Apr 1758; 9 Oct 1758; g-child. [Henry Milburne] &
Elizabeth, John and Mary, ch/o Lewis Griffin and dau. Francis [Frances
Slavin, d/o Edward Horn]; Richard, d/o dau. Elizabeth Melburn; nephew
William Aisquith; son Edward Horn & his dau. Ann (MCW 11.217) [SMW
TA1.372]

Horn, Edward; <u>will</u>; 9 Dec 1760; 4 Mar 1761; daus. Mary, Ann, Elizabeth; wife
Steasey; tract *Halfhead Folly* (MCW 12.37) [SMW TA1.409]; <u>inv.</u>; 1 Jun 1761; 5
May 1761; nok Mary Milburn, Susanna Clarke; exs. William Norris & wife
Statia (Annastatia] (I 74.284); <u>acct.</u>; 7 Jun 1763 (A 49.633)

HORRELL

Horrell, Christopher; <u>will</u>; 7 Jun 1703; 12 Aug 1703; sons Christopher, Giles;
daus. Frances, Ann; s-i-l Joseph Stratford; wife Eliza (MCW 3.19)

Horrell, John; *Horrell's Meadow*; 10 ac.; 23 Oct 1755 cert./pat. (COL)

Horrell, Isaac; <u>inv.</u>; 30 Jan 1769; 9 Nov 1769; nok John & Giles Horrell (I
102.182); <u>acct.</u>; 24 Nov 1769 (A 62.163); <u>dist.</u>; 24 Nov 1769 (BB 5.346)

Horril (Horrel), John Jr.; <u>will</u>; 9 Mar 1776; 15 Dec 1776; wife Monica (MCW
16.174)

HOSKINS

Hoskins (Haskins), William; planter; <u>will</u>; 25 Oct 1722; 10 Nov 1722; sons
William, John; daus. Sarah, Elizabeth; d-i-l Grace Knott; [d-i-l Ann Taylor];
wife Ann (MCW 5.122) [SMW PC1.270]

Hoskins, George; <u>acct.</u>; 10 Jun 1725; admx. Anne Hoskins (A 7.401)

Hoskins, John; <u>acct.</u>; 22 Sep 1703; extx. Rose, w/o Daniell Henly (I&A 24.172)
(SMAA p. 126)

Hoskins, William; <u>inv.</u>; 28 Jan 1722; nok John & George Hoskins (I 8.114); <u>acct.</u>;
8 Aug 1723; extx. Ann Hoskins (A 5.202)

HOULT

Hoult, John; <u>will</u>; 11 Sep 1751; 1 Nov 1751; child. Raphael, John, Susanna,
Mary, Sarah, Robert, Matthew; wife Lucretia (MCW 10.189) [SMW TA1.272];
<u>acct.</u>; 18 May 1753; orphans Ralph [age 18], Susannah [age 15], Mary [age
13], John [age 12], Sarah [age 8], Robert [age 5], Matthew [age 3], Aaron [age
1]; extx. Lucretia Hoult (A 34.151); <u>dist.</u>; 18 May 1753; extx. Lucretia; child.
Ralph [age 19 next Jan], Susannah [age 16 next Jan], Mary [age 14 next 5
Feb], John [age 13 next 15 Mar], Sarah [age 9 next Apr], Matthew [age 4 next
Feb], Aaron [age 2 next Sep] (BB 1.78)

HOWARD

Howard, John; age ca 22; 6 Feb 1649 (AM X.11)

Howard, Tho.; *Howards Mount*; 200 ac.; sur. 20 Dec 1653; 1707 poss. Peter
   Howard; New Town Hundred (RR p. 30) (TLC p. 29)
Howard, Edward; <u>inv.</u>; 14 Sep 1716; nok Will. & Rodel Howard (I&A 38a.1);
   <u>acct.</u>; 7 Aug 1718; admx. Mary, w/o William Shircliff (A 1.199) (SMAA p. 352)
Howard, Mary, age ca 50; d/o Thomas Melton; 20 Sep 1718; tract *St. Lawrence*
   (CCR p. 40)
Howard, William, Capt.; <u>inv.</u>; Mar 1720; 8 Jun 1721; admx. Mrs. Mary Howard
   (I 5.53)
Howard, Nathaniel; Capt.; <u>acct.</u>; 23 Mar 1721; admx. Mrs. Mary Howard (A
   4.189); <u>acct.</u>; 1 Mar 1722 (A 6.106)
Howard, William, Sr.; planter; <u>will</u>; 16 Aug 1729; 24 Nov 1730; sons William,
   Thomas, Peter, James, John; daus. Rachel Ford, Anne Dartt [Darth (?)],
   Margaret Shanks; wife Mary; tract *Twittnam* (MCW 6.176) [SMW PC1.328]; <u>inv.</u>;
   11 Jan 1730; 8 Mar 1730; nok Thomas Harrard, John Howard; admx./extx.
   Mary Howard (I 16.188); <u>acct.</u>; 9 Dec 1731 (A 11.320)
Howard, Ignatius, Mr.; <u>inv.</u>; 4 Jun 1752; 3 Oct 1752; nok William Howard,
   Elesabeth Willson; admx./exs. William Bradburn & wife Elisabeth (I 51.73);
   <u>acct.</u>; 2 Oct 1753; orphan George [age 14] (A 36.20); <u>dist.</u>; 2 Oct 1753; 1 child
   George Howard [age 15 next 1 Aug] (BB 1-89]
Howard, William; <u>will</u>; 28 Apr 1753; 15 Jun 1753; wife Sarrah; son Clement; s-
   i-l Hugh Wilson; dau. Sarra Newton; g-dau. Sarra Howard (MCW 10.269) [SMW
   TA1.300]
Howard, Joshua and Mary; child. Austin [b. 8 Oct 1755], Henrietta [b. 8 Oct
   1753] (SA p. 38)
Howard, Henry and Mary; child. Mary Ann [b. 24 Jul 1758], Charles [b. 24 Nov
   1762], Joseph [b. 3 May 1764] (SA p. 11, 45)
Howard, George and Ann [Annastatia Spink]; child. Sarah [b. 19 Jan 1761],
   Ignatius [b. 2 Mar 1765], Francis [b. 6 Mar 1767], Elizabeth, b. 14 Jun 1772
   (SA p. 15, 22, 49)
Howard, Thomas; <u>will</u>; 24 Dec 1773; 2 Mar 1774; sons Henry, Peter, Joshua,
   Martin Henry; daus. Mary Norris [Nevis], Ann; g-dau. Anastasia Payne; tract
   Gilmotts Hills (MCW 15.149) [SMW TA1.710]
Howard, Henry; <u>inv.</u>; 24 Aug 1775; 16 Sep 1776; nok Peter Howard, Margaret
   Nomes, Mary Wimsatt; admx. Mary Howard (I 125.292)
Howard, William; m. 4 Jul 1776 Eleanora Thompson (MM)

HOWELL
Howell, Owen; immigrated by 1670 (SK 12.551)
Howell, Evan; <u>inv.</u>; 2 Oct 1719; admx. ____ Howell (I 4.40); <u>acct.</u>; 26 Aug 1720;
   admn. Franciss Howell (f) (A 3.230); <u>acct.</u>; 26 Aug 1720 (SMAA p. 430)
Howell, Henry; <u>acct.</u>; 19 May 1740; exs. James Daniel (Daniell) & wife
   Elisabeth, Henry Howell (A 18.200)

HUDSON

Hudson, Edward; age ca 25; 23 Jun 1649 (AM X.17)

Hudson, Jeffery; 18 Feb 1677; 8 Apr 1678 (MCW 1.202) [SMW PC1.28]; inv.; 20 Apr 1678 (I&A 5.223); acct.; 29 Jul 1679 (I&A 6.233)

Hudson, Robert; acct.; 3 Aug 1687 (I&A 9.387)

Huttson, John; inv.; 4 Apr 1737 (I 22.208)

HULSE

Hull, Henry; will; 6 Nov 1675; 11 Dec 1675; bro. Humphry in Dorchester; mentions Eliza:, wife of William Hatton of St. George's (MCW 1.112); acct.; 21 May 1677; extx. Rebecca Addison, relict of Thomas Dent (I&A 4.74)

Hulse, Merwell; *Burrs Guilt*; 100 ac.; sur. 23 Mar 1680; 1707 poss. Philip Lock; Resurrection Hundred (RR p. 63) (TLC p. 61)

Hulston; 100 ac.; sur. 26 Mar 1680; 1707 poss. Giles Newman; Resurrection Hundred (RR p. 63) (TLC p. 61)

Hulse (Hules), William; will; 19 Dec 1725; 2 Mar 1725/6; sons James, William; wife Mary; tract *Hulse's Lott* (MCW 5.213) [SMW PC1.304]; inv.; 1726; 10 Jun 1726; nok James Hulse, Mary Lock; extx. Mary Hulse (I 11.375); acct.; 7 Aug 1728; extx. Mary, w/o Richard Shore (A 9.60)

Hulls [Hulse], Meverell; will; 19 Nov 1743; 27 Dec 1743; wife Elizabeth; her cousin Edward, s/o Luke Barber; sisters Rebecca, Sarah; bros. John and Luke Barber; dau. Elizabeth (MCW 8.241) [SMW TA1.138]; inv.; 28 Feb 1743; 7 Mar 1743; nok John Moran, Edward Barber; admx./extx. Elisabeth Hulls (I 28.447); acct.; 6 Nov 1745 (A 22.69)

Hulse, James; 5 Mar 1751; 7 Feb 1752; son Luke; wife Catherine; tract *Westham* [SMW TA1.301]

Hulls, Luke Barber; will; 5 Nov 1762; 18 Dec 1762; bro. John; cousins Elizabeth Green, Cornelius Barber; tract *Westham* (MCW 12.177) [SMW TA1.431]

HUNT

Hunt, Thomas; probate 10 Jan 1675 (MCW 1.114)

Hunt, Robert; will; 13 Apr 1676; 20 Apr 1676 (MCW 1.169) [SMW PC1.27]

Hunt, Thomas; gent.; will; 10 Dec 1733; 24 Feb 1735; mentions George Vaudery and sister Joanna; tract *Plimouth* (MCW 7.162) [SMW TA1.53]; inv.; 24 May 1736; 8 Jun 1737 (I 22.319); acct.; 4 Oct 1737 (A 14.523)

HUNTSMAN

Huntsman, Daniell; inv.; 30 Mar 1706 (I&A 25.172); acct.; 21 Apr 1707; admx. Katherine, w/o George Banks (I&A 26.303)

Huntsman, David (sic); admx. Catharine, wife of George Banks; 21 Apr 1707 (SMAA p. 146)

HUSCULAH

Husculaw [Husculow], Dennis; [planter]; <u>will</u>; 27 Nov 1687; 18 Mar 1687/8; wife Elizabeth; daus. Ann Willer, Jane (minor), son William; tracts *St. Ann's, St. Vincent's*; [tract *Bone*] (MCW 2.26) [SMW PC1.66]

Huscolah (Husculah), William; <u>will</u>; 29 Dec 1693; 29 May 1695; sister Jane, w/o John Nalle [Mall, Malle]; father Dennis Husculah [dec'd] (MCW 2.94) [SMW PC1.95]; <u>acct.</u>; [filed with 1696] (I&A 14.6)

HUTCHENS

Hutchings, Richard; <u>inv.</u>; [filed with 1679] (I&A 6.525)

Hutchings (Hutchins), William; <u>will</u>; 29 Nov 1708; 5 Mar 1708; sons Robert, John, Francis, William; wife Gallion [Gillion]; daus. Sarah, Katharine; g-son Robert Hutchins, Jr.; tract *Burditt's Neck* (MCW 3.134) [SMW PC1.153]; <u>inv.</u>; 8 Apr 1709 (I&A 30.292); <u>acct.</u>; 9 Sep 1710; one ex. was Robert Hutchins (SMAA p. 197) (I&A 31.359); <u>acct.</u>; 2 Jun 1716 (I&A 38b.4) (SMAA p. 294); <u>acct.</u>; 24 Sep 1719; unnamed widow; mentions Robert Hutchens (A 2.274) (SMAA p. 375)

Hutchens, William; <u>acct.</u>; 3 Jun 1725; admx. Sarah Hutchens (A 6.438)

Hutchings (Hutchins), Frances; <u>will</u>; 1 Jun 1719; 25 Sep 1719; sister Katharine Hassell [Hassett]; bros. Robert, William [& John] (MCW 4.216) [SMW PC1.251]; <u>inv.</u>; 27 Oct 1719; 4 Nov 1719; adm. Robert Hutchins (I 3.62); <u>acct.</u>; 8 Jun 1720 (A 2.503) (SMAA p. 450)

Hutchins (Hutchens), Robert; <u>will</u>; 14 Dec 1732; 20 May 1734; sons Aquily [Aquila], Francis, Robert; dau. Catherine; wife Frances; bro. John & his son Francis; tract *Resurrection Manner* (MCW 7.94) [SMW TA1.28]; Hutchens, <u>inv.</u>; 2 Jul 1734; 16 Sep 1734; nok Aquila Hutchins, James Wilkinson; admx./extx. Frances Hutchins (I 19.56); <u>acct.</u>; 16 Dec 1735; axtx. Frances, w/o John Abell (A 14.175)

Hutchings (Hutchens), Aquila; <u>inv.</u>; 16 Mar 1754; 1 Apr 1754; nok John & Francis Hutchings; admx./extx. Elisabeth Hutchings (I 58.69); <u>acct.</u>; 6 Oct 1755; orphans John [age 20], Sarah & Elisabeth [both of age], Robert [age 14], Frances [age 13], Mary [age 11], William [age 9], Aquillar [age 7], Thomas [age 5], Cathrine [age 3]; admx. Elisabeth Hutchings (A 38.192); <u>dist.</u>; 29 Jan 1756 (BB 2.8)

Hutchens, Robert and Ann; son Jane (sic) [b. 30 May 1763] (SA p. 5)

Hutchens, Francis and Susanna; child. Frances [b. 10 Oct 1763], Alathea [b. 16 Dec 1765] (SA p. 42)

Hutchens, John and Rachel; son John [b. 27 Jan 1777] (SA p. 29)

Hutchins, Bennett and Jane Stone; m. 7 Nov 1779 (SA p. 57)

HYDE

Hyde, Henry; 29 Oct 1675; 6 Nov 1675; daus. Ann, Margaret; wife Frances; son Robert; John and Joan Wachope, g-parents of Ann; bro. Thomas Hatton (MCW 1.110); <u>acct.</u>; 12 Oct 1677 (I&A 4.409)

Hide, Thomas; will; 9 Feb 1697; 13 Mar 1697; daus. Mary Killow, Eliza. Johnson; wife Hannah (MCW 2.141)

INGE

Inge, Vincent and Ann; dau. Mary [b. 29 Jun 1756] (SA p. 38)

Inge, Vincent and Susanna; child. Vincent [b. 31 Oct 1758], John [b. 29 Oct 1761], Ambrose [b. 23 Oct 1765], Ann Maria [b. 2 Apr 1768] (SA p. 13, 47, 48)

INNIS

Innis, Tho.; *Innis Choyce*; 100 ac.; sur. 21 Oct 1659; 1707 poss. by Caecilius Buttler, m. d/o Robt. Carvile; St. Mary's Hundred (RR p. 3) (TLC p. 3)

Innis Reserve; 25 ac.; sur. 9 Sep 1675; assgn. Rob. Carville; 1707 poss. Cecill Buttler by marrying d/o Rob. Carville; St. Mary's Hundred (RR p. 6) (TLC p. 7)

Innes, Thomas; wife Ann; convey *Innes Choice* on n. side of St. Inegoes Creek; 1676 (AM LXVI.189)

Innes [Junes], William; will; 4 Jan 1725; 3 Jul 1726 sons John, George; wife Elizabeth; tract *George's Content* (MCW 5.230) [SMW PC1.308]; inv.; 25 Aug 1726; 3 Nov 1726; nok Clemment Chenell, John Cole; extx. Elisabeth Innes (I 11.606); acct.; 12 Jul 1727; extx. Elisabeth, w/o Benjamin Woodward (A 8.280)

Innis, John; acct.; 9 Sep 1755 (A 38.177)

Innis, Thomas; inv.; 2 May 1757; nok Thomas Cune, William Innis (I 63.398) acct.; 24 Jul 1758; orphans Rebecca [age 11], John [age 7], Elisabeth [age 5] (A 41.489); dist.; 24 Jul 1758 (BB 2.90)

IRELAND

Ireland, Gilbert, Capt.; orignally *Edinborough*; resur. 30 Apr 1748 (TLC p. 111); *Edenbrough Addition*; 121 ac.; 20 Aug 1747 cert./pat. (COL)

Ireland, Gilbert; will; 17 Jan 1755; 6 Mar 1755; wife Anne; sons John, William Herbert, Gilbert; daus. Anne, Mary; tracts *Charing Cross, Swillenham* (MCW 11.82) [SMW TA1.331]; inv. 1 Mar 1756; [Capt.]; nok wife & child.; admx./extx. Ann Ireland (I 66.7, 16); acct.; 23 Nov 1768; extx. Ann, w/o Major Sweeney (A 60.185); acct.; 20 Mar 1759 (A 43.101)

JACKSON

Jackson, Barnaby; *Skrettons*; 650 ac.; sur. 1 Mar 1649; by 1707 included in survey of *Mason*; St. Mary's Hundred (RR p. 2)

Hawks Nest; 350 ac.; sur. 18 Aug 1661; 1707 incl. in resur. of *Masson*; St. Mary's Hundred (RR p. 3) (TLC p. 3)

Addition; 300 ac.; sur. 3 Mar 1665; incl. in resur. of *Mason*; St. Mary's Hundred (RR p. 3) (TLC p. 4)

Jackson, Thomas; will; 10 Jul 1687; 16 Jul 1687; child. George, Ann, Thomas, Margaret, Martha; wife Martha; tracts *Doxey's [Dorsey's] Plantation, Underwood's Choice, Rythine, Asquith's Folly, Pleasant Spring* in TA Co.,

Clarke's Forest in BA Co. (MCW 2.15) [SMW PC1.65]; <u>inv.</u>; 25 Jul 1687 (I&A
9.343); <u>acct.</u>; 14 Feb 1687 (I&A 9.465)
Jackson, George, Mr.; <u>inv.</u>; 25 Jul 1726; 24 Sep 1726; nok Thomas & James
Bisco (I 11.563)
Jackson, Theodorah; <u>acct.</u>; 15 Jan 1712 (SMAA p. 237)
Jackson, William; <u>inv.</u>; 18 Dec 1733; 11 Feb 1733; nok one minor (I 17.599);
<u>acct.</u>; 2 Dec 1734 (A 12.665)
Jackson, John; <u>acct.</u>; 17 Jan 1757; orphan Jane [age 10 mos.]; admx. Jane
Jackson (A 40.275); <u>dist.</u>; 7 Jan 1757 (BB 2.49)

JACOBSON
Jacobson, Christopher; service by 1673 (SK 17.545)
Jacobson, John; <u>inv.</u>; 5 Feb 1756; 3 May 1756; nok Jane Sword, Edward
Morgan; admx./extx. Jane Jacobson (I 60.580)

JAMES
James, Owen; *Hogg Neck*; 100 ac.; sur. 14 May 1650; 1707 poss. Peter Watts;
Poplar Hill Hundred (RR p. 22) (TLC p. 21)
James Land; 100 ac.; sur. 5 Oct 1650; 1707 no poss.; lies in Wolseley Manor;
Poplar Hill Hundred (RR p. 22); *Peters Holt* or *James Land* (TLC p. 21)
Mount Sinai; 100 ac.; sur. 1650; St. George's Hundred; 1704 RR
James, Abel; immigrated by 1670 with wife Diana (SK 16.88)
James, Abell; <u>will</u>; 24 Mar 1674/5; 13 Apr 1675; wife Diana; son Charles (MCW
1.88); <u>acct.</u>; 9 Jan 1676 (I&A 3.33); <u>acct.</u>; 15 Sep 1679 (I&A6.380)
James, Thomas and Mary Manning; m. 25 Sep 1752; child. George [b. 14 Jul
1753], Chloe [b. 2 May 1755] (SA p. 37, 57)
James, Thomas; *Cole's Addition* in FR Co.; 71 ac.; 3 Jan 1757 cert./pat. (COL)
Pasture Ground; 12 ac.;10 Jun 1758 cert./pat. (COL)
James, Champion, s/o Thomas and Mary James [b. 13 Jun 1757] (SA p. 38)
James, Mary, wife of Thomas, d. 25 Oct 1757 (SA p. 64)
James, Owen; <u>will</u>; 18 Sep 1659; 29 Sep 1659; mentions John, s/o John Lawson;
Rebecca, d/o Alexander Frizzell; Dorothy, d/o Robert Cager; kinsman Col.
John Price (MCW 1.14)
James, John; <u>inv.</u>; 13 Sep 1760; 13 Mar 1761; nok John Grey; admx./extx.
Margaret James (I 71.148); <u>acct.</u>; 4 Feb 1764 (A 51.4); <u>dist.</u>; 4 Feb 1764; child.
Hannah, Margaret, John, Jane (BB 4.29)

JAMESON
Jameson, John; <u>inv.</u>; 18 Mar 1716 (I&A 38b.112); <u>acct.</u>; 9 May 1719; adm. Thomas
Jameson (A 1.445) (SMAA p. 399)
Jameson (Jamestone), Anne; *Chapticoe Forest*; <u>will</u>; 3 Feb 1724; 1 Mar 1724;
nieces Margaret and Susannah, daus. of bro. William; bro. Thomas (MCW

5.189) [SMW PC1.295]; <u>inv.</u>; 19 May 1725; 6 Nov 1725; nok Thomas Jameson; ex. William Jameson (I 11.162); <u>acct.</u>; 2 Aug 1726 (A 7.509); <u>acct.</u>; 4 Jul 1727 (A 8.275)

Jamestone (Jameson), William, Mr.; <u>inv.</u>; 26 Mar 1733; 17 Apr 1734; nok Thomas & Joseph Jameson; admx./extx. Mary Jameston (I 18.111); <u>acct.</u>; 5 Jun 1735; orphan Margarett Jameson (A 13.229)

Jameson, Mary; <u>will</u>; 12 Feb 1741/2; 2 Jun 1742; sons Thomas and John Barber; g-son Bennett Taylor (MCW 8.184) [SMW TA1.119]

JANES

Janes, John, Mr.; <u>inv.</u>; 23 May 1733; 30 Jul 1733; nok Thomas Janes, Joannah Tennison; admx./extx. Sarah Janes (I 17.323); <u>acct.</u>; 26 Aug 1734; admx. Sarah, w/o Stephen Mackey (A 12.470)

Janes, Thomas; <u>inv.</u>; 20 Jan 1742; 4 Mar 1742; nok Mary & Sarah Wallet; admx./extx. Henrietta Janes (I 27.367)

Joans (Jeans, Janes), Ann; <u>inv.</u>; 5 Apr 1754; 17 Jan 1754; nok William Joan, William Langley; adm./ex. Thomas James (I 58.201); <u>acct.</u>; 24 May 1756; bro. William Jeans; ?wife, sister of William Langley (A 39.216); <u>dist.</u>; 25 Oct 1756; mentions Thomas & William Jeans (BB 2.33)

Jeanes, Thomas; *Pleasant Springs*; 100 ac.; 29 Sep 1758 cert./pat. (COL)

Jeanes, Thomas; *Pleasant Springs*; 178 ac.; 17 Jul 1770 cert./pat. (COL)

JARBOE

Jarboe, John, Lt. Col.; <u>will</u>; 4 Mar 1664; 9 Mar 1674; wife Mary; sons John, Peter, Henry; dau. Mary; sons Henry, Peter born later; tract *The Mill Land* (MCW 1.89)

Jarboe, John, Lt. Col.; <u>inv.</u>; 13 Jul 1675; 19 Jul 1675 (I&A 1.372)

Jarboe, Peter; <u>will</u>; 3 Mar 1697/8; 31 Mar 1698; wife Ann (MCW 2.137) [SMW PC1.101]; <u>inv.</u>; 13 Apr 1698 (I&A 16.203); <u>acct.</u>; 8 Nov 1699; relict Ann Nevitt, d/o John Nevitt (I&A 19½b.120)

Jarbo, John; <u>will</u>; 14 Oct 1704; 16 May 1705; sons John, Peter; bro. Henry; dau. Elizabeth; tract *St. Lawrence Freehold, Paul's March [Marsh]* (MCW 3.60) [SMW PC1.134]; <u>acct.</u>; 22 Sep 1707; ex. Henry Jarboe (I&A 27.148) (SMAA p. 142); <u>acct.</u>; 24 Aug 1708 (I&A 28.330) (SMAA p. 160)

Jarbo, John; *Jarboe*; sur. 17 Apr 1658; poss. Jarbo's heirs; widow m. Step'n Jarbo; not found; New Town Hundred (TLC p. 29)

Jarboe, Henry; <u>will</u>; 18 Mar 1708; 18 Apr 1709; sons Henry, Peter, Charles, Ignatius; daus. Mary, Monika; bro. Peter Joy (MCW 3.133) [SMW PC1.160]

Jarboo [Jarboe], Henry; <u>will</u>; 20 Feb 1742/3; 4 Mar 1742/3; child. Henry, Mary, James, Stephen (MCW 8.206) [SMW TA1.143]; <u>inv.</u>; 6 Sep 1743; 1 Dec 1743; nok Peter & Charles Jarboe; adm./ex. Henry Jarboe (I 28.356); <u>acct.</u>; 21 May 1744; mentions Charles Jarboe (A 20.231)

Jarboo [Jarboe], Peter; will; 12 Nov 1743; 7 Dec 1743; wife Monica; sons
Ignatius, Philip, Bennet, Garard [Jarrard], Peter, Clement, Henry [Henry
Barton]; tracts *St. Peters Hills, Hanover, Cross Manor* (MCW 8.241) [SMW
TA1.139]; inv.; 7 Dec 1743; 7 May 1744; nok Henry & Charles Jarboe;
admx./exs. Monica & Ignatius Jarboe (I 29.133); acct.; 5 Jun 1745 (A 21.360)
Jarboe, Joshua and Jean; child. Abner [b. 9 Dec 1763], Bennet [b. 2 Jan 1767],
Eleanor [b. 2 Nov 1768], Charles [b. 21 Jun 1773] (SA p. 24)
Jarboe, James; *Jarboe's Discovery*; 36 ac.; 29 Apr 1763 cert./pat. (COL)
Jarboe (Jerboe), Ignatius; *Pleasant Levels*; 239 ac.; 21 May 1759 cert./pat. (COL)
Jerboe's Ramble; 608 ac.; 30 Sep 1761 cert./pat. (COL)
Jarboe, Clement and Ann; child. Frances (m) [b. 15 Jun 1762], Eleanor [b. 30
Jul 1764], Monica [b. 26 May 1767] (SA p. 16, 50)
Jarboe, Mary; son Stephen [b. 7 Jan 1765] (SA p. 192)
Jarboe, Charles; m. 19 Oct 1772 Eliz. Stone (MM)
Jarboe, Rod; m. 17 Nov 1772 Monica Williams (MM)
Jarboe, Thomas; m. 28 Nov 1772 Ann Lucas (MM)
Jarboe, Peter and Nancy Jarboe; m. 16 Jan 1779 (SA p. 57)
Jarboe, Robert; d. 21 Mar 1803; age 51 yrs., 2 mos., 18 days (HGM)
Jarboe, Elizabeth; d. 6 Sep 1810; age 60 yrs., 11 mos., 2 days; w/o Robert, Jr.
(HGM)

JENIFER
Jenifer, Daniel; *Blewston Run*; 150 ac.; sur. 25 Oct 1665; 1707 poss. Cosmas
Parsons; St. Mary's Hundred (RR p. 4) (TLC p. 5)
Jenifers Gift; 100 ac.; sur. 4 Feb 1668; 1707 poss. Peter Watts; incl. in other
surveys; Poplar Hill Hundred (RR p. 25) (TLC p. 23)
The Cheat; 82 ac.; resur. 15 Dec 1671 called *Gardners Purchase*; 1704 no
mention; 1707 no poss.; St. Georges Hundred (RR p. 18) (TLC p. 19)
Jenifer, Daniell; m. Mary, extx. of William Smith; mentions John Brooke, wife
Katherine who m/2 Robt. Stevens; 1669 (CCR p. 8)
Jenifer, Daniel; wife Mary, extx. of William Smith; 1669 (AM LVII.460, 508)
Jenifer, Daniel; granted *Jenifer's Gift* 1672 (CCR p. 103)
Jenifer, Thomas; *Ripe*; 925 ac.; 1719 cert./pat. (COL)
Jenifer, Dan'l of St. Thomas; *The Ripe*; 925 ac.; resur. 11 Aug 1719 (TLC p. 80)
Jenifer, Daniel of St. Thomas; Gent.; will; 7 Sep 1722; 2 Jul 1730; wife
Elizabeth (MCW 6.155); inv.; 2 Jun 1731; nok Samuel & Ann Jenifer;
admx./extx. Elisabeth Jenifer (I 16.184)
Jenifer, Jacob; bro. of Daniel; m. aunt of James Pattison; age ca 65; 26 Aug
1723 (CCR p. 56)
Jenifer, Daniel; m/1 widow Smith; m/2 Mrs. Ann Toft of Accomack, VA; 26
Aug 1723 (CCR p. 56)
Jenifer (Jennifer), Michael; will; 10 Jul 1726; 2 Sep 1728; wife Mary; sons
Michael Parker, Daniel; bro. Daniel; tracts *Turvey, Forrest of Harvey* (MCW

6.77) [SMW PC1.318]; <u>inv.</u>; 23 Sep 1728; 9 Dec 1729; nok Elisabeth & Ann
Jenifer; extx. Mary Jenifer (I 13.382); <u>acct.</u>; 8 Dec 1729; extx. Mary, w/o James
Smith (A 10.177); <u>acct.</u>; 27 Jul 1730 (A 10.419)
Jenifer (Jenifers), Elizabeth; widow; <u>will</u>; 21 Oct 1734; 6 Jun 1735; dau. Ann;
son Samuel; dec'd husband Daniel of St. Thomas Jenifer (MCW 7.149) [SMW
TA1.40]; <u>inv.</u>; 24 Nov 1735; nok John Theobalds, Ann Jenifers; admn./extx.
Samuell Jenifers (I 21.208); <u>acct.</u>; Aug 1739 (A 17.248)
Jenifer, Samuel; <u>inv.</u>; 24 Dec 1754; nok Allexander Darran, Ann Taylor;
admx./extx. Ellen Jenifer (I 60.108); <u>acct.</u>; 12 May 1755; admx. Ellin, w/o John
Hopewell (A 37.161)
Jenifer, John Read; <u>inv.</u>; 10 Jun 1773; nok Samuel Jenifer, Ann Read; admx.
Elisabeth Jenifer (I 112.396)
Jenifer, Daniel of St. Thomas; <u>inv.</u>; 30 May 1774; 31 Aug 1774; adm. Samuel
Jenifer (I 119.157)

JENKINS
Jenkins, William; *Sheads*?; 424 ac.; 11 Jul 1725 cert./pat. (COL)
  Truth & Trust; 773 ac.; 12 Jul 1726 cert./pat. (COL)
  Salem; 215 ac.; sur. 23 Feb 1731 resur. 24 Aug 1727 (TLC p. 86); 23 Feb 1733
  cert./pat. (COL)
Jenkins, Joseph and Mary ____; m. 23 Jan 1742; child. John [b. 5 May 1744],
Agustine [b. 12 Jan 1746/7], Thomas [b. 28 Jun 1749], Edmund Courtney [b.
1 Oct 1752] (SA p. 35, 57)
Jenkins, Augustine [b. 12 Jan 1747]; d. 2 Feb 1800 Newtown; s/o Joseph
Jenkins and Mary ?Combs (JM p. 317)
Jenkins, William; <u>will</u>; 24 Feb 1755; 31 Mar 1755; wife Mary; sons Henry,
William, Ignatious, Michael, Joseph and Thomas Courtney Jenkins; daus.
Jane, Mary Hagar & her dau. Mary Ann; tracts *Tuesdays Work, Salem, St.
Thomas's, Truth and [or] Trust, Pyes Hardship, Foxes Range* (MCW 11.81)
[SMW TA1.321]; <u>inv.</u>; 14 Jun 1755; [planter]; nok Joseph & William Jenkins;
adm./ex. Henry Jenkins (I 60.316); <u>acct.</u>; 26 Jul 1756; orphans Joseph, William,
Thomas Cortenay, Henry [all of age], Mary Hagar, Jane, Michael [age 19],
Ign. [age 14] (A 39.228); <u>dist.</u>; 25 Oct 1756 (BB 2.37)
Jenkins, George, Mr.; <u>inv.</u>; 2 Jan 1759; 3 Aug 1759; nok Thomas Jenkins, Ann
Whitt; adms./exs. Thomas Jenking Ruker & wife Martha (I 67.93); <u>acct.</u>; 22 Sep
1760 (A 46.11); <u>dist.</u>; 22 Sep 1760 (BB 3.39)
Jenkins, Thomas; <u>will</u>; 22 Nov 1760; 5 Aug 1761; sons William, Thomas; daus.
Jean, Eleanor, Elizabeth (MCW 12.76); <u>inv.</u>; 9 __ 1761; 15 Aug 1761; nok
William Guyther, Jr., Robert Bean, Jr.; exs. Moses White & wife Jane,
William Jenkins (I 74.251); <u>acct.</u>; 4 Nov 1761 (A 47.232)
Jenkins, Edmund; m. 26 May 1773 Eliz. Milborn (MM)
Jenkins, William; planter; <u>will</u>; 9 Sep 1775; 17 Apr 1776; son Thomas; dau.
Mary; bro. Thomas; mother unnamed; wife Brittannia (MCW 16.116); <u>inv.</u>; 8

May 1776; 12 Mar 1777; nok Thomas Jenkins, Jane White; Bretannia Jenkins (I 125.286)

Jenkins, Joseph; will; 31 Oct 1774; 3 Jan 1775; sons John, Edmund, Augustine; wife Mary; tracts *Brushey Neck, Taylors Chance, St. Thomas's, Deer [Doe's] Park, Vaughn's Hills, Truth and Trust* (MCW 16.90) [SMW TA1.729]

Jenkins, Thomas and Mary Mackall; m. 13 Jan 1780 (SA p. 58)

Jenkins, George and Margaret Wise (by license); m. 31 Mar 1782 (SA p. 60)

Jenkins, Joseph; d. 16 Jan 1796; age 22 yrs, 4 mos., 12 days (HGM)

JERNINGHAM

Jenningham, Frances Henrietta; b. 1746; d. 17 Oct 1824 Bruges; d/o Henry Jerningham and Catherine _____ (JM p. 317)

Jerningham, Henry; will; 19 Nov 1772; 6 Jan 1773; uncle St. George Jerningham; wife Catharine; child. Charles Edward, Frances Henritta, Mary, Helloisa, Edwardinna, Olivia, Henry Tobias; bro. Nicholas; tract *Cannon Hill* [in Surrey] (MCW 15.30) [SMW TA1.363]; inv.; 20 Apr 1774; [Dr.]; extxs. Katharine & Frances Henrietta Jernigham (I 116.195); inv.; 10 Aug 1775; extx. Henrietta Jerningham (I 122.142, 143); acct.; 10 Oct 1775; extx. Katharine Jerningham (A 73.237)

JESSOP

Jessop, William; immigrated by 1677 (SK 15.434)

Jessup (Jesup), Joseph; will; 26 Dec 1717; 4 Mar 1718; wife Mary (MCW 4.199) [SMW PC1.244]; inv.; 10 May 1718; 9 Apr 1719; extx. Mary Jesup (I 1.498); acct.; 5 Nov 1719 (SMAA p. 383); acct.; 2 Nov 1720 (A 3.233) (SMAA p. 427)

Jessep (Jessop), William; will; 30 Sep 1726; 2 Nov 1727; bro. Richard Hopewell (MCW 6.41) [SMW PC1.326]; inv.; 26 Mar 1728; 23 May 1728 (I 13.95)

JOHNSON

Johnson, James; *Beans Point* or *Hatches Neck*; 100 ac.; sur. 23 Oct 1641; 1707 poss. Alice Mackay. & Tho. Heb; St. Georges Hundred (RR p. 17) (TLC p. 17) *Hunting Creek;* 200 ac.; sur. 14 Jul 1647; 1707 poss. James Johnson, now in VA; Poplar Hill Hundred (RR p. 22) *Latchford;* 200 ac.; sur. 14 Jul 1647; 1707 poss. James Johnson of VA; Poplar Hill Hundred (RR p. 21) (TLC p. 20) *Poplar Hill;* 200 ac.; sur. 28 May 1651; poss. James Johnson of VA; (TLC p. 21); sur. for Richard Banks [not James Johnson] Poplar Hill Hundred (RR p. 21) *Grapnell;* 200 ac.; sur. 28 May 1651; 1707 poss. James Johnson of VA; Poplar Hill Hundred (RR p. 22) (TLC p. 21) *Wilderpoole;* 300 ac.; sur. 14 Jun 1653; 1707 poss. James Johnson of VA; Poplar Hill Hundred (RR p. 22) (TLC p. 21)

Johnson, James; planter of *Poplar Hill;* agreement re the marriage of kinswoman Barbara Hatton and James Johnson; 31 May 1650 (AM X.12)

Johnson, James; *Poplar Hill*; <u>will</u>; written 31 May 1650; wife Barbara; mentions unnamed child. and postnuptial agreement between Barbara Hatton and her kinsman Thomas Hatton and James Johnson (MCW 1.4)

Johnson, William; *St. Wynefrid's*; <u>will</u>; written 7 Jun 1656; wife Emma; dau. Eliza:; neph. William, s/o bro. James Langworth; mentions Emma, d/o John Shanks; niece Mrs. Mary Langworth, sisters Agatha Langworth, Eliza: Price, Elisa: Morris; mother Mrs. Elisa: Morris (MCW 1.17)

Johnson, John; service by 1669; shoemaker (SK 12.357)

Johnson, John; <u>will</u>; 10 Apr 1687; 9 Dec 1687; child. John, Mary, James, Susan; wife Mary; mentions tract *Westham;* mentions Edward, s/o Luke Barber (MCW 2.21) [SMW PC1.60]; <u>inv.</u>; 23 Dec 1687; mentions dau. Mary (I&A 9.463); <u>acct.</u>; 27 Sep 1688; extx. Mary, w/o John Rose (I&A10.185)

Johnson, John; <u>inv.</u>; 3 Nov 1698 (I&A 12.21b)

Johnson, John; <u>acct.</u>; 10 Jun 1701; admx. Alice Johnson (I&A 20.207)

Johnson, Peter; <u>will</u>; 3 Jul 1701; 2 May 1705; son Leonard; dau.? Matthew [Mathue]; wife unnamed; tracts *The Plaines, Gardiner's Landing* (MCW 3.60) [SMW PC1.137]; <u>inv.</u>; 8 May 1705 (I&A 25.32); <u>acct.</u>; 13 May 1707; extx. Jane (relict), w/o Ethelbert Doyne (I&A 26.323); <u>acct.</u>; 27 May 1707 (SMAA p. 158)

Johnson, William; tailor; age ca 55; 11 May 1720 (CCR p. 46)

Johnson, William; age ca 52 in 1721 (MD p. 106)

Johnson, Joshuah; <u>inv.</u>; 6 Feb 1726; 7 Mar 1726; nok Francis Johnson, minors; widow; adm. John Johnson (I 11.728); <u>acct.</u>; 7 Jun 1727; widow dec'd (A 8.221)

Johnston (Johnson, Joneston), Samuel; <u>will</u>; 4 Aug 1729; 24 Nov 1729; dau. Susannah; son Samuel; tract *Redman's Hardship* (MCW 6.137) [SMW PC1.330]; <u>inv.</u>; 27 Nov 1729; 24 Dec 1729; exs. Samuel & Susannah Johnson (I 15.360); <u>acct.</u>; 24 Aug 1730 (A 10.424)

Johnson, Roger; <u>inv.</u>; 20 Jul 1733; 8 Aug 1733 (I 17.328); <u>acct.</u>; 13 Aug 1740 (A 18.55)

Johnson, John; *Additon to Peters Well*; 104 ac.; sur. 17 Jan 1726 (TLC p. 90); *Peter's Well Addition*; 10 Jun 1734 cert./pat. (COL)

Johnson, Samuel; *Redman's Hardship*; 100 ac.; 10 Jun 1734 cert./pat. (COL)

Johnson, Francis; <u>inv.</u>; 5 Nov 1734; nok John & Bar. Johnson; admx./extx. Hellen Johnson (I 20.99); <u>acct.</u>; 3 Jun 1735 (A 13.157)

Johnson, Archibald, Dr.; *Mossell Wells*; 138 ac.; sur. 8 May 1735 (TLC p. 92); *Moffatt's Wells*; 19 Nov 1736 cert./pat. (COL)

Johnson, John [Sr.]; <u>will</u>; 14 Jan 1744; 2 Apr 1745; child. Peter, Thomas, John, Leonard, Susanna; unnamed wife (MCW 9.44) [SMW TA1.166]; <u>inv.</u>; 7 Aug __; 26 Nov 1745; nok Thomas Johnson; adm./ex. Pricilla Burn (I 31.426)

Johnson, Peter; <u>will</u>; 2 Jan 1747; 8 Apr 1747; 2nd wife Grace, widow of John Mattenly; her child. James, Joseph and Luke Mattenly; child. of his m/1: John, Thomas, Leonard, Jess, Mary and Susanna Johnson, [& Peter]; bro. John; mentions Leonard, s/o John Johnson & Luke, s/o John Mattingly (MCW

9.100) [SMW TA1.188]; inv.; 8 Apr 1747; 19 May 1747; nok Thomas & John Johnson (I 35.103); inv.; 30 Mar 1748 (I 35.528); acct.; 20 Dec 1748 (A 26.11)

Johnson, John; will; 7 Apr 1763; 23 Apr 1767 wife Eleanor; sons Mile, John, Thomas Bennett, Leonard, Peter, Joseph; tract *Peter's Wells* (MCW 13.178); inv.; 21 May 1767; 11 Jan 1769; nok Mile Johnson, Mary Booth; exs. Eleanor & John Johnson (I 101.21); acct.; 9 May 1772 (A 67.136)

Johnson, Leonard; m. 31 Jan 1774 Mary Malohorn (MM)

Johnson, Leonard; oral; 19 Feb 1775; 30 Mar 1775; wife Winifred; child. unnamed (MCW 16.93) [SMW TA1.718]

JONES

Jones, Robert; *Bennets Purchase*; 100 ac.; sur. 15 Mar 1656; 1707 poss. Rich'd Vowles; New Town Hundred (RR p. 32) (TLC p. 31)
    Jones's Wood; 100 ac.; sur. 8 Jun 1658; 1707 poss. Thomas Cole; St. Georges Hundred (RR p. 18) (TLC p. 18)
    Jones; 100 ac.; sur. 16 Jun 1658; 1707 poss. Jos. Walker & Rich'd Clark; St. Georges Hundred (RR p. 19) (TLC p. 19)

Jones, Henry; service by 1673 (SK 17.416, 532)

Jones, Morrice; service by 1673 (SK 17.488; 7.559)

Jones, Edward; service by 1674 (SK 18.116; 15.402)

Jones, Jenkin [Jinkin] will; 15 Dec 1675; 21 Feb 1675 (MCW 1.168) [SMW PC1.19]

Jones, David; service by 1678 (SK 15.523)

Jones, John; will; 5 Oct 1677; 6 Nov 1677 (MCW 1.197) [SMW PC1.29]; inv.; 12 May 1678; [gent.] (I&A 5.112); acct.; 2 Sep 1680 (I&A 7a.219)

Jones, Robert; service by 1679 (SK WC2.67)

Jones, William; immigrated by 1680 (SK WC2.325)

Jones, Humphry; acct.; [filed with 1687] (I&A 9.356)

Jones, Robert; will; 9 Jan 1691; 29 Jul 1692; child. Avis & her dau. Sarah Dines, Sarah, Rebecca, Thomas, John; s-i-l Thomas Green (MCW 2.55); inv.; 29 Aug 1692; 3 Sep 1692 (I&A 10lc.2)

Jones, William; inv.; 7 Sep 1694 (I&A 13a.134); acct.; 26 Mar 1695 (I&A 13a.250) (SMAA p. 91)

Jones (Joannes), John; inv.; 6 Apr 1698 (I&A 16.188); acct.; [filed with 1697-8]; admx. Elisabeth Joans (relict) (I&A 16.242)

Jones, Solomon; will; 11 May 1710; 24 Jun 1710; sons William, Solomon; daus. Elinor, Katharine; tract *Scotland* (MCW 3.177) [SMW PC1.166]; inv.; 29 Dec 1710 (I&A 32b.26)

Jones, Catherine; *Maid's Right*; 100 ac.; resur. 23 Mar 1713 (TLC p. 71); 10 Apr 1715; from her father Robert cert./pat. (COL)

Jones, William; of PG Co.; *Poplar Point*; 90 ac.; 24 Apr 1717 cert./pat. (COL)

Jones, William; age ca 38; 11 May 1720 (CCR p. 46)

Jones, William; inv.; 12 Mar 1723; 14 Jun 1723; nok Robert Dorson, William Brewer; admx./extx. Elisabeth Jones (I 8.233)

Jones, John; innholder; <u>inv.</u>; 3 May 1725; 6 Aug 1725; nok Mary Jones; admx.
Ann Jones (I 11.89); <u>acct.</u>; 20 May 1726 (A 7.369); <u>acct.</u>; 26 Sep 1726 (A 8.3)

Jones, Ann; <u>inv.</u>; 17 Aug 1730; 25 Feb 1730; nok Mary Stewart, Anne Nevett (I
16.85); <u>acct.</u>; 4 Nov 1731 (A 11.258)

Jones, William; St. Michael's Hundred; <u>will</u>; 12 Jan 1734; 24 Feb 1734; sons
Solomon, John, William, Joseph; daus. Mary, Susanna; tracts *Scotland, Jones
Chance* (MCW 7.119) [SMW TA1.44]; <u>inv.</u>; 28 Mar 1735; 19 May 1735; nok
William Ashston, Johnathon Bissco; adms./exs. Mary & William Jones (I
20.400); <u>acct.</u>; 20 Jun 1738 (A 16.291)

Jones, John; *Poverty*; 64 ac.; 10 Jun 1734 cert./pat. (COL)

Jones, William; *Poplar Point*; 101 ac.; sur. 10 Oct 1715 for 90 ac. (TLC p. 74);
resur. for 101 ac.; undated (TLC p. 89); 13 Jun 1734 cert./pat. (COL)
Salter's Hall; 83 ac.; sur. 19 Jul 1735 (TLC p. 94); 16 Jul 1737 cert./pat. (COL)
Salter's Hall Addition; 34 ac.; sur. 4 Mar 1741 (TLC p. 97); 4 Nov 1742 cert./pat.
(COL)

Jones, William; s/o William, dec'd; *Jones's Fortune*; 112 ac.; sur 2 May 1722
for William Jones; pat. 10 Jul 1737 to his son William Jones (TLC p. 94); 18 Jul
1737 cert./pat. (COL)

Jones [Janes], Thomas; <u>will</u>; 2 Nov 1742; 3 Nov 1742; wife Henrietta; son John
(MCW 8.193) [SMW TA1.118]; <u>acct.</u>; 10 Aug 1744; extx. Henrietta, w/o Alexander
Anderson (A 20.427)

Jones, Mary; <u>will</u>; 4 Apr 1746; 12 May 1746; child. Susanna Bisscoe, Joseph,
John (MCW 9.69); Note error -SMW will for Mary Jones shows descendants of Eleanor Aston
[SMW TA1.210]; <u>inv.</u>; 14 Jul 1746; 23 Aug 1746; nok John & William Thomas;
William Jones; adm./ex. Joseph Jones (I 33.317, 319); <u>inv.</u>; 4 May 1747 (I 35.112)

Jones, William; *Jones's Conveniency*; 35½ ac.; sur. 20 Jan 1745 (TLC p. 111); 35
ac.; 30 Jul 1747 cert./pat. (COL)
Jones's Lane; 1¼ ac.; sur. 20 Jan 1745 (TLC p. 110); 1 ac. 18 Nov 1747 cert./pat.
(COL)

Jones, Sollomon; <u>will</u>; 6 Mar 1748/9; 14 Apr 1749; wife Cathrine; child. James,
Margaret, Monica [or Margaret Monica], Sollomon, Walter (MCW 10.4) [SMW
TA1.229]; <u>inv.</u>; 8 May 1749; 24 Jun 1749; nok Will & John Jones; admx./extx.
Catharine Jones (I 40.39)

Jones, Catherine; <u>will</u>; 3 Feb 1749; 28 Feb 1749; child. Solomon, Margreet,
Monocey, Walter, Bridgett; bros. Dennis and James Burne (MCW 10.72) [SMW
TA1.239]; <u>inv.</u>; 20 Mar 1750; 25 Jun 1750; nok Will & John Jones (I 43.280);
<u>acct.</u>; 17 Jun 1751 (A 30.193); <u>acct.</u>; 6 Dec 1752; orphans Margeret [age 14],
Monica [age 10], Solomon [age 9], Walter [age 4], Bridgett [age 2] (A 33.319);
<u>dist.</u>; 6 Dec 1752 (BB 1.61)

Jones, Aaron; <u>inv.</u>; 16 Jun 1750; 4 Sep 1750; nok minor child.; admx./extx. Ruth
Jones (I 43.389); <u>acct.</u>; 7 Mar 1751; orphans John [age 16], Elisabeth [age 13],
James [age 10], William [age 7], Thomas [age 4] Aaron [age 1] Moses [age
1]; admx. Ruth Jones (A 30.90)

Jones, John, Mr.; inv.; 15 Apr 1755; 6 May 1755; nok James & Dradon Mackdanby (I 60.214)

Jones, William; will; 15 Jan 1759; 12 Mar 1759; sons Mathious, Caleb, Mordicai, William, Thomas; daus. Mary Burns, Susanner, Sarah; [wife Mary] (MCW 11.232) [SMW TA1.452]

Jones, William; acct.; 1 Jul 1763; mentions Thomas Whitherinton m. d/o Sol. Jones; Joseph & Thomas (orphans of John Green); exs. William Williams & wife Ann (A 49.627)

Jones, Johnson and Elizabeth; son Uel [b. 19 Aug 1764] (SA p. 6)

Jones, Matthias & Susanna; *Pountney's Oversight*; 202 ac.; 8 Sep 1772 cert./pat. (COL)

Jones, James; inv.; 7 May 1774; 10 Aug 1774; nok John & Sarah Jones; admx. Susannah Jones (I 119.139)

JORDAN

Jourdein, John, Capt.; inv.; 9 Aug 1679; mentions Cutbert Scott and wife Sarah (I&A 6.368)

Jordayne (Jordain), John; will; 15 Aug 1678; 24 Oct 1678; wife Elizabeth (MCW 1.206) [SMW PC1.31] ; inv.; 9 Aug 1679; mentions Cutbert Scott and wife Elisabeth (I&A 6.368); inv.; 9 Aug 1679 (SMAA p. 68)

Jordan (Jordain, Gordan, Sr., Thomas; will; 15 Oct 1716; _ Nov 1716; sons Jesse, John, Thomas, Jerad [Jeard], Samuel, Theodor; wife Elizabeth (MCW 4.89) [SMW PC1.202]; inv.; 15 Jan 1716; nok Jns. Jordan, Samuell Williamson (I&A 38b.177); acct.; 25 Feb 1717; extx. Elisabeth Joardain (I&A 390b.79) (SMAA p. 339)

Jordan, Justinian; age ca 37; 27 May 1723 (CCR p. 52)

Jordan, Elizabeth; age a 78 in 1738 (MD p. 108)

Jordan, Justinian; will; 18 Feb 1748; 3 May 1749; wife Mary; sons Justinian, William, James, Jeremiah, Charles; bro. John; unnamed daus.; tracts *Langleys Endeavour, Constantinople* (MCW 10.4) [SMW TA1.230]; inv.; 1 Aug 1749; [Col.]; nok Justinian & William Jordan; admx./extx. Mary Jordan (I 40.345)

Jordan, Theodorus; inv.; 14 Mar 1750; 5 Jun 1751; nok Thomas Reeder, Samuel Jordan; admx./extx. Elisabeth Jordan (I 47.115); acct.; 12 Jun 1752; orphans Elisabeth [age 14], Susannah [age 12], Sarah [age 10], Jean (Jane) [age 7], Margaret [age 5], William [age 2] (A 32.347); dist.; 12 Jun 1752 (BB 1.45)

Jordan, Thomas; inv.; 19 Apr 1755; 18 Sep 1755; nok Samuel & William Jordan; admx./extx. Mary Jordan (I 59.199); acct.; 4 Mar 1756; orphans James [age 11], Thomas [age 11], Rebecca [age 9], John Skipper [age 7], Samuel [age 5], Mary [age 3]; admx. Mary Jordan (A 39.74); dist.; 28 May 1756 (BB 2.23)

Jordan, Justn.; will; Nov 1759; 11 Dec 1759; wife Elizabeth; child. Justn., Mary, James, John (MCW 11.253); testator Justinian [SMW TA1.378]; inv.; 18 Dec 1759;

1 Aug 1760; [Maj.]; nok William & James Jordan (I 70.67); <u>acct.</u>; 17 Dec 1763; minors Justinian, Mary Napler, James, John (A 50.181)

Jordan, Samuel; <u>inv.</u>; 25 Feb 1762; 5 Mar 1762; nok James Jordan, Thomas Ellis; admx. Lucretia Jordan (I 77.73); <u>inv.</u>; [filed with 1763] (I 80.156); <u>acct.</u>; 5 Apr 1763 (A 49.94); <u>dist.</u>; 5 Apr 1763 (BB 3.18)

Jordan, Mildred; <u>inv.</u>; 25 Oct 1768; 11 Nov 1771 (I 107.189); <u>acct.</u>; 7 Nov 1771 (A 66.79)

Jordin (Jordan), Lucretia; <u>will</u>; 18 Jul 1769; 12 Aug 1769; dau. Sarah Stevenson; sons John, Robert and Mathew Holts and Samuel Jordan (MCW 14.108) [SMW TA1.578]; <u>inv.</u>; 14 Sep 1769; 18 Dec 1769 (I 103.6); <u>acct.</u>; 3 Sep 1770; mentions James & Samuel Jordan (A 64.231)

Jordan, James; *All That's Left*; 4 ac.; 17 Dec 1771 cert./pat. (COL)

JOSEPH

Joseph, William; of PG Co.; *Chance*; 205 ac.; 1708 cert./pat. (COL)

Joseph, Joseph; <u>acct.</u>; 5 Nov 1719; extx. widow Mrs. Mary Joseph (A 2.305)

Joseph, William, Mr., Esq.; <u>inv.</u>; 14 Aug 1729; 16 Sep 1729; nok Nicholas Mills, John Joseph; adm./ex. William Joseph (I 15.104)

Joseph, William, Jr.; <u>inv.</u>; 20 Jan 1773; 17 Sep 1773; nok 20 Jan 1773; 17 Sep 1773; nok William & Clement Joseph (I 112.417)

JOWLES

Jowles, Henry, Col.; <u>inv.</u>; 8 May 1701; son Henry; dau. Sibbell (I&A 20.214); <u>acct.</u>; 7 Oct 1703; extx. Sibile Jowles (I&A 24.189) (SMAA p. 117)

Jowles, Henry Peregrine; Deputy Surveyor for SM Co.; *Jowles' Calf Pasture*; 112 ac.; sur. 16 Apr 1707 (TLC p. 65); 10 Oct 1708 cert./pat. (COL) *Greenfield*; 12 ac.; sur. 30 Apr 1705; (TLC p. 66); 13 May 1709 cert./pat. (COL)

Jowles, Henry, Col.; <u>acct.</u>; 22 Jul 1713; adm. Henry Peregrine Jowles (I&A 34.60) (SMAA p. 251)

Jowles, Henry Peregrine, Col.; d. 31 Mar 1720; age 38 (HGM)

Jowles, Henry Peregrine; <u>will</u>; 27 Mar 1720; 9 Jun 1720; wife Dryden; sons Henry Greenfield and Kenelm; daus. Mary, Rebecca, [& Sybill]; mother Mrs. Sybill Jowles; sister Sybill; tracts *Orphan's Gift, Brigade, Holbidge Town* (MCW 5.12) [SMW PC1.259]; <u>inv.</u>; 24 Aug 1720; nok T. T. Greenfield (I 4.228); <u>acct.</u>; 18 Jan 1721; mentions Sib. Jowles, Sr.; extx. Dryden Jowles (A 4.50); <u>acct.</u>; 29 Oct 1723 (A 5.414)

Jowles, Sybill (Sibill); <u>will</u>; 30 Aug 1730; 22 Dec 1730; bro. Richard Groome [Greene] (MCW 6.176) [SMW PC1.329]; <u>acct.</u>; 17 Sep 1735 (A 13.324)

Jowles, Kenelm Greenfield, Mr.; <u>inv.</u>; 4 Jun 1744; nok Henry G. Sothoron, Rebecca Jowles (I 29.231); <u>acct.</u>; 2 Apr 1746; admx. Mrs. Driden Forbes (A 22.173)

Jowles, Rebecca; <u>will</u>; written 21 Dec 1759; mother Dryden Forbes, niece Clarrissa; nephew John Forbes; bro. James Forbes (MCW 12.36) [SMW TA1.423]

JOY

Joy, Charles; <u>inv.</u>; 11 Jan 1700 (I&A 20.143); <u>acct.</u>; 17 Mar 1704 (I&A 8b.8)

Joy, Peter; age ca 50; Jun 1715 (CCR p. 33)

Joy, Peter; <u>will</u>; 13 Aug 1733; 12 Apr 1740; sons Charles, Ignatius, Enoch, John
    Baptist, Athanasius; daus. Sarah, Mary, Ellinor; wife unnamed; tract
    Bebergham [Sobergham] in TA Co. (MCW 8.76) [SMW TA1.113]; <u>acct.</u>; 17 Aug
    1741; ex. Ignatious Joy (A 18.376)

Joy, Peter; <u>inv.</u>; 16 Apr 1740; 7 Jul 1740; nok Charles & Enoch Joy; adm./ex.
    Ignatius Joy (I 25.78)

Joy, Enoch; <u>inv.</u>; 20 Aug 1746; 7 Oct 1746; nok Charles & Ignatius Joy;
    adm./ex. Techley Joy (I 33.321); <u>acct.</u>; 4 Aug 1747; orphans Ignatius, Enoch,
    Charles, Athanatius, Peter, Ann; admx. Tekela Joy (A 24.174)

Joy, Ann; <u>inv.</u>; 1 May 1747; 25 May 1747; nok John Basil & Athanatious Joye;
    adm./ex. Charles Joye (I 35.106)

Joy, John and Mary; child. Joseph [b. 20 Sep 1755], Mary [b. 20 Sep 1755] (SA
    p. 4, 5)

Joy, John and Eleanor; child. William [b. 18 Jul 1760], Benedict [b. 10 Apr
    1763] (SA p. 7)

Joy, John and Sarah; child. Winifred [b. 20 Feb 1762], Thomas Tarlton [b. 23
    May 1765], Elizabeth [b. 17 May 1768] (SA p. 5)

Joy, John, Jr. and Eleanor; dau. Henrietta [b. 3 Aug 1769] (SA p. 1)

Joy, William and Eleanor Armsworthy (by license); m. 24 Feb 1784 (SA p. 62)

JOYNER

Joyner, Robert; age ca 26 in 1660; mentions Samuel Harris & wife Elizabeth
    (MD p. 109)

Joyner, Robert; <u>will</u>; 28 Jan 1669; 12 Nov 1672; wife Mary; son Robert; daus.
    Mary and Katharine; tract *Scotland* (MCW 1.71)

KEECH

Keetch, James & John Price; *Good Luck*; 100 ac.; sur. 24 Jan 1678; assgn.
    Keetch; 1707 poss. James Keetch; Resurrection Hundred (RR p. 62) (TLC p. 59)

Keech (Keetch, Keeth), James; *Town Neck*; 200 ac.; sur. 10 Aug 1698; orig. sur.
    18 Apr 1659 for Cornelius Kennedy; 1707 poss. same Keetch; Resurrection
    Hundred (RR p. 64) (TLC p. 61); 10 Aug 1698 cert./pat. (COL)
    Satisfaction; 580 ac.; laid out 10 Mar 1704 (TLC p. 66); 10 Oct 1709 cert./pat.
    (COL)
    Recompense; 220 ac.; sur. 20 Mar 1705; 1707 poss. James Keetch;
    Resurrection Hundred (RR p. 65) (TLC p. 63); 30 May 1705 cert./pat. (COL)

Keech, Charles; *Charles' Lot*; 194 ac.; sur. 27 Mar 1704; 1707 poss. Charles
    Keetch; Resurrection Hundred (RR p. 65) (TLC p. 62); 20 Jul 1704 cert./pat. (COL)

Keech, James; <u>will</u>; probate 25 Mar 1708; wife Elizabeth; child. James, John,
    Courts & Margarett; tracts *Towne Neck, Charles Lott, Satisfaccon, Good*

Luck, Recompense (MCW 3.101) [SMW PC1.144]; inv.; 26 Apr 1708; [Capt.];
approvers James and John Keech (I&A 28.281); acct.; 8 Jun 1709; extx.
Elisabeth Keech (I&A 29.305) (SMAA p. 180); inv.; 28 Jun 1709 (I&A 29.294)

Keech, James; extx. Elisabeth; heir James; Sep 1712 (CCR p. 23)

Keech, James; inv. ; 20 Jul 1713; relict & extx. Elizabeth (SMAA p. 249); acct.; 20
Jul 1713 (I&A 35b.41)

Keech, James; *Remainder*; 19 ac.; 20 Apr 1715 cert./pat. (COL)
Hill Field; 96 ac.; sur. 28 Aug 1724 for Wm. Cumming & pat. by Keech (TLC
p. 82); 20 May 1725 cert./pat. (COL)

Keech, Elizabeth; will; 30 Oct 1718; 24 Nov 1730; son Courts; father John
Courts (MCW 6.177) [SMW PC1.330]

Keech, Dorothy; d/o Thomas Keech; 332½ ac.; *The Remainder of Charles' Lott*;
(TLC p. 97); *Charles Lot*; 332 ac.; 15 Dec 1741 cert./pat. (COL)

Keech, James; Gent.; will; 14 Jan 1725; 2 Mar 1725/6; wife Mary; sons Samuel,
James; daus. Mary, Dorothy, Elizabeth, Martha; bro. Courts Keech (MCW
5.218) [SMW PC1.305]; inv.; 6 Jul 1726; 4 Jul 1726; nok Elisabeth Keach,
Margarett Seager; extx. Mrs. Mary Keech (widow) (I 11.522); acct.; 26 Apr
1727 (A 8.187)

Keech, Samuel; will; 3 Jul 1750; 5 Jun 1751; wife Darcos; sons John, James;
tract *Prices Rest* (MCW 10.163) [SMW TA1.273]; inv.; 20 Jun 1751; 7 Aug 1751;
nok Mary Burroughes, William Cartwright; extx. Dorcus Keech (I 47.275);
acct.; 8 Jun 1753; admx. Darcus, w/o Benjamin Branson (A 34.145); acct.; 17
Mar 1755; orphans John [age 9], James [age 7], Susanah [age 4] (A 37.168);
dist.; 17 Mar 1755; child. John [age 10 next Apr], James [age 8 next Nov] &
Susannah Keech [age 5 next Dec] (BB 12.132)

Keach, James; acct.; 9 Nov 1756 (A 40.234); acct.; 28 Nov 1758; orphan Elisabeth
[age 5] (A 42.213); dist.; 28 Nov 1758 (BB 2.100)

Keech, John; *Keech's Lot*; 15 ac.; 20 Dec 1775 cert./pat. (COL)

Keech, Timothy and Araminta Uldra (by publication); m. 27 Feb 1783 (SA p. 61)

KEENE

Kene (Keefe), Arthur; inv.; 21 May [filed with 1698] (I&A 16.62); acct.; [filed
with 1698] (I&A 18.131) (SMAA p. 103)

Keen, John, Sr.; age ca 66; 26 Aug 1723 (CCR p. 56)

Keene, Thomas; *Keene's Rest*; 49 ac.; sur. 11 Dec ___ (TLC p. 95); 8 Dec 1738
cert./pat. (COL)

KEITH

Akeeth, Geo.; *Knightwood*; 50 ac.; sur. 7 Mar 1681; 1707 poss. George Keeth;
Harvey Hundred (RR p. 56) (TLC p. 54)

Keith, George; acct.; 1 May 1706 (I&A 25.175); acct.; admx. Ann Keeith (SMAA p.
132)

Keith, George; age ca 90; 25 Jun 1722 (CCR p. 50)

KELLEY

Kelee, John; transported by 1669 (SK 12.343)

Kelley, John; inv.; 20 Oct 1702 (I&A 1.613); acct.; 17 Jul 1703; widow Sisly, admx., m. William Blackman (SMAA p. 120); acct.; 6 Aug 1703 (I&A 24.210)

Kelley, Katherine; inv.; 30 Jun 1705 (I&A 25.36)

Kelley, Edward; inv.; 25 Sep 1705 (I&A 25.35)

Kelly, Phillip; inv.; 7 Feb 1709 (I&A 31.120); acct.; 19 Oct 1711 (I&A 33a.46) (SMAA p. 218)

Kelly, John; acct.; 23 Dec 1719 (A 2.415) (SMAA p. 365)

Kelly (Kelley), Daniell; inv.; 25 Feb 1726; 7 Jun 1727; nok Mary Kelly (I 12.10); acct.; 19 Feb 1727 (A 8.536)

Kelly, John; *Kelly's Luck*; 138 ac.; 10 May 1752 cert./pat. (COL)
Kelly's Fortune; 182 ac.; 29 Oct 1753 cert./pat. (COL)

Kelley, Joseph; will; 1 May 1765; 18 Jun 1765; daus. Elizabeth Morgan, Mary Kelly, Ann Price, Eleanor Kelley; sons John, Joseph; wife Mary (MCW 13.86) [SMW TA1.467]; acct.; 8 Sep 1767; exs. Mary & John Kelley (A 57.361)

Kelly, James; inv.; 13 Sep 1765; 26 Oct 1765; nok John Price, Joseph Keely; exs. Mary & John Kelly (I 87.322)

Kelly, John; *Kelly's Fortune*; 105 ac.; 12 Jun 1771 cert./pat. (COL)

KELSEY

Kelsey, Edward; acct.; 29 May 1707 (I&A 27.209); 29 May 1709 (sic) (SMAA p. 140)

Kelsey, Kathrine; acct.; 25 Sep 1707 (I&A 27.150) (SMAA p. 143)

KENDRICK

Kindrick (Kendrick), Edward; inv.; 5 Mar 1721; 1 May 1722; nok Mathew Kindrick, Mary Cruckson, Robert Francis; admx. Katherine Kendrick (I 7.149); acct.; 27 Nov 1723; admx. widow Kathrine Kendrick (A 5.346)

Kenderick (Kendrick), Richard; acct.; 8 Aug 1722; admx. Katherine Kinderick (Hendrick) (A 4.171) [NOTE: This acct. very possibly belongs to Edward, not Richard]

Kendrick, James; *Kendrick's Lane*; 80 ac.; 29 Sep 1752 cert./pat. (COL)

Kindrick, William and Diana; dau. Elizabeth [b. 23 Apr 1764] (SA p. 191)

Kindreck, James; inv.; 13 Jan 1775; 1 Oct 1775; nok Zachariah Kindreck, John Taylor; admx. Katharine Kindreck (I 122.196)

Kendrick. Benjamin and Mary Smith; m. 31 Dec 1779 (SA p. 58)

KEY

Key, Peter; immigrated by 1667; of VA (SK 11.247)

Key, Peter; *Edinburgh*; 100 ac.; sur. 10 Mar 1667; 707 no poss.; St. Mary's Hundred (RR p. 5) (TLC p. 6)

Key, Philip; s/o Richard and Mary Key; b. 21 Mar 1696 St. Paul's Parish, Covent Garden, London; will; 10 Mar 1764; 1 Sep 1764; sons John Key dec'd whose widow m. Thomas Bond, Richard Ward Key, Francis Key, Edmund

Key, Thomas Key; dau. Susanna Gardiner Bruce w/o Norman Bruce; g-child.
Philip Key (s/o John, dec'd), John Ross Key, Philip Barton Key; Susanna
Gardiner Key d/o John, dec'd; sis.-i-l Elizabeth Miles; mentions [g-dau.]
Elizabeth Scott Key; tract *Maiden Bower, Diniards and Finchley* (both in CH
Co.), *Melton's Hope, Weems, Epping Forrest, Terra Rubia, Paradise
Regained, Friendship* (latter 4 in FR Co.), *Bushwood Lodge, Addition to
Guiberts Chance, Penryn, Somerfield* (MCW 13.32) [SMW TA1.460]

Key, Philip, Esq.; *Covent Garden*; 200 ac.; resur. 19 Sep 1744; part of *Luck
Land* (TLC p. 107); 19 Sep 1744 cert./pat. (COL)
    Epping Forest; 1,070 ac.; 10 Oct 1750 cert./pat. (COL)
    Friendship; 206 ac.; 18 Oct 1750 cert./pat. (COL)
    Paradise Regained; 530 ac.; 19 Oct 1750 cert./pat. (COL)
    Melton's Hope; 144 ac.; 1 Jul 1758 cert./pat. (COL)
    Weems; 517 ac.; 30 Sep 1758 cert./pat. (COL)
    Good Hope; 729 ac.; 6 Feb 1760 cert./pat. (COL)
    Barron Doe; 93 ac.; 25 Mar 1762 cert./pat. (COL)

Key, John; will; 26 Mar 1755; 2 Sep 1755; wife unnamed; child. Philip, Susanna
(MCW 11.102) [SMW TA1.333]; inv.; 14 Dec 175; nok Philip & Philip B. Key;
admx./extx. Cecilia Key (I 62.190, 193); acct.; 5 Jul 1757; [Dr.]; orphans Philip
[age 6], Susanna Gardiner [age 5]; extx. Cecilia, w/o Thomas Bond (A 41.93);
dist.; 5 Jul 1757; widow & child. Philip & Susannah (BB 2.69)

Key, Philip; inv.; 2 Mar 1765; legatees Thomas, Philip s/o John, Susannah d/o
John, F., C., Richard Ward & Mrs. Key, Susannah Bruce (I 102.84, 101, 124);
acct.; 9 Dec 1769 (A 62.1); dist.; 9 Dec 1769; legatees (among others) widow,
Thomas, Richard Ward, Philip, Francis, John Ross, Philip Barton and Edmund
Key; also Susannah Gardiner, Elisabreth Scott, Susannah Gardiner Bruce,
Elisabeth Mills, Susannah Gardiner Key (BB 5.367)

Key, Richard Ward; will; 30 Nov 1764; 24 Apr 1765; daus. Frances Rebecca,
Mary; wife Hannah; bro. Francis; father Philip; g-father Philip; tracts *Wolf
Holes, Coles Adventure, Diniards* (MCW 13.73) [SMW TA1.473]; inv.; 31 Oct
1765; nok Ann Neale, Thomas Key; extx. Hannah Key (I 87.318)

Key, Philip; inv.; 18 Mar 1770; ex. Thomas Key (I 103.18)

Key, Thomas; inv.; 22 Mar 1773; nok Jane Briscoe, Susannah Gardiner Key;
adm. Philip Key (I 111.219)

Key, Theodosia, Mrs.; inv.; 24 Apr 1773; 29 Apr 1773; nok Phillip & Susanna
Gardiner Key (I 113.144)

Key, Philip; *Cambridge*; 96 ac.; 24 May 1776 cert./pat. (COL)
    Flower of the Forest; 39 ac.; 24 May 1776 cert./pat. (COL)
    Wee Bit; 7 ac.; 24 May 1776 cert./pat. (COL)

Key, Philip; m. 4 Mar 1778 Rebecca Sothoron (BRU 2.536)

KEYTING

Keyting, Nicho.; *Bulla Keyting*; 300 ac.; sur. 7 Mar 1658; n. side Deep Cr.; 1707 poss. Hen. Lowe [ex. Thos. Gruwin]; resur. into *Muggs Adventure*; St. Michael's Hundred (RR p. 14) (TLC p. 14)

Keyting, Thomas; wife Elizabeth; conveyed *Keyting's Plantation* to Thomas Doxey; 20 May 1676 (AM LXVI.191)

KING

King, Walter; will; probate 21 Oct 1653 (MCW 1._ [53-56])

King, Charles; *Charles's Park*; sur. 130 ac. 12 Sep 1706 (TLC p. 64); 120 ac.; 10 Oct 1707 cert./pat. (COL)
  Parks Addition; 110 ac. sur. 20 Jan 1718 (TLC); *Park Addition*; 100 ac.; 3 Nov 1722 cert./pat. (COL)

King, Margrett; will; 1 Mar 1709; 18 Mar 1709; mentions William and Mary, ch/o Thomas King; John, s/o Edward King; Susannah, w/o Charles King; sons John and James; mentions Henry King (MCW 3.168) [SMW PC1.163]; inv.; 25 Feb 1710; 16 Jan 1711 (I&A 33a.59); acct.; 12 Jul 1714; exs. John & James King (I&A 36b.41) (SMAA p. 267)

King, John; inv.; 31 Jul 1719; nok Charles & James King (I 2.155); acct.; 17 May 1720 (A 2.512) (SMAA p. 444); acct.; 9 Sep 1720 (A 3.223) (SMAA p. 424)

King, Edward; inv.; 4 Jun 1724; nok Charles & Jane King; admx. Sarah King (I 9.426); acct.; 30 Mar 1725; admx. Sarah, w/o Robert Newton (A 6.306)

King, James, Mr.; inv.; 25 Jul 1736; 1 Nov 1736; nok Charles & Thomas King; admx./extx. Sarah King (I 22.80); acct.; 22 Sep 1740; mentions Edward, James, John, Adam, Elisabeth, Anna, Mary & Sarah King; admx. Sarah King (A 18.64)

King, Charles; will; probate 5 Apr 1739; sons Charles, Richard; g-child. Samuel and Susannah Thomson; daus. Susannah Aisquith, Hellen, ___ Nuethall; tracts *Dedfort [Deaford], Charles' Park, Fox Grape Barron, Persimmon Branch, Parkee's [Peakes] Addition, T. B. [I. R.]* (MCW 8.22) [SMW TA1.84]; inv.; 20 Apr 1739; 18 Apr 1740; nok Richard King, Ann Hellen; adm./ex. Charles King (I 24.543); acct.; 16 Aug 1744 (A 20.436)

King, Richard; inv.; 20 Jan 1752; 29 May 1752; nok Susanna Diffin, Elisabeth Nutthall (I 48.454)

King, Edward and Eleanor; son Adam [b. 17 Oct 1757] (SA p. 17, 52)

King, Edward; will; 4 Feb 1758; 331 Jul 1758; wife Eleanor; son Adam (MCW 11.207) [SMW TA1.367]; inv.; 15 Jan 1759; 2 Jul 1759; nok John & Elisabeth King; admx./extx. Eleanor King (I 67.192); acct.; 26 Dec 1759 (A 44.226)

King, Ann; inv.; 7 Mar 1762; 7 Sep 1762; nok William & Jane King; adm. Thomas King (I 79.264)

King, Bennet, s/o Margaret King [b. 14 Jul 1764] (SA p. 25, 40)

King, Thomas and Eleanor; dau. Jane [b. 29 Jan 1772] (SA p. 21)

King, William; son James, bapt. 21 May 1780 (SA p. 30)

King, Henry and Catharine Watts (by license); m. 17 Jun 1784 (SA p. 62)

KIRBY

Kirby, William; service by 1673 (SK 17.478)

Kerby, Thomas; service by 1673 (SK 17.570)

Kirby, Willm.; *Kirby's Choyce*; 272 ac.; sur. 3 Dec 1680; 1707 poss. Col. Henry
  Lowe; St. Mary's Hundred (RR p. 8) (TLC p. 9)
  Kirby's Fortune; 106 ac.; undated; 1707 held by Wm. Kerby; St. Mary's
  Hundred (RR p. 7) (TLC p. 8)

Kerby, William; bricklayer; *Kerby's Choice*; 272 ac.; 3 Dec 1680 cert./pat. (COL)

Kirby, William; plasterer; will; 29 May 1710; 13 Apr 1720; sons Thomas,
  William; dau. Jane Adams; g-son William Adams (MCW 4.231) [SMW PC1.257]

Kirby (Kerby), William; planter; will; 30 Sep 1724; 26 Jan 1724; dau. Anne;
  wife Frances; wife's child. Thomas and William Loaker and James Watts
  (MCW 5.184) [SMW PC1.293]; inv.; 30 Mar 1725; 19 Apr 1725; nok Thomas
  Kirby, Hugh Hopewell; extx. Frances Kirby (I 10.357); acct.; 25 Apr 1726;
  mentions Thomas & William, sons of Thomas Loker; (A 7.327)

Kerby (Kirby), Thomas; will; 27 Jul 1725; 12 Jan 1755; wife Deborah; son
  Peter; dau. Susannah; tracts *Kerbys Lott, Kerbys Fortune* (MCW 11.82) [SMW
  TA1.330]

Kirby, Joseph; inv.; 15 Feb 1749; 2 Apr 1750; nok Thomas & William Kirby;
  admx./extx. Frances Kirby (I 42.8); acct.; 31 Oct 1750 (A 29.52)

Kirby, Peter and Henrietta; child. Richard [b. 22 Feb 1754], Rebecca [b. 4 Jan
  1762] (SA p. 5)

Kirby, Thomas; inv.; 30 Apr 1756; 3 Aug 1756; nok Susannah & Peter Kirby;
  admx.ex. Thomas Kirby (I 61.330)

Kirby, William and Elizabeth; son Hopewell [b. 22 Apr 1756] (SA p. 6)

Kirby, Thomas and Mary; dau. Elizabeth [b. 2 Jan 1764], Henrietta [b. 17 Apr
  1766] (SA p. 40, 42)

Kirby, Francis and Millburn Hagar (by license); m. 1 Jan 1782 (SA p. 59)

KIRK

Kirke, Martyn; admx. Maria; 19 Dec 1710 (SMAA p. 204)

Kirk, James; *Hillfield*; 96 ac.; 1724 cert./pat. (COL)

Kirk (Kirke), John; inv.; 29 Jan 1733; 15 Apr 1734; nok James & Joseph Keirk
  (I 17.719); acct.; 11 Aug 1735; orphans Zechariah, Katherine & Mary Kirk;
  admx. Dinah, w/o Richard Campbell (A 12.314)

Kirk, Mary; widow; will; 10 Dec 1734; 21 Jan 1734; dau. Mary; sons John,
  James; dau. Barbary Calvert (MCW 7.134) [SMW TA1.45]; inv.; 24 Jul 1735; 10
  Aug 1735; nok Mary Langlay, Barbray Joy; adms./ex. James Kerk (I 21.101);
  acct.; 11 Apr 1737 (A 15.300)

Kirk, Joseph; inv.; 1 Oct 1757; 9 May 1758; nok Elisabeth Kirk, William Faws;
  adm./ex. James Kirk (I 65.241)

KNEVETT

Knevet, Rich'd; *Redbud Thickett*; 100 ac.; sur. 14 Jul 1647; 1707 no poss.; New
   Town Hundred (RR p. 26) (TLC p. 25)
   Knevett; 300 ac.; sur. 12 May 1651; Choptico Hundred (RR p. 26) (TLC p. 25)
Knevett, Jno. *Nevets Beginning*; 100 ac. sur. 22 Oct 1681; 1707 poss. Jno.
   Heard; New Town Hundred (RR p. 38) (TLC p. 37)

KNOTT

Knott, Francis; will; 16 Mar 1704; 14 May 1705; sons Francis, William,
   Edward, John, James, Charles; daus. Elinor, Rebecca; wife Elinor (MCW 3.59)
   [SMW PC1.135]; inv.; 28 May 1705; [Sr.] (I&A 25.33); inv.; 15 Jan 1706 (I&A
   26.229); acct.; 9 Jul 1706; relict and extx. Elinor (SMAA p. 157)
Knot (Knott), Francis; inv.; 4 Apr 1724; 6 Jun 1724; nok Edward & William
   Knot; admx. Jene Knott (I 9.424)
Knott (Knot), Edward; planter; will; 22 Dec 1733; 6 Mar 1733/4; sons George,
   Clement, Edward, Lexius; dau. Monicke; bro. John (MCW 7.68) [SMW TA1.25];
   inv.; 2 Apr 1734; 4 Jun 1734; nok Charles & John Knott; adm./ex. Mary Knott
   (I 18.314); acct.; 17 Sep 1735; adm. George Knott (A 13.325)
Knot, James; planter; will; 31 Dec 1733; 6 Mar 1733/4; child. Francis,
   Susannah, Elizabeth, James, Mary Ann Knot; tract *Hazard* (MCW 7.69) [SMW
   TA1.26]; inv.; 2 Apr 1734; 4 Jun 1734; nok John & Charles Knott; admx./extx.
   Mary Knott (I 18.314); acct.; 4 Jun 1735 (A 13.228)
Knott, John; *Strap*; 44 ac.; sur. 27 Oct 1725 (TLC p. 91); 3 Dec 1735 cert./pat. (COL)
Knott, William; will; 30 Jan 1737; 7 Mar 1737; daus. Monekey, Mildred,
   Henareter, Wennefort; sons Benjamin, Thomas, John, Ignatius; wife Ann
   (MCW 7.242) [SMW TA1.78]; inv.; 7 Mar 1737; 7 Jun 1738; nok George & John
   Knott; admx./extx. Ann Knott (I 23.208); acct.; 7 Jul 1741 (A 18.273)
Knott, George; inv.; 5 Jul 1743; nok Lexsus & Edward Knott; admx./extx.
   Priscilla Knott (I 28.14); acct.; 29 Nov 1744; admx. Prissilla, w/o Luke
   Mattingly (A 21.137)
Knott, Ignatius, Mr.; inv.; 12 May 1747; 15 Sep 1748; nok Thomas Knott, Ann
   Hortlen (I 37.95); acct.; 8 May 1749; orphans Sarah [age 10], Richard Basil
   [age 6], Elisabeth [age 4] (A 27.15)
Knott, John; inv.; 18 Jun 1748; 5 Sep 1748; nok Thomas Knott, Monica Stewart;
   adm./ex. William Knott (I 37.101); acct.; 26 Jun 1749 (A 27.22)
Knott, Thomas; inv.; 4 May 1750; 3 Jul 1750; nok William & Benot Knott;
   admx./extx. Susannah Knott (I 43.288); acct.; 6 Dec 1750 (A 29.132)
Knott, John; inv.; 3 Sep 1753; nok Ann & Clement Knott; admx./extx. Elisabeth
   Knott (I 55.18); acct.; 7 Aug 1754 (A 36.402)
Knott, Bennett and Eleanor; sons [b. 18 Oct 1754], James [b. 6 Oct 1757] (SA p.
   40)
Knot (Knott), Elexander; inv.; 11 Feb 175_; nok Fairfax Compton (I 60.101);
   acct.; 4 Feb 1755 (A 37.76)

Knott, Clement; <u>inv.</u>; 22 May 1762; 16 Aug 1762; nok Samuel Makony, Ann Knott; admx. John Ethelbert Knott (I 79.249)

LAMB
Lamb, Richard; service by 1676 (SK 11.313)
Lamb, Anthony; <u>inv.</u>; 29 Jul 1683 (I&A 8.88)

LAND
Land, Phillip; *Fresh Pond Neck*; 500 ac.; sur. 15 Nov 1648; 1707 poss. Edward Miller. & Tho. Underwood; St. Michael's Hundred (RR p. 13) (TLC p. 13)
Land, Philip; <u>inv.</u>; 22 Jul 1680; admx. Rebeca Askins (I&A 7a.169)

LANE
Lane, Peter; service by 1679 (SK 15.537)
Lane, Charles; 100 ac.; *Rounton Ramour*; 100 ac.; sur. 27 Feb 1684; 1707 no poss.; St. Mary's Hundred (RR p. 11) (TLC p. 12); 27 Feb 1685 cert./pat. (COL)

LANGLEY
Langly, John; <u>inv.</u>; 10 May 1717 (I&A 37b.133); <u>acct.</u>; 14 Oct 1718; adm. Moore Langley (A 1.317) (SMAA p. 329); <u>acct.</u>; 6 Jun 1719 (A 2.220) (SMAA p. 385)
Langly, John, Sr.; <u>will</u>; 29 Feb 1723; 26 May 1729; wife Susannah; children John, Abraham, Susannah (MCW 6.110) [SMW PC1.342]; <u>inv.</u>; 17 Jul 1729; 5 Aug 1729; nok Abraham Langley, Anna Swift; admx./extx. Susanna Langley (I 14.283); <u>acct.</u>; 17 Aug 1730 (A 10.464)
Langley, Abram; <u>inv.</u>; 12 Jun 1741; 6 Aug 1741; nok. Susannah Wildman, John Langley; admx./extx. Elisa Langly (I 26.331)
Langley, John; 28 Aug 1755; 3 Apr 1758; wife Elizabeth; bro. William; sisters Elinor Daffin, Ann, Mary (MCW 11.370); also sister Susanna Hinds; father William [SMW TA1.370]; <u>inv.</u>; 15 Apr 1758; 3 Jul 1758; nok Joshua Tarlton, Thomas Langley; admx./extx. Elisabeth Langley (I 65.264)
Lang (Langley), John; <u>inv.</u>; 10 May 1756; 29 Aug 1756; nok William, Sr. & William Langley; admx./extx. Jane Langley (I 61.333); <u>acct.</u>; 20 Feb 1759; orphans John [at age], Josiah [age 12], John [dec'd] (A 43.98)
Langly, John; <u>inv.</u>; 30 Aug 1759; 5 Aug 1761; nok Hugh Hopewell, James Bisser, Jr.; admx. John Langly (I 74.273)
Langley, Jane; acct.; 23 Oct 1764; to Josias Langley; adm. John Langley (A 52.32); <u>dist.</u>; 28 Oct 1764 (BB 4.51)
Langley, John; <u>inv.</u>; 30 May 1768; 18 Jun 1768; nok Josiah Langley, Joseph Biscoe; admx. Mary Langley (I 95.244); <u>acct.</u>; 24 Dec 1769 (A 62.398); <u>acct.</u>; 10 Sep 1770 (A 64.247);<u>dist.</u>; 10 Sep 1770 (BB 5.387)
Langley, Josias and Susanna; son John Francis Xaviers [b. 22 Jun 1768] (SA p. 189)

Langley, William; 12 Oct 1775; 17 Apr 1776; son William; daus. Ann Smith, Mary Clark; s-i-l Thomas Clark (MCW 16.117)

LANGWORTH
Langworth, William; *Barbary's Addition*; 120 ac.; 4 Mar 1682 cert./pat. (COL)

Langworth, William; 7 Feb 1693; 1 May 1694; wife Ann; daus. Agatha, Elizabeth, Mary; bro. Sampel Lucket's 3 sons: Samuel, Thomas and Ignatius; f-i-l Thos. Hussey & his wife Mary; dec'd wife Mary Hussey; tracts *Mill's Marsh, Highpark, St. Barbaries Addition, Widow's Mite* in CH Co. (MCW 2.69) [SMW PC1.86]; acct.; 21 Aug 1695 (I&A 10.417) (SMAA p. 92)

LARGE
Large, Robert; service by 1669 (SK 12.376)

Large, Robert; inv.; [filed with 1696] (I&A 14.9); acct.; [filed with 1697] (I&A 15.224); acct.; 29 Jul 1698; 4 children; admx. Elisabeth, w/o William Morgan (I&A 16.184)

LATHAM
Latham, Matthew and Susanna; child.: Margaret Ann [b. 25 Dec 1761], William [b. 25 Jun 1765], Mary [b. 8 Mar 1767]; James [b. 27 Oct 1770] (SA p. 2, 8, 42)

Latham, John and Rebecca; son Jeremiah [b. 25 May 1763] (SA p. 195)

LAURENCE
Lawrence, Richard; written 26 Nov 1655; mentions Frances Peakes, w/o Walter Peakes (MCW 1.10)

Laurence, Henry; wife Frances, lately Frances Hyde; 23 Feb 1677 (AM LXVII.193)

Laurence, Henry; inv.; 1 Sep 1694 (I&A 13a.109); acct.; 30 Apr 1695; admx. Frances Lawrence (I&A 13a.290)

Lawrence, Thomas; 9 Mar 1699/1700; mentions unnamed father, mother, bros. & sisters (MCW 2. 203)

Lawrance (Laurence), Henry; inv.; 24 Feb 1718; 22 May 1719; nok Joseph Lawrance, Chris. Hammett; ex. Anne Lawrance (I 2.42); acct.; 22 Sep 1719; admx. widow Mrs. Anne Laurence (A 2.327) (SMAA p. 384); acct.; 2 Feb 1720; admx. Ann Lawrance alias Bayley (SMAA p. 452); acct.; 2 Feb 1720; legatees Joseph & William Laurence; dist. to widow; admx. Ann Lawrance, alias Ann Bayly (A 2.437)

Lawrence, William; inv.; 10 Jul 1736; 31 Jul 1736; nok Catherine Saellin, Frances Low; admx./extx. Victorius Larrence (I 21.419); acct.; 30 Jul 1737; orphan Barbara Larance; adms. John Manning & wife Victorious (A 14.425)

Lawrence, Joseph; will; 6 May 1750; 11 Mar 1750; sons Joseph, Henry, John Gose and William Lawrence; daus. Susannah, Dianna and Cathrine Lawrence and Elizabeth Thomas (MCW 10.143) [SMW TA1.277]; inv.; 16 May 1751; 1 Jun

1751; nok Henry & Catharine Lawrence; adm./ex. Joseph Lawrance (I 47.108); acct.; 14 Jun 1752; orphans Joseph, Henry, Elisabeth & Catherine [all at age], John Goos [age 19], William [age 17], Susannah [age 15], Diannah [age 13] (A 32.349); dist.; 14 Jun 1752 (BB 1.45)

Laurance, David; inv.; 20 Sep 1774 (I 119.146); acct.; 19 Aug 1775 (A 73.249); dist.; 19 Aug 1775 (BB 7.41)

LAWTON

Lawton (Laton, Latton), Thos.; will; probate 4 Mar 1718; sons John, Thomas, Joseph; daus. Mary, Anne; wife Jemine [Jemima] (MCW 4.199) [SMW PC1.244]; inv.; 10 Mar 1718; 10 Apr 1719; extx. Mary Jemmyme LacoLor (I 1.496, 529); acct.; 25 Apr 1720; extx. Jemyme, w/o Charles Brady (A 2.510) (SMAA p. 445)

Lowton, John; inv.; 30 Mar 1745; 7 Aug 1745; nok bro. John Lawton, Joseph Owens; admx./extx. Susanna Lowton (I 31.283)

Layton, John and Jane; children Joseph [b. 13 Jun 1762], Zachariah [b. 13 Jan 1765 (sic)], Ignatius [b. 24 Aug 1768], Susanna [b. 12 Mar 1765 (sic)] (SA p. 194)

LEACH

Leach, Charles; will; 19 Feb 1749/50; 3 Apr 1750; wife Sarah; children unnamed (MCW 10.73) [SMW TA1.261]; inv.; 7 Apr 1750; 5 Jun 1750; nok William Leach, Joseph Fowler; extx. Sarah Leach (I 43.271); acct.; 7 Aug 1751 (A 31.56); dist.; 7 Aug 1751 (BB 1.4)

Leach, Nehemiah; m. 1 May 1783 Elizab. Lyon (BRU 2.536)

LEAKE

Leeky, Alexander; age ca 40; 27 Oct 1721; tract *Watt's Lodge* (CCR p. 46) (MD p. 115)

Leckey, Alexander; acct.; 21 Mar 1723 (A 5.389)

Leake (Leak), John; innholder; Leonard Town; will; 2 Oct 1731; 14 Jan 1731; sons Richard, John, William; daus. Mary Brewer, Catherine; wife Katherine (MCW 6.210) [SMW PC1.347]; inv.; 14 Jan 1730 (sic); 11 Apr 1732; nok John & Catherine (Jr.) Lake; admx./extx. Catherine Leak (I 16.437)

Loak (Leak), John, Mr.; inv.; 20 Apr 1743; 11 Nov 1743; nok William Lake, Catharine Russell (I 28.357); acct.; 9 Aug 1744; mentions Richard, orphan of John Leak, Jr.; orphans Susanna, Elisabeth, Mary, Elinor (A 20.426)

LEE

Lee, Richard, St. John's; 31 Mar 1639; 17 Apr 1639 (MCW 1.1)

Lee, Hugh; age ca 41 in 1650 (MD p. 115)

Lee, Henry; *Lee*; 50 ac.; sur. 4 Dec 1640; esch.; Emanuell Ratcliff lives on it; St. Georges Hundred (RR p. 17) (TLC p. 16)

Legh (Lee), Charles; inv.; 9 Apr 1720; 6 Jun 1720; admx. Marry Lee (I 3.262); acct.; 28 Apr 1721 (A 3.425)

Lee, Luke; planter; will; 30 Sep 1736; 18 Oct 1737; wife Sarah (MCW 7.231) [SMW TA1.70]; inv.; 3 Dec 1737; 13 Feb 1737; Thomas & Nickleas Griffin; admx./extx. Sarah Lee (I 23.21); acct.; 24 Jul 1738 (A 16.294)

Lee, Robert; will; 28 Dec 1687; 4 Jan 1687; mentions Mrs. Ellinor Brookes, sister Mary Darnall, John Beall, Jr. s/o Thomas Beall; father and mother Michael and Christian Lee in Waterford, England; tract *Low's Gift* in DO Co. (MCW 2.20) [SMW PC1.61]; inv.; 7 Jan 1687 (I&A 9.459)

Lee, Samuel; planter; St. George's Hundred; will; 16 Nov 1706; 29 Apr 1713; son Luke (MCW 4.201) [SMW PC1.187]; inv.; 5 May 1713; nok Cassandre Lee, Thomas Griffin; mentions Samuell Lee (I&A 35b.65); acct.; 9 May 1716; ex. Luke Lee (SMAA p. 300); acct.; 7 May 1717 (I&A 38b.2)

Leigh, John; will; 8 Jul 1736; 15 Oct 1736; children Margaret Brooke, John, George, Joseph, Massey, William; wife Dorothy; tracts *Hills, Halley's Manner* (MCW 7.199) [SMW TA1.1]; inv.; 25 Mar 1737; nok Mary & George Leigh; admx./extx. Mrs. Dorothy Leigh (I 22.209); acct.; 30 Jun 1738 (A 16.214)

Lee, John, Sr.; inv.; 5 Nov 1742; nok John & Thomas Lee; adm./ex. Samuel Lee (I 27.227); acct.; 24 Apr 1744; orphans John, Samuel, Thomas; adm. Samuel Lee (A 20.309)

Lee, John; will; 17 Jan 1757; 9 Jul 1757; daus. Elizabeth Gibson, Susanna Bowling, Henerita Hobson, Sarah Tippit, Jane Tippit, Mary Fanning; sons Thomas Lee, John Lee; wife Mary (MCW 11.170) [SMW TA1.359]; inv.; 12 Jul 1757; 8 Mar 1758; nok Samuel & Thomas Lee; admx./extx. Mary Lee (I 65.143); acct.; 7 Mar 1758; orphans Thomas [age 8], John [age 11] (A 41.407); dist.; 7 Mar 1758; legatees Elisabeth Gibson, Susannah Bowling, Henrietta Hobson, Sarah Tippet, Jane Tippet, Mary Fanning, Thomas Lee, John Lee (BB 2.76)

Leigh, Massey; *Town Land*; 117 ac.; 12 Aug 1757 cert./pat. (COL)

Lee, Sarah; will; 25 Feb 1758; 4 Mar 1761; g-daus. Henrietta Hammitt, Elizabeth Bean (MCW 12.36) [SMW TA1.421]; inv.; 7 Apr 1761; nok William Calvie, J. Hammett (I 71.157)

Lee, Mary; will; 4 May 1761; 29 Sep 1761; sons Thomas and John; daus. Henrietta Hobson, Susanna Maddox, Jane Tippet, Sarah Tippet, Elizabeth Gibson, Mary Fanning (MCW 12.99); inv.; 2 Nov 1761; 1 Apr 1762; nok Thomas & Samuel Lee; ex. Thomas Lee, Jr. (I 79.265); acct.; 1 Mar 1763 (A 49.102); dist.; 1 Mar 1763; legatees Thomas, John, Jane Tippet, Sarah Tippet, Elisabeth Gibson, Henrietta Hobson, Susannah Maddox, Mary Fanning (BB 3.178)

Lee, Charles; will; 16 Dec 1769; 11 Apr 1770; children Aaron, Darke, Ezinar (f), Martha Cowne, Mary Ann Hart; wife Mary (MCW 14.135) [SMW TA1.612]; inv.; 4 Jun 1770; 3 Jul 1770; nok John Lee; extx. Mary Lee (I 103.332)

Lee, John; inv.; 8 Oct 1770; 1 Feb 1771; nok Ann Leigh, Charles Lee; admx. Ann Leigh (I 107.92)

Lee, Thomas; 20 Jan 1774; 10 Apr 1774; son Richard, William; wife Mary (MCW 15.150) [SMW TA1.707]

Leigh, Massey; will; 5 Sep 1775; 2 Apr 1776; children William Loaden Leigh, Christopher, Nicholas, Cecilia, Lewis, Edward and Richard; sister Margaret Brooke; bros. Joseph and William (MCW 16.116); inv.; 10 Apr 1776; 15 Jul 1776; nok George & James Leigh; ex. William Leigh (I 125.296)

Leigh, Walter; d. 26 Feb 1806, age 46 (HGM)

LEWELLIN

Lewellin, John; immigrated 1671 (SK WC2.124)

Lewellin, James; gent.; clerk; *Gallows Green*; 4 ac. 26 Apr 1681 cert./pat. (COL) *Enfield Chace*; 1,600 ac.; 4 Oct 1681 cert./pat. (COL)

Lewellin, John; inv.; 21 Apr 1698; admx. Audry Llewellin (I&A 16.11); acct.; 19 May 1699 (I&A 18.110)

Llewellin, Richard; *Fortune Addition*; resur. 25 Jun 1716(TLC p. 77); 250 ac.; 19 Jun 1719 cert./pat. (COL)

Llewellin (Lewellin), Justinian, Mr.; inv.; 23 Apr 1771; 1 Apr 1772; nok John Llewellin; adm. Ann Llewellin (I 109.9); acct.; 28 Apr 1774; adms. George Goldie, & wife Ann (A 72.10)

LEWGAR

Lewgar, John, Sr.; wife Ann, son John [age 9]; entered province in 1637 (PRPC)

Lewgar, John; unnamed; 300 ac.; sur. 4 Dec 1639; no poss. 1707; St. Mary's Hundred (RR p. 1) (TLC p. 1)
St. John's Freehold; 200 ac.; sur. 18 Feb 1640; poss. by His Lordship 1707; St. Mary's Hundred (RR p. 1) (TLC p. 2)
St. Anns; 1,000 ac.; sur. 18 Dec 1640; pat. surrendered by 1704; lay where New Patuxent Town once stood 1707; St. Mary's Hundred (RR p. 2) (TLC p. 1)
Scotland; 200 ac.; sur. 8 Jun 1657; 1707 poss. John Cecill & wife, Wm. Cecill, Adam Cecill; New Town Hundred (RR p. 31) (TLC p. 29)
Phillips Purchase; sur. 24 Apr 1658; assgn. Thomas Phillips; 1707 poss. Tho. Cecill; New Town Hundred (RR p. 31) (TLC p. 30)

LEWIS

Lewis, William; *Lewis Neck*; 30 ac.; sur. 4 Dec 1640; 1707 poss. Daniel Clocker; St. Mary's Hundred (RR p. 1) (TLC p. 1)

Lewis, Patrick; immigrated by 1674 (SK 18.144)

Lewis, John; acct.; 25 Jul 1678; orphans; admx. Katheren Shore (relict) (I&A 5.240)

Lewis, David; *Asquith's Folly*; 100 ac.; 5 Apr 1682; assigned from William Aisquith cert./pat. (COL)

Lewis, James; inv.; 15 Feb 1693 (I&A 13a.101)

Lewis, John; will; probate 19 Dec 1754; son Charles; daus. Mary Adams, Sarah
   Wise, Elenor Lewis; tract *Batchelor's Purchase* (MCW 11.67) [SMW TA1.314]
Lewis, Charles and Jane; son James [b. 13 Oct 1764] (SA p. 40)

LIDDELL
Liddell (Lydell), Robert; *Vennell's Chance*; 56 ac.; 17 Jul 1726 cert./pat. (COL)
Liddal, Robert; 2 Feb 1752; 24 Jul 1753; wife Mary (MCW 10.277) [SMW TA1.301]

LITTLE
Little, John; 22 Dec 1695; will; 22 Dec 1695; wife Mary; son John; dau.
   Johanna (MCW 2.99); inv.; 4 Feb 1695 (I&A 13b.52); acct.; 9 Sep 1696; extx.
   Mary, w/o Robert Thomas (I&A 14.89)
Litell (Little, Littell, Letell), John; will; 31 Mar 1729; 3 Jun 1729; wife Mary
   (MCW 6.119) [SMW PC1.344]; inv.; 2 Sep 1729; 16 Sep 1729; nok Luke Thomas,
   Mary Guillman; admx./extx. Mary Lettler (I 15.105); acct.; 30 Jun 1730; extx.
   Mary, w/o Thomas Balley (A 10.411)

LLOYD
Lloyd, John; will; 27 Jul 1658; wife Margaret; sis.-i-l Margery Molins (MCW
   1.219) (AM XLI.116)
Loyd, Roderick; acct.; 2 May 1704; extx. Martha Loyd (I&A 3.231)
Load, Roderick; inv.; 19 Mar 1716; nok bro. Edward Loyd (I&A 38a.2)
Loyn, Rotherick; acct.; 30 Jul 1718; admx. Sarah Lloyd (A 1.201) (SMAA p. 351)
Lloyd (Floyd), Francis; priest; 13 Nov 1729; age 37 (HGM)
Loyd, Rich'd; *Penamsez*; 100 ac.; sur. 18 Jan 1666; 1707 poss. Rob. Thomas;
   Poplar Hill Hundred (RR p. 24) (TLC p. 23)

LOCK
Lock, Philip; unnamed; 50 ac.; sur. 20 Jul 1714 (TLC, p. 71) *Good Pennyworth*; 50
   ac.; 10 Dec 1714 cert./pat. (COL)
Lock, Philip; 23 Mar 1717/8; 16 Aug 1722; sons William, Philip, Meverall
   [Mevewell] and James Hulse Lock; daus. Mary, Priscilla; wife Mary; tracts
   Good Pennyworth, Hulston (MCW 5.116) [SMW PC1.271]; inv.; 16 Nov 1722; nok
   William & Phillip Lock; extx. Mary Lock (I 9.21); acct.; 8 Aug 1723 (A 5.201)
Lock, William; Esq.; *Lock's Venture*; 49 ac.; sur. 4 Jan 1742 (TLC p. 101); 2 Sep
   1743 cert./pat. (COL)
Lock, William; inv.; 10 Mar 1761; 19 May 1761; adm./ex. Philip Lock (I 74.287)
Lock, Meverel; will; 20 Apr 1764; 5 May 1764; son Meverell, Jesse, George,
   Thomas; daus. Anne, Mary, Elizabeth; wife Elizabeth; tracts *St. Thomas with
   Addition, Dod Park, Heelstone [Houlstone], Truman's [Timmons's] Lodge,
   Keath [Keeth] and Price's Rest, John Edwards Discovery, Truman, Truman's
   [Timmons's] Hunting Quarter* (MCW 13.44) [SMW TA1.479]

Loch, Meverell; <u>inv.</u>; 6 May 1767; nok John Loche, John Oneale; exs. Elisabeth & Meveral Loch (I 94.21); <u>acct.</u>; 20 Jul 1767 (A 57.74)

Lock, Philip; *Pennyworth Addn.*; 43 ac.; 17 Aug 1765 cert./pat. (COL)

Lock, Meverell; *Narrow Chance*; 33 ac.; 13 Jul 1768 cert./pat. (COL)
    Lot; 35 ac.; 11 Nov 1769 cert./pat. (COL)

Lock, Jesse; s/o Meverel; approx. 1765; d. age 19 [SMW TA1.539.556]

Lock, Jesse; Deputy Surveyor for SM Co.; *Lock's Meadow*; 27 ac.; 22 Jul 1775 cert./pat. (COL)

LOKER

Loquer [Loquor]; Thomas; <u>will</u>; 26 Jan 1675; 21 Feb 1675; son Thomas (MCW 1.118) [SMW PC1.15]; <u>inv.</u>; 22 Feb 1675 (I&A 2.148); <u>acct.</u>; 14 May 1677; orphan (I&A 4.57)

Loquer, Thomas; s-i-l of Thomas Innes; 14 May 1677 (SMAA p. 78)

Locar (Loceux), Thomas; <u>inv.</u>; 8 Dec 1712 (I&A 33b.146); <u>acct.</u>; 14 Oct 1717; admx. Frances, w/o William Kerby (I&A 39c.118) (SMAA p. 313)

Loker, William, 14 Apr 1771; 3 Sep 1771; wife Elizabeth Parrot Loker; children Thomas, William, George, Arnold, Sevinia [Levina], Lorodia [Sorodia]; mentions James, s/o Mary Smith; [son Theodore] (MCW 14.182) [SMW TA1.630]; <u>inv.</u>; 1 Oct 1771; 5 Mar 1772; nok William Loke, William Bennett; exs. Elisabeth Parret Loker, Thomas Loker (I 109.12); <u>acct.</u>; 5 Jun 1773; exs. Thomas Loker, William Richardson & wife Elisabeth Parrott Loker (A 68.201)

LONG

Long, John; Charles Co.; <u>will</u>; 19 Nov 1697; 10 Jan 1697; wife Elenor; mentions Mary and Elizabeth [daus. of Clement Haly] and their g-father Edward Turner (MCW 2.132) [SMW PC1.97]; <u>inv.</u>; 24 Jan 1749; 6 Mar 1749; nok Robert Long, Elisabeth Hoskins; adm./ex. John Long (I 42.4); <u>acct.</u>; 2 Jul 1751 (A 30. 198)

Long, John and Barbara; children John Read [b. 23 Jul 1754], Reuben [b. 22 Dec 1756], Nicholas [b. 15 Dec 1759], Hannah [b. 10 Jan 1762], Gabriel [b. 1 Oct 1765], William [b. 28 Feb 1768], Margaret [b. 25 Oct 1769] (SA p. 1, 17, 51, 52)

Long, Peregrine; m. 12 Nov 1778 Rebecca Williams (BRU 2.535)

LORD

Lord, Thomas; <u>inv.</u>; 19 Nov 1702 (I&A 3.105)

Lord, Edwd.; <u>will</u>; 31 Dec 1718; 4 Mar 1718 (MCW 4.199) [SMW PC1.246]

Lord, William; <u>will</u>; 18 Jun 1726; 15 Aug 1726; son William; wife Susana (MCW 5.230) [SMW PC1.308]; <u>inv.</u>; 3 Jan 1726; extx. Susana Lord (I 11.721); <u>acct.</u>; 30 Sep 1727; extx. Susannah, w/o George Griggs (A 8.358)

LOVE

Love, Thomas; *Freestone Point*; 324 ac.; 5 Mar 1688 cert./pat. (COL)

Partnership; 260 ac.; 5 Oct 1695 cert./pat. (COL)
Love's Adventure; 136 ac.; 10 Nov 1695 cert./pat. (COL)
Love's Enjoyment; 311 ac.; 10 Nov 1695 cert./pat. (COL)
Love, Thomas, Capt.; age 53; 13 Oct 1714; tract *Norwood* (CCR p. 29)
Love, William, Mr.; inv.; 12 Jun 1755; 6 Apr 1756; nok Philip & Jesse Love; adms./exs. Elisabeth & Charles Love (I 60.568); acct.; 2 Nov 1756 (A 40.238)
Love, Jesse; *Love's Venture*; 40 ac.; 31 Jul 1776 cert./pat. (COL)

LOWE
Loe, Richard; dec'd by 2 May 1639 (AM IV.57)
Lowe, Henry; *Inclosure*; 200 ac.; 16 Aug 1694; poss. Hen. Lowe; Resurrection Hundred (TLC p. 63)
Low (Lowe), John; will; 30 May 1698; 15 Jul 1701; wife Rebecca; daus. Eliza., Alice, Ellinor, Rebecca; son John; kinsman Marshall Low; tracts *Brother's Joint Interest* [PG Co.], *The Guardian* (MCW 2.233); inv.; 16 Jul 1701 (I&A 21.208); acct.; 5 Apr 1709; ex. Rebecca Mudd (late Rebecca Wright), w/o Thomas Mudd; Rebecca d. by 5 Apr 1709 (I&A 29.177) (SMAA p. 182); acct.; 20 May 1709; (I&A 29.300); acct.; 30 May 1709 (SMAA p. 181)
Lowe, John; *Inclosure*; 75 ac.; sur. 8 May 1700; 1707 poss. Tho. Mudd, m. widow; St. Georges Hundred (RR p. 19) (TLC p. 19); 1 Jun 1700 cert./pat. (COL)
Lowe, Henry, Col. & wife Susannah Maria; ___ *Spring*; 244 ac.; 1703 cert./pat. (COL)
Low (Lowe), Thomas; acct.; 22 Mar 1706 (I&A 26.155); admx. Francis Lowe (SMAA p. 135)
Low, Margrett; will; 19 Feb 1711; 3 Apr 1711 (MCW 3.199) [SMW PC1.178]; inv.; 14 Apr 1711 (I&A 32c.92); acct.; 6 Mar 1711 (I&A33a.181) (SMAA p. 220)
Lowe, Susannah Maria; wife of Henry Lowe; d. 28 Jul 1714; age 47 (HGM)
Lowe, Henry, Col.; d-i-l ___ Darnall; June 1715 (CCR p. 33)
Lowe, Henry, Sr.; will; 25 Oct 1717; 6 Nov 1717; sons Henry, Jr., Bennett, Thomas, Nicholas; daus. Ann, Elizabeth, Henrietta Maria, Dorothy, Mary, Susanna Maria (w/o Charles Diggs); tracts *Golden Grove, New Design, Woods Quarter, Green Oak* (MCW 4.125); inv.; 3 Dec 1717 (I&A 39c.162); acct.; 22 Apr 1719; exs. Henry & Bennett Lowe (A 1.426) (SMAA p. 405)
Lowe, Bennett; inv.; 26 Nov 1722; mentions Eleanor & Mary Lowe (I 9.22); acct.; 19 Dec 1723; [Esq.]; sisters Mrs. Mary Lowe, Mrs. Dorothy Lowe, sister who m. Charles Diggs; adm. bro. Nicholas Lowe (A 5.287)
Lowe, Nicholas, Esq.; *Workington*; 350 ac. 18 Jan 1727 cert./pat. (COL)
Friends' Goodwill; 1,100 ac.; 16 May 1728 cert./pat. (COL)
Lowe, Nicholas; Gent.; will; probate 22 May 1729; sisters Susannah Diggs, Mary Neale, Elizabeth Darnall, Dorothy; tracts *Bennetts Lowe* and *Green Oak* in KE Co., *Spries [Spice] Hills* in CE Co, *Barbadoes* in CH Co., *Delabrook Mannor, Golden Grove* in DO Co., *Workinton*; mentions Christian Geist, Gent [30 years] and Philip Key [32 years] (MCW 6.113) [SMW PC1.345]; inv.; 20 Sep

1729; 22 Oct 1729; nok Henry Darnall, of Portland Manor, Edward Neale (I
15.110); acct.; 21 May 1730; sisters Susannah, w/o Charles Digges; Elizabeth,
w/o Henry Darnall; Mary, w/o Edward Neale; Dorothy, w/o Francis Hall (A
10.263); acct.; 23 May 1738 (A 16.133); acct.; 15 Jan 1742 (A 19.309)
Low, Ignatius; m. 20 Nov 1777 Priscilla Norris (MM)

LOWERY
Loury, Alexander; service by 1670 (SK 17,357)
Lowery, William. 28 Aug 1698; 9 Dec 1698 (MCW 2.167) [SMW PC1.118]

LUCAS
Lucas, William; will; 30 Nov 1675; 12 Jan 1675; wife Frances; son William
(MCW 1.114) [SMW PC1.13]; acct.; 29 Jan 1676 (I&A 3.65)
Lucas, Frances; 1678; husband d. 3 yrs. ago; mentions 2 children incl. crippled
female age 11 (MD p. 120)
Lucas, William, Jr.; inv.; 20 May 1749; 27 Jul 1749; nok William & Sofier
Lucas; admx./extx. Ann Lucas (I 40.42)
Lucas, William; planter; will; 27 Jun 1750; 16 Jul 1750; children Charles,
Henry, Jean, Suffiah, Mary; d-i-l Ann Lucas; g-children Charles, Ann, Mary,
Mathew and Thomas Drurys (?) (MCW 10.102) [SMW TA1.260]; inv.; 13 Aug
1750; 15 Oct 1750; nok John Baptist Lucas, Mary Power; adms./exs. Charles
& Henry Lucus (I 44.39); acct.; 7 Jul 1752; orphans Charles, Henry, Jean &
Sufiah [all at age], Mary [age 13] (A 32.412); dist.; 7 Jul 1753; children Charles,
Henry, Jane & Sufiah [all of age] & Mary [age ca 3 yrs.] (BB 1.71)
Lucas, William and Rachel; son Joshua [b. 9 Feb 1755] (SA p. 35)
Lucas, Mary; approx. 1765; age 24 [SMW TA1.539.556]
Lucas, Henry; inv.; 4 Apr 1769; nok Jean Spaldin, __dan Mahoney; admx. Ann
Lucas (I 98.356); inv.; 4 Apr 1769; nok Jean Spalding, Mary Mahoney, Monicia
Queen (I 101.18); acct.; 26 Feb 1771; adms. George Collins & wife Ann (A
66.169); dist.; 26 Feb 1771 (BB 6.93)
Lucas, John Baptie; inv.; 12 Jun 1772; 13 Sep 1772; nok Elisabeth & Eleanor
Lucas; admx./extx. Ann Lucas (I 110.95); acct.; 10 May 1775; admx. Ann, w/o
Thomas Jarboe (A 72.156); dist.; 10 May 1775 (BB 7.26)
Lucas, Stephen; inv.; 14 May 1774; 29 Nov 1774; nok Richard & Rachel
Sparks; admn. Michael Lucas (I 118.219); acct.; 15 Mar 1777 (A 74.28)

LURTY
Lurty, Patrick; inv.; 10 May 1724; 16 Jul 1724; admx. Elisabeth Lurty (I 10.11)
acct.; 4 Mar 1725; admx. Elisabeth, w/o Henry White (A 6.305)
Lurty, John and Susannah Nugent; m. 30 Apr 1780 (SA p. 58)

LYNCH
Lynch, Francis; acct.; 16 Jan 1711 (I&A 33a.170) (SMAA p. 221)

Lynch, John; inv.; 19 Apr 1742; 10 May 1742; nok John, Jr. & John Mackey; admx./extx. Catherine Lynch (I 26.543); acct.; 11.Jul 1743 (A 19.439)

Linch, Stephen; inv.; 24 Aug 1752; nok John & Benjamin McKay; admx./extx. Cathrine Lynch (I 49.107); acct.; 25 Jun 1753; mentions Francis (f), Christian, Ann, John & Richard Joyce Lynch, ch/o John Lynch; admx. Catherine Goldsberry (A 35.124)

Lynch, Francis; will; 2 Feb 1770; 6 Jun 1770; wife Jemima (MCW 14.135) [SMW TA1.613]; inv.; 1 Oct 1770; 13 Oct 1770; nok John McCleland, John Lynch; ex. Jemima Lynch (I 103.331); acct.; 20 Oct 1772 (A 67.144)

LYON

Lyon, Richard; inv.; 26 May 1735; 5 Jun 1735; nok John & Henry Lyon; admx./extx. Rachel Lyon (I 20.477); acct.; 2 Jun 1736; orphans John, Michaell & Susanna Lyon; adms. Bowles Billingsly & wife Rachell (A 15.81)

Lyon, John; m. 19 Jan 1783 Sarah Thompson (BRU 2.536)

MACDANIEL

Mackdaniel, Edward; inv.; 8 May 1711 (I&A 33a.44)

Macdaniel (Mackdanell), Edmund; acct.; 22 Feb 1711 (I&A 33a.157) (SMAA p. 223)

MACKALL

Mackall, George; St. George's Hundred [St. Mary's Hundred]; 30 Sep 1675; 3 Feb 1675; wife Ann; daus. Jane, Rachel, Hannah, Sarah; tracts *Pine [Piney] Point, Hepburne's Choice, Magys Jointure* in BA Co. (MCW 1.116) [SMW PC1.17]; inv.; 26 Apr 1676; 2 May 1676 (I&A 2.78)

Mecall, George; acct.; [filed with 1695]; admx. Hannah, w/o Philip Clarke; unadm. by extxs. Ann, w/o Robert Graham & Jane, w/o John Watson (I&A 13a.285)

Macall, James; acct.; 9 May 1716 (I&A 37c.156); acct.; 9 May 1716; drowned (SMAA p. 305)

MACKEY

Makey, John; records cattle mark for dau. Rebecca Makey; 13 Jul 1668 (AM LVII.345)

Mackey (Macky), John; St. George's Hundred; will; 27 Jan 1675; 26 Feb 1675; wife Eliza:; sons John and James (MCW 1.118); John Makey [SMW PC1.20]; acct.; 16 Oct 1677; extx. Elisabeth Spracklin (I&A 4.423)

Makey, James; inv.; Nov 1705 (I&A 25.175); mentions Alice Mackie; 22 Mar 1706 (SMAA p. 133) (I&A 26.158)

Mackey, John; acct.; 13 Sep 1706; admx. Alice Mackey (I&A 26.160) (SMAA p. 134)

Mackay (Mackey), John; *Beam Point*; 100 ac.; pat. *Bean Point* 23 Oct 1709; incl. in *Resurvey of Machie Neck* (TLC p. 66); 3 Oct 1709 cert./pat. (COL)

Mackay's Neck; 253 ac.; resur. 28 Nov 1713; pat. 25 Apr 1717 (TLC p. 73); 6
Jun 1719 cert./pat. (COL)

Mackey, Benjamin; inv.; 8 Jan 1727; 25 Mar 1728; nok John Lynch, John
Mackey; adm. Daniel Mackey (I 13.93); acct.; 16 Apr 1728 (A 9.165)

Mackey, Daniel; inv.; 19 Dec 1729; 26 Feb 1729; nok John Mackey, Stephen
McKey (I 15.371); acct.; 3 Jan 1731 (A 11.322)

Mackey, Patrick; inv.; 30 Mar 1730; 27 Jul 1730 (I 15.605); acct.; 27 Jul 1730 (A
10.418)

Mackey, Stephen; *Woodstock*; 127 ac.; sur. 29 Jul 1743 (TLC p. 103); 19 Oct 1743
cert./pat. (COL)

Mackey [Maukey], Sarah; will; 13 Feb 1747; 28 Mar 1748; children Thomas,
William Challener, Mary and Ann Jane [surname Jane] (MCW 9.143) [SMW
TA1.215]

Mackey, Stephen; inv.; 5 Apr 1748; 2 Aug 1748; nok John & Gilbert Mackey (I
36.114); acct.; 20 Jun 1749 (A 27.19); acct.; 20 Jul 1750; (testator m. widow of
John Jeans); orphans of John Jeans: Thomas, William, Mary (w/o Thomas
Bissco, Jr.), Ann; adm. Astin Sanford Smoote (A 28.230)

McKey (Mackey), John; inv.; 7 Nov 1751; 25 Nov 1751; nok Gilbert &
Benjamin McKeay; admx./extx. Elisabeth McKay (I 48.106); acct.; 9 Oct 1752;
dist. to Mary [age 10], Richard [age 3]; Elisabeth, w/o James Bissco (A 33.206)

McKey, John; inv.; 1 Dec 1760; 4 Mar 1761; nok John & Stephen McKay (I
71.173)

Mackey, John; dist.; 9 Oct 1752; admx. Elizabeth (BB 1.60)

McKay, Sarah; inv.; 10 Sep 1761; 13 Oct 1761; nok Roger Tolle, John Belt;
adm. George McKay (I 76.319)

McKay, John, Mr.; inv.; 10 Jun 1774; nok George & John McKay; adm.
Benjamin McKay (I 119.159)

MACKMURRY

Mackmurry, Bartholomew; [filed with 1674] (SMAA p.40)

MackMurree (Mackmorry) {Mackmurray], Batholomew; will.; 15 Feb 1697/8;
11 Apr 1698; son Adryan; son John Ruby; tract *Foxes Den* [*Forest Denn*]
(MCW 2.138) [SMW PC1.104]; inv. & acct.; Apr 1700 (I&A 19½a.153)

MADDOX

Maddox, Samuel; will; 18 Jan 1684; 9 Mar 1684/5; sons Notley, Samuel,
William, John (MCW 1.144) [SMW PC1.50]

Maddox, Notley; will; 24 Feb 1715; 3 Apr 1716; sons Samuel, Notley, John;
daus. Ann, Sarah, Jane; wife Margaret; bro. William Notley (MCW 4.43) [SMW
PC1.208]; inv.; 1 Jun 1716; nok Samuel & John Maddox (I&A 37a.167); acct.; 15
Mar 1717; extx. Margret Maddox (I&A 39b.78) (SMAA p. 338)

Maddox, Samuel; inv.; 11 Jun 1725; 4 Aug 1725; nok John Maddox, George
Wollis; admx. Margaret Maddox (I 11.17); acct.; 8 Jun 1727; admx. Margret,
w/o George Whetter (Whitter) (A 8.271)

Maddox, Margreter; will; 26 Sep 1739; 6 Nov 1739; sons Samuel, Notly, John;
daus. Anne Mugg, Sarah Sims, Jean Voidry (MCW 8.57) [SMW TA1.94]

Maddox (Madox), Samuel; will; 19 Nov 1739; 8 Dec 1739; nephew Samuel, s/o
bro. John; sisters Anne Mugg, Jane Vadry, Sarah Simms; bros. John, Notley
(MCW 8.57) [SMW TA1.91]; inv.; 16 Jan 1739; 6 Mar 1739; nok Peter Mugg,
George Vadrey; adm./ex. John Maddox (I 24.535); acct.; 9 Dec 1740 (A 18.99);
acct.; 13 Sep 1746 (A 22.265)

Maddox, Notley; will; 23 Apr 1761; 3 Nov 1761; wife Susanna; dau. Judith
Warren Maddox; bro. Townly [Tennely] (MCW 12.99) [SMW TA1.408]; acct.; 3
May 1763; extx. Susanna, w/o John Cartwright (A 49.623); dist.; 3 May 1763
dau. Judith Warner Maddox (BB 6.57)

Madox, Notley; inv.; 30 Mar 1762; 27 May 1762; nok John & William Maddox;
exs. John Cartwright & wife Susanna (I 78.93)

MAHONEY

Mahony, Timothy; inv.; 10 May 1710 (I&A 31.219); acct.; 7 Aug 1711 (I&A 32c.94);
acct.; admx. Elisabeth; 7 Aug 1711 (SMAA p. 217)

Mahany, Matthew; inv.; 1 Apr 1714 (I&A 35a.236); acct.; 13 Sep 1714 (SMAA p.
270)

Mahoney, Elizabeth; widow; age ca 58; d/o Susannah Cooksey; 25 Jun 1722
(CCR p. 50)

Mahany, Thomas; inv.; 5 Aug 1728; admx. Jane Mahany (I 13.174); acct.; 9 Jun
1729 (A 9.406)

Mahoney, Edward; will; 23 Jan 1749; 6 Mar 1749; children James, Edward, Ann
& others unnamed; tract *Piles Discovery* (MCW 10.72) [SMW TA1.240]

Mahoney, John; inv.; 15 Nov 1749; 6 Mar 1749; nok Richard & Ignatius
Mahony; admx./extx. Mildred Mahoney (I 42.5); acct.; 3 Apr 1750; orphans
Ignatious [age 12], Ann [age 8], Elinor [age 7], Mary [age 5], John Barton
[age 3], Bennett [age 1] (A 28.118)

Mahony (Honey), Edward; inv.; 1 May 1750; 5 Jun 1750; nok Samuel
Mahoney, Sr.; Elisabeth Fowler; admx./extx. Mary Mahoney (I 43.264); acct.; 8
Mar 1753; mentions Henry [at age], Joseph [age 14], Ann [age 12], Mary [age
9], John Baptis [d. since father] (A 33.411); dist.; 8 Mar 1753; children Henry
[of age], Joseph, [age 15 next June], Ann [age 13 next May], Mary [age 10
next Aug] & John [d. after his father] (BB 1.72)

Mahoney, Basil; *Haphazard*; 18 ac.; 28 Sep 1763 cert./pat. (COL)

Mahoney, Samuel; will; 31 Oct 1766; 20 Jul 1767; sons Clement, Samuel, Basil;
dau. Monica Hodgkin; g-dau. Allitasia, d/o dau. Ann Mahoney; [dau. Jean
Thompson]; wife Monica (MCW 14.2) [SMW TA1.523]; inv. 27 Oct 1767; 10 Nov

1767; nok Monicca Mahony, Jean Thompson; ex. Basil Mahoney (I 94.200); acct.; 4 Aug 1768 (A 58.256)

MALONE
Melone (Malone), Margaret; inv.; 2 Jun 1724; nok Elisabeth Hastie; adm. John Hastey (I 9.452); acct.; 2 Jun 1724 (A 6.36); acct.; 3 Jul 1725 (A 6.440)
Mallahone, John; acct.; 26 Nov 1728; admx. Anne Woods (A 9.263)
Malohone, Jac.; m. 21 Apr 1771 Maria Langley (MM)

MANLEY
Manley, John; Deputy Surveyor for SM Co.; *Basford Manor*; 4,000 ac.; 21 Jul 1679 cert./pat. (COL)
Manley, Thomas; *Thomas's Conclusion*; 123 ac.; 18 Dec 1747 cert./pat. (COL) *Chances Conclusion with Amendment* [orig. *Chances Conclusion*]; resur. 18 Dec 1747 (TLC p. 75)
Manley, Thomas; inv.; 9 Nov 1772; 9 Mar 1772; nok Priscilla Hernson, Mary Allison; admx. Ann Manley (I 114.13)

MANNING
Manning, Elizabeth; age ca 35 in 1678 (MD p. 134)
Manning, Susannah; inv.; 24 Nov 1717; 24 Feb 1758; nok Ann & James Manning (I 65.72)
Manning, John; acct.; 17 May 1718; adm. Cornelius Manning (A 1.49) (SMAA p. 354); acct.; 17 Jun 1719; children Mark, Mary, John (A 2.50) (SMAA p. 400); acct.; 25 Jul 1719 (A 2.136) (SMAA p. 386); acct.; 23 Sep 1720 (A 3.185) (SMAA p. 414)
Maning (Manning), Cornelius; will; 10 Apr 1721; 15 Aug 1721; son Cornelius; daus. Mary Mills and Ann; wife Elizabeth; ___ Shurley, g-mother of Ann; mentions John, s/o John Maning and William, s/o Edward Morgan; tracts *Maning's Hold, Porkhall Neck, Riggs, Cornelius' Swamp, Hatton's* (MCW 5.67) [SMW PC1.263]; inv.; 14 Oct 1721; 4 Dec 1721; nok Mary Morgan, Mary Simes; ex. Mary Manning (I 6.238); acct.; 13 Aug 1722; exs. William Coombs and wife Elizabeth [probate calls her Mary] (A 4.237); acct.; 18 Mar 1723; exs. William Coombs & wife Elisabeth (A 5.393)
Manning, Marke; inv.; 22 Apr 1726; 2 Nov 1726; nok Mary Mills, Mary Sikes (I 11.603, 604); acct.; 10 Jul 1727; admx. Mary Morgan (A 8.278, 279)
Manning, Cornelius; *Broad Neck*; 83 ac.; resur. 23 Apr 1735 (TLC p. 94); 26 Nov 1737 cert./pat. (COL)
Manning, John; will; probate 3 Jul 1750; sons James, John, Joseph; daus. Ann, Susana; wife Mary; tracts *Marks Delight, Fortune, Tanton Dane* (MCW 10.97) [SMW TA1.259]; inv.; 25 Aug 1750; 9 Oct 1750; nok Cornelius Manning, John Cole; admx./extx. Mary Manning (I 44.35); acct.; 9 Sep 1751; orphans Owen

[age 14], James [age 10], John [age 8], Susannah [age 5], Joseph [age 2], Mark [age 8 mos.] (A 31.67); <u>dist.</u>; 9 Sep 1751 (BB 1.4)

Manning, Cornelius and [?Jane] his wife; [microfilm shows ditto of Jane under name for wife Cornelius Manning; some sources question that his wife was named Jane and list Ignatius as Ignatius Greenwell]; children Ignatius [b. 23 Dec 1754], Monica [b. 26 Oct 1759], Frances [b. 10 Jan 1762] (SA p. 54)

Manning, Cornelius and Jane; daus. Monica [b. 26 Oct 1759], Frances [b. 10 Jan 1762] (SA p. 19)

Manning, Cornelius; <u>will</u>; 2 Aug 1764; 3 Sep 1764; sons John, Robert; daus. Monica, Mary, Anne Elizabeth Fenwick; child Francis [dau.]; wife Jane; g-son Cornelius Fenwick; s-i-l John Greenwell; tract *Nun's Oak* (MCW 13.43) [SMW TA1.459]; <u>inv.</u>; Oct 1764; 24 Apr 1765; nok Athanathus Ford, Mary Combs, Ann Elisabeth Fenwick; extx. Jane Manning (I 87.8); <u>acct.</u>; 15 Dec 1766 (A 55.326); <u>dist.</u>; 15 Dec 1766 (BB 5.11)

Manning, James and Margaret; children William [b. 22 Jun 1762], Mary [b. 17 Sep 1765], John, [b. 27 Mar 1767] (SA p. 194)

Manning, John and Susanna; son Joseph [b. 2 Oct 1767] (SA p. 193)

Manning, James; planter; <u>will</u>; 4 May 1768; 18 Jun 1768; sons William, John; dau. Mary; wife Margaret; f-i-l John Fenwick; bro. John; tracts *Revells, Tauton Dean, Marks Adventure* (MCW 14.44) [SMW TA1.565]; <u>inv.</u>; 20 Sep 1768; nok John Wiseman Greenwell, John Manning; exs. Margaret & John Manning (I 98.110); <u>acct.</u>; 12 Apr 1769 (A 60.363); <u>acct.</u>; 13 Aug 1771; exs. Philip Coombs & wife Margaret, John Manning (A 66.173); <u>dist.</u>; 13 Aug 1771 (BB 6.91)

Manning, Joseph; <u>acct.</u>; 25 Nov 1771; adm. John Manning (A 66.71); <u>dist.</u>; 25 Nov 1771 (BB 6.84)

Manning, Mark; <u>will</u>; 17 Feb 1774; 14 Jun 1774; bro. John (MCW 16.34) [SMW TA1.681]

MANSELL

Mansell, John; *Gilmots Hill*; 600 ac.; sur. 17 Mar 1650; 1707 poss. Henry Spink, Edw'd Spink, Tho. Walker; New Town Hundred (RR p. 29) (TLC p. 27)
St. Johns; 100 ac.; sur. 24 Jan 1648; New Town Hundred (RR p. 27) (TLC p. 26)

Mansfield, Philip; service by 1674 (SK 18.102)

Mansell (Mansfield), Vincent; *Chester*; 300 ac.; 2 tracts sur. 18 Apr 1678; 1707 poss. His Lordship; St. Clements Hundred (RR p.) (TLC p. 45); 6 Aug 1683 cert./pat. (COL)
Gloster; 4 Jun 1683 cert./pat. (COL)

Mansell, Vincent; <u>inv.</u>; 31 Dec 1686 (I&A 9.469); <u>inv.</u>; 31 Dec 1686; 9 Jul 1687 (I&A 9.350)

Mansell, Robert; taylor; <u>will</u>; 16 Apr 1716; 5 Oct 1717; cous. Robert Mansell and his sister Grace of Devonshire (MCW 4.113)

Mansfield, Walter; <u>acct.</u>; 29 Nov 1731 (A 11.316)

MAREMAN

Mareman, John and Ann; son Zachariah [b. 16 Dec 1751], Joseph [b. 6 Jul 1748], Joshua [b. 15 Jun 1746] (SA p. 36, 37)

Mairman, John; will; 2 Oct 1764; 26 Aug 1766; wife Ann; sons William, Joshua, Joseph, Zachariah; daus.? Elinor Nichols, Lotte Mason, Sarah Mason, Elizabeth Carpenter, Susannah Wells, Lidia Linseyward (MCW 13.151) [SMW TA1.500]; inv.; 20 Feb 1767; nok William & Joshua Mareman; extx. Ann Mareman (I 91.86); acct.; 7 Jun 1769 (A 62.155); dist.; 7 Jun 1769 (BB 5.228)

Mareman, Joshua and Susanna; children James [b. 18 May 1767], Mary [b. 29 Oct 1769], John Baptist [b. 27 Mar 1771], Mary Attaway [b. 6 Apr 1773], Joseph [b. 12 Aug 1775] (SA p. 24, 27)

Mareman, Joseph and Elizabeth; children Richard [b. 3 Feb 1768], Ann [b. 18 May 1775] (SA p. 11, 26, 45)

Mareman, William and Mary; dau. Lydda [b. 23 Jun 1773], Elizabeth [b. 3 Jul 1776] (SA p. 23, 27)

Mareman, Ann; widow of John Mareman; will; 8 Oct 1774; 12 Nov 1774; children Susanna Wells, Lydda Ward, Eleanor Rainy, William, Joshua, Joseph, Zachariah; mentions William Clarke's children; gr-dau. Sarah Mason (MCW 16.1) [SMW TA1.678]

Mareman, Zachariah and Ann; son William [b. 26 Nov 1775] (SA p. 27)

MARLOE

Marloe, Wm.; *Adjoynder*; 50 ac.; sur. 22 Oct 1667; 1707 poss. Rob. Tunnell; Poplar Hill Hundred (RR p. 24) (TLC p. 23)

Hogg Confusion; 100 ac.; sur. 22 Oct 1667; 1707 poss. Widow Jones; land not found; Poplar Hill Hundred (RR p. 24) (TLC p. 23)

MARRITT

Marrett, John; acct.; 13 Mar 1718; ex. Francis Marrett (A 1.38)

Marritt (Marett), John; cordwinder; will; 9 Apr 1717; 1 May 1717; son John; dau. Alice Gibson; d-i-l Mary Christian; wife Frances (MCW 4.98) [SMW PC1.215]

Maritt, Francis; widow; 23 Oct 1721; 9 Oct 1721; sons John Marritt and John Price; daus. Hoopswell [Hopewell] Marritt and Francis Beech (MCW 5.75) [SMW PC1.268]

MARSHALL

Marshall, George; 21 Sep 1675; 21 Dec 1675; son Adriaen, [son Doryien] (MCW 1.117) [SMW PC1.24]; acct.; 21 Apr 1677; mentions Christopher Spry m. widow of Thomas Brinson (I&A 4.1); mentions Elizabeth, extx. of Charles DelaRoche; 21 Apr 1677 (SMAA p. 47)

MARTIN

Martin, Eleanor; widow of Christopher Martin; tailor; 8 Oct 1641 (AM IV.66, 92)

Martyn (Martin), Elionor; wife of Francis; vs Patience Martyn (widow of William, heir of Francis); all of *St. Hiermoms*; sons Lodowicke, William; Francis father of William; children of Patience: Margarett, Martha and Dorothy Needham; 21 Jan 1662 (AM XLIX.30)

Martin, James; *Rollery*; 100 ac.; sur. 3 Apr 1665; 1707 poss. son James Martin; New Town Hundred (RR p. 33) (TLC p. 32)

Martin, James; *Cole Park*; 150 ac.; sur. 13 Apr 1665; 1707 poss. James Martin; St. Clements Hundred (RR p. 44) (TLC p. 43)

Martin, James; records cattle mark for son James; 14 Jan 1667/8 (AM LVII.232)

Martin, James; [St. Clement's Bay]; will; 3 Aug 1669; 4 Sep 1669; wife Ann; dau. Ann; son James; tracts *Edinborough, Ralley* [*Rolley*], *Cole Parke*; mentions Charles Maynard and his sisters Elizabeth and Agnes Maynard (MCW 1.48) [SMW PC1.9]

Martin, Ann; widow; *St. James's*; 100 ac.; 20 Oct 1682 cert./pat. (COL)
   Widow (bounds of); 100 ac.; undated cert./pat. (COL)
   Witham [*Witcham*]; 1707 poss. James Martin; no land; Choptico Hundred (RR p. 53) (TLC p. 51)

Martin, James; *Wolf Holes*; 258 ac.; sur. 8 Apr 1703; 1707 poss. James Martin; St. Clements Hundred (RR p. 48) (TLC p. 47); 10 Nov 1703 cert./pat. (COL)

Martin (Martyn), James; inv.; 6 Jun [filed with 1716] (I&A 38b.54); acct.; 30 Jul 1718; admx. Elizabeth Burrell (A 1.203) (SMAA p. 350)

Marten (Martin, Martan, Martain), William; will; 21 Oct 1745; 5 Dec 1750; sons William, John, Thomas; daus. Hanah Johneston, Elisabeth Taylor, Wineford Woodward (MCW 10.124); dau. called Elizabeth Raylen [SMW TA1.244]; inv.; 11 Nov 1751; nok Janet Artos, Thomas Marten; adm./ex. William Marten (I 48.104); acct.; 27 Nov 1752; orphans William, Jenett, Ann [all of age], Thomas [age 10] (A 33.317); dist.; 27 Nov 1752 (BB 1.61)

Martin, William and Mary Ann; children Thomas [b. 13 Jun 1757], William [b. 13 Feb 1759], George [b. 10 May 1761] (SA p. 7)

Martin, Thomas and Jane; children Ann [b. 27 Mar 1759], John Curry [b. 17 Feb 1761], Jane Dorothy [b. 17 Feb 1764] (SA p. 7)

Martin, Thomas Green; will; probate 2 Aug 1773; wife and children unnamed (MCW 15.69); inv.; 22 Nov 1773; nok Thomas Lee, Jr. & Sr. (I 114.11); acct.; 10 Oct 1775 (A 73.241); dist.; 10 Oct 1775 (BB 7.42); inv.; 20 Oct 1775 (I 122.189)

Martin, William and Anne Thompson; m. 3 Feb 1780 (SA p. 58)

Martin, Stephen and Elizabeth; dau. Laura Sophia [b. 21 Jan 1816; bapt. 19 May 1816] (SA p. 34)

MASON

Mason, Susan; transported by 1677 (SK 15.433)

Mason, Robert; gent.; *Ambersley*; 65 ac.; 3 Jan 1682 cert./pat. (COL)

Mason, Robert; High Sheriff; age ca 40 in 1693 (MD p. 126)

Mason (Mecens), William; inv.; 20 Jun 1698 (I&A 16.206)

Mason, Robert; will; 1 Mar 1697; 17 Sep 1701; wife Susannah; sons Robert, John, Matthew, Rodham; dau. Mary [other daus. unnamed]; tracts *Sewell, Cook's Folly, Amhersley, Stimhope's Neglect, Grime's Ditch, Paradise* in BA Co., *Bloomberry, Dunbarr, Salop* [PG Co.] (MCW 2.227) [SMW PC1.126]; acct.; 20 Mar 1706; extx. Susanna Mason; acct.; 20 Mar 1706/7 (SMAA p. 148) (I&A 26.275); inv.; 25 Mar 1706 (I&A 25.174; 29.157)

Mason, Robert; acct.; undated [1709]; mother Susanna, extx.; her children Matthew, Rodham, John, Elizabeth (SMAA p. 175); acct.; 25 Sep 1710; extx. Susanna Mason (I&A 32b.241) (SMAA p. 194); acct.; 11 May 1716 (I&A 37c.157); acct.; 31 May 1716 (SMAA p. 293, 302) (I&A 38b.6)

Mason, George; will; 14 Oct 1722; 21 Nov 1722 (MCW 5.122) [SMW PC1.270]; inv.; 1 Feb 1722; 4 Feb 1722 (I 8.53); acct.; 8 Feb 1723 (A 5.344)

Mason, John; will; 30 Sep 1717; 29 Oct 1717; sisters Susannah w/o George Clarke, Elizabeth Rogers, Mary Mason; nephew Robert [Rodham] Mason and his bro. Stratford; bro Mathew; nephew Rodham Rogers; tracts *Mason's Purchase, Cooke's Folly, Dunbar and Bloonsberry* (MCW 4.171) [SMW PC1.222]; inv.; 25 Nov 1717; nok George Clarke; ex. Matt. Mason (I&A 39c.173); acct.; 26 Nov 1719; legatees Robert Mason, Mrs. Ann Waughope (A 2.408)

Mason, Susanna; widow of Robert Mason, gent.; will; 14 Jan 1716; 13 Feb 1716; sons John, Mathew; daus. Elizabeth Rogers, Susanna Clarke, Mary; g-son Robert Mason (MCW 4.99) [SMW PC1.214]; inv.; 17 Jun 1717 (I&A 37b.229); acct.; 7 Aug 1719; mentions Elisabeth, w/o Mr. John Rogers & Susanna, w/o Mr. George Clark]; ex. Mathew Mason, ex. of John Mason, ex. of dec'd] (A 2.309); acct.; 7 Aug 1719 (SMAA p. 381)

Mason, John; *Dunbar*; 190 ac.; resur. 8 Dec 1715; (TLC p. 72); 11 Apr 1716 cert./pat. (COL)

Mason, John; acct.; ex. Matthew; 26 Nov 1719 (SMAA p. 369)

Mason, Mathew; acct.; 22 Apr 1720; exs. Johanna & William Price (A 10.231)

Mason, Mathew; Gent.; acct.; 12 Feb 1722; 27 Mar 1729; wife Mary; children of Mary and Mathew: John, Elizabeth, Susannah, Mary; son Robert; tracts *Paradise* in BA Co., *Paradise* (part of *Christian Temple Manor* in CH Co. (MCW 6.98) [SMW PC1.333]; inv.; 3 May 1729; 4 Jun 1729; nok Thomas Gardiner, Ann Blakiston; extx. Mrs. Mary Mason (I 14.164); acct.; 1 Sep 1730 (A 10.423)

Mason, Matthew; inv.; 12 Mar 1770; 14 Aug 1770; nok William Bowling, Caleb Mason; admx. Elisabeth Mason (I 103.322); inv.; 8 Jul 1771 (I 106.387); acct.; 24 Jul 1771 (A 66.172)

Mason, John; planter; will; 6 Nov 1776; 1 Apr 1777; nephews Clement Gardener (& his child. Jean, John), John Mason Goldsmith, John Gardener (& his son John), John Roberts, Nehemiah Mason (& his sons Robert and John), William Gardener (& wife Mary & her dau. Sary); nieces Rebeckah

Goldsmith, Susanah Shanks, Elizabeth Brothers, Mary Ann Leek, Susanah
Hilton, Abigal Jordan, Mary Goldsmith, Sarah Davice; mentions Nehemiah
Rodham Mason and Henritta Gardener; tract *Eandfields* (MCW 16.215)

MATTHEWS
Matthews, Thomas; gent.; age ca 37 in 1659 (MD p. 127)
Mathews, Love; service by 1671; widow (SK 16.115)
Mathewes, William; immigrated by 1674 (SK17.634)
Matthews, Thomas; will; probate 29 Jan 1676; wife and child. unnamed (MCW
    1.185) [SMW PC1.24]
Mathews, Ignatius; infant s/o Thomas Mathews, the younger, who was s/o
    Thomas Mathews, the elder; mentions William Guyther, s/o Nicholas & wife
    Mary; 1677 (CCR p. 9)
Matthews, James; priest; d. 8 Dec 1694; age 36 (HGM)

MATTINGLY
Mattenly, Tho.; *Mattenly's Hope*; 200 ac.; sur. 17 Jul 1680; 1707 poss.
    Thomas Mattenly [in New Town Hundred]; St. Clements Hundred (RR p. 47)
    (TLC p. 46); 28 Sep 1680 cert./pat. (COL)
    Mount Misery; 100 ac.; sur. 28 May 1680; 1707 poss. Thomas Mattenly; St.
    Clements Hundred (RR p.) (TLC p. 47); 28 Sep 1680 cert./pat. (COL)
Mattingly, Thomas, Sr.; will; planter; 9 Oct 1714; 12 Jan 1714; sons Thomas,
    James, Charles, William, Luke, Ignatius; daus. Elizabeth Clark, Judith Parker,
    Ann; wife Elizabeth; g-son James Clark; tracts *Mount Misery, Matingly's
    Purchase* (MCW 4.68) [SMW PC1.192]; acct.; 8 Apr 1717; extx. Elisabeth
    Mattingly (I&A 39b.61) (SMAA p. 320)
Matt___, Matthew; acct.; 28 Dec 1714 (I&A 36b.35)
Mattingsly, Cezar; age ca 64; his m-i-l was sister of John Sattle; 1 Dec 1718;
    tract *St. Lawrence* (CCR p. 41)
Mattinly, Thomas; age ca 30 in 1718 (MD p. 127)
Mattingly, Clement and _____; son Thomas [b. 28 Mar 1738], John Baptist [b.
    28 Jan 1745], Elisabeth [b. 7 Jun 1736], Mary Ann [b. 6 Oct 1741], Ann [b. 6
    May 1747], Ruth [b. 23 Jun 1749] (SA p. 37)
Mattingley, Edward; *Mattingley's Lane*; 25 ac.; sur. 15 Dec 1744 (TLC p. 105); 29
    Jan 1745 cert./pat. (COL)
Mattingly, John; will; 28 Feb 1759; 3 Apr 1759; wife unnamed; son John
    Baptist; tract *Phems* (MCW 11.231) [SMW TA1.382]
Mattingly (Mattenly), John, Mr; inv.; 1 May 1744; 5 Jun 1744; nok John &
    Ignatius Mattingly; admx./extx. Grace Mattingly (I 29.225); acct.; 21 Jun 1745;
    orphans John, Ignatius, Richard, Luke, Joseph, Elisabeth, Susanna; admx.
    Grace, w/o Peter Johnson (A 21.366)
Mattenly (Mattingly), James; 3 May 1745; 28 May 1745; children Anne, Robert,
    Peter, John, James, Thomas; bros. Thomas and Luke Mattenly; [dau. Monica]

(MCW 9.29) [SMW TA1.175]; <u>inv.</u>; 19 May 1745; 2 Sep 1745; nok William &
Luke Mattingly (I 31.276); <u>acct.</u>; 21 Apr 1746 (A 22.175); <u>inv.</u>; 30 Aug 1746; 1
Sep 1746 (I 33.94); <u>acct.</u>; 1 Sep 1746 (A22.293)

Mattingly, Thomas, Mr.; <u>inv.</u>; 4 Aug 1756; 1 Mar 1757; nok Vincent Taylor,
John Baptist Mattingly; admx./ex. Thomas Mattingly (I 62.246); <u>acct.</u>; 20 Sep
1757 (A 41.250); <u>acct.</u>; 4 Jul 1758; [Jr.]; to Dorothy & Mary [of age], Elisabeth
[age 14], Sarah [age 12], Edward [age 8], Thomas [age 3]; adm. Thomas
Mattingly (A 41.597); <u>dist.</u>; 4 Jul 1758 (BB 2.91)

Matingly, John; <u>inv.</u>; 28 Apr 1759; 7 Jun 1759; nok Richard & Ignatius
Mattingly; admx./extx. Elisabeth Matingley (I 67.182); <u>acct.</u>; 6 May 1760;
orphans John Baptist [age 18], John [age 14], James Bartin [age 17], William
[age 12], Jane [age 13], Henry [age 8], Margaret [age 6], Elisabeth [age 4],
Bennett [age 2] (A 44.272); <u>dist.</u>; 6 May 1760 (BB 3.27)

Mattingley, James; *Mattingley's Slipe*; 372 ac.; 20 Feb 1762 cert./pat. (COL)

Mattingly, Thomas; <u>inv.</u>; 21 Jun 1762; 4 Oct 1762; nok Robert & Peter
Mattingly; admx. Margaret Mattingly (I 79.262); <u>acct.</u>; 7 Jun 1763; minors
James, Richard (A 49.597)

Mattingley, John Baptist; *Grave's Swamp*; 46 ac.; 29 Sep 1762 cert./pat. (COL)

Mattingly, William; <u>will</u>; 28 Nov 1771; 13 Dec 1771; daus. Dolly, Polly; sons-i-
l Leonard Wathing, Robert Saxon (MCW 14.212) [SMW TA1.645]; <u>inv.</u>; 21 Jul
1772; nok Luke & Ignatius Mattingly (I 109.355); <u>acct.</u>; 10 Oct 1773 (A 69.208);
<u>dist.</u>; 10 Oct 1773; daus. Polly, Dolly (BB 6.277)

Mattingly, Luke; m. 11 Feb 1772 Eliz. Thompson (MM)

Mattingly, Elizabeth; <u>will</u>; 12 Apr 1773; 1 Jul 1773; 3 daus.-i-l Ann, Elizabeth,
Mary; sisters-i-l Ann, Ruthy and Elizabeth Mattingly, Mary McWilliams;
sisters Lendenfin Wick [Lender Fenwick], Elinor Miles, Bitha Wildman,
Beckey Hill; f-i-l Clement Mattingly; m-i-l Ann Mattingly; [s-i-l Elizabeth
McWilliams] (MCW 15.69) [SMW TA1.650]

Mattingly, Thomas; <u>will</u>; 10 Apr 1773; 10 Jul 1773; children Ann, Elizabeth,
Mary and John; wife unnamed; father Clement (MCW 15.70) [SMW TA1.672];
<u>inv.</u>; 20 Jul 1773; [Jr.]; nok Ann & Ruth Mattingly; ex. Clement Mattingly (I
116.216)

Mattingly, John; <u>inv.</u>; 9 Jul 1773; 5 Nov 1773; nok John & Robert Mattingly;
admx./extx. Ann Matting (I 114.34)

Mattingly, Thomas; <u>will</u>; 11 Apr 1774; 10 Sep 1774; sons Leonard, Edward,
John [John Baptist], Clement (MCW 16.21) [SMW TA1.679]

Mattingly, Robert; <u>will</u>; 27 Jun 1776; 14 Dec 1776; wife unnamed; mentions
Gabriah, Annastatia, Charles and Katharine Mattingly (MCW 16.175); <u>inv.</u>; 14
Feb 1777; nok James & Mr. Luke Mattingly; ex. Bazel Mattingly (I 125.295)

Mattingly, Robert and Mary Ann; dau. Catharine [b. 29 Mar 1778] (SA p. 29)

Mattingly, Edward; m. 17 Sep 1779 Martha Sym (BRU p. 535)

MAYNARD

Maynard, Charles; *Maynards Comfort*; 100 ac.; sur. 6. Feb 1649; 1707 poss.
Tho. Davis; New Town Hundred (RR p. 28) (TLC p. 27)

Maynard, Charles; will; 2 May 1661; wife Ann; daus. Agnes, Elizabeth
Maynard (MCW 1.43) [SMW PC1.1]

Maynard, Char.; *Edenburgh*; 100 ac.; sur. 2 Jun 1657; 1707 poss. James Martin;
New Town Hundred (RR p. 30) (TLC p. 29)

Leith; 100 ac.; sur. 14 Feb 1666; 1707 poss. James Thos. Stratford; New
Town Hundred (RR p. 34) (TLC p. 33)

Maynards Comfort; 100 ac.; sur. 17 Aug 1668; 1707 poss. David Parson,
tenant to James Martin; St. Clements Hundred (RR p. 45) (TLC p. 43)

McCAVE

McCave, Simon; inv.; 7 Mar 1754; nok minors; admx./extx. Mary McCave (I
58.67)

McCave, Alice; children John Bond [b. 23 Nov 1760], Eleanor Ann [b. 5 Aug
1764] Margaret Ann [b. 20 Nov 1767] (SA p. 190)

McCLANE

Mackelan (Macklain, Mackelaine), Hector; will; 17 Oct 1721; 8 Oct 1721/2;
sons William and Hector; wife Anne (MCW 5.76) [SMW PC1.266]; inv.; 15 Nov
1721; 30 Jan 1721; nok William Banister; admx. Ann Mackclain (I 7.30); acct.;
30 Jan 1722; admx. Ann, w/o John Hall (A 5.36)

McClane, William and Mary; children Enoch [b. 26 Feb 1758], William [b. 23
Apr 1760], Arthur [b. 22 Dec 1763], Richard [b. 14 Apr 1765], John Vowles
[b. 25 Dec 1767] (SA p. 8, 41, 42)

Maclane, William; inv.; 11 Aug 1774; 13 Jan 1771 (sic); admx./extx. Mary
McLean (I 121.417)

McClain, John and Elizabeth Clarke (by license); m. 14 Jan 1782 (SA p. 60)

McGILL

McGill, David; inv.; 18 Apr 1744; 3 Jul 1744; nok Mary Wilkeson, Mararel
Abell; admx./extx. Grace Macgill (I 29.248)

McGill, Abell and Marianne; dau. Jannett [b. 4 Dec 1765] (SA p. 42)

Macgill (McGill), Mary; inv.; 29 Nov 1766; 27 Feb 1767; nok Samuel, Jr. &
John, s/o Samuel Abell; adms. Ann & Winnifred McGill (I 91.83); acct.; 13 Jul
1768; admx. Ann McGill (A 58.254)

Magill (Macgill), Abell; inv.; 22 Apr 1767; 30 Apr 1768; nok John Abell of
Samuel, Margaret Mackgill; admx. Mariamne McGill (I 95.247)

McGil, Charles and Mary Bradford (by publication); m. 11 May 1784 (SA p. 62)

McGRAW

Magraw (Magrah), Andrew; inv.; 15 Jun 1699 (I&A 19½a.151); acct.; 14 Mar 1700 (I&A 10.186)

McGra (Magrah), John; inv.; 5 Nov 1737 (I 23.77); acct.; 24 Feb 1740 (A 18.123)

McKELVEY

McKelravey, Daniel; inv.; 30 Mr 1732 (I 16.436)

McKelvey, Andrew; acct.; 3 May 1746; mentions John Mckelvery; orphan William; admx. Ann McKelvey (A 22.176)

McKellvie, John; will; 28 May 1750; 6 Oct 1750; g-son William, s/o Andrew and Ann; wife Catharine (MCW 10.112) [SMW TA1.252]

McKENZIE

Mackenzie, Collen; immigrated from VA by 1680 (SK WC2.378-379)

Mackenzie (Mackensey), Collins (Collen); will; oral; St. Clements; 31 Dec 1682; 11 Jan 1682 (MCW 1.121) [SMW PC1.46]; acct.; 7 Jul 1686 (I&A 9.42)

McKenzie, James and Casandra Magruder (by license); m. 1 Apr 1781 (SA p. 59)

McKenzie, Alexander and Sarah Anderson (by license); m. 8 Nov 1781 (SA p. 59)

McWILLIAMS

McWilliams (MacWilliams), Thomas; inv.; [filed with 1737]; nok W. McWilliams, George Forbes; admx./extx. Mary MacWilliams (I 22.399, 402); acct.; 23 Apr 1739 (A 17.104)

McWilliams, Mary; will; 23 Mar 1757; 8 Mar 1759; sons William, Keneton [Kenelm], Thomas; dau. Mary (MCW 11.232) [SMW TA1.375]; inv.; 2 Apr 1759; 8 Aug 1759; nok William & Kenelm McWilliams; ex. Thoms McWilliams (I 67.327); acct.; 14 Sep 1759 (A 43.306)

MacWilliams, William, Dr.; inv.; 12 May 1758; 20 Nov 1758; nok Thomas & Janet MacWilliams; admx./extx. Sarah MacWilliams (I 66.69, 76); acct.; 10 Aug 1763; 5 daus. (A 49.517)

MEDCALF

Medcalfe, George; inv.; 4 Jul 1702 (I&A 23.160); acct.; 17 Mar 1702 admx. Elisabeth Medcalfe (I&A 24.12); acct. ; 10 Mar 1702/3 (SMAA p. 125); acct.; 22 Apr 1703 (I&A23.19)

Medcalf, John; inv.; 17 Dec 1706 (I&A 26.252); acct.; 8 Jul 1707; admx. Mary, w/o John Johnson (I&A 27.151) (SMAA p. 141)

Madcalf, William; will; 18 Jan 1733/4; 1 Mar 1733/4; sons George, John, William, Ignatius; wife Susannah (MCW 7.59) [SMW TA1.20]; inv.; 1 Mar 1733; 4 Jun 1734; nok Peter Peake, Ann Vincent; admx./extx. Susanna Medcalf (I 18.317); acct.; 16 Nov 1737; extx. Susannah, w/o Ignatius Thompson (A 14.529)

Medcalf, Ignatius and Sarah; son John Kenelin [b. 25 Oct 1760] (SA p. 8, 42)

Medcalf, Ignatius; <u>inv.</u>; 20 Nov 1762; 1 Feb 1763; nok William Medcalf; admx. Sarah Medcalf (I 80.163); <u>acct.</u>; 31 Mar 1763 (A 49.98)

Metcalfe, Francis; surgeon; <u>will</u>; 5 Aug 1773; 1 Sep 1773; bro. John of London; father William of York (MCW 15.71) [SMW TA1.659]

Medcaff, John; <u>inv.</u>; 7 Aug 1773; 10 Oct 1773; nok George Howard, John Wimsatt; admx. Elisabeth Medcaff (I 114.29)

MEDLEY

Medley, John; *Pococomoco Point*; 100 ac.; sur. 14 Dec 1641 with 50 unnamed acres; resur. into *Medleys Neck*; New Town Hundred (RR p. 26) (TLC p. 25)

Medly, John; *Medley*; 150 ac.; sur. 28 May 1651; 1707 no poss.; in *Resurvey of Medly*; New Town Hundred (RR p. 29) (TLC p. 28)

Medley, John (?); *Medley*; 1,250 ac.; [undated]; resur. of several tracts;New Town Hundred (RR p. 40) (TLC p. 40)

Medly, John; *Robert's Neck*; 100 ac.; sur. 20 Jun 1651; in *Resurvey of Medly*; New Town Hundred (RR p. 29) (TLC p. 28)

Medley, John; <u>inv.</u>; 19 Aug 1676; 16 Nov 1676 (I&A 2.317); <u>acct.</u>; 9 Mar 1677; admx. Ann Cole, wife of Robert (I&A 4.624)

Medley, George; <u>will</u>; probate 22 May 1678; bro. William; sis. Anne (MCW 1.170)

Medley, William; 4 Jun 1679; age 26 and upwards; s/o John Medley (CCR p. 6)

Medley, Thomas; <u>inv.</u>; 14 Jan 1683 (I&A 8.121)

Medly (Medley), William; <u>acct.</u>; 9 Aug 1686; adm. Thomas Medly (I&A 9.146) (SMAA p. 88)

Medly, William; <u>inv.</u>; 1 May 1695 (I&A 13a.319); <u>acct.</u>; [filed with 1696] (I&A 14.8]

Medly, William; <u>inv.</u>; 17 Mar 1697 (I&A 16.197); <u>acct.</u>; 20 Sep 1699 (I&A 19½b.115)

Medly, William; <u>acct.</u>; 1 Aug 1711 (I&A 32c.93) (SMAA p. 217)

Medly (Medley), William; <u>will</u>; 22 Sep 1725; 30 Nov 1725; bro. John & his son George; cous. John & his son John; cousins William, Thomas, James and Ann Medley (MCW 5.205) [SMW PC1.298]; <u>inv.</u>; 9 Dec 1725; 3 Apr 1726; nok John Midlay, Jr., Rebecca Thompson; exs. John & George Medley (I 11.260); <u>acct.</u>; 2 Apr 1727 (A 8.219)

Medley, John, gent.; *Medley's Hope*; 420 ac.; [28 Jun 1726] cert./pat. (COL) *Medley's Neck*; 315 ac.; resur. 18 Jan 1737 for John Medley, s/o John (TLC p. 95); 6 Dec 1738 cert./pat. (COL)

Medley, George; <u>will</u>; 1 Apr 1731; 1 Jun 1731; sons Clemant, Often [Oston], Bennet, George; wife Ann (MCW 6.192) [SMW PC1.357]; <u>inv.</u>; 1 Jun 1731; 17 Nov 1731; nok John, Jr. & William Meadley; admx./extx. Ann Medley (I 16.317); <u>acct.</u>; 12 Jun 1733; extx. Ann, w/o William Williams (A 12.32)

Medley, Clement; bro. of John, s/o George, gs/o William; *Robert's Neck*; 95 ac.; 9 Oct 1736 cert./pat. (COL) *Part of Roberts Neck*; sur. 19 Feb 1719 for William Medley (TLC p. 92)

Medley, John, Sr.; <u>will</u>; 2 Dec 1743; 5 Apr 1748; children John, George, William, Thomas, James & his son James, Mary (dec'd), Ann Cole, Clement, Jean, Henrietta; wife Sarah; s-i-l Thomas Greenwell & his son George (MCW 9.156) [SMW TA1.219]; <u>inv.</u>; 5 Sep 1748; nok John & William Medley; adms./exs. Sarah & Clement Medley (I 37.103); <u>acct.</u>; 2 Aug 1749; children Clement & Jane [both of age], Henreitta [age 12] (A 27.106)

Medley, John, Jr.; oral; <u>will</u>; 11 Jan 1749; wife Frances (MCW 10.70) [SMW TA1.232]

Medley, John; <u>inv.</u>; 2 Jul 1750; nok John Cole, William Medley; adms./exs. Basil Peake & wife Elisabeth (I 43.380); <u>acct.</u>; 19 Sep 1751; orphans Philip [age 18], Elisabeth [of age], Joseph [age 13], Anistacia [age 9], Ignatius [age 6] (A 31.219); <u>dist.</u>; 19 Sep 1751 (BB 1.16); <u>inv.</u>; 18 May 1754; 14 Jun 1754; [Jr.]; nok Clement & George Medley (I 58.188)

Medly, Francis (Frances); <u>inv.</u>; 16 Jul 1750; 17 Jul 1750; nok James Pike, Ann Wheeler (I 43.298); <u>acct.</u>; 13 Apr 1752; sisters Ann Wheler & w/o Thomas Viliner & w/o James Pike (A 32.232); <u>dist.</u>; 13 Apr 1752 (BB 1.37)

Medley, William; <u>will</u>; 24 Aug 1752; 29 Nov 1752; wife Elioner; daus. Mary, Elioner (MCW 10.246) [SMW TA1.292]; <u>inv.</u>; 22 Dec 1750 (sic); 5 Feb 1754; nok Philip & Augustine Medley; admx./extx. Elenor Medley (I 58.63); <u>acct.</u>; 17 Dec 1753 (A 36.13); <u>acct.</u>; 20 Apr 1755; dau. Elisabeth [age 7] (A 37.166); <u>dist.</u>; 28 Apr 1755; legatees at full age except for dau. Eliz'a [age 8 next Feb] (BB 1.131)

Medly, William; <u>inv.</u>; 30 May 1753; 6 Jun 1753; nok Clement & Philip Medley; admx./extx. Elisabeth Medley (I 54.52)

Medley, John; <u>acct.</u>; 22 Jul 1754; mother Elisabeth; siblings Philip & Elisabeth [both of age], Joseph [age 15], Anislasia [age 12], Ignatius [age 9]; admx. Elisabeth, w/o Basil Peak (A 36.399); <u>dist.</u>; 22 Jul 1754; mentions Basil Peake & his wife [mother of dec'd]; bros. & sisters Philip & Elizabeth [of age], Joseph [age 15 next 19 Mar], Anistasia [age 12 next 2 Feb], Ignatius [age 9]; bros. & sis. of dec'd widow [dec'd] John Smith, James Pike, Thomas Vilener, Ann Wheeler & Christian Smith (BB 1.114)

Medley, Clement and Mary Ann; children Ann [b. 28 Mar 1755], William [b. 20 Apr 1757], Catharine [b. 20 Jan 1760], Sarah, [b. 29 Jul 1763], Charles [b. 29 Jul 1763], Mary [b. 14 Nov 1768] (SA p. 192, 193)

Medley, Clement and Mary; children Eleanor [b. 27 Feb 1761 or 1762], Joseph [b. 3 Nov 1764], Matthew [b. 16 Feb 1766], Ann Elizabeth [b. 1 Feb 1768], Mary [b. 9 Mar 1770] (SA p. 19, 25, 53, 54)

Medley, Augustine; <u>will</u>; 4 Oct 1761; 13 Oct 1761; bros. George, Bennitt, Clement; Bennett and George [sons of bro. Clement]; mentions Catey Medley (MCW 12.98) [SMW TA1.450]; <u>inv.</u>; 9 Nov 1762; 21 Dec 1763; nok Clement & Bennet Medley; ex. George Medley (I 80.143)

Medley, Joseph and Anastatia; children Eleanor [b. 14 Dec 1764], Joseph [b. 22 Mar 1766], Bernard [b. 22 Dec 1768] (SA p. 194)

Medley, George and Ann; son Augustine [b. 26 Sep 1763] (SA p. 10, 44)

Medley, Thomas; inv.; 23 Sep 1764; 22 Oct 1764; nok Ann Cole, Clement Medley, Jr.; admx. Mary Medley (I 86.56)

Medley (Medly), Clement; will; 31 Oct 1771; 10 Feb 1772; wife Mary; children Bennett, Joseph, Matthew, Eleanor, Mary, Anne Eliz., Eleanor Nottingham; bro. Bennett (MCW 14.212) [SMW TA1.641]; inv.; 12 Dec 1771; 19 Mar 1772; nok Bennett Medley, Jr. & Sr.; admx. Mary Medley (I 109.20)

Medley, Clement; of *Medley's Neck*; planter; will; 31 Mar 1772; 10 Mar 1774; daus. Ann, Catharine, Salley; sons William, Charles (MCW 15.150) [SMW TA1.709]; inv.; 30 Jul 1774; nok Philip & George Medley (I 119.162)

Medley, Clement; acct.; 26 Apr 1774; admx. Mary, w/o Ignatius Wimsatt (A 70.146)

Medley, Ignatius; inv.; 3 Aug 1774; nok Philip Medley, Elisabeth Peak; admx. Mary Medley (I 119.190)

Medley, Bennet; will; 25 Sep 1774; 29 Nov 1774; bros. Matthew & Joseph; sisters Eleanor, Elizabeth, Mary; uncles George and Bennett Medley; Mary, widow of Robert Drury; tract *Dry Docking* (MCW 16.2) [SMW TA1.689]; inv.; 1 Dec 1774; 17 Feb 1775; nok Mary ReshWick, Elisabeth "not on ham" [?Nottingham]; adms./exs. George & Bennet Medley (I 121.399)

Medley, Mary; will; 15 Nov 1774; 3 Mar 1775; son John; bro. John Fenwick (MCW 16.90) [SMW TA1.731]

MEEKEN

Meeken, William; *Wolverhampton*; 150 ac.; sur. 3 May 1681; 1707 poss. James French; New Town Hundred (RR p. 39) (TLC p. 39); 3 May 1681 cert./pat. (COL) *St. Williams*; 50 ac.; sur. 15 Apr 1683; 1707 poss. John Meaken in New Town Hundred; St. Clements Hundred (RR p. 48) (TLC p. 46); 50 ac.; 16 Apr 1683 cert./pat. (COL)

Meakin (Meekin), James; acct.; 8 Jun 1720; admx. Mrs. Ann Read (A 2.505) (SMAA p. 449)

Meken, William, Mr.; inv.; 5 Sep 1748; 12 Dec 1748; nok William, s/o John & John Meken; admx./extx. Teresia (I 37.377)

Meken, William; inv.; 2 May 1750; 5 Jun 1750; nok Tersa & William Meken, Catharine Pye; admx./extx Elisabeth Medley (I 43.269)

Mekin, Augustine and Margaret; daus. Susanna [b. 4 May 1761], Margaret [b. 26 Aug 1764] (SA p. 9, 43)

Meekins (Meekin), Augustine; will; 21 Feb 1767; 9 Mar 1767; wife [Margaret] and children unnamed; [dau. Teresa]; extx. Margaret; sisters Margarett and Teresa; extx. Margaret (MCW 13.178) [SMW TA1.514]; inv.; 27 Apr 1767; 2 Jun 1767; nok William Thompson, Teresa Meekin (I 93.122); acct.; 8 Sep 1767; admx. Margaret Meekin (A 57.359); acct.; 30 Jun 1768 (A 58.265); acct.; 4 Apr 1769 (A 61.106)

MELTON

Melton, Thomas; *Boston*; 200 ac.; sur. 21 May 1664; 1707 poss. Thos. Melton, Ralph Foster; Choptico Hundred (RR p. 50) (TLC p. 48)

Melton's Hope; 150 ac.; sur. 23 Sep 1667; assgn. Samuell Harris; 1707 poss. for Harris' orphan; Choptico Hundred (RR p.) (TLC p. 49)

St. Johns; 100 ac.; sur. 23 Nov 1671; 1707 poss. Thos. Melton; St. Clements Hundred (RR p. 45) (TLC p.)

St. Thomas; 190 ac.; sur. 16 Mar 1672; 1707 poss. Rob. Strutton; St. Clements Hundred (RR p. 45) (TLC p.)

St. Peters Well; 100 ac.; sur. 30 Jul 1678; 1707 poss. widow Alice Johnson; Choptico Hundred (RR p. 53) (TLC p.)

Melton, Thomas, Sr.; will; 24 Sep 1705; 1 May 1706; son Thomas; dau. Mary Howard; g-son Thomas Adams; g-dau. [dau] Rachel Adams; tracts *Boston, Cuckold's Haven, St. John's* (MCW 3.79) [SMW PC1.143]; inv.; 20 Jun 1706 (I&A 25.344); acct.; 1 Aug 1707; legatees Mary Howard, Rachaell Addams, Thomas Addams; ex. Thomas Melton (I&A 27.153)

Melton, Thomas; planter; will; 8 Jul 1724; 16 Sep 1724; sons Richard, Thomas, Adam, John; dau. Elizabeth; wife Mary; f-i-l Richard Millard; tracts *St. John's, Boston* (MCW 5.174) [SMW PC1.291]; inv.; 21 Sep 1724; 3 Nov 1724; nok Mary & William Howard; ex. Mary Meton (I 10.165); acct.; 5 Jul 1726; adm. Mary, w/o Thomas Walker (A 7.404)

Melton, Joshua; m. 10 Nov 1772 Sarah Molohorn (MM)

MERRILL

Merrell, William; inv.; [filed with 1714] (I&A 36a.225); acct.; 10 Aug 1715; admx. Anne, w/o John Carmichael (I&A 36c.280) (SMAA p. 281); acct.; 26 Oct 1719 (SMAA p. 374); acct.; 26 Oct 1719; mentions Magdilen, Susanah & Eliner Merrill (A 2.279)

Merrill, Catherine; inv.; 1736; 27 Nov 1738; nok John Carmichall, Luke Merrill; adm./ex. Philip Merrell (I 23.502)

Merrell, Joshua and Mary; children Mary Ann [b. 21 Dec 1769], Philip [b. 22 Oct 1762] (SA p. 26)

Merrell, Joshua and Mary Ann; dau. Eleanor Mills [b. 4 Nov 1775] (SA p. 28)

MERRITT

Merritt (Meoritt), Frances; inv.; 14 Feb 1721; nok Frances Beach, Francis Horn (I 7.24); acct.; 8 Aug 1722 (A 4.170)

Merritt (Merett), John; 28 Dec 1734; 23 Jan 1734; sister Hopewell Merritt; wife Jane; mentions William, s/o John Gibson; also John Gibson and John, Jr. (MCW 7.120) [SMW TA1.44]; inv.; 7 Jan 1734; 16 Apr 1735; nok John & Aelz Gibson; admx./extx. Jane Merritt (I 20.405); acct.; 15 Nov 1737; extx. Jane, w/o George Vaudrey (A 14.528)

MICKELL

Mickell, John; inv.; 15 Aug 1749; 29 Oct 1749; nok William & Ann Mickell (I 41.459)

Mickell, William; 17 Feb 1749; 8 Mar 1749; sister Ann, mother of Willibe Varnon Wots [William Varmon Wats]; mentions Elizabeth, w/o John Maddly, dec'd & John [Samuel], s/o John Thompson (MCW 10.73) [SMW TA1.238]

Mickell (Mickel), William; acct.; 27 Jul 1749; children Margaret, William, Susanna & Tereasia [all of age], Peter Augusta [age 14]; admx. Tereasia Mickell (A 27.103); acct.; 18 Mar 1750; extx. Elisabeth,w/o Basil Peak (A 30.15)

MIDDLETON

Middleton, John; age ca 25 in 1702 (MD p. 130)

Middleton, George, Mr.; inv.; 6 Apr 1724; 5 Aug 1724; admx. Katherine Palmer (I 10.13); acct.; 7 Jul 1725 (A 6.439)

MILBURN

Millburn (Milburn), will; Stephen; 8 Apr 1720; 27 Apr 1723; sons Joseph, John, (?) Joshua [or Stephen]; daus. Sarah Nilson [Hilton] and ____ Sweny [Jeeny Milburn] (MCW 5.132) [SMW PC1.276]; acct.; 28 May 1724; ex. Joseph Millbourne (A 6.35); inv.; 18 Jun 1723; 29 Jun 1723; nok Stephen & John Milburn; adm. John Milbourne (I 8.235)

Millburn, Joseph; will; 24 Nov 1734; 13 Jan 1734; wife Elizabeth; sons Jeremiah, Stephen (MCW 7.120) [SMW TA1.42]; inv.; 4 Mar 1734; 7 Apr 1735; nok John & Sarah Milburn; adms./exs. John Mackey & wife Elisabeth (I 20.403); acct.; 17 May 1736 (A 15.75)

Milbourn, Richard; *Milbourn's Chance*; 178 ac.; sur. 13 Sep 1750 (TLC p. 116); 13 Sep 1750 cert./pat. (COL)

Milbourne Jeremiah and Elizabeth; dau. Eleanor [b. 10 Feb 1757] (SA p. 193)

Milbourn [Milburn], John; will; 19 Nov 1764; 22 Apr 1765; daus. Elizabeth Barnhouse, Jane Barnhouse, Susanna, Frances, Ann, Kezia, Milacent; sons Ignatius, John, [& Richard]; wife Mary (MCW 13.73) [SMW TA1.476]; inv.; 1 Jul 1765; 24 Jul 1765; nok Stephen & Aaron Milburn; extx. Mary Ann Milburn; (I 88.64)

Milburn, John; will; 6 Oct 1765; 9 Jun 1766; 5 children Ann, John, Salley, Susanah, Sophiah; wife Ann; bro. Joseph (MCW 13.109) [SMW TA1.495]; inv.; 9 Dec 1766; [Jr.]; nok Joseph & Aaron Milburn; extx. Ann Milburn (I 91.99, 101); acct.; 9 Dec 1766 (A 55.324); acct.; 14 Jul 1767 (A 57.78); dist.; 14 Jul 1767; children Ann, John, Sally, Susannah, Sophia (BB 5.72)

Milburn, Stephen; will; 3 May 1767; 11 Aug 1769; children Elizabeth Smith, Aaron, Austin, Stephen, Britani, Joseph, Rebecca Clocker, Mary Wise, Ann Morgan, Peter, Sarah Herbert, William, [& Adam]; g-ch. Ann and John Milburn, ch/o son John (MCW 14.108) [SMW TA1.576]; inv.; 11 May 1770; nok Peter & Joseph Milburn; exs. Aaron, Austin & Stephen Milburn (I 103.239);

acct.; 4 Apr 1772; ex. Aaron & Austin Milburn (A 66.277); dist.; 4 Apr 1772; children Elisabeth, Aaron, Austin, Brittania, Rebecca, Mary, Ann, Peter, Sarah, Stephen, William; g-ch Ann, John & Joseph Milbourn (BB 6.108)

Milburn, Richard; *Milburn's Folly*; 51 ac.; 17 Jul 1767 cert./pat. (COL)

Milburn, John; boatwright; will; 15 Apr 1773; 21 Sep 1774; daus. Ignatius (sic), Millsson; sons, William, Jonathan; unnamed mother living; [bro. Ignatius] (MCW 15.150) [SMW TA1.707]

Milburn, Henry; will; 1 Nov 1775; 4 Apr 1776; wife Sarah; sons Richard, William, Thomas (MCW 16.117); inv.; 14 Oct 1776; nok Angelica Milburn, Richard Clarke; ex. Sarah Milburn (I 125.271)

Milburn, Aaron; inv.; 24 Jan 1776; 29 Jul 1776; nok Joseph Milburn; admx. Angela Milburn (I 125.282)

MILES

Miles, Morris; service by 1667 (SK 11.186)

Miles, Francis; *Miles Meadow*; 150 ac.; sur. 13 Mar 1674; 1707 poss. Wm. Asquith; St. Mary's Hundred (RR p. 6) (TLC p. 7)
 The Back Acres Beginning; 100 ac.; sur. 10 Jan 1681; 1707 poss. Wm. Asquith, ex. of Miles ; St. Mary's Hundred (RR p. 8) (TLC p. 9); *Back Acres*; 100 ac.; [7 Jan 1682] cert./pat. (COL)

Miles, Peter; acct.; 9 Apr 1688 (I&A 9.505)

Miles, Thomas; inv.; 8 Feb 1697 (I&A 15.325); acct.; 1 Dec 1698; extx. Susannah Miles (I&A 18.126) (SMAA p.98)

Miles [Myles], John; will; 30 Feb 1697; 16 Mar 1697; children James, John, Nicholas, Henry, Edward & unnamed dau. (MCW 2.133) [SMW PC1.96]; inv.; 4 Apr 1698 (I&A 16.192); inv.; 30 May 1698 (I&A 16.31); inv.; 9 Dec 1699 (I&A 11b.2); inv.; 26 Mar 1700 (I&A 11b.3)

Miles, Francis; will; probate 23 Sep 1700; g-son Francis, s/o John Miles; Robert, s/o John Wiseman; Mary, d/o John Miles; dau. Catherine Wiseman; tracts *Back Acres, Miles Meadow* (MCW 2.197); inv.; 11 Nov 1700 (I&A 21.52); acct.; 4 Oct 1704 (I&A 3.379) (SMAA p. 129)

Miles, Susanna; will; 22 Feb 1701/2; 2 Jun 1702; daus. Sarah w/o Edward Horne, Winnifrede; mentions Robert, s/o Jno. Wiseman; Mary d/o Jno. & Margery Miles; tract *Halford's Folly* (MCW 2.239); inv.; [filed with 1702-3] (I&A 23.185)

Miles (Myles), Francis; inv.; 1 Jun 1719; 3 Jun 1719 (I 2.102); acct.; 24 Mar 1720 (A 2.430) (SMAA p. 456)

Miles, John; will; 3 Jan 1726/7; 23 Jan 1726/7; wife Mary; sons John, Jr., Henry; daus. Mary, Margaret, Elizabeth, Priscilla and Anne; bros. Nicholas, Edward; dau. Elineor Sinnott; *Summerfield, Westfield, Cornelius's* (MCW 6.6) [SMW PC1.311]

Miles, John, Sr.; acct.; 5 Sep 1727; ex. John Miles (A 8.322)

Miles, Margaret; will; 12 Dec 1745; 11 Aug 1746 (MCW 9.86) [SMW TA1.208]

Miles, Dorothy; will; 11 Jan 1761; 8 Jun 1761; mother Elizabeth Miles (MCW 12.76) [SMW TA1.417]

Miles, John Barton; inv.; 19 Jun 1765; nok Philip Miles, Belinder Fenwick; admx. Elisabeth Miles (I 88.74); acct.; 24 Nov 1767 (A 57.340)

Miles, John; inv.; 19 Apr 1727; 56 Jun 1727; nok Mary, Margrett & Elisabeth Miles; ex. John Miles (I 12.3); acct.; 19 May 1730; [Sr.] (A 10.257)

Miles, Henry; inv.; 22 Jun 1727; 29 Jun 1727; nok Mary Miles, Mary Mils; adm. John Miles (I 12.139); acct.; 19 May 1730 (A 10.259)

Miles, Mary; widow; will; 3 Apr 1734; 15 May 1734; daus. Margret, Priscilla, Ann; g-dau. Mary Sinnett; s-i-l Joseph Stone (MCW 7.85) [SMW TA1.27]

Miles, John; inv.; 14 Aug 1761; nok John Barton & Belindar Miles; admx./extx. Elisabeth Miles (I 74.267); acct.; 3 Feb 1764 (A 51.3)

Miles, Elizabeth; will; 3 Nov 1771; 12 May 1772; children Phillip, Elizabeth, Rebecca Hill, John, Eleanor; Henry Richard; g-dau. Dorothy and Elesabet Wildman (MCW 14.238) [SMW TA1.642]

Miles, John; dist.; 28 Apr 1774; adm. Mr. John Miles (BB 6.266)

MILLARD

Millard, Richard; planter; age ca 55; 3 Jan 1723 (CCR p. 57)

Millard (Miller), Richard; will; 27 Feb 1725/6; 20 Apr 1726; wife Anne; daus. Monica, Elizabeth, Elinor and Mary Melton [Matton], Margrett Boyde, Anne Shirkilift; sons Richard, Joseph [?Joshua]; tracts *Little St. Thomas, Turners Plaine, Gloster* (MCW 5.219) [SMW PC1.307]; inv.; 10 May 1726; 4 Jul 1726; nok Adam Boyd, John Shurcleff; exs. Ann, Richard & Joshua Millard (I 11.490); acct.; 19 Apr 1727; exs. Ann, Richard & John Millard (A 8.222)

Millard, Theophilus; inv.; 19 Jun 1733; 20 Aug 1733; nok Richard Griffin, Charles Kerwick; admx./extx. Parthenia Millard (I 17.336)

Milliard, Joshua; *Neale's Lot*; 455 ac.; 6 Sep 1757 cert./pat. (COL)

Millard, Joshua; acct.; 22 Nov 1757; mentions Richard [age 18], Joseph [age 15], Joshua [age 13], Mary w/o William Wheeler; admx. Mary, w/o Peter Ford (A 41.325); dist.; 22 Nov 1757; mentions Richard, Joseph, Joshua, William and Mary w/o William Wheler (BB 2.74)

Millard, Richard; will; 26 Jun 1764; 30 Apr 1765; wife Mary; son Francis Austin Millard; daus. Jane w/o Bennet Wheeler, Mary Ann, Ann, Eleanor, Elizabeth w/o Henry How & their dau. Mary Ann (MCW 13.72) [SMW TA1.470]; inv.; 1 Jun 1765; 22 Apr 1767; nok Joshua Mills, John Sheircliff; extx. Mary Millard (I 91.343); acct.; 22 Apr 1767 (A 56.77); dist.; 22 Apr 1767 (BB 5.27)

MILLER

Miller, John; Poplar Hill Hundred; will; 28 Feb 1687/8; 2 Apr 1688; mentions Susanna, d/o John Little (MCW 2.22) [SMW PC1.71]; inv.; 16 Apr 1688 (I&A 9.517); inv.; [filed with 1710] (I&A 31.349); acct.; 9 Oct 1711 (I&A 33a.45); acct.; 19 Oct 1711; adm. Francis Miller (f); 19 Oct 1711 (SMAA p. 214)

Miller, John; planter; will; 15 Feb 1717; 17 Feb 1717; wife Ann; daus. Rebecca,
Priscilla, w/o William Hebb [Hobb] & their son John; tracts *Farnham,
Chelsey, Forest of Dane, Gardiner's [Garner's] Purchase; Strife* (MCW 4.126)
[SMW PC1.234]; inv.; 22 Feb 1717; nok Francis Lowe, Barbery Fidder (I 1.45)

Miller, Edward, Jr.; inv.; 2 Sep 1719; 9 Dec 1719; nok Edward Miller, John
Green; admx. Mary Miller (I 3.222)

Miller, Edward, Jr.; acct.; 2 Jul 1720; admx. Marry, w/o Daniell Duggins (A 3.97)

Miller, Edward; planter; will; written 22 Mar 1721; g-ch Thomas and Anne
Miller; g-daus. Sarah and Laurena, ch/o Robert Perry; tracts *Bay Side, Locust
Thickett* (MCW 5.147) [SMW PC1.275]; inv.; 19 Nov 1723; nok John & Elisabeth
Green; extx. Mary Miller (I 9.215); acct.; 12 Sep 1724 (A 6.124)

Miller, Joshua, Mr.; inv. 23 May 1756; 2 Jun 1756; nok Richard Millard,
Nicholas Mills; admx./extx. Mary Miller (I 61.326)

Miller, Mary; inv.; Feb 1725; 2 Mar 1725; nok minors (I 11.224); acct.; 21 Nov
1726 (A 8.154)

MILLMAN

Milman, John; *Milman's Adventure*; 123 ac.; sur. 6 Feb 1728 (TLC p. 85); 20 Aug
1731 cert./pat. (COL)

Millman, John; 31 Jan 1738/9; 6 Mar 1738/9; wife Mary (MCW 8.21) [SMW TA1.86]

Millman, Mary; will; 4 Dec 1740; 21 Feb 1740/1; g-ch Mary, Robert and James
Thomas; dau. Prudence, w/o John Taylor (MCW 8.115) [SMW TA1.98]; inv.; 1
May 1741; 4 Aug 1741; nok Richard Shirly, Catherine Greenwell (I 26.332)

MILLS

Mills, Nicho.; *Ann Langworth*; 150 ac.; sur. 8 Apr 1653; 1707 poss. James
Martin; St. Clements Hundred (RR p. 43) (TLC p. 42)

Mills, Peter; *Hatfield Hill*; 200 ac.; sur. 19 Nov 1664; to Mich'l Thompson;
listed 1704, not in 1707; poss. Wm. Langhorn; New Town Hundred (TLC p. 34)

Mills (Miles), Peter; *Anstruther*; 30 ac.; sur. 29 Apr 1667; 1707 poss. Mary
Dant; New Town Hundred (RR p. 34) (TLC p. 33)
Minsterdam; 64 ac.; sur. 29 Apr 1667; 1707 Peter Mills; New Town Hundred
(RR p. 34) (TLC p. 33)
Pomfreit Field; 150 ac.; sur. 5 Jun 1667; 1707 poss. Nicho. Mills; New Town
Hundred (RR p. 35) (TLC p. 34)

Mills, Peter; Bretton's Bay; carpenter; wife Mary; convey land; 31 May 1667
(AM LVII.211)

Mills, Peter; 19 Apr 1671; Dutch; naturalized (CMN N5)

Mills, Peter; [carpenter]; will; 3 Sep 1684; 17 Mar 1684/5; wife Mary; dau.
Eliza.; sons Nicholas and Peter; tracts *Minsterdam, Pomfrett Field* (MCW
1.144) [SMW PC1.52]; inv.; 18 Mar 1685 (I&A 8.351); acct.; Jul 1686 (I&A 9.41)

Mills, John; acct.; 25 Oct 1700 (I&A 20.53); acct.; [filed with 1701-2] (I&A 21.387)

Mills, Charles; inv.; 24 Nov 1716; 8 Mar 1716; nok James Mills, William
Meken (I&A 38b.179); acct.; 24 Jul 1718 (A 1.39) (SMAA p. 372)

Mills, Nicholas; *Strife*; 200 ac.; sur. 15 Oct 1713 for Will'm Marya Farthing;
pat. 2 Sep 1714 (TLC p. 11); 12 May 1719 cert./pat. (COL)
Strife Addition; 109 ac.; sur. 13 Jun 1720 (TLC p. 81); 10 Sep 1724 cert./pat. (COL)
Neal's Lot; 419 ac.; sur. 16 Jun 1720 (TLC p. 82); 10 Dec 1724 cert./pat. (COL)

Mills, Peter, Mr.; *Poplar Neck*; 109 ac.; 1720 cert./pat. (COL)

Mills, Frances; age ca 50; 12 Apr 1725 (CCR p. 59)

Mills, Justinian, s/o Nicholas Mills [b. 2 Apr 1728] (SA p. 20)

Mills, John; will; 31 Aug 1728; 6 Nov 1728; dau. Mary, son John; wife Mary
(MCW 6. 79) [SMW PC1.321]; inv.; 6 Nov 1728; 4 Feb 1728; nok Nicholas &
Susanna Mills; extx. Mary Mills (I 13.422); acct.; 20 Jan 1729; extx. Mary w/o
Enoch Combs (A 10.180)

Mills, Nicholas; will; 11 Nov 1728; 18 Mar 1728/9; g-son John; gr-dau. Mary;
son Nicholas; daus. Mary Millard, Susannah; d-i-l Mary Mills; wife Elizabeth;
tracts *Strife, Strife's Addition, Neals Lott* (MCW 6.98) [SMW PC1.334]; inv.; 18
Mar 1728; 4 Jun 1729; nok Nicholas & Susanna; exs. Mrs. Elisabeth &
Nicholas Mills (I 14.168); acct.; 5 Nov 1729 (A 10.176)

Mills, Mary; inv.; 7 Oct 1734; nok John & Margarett Miles (I 19.140); acct.; 8 Jan
1735 (A 14.177)

Mills, Charles; inv.; 26 Feb 1736; 4 Apr 1737; nok A. & John Mills; admx./extx.
Elisabeth Mills (I 22.206); acct.; 11 Nov 1737; orphan Mary Mills; admx.
Elisabeth, w/o Theodorus Jordan (A 14.525)

Mills, Mary, wife of Justinian Mills [b. 1 Sep 1736] (SA p. 20)

Mills, Peter; age ca 62 in 1738 (MD p. 131)

Mills, Peter; will; 4 Apr 1741; 6 Jun 1744; wife Margaret; sons Peter, William;
g-sons William, Joshua; tract *St. Johns* (MCW 8.271) [SMW TA1.135]

Mills, William; will; 26 Sep 1750; 7 Nov 1750; nephews William Whealor,
William Mills; cousin Henerater Whealor; bro. Ignatious Whealor (MCW
10.124) [SMW TA1.243]; inv.; 6 Mar 1750; nok Peter & Ignatius Mills; adm./ex.
William Mills (I 45.76); acct.; 3 Mar 1752 (A 32.105)

Mills, Justinian and Mary Dant; m. 26 Oct 1751 (SA p. 57)

Mills, Justinian and Mary; children John [b. 5 Feb 1753], Elizabeth [b. 9 May
1755], Winifred [b. 30 Oct 1757], Margaret [b. 30 Jan 1760], Joseph [b. 26
Feb 1762] Justinian and Mary [b. 7 Oct 1764], Ann [b. 3 Dec 1767], Charles
[b. 24 Aug 1770] (SA p. 20, 54, 55)

Mills, Nicholas and Anastatia; children Ignatius [b. 16 Nov 1758], Bernard [b.
27 Sep 1760], Ethelbert [b. 12 Nov 1764], Stephen [b. 2 Jan 1767], Nicholas
[b. 9 Mar 1769] (SA p. 189)

Mills, Nicholas; will; 2 Sep 1760; 26 Apr 1768; son Justenian, Nicholas; dau.
Jean; other unnamed children; tracts *Strife, Strife Addition* (MCW 14.33) [SMW
TA1.566]; inv.; 26 Ar 1768; nok George Greenwell, Clement Medley; exs.
Justinian & Nicholas Mills (I 97.272); acct.; 12 Apr 1769 (A 60.365)

Mills, James; *Weems Addition*; 23 ac.; 23 Sep 1761 cert./pat. (COL)

Mills, Peter; will; 28 Mar 1762; 24 Aug 1762; sons William, Joshua; wife Monica (MCW 12.160) [SMW TA1.430]

Mills, James; will; 27 Dec 1763; 1 Mar 1764; g-sons James, John and Thomas and Townshend Eden, also John Gordan [Jordan], James and Justinian Jordan; bros. George, Andrew & wife Nappler; daus. Elizabeth Jordan, Mary Eden; tract *The Wembs* (?) (MCW 13.5) [SMW TA1.482]; inv.; 11 Feb 1765; nok John & James Mills; ex. Nayler Mills (I 87.30)

Mills, Mary; b. 1764; d. 14 Jul 1800 Canford House, Dorset; d/o Justinian Mills and Mary Dant (JM p. 318)

Mills, George; inv.; 20 Feb 1765; nok John, Sr. & Andrew Mills; admx. Elisabeth Mills (I 87.19); acct.; 8 Sep 1765 (A 53.96)

Mills, Andrew; will; 28 Sep 1771; 20 Jan 1772; wife unnamed; children, John, James, Elizabeth Tippitt, Charles (MCW 14.213) [SMW TA1.649]; inv.; 29 Apr 1773; nok Zachariah & Thomas Bond; exs. James & Charles Mills (I 116.1); acct.; 10 Jul 1774 (A 71.366)

Mills, John, Sr.; inv.; 16 Dec 1774; 28 Apr 1774; nok James & Susanna Mills; adm./ex. John Mills (youngest) (I 116.191); acct.; 28 Apr 1774; adm. John Mills youngest (A 69.374)

Mills, Charles Nathl.; m. 17 Jan 1778 (BRU p. 536)

MITCHELL

Mitchell, John; age ca 35-36 in 1684 (MD p. 132)

Mitchell, John; inv.; 12 Feb 1686 (I&A 9.442)

Mitchell, John; *Mitchell Choyce*; 47 ac.; sur. 7 Jul 1686; in 1704 RR not in 1707; poss. undated John Mitchell; Poplar Hill Hundred (TLC p. 24)

Mitchell, John; acct.; 2 Oct 1688; admx. Elisabeth (I&A 10.161)

Mitchell, Darby; inv.; 16 Mar 1713 (I&A 34.175); acct.; 16 Jun 1716; admx. Ursula, w/o Thomas England (I&A 38b.13); acct.; 10 Jun 1716 (SMAA p. 298)

Mitchell, William; inv.; 10 Feb 1735; 8 Mar 1735; nok James Mitchell, Margrett Tanhill; admx./extx. Martha Mitchell (I 21.239); acct.; 13 Apr 1741; orphans Benjamin, John, William, Ann, Margrett, Mary, Martha, Jane, Tabitha; admx. Martha, w/o Benjamin Highfield (Hifield)] (A 18.168)

Metchel, Joseph; inv.; 28 May 1744; 6 Mar 1744; admx./extx. Mary Mitchel (I 30.306)

Mitchell, William; inv.; 18 Jun 1750; nok William Mitchell, minors; admx./extx. Perthena Mitchell (I 43.277); acct.; 28 Jul 1750 (A 28.231)

Mitchell, John; will; 1 Feb 1775; 28 Aug 1775; sons Benjamin, William; wife Elizabeth (MCW 16.111) [SMW TA1.727]

MITFORD

Mitford, Bulmer; written 23 Jul 1665; wife Fortune; son Thomas; cousin John Morecroft (MCW 1.32)

Mittford, Fortune; widow; records cattle marks for sons Thomas and Joseph; 7 Jul 1668 (AM LVII.343)

MOLLEHONE
Mollohoan, John; <u>inv.</u>; 14 Mar 1726; 6 Jun 1727; nok Edmond Boling, Owin Brady, William & Ellind Mollohoan; admx. Anne Woods (I 12.6)

Mollehone, John; <u>inv.</u>; 5 Jun 1745; 5 Aug 1745; nok Thomas & William Mollehone; admx./extx. Mary Mollehone (I 31.282); <u>acct.</u>; 7 Apr 1747; orphans William, Samuel, John, Baptis; admx. Mary, w/o William Hambleton (A 23.302)

MOLTON
Molton, Thomas; <u>acct.</u>; 1 Aug 1707 (SMAA p. 144)

Molton (Moltan), Benony; <u>acct.</u>; 17 Sep 1757; admx. Mary Molton (A 41.257); <u>inv.</u>; 16 Feb 1757; 1 Mar 1757; admx. Mary Molton (I 62.243); <u>acct.</u>; 31 May 1759 (A 43.170)

MOONEY
Mooney (Money), Thomas; <u>inv.</u>; 28 Apr 1697; unnamed relict (I&A 15.85); <u>acct.</u>; 9 Oct 1697; admx. Rose Mooney (relict) (I&A 15.257) (I&A 18.139) (SMAA p. 95, 104)

Moonne, Thomas; *Valentine's Grove*; 96 ac.; sur. 14 Feb 1739 (TLC p. 96); 20 Dec 1740 cert./pat. (COL)

Moony (Money), Thomas; 12 Aug 1756; 18 Oct 1756; <u>will</u>; cousins Mark Brewer & his son James, Edward Spink, Mary Clarke; wife Mary; sister Mary Spalding (MCW 11.149) [SMW TA1.349]; <u>acct.</u>; 6 Jun 1757 (A 41.90); 13 Mar 1758 (A 41.404); <u>inv.</u>; 12 Nov 1756; 1 Sep 1757; nok Mary Spalding, Mark Brews (I 63.139a); <u>dist.</u>; 13 Mar 1758; to Mary Mooney (BB 2.76)

Mooney (Moony), Mary; widow; <u>will</u>; 22 May 1760; 8 Jun 1761; bros. Josias & John Barton Miles; nephew Henry Hill; niece Elizabeth Gardiner Hill [d/o bro. Henry Hill]; sisters Elizabeth, Verlinda and Dorothy Miles; mother & father unnamed (MCW 12.76) [SMW TA1.415]; <u>inv.</u>; 14 Sep 1761; 5 Nov 1761; nok Belender & John Barton Miles (I 76.310)

MOORE
Moore, Thomas; immigrated by 1667 (SK 13.121)

Moor, Leonard; <u>inv.</u>; 5 Dec 1750; 4 Mar 1750; nok John, Sr. & Jese Moor; adm./ex. John Moore (I 45.73)

Moore, John; <u>inv.</u>; 2 Mar 1757; nok William Price, Mary Milburn; admx./extx. Elisabeth Moore (I 63.20, 21); <u>acct.</u>; 27 Oct 1760 (A 46.9); <u>dist.</u>; 27 Oct 1760; mentions James, Elizabeth [both of full age] (BB 3.39)

Moore, William; <u>inv.</u>; 8 Mar 1774; 10 Apr 1774; mentions John & Elisabeth Moore; adm./ex. William Moore (I 116.209)

More, Jacob; m. 4 May 1776 Ann Dorsey (MM)
More, Thomas; m. 23 Feb 1783 Mary Burroughs (BRU p. 536)

MORAN

Mooran, John, Peter, Andrew & William; *Four Brothers*; 858 ac.; 16 Sep 1747
cert./pat. (COL)
Moran, Hezekiah; m. 11 Feb 1778 Rachel Lyon (BRU p. 536)
Moran, Peregrine; m. 8 Jan 1784 Eleanor Barber (BRU p. 536)

MORGAN

Morgan, James; inv.; 27 Apr 1699 (I&A 20.21)
Morgin (Morgan, Morgaine), William; will; 24 Aug __; 5 Nov 1720 (MCW 5.28)
[SMW PC1.254]; inv.; 27 Apr 1722; 19 Jun 1722; nok William Morgaine; admx.
Mary Morgaine (I 7.221); acct.; 21 Sep 1723; admx. Mary, w/o William Griggs
(A 4.290)
Morgan, Edward; will; 20 Apr 1718; 18 Jul 1722; sons John, Benjamin, Edward,
William; daus. Mary, Sarah, Elizabeth, Elinor; g-dau. Jane Chirrel [Cliviol];
wife Mary; tract *Parish* (MCW 5.109) [SMW PC1.272]; acct.; 17 Jun 1723; extx.
Mary Morgaine (A 4.290)
Morgin (Morgan), Mary; will; 12 Nov 1726; 1 Jun 1728; daus. Elizabeth,
Elender; son William;; s-i-l John Sikes (MCW 6.70) [SMW PC1.317]; inv.; 30 Jul
1728; 23 Oct 1728; nok Elisabeth & Elenor Morgan (I 13.283); acct.; 14 Jul
1729 (A 9.443)
Morgan, Benjamin; oral; will; 6 Jan 1733; sons William, Benjamin; mentions
"Daster Margaret Morgin" [SMW TA1.18]; inv.; 24 Jan 1733; 17 Jun 1734; nok
John Morgan, James Dosson (I 18.332); acct.; 22 Jan 1734 (A 12.750)
Morgan, John; will; 28 Feb 1741/2; 17 May 1742; wife unnamed [Mary] (MCW
8.170) [SMW TA1.127]; inv.; 27 May 1742; nok William Morgan, Mary Sikes;
adms./exs. George Cromwell & wife Mary (I 27.59); acct.; 9 Jun 1743;
mentions Mary, orphan of James Green (A 19.437)
Morgan, William; *Hazard*; 73 ac.; sur. 24 Aug 1745 (TLC p. 108); 24 Aug 1745
cert./pat. (COL)
White Birch Freehold with Addition; sur. 16 Apr 1744 (TLC p. 110)
White Birch Freehold; 153 ac.; 4 Dec 1745 cert./pat. (COL)
Morgan, William; *Boats Landing*; 108 ac.; [1748] cert./pat. (COL)
Morgan (Morgane), William; will; 21 Sep 1751; 25 May 1752; wife Mary; daus.
Ann Bailey, Mary, Sarah; tracts *White Burah [Burch] Freehold, Hazzard*
(MCW 10.223) [SMW TA1.292]; inv.; 1 Aug 1752; 24 Aug 1752; nok Ann Stevens,
Ann Barryman; admx./extx Mary Morgan (I 49.105); acct.; 22 May 1753;
mentions Ann & Mary (both at age), Sarah (age 13) (A 34.155); dist.; 22 May
1753; extx. Mary; children Ann & Mary [of full age], Sarah [age 14 next Apr]
(BB 1.78)

Morgan, John; <u>inv.</u>; 18 May 1752; 25 Sep 1752; nok James & Elisabeth
    Morgan; admx./extx. Mary Morgan (I 51.64); <u>acct.</u>; 22 Oct 1753 (A 36.36)

Morgan, John; <u>inv.</u>; 1 Sep 1772; nok William & Keziah Morgan (I 109.362); <u>acct.</u>;
    12 Apr 1774 (A 69.378); 18 Apr 1774 (A 70.136)

Morgan, William; <u>inv.</u>; 10 Sep 1774; admx. Charity Morgan (I 119.136); <u>acct.</u>;
    1775 (A 72.158); <u>dist.</u>; 1775 (BB 7.26)

MORRIS

Morrice, Jacob; immigrated by 1672 (SK 16.637); <u>acct.</u>; admx. Mary Morris; Aug
    14 __ [1674] (SMAA p. 40)

Morris, John; <u>inv.</u>; 10 Nov 1686 (I&A 9.222)

Morris, Jacob; <u>inv.</u>; 19 Jul 1703 (I&A 24.86)

Morris, Robert; <u>inv.</u>; 25 Mar 1715; 25 Mar 1715 (I&A 36c.129)

Morris, Thomas; <u>inv.</u>; 25 Aug 1725; 2 Nov 1725; nok Joseph & Catherine
    Chunn; admxs. Jane Rice, Ann Morris (I 11.136)

Morris, Dabry; <u>inv.</u>; 17 Nov 1726; nok Timothy Tolle, Robert Taylor; admx.
    Elisabeth Morris (I 11.712); <u>acct.</u>; 22 Jul 1727; admx. Elisabeth, w/o John
    Downe (A 8.286)

Morris, Thomas; <u>acct.</u>; 2 Aug 1729; admx. Jane Price, Ann Morris (A 9.447)

Morris, Ann; <u>inv.</u>; 5 Jul 1733; 5 Aug 1733; nok minors; adm./ex. Joseph
    Fitzjeffery (I 17.326); <u>acct.</u>; 12 Aug 1734 (A 12.462)

Morris, Jacob; <u>inv.</u>; 3 May 1736; 4 Aug 1736; nok Thomas Morris, Anne Lyon;
    admx./extx. Elinor Morris (I 21.514)

Morriss, Thomas; <u>inv.</u>; 21 Jun 1744; 6 Sep 1744; nok John & Catherine Chunn (I
    29.418); <u>acct.</u>; 7 Jul 1747; orphans Henry, James, Jane (A 24.18)

Morris, John; <u>inv.</u>; 22 Apr 1751; 5 Jun 1751; nok Darby Morris, David Downie;
    admx./extx. Ann Morriss (I 47.118); <u>acct.</u>; 9 Mar 1752; orphans Elisabeth [age
    4], Mary [age 2]; admx. Ann, w/o Thomas Crane (A 32.116); <u>dist.</u>; 9 Mar 1752;
    daus. Eliz'a & Mary (BB 1.29)

MOSLEY

Mosley, Thomas; service by 1673 (SK 17.556)

Mosely (Mosley, Mozley), Robert; Poplar Hill; <u>will</u>; 17 Dec 1721; 6 Feb 1721;
    son Robert; daus. Patience, Elizabeth; wife Margaret [step-mother] (MCW 5.82)
    [SMW PC1.260]; <u>inv.</u>; 23 Feb 1721; 23 Apr 1722; nok Thomas Cook, Robert
    Tunnell (I 7.148); <u>acct.</u>; 6 Feb 1722; extx. Margarett, w/o Jaffell Bloomfild (A
    5.37); <u>acct.</u>; 7 Feb 1723 (A 5.341); <u>acct.</u>; 6 Feb 1726 (A 8.157)

Mosely, Elisabeth; <u>inv.</u>; 1 Oct 1734; 18 Nov 1734; nok Ann Sikes, John
    Shenboton; admx./ex. Robert Mosely (I 20.110); <u>acct.</u>; 3 Nov 1735 (A 14.109)

MOY

Moy, Roger; oath 24 Nov 1638; contract to marry Ann Phillipson (AM IV.51.52)

Moy; Elizabeth; wife of Richard, innholder; 1670/1 (AM LXV.1)

Moy, Richard; will; 19 Feb 1670; 13 Dec 1675; wife Eliza:; son Daniel (MCW 1.112)

Moy, Richard; 2nd will [codicil]; 9 Dec 1675; 13 Dec 1675; wife Eliza:; son Daniel; tracts *The Vineyard;* rights in KE Co. plantation *Kentfort* (MCW 1.113) [SMW PC1.23]

Moy, Elizabeth; widow of Richard Moy; will; 8 Jan 1675; 14 Feb 1675; son Daniel; bros. & sisters Symon, William, Robert and Jane Turpine of Bantford, near London; mentions Thomas and Richard, sons of Thomas Griffin and Eliza; Winifred, d/o William Osbaldston; Margaret, d/o of Thomas Wynne; Eliza, w/o Thomas Hatton (MCW 1.118); acct.; 26 Aug 1679; mentions Thomas and Richard, sons of Richard Griffin (I&A 6.319)

Moy, Richard & Elisabeth; inv.; 14 Feb 1675; 22 Jan 1676 (I&A 3.43)

Moy, Daniell; *Towles Discovery;* 100 ac.; sur. 26 Oct 1680 & assgn. from Roger Towle & John Saxon; resurved into *Vineyard;* 1707 no poss.; St. Mary's Hundred (RR p. 7) (TLC p. 8)

Moy, Daniel; s/o Richard; *Fowle's Discovery;* 100 ac.; 7 Apr 1682 cert./pat. (COL)

Moy, Dan.; *Vineyard;* 340 ac.; sur. 6 Jun 1681; orphan s/o R'd Moy; 1704 says see *Gerrards Freehold;* 1707 poss. Tho. Taylor; St. Mary's Hundred (RR p. 10) (TLC p. 11)

Moy, Daniel; inv.; 3 Dec 1698 (I&A 18.25); acct.; 20 Aug 1699 (I&A 19½v.118)

Moye, Richard; age ca 23; 9 Feb 1721 (CCR p. 44)

MUDD

Mudd, Thomas; immigrated by 1680 (SK WC2.402)

Mudd, Thomas; *Jarvis;* 120 ac.; sur. 13 Apr 1681; 1707 poss. Tho. Clark; lies in CH Co.; Choptico Hundred (RR p. 53) (TLC p. 51); 120 ac.; 13 Apr 1681 cert./pat. (COL)
Mudd's Rest; 200 ac.; 12 Jul 1686 cert./pat. (COL)

MUGG

Mugg, Peter; inv.; 9 Nov 1750; 4 Jun 1751; nok John Maddox, Anthony Simms; admx. Ann Mugg (I 47.110); acct.; 10 Jun 1751 (A 30.189)

Magg (Mugg), Ann, Mrs.; inv.; 22 Sep 1755; 17 Dec 1755; nok Notley & Samuel Maddox (I 60.360, 362); acct.; 13 Jun 1757; orphans John [age 19], Walter [age 18], Thomas [age 16], Peter [age 12], Notley [age 10] (A 41.88); dist.; 13 Jun 1757 (BB 2.63)

Mugg, Walter and Priscilla; children Ann [b. 12 Dec 1766], Elizabeth [b. 10 Jan 1770], Peter [b. 6 May 1773] (SA p. 25, 191)

MURPHY

Murphey, Daniell; inv.; Jan 1675; 22 Mar 1675 (I&A 1.592); acct.; [filed with 1677]; admx. Ann Edwards (relict) (I&A 4.206)

Murphy, David; relict & admx. Anne Edwards; 28 Jul 1677 (SMAA p. 76)

Murphey, John; inv.; 27 Jul 1698 (I&A 16.193)

Murphey, James; inv.; 28 Feb [filed with 1717-8] (I 1.52)

Murphy?, ____; acct.; 18 Nov 1718; admx./extx. Margret Murtagh (Murphy) (A 1.325)

Murtagh, James; relict and extx. Margaret; 18 Nov 1718 (SMAA p. 344)

Murphy (Murphey), James; inv.; 26 Apr 1725; 22 Sep 1725; nok William & John Lukes (I 11.128); acct.; 4 May 1726 (A 7.335); acct.; 5 Jul 1726 (A 7.405)

Murphy, Michael; priest; 8 Jul 1759; age 34 (HGM)

Murphey, Zekhaniah; m. 6 Jan 1778 Elianor Gray (BRU p. 535)

Murphy, Hezekiah; m. 13 Feb 1778 Mary Robinson (BRU p. 536)

MURTY

Murty, Step'n; *Waterford*; 800 ac.; resur. 24 May 1676; 1707 Clement Hill, atty. for Step'n Murty; land not found; New Town Hundred (RR p. 37) (TLC p. 36)

Murty, Stephen; will; 18 Apr 1684; 4 Jun 1684; wife Elizabeth; in Waterford, Ireland; sons John, Anthony; tracts *New Waterford, New Passage* (MCW 1.131) [SMW PC1.49]; inv.; 19 Jun 1684 (I&A 8.208); acct.; 12 Mar 1687 (I&A 9.470); acct.; 4 Dec 1688 (I&A 10.185)

Murty, Anthony; inv.; 19 May 1687 (I&A 9.284)

NEALE

Neale (Neall), Henry; New Towne; will; oral; probate 22 Jan 1672; wife Anne; son Henry (MCW 1.71) [SMW PC1.11]; inv.; 7 Feb 1674 (I&A 1.20); acct.; 12 Jun 1674; extx. Anne Neall; 2 children (I&A 1.22)

Neale, Samuel; acct. ; 27 Jul 1674; ex. Thomas Spinke of St. Inegoes; dau. Rebecca (SMAA p. 44)

Neale (O'Neal), Henry; will; 22 Mar 1721; 4 Apr 1721; bros. Arthur and Henry; cousin Catherine Bisco; wife Elinor (MCW 5.48) [SMW PC1.267]; inv.; 11 May 1721; 30 Jun 1721; admx. Ellenor Oneal (I 5.149); acct.; 13 Aug 1722; extx. Elinor, w/o Thomas Ryon (A 4.287)

Neale, Roswell; *St. Winifred's Freehold*; 952 ac.; resur. 18 Jul 1714 for Ozwell Neale (TLC p. 41); 3 Apr 1736 cert./pat. (COL)

Oneale, Peter; will; 17 Apr 1745; 16 Sep 1747; wife Ann; sons John, Peter Lamar, James; daus. Elizabeth, Mary; tract *Crachbone [Crackbone]* (MCW 9.122) [SMW TA1.196]

Oneal, Peter; *Hard Fortune*; 62 ac.; 30 Mar 1747 cert./pat. (COL)

Neale, Roswell; 24 Mar 1751; 7 May 1751; wife Elizabeth; sons James, Raphael, Bennett, Jeremiah, William, Henry; daus. Anne w/o William Gibson, Mary Wheeler, Elizabeth Neale; tract *St. Winifred's Free Hold* (MCW 10.153) [SMW TA1.268]; inv.; [filed with 1752]; nok Ann Thompson, Henry Neall; adms./exs. James, Raphael & Bennett Neall (I 51.78); dist.; 2 Sep 1752 (BB 1.71)

Neale, Bozwell; acct.; 2 Sep 1752 exs. James, Raphael & Bennitt Neal (A 33.202); acct.; 10 Oct 1753; exs. Raphael, Bennitt Neale (A 36.25)

Neal, Charles; inv.; 27 Mar 1756; 16 May 1757; nok Mary & Anne Neale; admx./ex. Daniel Neale (I 63.173); dist.; 16 May 1757; widow; orphans Mary Branson and Charles, Daniel & Ann Neale (BB 2.58)

Neal, James; acct.; 25 Oct 1753 (A 35.238)

Neale, Mary; widow of Raphael Neale of Charles Co.; will; 29 Sep 1760; 24 May 1763; daus. Ann Thompson, Mary Tawny, Henerite Brook; g-ch. Rapheal and Eleanor Thompson, Mary Eleanor Comb [Thompson], John Frances Towney, John Diggs, Repheal Brook, Eleanor Diggs; sons-i-l Edward Diggs, Thomas Tawny, Bazil Brooke, John Tankester (or Lankester) (MCW 12.205) [SMW TA1.443]; inv. 6 Sep 1763; nok George Slye, Mary Taney (I 81.241)

Neale, Henry; will; 20 Nov 1766; 9 Feb 1767; sons Wilfred, Henry; daus. Mary Roach and Henrietta Ford (MCW 13.151) [SMW TA1.532]; inv.; 10 Mar 1767; 3 Jun 1767; nok Raphael & Jeremiah Neal; ex. Wilfred Neale (I 93.99); inv.; 20 Sep 1767 (I 95.24, 25); acct.; 12 Aug 1768 (A 58.266)

Neale, Bennett; will; 23 Feb 1771; 3 May 1771; wife Mary; children Benone, Charles, Elizabeth, w/o Kenelmn Chesold [Cheseldyne], Sarah, Anne, Elenor; tracts *Wee Bitt, Mile* (MCW 14.180) [SMW TA1.622]; inv.; 18 Jun 1771; 9 Sep 1771; nok Raphael Neale, Ann Gibson; extx. Mary Neale (I 106.385, 387); dist.; [filed with 1774-5]; children Sarah, Ann, Eleanor, Benoni, Charles (BB 7.11)

NELSON

Nelson, Joshua; Northumberland Co.; will; 11 May 1744; 9 Jul 1744; wife Elizabeth daus. Mary Ann, Chloe; sons Seneca, Lancelot [SMW TA1.186]; inv.; 5 Jun 1745; 6 Aug 1745; admx./extx. Elisabeth Nelson (I 31.288); acct.; 6 Oct 1747 (A 24.235)

Nelson, Elizabeth; her son Seneca Nelson; *Doe Park*; 261 ac.; 14 Jul 1768 cert./pat. (COL)

NEVETT

Nevell, Rich'd; unnamed; 100 ac.; sur. 10 Dec 1641; surrendered; New Town Hundred (RR p. 26) (TLC p. 25)

Nevill, John; 50 ac.; unnamed; sur. 14 Jul 1647; esch.; [1704 says John Nevitt]; Poplar Hill Hundred (RR p. 22) (TLC p. 21); also see RR 21 re 200 ac. unclaimed

Nevett, John; *Nevett's Beginning*; 100 ac.; 22 Oct 1681 cert./pat. (COL)

Nevit, Nicholas; inv.; [filed with 1709] (I&A 30.298); acct.; 15 Jul 1711 (I&A 32c.96) (SMAA p. 216)

Neavitt (Nevett), Francis; planter; will; 20 Feb 1723; 17 Mar 1723; daus. Elizabeth and Mary; wife Elinor (MCW 5.161) [SMW PC1.286]; acct.; 4 Aug 1725 (A 7.96); acct.; 3 Aug 1726 (A 7.512)

Neavett (Neavitt), Francis, Mrs.; inv.; 17 Mar 1723; 5 Jun 1724; nok Margaret Neavett, John Realy (I 9.446)

NEWMAN

Newman, Richard; service by 1679 (SK WC2.67)

Newman, William; *Monmouth*; 87 ac.; 15 Jun 1687 cert./pat. (COL)
Newman, Richard; inv.; 25 Feb 1701 (I&A 21.370); acct.; 9 Oct 1702; unnamed
son; adm. Annastatia Newman (I&A 23.91) (SMAA p. 108)
Newman, Thomas; acct.; 5 Aug 1720 (SMAA p. 435)

NEWTON
Newton, Thomas; *Nutons Rest with Addition*; 37 ac.; sur. 14 Jun 1720; (TLC p.
90); *Newton's Addition*; 10 Jun 1734 cert./pat. (COL)
Newton's Rest; 63 ac.; sur. 20 May 1716 (TLC p. 88); 10 Jun 1734 cert./pat. (COL)
Andrew's Wood; 142 ac.; 29 Nov 1759 cert./pat. (COL)
Newton, Thomas, Sr.; will; 4 Dec 1741; 6 Dec 1741; son Thomas; d-i-l
Elizabeth; g-sons Clement & Joseph; wife Katherine (MCW 8.155) [SMW
TA1.128]; inv.; 14 Dec 1741; 22 Dec 1741; nok John & Richard Newton;
admx./extx. Catherine Newton (I 26.428); acct.; 5 Jul 1743 (A 19.438)
Newton, Clement; will; 30 Jun 1760; 4 Nov 1760; sons Joseph, Clement. Albane
[Alleane], Barnard, Gabriel, Adelbert; daus. Ann, Mary, Bibiana,
Immaranchaanner [Junmarauchanner] (MCW 12.21) [SMW TA1.399]; inv.; 4 Nov
1760; 4 Mar 1761; nok Richard & John Newton; admx./ex. Joseph Newton (I
71.166); acct.; 8 Aug 1762 (A 48.394)
Newton, John; inv.; 24 Nov 1762; 8 Feb 1763; nok Richard & Thomas Newton;
admx. Monica Newton (I 80.140); acct.; 8 Jun 1763 (A 49.601)
Newton, Joseph and Mildred; children Rhodolph [b. 13 May 1763]; John
Shadrach [b. 1 Jan 1767], James [b. 11 Feb 1769] (SA p. 191)
Newton, John; will; 14 Mar 1764; 24 Jan 1765; mentions Catharine and John,
ch/o Robert Newton and Elizabeth; bro. Leonard; wife Frances; [b-i-l
Matthew Wise] (MCW 13.74) [SMW TA1.470]; inv.; 23 Apr 1765; nok Catharine
Newton, Adam Wise; exs. Frances Newton & wife Mathes (I 87.15); acct.; 13
Apr 1767; ex. Frances Newton (A56.82); dist.; 19 Apr 1767; legatees Catharine,
d/o Robert Newton and Elisabeth; widow Frances (BB 5.27)
Newton, Monica; inv.; 1 Nov 1766; mentions John Baptis & James Newton (I
91.81, 82)
Newton, Bernaar; m. 11 Dec 1769 Mary Pain (MM)
Newton, Bernard and Mary Ann; dau. Elizabeth [b. 24 Jul 1771] (SA p. 26)
Newton, Thomas, Sr.; joyner; will; 27 Mar 1772; 15 Sep 1772; children Arnold,
Henry Thomas, William, Ignatius, Sarah, Susannah Poole, Elizabeth,
Clement, Mary; wife Susannah; tracts *Andrews Wood, Newtons Property*
(MCW 14.237) [SMW TA1.639]; inv.; 15 Sep 1772; 11 Jan 1773; nok Elender
Howard, Joseph New; ex. Susannah & William Newton (I 114.36); acct.; 1 Apr
1775 (A 72.155); acct.; 20 Oct 1775 (A 73.251)
Newton, Alban; m. 30 Mar 1773 Marion Pike (MM)
Newton, Bernard; m. 8 Feb 1775 Mary Pike (MM)
Newton, Gabriel; m. 24 Oct 1775 Henrietta Wheatley (MM)

NICHOLS

Nicholls, Thomas; <u>inv.</u>; 27 Feb 1702 (I&A 24.1); <u>inv.</u>; 27 Feb 1702 (I&A 24.1)

Nicholas, Mary; <u>acct.</u>; 11 Nov 1706; adm. Thomas Nichols (I&A 26.159) (SMAA p. 134)

Nichols, William; <u>inv.</u>; 17 Apr 1714; wido Sarah Cartwright (I&A 36a.99)

Nickolls (Nicholls, Nicols), Henry; <u>will</u>; probate 18 Mar 1728/9; sister Mary (MCW 6.113); wife Elizabeth [SMW PC1.322]; <u>inv.</u>; 22 Mar 1728; nok Thomas & Elisabeth; admx. Elisabeth Nicholls (I 14.9)

Nichols, Thomas; <u>will</u>; 10 Oct 1740; 5 Nov 1740; wife Ann; children Thomas, Luke, Henry, James, Ann, Sarah; tract *Nichols Adventure* (MCW 8.111) [SMW TA1.99]; <u>inv.</u>; 23 Mar 1740; adm./ex. Thomas Nicholas (I 25.432)

NOBLE

Noble, John; *Nobles Victor*; 50 ac.; sur. 17 Aug 1682; 1707 poss. Widow Tant; New Town Hundred (RR p. 39) (TLC p. 38); 6 Mar 1686 cert./pat. (COL)

Noble, John; <u>inv.</u>; 12 Apr 1698 (I&A 18.21a)

Noble, John; <u>inv.</u>; 30 Apr 1717; nok Ann Noble (I&A 39b.68); <u>acct.</u>; 13 Jun 1720; admx. Ann, w/o Pattrick Fisher (A 3.94) (SMAA p. 413)

Noble, Mary; <u>inv.</u>; 8 Jun 1743; nok minors; admx./extx. Rachel Noble (I 28.9)

Noble, John; <u>will</u>; 21 Feb 1749/50; 18 Sep 1758; cousin Mazerdin Fergoe [Forgee]; wife Elizabeth (MCW 11.214) [SMW TA1.369]

NORMAN

Norman, John; *Yeilding*; 300 ac.; sur. 8 Mar 1653; 1707 poss. John Bayly; New Town Hundred (RR p. 30) (TLC p. 29)

Norman, Thomas; <u>inv.</u>; 11 Mar 1718; 10 Sep 1719 (I 3.52)

NORRIS

Norris, Jacob; <u>acct.</u>; 4 Sep [filed with 1704]; admx. Mary Norris (I&A 3.368)

Norris (Norriss), John; <u>will</u>; 13 Apr 1709; 2 Aug 1710; sons Thomas, Luke, John, Marke; wife Susannah; daus. Monica, Elizabeth and Mary (MCW 3.174) [SMW PC1.165]; <u>acct.</u>; 8 Jun 1711; admx. Susannah Norris (I&A 32c.90) (SMAA p. 216)

Norrice, John; <u>inv.</u>; 30 Aug 1710; nok Nicholas Mills, John Heard (I&A 32b.1)

Norris, Clement; *Norris's Frolic*; 3 ac.; 3½ ac.; sur. 13 Aug 1740 (TLC p. 96); 17 Dec 1740 cert./pat. (COL)

Norris (Norriss), John; <u>inv.</u>; 6 May 1748; nok Mark & Clement Norriss; admx./extx. Ann Norris (I 35.525); <u>acct.</u>; 2 May 1749; orphans Thomas (age 20), John (age 19), Susanna (age 15), William (age 14), Matthew (age 11), Monica (age 8), Clement (age 6), Stephen (age 4), John Baptis (newborn) (A 26.52)

Norris, Clement and Elizabeth; sons Thomas [b. 1 May 1753], Vincent [b. 5 Apr 1755] (SA p. 190)

Norris, Thomas and Ann; child. Mary Ann [b. 1 Nov 1756], Philip [b. 1 May 1758], Mary [b. 22 Oct 1759], William [b. 7 Jun 1761], Joseph [b. 29 Jul 1764] (SA p. 12, 13, 47)

Norris, John and Mary; child. Philip [b. 25 Dec 1754], Henry Elijah [b. 14 Mar 1758], Arnold [b. 26 Jun 1761], Barbara [b. 17 Mar 1766], Susanna [b. 14 Mar 1771] (SA p. 15, 55)

Norris, Thomas; *Norris's Venture*; 58 ac.; 9 Jan 1759 cert./pat. (COL)
Sandy Levels; 11 ac.; 22 Jan 1762 cert./pat. (COL)

Norris, Mark and Elizabeth; child. Cuthbert [b. 26 Jun 1760], John [b. 6 May 1762], Henrietta [b. 9 Jul 1765], Mathias [b. 1 Sep 1767], Mary [b. 20 Jul 1769] (SA p. 191)

Norris, Thomas;[planter]; will; 19 Oct 1761; 1 Dec 1761; sons Ignatius, Rodelphus, Thomas, Clement, John; daus. Monica, Priscilla, Henrietta; wife Jane; tracts *Sugar Rains [Lugous Plains], Wheatley's Content* (MCW 12.98) [SMW TA1.4254]; inv.; 31 May 1762; 1 Jun 1762; nok Mar. & Luke Norris; exs. Jane & Rodolphus Norriss (I 78.86); acct.; 9 Feb 1763 (A 49.100); dist.; 9 Feb 1763; Clement, John, Thomas, Ignatius, Rodolphus, Maria, Priscilla, Henrietta (BB 3.179)

Norris, Philip and Monica; child. Susannah [b. 24 Dec 1761], Henrietta [b. 13 Sep 1764], Eleanor [b. 13 Nov 1767] (SA p. 190)

Norris, Ann; 27 Nov 1764; 10 Jun 1766; sons Thomas, John, William, Matthew, Clement, Stephen, John Baptist; daus. Susannah Gough, Monica Stone (MCW 13.110) [SMW TA1.491]; acct.; 4 May 1767; exs. Matthew & Clement Norris (A 56.75)

Norris, Joseph and Elizabeth; child. Enoch [b. 27 Feb 1765], Luke [b. 3 Jan 1767], Susanna [b. 27 Sep 1768] (SA p. 16, 50)

Norriss, Ann; inv.; 4 Sep 1766; 28 Oct 1766; nok Thomas & Mark Norriss; exs. Thomas & Clement Norriss (I 91..79); dist.; 4 May 1767; Thomas, John, William, Mathew, John Baptist, Susannah Gough, Monica Stone (BB 5.26)

Norris, Luke; will; probate 1 May 1767; sons John, Mackelvey, Joseph; dau. Susaner Pool, Jane; wife unnamed; tract *Whealey's Contentment* (MCW 13.177); inv.; 10 Nov 1767; nok John & Joseph Norris; extx. Catharine Norris (I 94.206)

Norris, Bennet and Frances; dau. Winifred [b. 3 Apr 1768] (SA p. 195)

Norris, Thomas and Mary; child. Elizabeth [b. 26 Oct 1768], Rebecca [b. 18 Sep 1771], Dorothy [b. 24 Aug 1773] (SA p. 24, 190)

Norris, William; inv.; 6 Dec 1768; nok Clement & Thomas Norris; extx. Annastatia Norris (I 98.114); acct.; 9 May 1770 (A 64.103)

Norris, Rhodolph and Dorothy; dau. Mary Ann [b. 22 Apr 1768] (SA p. 189)

Norris, Ignatius; m. 22 Mar 1770 Lucia Pike (MM)

Norris, John Baptist; m. 18 Aug 1770 M. Woodward (MM)

Norriss, William; acct.; 14 May 1771; admx. Anastatia Norriss (A 66.164)

Norris, Jac.; m. 6 Mar 1773 Monica Greenwell (MM)

Norriss, John; inv.; 16 Mar 1774; 10 Sep 1774; nok McKelvie & Mar Norriss; admx. Ann Draden Norriss (I 119.147); acct.; 13 Sep 1774 (A 72.16)

Norris (Norriss), Annastatia; will; 19 Oct 1774; 1 Nov 1774; daus. Henneriatta, Wrancher, Elezabeth Belwood, Mary Rhodes; son Matthew; bro. Philip (MCW 16.1) [SMW TA1.692]; inv.; 1 Dec 1774; 20 Aug 1775 (I 122.184)

Norris, Thomas; m. 1 Jun 1776 Catherine Mattingly (MM)

Norris, William and Dorothy White; m. 22 Nov 1778 (SA p. 57)

NOTLEY

Notley, Tho.; *Notleys Addition*; 450 ac.; sur. 28 Sep 1672; 1707 poss. Ethelbert Doyne; St. Clements Hundred (RR p. 45) (TLC p. 44)

Notley, John; acct; 13 Nov 1675; admn. Thomas Notley (I&A 1.459); inv.; 2 Oct 1675; 15 Oct 1675 (I&A 1.447)

Notley (Nottley), Thomas; will; 3 Apr 1679; 6 Apr 1679; sister Katharine Grudgefield of London; mentions Capt. Gerrard Slye & wife Jane, Notley s/o Benjamin Rozer; tract *Cerneabdy Manor*; [sons Notley Maddux and Nathan Gouldsmith] (MCW 1.211) [SMW PC1.34]; inv.; 12 Apr 1679 (I&A 6.576)

NOTTINGHAM

Nottingham, Thomas; inv.; 26 __ 1713; nok John Wheatley, Sr. & Jr. (I&A 35a.329); acct.; 5 Jul 1716; adm. Stephen Nottingham (I&A 38b.12); acct.; 6 Jul 1716 (SMAA p. 297)

Nottingham, Stephen; will; 23 Apr 1745; 7 May 1745; children Atahanatius, Mary, Anne, Mathias; tracts *Nevet's* (?), *St. Anns* (MCW 9.28) [SMW TA1.173]; inv.; 22 Jun 1745; 1 Jul 1745; nok Thomas & Francis Wheetley; adm./ex. Athanatius Nottingham (I 31.163); acct.; 10 Nov 1746 (A 23.127)

Nottingham, Mathias and Mary; children Raphael Ignatius [b. 9 Jun 1754], Mary Ann [b. 2 Aug 1757], Elizabeth [b. 5 Jan 1751], Ignatius [b. 21 Apr 1763 - 1765] (SA p. 11, 46)

Nottingham, Athana and Mary; children Mary Ann [b. 18 Nov 1762], Ann [b. 3 Sep 1763], Enoch [b. 25 Dec 1766] (SA p. 19, 54)

Nottingham, Athanasius; will; 11 Jul 1767; 18 Aug 1767; bro. Matthias; children Philip, Basil, Catherine, Eleanor, Bennett, Barbary, Elizabeth, Mary Ann, Ann, Enoch; wife Mary; tract *Nivitts St. Ann* (MCW 14.19) [SMW TA1.516]; inv.; 8 Jan 1768; 30 Apr 1768; nok Philip Nottingham, Ann David; ex. Mary Nottingham (I 96.172); acct.; 12 Apr 1769 (A 60.365); acct.; 20 Oct 1770 (A 64.254); dist.; 20 Oct 1770 (BB 5.396)

Nottingham, Matthias; will; 28 Sep 1767; 17 Nov 1767; wife Mary; sons Raphel Ignacius, Ignatius, Stephen; daus. Mary, Elizabeth; tracts *Salmon, Nibitts St. Ann* (MCW 14.19); calls dau. Mary Ann [SMW TA1.418]; inv.; 1 Dec 1767; 12 Apr 1768; nok An Payne, Stephen Nottingham; extx. Mary, w/o Leonard Payne, Jr. (I 97.90); inv.; 4 Apr 1769 (I 100.128); acct.; 4 Apr 1769 (A 61.106)

Nottingham, Basil; m. 31 Dec 1774 Joanna Stone (MM)

NOWELL

Nowell [Newele], Henry; <u>will</u>; 28 Nov 1734; 5 Nov 1735; wife Elizabeth; son
Henry; dau. Frances Taylor (MCW 7.157) [SMW TA1.41]; <u>inv.</u>; 30 Dec 1735; 23
Feb 1735; nok James & Oliver Tayler; adms./exs. James Darnel & wife
Elisabeth, Henry Nowel (I 21.235)

Nowel, Henry; <u>inv.</u>; 27 Aug 1764; nok Susannar & Mathew Hagur; admx. Lydia
Nowel (I 84.290); <u>acct.</u>; 31 Oct 1765 (A 54.6)

Nowell, Edward; <u>dist.</u>; 31 Oct 1765; admx. Lydia Nowell (BB 4.151)

NUGENT

Newgent, Wm.; *Newgent*; 100 ac.; sur. 2 Nov 1650;1707 no poss.; New Town
Hundred (RR p. 29) (TLC p. 27)

Nugent, Edmond; *St. Katharine's*; 180 ac.; 5 Oct 1695 cert./pat. (COL)

Nugen, Robert; *Nugen's Venture*; 50 ac.; sur. 19 Feb 1728 (TLC p. 93); 17 Nov
1737 cert./pat. (COL)

Nugent (Nugen), Robert; *Foxes' Den*; 87 ac.; 17 Mar 1758 cert./pat. (COL)
Nugen's Folly; 19 ac.; 29 Sep 1762 cert./pat. (COL)

Nugent, Robert; <u>will</u>; 26 Dec 1775; 10 Feb 1775; wife Ann; children Robert,
Williba, Mary Ennis, Susannah, Elizabeth (MCW 16.93) [SMW TA1.718]

NUNN

Nunn, John; *Nunns Oak*; 300 ac.; sur. 14 Jul 1647; 1707 poss. John Fossey &
Daniel Smith; 150 ac. incl. in *Resurvey of Radnor*; New Town Hundred (RR p.
27) (TLC p. 25)

Nunn, John; <u>will</u>; probate 4 Apr 1653 (MCW 1.7)

NUTHALL

Nuthall, John; b. Mar 1651; father of John; g-father of Brent; 8 Oct 1721; tract
Crop Manor (CCR p. 50)

Nutthall, John, Jr.; m. ca 1693 Mary Brent of Stafford Co., VA (siblings:
Margaret Brent, w/o George Plowden, & William Brent); son Brent [b. ca
1697]; 3 Aug 1717 (CCR p. 39)

Nuthall, John, Sr.; Gent.; <u>will</u>; 22 Nov 1713; 28 Sep 1714; son John; g-son
Breaht Nuthall; g-dau. Elinor Nuthall (MCW 4.18) [SMW PC1.185]

Nuthall, John, Jr.; extx. Ellinor; 13 Sep 1716 (SMAA p. 296)

Nuthall, John; wife Barbara; 11 May 1720; tract *St. Mary's Hill* (CCR p. 46)

Nuthall, Margaret; dau. Ann Roach [b. 28 Feb 1761] (SA p. 8, 45)

Nutthill [Nuthall], Elizabeth; <u>will</u>; 18 Jun 1762; 21 Dec 1762; daus. Mary Brent
Atkinson, Mary Brent Nutthill and Ariminta Nutthill; g-dau. Ann Nutthill;
s-i-l Joshua Atkison (MCW 12.177) [SMW TA1.440]; <u>inv.</u>; 21 Dec 1762; nok
Charles King, Susanna Daffin; exs. Mary Brent Nuthall (I 81.228; 82.206)

OAKELY

Oakeley, Ann; d/o Thomas Oakeley; records cattle mark; 14 Feb 1669 (AM
   LVII.497)

Oakely, Lyonell; will; 7 Jun 1688; 27 Jul 1688; sisters Ann, Elizabeth & Mary
   (MCW 2.29) [SMW PC1.74]; inv.; 20 Aug 1688 (I&A 10.110)

OLIVER

Oliver, Blanch; widow of Roger; son William; dau. Mary Harrison; 22 Sep 1647
   (AM IV.209, 329)

Oliver, Luis (Lewis); inv.; 15 Aug 1718 (I 1.407); acct.; 9 Apr 1720; admx.
   Elisabeth Oliver (A 3.30) (SMAA p. 418)

Oliver (Olever), Clement; inv.; 4 Mar 1731; 3 Jun 1732; nok Lewis & John
   Oliver (I 16.443); acct.; 2 Dec 1732 (A 11.528)

Oliver, John; *Archie's Hills*; 65 ac.; 4 May 1752 cert./pat. (COL)

Oliver, John; will; 1 Feb 1762; 22 Feb 1763; wife Mary; tract *Archers Hill* (MCW
   12.175) [SMW TA1.431]; inv.; 22 Feb 1763; 22 Feb 1763; extx. Mary Oliver (I
   80.170); acct.; 22 Feb 1763 (A 49.103); dist.; 22 Feb 1763 (BB 3.178)

ORION

Orion (Orian, Orior), Thomas; 24 Nov 1720; 1 May 1720; sons Edward,
   Thomas; dau. Ann (MCW 5.23) [SMW PC1.252]; inv.; 30 Mar 1721; 8 Jun 1721 (I
   5.52); acct.; 10 Mar 1721 (A 4.73)

Oryon. Malligo (Mallygo); inv.; 24 Aug 1732; nok dau. Ann & son William
   Orion; admx./extx. Ann Oryon (I 16.576); acct.; 4 Nov 1736; mentions William
   & Elisabeth Oryon; admx. Ann Hinkson, w/o John Hinkson (A 15.230)

OSBORN

Osborn, Henry; Leonard's Creek; St. Mary's Co.; will; 26 Aug 1664; 22 Apr
   1665; wife Catharine; mentions "my" child. (MCW 1.31)

Osbourne, John; service by 1680 (SK WC2.315, 341)

Osburn, Richard; acct.; 18 Mar [filed with 1722] (A 5.112)

OWENS

Owen, Patrick; will; oral; probate 7 Jan 1733; bro. James (MCW 7.53) [SMW
   TA1.19]; inv.; Mar 1733; 6 Nov 1734; ex. James Owen (I 20.100); inv.; 4 May
   1734; 4 Jun 1734 (I 18.321)

Owens, John; inv.; 18 Jun 1733; 8 Aug 1733; nok minors; admx./extx. Sarah
   Owens (I 17.331)

Owens, Joseph; inv.; 23 Jan 1745; 7 Aug 1746; nok Josep Illing, John Owens (I
   33.310)

Owens, John and Sarah Saunders; m. 3 Oct 1779 (SA p. 57)

PACE

Peace (Pace), Thomas; inv.; 16 May 1698 (I&A 16.205)

Pace [Perce], John; <u>will</u>; 23 Mar 1746; 11 May 1747; sons Jonathan, Stephen; dau. Mildred; child.'s uncle Benjamin Williams; wife Ann Perce (MCW 9.111) [SMW TA1.201]

PAKE

Pake, Walter; *The Hills*; 100 ac.; sur. 15 Nov 1648; 1707 poss. James Tant; New Town Hundred (RR p. 27) (TLC p. 26)
Pake; sur. 29 Jan 1649; 1707 poss. Henry Jarbo; New Town Hundred (RR p. 28) (TLC p. 27)
Rocky Point; 200 ac.; sur. 15 Jun 1652; assgn. Rich'd Knevett; 1707 poss. Sam. Davis who m. relict of Geo. Midcalf; New Town Hundred (RR p. 31) (TLC p. 30)
Redbud Thickett; 100 ac.; sur. 1 Mar 1657; assgn. Wm. Styles; 1707 poss. Rich'd Vowles; New Town Hundred (RR p. 31) (TLC p. 30)
St. Peters Hill; 500 ac.; sur. 19 Apr 1662; 1707 poss. Henry Jarbo; mentions Henry, Peter, Charles, Ignatius, Mary & Monica Jarboe; New Town Hundred (RR p. 32) (TLC p. 31)
St. Francis's; 500 ac.; sur. 19 Oct 1665; 1707 no poss.; incl. *Resurvey of Hanover Addition*; New Town Hundred (RR p. 33) (TLC p. 32)
St. Margrets; 300 ac.; sur. 7 May 1666; eschild. and granted Margaret Noble, d/o Pake; 1707 poss. James Gough; New Town Hundred (RR p. 33) (TLC p. 32)
Pakes, Walter; f/o Mary; give of 300 a. in St. Lawrence Neck in consideration of her marriage to Henry Aspinall; 2 Mar 1663/4 (AM XLIX.168); from Walter Pakes to s-i-l Henry Aspinall; 100 a. called *St. Peter's Hill* (AM XLIX.224)
Pakes, Walter; age ca 43 on 7 Jun 1653; age ca 53 on 12 Nov 1661; age 54 on Aug 1662 (AM X.276; XLI.528, 590)
Pake, Walter; s-i-l Henry Aspinall; 25 Dec 1665 (CCR p. 2)
Pake, Walter; innholder of St. Lawrences in Brittons Bay; indicted for murder; 23 Oct 1668 (AM LVII.352)

PALMER

Palmer, Katherine; widow; <u>will</u>; 4 Mar 1722; 1 Nov 1726; nephew Peter, s/o bro. Peter Cantancean; father John Cantancean; uncle William Cantancean; sons Thomas, James and John Waughop; daus. Ann Waughop, Katherine Kennedy w/o William Kennedy; g-son Thomas Palmer Waughop, s/o James; tract *The Wine Yard* (MCW 5.233) [SMW PC1.313]; <u>inv.</u>; 1 Mar 1726; 27 Apr 1727; nok James Waughop; exs. Thomas & James Waughop (I 11.866)
Palmer, William; <u>inv.</u>; 15 Jun 1726; 8 Sep 1726; admx. Elisabeth Williams (I 11.501); <u>acct.</u>; 8 Sep 1726 (A 7.516)

PARKER

Parker, Edward; <u>will</u>; probate 20 Jul 1644 (MCW 1.2)
Parker, Edward; St. Inigoes Manor; <u>will</u>; 3 Jan 1669; 29 Jan 1669; f-i-l Nicholas Young; tracts *Fresh Pond Neck, Parker's Land*; mother unnamed; bros.

Samuel and Edward; sister Eliza; kinsman William Bretton (MCW 1.51) [SMW PC1.8]

Parker, Edward; St. Inigoes Manor; <u>will</u>; 3 Jan 1669; 29 Jan 1669; to f-i-l Nicholas Young, *Fresh Pond Neck*; to mother [unnamed] *Cedar Point* in CH Co.; bros. Samuel and Philip, 800 ac. *Parker's Delight* (*Parker's Land*) in BA Co.; sis. Eliza. (MCW 1.40)

Parker, George; immigrated by 1672 (SK 17.397)

Parker, Richard; surgeon; <u>acct.</u>; 26 Jul 1673 (SMAA p. 122)

Parker, Robert; 28 Jan 1754; 14 May 1755; wife Judea; daus. Elizabeth, Sarah, Margaret [SMW TA1.335]

PARKS

Parks, William Thomas; <u>acct.</u>; 28 Jul 1703; adm. William Parks (I&A 3.98)

Park, Rally & Cole; *Clarks East Discovery*; 99 ac.; incl. 2 parcels escheat land; resur. 16 Aug 1727 (TLC p. 89)

Clarks West Discovery; 212 ac.; 2 tracts escheat land; resur. 16 Aug 1727 for Joseph Clark (TLC p. 90)

PARRAN

Parran, Charles Somersett & Margaret Ireland (by license); m. 17 Dec 1782 (SA p. 60)

Parran, Thomas and Jane Mackall (by license); m. 6 Feb 1783 (SA p. 61)

PARSONS

Parsons, John; unnamed; 150 ac.; 150 ac.; 1 Sep 1687 cert./pat. (COL)

Parsons, John; *Barnscott*; 50 ac.; 1 Sep 1687 cert./pat. (COL)

Parsons (Persons), John; <u>will</u>; 5 May 1688; 9 Jul 1688; sons Edward, John, Cosine [Cesure]; wife Mary; dau. (unnamed) (MCW 2.28) [SMW PC1.70); <u>inv.</u>; 10 Dec 1688 (I&A 10.136)

Parsons, John; <u>inv.</u>; 5 Apr 1703 (I&A 1.639)

Parsons, Edward; <u>will</u>; 12 Dec 1715; 21 Apr 1716; wife Mary; child. Robert, John, Charles, Elizabeth, Edward, Mary; wife Mary; former wife Phillis; bro. Robert Hopkins; tract *Worrell* [*Maxwell*] (MCW 4.70) [SMW PC1.206]; <u>inv.</u>; 5 Feb 1705 (I&A 25.173); <u>acct.</u>; 25 Sep 1707; adm. Cosmas (Casmus) Pearsons (I&A 27.152) (SMAA p. 145)

Parsons, Robert; <u>inv.</u>; 18 Nov 1726; 7 Mar 1726; nok William & Eallis Brewer; admx. Elisabeth Parsons (I 11.726); <u>acct.</u>; 1 Aug 1727 (A 8.353)

Parsons (Persons), Causmay (Cosmos, Cosmas); <u>will</u>; planter; 17 Nov 1733; 11 Dec 1733; child. John, Mary Mahoney, James, Anna, Joseph, Edward, Clement (MCW 7.49) [SMW TA1.13]; <u>inv.</u>; 22 Jul 1734; 8 Nov 1734; nok Mary Massy, John Brady; adm./ex. John Parsons (I 20.105); <u>acct.</u>; 13 Sep 1735 (A 13.319)

Parsons, James [b. 1 Apr 1744]; orphan (SA p. 36)

Parsons, Edward; *Small Addition*; 19½ ac.; sur. 30 May 1748 (TLC p. 114); 19 ac.; 30 May 1748 cert./pat. (COL)

Parson, Edward; <u>will</u>; 28 Feb 1770; 17 Jul 1770; wife Elizabeth; tract *Greens*
(MCW 14.143) [SMW TA1.595]; <u>inv.</u>; 9 Aug 1770; 10 Feb 1771; nok Ann
Wellenner, Jonathon Sharp; ex. Elisabeth Parsons (I 107.90)

PATTISON
Pattison, James; <u>will</u>; 23 Sep 1697; 1 Apr 1698; dau. Elinor Harbert, now w/o
William Herbert, formerly wife of John Angell; g-child. James, John &
Angelor Angell; Vitires [Vitius], Luke, Michael, Francis & Mark Harbert; g-
son John s/o Daniel Hammond, dec'd; mentions Ann Angell; tracts *Churchill,
The New Ground* (MCW 2.142) [SMW PC1.106]; <u>acct.</u>; 11 Oct 1700 (I&A 20.54);
<u>acct.</u>; 30 Apr 1702 (I&A 21.328)
Pattison, James; constable of Newtown in 1655; mentions Pope Alvey (cooper)
(MD p. 145)
Pattison, James; wife Margaret, extx. of Walter Hall; 1680 (AM LXIX.387)

PAVATT
Pavett, James; <u>inv.</u>; 6 Aug 1740; 29 Aug 1740; nok Isaac & John Pavett;
admx./extx. Elisabeth Pavett (I 25.197)
Pavet, Joseph; <u>inv.</u>; 26 Jan 1745; 7 Apr 1746; mentions Elisabeth Pavett;
adm./ex. Isaac Prevatt (Pavett) (I 32.221); <u>acct.</u>; [filed with 1747] (A 23.197)
Pavatt, Isaac; St. Inegoes Hundred; <u>will</u>; 9 Dec 1754; 27 Jan 1755; wife
Margaret; sons James, John, Isaac (MCW 11.82) [SMW TA1.329]; <u>inv.</u>; 30 Jun
1755; nok John Pavett, Mary Richardson; admx./extx. Margaret Pavott (I 59.8);
<u>acct.</u>; 21 Mar 1756; orphans James [age 14], John [age 11], Isaac [age 9] (A
40.16); <u>dist.</u>; 28 May 1756 (BB 2.23)
Pavett (Pavell, Pravett), Margaret; <u>will</u>; 27 Mar 1769; 1 Feb 1770 son Isaac; g-
dau. Margaret; unnamed child. (MCW 14.134) [SMW TA1.597]; <u>inv.</u>; 6 Jun 1770;
nok Susanna Pavatt, Mary Biscoe; ex. Isaac Pavatt (I 103.220); <u>inv.</u>; 14 Mar
1771 (I 197.187, 188); <u>acct.</u>; 14 Mar 1771 (A 66.178); <u>dist.</u>; [filed with 1771] (BB
6.90)
Pavat, John; <u>inv.</u>; 22 Nov 1773; 1 Mar 1774 (I 116.198)

PAYNE
Payne, Thomas; <u>will</u>; 8 Apr 1648; 25 Aug 1648 (MCW 1..3); ex. appointed 25
Aug 1648; <u>inv.</u> 31 Aug 1648 (AM IV.407. 408)
Paine, Thomas; *Paines Range*; 50 ac.; sur. 15 Sep 1667; sur. within *St. Jeroms
Mannour*; 1707 no poss; St. Michael's Hundred (RR p. 14) (TLC p. 14)
Paine, Thomas; *St. Jerome's*; <u>will</u>; 12 Mar 1672; 23 May 1673; sons Isaac,
Joseph; daus. Mary, Sarah, Elizabeth, Hannah and Rachel; wife Jane; tracts
Paine's Lott and *Holt* in BA Co. (MCW 1.73)
Payn, Charles; <u>acct.</u>; 3 Feb 1756; adm. Richard Payn (A 39.72)
Paine, Jane; <u>inv.</u>; 17 Feb 1675; 6 Mar 1675; mentions *Paine's Range, Paine's
Lott, Hoult, St. Jermo's Thickett* (I&A 1.567); <u>inv.</u>; 9 Jun 1675 (I&A 1.340); <u>acct.</u>;

16 May 1678; mentions Jane Gray, admx. of Alexander Winsore, m. Thomas
Jones; adm. Thomas Spinke (I&A 5.99)

Paine, Jane; d. 5 Jun 1675; 7 young child. (AM LXVIII.154)

Payne, Henry; acct.; [filed with 1693-5]; admx. Mary Payne (widow) (I&A 10.367)

Payne, Jane; acct.; 4 Oct 1695; mentions Jane, w/o John Wattson & extx. of
Thomas Spink (I&A 10.481)

Payne (Paine), Isaak (Isaac); will; 14 Mar 1712/3; 28 Mar 1713; son Thomas;
daus. Hannah, Sarah; tracts *Riders, Broadneck* (MCW 4.201) [SMW PC1.187]; inv.;
6 May 1713; nok Thomas Griffin, William Coller, John Arthee (I&A 34.120);
acct.; 20 May 1715 (I&A 36c.64)

Payne (Paine), Charles; *Strife*; 50 ac.; sur. 29 Apr 1714 (TLC p. 69); 2 Sep 1714
cert./pat. (COL)

Payn, Jack; acct.; 20 May 1715 (SMAA p. 283)

Payne (Paine, Payn), Charles; Brittain's Bay; will; 11 Dec 1717; 7 Jan 1717/8;
sons Peter, Charles, Leonard; dau. Mary; bros. Ezekiel and Thomas & his
child. Henry, Charles, James; niece Mary, d/o b-i-l Alexander Heathman; b-i-l
John Meekin; tracts *Howard's Gift, Howard's Mount, The Fox, Strife* (MCW
4.173) [SMW PC1.233]; inv.; 11 Jan 1717; nok Ezekiel Payne, John Drurey (I&A
39c.187); acct.; 5 Nov 1718; ex. Thomas Payn (A 1.308) (SMAA p. 327); 8 Mar
1722 (A 5.32)

Pain, Thomas; will; 31 May 1731; 16 Nov 1731; sons Henry, Thomas, James;
wife Tecla [Teday] (MCW 6.199) [SMW PC1.359]; inv.; 7 Feb 1731; 8 Mar 1731;
nok Henry & Thomas Payne; admx./extx. Trelay Pain (I 16.434); acct.; 8 Mar
1732; mentions Henry, Thomas, James, Elisabeth, Jane, Elleanor & Terrisa
Pain; extx. Teely Pain (A 11.591)

Pain, Henry; inv.; 9 Nov 1741; 6 Apr 1742; nok Thomas & James Payne;
admx./extx. Ann Payne (I 26.489); acct.; 4 Aug 1743; orphans Henry, Mary,
Elisabeth, Pricila, Elisabeth? (A 19.537)

Payne (Pain), Ezekiel; inv.; 2 Aug 1743; 5 Nov 1743; nok Charles & Leonard
Payne; admx./extx. Catharine Paine (I 28.359); acct.; 28 Aug 1744; orphans Jan
Baptist, An (A 20.437)

Payn, Thomas; will; 18 Jan 1747; 19 Apr 1748; child. Mary, Isaac, Joseph,
Thomas, John, Diana, Elizabeth; wife Elizabeth (MCW 9.143) [SMW TA1.217];
inv.; 28 Jul 1748; nok Thomas & Isaac Payn; admx./extx. Elisabeth Payn (I
37.91); acct.; 17 Apr 1749; child. Joseph (age 27), Isaac (age 25), Thomas (age
21), John (age 8), Mary (age 19), Elisabeth (16), Dinnah (age 14) (A 26.46)

Payne, Charles; inv.; 25 Aug 1753; 7 Mar 1754; nok Peter & Leonard Payne;
adm./ex. Richard Payne (I 57.126)

Payne, Richard and Priscilla; sons John Barton [b. 3 Aug 1754], Francis
Exlinerus (Exhuerus) [b. 12 Sep 1756], James [b. 28 Feb 1759] (SA p. 10, 37, 44)

Payne, Leonard and Monica; child. Priscilla [b. 19 May 1753], Henry Berryman
[b. 21 Mar 1756], Elizabeth [b. 18 Aug 1758], Monica [b. 13 Mar 1763] (SA p.
10, 37, 45);

Payne, Leonard and Monica; son Jeremiah [b. 29 Sep 1760] (SA p. 39)

Payne, Henry and Jane; child. Bernard [b. 27 Nov 1762], Allelusia [b. 17 Apr 1765] (SA p. 14, 48)

Payn, John; St. Michaels Hundred; will; 20 Jan 1763; 8 Feb 1763; mother Elizabeth (MCW 12.175) [SMW TA1.443 (sic) ?434]; inv.; 10 Feb 1763; 18 Jun 1763; nok George Smoot, Aacia Payn (I 81.243)

Payne, Baptist and Ann; child. Winifred [b. 14 Apr 1763], Mary Ann [b. 22 Sep 1765] Elizabeth [b. 17 Apr 1768] (SA p.15, 49)

Payne, Charles and Monica; dau. Ann [b. 15 Sep 1767] (SA p. 9, 44)

Payn, Jos.; m. 11 Dec 1769 Binnie Stuart (MM)

Payne, Vincent and Mary; son Joseph [b. 8 Dec 1771] (SA p. 21)

Payne, John Baptist and Ann; dau. Eleanor [b. 30 May 1771], Rosa Ann [b. 12 Sep 1773] (SA p. 22, 24)

Payne (Pain), Pater; inv.; 16 Feb 1772; 16 May 1772; nok Joseph Melton, Ann Mackbridge; admx. Sabina Pain (I 109.360)

Payne, Raphael and Tabitha; dau. Elizabeth [b. 9 Apr 1772], Sarah [b. 26 Jan 1775], Anastatia [b. 23 Dec 1777] (SA p. 25, 29)

Payne, Leonard and Teresia; dau. Frances [b. 12 Sep 1772] (SA p. 21)

Payne, Leonard, Sr.; planter; will; 6 Oct 1775; 22 Nov 1775; sons Vincent, John, Raphael, Jeremiah, Benjamin, Leonard; daus. Elizabeth, Monica, Priscilla Vowles, Ann Cissell, Monica; g-ch Elizabeth Newton and Anastatia, Philip, Elizabeth, Mary & Susanna Payne (MCW 16.109) [SMW TA1.726]

PEACOCK

Peacock, Paul; will; 9 Jun 1709; 13 Aug 1709; wife Eleanor; dau. Mary, [dau. Eleanor], son Paul (MCW 3.148) [SMW PC1.163]; inv.; 22 Aug 1709 (I&A 30.299)

Peacock, Elinor (Ellenor); inv.; 22 Dec 1709 (I&A 31.12); acct.; 29 Jun 1714 (I&A 36a.159)

Peacock, Paul; inv.; 9 May 1743; 1743; nok Thomas Cumpton; admx./extx. Ann Peacock (I 28.194); acct.; 10 Sep 1744 (A 20.439)

Peacock, Philip; planter; will; 1 Dec 1771; 24 Nov 1773; wife Sasannah (MCW 15.91) [SMW TA1.662]

Peacock, Ignatius and Ann; son John Barton [b. 12 Dec 1774] (SA p. 25)

PEAKE

Pek (Peake, Peak), William; inv.; 8 Apr 1714; nok Peter Becker, John Ford (I&A 36a.100); acct.; 4 Aug 1715; admx. Elisabeth Peake (I&A 36c.59) (SMAA p. 292)

Peake, Edward and Ann; child. Henry Barton [b. 7 Nov 1754], Henrietta [b. 3 Feb 1757], Kenelm [b. 11 Mar 1760], Mary [b. 4 Apr 1762], Francis [b. 4 Feb 1764], Charles [b. 8 Oct 1767], John [b. 8 Oct 1771] (SA p. 13, 21, 47)

Peake, John and Susanna; child. Augustine [b. 23 Jan 1757], Robert [b. 23 Nov 1755] (SA p. 9, 43)

Peake, Peter; will; 28 Oct 1755; 16 Feb 1756; wife Catharine; child. Susanna, John, Peter and Ignatious Peake; dau. Anastatia Browne (MCW 11.123) [SMW TA1.354]; acct.; 18 Apr 1757; orphans John, Peter, Ignatious, Anastatia Brown,

Susannah; extx. Catherine Peak (A 41.27); <u>dist.</u>; 10 Apr 1757; orphans John, Peter, Ignatius, AnnStatia Brown, Susannah (BB 2.59)

Peake, Peter and Mary; dau. Mary [b. 6 Nov 1755] (SA p. 195)

Peeke, Porter; <u>inv.</u>; 30 Mar 1756; 26 Apr 1756; nok John Peak, Jr. & Sr.; admx./extx. Catharine Peak (I 60.576)

Peake (Peak), Bazil; <u>will</u>; 8 Sep 1760; 31 Oct 1760; bro. John Baptist; d-i-l Elizabeth Medley, s-i-l Joseph Medley; father William; wife Elizabeth & her son Joseph Medley; bros. and sisters Philip, Bennet, Ignatius, Dorothy and Rebecca Peake (MCW 12.2) [SMW TA1.397]; <u>inv.</u>; 1 Jan 1761; 3 Mar 1761; nok Peter Peek, William Peak; adm./ex. Mrs. Elisabeth Peak (I 71.140); <u>acct.</u>; 29 Feb 1762 (A 47.377); <u>dist.</u>; 19 Feb 1762 (BB 3.115)

Peake (Peak), William; <u>will</u>; 8 Dec 1760; 7 Apr 1761; bro. Peter; sons William, Phillip, Ignatius, Bennet; daus. Dorothy, Rebecca; wife Mary (MCW 12.36) [SMW TA1.422]; <u>inv.</u>; 28 Apr 1761; 3 Jun 1761; nok John, Sr. & Peter Peake; extx. Mary Peake (I 74.276)

Peak, Peter; *Poverty Level*; 15 ac.; 28 Jan 1762 cert./pat. (COL)

Peake (Peak), John; <u>will</u>; 5 Mar 1761; 3 Nov 1761; sons Robert, Augustine; wife Elizabeth (MCW 12.98); <u>acct.</u>; 10 May 1763; extx. Elisabeth Peak (A 49.607)

Peake, William and Henrietta; child. Ann [b. 19 Nov 1761], Raphael [b. 20 Feb 1765], Eleanor [b. 5 Jun 1767], Joshua [b. 28 Sep 1769] (SA p. 195)

Peake (Peeke), John; <u>inv.</u>; 2 Jun 1762; nok Ignatius & Susanna Peeke; extx. Elisabeth Peeke (I 78.84)

Peake, William; <u>acct.</u>; 19 Oct 1766; extx. Mary Peake (A 55.321)

Peake, Monica; dau. Eleanor [b. 5 Apr 1767] (SA p. 193)

Peek, John Baptist; m. 16 Feb 1768 Grace Craghill (MM)

Peake, Peter; <u>inv.</u>; 2 Aug 1768; 4 Aug 1768; nok James Wheatly, William Peeke; admx. Mary Peake (I 97.271); <u>acct.</u>; 9 Jul 1770 (A 64.221); <u>dist.</u>; 9 Jul 1770 (BB 5.386)

Peak, Jos.; m. 11 Dec 1769 Susan Yets (Yates?) (MM)

Peeke, Catharine; <u>will</u>; 17 Nov 1770; 24 Nov 1770; child. John Baptist Payne, Ann Cole; g-daus. Susanna, Winefort & Mary Cole, Winefort, Mary & Elizabeth Payne (MCW 14.149) [SMW TA1.594]

Peake, John and Susanna; son Joseph [b. 11 Dec 1772] (SA p. 23)

PEIRCE

Peirce, Thomas; immigrated by 1667 (SK 13.121)

Pierce (Pearce), Thomas; <u>inv.</u>; 6 Mar 1675 (I&A 1.564); <u>acct.</u>; 11 Oct 1677; mentions Rebecca, relict of Thomas Dent, now w/o John Addison; John Steevens m. widow of Edward Jolley; admx. Lidia Turbervile (relict) (I&A 4.398); <u>acct.</u>; 6 Feb 1694; admx. Lidia (relict), w/o Gilbert Turberville (I&A 13a.221)

Pierce (Pearce), Edward; *Pierce's Chance*; 50 ac.; sur. 26 Aug 1701; 1707 poss. widow Mary Courtney; poss. Edward Pierce; St. Mary's Hundred (RR p. 10) (TLC p. 11); 50 ac.; Apr 1702 cert./pat. (COL)

Pearce (Perce), Thomas; inv.; 20 Sep 1707 (I&A 27.245); acct.; admx. Jane, wife of John Noble; 7 Dec 1708 (SMAA p. 171) (I&A 28.70)

Peirce (Pierce, Peirse), Edward; will; planter; 31 Dec 1720; 24 Apr 1732; wife Elinor; sons Edward, John, Robert, Thomas; dau. Mary; tracts *Chance, Courtney's Fancy* (MCW 6.219) [SMW PC1.352]; inv.; 10 Jul 1731; 24 Jul 1732; nok John & Thomas Peirce; admx./extx. Elinor Peirce (I 16.551); acct.; 1 Apr 1734 (A 12.217)

Peirce (Pairce) [Pierce], Edward; planter; will; 29 Jan 1739/40; 23 Jun 1740; bros. John, Thomas, Robert; niece Millard & nephew Jonathan, ch/o John; mother Eleanor; tracts *Baker's Fancy, Baker's New Fancy* (MCW 8.99) [SMW TA1.102]; acct.; 19 Oct 1741; ex. John Pairce (A 18.382)

Pearce, Elinor (Elenor); inv.; 25 Feb 1744; 7 May 1745; nok John & Lydia Pearce; adm./ex. Thomas Pearce (I 30.424); acct.; 23 Jun 1746; mentions Thomas, John & Robert Pearce (A 22.254)

Peirce, John; inv.; 27 Oct 1747; nok Robert and Thomas Pearce; adms./exs. William Lucus & wife Ann (I 35.522); acct.; 26 Aug 1751; orphans Mildred [age 14], John [age 12], Susanna [age 6], Stephen [dec'd]; extx. Ann, w/o James Compton (A 31.61); dist.; 26 Aug 1751 (BB 1.4)

Peirce, John; acct.; 15 Oct 1750; extx. Ann Lucus, late Ann Pierce (A 29.48)

Peirce (Pierce, Pearce), Robert; inv.; 30 Oct 1754; 55 May 1744; nok Inashe Perce (?), Ledis Stuberors; admx./extx. Ellinor Peirce (I 58.324); acct.; 21 Oct 1755 (A 38.295); acct.; 27 Aug 1759; orphans Tiriasea & William [both at age], Ign. [age 18], Susannah [age 14], Joseph [age 12]; admx. Eleanor Rea (A 43.270)

Pearce, Joseph Vanswearingen; will; 1 Jul 1772; 45 Nov 1772; sisters Tenesia & Susannah Pearce; tract *Courtneys Fancy* (MCW 15.6) [SMW TA1.647] [listed as Joseph Vanswearingen's will]

PENNY

Penny, John; inv.; 30 Mar 1720; 19 May 1721; admx. Agnuss Penny (I 5.69); acct.; 13 Feb 1720; [smith]; admx. Agnuss Penny (A 3.287) (SMAA p. 439)

Peny (Peney, Penny), Catherine; will; 30 May 1742; 6 Jul 1742; son William More; g-dau. Mary Moore (MCW 8.178) [SMW TA1.120]; inv.; 5 Nov 1743; nok Mary Shaw (I 28.361)

PERCH

Pearch, Simon; *Hard Adventure*; 276 ac.; 276 ac.; sur. 30 May 1694;1707 no poss.; New Town Hundred (RR p. 40) (TLC p. 39); 20 Feb 1695 cert./pat. (COL)

Perch, Symon (Simon); inv.; 2 Aug 1712 (I&A 33b.204); acct.; 2 Aug 1713 (I&A 35b.72); 22 Aug 1713 (SMAA p. 247)

PERRY

Perry, Robert; inv.; 6 Jan 1675 (I&A 2.188); acct.; 31 Aug 1676 (I&A 2.186)

Perry, Rich'd; *The Tavern*; 200 ac.; sur. 10 Mar 1679; 1707 poss. George
  Plowden; Resurrection Hundred (RR p. 61) (TLC p. 58)
Perry, Hugh; inv.; 14 Jul 1728; 12 Aug 1728; nok John Teare, one child; admx.
  Elisabeth Perry (I 13.190); acct.; 19 Apr 1729 (A 9.360)
Perry, Robert; will; 10 Sep 1724; 19 Jun 1725; daus. Sarah, Lurenia, Lidia,
  Mary, Elizabeth, Katherine, Penelope, and Charity Perry; dau. Mary Batson;
  wife Mary (MCW 5.193) [SMW PC1.296]; inv.; 6 Jul 1725; 31 Jul 1725; nok Sarah
  Perry, Mary Madson; extx. Mary Perry (I 11.9)

PHENIX

Phenix George; immigrated by 1668; tailor (SK 16.74)
Phoenix (Phenix), George; acct.; 22 Jan 1683 (I&A 8.121) (SMAA p. 80)
Phunex, John; 28 Jul 1707 (SMAA p. 140)

PHEPO

Phepo, Mark; *Phepos Fort*; 100 ac.; sur. 8 Mar 1658; 1707 pos. John Symons;
  St. Michael's Hundred (RR p. 14) (TLC p. 14)
  Cornelius Swamp; 100 ac.; sur. 16 Aug 1668; 1707 poss. Eliza. Savage; St.
  Michael's Hundred (RR p. 14) (TLC p. 14)
Phepo, Marke; will; 19 Jan 1669; 8 Feb 1669; sons Philip, Thomas, and William
  Land (MCW 1.51)

PHILLIPS

Phillips, John; orphan of Thomas; 1668 (AM LVII.420)
Phillips, Martin; immigrated by 1678 (SK 15.523)
Phillips, Henry; inv.; 6 Sep 1684 (I&A 8.211)
Philips, Margaret; widow of Bartholomew; 26 Jun 1719 (CCR p. 41)
Philipps, John; acct.; 2 Mar 1730; mentions Hilton John, Elisabeth, Hannah &
  Ann Philipps; admx. Hannah Philips (A 11.59)
Philips, Hanah (Hannah); inv.; 17 Sep 1734; 6 Nov 1734; nok Philip Tippitt,
  James Fanning (I 20.103); acct.; 7 Aug 1735; mentions Hilton John, Elisabeth,
  Hannah & Ann Philips (A 13.312)
Phillips, John; inv.; 13 Mar 1729; 22 Apr 1730; nok John & Benjamin Fanning;
  admx./extx. Hannah Phillips (I 15.423)
Phillips (Philips), Robert; will; 29 Aug 1733; 17 Jan 1736; sons James, Robert;
  dau. Mary Miller & her son John Anthers [Author]; wife Mary (MCW 7.205)
  [SMW TA1.73]; inv.; 12 Mar 1736; 31 May 1737; nok James Phillips, Mary
  Miller; admx./extx. Mary Phillips (I 22.318); acct.; 20 Aug 1739 (A 17.243)
Phillips, Ann; oral; will; 11 Nov 1755; son John; g-son John Barnes (MCW 11.112)
  [SMW TA1.336]; inv.; 21 Dec 1755; 4 Aug 1756; nok John & Isabel Philips (I
  61.337)
Phillips, Thomas; inv.; 28 Nov 1757; 9 Mar 1758; nok George Carpenter, James
  Mardaw; admx./extx. Henrietta Phillips (I 65.149); acct.; 1 May 1758 (A 42.146);

<u>acct.</u>; 6 Jun 1758 (A 41.484); <u>acct.</u>; 3 Jun 1760; orphans Elisabeth [age 8],
George [age 3] (A 44.274); <u>dist.</u>; 3 Jun 1760 (BB 3.27)

Phillips (Philips), Thomas; <u>inv.</u>; 13 Jun 1758; 8 Mar 1759; nok Clement Hill,
Rebakah Phillips; admx./extx. Ann Phillips (I 66.230, 234)

Phillips, Henry; m. 23 Feb 1784 Elizab. Walker (BRU p. 536)

PHIPPARD

Phippard [Shippard], Anne (Anner); <u>will</u>; 7 Feb 1738/9; 7 Jun 1739; sons
Thomas and John Blackiston; husband William Phippard; niece Susanna, w/o
John Coode; bro. Mathew Guibert; daus. Elizabeth Neale, Susanna Mason; g-
daus. Anne, Elizabeth and Mary Mason; s-i-l Roswell Neale (MCW 8.39) [SMW
TA1.75]; <u>inv.</u>; 15 Jun 1739; 9 Aug 1739; nok Robert & Susanna Mason (I
24.177); <u>acct.</u>; 1 Sep 1740 (A 18.58)

Phippard [Shippard], William, <u>will</u>; 22 Aug 1745; 4 Apr 1745; dau. Susanna;
niece Mary; sister Ursula Haskins; wife Mary (MCW 9.61) [SMW TA1.181]; <u>inv.</u>
18 Mar 1745; 3 Jun 1746; nok John & Ursular Haskins; admx.extx. Mary
Phippard (I 33.39, 54); <u>acct.</u>; 19 May 1747 (A 23.307)

PIERCY

Piercey, Richard; *Foxes Range*; 70 ac.; sur. 28 Apr 1743 (TLC p. 103); *Fox Range*;
17 Mar 1744 cert./pat. (COL)

Piercy, Mary; <u>will</u>; 4 Jan 1768; 2 Aug 1769; child. William, Susannah, George,
3 unnamed; d-i-l Ann Piercy; mother Susannah Daffin; sis. Susannah Hellen;
bros. William and Thomas Aisquith (MCW 14.109) [SMW TA1.574]

PIKE

Pike, Archibald; planter; <u>will</u>; 31 Jan 1750; 3 Apr 1750; sons James, Archibald,
John; dau. Mary Greenwell; wife Lucy; tracts *Forest Ordain, Farney Branch*
(MCW 10.73) [SMW TA1.261]; <u>inv.</u>; 19 Apr 1750; 7 Nov 1750; nok John Pike,
John Wiseman Greenwell; adms./exs. Lucy & James Pike (I 44.229); <u>acct.</u>; 28
May 1751; Archbold [age 17] (A 30.185)

Pyke, James and Ann; child. Mary Ann [b. 14 May 1753], Henry [b. 5 Feb
1756], James [b. 18 Apr 1759] (SA p. 18, 53)

Pyke, John and Kezia; child. Mary Ann [b. 17 May 1757], John [b. 1 Jun 1759],
William [b. 18 Sep 1761] (SA p. 194)

Pike, James; *Forest of Dean*; 337 ac.; 28 Sep 1761 cert./pat. (COL)

Pike, John; <u>will</u>; 11 Feb 1762; 1 Jun 1762; child. Archibald, Mary, Lucy, Ann,
Mary Ann, John; wife Kezia; [tract *Feney (?) Branch*] (MCW 12.134) [SMW
TA1.429]; <u>inv.</u>; 7 Sep 1762; nok James Pike, John Wiseman Greenwell; extx.
Kezia Pike (I 79.275)

Pike, James; planter; <u>will</u>; 13 Feb 1774; 20 Mar 1774; sons Henry, James; wife
Mary Ann; mentions [child.] Mary Ann Newton, Elizabeth Pike, Archibald

Pike; tract *Forrester Den* (MCW 15.149) [SMW TA1.712]; inv.; 20 Aug 1774; nok Mary & Archibald Greenwell; extx. Mary Ann Pike (I 119.186)

PILBOROUGH

Pilborough, Robert; inv.; 24 Jul 1741; 16 Nov 1741; nok Eliza Crust, William Bull; admx./extx. Eliza Pilborough (I 26.426)

Pilbroe (Pilborough), Thomas; inv.; 12 Jun 1758; 6 Feb 1759; nok Susanna Pilborough (I 66.227); acct.; 20 Mar 1759 (A 43.100)

PILE

Piles, John; *Piles's Woodlane*; 200 ac.; sur. 22 Sep 1653; 1707 poss. James Greenwell, Sr.; New Town Hundred (RR p. 30) (TLC p. 28)

Piles, Joseph; wife dec'd; eld. dau. Sarah, wife of Nicholas Pewes (?)]; [1674] (SMAA p. 41)

Pille, John; inv.; 20 May 1676 (I&A 2.156); acct.; [filed with 1676]; admx. Sarah Pile (widow) (I&A 2.158)

Pile, Joseph; s/o John, dec'd; *Baltimore's Bounty*; 1,150 ac.; 20 Nov 1680; bro. John; mother Sarah cert./pat. (COL)
    Ferne; 100 ac.; 11 Apr 1683 cert./pat. (COL)

Pile, Joseph; gent.; *Sarum*; 2,600 ac.; [12 Nov 1680] cert./pat. (COL)

Pile, Joseph, Capt.; *Salisbury*; 191 ac.; 2 Jul 1688 cert./pat. (COL)

Pile, Joseph; will; 16 Jan 1691; 8 Nov 1692; son Joseph; daus. Sarah, Mary, Ann, Elizabeth; bros. Anthony Neale, Thomas Turner; tracts *Sarum, St. Barbaries, Pile's Discovery, Baltimore's Gift, Ferne, Salsbury* (MCW 2.49); inv.; 10 Nov 1692; 28 Jan 1692; exs. Anthony Neale, Thomas Turner (I&A 10lc.22); acct.; 1 May 1695 (I&A13a.286); acct.; [filed with 1697] (I&A 14.98); acct.; 11 Oct 1701 (I&A21.149); acct.; 18 Feb 1706; daus. Sarah, w/o Nicholas Power; Mary, w/o William Boarman, Jr.; Ann, w/o Luke Gardener; Elisabeth; son Joseph (I&A 26.192)

PILKINTON

Pilkinton, Hugh; acct.; 14 Aug 1744; orphans Richard, Margaret, Susanna; admx. Mary, w/o William Leak (A 20.432)

Pilkinton, Richard; *Pilkinton's Venture*; 82 ac.; 22 May 1759 cert./pat. (COL)

Pikleton, Richard; m. 28 Feb 1775 Anna Hutchings (MM)

PLATER

Plater, George; of Annapolis; *St. Joseph's Manor*; 1.250 ac.; 9 Dec 1727 cert./pat. (COL)

Plater, George; *Hazzard*; 234½ ac.; orig. called *Thorp* (TLC p. 102); 234 ac.; 10 Nov 1743 cert./pat. (COL)

Plater, George; age ca 40; 28 Oct 1745 (CCR p. 91)

Plater, George; will; 9 Aug 1751; 6 Jun 1755; sons George, [s-i-l] John Taylor; daus. Ann, Elizabeth; tracts *Joseph's Manner, Resurrection Mannor, Fenwick*

Mannor, Stewarts Hope, Swan all in SM Co.; *Batchellors Harbou r* in PG
Co.; *Tasker's Camp* in BA Co.; *Burford's Choice* in DO Co.; *The Sugar
Land, Brightwells Hunting Quarter, Bradfords Rest* in FR Co. (MCW 11.95)
[SMW TA1.336]

PLOWDEN
Plowden, George; will; 5 Feb 1708/9; 26 Nov 1713; sons Edmond, George;
  daus. Dorothy, Winifred; tracts *The Farm, Resurrection Manor, The Tavern*
  (MCW 3.257) [SMW PC1.185]; inv.; 13 Jul 1713 (I&A 35a.16); acct.; 28 Sep 1714;
  admn. Edmond Plowden (I&A 36a.233) (SMAA p. 260)
Plowden, Edmund; *Plowden's Discovery*; 66 ac.; sur. 29 Mar 1742 (TLC p. 98); 8
  Aug 1742 cert./pat. (COL)
Plowden, Edmond; All Faiths Parish; will; 1 Sep 1757; 2 Aug 1758; sons
  Edmond, George, [& Francis Jarret]; wife Henrietta; tracts *Resurrection
  Manner, Scotch Neck, Plowden's Discovery* (MCW 11.213) [SMW TA1.447]
Plowden, Edmund; s/o George Plowden & Margaret Brent; 3 Aug 1717 (CCR p.
  39)

PLUMMER
Plummer, John; inv.; 11 Oct 1706 (I&A 26.154)
Plummer, Thomas; *Hopson's Choice*; 30 ac.; sur. 1 Dec 1731 (TLC p. 89); 10 Jun
  1734 cert./pat. (COL)
Plummer, Thomas; planter; will; 28 Mar 1738; 14 Sep 1738; wife Margaret;
  cous. John; bro. William Cuttler; tracts *Hopston's Choice, Arbuston's
  [Arbungtong] Oak* (MCW 7.256) [SMW TA1.60]; inv.; 13 Dec 1738; 5 Feb 1738;
  nok William Cutler, John Plummer; admx./extx. Margrett Plummer (I 23.534);
  acct.; 15 Nov 1739 (A 17.347)
Plummer, Margaret; will; probate 21 Jun 1756; sister's child. Ann Hall & James
  Greenwell; Jestenuall, s/o John Hall; Mary Peack's unnamed child.; tract
  Asbuston [Arbuster's Oak] (MCW 11.136) [SMW TA1.346]

POPE
Pope, Nathaniel; immigrated by 1639 of St. Mary's Hundred (SK 1.53-55)
Pope, Francis & John Courts; *Courts Freehold*; 200 ac.; 3 Aug 1647; 1707 poss.
  Tho. Cambell; St. Georges Hundred (RR p. 17); *Courts Freehold* or *Harts Hall*
  (TLC p. 17)
Pope, Nathaniel; *Popes Freehold*; 100 ac.; sur. 26 Feb 1649; St. Maryes City by
  1707; St. Mary's Hundred (RR p. 1) (TLC p. 2)

PORTWOOD
Portwood, John; *Grantham*; 100 ac.; sur. 3 Oct 1672; 1707 poss. Ralph Forster;
  escheat; Choptico Hundred (RR p. 53) (TLC p. 51)
  Wales; 200 ac.; sur. 26 Mar 1680; 1707 poss. Thomas Reeves; St. Clements
  Hundred (RR p. 47) (TLC p. 45)

Porttwood, John; <u>inv.</u>; 8 Feb 1688 (I&A 10.196)

POTTER

Potter, Henry; age 40 yrs.; 22 Dec 1659; 23 Jun 1662; dau. Audry (MCW 1.19)
Potter, Robert; <u>acct.</u>; 11 May 1752; daus. Cathrine, w/o Ralph Stocken; Mary,
    w/o Thomas Smith; Ann, w/o James Rigg; Susannah [at full age], Elisabeth
    [age 15], Jean [age 13], Elenor [age 11]; admx. Ann Potter (A 32.235); <u>inv.</u>; 21
    May 1751; 19 Jun 1751; nok Catharine Stocken, Mary Smith (I 47.122); <u>dist.</u>;
    11 May 1752; daus. Catherine, w/o Ralph Hocker; Mary, w/o Thomas Smith;
    Ann, w/o James Rigg; Susanna, Eliza, Jane, Eleanor (BB 1.37)
Potter, Ann; <u>inv.</u>; 27 Mar 1760; nok Minder & Jonas Potter (I 69.132)
Potter, Jane; <u>inv.</u>; 27 Jan 1768; 4 Jul 1768 (I 97.285)

POULTER

Poulton, Ferdinando; *St. Inigos Mannour & St. George's Island*; 1,000 ac.; sur. 9
    Nov 1639; 1707 poss. Robert Brook; St. Inigoes Hundred (RR p. 15) (TLC p. 15)
Poulter, Henry; <u>will</u>; 12 Dec 1704; 20 Apr 1705; wife Mary (MCW 3.59) [SMW
    PC1.133]; <u>inv.</u>; 8 Jun 1705 (I&A 26.221); <u>acct.</u>; 19 May 1709; extx. Mary, w/o
    William Hardy (I&A 29.299) (SMAA p. 185)
Poulton, Henry; priest; d. 27 Sep 1712; age 33 (HGM)
Poulton, John; planter; <u>inv.</u>; 28 Sep 1727; 20 Sep 1727 (I 12.262)

POWELL

Powell, George; *The Ridge*; 50 ac.; sur. 7 Sep 1666; 1707 poss. Sam. Warren;
    Resurrection Hundred (RR p. 60) (TLC p. 57)
    Ludgate; 50 ac.; sur. 1 Mar 1674; 1707 poss. Sam'l Warren; Resurrection
    Hundred (TLC p. 59)
Powell, John; service by 1670 (SK 16.60; 17.57)
Powell, George; immigrated by 1673 (SK 17.574; 18.163; 15.310)
Powell, John; *Addition*; 50 ac.; sur. 18 Jun 1695; 1707 poss. Cosmus Parsons;
    Resurrection Hundred (RR p. 65) (TLC p. 62)
Powell, John; <u>inv.</u>; 19 Apr 1698 (I&A 16.204); <u>acct.</u>; 6 Aug 1698; mentions 1
    orphan (I&A 16.184); <u>acct.</u>; [filed with 1699]; admx. Susanna (widow), w/o
    William Whitter (I&A 19.59)
Powell, Joseph; <u>inv.</u>; 23 Apr 1711 (I&A 32c.91); <u>acct.</u>; 7 Mar 1711; admx.
    Elisabeth, w/o Oswell Dash (I&A 33a.181) (SMAA p. 219)

POORE

Poure, John; service by 1674 (SK 18.111)
Poore (Power), Patience; <u>inv.</u>; 10 Feb 1701; adm. Daniell Clocker (I&A 21.362);
    <u>acct.</u>; 15 Dec 1707 (I&A 28.8)
Poore, Sarah; *Pyles Discovery*; 244 ac.; sur. 24 Jun 1689; 1707 poss. Nicho.
    Poore; St. Clements Hundred (RR p. 48) (TLC p. 47)

Poore, Mary; d/o Capt. Joseph Pile; *Pyles Discovery*; 245 ac. 10 Nov 1695
   cert./pat. (COL)
Poor (Poore, Power), James; <u>inv.</u>; 15 Aug 1720; admx. Marry Poore (I 342); <u>acct.</u>;
   21 Apr 1721 (A 3.424)

POWERS

Power (Powers, Poor), Nicholas; <u>will</u>; 27 Mar 1712; 12 Jun 1712; sons Nicholas
   and Joseph; dau. Mary (MCW 3.228) [SMW PC1.172]; <u>inv.</u>; 2 Mar 1712 (I&A
   33b.232); <u>acct.</u>; 23 May 1713 (SMAA p. 243); <u>acct.</u>; 3 Sep 1713 (I&A 35b.112); 13
   Sep 1713 (SMAA p. 239); <u>acct.</u>; 12 Nov 1713; mentions child. Nicholas, Mary &
   Joseph Power (I&A 35a.19, 29) (SMAA p. 256); <u>inv.</u>; 3 Dec 1713; mentions Mary,
   w/o Joshua Doyne; ex. Edward Cole (I&A 35a.15); <u>acct.</u>; 8 Dec 1713 (SMAA p.
   255); <u>acct.</u>; 30 Aug 1715; dau.; mentions Edward, s/o Edward Cole (SMAA p.
   277) (I&A 36c.285)
Powers, Nicholas; s/o Nicholas Powers; 1 Dec 1718 (CCR p. 41)
Power, Joseph; <u>will</u>; 31 Jan 1724/5; 31 Mar 1724; nephews Nicholas, Jr. and
   John Power; niece Sarah Doyne; b-i-l Joshua Doyne; cous. Clement Gardiner
   (MCW 5.190); calls b-i-l Justinian Doyne [SMW PC1.296]; <u>inv.</u>; 24 Jul 1725; 29
   Apr 1728 (sic); nok Mary Power, Clement Gardiner (I 11.146); <u>acct.</u>; 2 Mar 1725
   (A 7.233)
Poore (Power), Nicholas, Jr.; oral; <u>will</u>; 9 Jun 1742; wife unnamed (MCW 8.212)
   [SMW TA1.122]; <u>inv.</u>; 12 Jul 1743; 6 Sep 1743; nok mother Mary Power, John
   Sanders Power; admx./extx. Elisabeth Power (I 28.197); <u>acct.</u>; 18 Dec 1744;
   admx. Elisabeth, w/o Thomas Aprice (A 21.145)
Power, John Sanders; <u>will</u>; 19 Apr 1775; 24 Jul 1775; son Clement; daus. w/o
   John Johnson, Dorothy Wathing; bros. Edward and Joseph Power; wife Jane;
   8 (sic) unmarried child. John Evangelist, Philip and James, Thomas, Mary,
   Ann, Jane, Elizabeth, Eleonar (MCW 16.91) [SMW TA1.733]; <u>inv.</u>; 16 Aug 1775;
   10 Oct 1775; nok Clement Power, Catharine Johnson; extx. Jane Power (I
   122.178)

PRATT

Pratt, John; <u>inv.</u>; 5 Mar 1739; nok John & Edward Pratt; admx./extx. Hannah
   Pratt (I 24.533); <u>acct.</u>; 2 Sep 1740; admx. Hannah, w/o Mathew Chesher (A
   18.59)
Pratt, Samuel; <u>inv.</u>; 15 Jul 1749; 3 Oct 1749; nok Edward & Elisabeth Pratt;
   adm./ex. William Pratt (I 40.359); <u>inv.</u>; 20 Jun 1750; 8 Nov 1750; nok Edward
   & Jane Pratt (I 44.237); <u>acct.</u>; 2 Jul 1751 (A 30.199)
Pratt, William; <u>inv.</u>; 19 Jun 1750; 8 Nov 1750; nok Edward & Joseph Pratt;
   adm.ex. Jane Pratt (I 44.236); <u>acct.</u>; 2 Apr 1751 (A 30.17)

PRICE

Price, John, Col.; <u>will</u>; 10 Feb 1660; 11 Mar 1660/1; s-i-l Joseph Bullett; dau.
   Anne Price (MCW 1.18)

Price William; age ca 24 in 1662 (MD p. 153)

Price, Joane; immigrated by 1669; wife of Thomas (SK 15.548)

Price, John & James Keitch; *Price's Lott*; 100 ac., 64 ac.; sur. 24 Jan 1673; assgn. Price; resur. 2 May 1680 for 164 ac.; poss. Jos. Edwards; 1704 RR says sur. 1678; Resurrection Hundred (TLC p. 60)

Price, Ann; d/o John ; m. Rich'd Hatton prior to 1674; both dead prior to 1676 (SK 19.375)

Price, John; *The Refuse*; 50 ac.; sur. 16 Jul 1682; 1707 poss. Jone Price; Resurrection Hundred (RR p. 63) (TLC p. 61)

Price, Tho.; *The Grove*; 50 ac.; sur. 6 Nov 1682; 1707 poss. Paul Price; St. Mary's Hundred (RR p. 9) (TLC p. 10)

Price, John; [carpenter]; age 64; will; 15 Nov 1697; 28 May 1698; wife Joan [Jane]; dau. Elizabeth; dau. Ann Roberts (MCW 2.137) [SMW PC1.103]

Price, Thomas, Sr.; inv. & acct.; 9 Apr 1703; adm. Thomas Price (I&A 22.79)

Price, John; inv.; 16 Aug 1705 (I&A 25.41); acct.; 10 Sep 1707; admx. Francis (widow), w/o John Meritt (I&A 27.154) (SMAA p. 145); acct.; 29 May 1708 (I&A 28.222) (SMAA p. 165)

Price, Paul; inv.; 19 Feb 1708 (I&A 29.53); acct.; 16 Sep 1710; admx. Alice Hogan (Hoggan), alias Alice Price (I&A 31.370) (SMAA p. 204)

Prise (Price), William; inv.; 1 May 1713 (I&A 34.119); acct.; 25 Apr 1715; adms. John Wellburne and wife Ann (I&A 36c.61) (SMAA p. 286)

Price, Abraham; acct.; 8 Apr 1714; admx. Jane Price (I&A 36b. 166) (SMAA p. 272)

Price (Aprice), Edward; age ca 54; 20 Sep 1718; tract *St. Lawrence* (CCR p. 40); age ca 72; 1736 (MD p. 4)

Price, William; *Brick Kiln*; 217 ac.; escheat; resurvey 17 Jun 1718 (TLC p. 79); 5 Aug 1721 cert./pat. (COL)

Price, John; inv.; 5 Apr 1726; 7 Jul 1726; nok Joseph Chunn, John Branson; admx. Elisabeth Price (I 11.377); acct.; 2 Aug 1727; admx. Elisabeth, w/o Robert Clarke (A 8.354); acct.; 1 Jul 1729 (A 9.406)

Price, William; will; 20 Feb 1728/9; 29 Apr 1729; planter; wife Johana; sons William, Henry; daus. Susan [Susannah] Hook, Frances (MCW 6.105) [SMW PC1.335]; inv.; 1 May 1729; 28 Jul 1729; nok Johana Cook, Mary Price; adms./exs. Johana & William Price (I 14.277)

Price, John; inv.; 14 Mar 1733; 6 Nov 1734; nok John Merritt, Thomas Beach; admx./extx. Mary Price (I 20.101)

Price, Thomas; inv.; 18 Mar 1733; nok Joseph & Clair Price; admx. Clare Price (I 17.716); acct.; 30 Dec 1734 (A 12.741)

Price, Jane; inv.; 27 May 1735; 3 Jun 1735; nok Thomas Morris, Ann Lyon (I 20.467); acct.; 3 Nov 1736 (A 15.226)

Price, John; acct.; 2 Jun 1736; orphans John, Hopewell, Francis, Mary, Jane, Susana & Elisabeth Price; admx. Mary, w/o Charles Taylor (A 15.82)

A'Price, Edward A., Jr.; will; 7 Oct 1744; 8 Nov 1744; wife Ann; bros. Thomas, James (MCW 9.12) [SMW TA1.161] inv.; 8 Nov 1744; 6 Mar 1744; nok James Aprice, Anthony Brown, Jr.; admx./extx. Ann Aprice (I 30.301); acct.; 3 Nov 1747; extx. Ann, w/o Richard Ford (A 24.244)

Price, Henry; will; 14 Jul 1746; 15 Aug 1748; nephews Thomas Cook, William Price; sister Frances; bro. William; mother Johannah (MCW 9.170) [SMW TA1.219]

Apprice, James; *Swamp*; 17 ac.; 25 Mar 1758 cert./pat. (COL)

Price, Ralph [Ralphael]; will; 24 Sep 1760; 13 Oct 1760 (MCW 12.2) [SMW TA1.398]; inv.; 17 Oct 1760; 4 Mar 1760 (I 71.138)

Price, William; *Buck Hills*; 400 ac.; 29 Sep 1763 cert./pat. (COL)

Price, John; inv.; 24 Jul 1765; nok Paul & John Price; mentions William Price; admx. Barbara Price (I 88.81)

Price, William; will; 22 Mar 1766; 17 Nov 1767; wife Ann; sons William, Archabald, Jesse, John, Henry, Bennett, Ignasius; daus. Elizabeth Massey, Ann; tracts *Birch Hills, Gagesed* (MCW 14.18) [SMW TA1.530]

Price, William, Mr.; inv.; 8 Feb 1768; 24 Feb 1768; nok Henry & Bennett Price; extx. Susannah Price (I 97.93); inv.; 16 Feb 1768; 18 Jun 1768 (I 95.248)

Price, Ann; will; 7 Jun 1771; 7Aug 1771; child. Ann, Bennet, Archibald, Henry; g-dau. Elizabeth Massey (MCW 14.182) [SMW TA1.628]

Price, Jesse; inv.;. 3 Aug 1774; adm. Bennett Price (I 119.126)

Price, William and Elizabeth Carter; m. 31 Oct 1779 (SA p. 57)

PRITCHARD

Prichard, John; *Wiccohandick*; 350 ac.; sur. 19 Apr 1648; 1707 poss. Widow Brown; St. Georges Hundred (RR p. 18) (TLC p. 18)
Tinkerly; 350 ac. sur. 1648; St. George's Hundred; 1704 RR

Pritchard, Wm.; *Bedford*; 100 ac.; sur. 24 Nov 1671; 1707 no poss.; Choptico Hundred (RR p. 52) (TLC p. 50)

Pritchet (Prichard), William; inv.; 17 Mar 1725; 8 Jun 1726; nok Thomas, Sr. & James Boult; admx. Mary Pritchet (I 11.339); acct.; 27 Apr 1727 (A 8.223)

PYE

Pye, George; 50 ac. unnamed; sur. 12 Nov 1640; assgn. Tho. Weston; made part of *Westbury Mannour*; St. Georges Hundred (TLC p. 16)

Pye, Edward; wife Ann, admx. of Benjamin Rozer of CH Co.; 1682] (AM LXX.276)

QUEEN

Queen, Henry; will; 21 Dec 1767; 2 Feb 1768; sisters Catherine Edelin, Sarah Jeamson [Tenneson]; bro. Samuel & his son Edward; sis.-i-l Margret Meawthis; d-i-i Clare Brooks; b-i-l Walter Pye; wife unnamed [Monica]; tracts *Pinner [Tinner], Delebroke Manner, Hardship, Woolleston Mannor, Shaws, St. Johns* (MCW 14.32) [SMW TA1.564]; inv.; 17 Feb 1768; 4 Jul 1768;

nok Walter Pye, Benjamin Jameson; extx. Monica Queen (I 97.279); inv.; 3 Sep 1770 (I 104.289); acct.; 3 Sep 1770 (A 64.235)

Queen, Monica; will; 24 Nov 1772; 1 Dec 1772; dau. Ann Hill; g-son Henry Hill; sisters Ann & Mary Boarman (MCW 15.7) [SMW TA1.648]; inv.; 1 Dec 1772; 10 Aug 1774; nok Ann Lucas, John Smith (I 119.151)

Queen, Samuel; will; 10 Jan 1711; 18 Mar 177/2; sons Samuel, Marsham, William; daus. Katharine, Margret; s-i-l Richard Brooke; wife Katharine; f-i-l Richard Marsham; tracts *Underwood, Hudson's Range, Acchomac* [*Achamack*] (MCW 3.222); Gent.; tract *Achamack* [SMW PC1.176]; inv.; 20 Mar 1711 (I&A 33a.146); acct.; 7 Aug 1712; widow dec'd (I&A 33b.34); mentions funeral charges for " he and his wife"; 7 Aug 1712 (SMAA p. 233)

RABLING

Rabling, Thomas; inv.; 28 Aug 1720; extx. Mary Rabling (I 4.233)

Rabling, Thomas; inv.; 8 Oct 1750; 2 Apr 1751; nok Ruth Davis, Anne Scot (I 45.84); dist.; 2 Oct 1753; 1 child Ruth Rabling [age 6 next Feb] (BB 1.89)

RAMSEY

Ramsey, William; age ca 43 in 1682 (MD p. 154)

Ramsay, Charles and Anne Taylor (by license); m. 1 Aug 1784 (SA p. 62)

RAPHER

Rapour, Richard; will; 18 Mar 1752; 2 Jun 1752; daus. Mary [d-i-l], Ann Dianna, Sarah Shanke; wife Teresia; 3 sons Richard [ca 15 yrs. old], William and Richard James; s-i-l Thomas Shanke; [*Gullmot Hills*] (MCW 10.223) [SMW TA1.293]

Rapher [Raper], Richard; will;11 Feb 1759; 1 May 1759; sisters Ann Diana, Sarey Shanks (MCW 11.237) [SMW TA1.380]

RATCLIFF

Ratcliff, Emanuel; immigrated by 1669 of VA (SK 12.262; 16.18)

Ratclif, Francis; will; 6 Oct 1747; 4 Mar 1747; wife Mary; son John; g-dau. Mary Ann Ratcliff; dau. Ann Wilson; [g-sons Francis Ratclif, William Wilson]; tract *Ratcliffs Hope* (MCW 9.143) [SMW TA1.189]

RAWLINGS

Rawlins, Anthony; *White Birch Freehold*; 100 ac.; sur. 12 Mar 1648; 1707 poss. Wm. Morgan; St. Michael's Hundred (RR p. 13) (TLC p. 13)

Rawlings, Nicholas; age ca 26; 20 Dec 1664 (AM XLIX.318)

Rawlings, Nicholas; immigrated by 1666; cooper (SK 10.265)

Rawlins, Elisabeth; inv.; 26 Apr 1676 (I&A 2.125); acct.; 16 Oct 1677; extx. Elisabeth Spracklin (late Elisabeth Mackye) (I&A 4.425)

RAY

Ray, Abraham; immigrated by 1671 (SK 16.122)

Ray, Alexander; immigrated by 1671 (SK 16.122)

Ray, John; service by 1680 (SK WC2.278-279)

Reay (Raye), Daniel; inv.; 10 May 1732; 17 Jul 1732; nok John Sledmore, Mary
Morgain; admx.extx. Jane Sword (I 16.550); acct.; 4 Dec 1732; orphans
William, Margaret & Ann Raye; admx. Jane, w/o William Sword (A 11.530)

REED

Read, Abra.; *Dunsmore Heath*; 40 ac.; sur. 22 Jun 1681; 1707 eschild. for want
of heirs; St. Mary's Hundred (RR p. 8) (TLC p. 9)

Reed, John; inv.; 13 Dec 1696 (I&A 15.69)

Read, Robert; acct.; 6 Jun 1711 (SMAA p. 221)

Read, John; wife Hannah; Nov 1712 (CCR p. 23)

Read (Reed), William; will; 18 Mar 1717/8; 22 Apr 1718; sons John, William;
wife Ann (MCW 4.132) [SMW PC1.237]; acct.; 2 Nov 1720; extx. Ann Read (A
3.232); acct.; 10 Jun 1722; extx. Ann, w/o Henry Rayly (A 4.248)

Read, William; will; extx. Ann; 2 Nov 1720 (SMAA p. 428)

Reed, George; planter; age ca 39; 21 Sep 1722 (CCR p. 51)

Read, George; inv.; 16 Mar 1735; 2 May 1744 (I 28.509); inv.; 30 Apr 1744; nok
Margaret Read, Henry Williams; admx./extx. Elinor Read (I 28.512); acct.; 2
May 1744 (A 10.147); acct.; 1 Jul 1745; orphans Margaret, Elisabeth (A 21.367)

Read, William; will; 31 Oct 1739; 17 Dec 1739; bro. John; wife Ann (MCW 8.65)
[SMW TA1.88]; inv.; 3 Jan 1739; 14 Apr 1740; nok John, Jr. & John Read;
admx./extx. Ann Read (I 24.251)

Read, Clarke (Charles (sic)); inv.; 17 Dec 1751; 13 Jul 1752; nok John & Philip
Read; admx./extx. Mary Read (I 49.100); acct.; 21 May 1753; nok Amey Clarke
Read [age 1]; adms. George Rogers & wife Mary (A 34.172); dist.; 21 May
1753; [Charles (sic)]; 1 child Amy Clarke Read [age 2 next 12 Sep] (BB 1.79)

Read, George; inv.; 10 May 1752; 2 Jun 1752; nok John & Phil Read;
admx./extx. Elenor Read (I 49.23); acct.; 2 Mar 1753; admx. Elinor, w/o
Richard Wimsatt (A 33.328); dist.; 2 Mar 1753 (BB 1.72); acct.; 17 Dec 1759 (A
44.173)

Read, Philip; inv.; 29 Jun 1758; 19 Sep 1758; nok John Read, Elianor Hopewell;
admx./extx. Ann Read (I 65.426); acct.; 25 Sep 1759; orphans Mary Ann [at
age], Cane [age 15], John Hatten [age 12], Philip [age 7] (A 43.359)

Read (Reed), John; will; 6 Sep 1761; 9 Mar 1770; g-sons John Hatton Read,
John Read Jenifer, Philip Read, John Read Long; daus. Gemima King, Ellen
Hopewell & her sons Samuel, John Read & Daniel Jenifer, Barbara Long; g-
dau. Amy Clark Read; tract *Orchard Neck* (MCW 14.133) [SMW TA1.587]; inv.; 20
Apr 1770; 1 Mar 1771; ex. John Hatton Read (I 106.367); inv.; 8 Oct 1771 (I 107,
188); acct.; 8 Oct 1771 (A 66.78); dist.; 8 Oct 1771; g-ch Hopewell, Barbarah
Long; mentions Elisabeth King (BB 6.83)

Read, Ann; <u>will</u>; 20 Sep 1774; 3 Mar 1775; g-ch Ignatius & Ann Biscoe and
    Francis, Ann & Ignatius Taylor; sons Ignatius, Jenifer (sic) (MCW 16.92)

Reed, John; m. 10 Jul 1775 Rebecca Latham (MM)

Reed, Philip; m. 16 Jul 1776 Ann Smith (MM)

Read, Philip and Eleanor Tawney (by license); m. 1 Oct 1781 (SA p. 59)

REDMAN

Redmond, John; immigrated by 1678 (SK 15.539)

Redman, John; <u>inv.</u>; 25 Apr 1701 (I&A 21.1); <u>acct.</u>; 15 Jul 1702; [Sr.]; adm. John
    Redman, Jr. (I&A 23.92)

Redman, John; planter; <u>will</u>; 20 Jan 1731; 18 Feb 1731; sons Jeremiah, Thomas,
    Daniel, Vincent, Solomon, John; daus. Anne Leake, Sarah Robinson, Frances
    Fryer, Elizabeth; g-son John Lake (Leake) (MCW 6.210) [SMW PC1.348]; <u>inv.</u>; 18
    Feb 1731; 20 Sep 1732; nok Anne Leake, John Readman; adms./extx.
    Jeremiah & Daniel Redman (I 16.577); <u>acct.</u>; 17 Aug 1733; adm. Jeremiah
    Redman (A 12.41)

Redman, James; <u>inv.</u>; 1 Feb 1733; 5 Jun 1734; nok John & John Redman;
    admx./extx. Rose Redman (I 18.324)

Redman, John; *Redman's Hardship*; sur. 1722 for John Redman & Samuel
    Johnson (TLC p. 90); 100 ac.; 10 Jun 1734 cert./pat. (COL)
    Small Hopes; 159 ac.; sur. 19 Jul 1728 (TLC p. 89); 10 Jun 1734 cert./pat. (COL)
    Small Hopes Addition; 142 ac.; sur. 23 Mar 1729 (TLC p.); 10 Jun 1734 cert./pat.
    (COL)

Redman, Danniell; <u>inv.</u>; 14 Nov 1734; 17 Sep 1735; nok Elisabeth & John
    Redman; adm./ex. Jeremiah Redman (I 21.102); <u>acct.</u>; 27 Aug 1739; mentions
    Vincent, Jeremiah, Thomas, & Elisabeth Redman (A 17.244)

Redman (Readman), John; <u>will</u>; 6 Sep 1736; 4 Oct 1736; child. Priscilla
    Hoskins, John, Sarah; tract *The New Design* (MCW 7.191) [SMW TA1.52]; <u>inv.</u>; 17
    Dec 1736; 2 Mar 1736; nok Vincent & Jeremiah Redman (I 22.205); <u>acct.</u>; 20
    Apr 1738 (A 16.89); <u>acct.</u>; 22 Nov 1738 (A 17.34)

Redman, Vincent; <u>will</u>; 30 Jan 1738/9; 7 Aug 1740; dau. Hannah (MCW 8.100)
    [SMW TA1.102]; <u>inv.</u>; 6 Nov 1740; 26 Mar 1760; nok Will Lak, Elisabeth
    Redman; adm./ex. Jeremiah Redman (I 25.438); <u>inv.</u>; [filed with 1743] (I 28.13)

Redman, John, Jr.; <u>will</u>; 9 Aug 1744; 11 Nov 1744; child. unnamed (MCW 9.12)
    [SMW TA1.161]; <u>inv.</u>; 21 Nov 1744; 4 Feb 1744; nok John Redmon, Benjamin
    Readmon; admx./extx. Sarah Redmon (I 30.219)

Readman, John; <u>will</u>; 4 Mar 1745; 8 Mar 1745; child. James, Jeremiah, John,
    Benjamin, Martha, Mary Lurty, Elizabeth Adams, Thomas, Eleanor Cox; wife
    Rebecca; tract *Small Hopes* (MCW 9.28) [SMW TA1.171]; <u>inv.</u>; 28 Mar 1745; 13
    May 1745; nok Benjamin & Thomas Redman; admx./extx. Rebecca Redman
    (I 30.426)

Redman, John, Sr.; <u>acct.</u>; [filed with 1746]; orphans James, Jeremiah, Nassey,
    Rodam, Ledia; extx. Rebecca, w/o Alexander Forguson (A 22.252)

Redman, John, Jr.; acct.; 30 Jun 1746; orphans John & Elisabeth; admx. Sarah, w/o Edward Caster (A 22.259)

Redmon, Benjamin; inv.; 2 Jun 1755; 22 Uul 1755; nok Elenor Cox, Marey Lurtey; admx./extx. Cathrine Redman (I 59.204)

Redman, Benjamin; acct.; 30 Aug 1756; orphans Benjamin [age 15], William [age 13], Joshua [age 12], Jonathon [age 10], Isaac [age 7], Catey [age 5], Heneritta [age 1]; admx. Catherine Redman (A 40.188); dist.; 2 Nov 1756 (BB 2.37)

Redman, William and Ann; child. George [b. 7 Oct 1763], John [b. 11 Apr 1765], William [b. 6 Aug 1767], Britannia [b. 5 Feb 1769], Benjamin [b. 8 Jun 1770] (SA p. 41, 190)

Redman, Thomas; *Small Hopes*; 151 ac; 23 Mar 1770 cert./pat. (COL)

Redman, Thomas; inv.; 14 Jan 1773; 10 Jul 17; nok William Gaulsbery; admx. Sarah Redman (I 112.409); acct.; 8 Feb 1774 (A 69.371); dist.; 8 Feb 1774 (BB 6.265); inv.; 18 Feb 1774 (I 116.188, 190)

Redman, Zachariah and Fanny Mattingly (by license); m. 7 Sep 1815 (SA p. 64); dau. Rosanna [b. 1 Jan 1816; bapt. 17 Mar 1816] (SA p. 34)

REEDER

Reader (Reeder), Simon; will; 6 Apr 1685; 17 Jun 1685; sons John, Benjamin, Richard; dau. Mary Bridgin; wife Virtue (MCW 1.155) [SMW PC1.56]; inv.; 7 Aug 1685 (I&A 8.439)

Reeder, Benjamin; *Reeders Adventure*; 350 ac.; sur. 22 Feb 1703; 1707 poss. same Reeder; St. Clements Hundred (RR p. 48) (TLC p. 47); 350 ac.; 9 Jul 1704 cert./pat. (COL)
   Reeders A_____; 350 ac.; sur. 27 Feb 1703; [in St. Clements Hundred]; 1707 no poss.; within lines of *Trent Neck*; Resurrection Hundred (RR p. 65)

Reeder, Benjamin & Rich'd Vowles; *Basford Gleaning*; 400 ac.; sur. 12 Mar 1703; 1707 poss. Reeder & Voles; St. Clements Hundred (RR p. 48) (TLC p. 47)

Reader, (Reader), Richard; will; probate 5 Mar 1717/8; bro. Benj.; wife Elizabeth; father Seimon [Simon] Reeder; dau. Elizabeth (MCW 4.128) [SMW PC1.238]; inv.; 12 May 1717 (I&A 37b.10); inv.; 4 Jul 1718; nok Oswald Dash, Mary Bull (I 1.308); acct.; 22 Apr 1720; extx. Elisabeth, w/o George Creffit (Crafft) (A 2.509); acct.; 22 Apr 1720 (SMAA p. 446)

Reader, Benjamin; age ca 52; 26 Jun 1719; tract *Bodle ats Knight* (CCR p. 41)

Reeder, Benjamin; planter; will; 22 Mar 1719/20; 7 Jun 1720; sons Simon, Thomas, John, Benjamin; daus. Elizabeth Aullstan, Ann Davis; wife Elizabeth; tracts *Bashfordbery Gleaning, Tattershals Gift, Reeders Adventure* (MCW 5.12); names Ann Davis as Ann Reeder [SMW PC1.258]; inv.; 4 Aug 1720; nok Elisabeth Scott, Elisabeth Gilstan; admx./extx. Elisabeth Reeder (I 4.41); acct.; 8 Jun 1721; exs. Elisabeth & Simon Reader (A 3.376); acct.; 10 Nov 1722; exs. John Baggley & wife Elisabeth, Simon Reader (A 5.111)

Reader (Reeder), Thomas; *Bogue's Increase*; 273 ac.; sur. 25 Nov 1737 (TLC p. 95); 30 Nov 1738 cert./pat. (COL)

Thomas & Henry; 113 ac.; sur. 20 Jul 1743 (TLC p. 102); 14 Nov 1743 cert./pat. (COL)

Workinton Park; 1,539 ac.; resur. 19 Nov 1745; orig. *Workington* (TLC p. 107); 19 Nov 1745 cert./pat. (COL)

Rose Land; 133 ac.; *Roseland with Addition*; resur. 9 May 1744 (TLC p. 109); 1 Feb 1746 cert./pat. (COL)

Reeder, Judith Townley; b. 26 Jan 1744; d. 24 Oct 1771; age 27; w/o Henry Reeder; child. Jane, Thomas, Susannah (HGM)

Reeder (Reader), Thomas; *Row Land*; 133 ac.; 1 Feb 1746 cert./pat. (COL)

Fourth Addition; 209 ac.; 10 Mar 1756 cert./pat. (COL)

Reeder's Purchase; 98 ac.; 23 Apr 1764 cert./pat. (COL)

Reeder, Benjamin; inv.; 25 Jul __; 29 Nov 1749; nok Thomas & John Reeder; admx./extx. Margaret Reeder (I 41.456); acct.; 2 Apr 1753 (A 33.414); acct.; 3 Sep 1753 (A 35.121); dist.; 2 Apr 1753 (BB 1.72)

Reeder, Simon; will; 23 Oct 1754; 18 Nov 1754; mentions Mary, w/o Peter Hart; nephew Simon, s/o bro. Benjamin of CH Co.; tract *Wentworth* (MCW 11.60) [SMW TA1.322]; inv.; 20 Nov 1754; 4 Feb 1755; nok Richard Robert Reeder, Anne Davis; adm./ex. Benjamin Reeder (I 60.103); acct.; 22 Jul 1755 (A 38.190); dist.; 29 Jan 1756 (BB 2.7)

Reeder, John, Jr.; age 32 in 1764 (MD p. 155)

Reeder, John, Jr.; *Wales*; 784 ac.; 25 Mar 1765 cert./pat. (COL)

Susanna; 203 ac.; 5 Aug 1771 cert./pat. (COL)

Summer Seat; 415 ac.; 2 May 1775 cert./pat. (COL)

Reeder, John, Jr.; approx. 1765; age 30-32-35 [SMW TA1.539.556]

Reeder, Thomas; approx. 1765; age 50-53 [SMW TA1.539-556]

Reeder, Thomas; *Stewart's Hope*; 89 ac.; 6 Mar 1768 cert./pat. (COL)

Reeder, Thomas, Sr.; will; 11 Oct 1773; 9 Nov 1773; sons John (Johns), Henry & Thomas Attaway Reeder; daus. Henrietta Egan, Elizabeth Bruce, Elizabeth Attaway Stephen, Daiden; g-child. Sophia & Thomas Attaway Reeder; mentions Thomas & Catharine Spalding; tracts *Bashford Berry Gleening, Bennits Delight, Parrish Beedle, Great St. Thomas* (MCW 15.90) [SMW TA1.664)

Reeder, Thomas Attaway; s/o Thomas, dec'd; *Middle Ground*; 175 ac.; 29 Jun 1774 cert./pat. (COL)

Reeder, Benjamin and Susannah Bond (by license); m. 29 Sep 1782 (SA p. 60)

REEVES

Reeves, Thomas; planter; age ca 70; 22 Dec 1714/5; tract *Clear Doubt* (CCR p. 32)

Reves (Reeves, Rives), Thomas; planter; will; 8 Dec __; 7 Jun 1719; sons Ubgate, Thomas, William; dau. Anne Hoskins; g-son Thomas [s/o Upgate]; wife Mary; tracts *Walles, Leeth* (MCW 4.227); acct.; 4 May 1720; ex. Ubgate Reeves (A 3.21) (SMAA p. 419); acct.; 16 Dec 1720 (SMAA p. 423); acct.; 16 Dec 1720 (A 3.183); acct.; 15 Oct 1722 (A 4.247)

Reeves (Reves), Thomas, Sr., Mr.; inv.; 6 Apr 1720; nok Thomas Reves, Jr.; ex. Ubete Reves (I 3.288)

Reeves (Reaves), Ubgatt (Ubgate); Gent.; will; 9 Jan 1724; 6 Feb 1738; sons Thomas, John; dau. Mary; wife Jane; tracts *Casheans Manor, Reave's Range* (MCW 8.20) [SMW TA1.106]; inv.; Mar 1738; 9 Aug 1739; nok Thomas Reeves, Napper Mills; admx./ex. Thomas Reeves (I 24.175); acct.; 10 Feb 1742 (A 19.287); acct.; 26 Feb 1739; widow dec'd (A 17.393)

Reeves, Ubgat; age ca 57 in 1726; age ca 69 in 1738 (MD p. 156)

Reeves, Thomas; *Wales Addition;* 91 ac.; sur. 22 Nov 1731 (TLC p. 91); 10 Jun 1734 cert./pat. (COL)

Reeves, Mary; will; 12 Jun 1740; 6 Aug 1740; sister Susanna; bro. John (MCW 8.100) [SMW TA1.106]

Reeves, Thomas; will; 14 Dec 1751; 13 Jan 1752; wife Mary; g-son John Hobson; dau. Elizabeth Thomas; cousin Susaner Reeves, Sr.; s-i-l Thomas Hobson; bro. William & his son Thomas Reeves, Jr.; tract *Coston* (MCW 10.198); tracts *Wails D__, Boston* [SMW TA1.266]; inv.; 21 Nov 1753; 5 Dec 1753; nok John Reeves, Susannah Cook; adms.exs. William Thomas & wife Elisabeth (I 57.31]; acct.; 27 Nov 1754 (A 36.516); dist.; 27 Nov 1754 (BB 1.123)

Reeves, Edward; inv.; 12 Apr 1769; 14 Feb 1770; nok Elisabeth & John Hendley; admx. Jane, w/o Michael Cusack (I 103.223); acct.; 14 Feb 1770 (A 64.99); acct.; 17 Jul 1770 (A 64.223); dist.; 11 Jul 1770 (BB 5.384)

Reeves, George and Mary; dau. Susanna [b. 7 Aug 1771] (SA p. 20, 55)

REYNOLDS

Raynalds, William; age ca 42 in 1650 (MD p. 155)

Reynolds, George; *The Fox*; 100 ac.; sur. 15 Mar 1657; 1707 poss. James Martin; TLC says poss. Widow Eagle; New Town Hundred (RR p. 30) (TLC p. 29)

Reynolds, George; Brettons Bay; wife Dorothy; convey 100 a. to Thomas Covant, carpenter; 1 Dec 1666 (AM LVII.209)

Reynolds, George; will; written 11 Jan 1668; wife Dorothy; son George; mentions *Fox, Bennett's Purchase* and *Tomson* (MCW 1.46)

Reynolds, John; *St. Jerome's*; will; 24 Aug 1673; 3 Oct 1673 (MCW 1.75)

Reynolds, Thomas and Ann his wife; service by 1674 (SK 18.130)

Reynolds, John; acct.; 30 Sep 1682; mentions Sarah, admx. of William Claw (I&A 7c.351)

Reynolds, John; age ca 33 in 1684 (MD p. 157)

Renalls, George; inv.; 26 Jan 1692 (I&A 13a.113); acct.; 30 Apr 1695; admx. sister Ann Darft (alias Ann Medley, w/o Charles Darft) (I&A 13a.293)

Rennolds (Rennalds), Thomas; acct.; 15 Mar 1706; admx. Elisabeth, w/o John Browne (I&A 26.158) (SMAA p. 133)

RHODES

Rodes, Abraham; wife Frances; from England ca 1670; 25 Jun 1722 (CCR p. 50)

Rhodes, Abraham; service by 1673 (SK 18.313)

Roades (Rhodes), Abraham; [carpenter]; will; 29 Apr 1705; 15 Aug 1705; wife
Frances; cousin Blooer Goodacres [Goodard]; mentions John, s/o Francis
Rhodes; tract *Rhode's Rest* (MCW 3.65) [SMW PC1.140]; inv.; 6 Sep 1705 (I 25.37);
acct.; 12 May 1708; extx. Frances Rhoades (I&A 28.216) (SMAA p. 167)

Rhodes (Rodes, Roades), Frances; acct.; 26 Mar 1710 (I&A 32c.26) (SMAA p. 207);
acct.; 20 May 1707; 6 Dec 1710 (SMAA p. 212); inv.; [filed with 1710] nok John
Rodes (I&A 31.356); inv.; 6 Dec 1710 (I&A 34.6)

Rhoades, Jeremiah; *Rhodes' Adventure*; 125 ac.; 6 Aug 1761 cert./pat. (COL)

Rodes (Rhodes), John; will; 1 Sep 1761; 30 Oct 1764; sons Abraham, John,
Barnaby, Mark, Jeremiah, Michael, Basil, Nicholas, Ignatius; dau. Elizabeth
Metchel; wife Eleanor; tracts *Tesberry Plains, Sharedons Reserve* (MCW 13.58)
[SMW TA1.487]; inv.; 25 Jan 1765; 10 Feb 1765; nok John & Jeremiah Rodes;
ex. Abraham Rodes (I 87.3)

Rodes (Rhoades), Mark; inv.; 3 Sep 1772; 16 Sep 1772 (I 109.348); acct.; 15 Sep
1772 (A 67.140)

Rhodes (Rhoades); will; 6 Jan 1776; 19 Feb 1776; bros. Abraham, Jeremiah,
Basel, John, Barnaby; sister's child Ann Dawsey; father John (MCW 16.130)

RICHARDSON

Richardson, Nicholas; immigrated by 1664 (SK 17.482)

Richardson, Francis; age ca 23 in 1665 (MD p. 157)

Richardson, Nicholas; acct.; 11 Oct 1677 (I&A 4.408)

Richardson, Nicholas; Dr.; will; 2 Nov 1716; 8 Jan 1716; son Nicholas; daus.
Bridgett Charmes and Elener and Ann; wife Bridgett; tract *Hunting Quarter*
(MCW 4.90) [SMW PC1.201]; inv.; 27 Mar 1717; nok William Sanders, Bridge
Charmes (I&A 37b.3); acct.; 26 May 1718; extx. Bridgett Richardson (A 1.46)
(SMAA p. 357); acct.; 23 Jul 1720 (A 3.76) (SMAA p. 437)

Richardson, Thomas; Deputy Surveyor for BA Co.; *Richardson's Fancy*; 38 ac.;
sur. 29 Nov 1722 (TLC p. 82); 1722 cert./pat. (COL)

Richardson, Bridgitt; widow; will; 7 Feb 1723/4; 16 Mar 1723; daus. Bridgitt
Warran, Anne, Elinor; son Nicholas; son John Warren (MCW 5.161) [SMW
PC1.287]; inv.; 20 Apr 1724; 2 May 1724; nok Nicholas & Anne Richardson (I
9.380); acct.; 14 Apr 1725 (A 6.308); acct.; 28 May 1726 (A 7.377)

Richardson, Thomas; inv.; 9 Oct 1732; nok William & Ann Richason;
admx./extx. Ann Richardson (I 16.615); acct.; 21 May 1733; admx. Ann, dec'd
w/o Thomas Griffin (A 11.698); acct.; 17 Jun 1734; orphans Elisabeth &
Thomas Richardson (A 12.349)

Richardson, William; inv.; 6 Jun 1733; 9 Jul 1733; nok Jonathon Bisco, Thomas
Rishon (I 17.177); acct.; 14 Apr 1735; mentions Thomas Richardson; admx.
Elisabeth, w/o Marke Stephens (A 13.125)

Richardson, James; adm. of estate of Ann ____; 3 Nov 1761 (A 47.225)

Richardson, Nicholas and Elizabeth Collison (by publication); m. 19 Dec 1784 (SA
p. 63)

RIDER

Rider, Henry; immigrated by 1671 (SK 16.113)

Rider (Ridor), Daniel; inv.; will; 22 Sep 1755; 26 Apr 1756; nok Elisabeth
Corbin, Jean Rider; admx./extx. Sarah Corbin, w/o William Corbin (I 60.574);
acct.; 19 Dec 1757 (A 41.329)

RIDGELY

Ridgely, Martha; service by 1671; wife of Robert (SK 16.400)

Ridgely, Robert; clerk, ca 1671; residing in City of St. Mary's; grant from Lord
Baltimore of *Gallowes Greene;* site for office (SK 16.594; 20.269)

Ridgely, Thomas; unnamed; 1 ac.; 9 Jun 1678 cert./pat. (COL)

Ridgely, Robert; rights by 1680 (SK WC2.255, 340, 359, 377)

Ridgely, Robert; St. Inigoes; will; 20 Dec 1680; 24 Dec 1680; wife Martha; sons
Robert, Charles, William; only dau. Mary [Martha]; tracts *Little Beleau;
Friend's Choice* in WO Co.; *Belleon* and *Western Fields* in SO Co.; *General
Gift* and *Timberle* in CA Co.; [*Vanswearingen's Point*]; mentions William
Stevens and wife Eliza: of SO Co. (MCW 1.102) [SMW PC1.36]; inv.; 17 Dec 1682
(I&A 8.295)

Ridgley (Ridgly), Robert; inv.; 1 Jun 1702; extx. Elisabeth Ridgley (I&A 22.15);
acct.; 28 Jul 1704 (I&A 3.406) (SMAA p. 128); acct.; 4 Dec 1707; extx. Elisabeth,
w/o William Gouldsmith (I&A 28.74); 26 Feb 1707 (SMAA p. 148)

RIGILL

Rigill, Charles; acct.; 10 Jan 1757; admx. Mary Rigill (A 40.278)

Rigill, Thomas and Statia; dau. Mary, bapt. 21 Oct 1781 (SA p. 30)

RILEY

Reyley; service by 1675 (SK 15.302)

Rylay (Ryly, Riley), [of Breton's Bay]; John; Brittaines Bay; will; 3 Apr 1708;
23 Apr 1709; son John; 5 daus. Frances and Winifred Ryly & Mary Bright,
Elizabth Peak, Margaret Tomson [Towson]; g-son William Peake; tract;
Green Hill (MCW 3.132) [SMW PC1.162]; inv.; 4 May 1709 (I&A 28.437); acct.; 23
Sep 1710; ex. John Ryly (I&A 32b.10) (SMAA p. 205)

Reyley, John; inv.; 14 Jan 1712; nok William Peach, Samuell Abell (I&A 33b.199)

Riley, John, Sr.; acct.; 20 Aug 1713; legatee John Riley, Jr. (I&A 35b.30)

Riley, John, Jr.; acct.; 26 Aug 1713 (SMAA p. 301)

Realy, Micheall; inv.; 8 Jun 1714; nok John Realy, John Neavil (I&A 36a.100)

Reyley, Michael, Sr.; acct.; 4 Oct 1716; adm. Henry Reyley (I&A 38b.5) (SMAA p.
294)

Rayly, John, Jr.; acct.; 2 Apr 1723; admn. John Forde, Jr. (A 5.191)

Realy, John, Sr.; acct.; 2 Apr 1723; mentions Frances, w/o John Forde, Jr. (A
5.108)

238   *Colonial Settlers of St. Mary's County, Maryland*

Raily, Richard; <u>will</u>; 25 Apr 1727; 19 Jul 1727; bros. William, John, Henry, Michael (MCW 6.31) [SMW PC1.323]; <u>inv.</u>; 6 Oct 1727; 28 Feb 1727; nok Henry & John Raley; ex. Michael Raley (I 13.8); <u>acct.</u>; 29 Oct 1729; legatees Henry, John & William Raley; orphan almost at age (A 9.492)

Riley (Rylery), Henry; *Saturday's Work*; 21 ac.; 27 Nov 1738 cert./pat. (COL)

Rile (Raley), Michel (Michael); <u>will</u>; 31 Aug 1738; 8 Nov 1738; son Joseph; wife Grace (MCW 8.7) [SMW TA1.58]; <u>inv.</u>; 8 Nov 1738; 6 Mar 1738; nok Michael & John Raley; admx./extx. Grace Raley (I 24.50); <u>inv.</u>; Michael Realy, Jr.; list of debts (I 24.50); <u>acct.</u>; 14 Jun 1740 (A 17.529)

Riley, Robert; <u>inv.</u>; 24 Mar 1739; admx./extx. Ann Realey (I 24.540)

Riley (Realy), John; <u>will</u>; 22 Dec 1743; 7 Mar 1743/4; daus. Anne, Elizabeth; son Bennet; wife Mary (MCW 8.261) [SMW TA1.154]; <u>inv.</u>; 10 Apr 1744; 5 Jun 1744; nok John & Peter Ford, Sr.; admx. & extx. ___ & wife Mary (I 29.221); <u>inv.</u>; 19 Sep 1746; 16 Nov 1746; nok John Realey, Jonathon Seel; admx./extx. Mary Railey (I 34.148)

Reileigh, Henry; <u>will</u>; 19 Apr 1751; 4 Mar 1754; bros. Michael & his son John, John, William; mentions Elizabeth [d/o Benjamin Williams] (MCW 11.20) [SMW TA1.320]

Raley, Michael; <u>inv.</u>; 18 Jun 1754; 5 Sep 1754; nok John & Michael Raly (I 57.331)

Raley, Henry; <u>dist.</u>; 6 May 1755; extx. Margaret, w/o Nicholas Mills (BB 1.132)

Realy, John; *Hammer*; 16 ac.; 14 Dec 1757 cert./pat. (COL)

Reiley, John; <u>will</u>; 1 May 1765; 18 Jun 1765; dau. Jean Able; sons John & his son John, Henry ___; s-i-l Thomas Forrest (MCW 13.86) [SMW TA1.468]

Realy [Reilly], John, Sr.; <u>will</u>; 31 Mar 1773; 26 Apr 1774; wife Lyde; son Gabriel; dau. Jane Stone; g-son John Michael Stone (MCW 15.130) [SMW TA1.704]

Raley, (Raily), James; <u>inv.</u>; Apr 1774; 16 May 1775; nok Lydia Williams, Marget Gree Will (sic); extx. Jane, w/o John Bazil Nottingham (I 122.190)

RISHWICK

Van Reswick, John; <u>inv.</u>; 1 May 1697 (I&A 15.213)

Reswick, Thos.; unnamed; 111 ac.; escheat land; resur. 15 Nov 1713 (TLC p. 74)

Reswick, Thomas; *Riswick's First Purchase*; 111 ac.; 25 Apr 1717 cert./pat. (COL)

Vanrishwick, Thomas, Sr.; <u>will</u>; 2 Jul 1751; 11 Mar 1751; sons John, Thomas; wife Anne; tract *White Acor*[Acre] (MCW 10.177) [SMW TA1.283]; <u>acct.</u>; 28 Oct 1752; Ann Vanrishwick (A 33.203, 205); <u>dist.</u>; 28 Oct 1752 (BB 1.71); <u>acct.</u>; 13 Feb 1756 (A 39.62); <u>dist.</u>; 28 May 1756 (BB 2.23)

Vanrishwick, Thomas, Mr.; <u>inv.</u>; 3 Sep 1751; 5 Mar 1752; nok John B. & An Rishwick; admx./extx. Ann Vanrishwick (I 48.296)

Reswick (Vanreshwick), John and Appolonia; child. Thomas [b. 15 Oct 1752], Mary [b. 23 Mar 1755], Joseph [b. 15 Aug 1757], Francis [b. 4 Nov 1763], George [b. 10 May 1756], John Basil [b. 12 Oct 1762] (SA p. 16, 51)

Reshwick, Thomas and Ann; child.. Monica [b. 19 Aug 1753], Wilford [b. 12 Jan 1756] (SA p. 38)

Vennsweek (Vanrish) [Variswick], Ann; will; 3 Jan 1759; 6 Mar 1759; 8 child. John, Thomas, Elizabeth Norris, Mary Serkliff, Monica Spink, Ann, Elloner, Winifed (MCW 11.232) [SMW TA1.376); inv.; 15 Mar 1759; 7 Jun 1759; nok Thomas V. Ratwick; admxs./extxs. Ann, Eleanor & Winifred Vanriswick (I 67.184)

Van Riswick, Thomas; inv.; 9 Mar 1762; nok John Bapt. & Elender Rishwick; admx./extx. Ann Riswick (I 79.270); acct.; 25 May 1763; admx. Ann, w/o George Medley (A 49.609)

Reswick, John; gent.; will; 18 Nov 1766; 5 Mar 1767; child. Thomas, Joseph, Francis, Elizabeth, Mary; wife Appalonia; tracts *Brough, White Acre* (MCW 13.177) [SMW TA1.534]; inv.; 26 Mar 1767; 3 Jun 1767; nok Monica Spink; extx. Appolana Riswick (I 93.120); acct.; 9 Nov 1768 (A 60.183)

Riswick (Beswick), Monica; will; probate 5 Aug 1773; bro. Wilford; both child. of Thomas and Ann (MCW 15.69) [SMW TA1.660]

Rishwick, Thomas and Mary; son Joseph [b. 19 Sep 1774] (SA p. 26)

ROACH

Roach, William; *Roach's Discovery*; 157 ac.; 3 Nov 1722 cert./pat. (COL); sur. 30 Mar 1719 (TLC p. 84); 235 ac.; 1710 cert./pat. (COL)

Rocke (Roach), William; inv.; 28 Sep 1724; 4 Nov 1724; nok son William Roach; admx. Elisabeth Roach (I 10.169); acct.; 5 Oct 1725; admx. Elisabeth, w/o Henry Nicholls (A 7.181); acct.; 2 Nov 1726 (A 8.152)

Roach, William; *St. John's Addition*; 190 ac.; sur. 17 Jul 1723; pat. to Roach's s-i-l (TLC p. 91); 18 Oct 1734 cert./pat. (COL)

Roach, James; *Roach's Privilege*; 32 ac.; 24 Mar 1760 cert./pat. (COL)

Roach, William; *St. James*; 100 ac.; 29 Apr 1761 cert./pat. (COL)

Roach, James; s/o William, dec'd; *St. John's Landing*; 372 ac.; 16 Oct 1782 cert./pat. (COL)

ROBERTS

Roberts, Peter; immigrated by 1666 with wife (SK 10.341)

Roberts, Peter; *Copt Hall*; 100 ac.; sur. 3 Feb 1669; 1707 poss. Joseph Pe__ [TLC says Peters]; Choptico Hundred (RR p. 52) (TLC p. 50)

Roberts, Phobby; immigrated by 1671 with wife Grace (SK 16.395)

Roberts, John; will; 9 Apr 1675; 4 May 1675; mentions John s/o Peter Roberts (MCW 1.88); inv.; 10 Jun 1675; 4 Aug 1675 (I&A 1.398)

Roberts, Mary; service by 1677; wife of John (SK 15.434)

Robert, Fobbe; will; 10 Jun 1692; 22 Oct 1692; niece Ellinor Courtney; nephew John Johnson (MCW 2.55)

Robarts, John; inv.; 28 May 1698 (I&A 19½a.27); acct.; 6 Sep 1699 (I&A 19½b.117)

Roberts, William; will; 1 Sep 1762; 11 Sep 1766; wife Henrietta; sister Ann (MCW 13.137) [SMW TA1.499]; inv.; 10 Feb 1767; nok Hon. & Ann Robarts

(Robbearts); adms. James Hendley & wife Henretta (I 91.84); <u>acct.</u>; 27 May
1769 (A 62.160)

Roberts, John; <u>inv.</u>; 1 Feb 1777 (I 125.265)

ROBINSON

Robinson, John; *Poultshelly*; 100 ac.; sur. 22 Oct 1640; eschild.; 1707 no poss.;
St. Georges Hundred (RR p. 17) (TLC p. 17)

Robinson, Andrew; *New Designe*; 350 ac.; sur. 4 Oct 1666; 1707 poss. Sam'l
Queen; Harvey Hundred (RR p. 56) (TLC p. 53)

Robinson, John; service by 1671 (SK 16.123)

Robinson, John; mariner; <u>will</u>; 13 Dec 1739; 24 Aug 1741; mentions William
Harrison, Jr. and Sr. (MCW 8.148) [SMW TA1.1130]; <u>inv.</u>; 5 Mar 1742 (I 27.368)

ROCHFORD

Rochford, Michael; <u>will</u>; 13 Aug 1678; 30 Aug 1678; wife Margaret; mother
Helena Rochford; bro. Patrick Christian; sis. Katharine Rochford of Limerick,
Ireland (MCW 1.205) [SMW PC1.32]; <u>inv.</u>; 17 Sep 1678 (I&A 6.26); <u>acct.</u>; 15 Feb
1680; ex. Arthur Taylor, son (I&A 7a.374)

Rochford, Michaell; [?SM Co.]; <u>will</u>; 1 Nov 1705; 13 Nov 1705; bro. John Cole;
tracts *Phames (Thames?) Street, Tower Dock* (MCW 3.71)

ROSE

Rose, John; <u>inv.</u>; 23 Jun 1710; mentions Mary Rose; dau. Mary Clarke (I&A
31.217); <u>acct.</u>; 4 Aug 1713; admx. Mary Rose (I&A 35b.93) (SMAA p. 247)

Rose, Thomas; <u>inv.</u>; 5 Feb 1712; nok Jane Rose; (I&A 33b.231); <u>acct.</u>; 27 Jan 1712
(I&A 33b.165)

Rose, Mary; Chaptico Hundred; <u>will</u>; 10 Mar 1716/7; 18 Dec 1719; daus. Mary
Clarke, Mary Birch; g-sons John Johnson , Samuel, Richard and Benjamin
Sothoron, Harman Clark; g-daus. Ann and Mary Sothoron (MCW 4.221) [SMW
PC1.228]; <u>inv.</u>; 29 Jan 1719; 3 Mar 1720 (I 3.223); <u>acct.</u>; Feb 1723; mentions
Anne, w/o James Briscoe; Harman, s/o Mary & Fran. Clark; Mary, w/o John
Birch; others (A 5.360)

ROSEWELL

Rosewell, Will'm; *Engsbatch*; 300 ac.; sur. 8 Jan 1665; 1707 poss. Jno. Bowling
[by marrying d/o Wm. Langworth]; St. Clements Hundred (RR p. 44) (TLC p. 43)
Weston; 200 ac.; sur. 8 Jan 1665;1707 poss. 100 ac. ea. John & Math.
Cartwright; St. Clements Hundred (RR p. 44) (TLC p. 43)
New Town; 200 ac.; sur. 10 Jan 1665; 1707 no poss.; Choptico Hundred (RR p.
50) (TLC p. 48)
St. John's; 300 ac.; sur. 10 Jan 1665; 1707 no poss.; Choptico Hundred (RR p.
50) (TLC p. 48)
Engsbatch Addition; 140 ac.; sur. 15 Dec 1673; 1707 poss. John Bowling of
CH Co. [m. Langworth's dau.]; St. Clements Hundred (RR p. 45) (TLC p. 44)

Clarken; 200 ac.; sur. 26 May 1680; 1707 poss. Wm. Hayden; New Town Hundred (RR p. 38) (TLC p. 37)

Clarken Addition; 75 ac.; sur. 2 Dec 1680; 1707 no poss.; New Town Hundred (RR p. 38) (TLC p. 37); 2 Dec 1680 cert./pat. (COL)

St. Barbaras Addition; 120 ac.; sur. 28 Dec 1680; 1707 poss. James Hagor of CH Co. who m. d/o Wm. Langworth; St. Clements Hundred (RR p. 47) (TLC p. 46); 28 Dec 1680 cert./pat. (COL)

Green Meadow; 200 ac.; sur. 17 Apr 1682; 1707 poss. exs. Wm. Rosewell; St. Clements Hundred (RR p. 48) (TLC p. 46); 200 ac.; 17 Apr 1682 cert./pat. (COL)

Roswell [Rosewell], William; will; 17 Sep 1694; 14 May 1695; g-sons Roswell, Thomas & Anthony, sons of Anthony Neale [mentions his son James]; wife Ema [Eva]; dau. Eliza.; g-son of testator's wife Thomas, s/o Thomas Turner; tracts *St. Winifred's, William's Folly, The Meadows, Little St. Thomases* (MCW 2.94) [SMW PC1.94]

Roswell, William, Mr.; inv.; 27 May 1695; 3 Jul 1695 (I&A 13a.383); acct.; 3 Jul 1695; extx. Anna Roswell (I&A 13a.385); acct.; 2 Aug 1696 (I&A 14.4); acct.; May 1697 (I&A 14.101)

ROSS

Ross, Alexander; inv.; 21 Jun 1750; 21 Oct 1751; adm./ex. Duanda Ross (I 48.102, 103); acct.; 30 Jun 1753; [Dr.]; admx. Dicanda Ross (A 35.124)

Ross, Lazarus and Jane Cox (by license); m. 28 Nov 1780 (SA p. 58)

ROSSON

Rosson, Robert; joiner; will: 10 Feb 1732/3; 14 May 1733; wife Whinnifrit; daus. Elizabeth, Ann, Mary; tract *Burwastcoat* (MCW 7.16) [SMW TA1.2]; inv.; 14 Aug 1733; 27 Aug 1733; nok Joseph Weathey, Ann Rosson; admx./extx. Winifred Rosson (I 17.533); acct.; 6 Aug 1734 (A 12.460)

Rosson, Winifred; widow; *Winifred's Chance*; 36 ac.; sur. 13 Sep 1742 (TLC p. 103); 14 Sep 1743 cert./pat. (COL)

ROUSBY

Rousby, Christopher; gent.; unnamed; 1 ac.; 9 Jun 1678 cert./pat. (COL)

Rousby, John; *Susquehannah P't & Edloes Addition*; 205 ac.; resur. 2 Dec 1716 (TLC p. 76); *Susquehannah Point*; 205 ac. CA Co.; 5 Apr 1717 cert./pat. (COL)

Rousby, John, Hon., Esq.; inv.; 11 Jul 1747; nok Walter Smith, Barbara Mackall (I 35.83)

RULE

Rull, Stamp; inv.; 7 Feb 1697 (I&A 15.313)

Rule, Peter; will; 12 Oct 1728; 5 Nov 1728; sister Rebecca Thomas; bros. William, John and Thomas Wherrit; sisters Rebecca Thomas, Mary Wherrit; wife Elizabeth; tract *Wattses Lodge* (MCW 6.79) [SMW PC1.320]; inv.; 20 Dec

1728; 27 Jan 1728; nok Rebecca Thomas, Eales Genkins; extx. Elisabeth Rule (I 13.384); acct.; 21 Jul 1729 (A 9.445)

Rule, Elizabeth; will; 2 Dec 1746; 10 May 1758; g-dau. Elizabeth Watts; sons, Daniel and Thomas Watts; g-son Jeremiah Cole (MCW 11.202) [SMW TA1.363]

RUSSELL

Russell, Christopher; will; 30 Mar 1662; 30 Jul 1662; 2nd son Walter, dau. Eliza Russell, eld. son William (MCW 1.21)

Russell, Richard; acct.; 13 Dec 1674; adms. Sarah Vaughn (relict) (I&A1.145)

Russell, William; acct.; 16 Feb 1714 (I&A 36b.267) (SMAA p. 276)

Russell, John; inv.; 6 Aug 1715 (I&A 36c.214); acct.; 27 Feb 1716; admx. Dorothy, w/o John Fathery (I&A 39b.57) (SMAA p. 304); acct.; 7 Jul 1717 (I&A 37c.160)

Russel (Russell), Luke; will; 15 Mar 1728/9; 3 Jun 1729; sons Luke, Thomas and Robert Russell and Joseph Watkins; wife Mary; tracts *Brough, Golden Springs* (MCW 6.119); tract *Brough and Cooks Race* [SMW PC1.344]; inv.; 29 Jun 1729; 13 Oct 1729; nok Thomas & Sarah Russell; extx. Mary Russell (I 15.142); acct.; 9 Mar 1729; extx. Mary, w/o William Watson (A 10.226)

Russell, Luke; *Poverty*; 64 ac.; sur. 7 Oct 1720; pat. John Jones; (TLC p. 88); 13 Jun 1734 cert./pat. (COL)

Russell, John; inv.; 13 Mar 1738; 4 Jul 1738; nok minors (I 23.197); acct.; 1 May 1744 (A 10.146)

Russell, William and Ann; child. William [b. 29 Apr 1747] Ignatius [b. 10 Mar 1748/9], James [b. 6 Dec 1755], Mary Ann [b. 20 Mar 1757], Charles [b. 12 Oct 1759] (SA p. 35, 36, 37, 39)

Russell, John; m. 6 Sep 1770 Susan French (MM)

Russell, John and Susanna; dau. Catharine [b. 27 Jun 1771] (SA p. 12, 47)

Russell, Ignatius and Mildred; dau. Eleanor [b. 22 May 1773], Philip [b. 15 Sep 1775]; Allusia [b. 24 Dec 1777] (SA p. 23, 28, 29)

Russel, G.; m. 27 May 1774 Ann Draden Abell (MM)

Russell, John Baptist, s/o William and Dryden [b. 14 Feb 1776] (SA p. 28)

SALMON

Salmon, Stephen; *Salmon*; 50 ac.; sur. 24 Jan 1648; assgn. Thos. Honard, sold to Will'm Spink; 1707 poss. by Charles Daft for Spink orphans; New Town Hundred (RR p. 27) (TLC p. 26)

Solman, Thomas; immigrated by 1670 (SK 12.611)

Salmon, Thomas; *Thames*; 150 ac.; sur. 14 Nov 1670; 1707 poss. Cesar Mattingly; St. Clements Hundred (RR p. 45) (TLC p. 43)
Rochester; 200 ac.; sur. 8 Sep 1673; 1707 poss. James Greenwell; New Town Hundred (RR p. 36) (TLC p. 35)

Salmon, Tho.; *The Poole*; 120 ac.; sur. 17 Oct 1675; 1707 poss. widow Susanna Heard; New Town Hundred (RR p. 37) (TLC p. 36)

Sallmon, Thomas; Newtowne; <u>will</u>; 3 Nov 1695; 14 Nov 1695; mentions John
and Justinian, sons of Jas. Greenwell; tract *Rochester* (MCW 2.99); SMW says this
is will of Thomas Johnson [SMW PC1.91]; <u>inv.</u>; 15 Nov [filed with 1694-5]; cooper;
(I&A 10.475); <u>acct.</u>; 13 Dec 1695; mentions James and John, sons of James
Grenwell, Sr. (I&A 14.52)

Solomon, Robert; <u>inv.</u>; 17 Jun 1703 (I&A 24.91)

Salmond (Salmon), Robert, Mr.; <u>inv.</u>; 2 Nov 1737; 7 Mar 1737; adms./exs.
Thomas Bold & wife Elisabeth (I 23.78); <u>acct.</u>; 20 Oct 1739; mentions James
Salmon, resident of Antigou (A 17.399)

SAMPSON

Sampson, Thomas; Mariner; immigrated by 1667 (SK 11.110)

Sampson, Absalom; *Enclosure*; 62 ac.; 27 May 1748 cert./pat. (COL)

Samson, Edward; <u>will</u>; 3 Apr 1764; 7 Apr 1764 (MCW 13.43) [SMW TA1.481]

SANDERS

Sanders, John of Charles Co.; age ca 50; m. ca 1692 Sarah Matthews; 11 May
1720; tract *St. Mary's Hill* (CCR p.46)

Sanders, John; <u>inv.</u>; [filed with 1716] (I&A 38b.145)

Sanders, John; <u>will</u>; 3 Aug 1741; 11 Jan 1741; wife Mary; her child. Joseph and
Ann Hartly (MCW 8.156) [SMW TA1.129]; <u>inv.</u>; 3 Feb 1741; 4 Jun 1742; nok
Jonathon & Ann Hartley; admx./extx. Mary Sanders (I 26.582); <u>acct.</u>; 19 Sep
1743 (A 19.538)

Sanders, William; <u>inv.</u>; 24 Nov 1720; 10 Feb 1720; admx. Leydia Sanders (I
4.269); <u>acct.</u>; 27 Jan 1721; admx. Lidia, w/o John Edwards (A 4.77)

Sanders, William; <u>inv.</u>; 30 Nov 1758; 5 Mar 1759; nok Lydia Nowell, Thomas
Saunders; admx./ext. Elisabeth Saunders (I 66.229); <u>acct.</u>; 5 Mar 1759 (A 43.99)

Saunders, Sinnot and Ann; dau. Elizabeth [b. 24 Jan 1768] (SA p. 6)

Sanders, Mary; <u>will</u>; 4 Dec 1775; 15 Sep 1776; sons Igantius, Enoch (MCW
16.174)

SANNER

Sanner, John; service by 1680 (SK WC2.276)

Sanner, John; *Salisbury Plain*; 100 ac.; sur. 29 Nov 1680; 1707 poss. Daniell
Berry; St. Mary's Hundred (RR p. 9) (TLC p. 10)

Sanner, Thomas; planter; age ca 49; 20 Apr 1737 (CCR p. 81)

Sanner, Nicholas; <u>inv.</u>; 1 Oct 1770; nok John & Jonathon Sanner; admx. John
Sanner (I 103.336); <u>acct.</u>; 3 Sep 1771; adm. John Sanner; admx. Susannah
Sanner (A 66.163)

Samner, Thomas, Sr.; s/o John, dec'd; *Salisbury Plains*; 100 ac.; 25 Sep 1773
cert./pat. (COL)

Sanner, Thomas; <u>will</u>; 9 Oct 1773; 25 Nov 1773; sons Thomas, Joseph; wife
Ann; tract *Salsbery* (MCW 15.91) [SMW TA1.662]

Samner, Thomas & Joseph; sons of Thomas, dec'd; *Salisbury Plains*; 252 ac.;
20 Sep 1775 cert./pat. (COL)
Sanner, Isaac and Eleanor Price (by license); m. 12 Dec 1782 (SA p. 60)
Sanner, Thomas and Mary Collason (by license); m. 23 Dec 1783 (SA p. 61)
Sanner, John and Susannah Goodin (by license); m. 17 Oct 1784 (SA p. 63)
Sanner, John and Elizabeth Abell (by license); m. 1 May 1785 (SA p. 63)

SARGENT
Serjeant, Seth; immigrated by 1680 (SK WC2.358-369)
Sargent, Jasper; inv.; 18 Dec 1729; 4 Mar 1729 (I 15.372); acct.; 6 Jul 1730 (A
10.415)

SCOTT
Scott, William; m. by 22 Apr 1650 Sarah ___, widow of Wm. Bruff (MM)
Scott, Richard; service by 1679 (SK WC2.125)
Scott, Cuthbert; immigrated by 1679 (SK WC2.99)
Scot, Cuthbert; *Hopton Park*; 2,100 ac.; resur. 23 Mar 1680; contains 3 tracts:
part of *Indian Quarter, Evans Quarter, Evans Freehold* & remaining 1,200 ac.
new rent; 1707 poss. John Bap. Carbery, James French, Arthur Thompson's
heirs; mentions John Baptist Carberry's wife Eliza.; New Town Hundred (RR
p. 37) (TLC p. 36); *Hopton's Park*; 1,680 ac.; 27 Feb 1682 cert./pat. (COL)
Scott, Cuthbert; inv.; 8 Aug 1691; 5 Jul 1697; unnamed relict,w/o Mr. John
Baptista Carberry (I&A 15.38)
Scott, Richard; inv.; 25 Jun 1702 (I&A 22.30)
Scott, Simon; inv.; 26 Feb 1717 (I 1.28); acct.; 3 Jun 1718; admx. Ann Scott (A
1.30) (SMAA p. 332)
Scott, Thomas; *Peach Blossom*; 55 ac.; sur. 2 Jan 1718; poss. Thomas Reeves
(TLC p. 78); 21 Jul 1720 cert./pat. (COL)
Scott, Robert, Rev.; age 55 in 1722; age ca 62 in 1729 (MD p.164)
Scott, Robert; clerk; will; 7 Nov 1733; 11 Dec 1733; niece Susanna Murray;
sister Margaret Gutherie and sister Ann Scott of Dundee, North Britain; tract
Fanskirk (MCW 7. 49) [SMW TA1.13]; inv.; 11 Dec 1733; 20 May 1734; nok Su.
Murray (I 18.84); acct.; 16 Apr 1735; legatee niece Susanna Murray (A 13.18)
Scott, Thomas; Chaptico; will; 24 Oct 1734; 16 Nov 1734; daus. Mary Hoskins,
Henrietta, Sarah; son Thomas; tract *Walkers* (MCW 7.114); track called *Walken*
[SMW TA1.30]
Scott, Thomas; inv.; 4 May 1734; 5 Jun 1735; nok ___ & Andrew Mill (I 20.472);
acct.; 1 Mar 1736 (A 15.263); acct.; 30 Oct 1736 (A 15.209)
Scott, Thomas; inv.; 8 May 1760; 17 Dec 1761; nok Ann Scott, Ruth White;
admx. Margaret Scott (I 76.306)
Scott, James; m. 18 Nov 1783 Peggy Edwards (BRU p. 536)

SEALE

Seal, Jonathan; *Chance*; 205 ac.; sur. 19 Dec 1706; resur. 22 Apr 1731 (TLC p. 64); 10 Oct 1707 cert./pat. (COL)

Seale, Jonathon; inv.; 10 Apr 1711; nok Robert & John Ford (I&A 32b.149)

Seale (Seal), Jonathon; acct.; 30 Oct 1758; mentions Jonathon, Leonard, Elisabeth Goldsboroug, Eleanor Baily, Lydia Raily, Monica How; admx. Lydia, w/o John Raily (Railey) (A 42.158); dist.; 30 Oct 1758; mentions Jonathon & Leonard Seal, Elisabeth Goldsbery, Eleanor Bailey, Lydia Bailey, Monaca Hews (BB 2.99)

SERGESON

Sergeson, William; *Wills Swamp*; 150 ac.; sur. 6 Mar 1674; 1707 poss. Robt. Baker; St. Mary's Hundred (RR p. 6) (TLC p. 7)
Sergesons Folly; 50 ac.; sur. 18 Dec 1680; 1707 pos. Robert Baker; St. Mary's Hundred (RR p. 8) (TLC p. 9); 18 Dec 1680 cert./pat. (COL)

SERSON

Serson, Francis; acct.; 2 Jul 1711; admx. Ailce (SMAA p. 331); inv.; 23 Dec 1715 (Dr.) (I&A 36c.218); acct.; 2 Jul 1718; admx. Ailce Serson (A 1.33)

Searson (Serson, Sarson), Alice; oral; 4 Apr 1731; g-son Thomas Jordan (MCW 6.185) [SMW PC1.357]; inv.; 22 May 1731; 3 Aug 1731; nok one minor (I 16.291); acct.; 14 Jan 1731 (A 11.324)

SEWALL

Sewell, Nicholas; great-g-son of Henry Sewell who was granted *Wiccomico* 17 May 1664 (CCR p. 100)

Sewall, Thomas; service by 1667 (SK 11.236)

Sewall, Nicholas; unnamed; [1683 survey]; 2,000 ac.; [18 Nov 1735] cert./pat. (COL)

Sewall, John; *Cuthberts Fortune*; 100 ac.; sur. 7 Nov 1694; 1707 poss. Adam Head (m. John Sewall's widow); lies in *Fenwick Manor*; Resurrection Hundred (RR p. 64) (TLC p. 62)
Addition to Cuthberts Fortune; 100 ac.; sur. 19 Aug 1695; 1707 poss. Adam Head (m. John Sewall's widow); lies in *Fenwick Manor*; Resurrection Hundred (RR p. 65) (TLC p. 62)

Sewell, Nicholas, Maj.; of CA Co.; *Partnership*; 1,878 ac.; 13 Dec 1697 cert./pat. (COL)

Sewell, John; acct.; 14 Jun 1699 (I&A 19.58)

Sewell, Nicholas; wife Susannah; son Henry; 11 May 1720; *St. Mary's Hill* (CCR p. 46)

Sewell, Mordecai; will; 11 Jan [1721]; 18 Jan 1721; uncle Thomas Gosling; mentions Thomas Gosling Hutchins [s/o John]; tract *Mackgrinday* [CA Co.] (MCW 5.82) [SMW PC1.268]

Sewell, Henry; <u>will</u>; 19 Mar 1721/2; 7 May 1722; father Maj. Nicholas Sewell; sons Henry, Nicholas; bro. Nicholas (MCW 5.91) [SMW PC1.272]; <u>acct.</u>; 14 May 1726; mentions child of relict Elisabeth Sewall who m. Phill. Lee; ex. Mr. Nicholas Sewell (A 7.340); <u>acct.</u>; 2 Jul 1728; ex. Mr. Nicholas Sewell (A 9.231)

Sewell, Nicholas; Maj.; age ca 67; 25 Jun 1722 (CCR p. 50)

Sewall, Henry, Mr.; <u>inv.</u>; 30 Aug 1722; 17 Dec 1722; nok Clement & Ann Sewall; extx. Mrs. Elisabeth Sewall (I 9.19); <u>acct.</u>; 13 Aug 1723; adms./exs. Elisabeth & Nicholas Sewall (A 5.206)

Sewell (Sewall), Nicholas, Maj.; *Mattapany Sewall*; 1,200 ac.; 2 Oct 1722 cert./pat. (COL)

   St. Peter's; 150 ac.; 10 Sep 1724 cert./pat. (COL)

Sewell (Sawell, Sawall), Cuthbert; <u>will</u>; 31 Jan 1723/4; 7 Mar 1723; sisters Mary Green, Priscilla Head, Elizabeth Harbert; f-i-l Adam Head; bro. Leonard Green; tracts *Fenwick's Maner, Cudbirt's Fortune, Addition to Cudbirt's Fortnue* (MCW 5.160) [SMW PC1.274]; <u>inv.</u>; 4 May 1724; 4 Jun 1724 (I 9.443); <u>acct.</u>; 4 Aug 1725 (A 7.98); <u>acct.</u>; 3 Nov 1726 (A 8.69)

Sewall, Nicholas, Jr.; <u>will</u>; 28 Oct 1727; 11 Apr 1732; nephew Nicholas Lewis and Charles Sewall; sons of bro. Charles; nephew Nicholas, s/o Peregrine Frisby; Elizabeth, widow of bro. Henry now wife of Philip Lee, Esq.; tract *Mattapany Sewll* (MCW 6.220) [SMW PC1.350]; <u>inv.</u>; 7 Aug 1732; mentions Clement & Ann Sewall; adm./ex. Charles Sewall (I 16.554); <u>acct.</u>; 18 May 1733 (A 11.689)

Sewall, Nicholas; <u>will</u>; 16 Apr 1737; 9 May 1737; daus. Ann, Sophia, Jane Brooke, Claire Young, Elizabeth Frisby, Susanna Douglas, [Mary Carroll]; sons Charles, Clement; g-sons Nicholas, Charles, Henry; tracts *Lady's Gift, Sewall's Range, Sewall's Manor, The Cross* in BA Co., *Darby* in DO Co. (MCW 7.214) [SMW TA1.66]; <u>inv.</u>; 30 Jun 1737, 16 Aug 1737; [Maj.]; nok Ann & Sophia Sewall; admx./ex. Mr. Charles Sewall (I 22.402); <u>acct.</u>; 24 May [filed with 1738] (A 16.138)

Sewall (Sewell), Charles; <u>will</u>; 8 Aug 1741; 27 Apr 1742; wife Eleanor; bro. Clement; sons Nicholas, Charles; tract *Darby* (MCW 8.170) [SMW TA1.124]

Sewall, Nicholas Lewis; gent.; *Sewall's Discovery*; 108 ac.; sur. 6 May 1743 (TLC p. 106); 15 Nov 1744 cert./pat. (COL)

   Fishing Point; 13 ac.; sur. 23 Apr 1745 (TLC p. 112); 18 Mar 1747 cert./pat. (COL)

Sewall, Nicholas; b. 9 Dec 1745; d. 23 Mar 1834 Worcester, England; s/o Nicholas Louis Sewall (JM p.320)

Sewall, Charles, Jr.; gent.; *Friend's Discovery*; 117 ac.; 29 Sep 1756 cert./pat. (COL)

Sewall, Henry and Mary; child. Element [b. 10 Jun 1757], Mary Smith [b. 7 Jul 1762], Henry [b. 3 Jun 1764], Charles [b. 20 Jul 1767] (SA p.16, 51)

Sewall, Harry; m. 28 Jan 1770 Sarah Roach (MM)

SHADRICK
Shadrick, Mark; *Caterpillar Spite*; 84 ac.; 25 Mar 1765 cert./pat. (COL)
Shadrick, Mark; will; 15 Jul 1772; 10 Aug 1772; child. John, Thomas, Mary,
Sarah, Elenor; wife Margaret; tract *Shadrick's Purchase* (MCW 14.237) [SMW
TA1.638]; inv.; 8 Sep 1772; 3 Nov 1772; nok Mary & Elenor Shadrick; exs.
Margaret & John Shadrick (I 109.390); acct.; 25 Mar 1774 (A 69.369); dist.; 25
Mar 1774; legatees John, Sarah, Thomas, Mary & Eleanor Shaderich; widow
(BB 6.272)

SHAMWELL
Shamwell, Isaac; *Darbyshire*; 130 ac.; sur. 9 Jul 1744 (TLC p. 104); *Darby Lux*; 13
Oct 1744 cert./pat. (COL)
Shamwell, Joseph; inv.; 17 Jul 1766; 14 Oct 1766; nok Benjamin Stevens, Sarah
Biggs; admx. Susanna Shamwell (I 91.98); acct.; 14 Oct 1766 (A 55.326)
Shemwell, William; will; 11 Nov 1774; 2 Jan 1775; wife Priscilla; sons Joseph,
William, Elisha; daus. Rebeckah, Mary, Priscilla; tract *Derbey Sheir, Clarkes
Hope* (MCW 16.92); tract called *Derbyshire* [SMW TA1.737]; inv.; 4 Jan 1775; 10
Sep 1775; nok James & Isaac Shamwell; extx. Priscila Shamwell (I 122.146)
Shamwell, Joseph; m. 20 Nov 1783 Nancy Billingsly (BRU p. 536)

SHANKS
Shanks, John; *Shanks*; 200 ac.; sur. 8 Dec 1652; 1707 poss. James Martin; incl.
in other sur.; New Town Hundred (RR p. 29) (TLC p. 28)
Shank, John; will; 19 Jun 1683; 16 Feb 1684; wife Abigall; son John; daus.
Mary Shank, Elizabeth Tennison; g-son Charles Watts; tract *Little Hackley
[Haikley]* (MCW 1.143) [SMW PC1.45]; inv.; 3 Mar 1684; d. 26 Jan 1684 (I&A
8.373); acct.; 4 Sep 1686; extx. Abigall Simons (I&A 9.83)
Shankes (Shanks), Thomas; planter; inv.; 12 May 1698 (I&A 16.191); acct.; 10
Mar 1698 (I&A 18.123); admx. Margaret (SMAA p. 99)
Shanks, John; inv.; 18 Feb 1716 (I&A 38b.175); acct.; 25 May 1718 (A 1.47) (SMAA
p. 337); inv.; 5 Jun 1719 (I 3.96); acct.; 3 Mar 1720 (A 2.433) (SMAA p. 455)
Shanks, Robert; *Shanks' Adventure*; 101 ac.; sur. 1 Apr 1718 (TLC p. 77); 6 Aug
1719 cert./pat. (COL)
Shanks' Risque; 102 ac.; sur. 31 Mar 1719 (TLC p. 79); 1720 cert./pat. (COL)
Shankes (Shenks), Thomas; oral; will; 8 Jan 1749; daus. Mary, w/o Thomas
Jordan; Susanna, w/o Edward Healard Hebb; son Thomas (MCW 10.70) [SMW
TA1.231]; inv.; 15 Feb 1749; 1 May 1750; nok Thomas Jordan, Mathew
Mason; admx./exs. John Mason & wife Judith (I 42.209); acct.; 30 Apr 1751;
orphans w/o Thomas Jordan, w/o Edward Hilliard Hebb, w/o Matthew Mason,
Heneritta [age 15], Abigall [age 12], Ann [age 10], John [age 10], Thomas
[age 4] (A 30.87)
Shanks, Thomas; *Shanks's Risk*; 102 ac.; 13 Nov 1752 cert./pat. (COL)

Shanks, Joseph; oral; <u>will</u>; 24 Feb 1757; child., Sarah, Diana, Susanna, Lettice, Alexander; wife Mary Ann (MCW 11.176) [SMW TA1.361]; <u>inv.</u>; 24 Aug 1757; 2 Nov 1757; nok John Hanks, Lazarus Maddox; admx./extx. Maryann Shanks (I 64.6b)

Shanks, Thomas; planter; <u>will</u>; 1 May 1771; 3 Jun 1771; sons Robert, Thomas, 5 unnamed child.; tract *St. Oswells* (MCW 14.181) [SMW TA1.619]; <u>inv.</u>; 8 Jun 1771; 3 Sep 1772; nok William Rapour, John Shanks; adm./ex. Robert Shanks (I 109.352)

Shanks, Joseph; m. 18 Feb 1772 Susanna Goldsmith (MM)

SHEPEY

Shepey (Shipey), Rich'd; *Hopewell*; 100 ac.; sur. 15 Jun 1666; 1707 poss. Rob. Strutton; New Town Hundred (RR p. 34) (TLC p. 33)

Shepey (Shipey), Rich'd; *Hopewell*; 100 ac.; sur. 12 Nov 1666; 1707 no poss.; New Town Hundred (RR p. 34) (TLC p. 33)

Shepey (Shipey), Rich'd; *Assurance*; 60 ac.; sur. 3 Aug 1670; 1707 poss. John Bayly; New Town Hundred (RR p. 35) (TLC p. 34)

SHEPPARD

Sheppard, John; immigrated by 1669 (SK 12.375)

Sheppard, John; <u>will</u>; 22 May 1699; 6 Mar 1699; son Richard; dau. Eliza. Reete (MCW 2.173); wife Mary [SMW PC1.111]

Shepheard, John; *Formby*; 200 ac.; sur. 15 Nov 1669; 1707 poss. Phil Lynes [of CH Co.]; 4 Oct 1726 from Richard Sheppard 200 ac. to Richard Edlin; charged in CH Co.; Choptico Hundred (RR p. 52) (TLC p. 50)

Sheppard (Shepard), Catherine; <u>will</u>; 10 May 1714; 26 May 1714; sons William and John Wilkisson; dau. Catherine Taney; g-son Robert Hutchins; g-dau. Catherine Hutchins (MCW 4.22) [SMW PC1.197]; <u>inv.</u>; 22 May 1714 (I&A 36a.146); <u>acct.</u> 24 May 1715 (I&A 36c.54)

SHERCLIFFE

Shertcliff, Wm.; *Favour*; 100 ac.; sur. 24 Jan 1648; escheat; granted John Dansey in *Radnor*; 1707 no poss.; New Town Hundred (RR p. 27) (TLC p. 26)

Shertcliff, John; *Gilmot*; 200 ac.; sur. 15 Jul 1659; 1707 poss. son William Shertcliff; land not found; New Town Hundred (RR p. 32) (TLC p. 31)

Horton Hayes; 150 ac.; sur. 16 May 1650; resur. 30 Aug 1658 this tract and another unnamed into *Ferny Hill* of 300 ac.; 1707 poss. Fran. Spink; 18 Jul 1717 mentions Dennis Mahany & wife Mildred; New Town Hundred (RR p. 29) (TLC p. 27)

Small Hopes; 100 ac.; sur. 13 Nov 1652; esch. as no heirs of Matt. Rowse; granted John Jordain 1677; 1707 poss. James Thomson; resur.; St. Clements Hundred (RR p. 43) (TLC p. 42)

Shertcliff; 100 ac.; sur. 25 Aug 1653; 1707 son William Shertcliff; New Town
Hundred (RR p. 30) (TLC p. 28)

Shertcliff; 200 ac.; pat. 22 Jun 1662; 1707 poss. William Shertcliff; New
Town Hundred (RR p. 32) (TLC p. 31)

St. Williams; 90 ac.; sur. 11 Apr 1686; 1707 poss. Wm. Shertcliff; New Town
Hundred (RR p. 40) (TLC p. 39); 3 Jun 1685 cert./pat. (COL)

Shirtcliffe, John; will; 2 Dec 1661; 26 Mar 1663; wife Anne; eld. son John,
young. son William, dau. Anne, cous. Thomas Spalding; b-i-l Henry Spinke
(MCW 1.24)

Sheircliffe (Shercliff), John; inv.; 26 Mar 1677 (I&A 4.140); acct.; 21 Aug 1678
(I&A 5.252)

Sheircliffe (Shercliff), Anne; inv.; 26 Mar 1677 (I&A 4.141); acct.; 21 Aug 1678
(I&A 5.249)

Shercliffe, William; will; 25 Mar 1707; 1 Jul 1707; dau. Mildred, w/o Dennis
Mohawny; wife Mildred; sons John, William, Thomas, Peter; daus. Mary
Melton w/o Thomas Melton, Anna, Elizabeth and Ticia; mentions Ellinor, d/o
Thomas Spinke; tract *Ferny Hill* (MCW 3.92); names daus. Mary Mothon, Tecla
[SMW PC1.149]; acct.; 22 Feb 1709; extx. Mildred, w/o Thomas Green (I&A
31.40) (SMAA p. 182)

Shierclieff (Shircliff), Peter; will; 4 May 1730; 25 Feb 1730; bros. John,Thomas,
William (MCW 6.184) [SMW PC1.356]

Shercliffe (Shierclieffe), Thomas; will; 26 Aug 1738; 20 Nov 1738; sons Henry,
Thomas; wife Monica (MCW 8.7) [SMW TA1.58]; inv.; 28 Nov 1738; 8 Mar 1738;
nok John Sheircliff, Jr. & Sr.; admx./extx. Monica Sheircliff (I 24.51); acct.; 15
Dec 1739 (A 17.402)

Shircliff, Henry; *Linstead's Addition*; 100 ac.; 29 Sep 1745 cert./pat. (COL)

Sheirclife, John; will; 29 Dec 1749/50; 6 Feb 1749; sons Joseph, John, Richard;
wife Ann; bros. William, Thomas, Peter [dec'd] (MCW 10.71) [SMW TA1.235]

Shircliff, John & Richard; *Cole's Adventure*; 145 ac.; 2 Mar 1758 cert./pat. (COL)

Sheircliff, Richard; inv.; 13 Mar 1762; nok Susanna & John Heard; adm. John
Sheircliff (I 79.272)

Sheircliff, Henry; [planter]; will; 24 Mar 1767; 5 May 1767; child. Joseph,
Thomas, Mary; wife Mary (MCW 14.1) [SMW TA1.524]; inv.; 10 Nov 1767; nok
Eleanor Bryan, Ann King; extx. Mary Sheircliff (I 94.201); acct.; 27 May 1769
(A 62.161); dist.; 7 May 1769; child. Joseph, Thomas, Mary (BB 5.228)

Shircliff, Henry; inv.; 10 Nov 1767; extx. Mary Shircliff (I 95.24)

SHIRBURN

Shireburn (Shirburn), Richard, Dr.; inv.; 3 Feb 1725; 3 Mar 1725; nok Benedict
& John Boarman; admx. Clare Shirebun (I 11.227); acct.; 11 Dec 1727 (A 8.468)

Chirburn (Shierburn), Clare (Clear); will; 21 Feb 1745; 6 Aug 1747; sons
Richard Brooks, Baker Brooks and Nicholas Shirburn (MCW 9.122) [SMW

TA1.194]; <u>inv.</u>; May 1747; 22 Sep 1748; nok John & Benedict Boarman;
   adm.ex. Nicholas Sheirbine (I 37.380)
Shirobum, Nicholas, Mr.; <u>inv.</u>; 4 Feb 1754; 9 Dec 1754 (I 60.107)

SHIRLEY
Shirly, Richard, Sr.; <u>will</u>; 4 Apr 1737; 19 Nov 1737; wife Sarah; sons Richard,
   George, William, John (MCW 7.231); does not mention son Richard [SMW
   TA1.72]; <u>inv.</u>; Jan 1737; 13 Feb 1737; nok Richard Shirley, minors; adms./extx.
   John Diall & wife Sarah (I 23.22); <u>acct.</u>; 23 Apr 1738 (A 17.11)
Shirley (Shirly), Richard; <u>will</u>; 16 Apr 1747; 15 Jul 1747; son Robert; wife
   unnamed (MCW 9.113) [SMW TA1.198]; <u>inv.</u>; 15 Jul 1747; 16 Oct 1747; nok John
   Wiseman Greenwell, John Wiseman; admx./extx. Grace Shirly (I 35.371)
Shirly, Ignatius; m. Nov 1775 Mary Norris (MM)

SHOARE
Shoare, Thomas; service by 1679 (SK WC2.46)
Shore, Tho.; *Shores Delight*; 175 ac.; sur. 24 Jan 1680; pat. by Caleb Osborn
   who m. widow of Shore in behalf of his dau.; 1707 no poss.; St. Georges
   Hundred (RR p. 19) (TLC p. 19); 75 ac.; 19 Jan 1681 cert./pat. (COL)

SIKES
Sikes, John; <u>inv.</u>; [filed with 1711] (I&A 33a.147)
Sikes, John; *Friends in Conjunction*; 250 ac.; 7 Sep 1738 cert./pat. (COL)
Sikes, John; <u>will</u>; 4 Aug 1749; 4 Nov 1749; wife Mary; mentions Joshua
   Morgan, s/o Elizabeth Griffin, also Benjamin, s/o William Morgan (MCW
   10.66) [SMW TA1.225]; <u>inv.</u>; 31 Jan 1749; 31 Mar 1750 (I 42.7); <u>acct.</u>; 3 Aug 1751
   (A 31.52) (BB 1.4)
Sikes, Thomas; <u>will</u>; 27 Feb 1728; 7 Aug 1728; wife Mary; dau. Ann Hoskins
   (MCW 6.77) [SMW PC1.317]; <u>inv.</u>; 13 Aug 1728; 6 Nov 1728; nok Anne
   Hawskins, Thomas Bond; extx. Mary Sikes (I 13.284); <u>acct.</u>; 7 May 1729 (A
   9.361)
Sikes, Thomas; age ca 80; 12 Apr 1725 (CCR p. 59)

SILENCE
Silence, John; <u>inv.</u>; 11 Mar 1717 (I 1.51)
Silence, John, Sr. and Mary; child. Enoch [b. 6 Mar 1760], Jeremiah [b. 19 Oct
   1762], Austin [b. 11 Apr 1765] (SA p. 3)
Silence, John, Jr. and Elizabeth; child. John [b. 24 Mar 1761], Ann [b. 27 Dec
   1766], Edmund [b. 9 Mar 1771] (SA p. 3, 20, 55)
Silance, Enoch and Eleanor Rhodes (by license); m. 14 Sep 1784 (SA p. 62)

SIMMONS

Simmons, John; <u>inv.</u>; 20 Jul 1708 (I&A 28.284); <u>acct.</u>; 26 Jul 1712; admx. Helen, w/o Gilbert Hart (I&A 33b.135); 20 Jul 1712 (SMAA p. 228)

Symons, Mary; relict & admx. of George Simmons; <u>inv.</u>; 11 Jun 1716; nok underage child. (I&A 37a.169)

Simonds, James; <u>inv.</u>; 7 Aug 1736; 3 Dec 1736 (I 22.81); <u>acct.</u>; 13 Jun 1737 (A 14.295)

Simmons, Able; <u>will</u>; 5 Oct 1755; 24 Nov 1755; wife Mary; mentions John Horne Milburn [s/o Rebecka Cloker] (MCW 11.112) [SMW TA1.335]

Simmonds, John; *Stratford Addition*; 32 ac.; 19 Sep 1763 cert./pat. (COL)

Simmons, John; <u>will</u>; 5 Mar 1773; 15 Jul 1773; child. Mathew Wise, John, Abell and Mary Milbren Simmons; f-i-l Mathew Wise; wife unnamed; tracts *Cole Harbour, The Addition of Stradford* (MCW 15.70); name given as Mary Milburn [SMW TA1.672]; <u>inv.</u>; 21 Sep 1773; nok James & A. Milbourne; ?extx. Elisabeth Simmons (I 112.402)

SIMMS

Simm, Marmaduke; m. Fortune Mittford, extx. of Dr. William Champ, dec'd; 1668 (AM LVII.358)

Simms (Seemms), Marmaduke; 17 Aug 1690; 20 Mar 1692/3; sons Anthony, James, John, Marmaduke; wife Fortune; tracts *Simms' Forest, Middle Plantation* (MCW 2.63); <u>acct.</u>; 14 Apr 1695; extx. Fortune Seemes (I&A 13a.257)

Simms, Anthony; *Itchcomb's Freehold*; 344 ac.; 10 Sep 1744 cert./pat. (COL)

Simmes, Anthony; <u>will</u>; 14 Oct 1749; 20 Feb 1749; dau. Jane Baxter; "son" George Baxter; son Anthony; g-child. John and Ann Simmes Baxter, Anthony and Elenor Baxter; tract *Batchelors Comfort* (MCW 10.72) [SMW TA1.237]

Simms, Anthony, Mr.; <u>inv.</u>; 14 May 1750; 25 Jun 1750; nok Athony Simms, Joseph Sikes (I 43.279); <u>acct.</u>; 8 Jul 1751 (A 30.201)

Semmes, Teresa; b. 1750; d. 2 Jun 1769 Liege; d/o Joseph Milburn Semmes and Rachel Prather (JM p.320)

Sims, Anthony and Mary; dau. Elizabeth [b. 28 Oct 1768] (SA p. 191)

Simms, Anthony; <u>will</u>; 11 Apr 1769; 7 Mar 1770; wife Sarah; child. Bennett, James, Ignatius, Ann, Sarah, Patty, Jane w/o Charles Green, Anthony (MCW 14.134) [SMW TA1.609]

Simms, Bennett; <u>will</u>; 6 Nov 1769; 7 Jun 1770; mother Sarah Simms; bros. James, Ignatius; sisters Ann, Sarah, Pattey (MCW 14.132) [SMW TA1.613]; <u>inv.</u>; 4 Oct 1770; 1 Sep 1771; nok Ann & Sarah Simms; ex. James Simms (I 107.188)

SIMPSON

Simson, Paul; *Crackbourns Purchase*; 200 ac.; sur. 11 Dec 1652; assgn. Rich'd Crackbourn; 1707 poss. Tho. Cooper by m. widow of Hugh Benson; New Town Hundred (RR p. 32) (TLC p. 30)

Simpson, Thomas; planter; kinsman Richard Willan; 1661 (AM XLI.556)

Simpson, Thomas; age ca 66 in 1682 (MD p. 168)

Simpson, Thomas; age 66 in 1723 (MD p. 168)

Simpson, Thomas, Mr.; <u>inv.</u>; 29 Nov 1750; 6 Mar 1750; nok Josias Simpson, Elisabeth Mackhon; adms./exs. Benjamin Molten & wife Mary (I 45.74); <u>acct.</u>; 1 Sep 1751; mentions Philip s/o Philip Tippett, also Josias, John, Elisabeth, 3 orphans of John Faning; adms. Benony Moltan & wife Mary (A 31.65)

Simpson, Jos.; m. 28 Jan 1770 Mary Jarboe (MM)

SINGER

Singer, Thomas; <u>acct.</u>; 1 Nov 1718 (A 2.440); 20 Jan 1719 (SMAA p. 451)

Singer (Singler), Philip; <u>inv.</u>; 7 Jan 1740; 14 Apr 1741; nok Mary & Charles Singer; admx./extx. Ann Singer (I 25.441); <u>acct.</u>; 3 Dec 1741; orphans Charles, Philip, John, Mary; admx. Ann Singer (A 18.461)

SINNOT

Sinnot, John; <u>inv.</u>; 23 Oct 1721; 9 Dec 1721; nok Catherine Sinnett, Stephen Mackey; adm. Sunnion Sinnot (I 6.243); <u>acct.</u>; 13 Feb 1721; child. at age; admx. Simon Sinnot (A 5.11, 12)

Sinnott (Sinnot), Simon, Mr.; <u>inv.</u>; 26 Jul 1733; 10 Dec 1733; nok Thomas Sanders (I 17.544), <u>acct.</u>; 29 Jul 1734; admx. Eleanor, w/o James Burn (Burne) (A 12.357)

SISSONS

Sisons [Sissons], Alice; widow of Edward Sisons; <u>will</u>; 12 Dec 1706; 3 Jan 1706; g-dau. Alice, d/o Richard Shonburt [Shoubert]; dau. Hannah Jackson; g-son John Strautran; sons Robert and William Tunill [Turill]; [g-dau. Mary Jamson, g-son John Phanham; dau. Anne Simes] (MCW 3.84) [SMW PC1.173]

Sison (Sissons), Allis; <u>inv.</u>; 3 Jan 1706 (I&A 26.163); <u>acct.</u>; 18 Oct 1709 (I&A 30.160); 10 Oct 1709 (SMAA p. 180)

SLEDMORE

Sledmore, John; <u>inv.</u>; 25 Feb 1745; 3 May 1746; nok William Sword, Peter Hilburn; admx./extx. Mary Sledmore (I 32.224); <u>acct.</u> 13 Apr 1747; mentions William Sledmore (A 23.303)

Sledmore, Mary; <u>inv.</u>; 17 Aug 1750; nok Mary Rusell, Mary Stokings (I 44.245); <u>acct.</u>; 22 Jul 1751; child. Matthew Broomer, Mary, w/o Thomas Russill, Jane Watson & her daus. Mary & Martha Hawkins & Elisabeth Watson; adm. Matthew Broomer (A 30.205)

SLYE

Slye, Robert; age ca 38 in 1666 (MD p. 169)

Slye, Robert; St. Clement's Manor; <u>will</u>; 18 Jan 1670; 13 Mar 1670; wife Susannah; young. son Robert; daus. Eliza, Frances; eld. son Gerard; b-i-l

Thomas and John Gerard; sis.-i-l Mary Gerard; sis. Eliza: Russell; nephews Timothy and Thomas Cooper of New England; bros. Justinian Gerard and Nehemiah Blackstone; tracts *Bushwood, Lapworth, Norwood Lapworth Lodge, Clear Doute, Rich Neck* (MCW 1.59)

Slye, Gerrard, Capt.; of *Bushwood*; m. Jane Saunders; she came from England ca 1670-80; sons Gerrard & Charles; 25 Jun 1722 (CCR p. 50)

Slye, Gerrard; *Bastard Bury*; 829 ac.; sur. 16 Oct 1678; tract let fall; resur. 14 Mar 1704 by Slye for 606 ac. called *Bushwood Lodge*; 1707 poss. Gerrard Slye, son; St. Clements Hundred (RR p. 49) (TLC p. 47); *Bastard Berry's*; 829 ac.; [1679] cert./pat. (COL)

Slye, Robert; [Capt., merchant]; will; 18 Apr 1698; 12 Oct 1698; wife Priscilla; child. John, Judith, Susanna, Sarah; bro. Luke Gardner; tracts *Lapwood [Sapwood], Norwood* (MCW 2.167) [SMW PC1.114]; inv.; 4 May 1703; 8 Jun 1703 (I&A 24.147); acct.; 24 May 1704; adm. Gerard Sly (I&A 3.174); inv.; 21 Jul 1705 (I&A 25.185)

Slye, Gerard; gent.; *Bushwood Lodge*; 606 ac.; 20 May 1705 cert./pat. (COL)

Slye, Gerard; *Weebit*; 62 ac.; surv. 25 Apr 1705; 1707 poss. Gerard Slye, son; lies in *St. Clements Manor* or *Bushwood Lodge*; Choptico Hundred (RR p. 54) (TLC p. 52); *Wee Bit*; 62 ac.; 30 May 1705 cert./pat. (COL)

Slye, Robert; m. sister of Thomas Love prior to 1714 (CCR p. 29)

Slye, Ger'd & wife Mary; *Gardiners Grove*; 247 ac.; sur. 9 Jan 1719 (TLC p. 78)

Slye, Robert; of *Bushwood;* m. Susanna, d/o Thomas Gerrard; sons Gerrard & Robert Slye; 25 Jun 1722 (CCR p. 50)

Slye, Gerrard; age ca 43; 27 May 1723 (CCR p. 52)

Slye, Gerrard; Gent; Bushwood; will; 23 Jul 1733; 23 Nov 1733; wife Mary; child. Henrietta, George, Elizabeth, Mary Neale, Susannah Key [Slye], Ann Boarman, Susannah Craycroft, Jane; tracts *Wee Bit, Bushwood Lodge, Piper Hill* (MCW 7.48) [SMW TA1.1]; inv.; 16 Feb 1733; 17 Apr 1734; nok Henry Neale, Thomas Gardiner; extx. Mary Slye (I 18.117)

Slye, Charles; inv.; 8 Jun 1736; 4 Aug 1737; nok Thomas Gardiner, Henry Neale (I 33.402)

Slye, Mary; will; 10 Dec 1744; 7 May 1744; daus. Mary Lancaster, Henrietta Plowden, Anne Nealle; son George; g-dau. Mary Nealle, Jr. (MCW 9.38) [SMW TA1.157]

Slye (Sly), George; will; 21 May 1773; 20 Jun 1773; nieces & nephews Jean, Nancy [Nacy] and Nicholas Craycroft, Wilfred and Henry Neale, Nicholas Craycroft, Edward [Edmond] Plowden; sister ____ Plowden; wife Clare; tracts *Stones Rest, Lincey* (MCW 15.70) [SMW TA1.657]; inv.; 28 Jul 1773; 20 Apr 1774; extx. Clare Sly (I 115.425)

SMITH

Smith, Anne; wife of William; his will made Augusta Carolina 1635; inv. & accts. 1638 (AM IV.16.48)

Smith, William; dec'd; widow Ann; recorded 21 Sep 1638 (PRPC)

Smith, Peter; immigrated by 1660 of Herring Creek (SK 9.33)

Smyth, William; innholder; wife Mary; convey *Smyths Delight* on Transquaking River; 1 Apr 1665 (AM XLIX.428)

Smith, William; *Smiths Town House*; 1 ac.; sur. 25 Sep 1666 St. Marys Citty; incl. in *Pope's Freehold*; 1707 no poss.; St. Mary's Hundred (RR p. 5) (TLC p. 6)

Smyth, John; records cattle mark for dau. Elizabeth; 10 Jan 1667/8 (AM LVII.232)

Smith, Henry; immigrated by 1672 with wife Sarah (SK 17.47)

Smith, John; service by 1674 (SK 18.72, 84)

Smith, John; will; 12 Feb 1676; 28 Apr 1677; wife Susanna; sons John and Notley; dau. Eliza:, Susanna, Jane; tracts *Smith's Addition, Addition by Patent, Hope, Smith's Reserve, Coventry, Smith's Purchase, Church Over* (MCW 1.191); inv.; 18 Jul 1677; 28 Jul 1677 (I&A 4.204)

Smith, Thomas; immigrated by 1677 (SK 15.417)

Smith, Thomas; service by 1680 (SK WC2.325)

Smith, Thomas; will; 19 Dec 1684; 11 Feb 1685; wife Eliza: (MCW 1.141) [SMW PC1.67]

Smith, Daniel; *Buck Branch*; 50 ac.; 10 Jan 1687 cert./pat. (COL) *Smiths Rest*; 35 ac.; sur. 8 Aug 1698; 1707 poss. Daniel Smith; land not found; Poplar Hill Hundred (RR p. 24) (TLC p. 25)

Smith, Richard; *Industry*; 153 ac.; sur. 10 Nov 1694; assgn. Wm. Wilkinson; 1707 poss. same Wilkinson; Resurrection Hundred (RR p. 65) (TLC p. 62) *Susquehannah Point*; 195 ac.; resur. 17 Jul 1700; 1707 poss. Rich'd Smith; resur. 2 Dec 1716; Harvey Hundred (RR p. 57) (TLC p. 55)

Smith, Henry; *Smiths Rest*; 100 ac.; sur. 10 Dec 1694; 1707 poss. same Smith; St. Michael's Hundred (RR p. 14) (TLC p. 15); 5 Oct 1695 cert./pat. (COL)

Smith, Peter; carpenter; age ca 41; 24 Aug 1698 (CCR p. 12)

Smith, John; will; 30 Jul 1701; 6 Sep 1701; sons John, Richard; wife Ann (MCW 2.224); inv.; 12 Sep 1701 (I&A 21.43); acct.; 14 Jan 1702; relict unnamed, w/o Michael Cusack (I&A 23.35)

Smith, John; widow m. Micahel Cusack; 14 Jan 1702/3 (SMAA p. 107, 213)

Smith, Richard, Capt.; of CA Co.; *Smith's Discovery*; 258 ac.; sur. 9 Mar 1705 (TLC p. 63); 1 Aug 1706 cert./pat. (COL)

Smith, William of CH Co.; *Stoney Hills*; 96 ac.; sur. 10 May 1706; now lies in CH Co. (TLC p. 64); 10 Oct 1707; cert./pat. (COL)

Smith, Henry; will; 9 Dec 1707; 7 Feb 1712; dau. Sarah [Catah], Mary; wife Ann; s-i-l Thomas Griffin (MCW 3.237) [SMW PC1.184]; acct.; 20 May 1714; exs. John Authors and wife Anne (I&A 36b.42); 21 May 1714 (SMAA p. 263)

Smith, Richard; St. Leonards; will; 31 Jul 1710; 19 Mar 1714; sons Richard, Walter, Rousby; daus. Elizabeth w/o William Tom, Ann w/o William Dawkins, Barbary ?w/o Charles Somerset Smith who is called "son"; mentions Thomas Johnson & wife Mary; bro. Walter Smith; tracts *Smith's Fort, Smith's Forrest, Locust Thicket, Brook Ridge, Valley of Jehosophat,*

Addition to the Valley of Jehosophat, Hogg Pen, Blinkhorne, Wolfe's Quarter, Stedmore, Brook Partition, Upper Cock Town, Vines Neck, Cock's Comb, Cock's Head, Smith's Conveniency, First Part of Free Gift, Beaver Dam, Calverton Manor (MCW 4.37)

Smith (Smyth), Charles; inv.; 23 Oct 1710 (I&A 32c.10); acct.; 15 Dec 1712; admx. Susannah Smyth (I&A 33b.170) (SMAA p. 227)

Smith, Peter, Sr.; carpenter; 30 Dec 1717; 8 Jan 1717; son Peter; daus. Sarah Howard, Mary Johnson, Elizabeth, Susannah; g-son Joseph Johnson; wife Dorothy; *Dansburry [Dousbury] Hill* (MCW 4.173) [SMW PC1.223]; inv.; 26 Feb 1717 (I&A 39a.25); acct.; 12 Jun 1719; widow Dorothy; legatees John, Elisabeth w/o Robert Persons, Susannah, Peter; ex. Robert Ford (A 2.28) (SMAA p. 390); acct.; 9 Mar 1720 (A 3.287) (SMAA p. 431)

Smith, Daniel; shipwright; will; 1 Feb 1718; 1 Feb 1719; sons John, Jeremiah, Richard, Jeremiah; daus. Anne, Jenne [Jane]; wife Elizabeth (MCW 5.31) [SMW PC1.252]; inv.; 8 Mar 1720; 8 Jun 1721; nok Mary Cruckson; mentions James Crackson; extx. Elisabeth Smith (I 5.50); acct.; 8 Jan 1721 (A 4.53); acct.; 11 Feb 1722 (A 5.34)

Smith, John; age ca 33; 11 May 1720 (CCR p. 46)

Smith, Edward, age ca 39; wife Mary; age ca 31; 19 Sep 1722 (CCR p. 51)

Smith, John; inv.; 29 Oct 1725; 2 Nov 1725; nok Richard Smith, Lawrence Bateman (I 11.136); acct.; 8 Jun 1726; mentions dec'd child (A 7.374)

Smith, Dorothy; *Edenbrough*; 167 ac.; resur. 14 Aug 1727 into *Edinburgh with Addition* (TLC p. 83); 14 Oct 1727 cert./pat. (COL)

Smith, Henry; acct.; 20 Nov 1727; 20 Nov 1727; extx. Ann, w/o John Arters (A 8.467)

Smith, Charles; inv.; 4 Mar 1728; 31 Mar 1729; admx. Elisabeth Smith (I 14.7); acct.; 29 May 1729 (A 9.442)

Smith, James; *Treble Defence*; 230 ac.; 17 Oct 1732 cert./pat. (COL)
Triple Defence Addn.; 34 ac.; 3 Apr 1743 cert./pat. (COL)
Treeple Defence; 206 ac.; sur. undated; 259 ac. resur. 28 Aug 1744 into *Triple Defence Rectified* (TLC p. 87); *Triple Defence*; 259 ac.; 29 Sep 1749 cert./pat. (COL)
Puntney's Oversight; 219 ac.; sur. 31 Mar 1738 (TLC p. 95); *Pountney's Oversight*; 27 Jun 1739 cert./pat. (COL)
Staple Addition; 34 ac.; 8 Apr 1742 cert./pat. (COL)
Pountney's Oversight; 198 ac.; 10 Aug 1753 cert./pat. (COL)
Pine Land; 370 ac.; 29 Sep 1755 cert./pat. (COL)

Smith, John; will; 19 Mar 1733 [or 1735]; 6 May 1761; sons George, Thomas, Edward, Simmons, John; dau. Mary Saunder [Lundy (?)]; s-i-l Hopewell Adams; wife Mary; tracts *Round Pond, Piney Hill* (MCW 12.75) [SMW TA1.419]

Smith, Richard; inv.; 10 May 1734; 7 Jun 1734; nok John Wheeler, Jane Smith; adm./ex. John Smith (I 18.328); acct.; 9 Dec 1735; mentions John, Ruth, Anne & Jane Smith, and Henry & Frances Bacon (A 14.106)

Smith, John; will; 11 Aug 1735; 3 Mar 1735; sons Benjamin, Leonard; bros.
Basil and Clement Gardner; wife Jean; tracts *Sharp, Letchworth* (MCW 7.163);
inv.; 29 Mar 1737; nok Ba. & Roger Smith; admx./extx. Jane Smith (I 22.315);
acct.; 22 Aug 1738 (A 16.299)

Smith, Charles; inv.; 20 Apr 1738; 19 Jun 1738; nok Anthony & Charles Smith;
admx./extx. Ann Smith (I 23.202, 203); acct.; 27 Aug 1739; orphans William,
Charles, Joshua, Elisabeth, Ann & Mary Smith (A 17.246)

Smith, Dorothy; will; 3 Jan 1742; 21 Apr 1743; g-child. Henry, Ruth, Margaret,
Michael, Joshua and Susanna Winstread; husband Thomas Roson, dec'd; s-i-l
Thomas Winstead (MCW 8.217) [SMW TA1.147]; inv. 9 Jul 1743; nok Thomas, Jr.
& Henry Winstead (I 28.353, 354); acct.; 29 Dec 1744 (A 21.146)

Smith, William; inv.; 30 Aug 1742; nok Charles & Anthony Smith; admx./extx.
Mary Smith (I 27.58); acct.; 30 Apr 1744 (A 20.145)

Smith, William; inv.; 4 Jun 1744; nok Mary & Jane Smith (I 29.237); acct.; 22
Apr 1745 (A 21.220)

Smith, Daniel; inv.; 8 Feb 1751; 20 May 1751; nok George Smith, Elisabeth
Adams; adms./exs. Edward & Thomas Smith (I 48.22); acct.; 13 May 1752;
siblings: Thomas, Edward, George, Simmons, Solomon & Jobe Smith, Mary
Lander, Elisabeth w/o Hopewell Adams (A 32.238)

Smith, James; *Trinity Mannor*; will; 21 Nov 1753; 18 Mar 1754; wife Mary;
child. John, Elizabeth Parrott now w/o William Loker, Mary, Martha,
Susannah, James, John & his son John; tracts *St. Gabriel Mannor, Narrows,
Point Lookout, Pountneys Oversight, Pountnay Marsh, Trinity St. Gabriels,
St. Michaels Manor, Turvey* (MCW 11.19); Elizabeth "now wife of Sekoe (?)"
[SMW TA1.311]; inv.; 24 Apr 1754; 17 Jun 1754; mentions John Smith;
adms./exs. Mary Smith, James Smith (I 57.242, 251)

Smith, John and Elizabeth; dau. Ann [b. 3 May 1756] (SA p. 19)

Smith, James; inv.; 13 Oct 1758; 6 Dec 1758 (I 66.16); acct.; 30 Apr 1759;
mentions John, Elisabeth w/o William Locker, Mary w/o Samuel Tibbles,
Martha w/o Samuel Culeseall, James, Susanah; exs. Mary & James Smith (A
43.149); acct.; 29 Oct 1759 (A43.357)

Smith, William; inv.; 12 Jan 1759; 30 Apr 1759; nok Ann Coleman, Mary
Smith; adm./ex. James Smith (I 67.95)

Smith, Joseph; inv.; 27 May 1761; 10 Mar 1762; nok Susanna Smith, John
Baptist Buckman (I 77.66)

Smith, John; inv.; 2 Jun 1761; 5 Aug 1761; nok Thomas & Elisabeth Smith; ex.
Mary Smith (I 74.254)

Smith, James; acct.; 11 Jul 1763; exs. William & Rebecca Walter (A 49.540)

Smith, John; inv.; 25 Jun 1765; 6 Aug 1765; nok Paul & Rachel Smith; admx.
Elisabeth Smith (I 88.82)

Smith, Henry Bacon; inv.; 14 Jul 1765; nok John & Margaret Smith; admx.
Manica Smith (I 88.80); acct.; 6 Apr 1767; adms. William Baker & wife
Monica (A56.79)

Smith, James, gent.; s/o James, dec'd; *Turvey*; 383 ac.; 21 Mar 1770 cert./pat. (COL)

Smith, John; acct.; 10 Sep 1770; admx. Elisabeth Smith (A 64.244); dist.; 10 Sep 1770 (BB 5.387)

Smith, Mary; will; 22 Oct 1770; 10 Jan 1772; child. Daniel Jenifer, John Smith, Elizabeth Locker, Mary Theobalds, Martha Edwards, Susanna Jones, Michael Parker [Tasker] Jenifer, James Smith; g-child. Elisha, Daniel, Ann, Margaret and Elizabeth Jenifer and Elizabeth and Mary Stone Smith (MCW 14.212) [SMW TA1.633]; inv.; 19 Feb 1772; Sep 1772; nok Elisabeth Parrot Loker (I 110.102); acct.; 10 Sep 1773 (A 69.209)

Smith, James; Gent.; will; 15 Nov 1771; 2 Apr 1772; daus. Mary, Margery (MCW 14.213) [SMW TA1.646]; inv.; 19 Jun 1772; 23 Jun 1772; nok Elisabeth Plocker, Susannah Jones; ex. John Smith (I 109.359)

Smith, Jos.; m. 13 Nov 1773 Joanna Manning (MM)

Smith, Peter; will; 20 Dec 1773; 10 Apr 1774; wife Ann; sons Varnan (Vernon), Peter, Abner; daus. Melonday, Ann, Mary Boyle; [son Oliver] (MCW 15.129) [SMW TA1.705]; inv.; 3 Aug 1774; nok Charles & Arthur Smith; exs. Ann & Varnon Smith (I 119.168)

Smith, John; will; 17 Dec 1775; 14 Dec 1776; g-dau. Ann Edwards; g-sons John and Charles Smith; wife Elizabeth; daus. Ann, Margret (MCW 16.173)

Smith, James; acct.; 20 Aug 1776; adm. John Smith (A 74.7)

Smith, Mary; about to m. Garret Vansweringen, Gent. of St. Mary's City 5 Oct 1776 (SK 19.382)

Smith, Walter and Mary Hendley; m. 19 Sep 1779 (SA p. 57)

Smith, Walter and ____ King (by publication); m. 31 Mar 1785 (SA p. 63)

SMITHSON

Smithson, John; will; probate 22 Mar 1637; wife Anne, extx. (MCW 1.1)

Smithson, Owen; acct.; 2 May 1737; admx. Ann Smithson (A 14.292)

Smithson, Anne; widow & extx. of John; 1638 (AM IV.43, 46)

Smithson, Martin; inv.; 1 Jul 1732; 1 Aug 1732 (I 16.553); acct.; 3 Jul 1733 (A 11.716)

Smithson, Owen; acct.; 2 Aug 1736; admx. Anne Smithson (A 15.192); inv.; 3 May 1736; 12 Jul 1736; nok Thomas & John Guyther (I 21.418); inv.; 15 Nov 1736 (I 22.324)

SMOOT

Smoote, Wm.; *Smoote*; 300 ac.; sur. undated; pat. 12 Jun 1646; 1707 Camas Parsons, Wm. Kenedy; Poplar Hill Hundred (RR p. 21) (TLC p. 20))

Smoot, Barton; will; 19 Jan 1760; 7 Mar 1760; wife and child. unnamed (MCW 11.259) [SMW TA1.384]; inv.; 26 Sep 1761; 21 Aug 1761; nok William, Jr. &

George Guyther; extx. Susanna Smoot (I 74.262); <u>acct.</u>; 30 Oct 1765; extx. Susanna McCaul Smoot (A 53.234)

Smoot, John; *Smoot's March*; 31 ac.; sur. 30 Nov 1737 (TLC p. 95); 28 Nov 1738 cert./pat. (COL)

Smoot, Alexander and Abigail H. Tabbs (by license); m. 4 Nov 1784 (SA p. 63)

SNOW

Snow, Justinian; dec'd; bro. of Marmadue; 19 Mar 1638 (AM IV.55); b-i-l Thomas Gerard, surgeon; <u>inv.</u> 24 May 1639; <u>acct.</u> 21 Mar 1639 (AM IV.79)

Snow, Abell; *Snow Hill Mannour*; 1,000 ac.; sur. 10 Feb 1640; poss. 200 ac. Richard Calvert; remainder leased by His Lordship 1707; St. Mary's Hundred (RR p. 1) (TLC p. 1)

Snow, Justinian; died at sea on way to MD; bros. Marmaduke; b-i-l Thomas Gerard (surgeon); recorded 19 Mar 1638 & 22 Mar 1639 (AM IV.79)

Snow, Marmaduke; <u>inv.</u>; 6 Dec 1675; 17 Apr 1676 (I&A 2.132)

SOLLEY

Solly, Benja.; *Birch Hanger*; 664 ac.; sur. 18 Mar 1671; 1707 poss. Clement Hill, Solly's atty.; Choptico Hundred (RR p. 52) (TLC p. 50)
Helagh or *Hatagh*; 260 ac.; sur. 29 Apr 1673; 1707 poss. Clement Hill, atty. for Solly; in. bounds of *Birch Hanger*; Choptico Hundred (RR p. 53) (TLC p.)

Solley, Benjamin; gent.; <u>inv.</u>; 23 Mar 1674 (I&A 1.325); <u>acct.</u>; [filed with 1676]; admx. Lydia Solley (I&A 2.153)

SOMERHILL

Somerhill (Summerhill), James; *Partnership*; 200 ac.; sur. 10 Sep 1706 for Somerhill & Francis Graham (TLC p. 64); 10 Oct 1707 cert./pat. (COL)

Somerhill (Summerhill), James; *Release*; 50 ac.; sur. 2 Aug 1714; not clear of elder surveys (TLC p. 69); 2 Sep 1714 cert./pat. (COL)

Somerhill, William; <u>acct.</u>; 7 Jun 1715; adm. James Somerhill (I&A 36c.50); 17 Jun 1715 (SMAA p. 286)

Somerhill [Sumerhill], James; <u>inv.</u>; 3 Mar 1725; 4 May 1726; nok Elinor Briscoe, Mary Keech, Gunder Erickson, John Cornwell; extx. Elisha Sumerhill (I 11.262); <u>acct.</u>; 7 Jun 1727 (A 8.230)

Sumerhill, James; <u>will</u>; probate 3 Feb 1725; wife unnamed; sons Samuel and James; tracts *Partnership, Releife, Westham* (MCW 5.200) [SMW PC1.299]

Summerhill, William; <u>inv.</u>; 23 Jun 1714; nok John Somerhill, Mary Keech (I&A 36a.211)

SOMERVILL

Somervill (Somervell), John; *Sommerfield*; 33 ac.; 10 Apr 1760 cert./pat. (COL)

West Hopewell; 247 ac.; 27 Sep 1762 cert./pat. (COL)
Hog's Confusion; 304 ac.; 29 Sep 1764 cert./pat. (COL)
Somervel, William and Elizabeth Chesley; m. 7 Sep 1779 (SA p. 57)

SOTHORON

Southern, Rich'd; *Littleworth*; 25 ac.; sur. 28 Jul 1679; 1707 poss. John
Southern; Resurrection Hundred (RR p. 63) (TLC p. 61)
Southern's Desire; 125 ac.; sur. 28 Dec 1680; 1707 poss. John Southern;
Resurrection Hundred (RR p. 63) (TLC p. 61)
Southern's Hills; 50 ac.; sur. 28 Jul 1679; 1707 poss. John Southern;
Resurrection Hundred (RR p. 63) (TLC p. 61)
Southeron (Sothoron), Richard, Capt.; inv.; 28 Sep 1702 (I&A 23.173); son John,
admn.; 7 Oct 1703 (SMAA p. 118)
Southern (Sothoron), John; of CH Co.; *Long Yorkshire*; 134 ac.; 10 Jan 1706
cert./pat. (COL)
Sothoron (Southern), Samuel; will; 6 Jan 1711; 5 Feb 1711; wife Margaret;
tracts *Two Brother's Friendship, Southerne's Desire, Tower Hill* (MCW 3.224)
[SMW PC1.177]; inv.; 4 Mar 1711; nok Elisabeth Price, William Wells (I&A
33b.204); acct.; extx. Margaret; 5 Aug 1713 (I&A 35b.94) (SMAA p. 248); acct.;
extx. Margaret, wife of John Segar; 27 Sep 1714 (I&A 36c.57) (SMAA p. 264)
Sothoron, John & Samuel; *Brotherhood*; 220 ac.; sur. 2 Apr 1727 (TLC p. 87); 16
Jul 1733 cert./pat. (COL)
Sotheron (Sothern), John Johnson; will; 9 Oct 1744; 5 Dec 1744; wife Elizabeth;
her son Greenfield; son Henry G.; bros. Samuel and Richard Sotheren (MCW
9.13) [SMW TA1.158]; inv.; [filed with 1746]; exs. Samuel & Richard Sothoron (I
34.154); acct.; 6 Sep 1746 (A 22.317)
Sothoron, Samuel; will; 2 Dec 1767; 15 Jun 1758 (sic); wife Jane or Jean; sons
Richard, Samuel, Levin, John Johnson Sothoron; daus. Ann Burroughs,
Susanah, Mary, Margaret, Jane, Elizabeth; tracts *Little Worth, Truemans Lot,
Sotherons Supply, Sothorons Hills* (MCW 14.44) [SMW TA1.557]
Sotheron, Mary; b. 14 Jan 1736; d. 11 Oct 1763; age 26; w/o Henry Greenfield
Sotheron; d/o Maj. Zachariah Bond (HGM)
Sothoron, John Johnson; acct.; 10 Mar 1746; mentions Benjamin Sothoron, g-
son of Mary Rose; exs. Samuel & Richard Sothoron (A 23.157); acct.; 21 Oct
1747; orphan Henry Greenfield Sothoron; exs. Samuel & Richard Sothoron (A
24.239)
Sothoron, Samuel; *Sothoron's Supply*; 21 ac.; 10 Aug 1753 cert./pat. (COL)
Sothoron (Southeron), Richard; *Southeron's Venture*; 27 ac.; 25 Mar 1767
cert./pat. (COL)
Sothoron's Discovery; 138 ac.; 31 Mar 1775 cert./pat. (COL)
Sothoron, Samuel; inv.; 2 Jul 1768; 17 Aug 1768; nok Richard & John J.
Sotheron; exs. Jean & Levin Sotheron (I 98.129)
Sothoron, John; acct.; 10 Sep 1770; exs. Jean & Levin Sothoron (A 64.251)

Sotheron, John Johnson; *Bruce's Neglect*; 10 ac.; 23 Jul 1770 cert./pat. (COL)
Sothon, Samuel; m. 9 Jan 1783 Henrietta Bruce (BRU p. 536)

SPALDING

Spalding, Tho.; *St. Giles*; 116 ac.; sur. 22 May 1667; poss. Tho. Spalding, Jr.; in
1704 RR, not in 1707; New Town Hundred (TLC p. 36)
Spalding, Thomas; *Spaldings Addition*; 42 ac.; sur. 21 Aug 1674; in 1704 not in
1707; poss. Tho. Spalding; Choptico Hundred (TLC p. 50)
William's Hermitage; 109 ac.; 21 Sep 1688 cert./pat. (COL)
Spalding, William & John; *Two Brothers*; 165 ac.; sur. 8 Jun 1704 (TLC p. 70); 10
Dec 1714 cert./pat. (COL);
Spalding, William; gent.; *St. Joseph's*; 142½ ac.; resur. 25 Oct 1722 (TLC p. 86);
142 ac.; 28 Aug 1726 cert./pat. (COL)
Heart's Delight Addition; 152 ac.; sur. 3 Sep 1720 (TLC p. 80); 192 ac.; 29 Aug
1726 cert./pat. (COL)
Spalding, Thomas, Jr.; *Wranglefield*; 260 ac.; sur. 10 Feb 1733; incl. into
Resurvey America Felix Secundus; pat. vacated 2 Dec 1746 (TLC p. 92); 19 Aug
1736 cert./pat. (COL)
Spalding, Peter; inv. 16 Apr 1740; 6 Aug 1740; nok William, Sr. & Edward
Spalding; admx./extx. Elisabeth Spalding (I 25.192); acct.; 21 Jul 1741; orphans
Thomas, Peter, James, Michael, Edmund, Mary, Ann & Elisabeth Spalding,
Catherine Anderson (A 18.277)
Spalding, William, Sr.; will; 6 Dec 1740; 9 Jan 1740/1; sons Thomas, William,
Henry, Benedict, John; wife Ann; daus. Jean Plowden, Ann Joseph, dec'd,
Mary Seale; tracts *St. Barbery, The Mill Land, The Water Mill, Spalding
Attition, St. Gilesses, Addition to Heart-Delight, New Cassell, St. Joseph, The
Two Brothers* (MCW 8.115) [SMW TA1.95]; inv.; 4 Mar 1740; 16 Nov 1741; nok
Edward & Thomas Spalding; adms./exs. Thomas, William, Bennedict &
Henry Spalding (I 26.423); acct.; 8 May 1744 (A 20.160)
Spalding, Thomas; *Spalding Adventure*; 207 ac.; sur. 20 Aug 1740 (TLC p. 98); 24
Aug 1742 cert./pat. (COL)
Spalding. Clement; *Spalding's Adventure*; 729 ac.; 22 Dec 1752 cert./pat. (COL)
Spalding (Spaulding), John; inv.; 3 Nov 1758; 26 Mar 1759; nok William
Spalding, Edward Field; admx./extx. Elisabeth Spalding (I 66.217); acct.; 4 Sep
1759; dau. Ann, w/o John Baptist Mattingley; admx. Elisabeth Spaulding (A
43.304)
Spalding, Elizabeth; will; 20 Mar 1760; 24 Jun 1760; sons Robert and Benjamin
Fenwick; dau. Ann Mattanly; g-dau. Ann Burn; g-son John Taney [Janey]
(MCW 12.227) [SMW TA1.385]
Spalding, Ann; widow; will; 10 Nov 1760; 17 Feb 1761; sons Thomas, Henry,
John Baptist, William, Benedick; daus. Mary Seale, Ann Joseph & her
unnamed child.; g-dau. Elizabeth Bradford (MCW 12.35) [SMW TA1.418]

Spalding, William; <u>inv.</u>; 29 May 1765; nok Henry Spalding, Bennet Fenwick; admx. Elisabeth Spalding (I 88.72); <u>dist.</u>; 14 Apr 1767 (BB 5.21)

Spalding (Spauldling), William; <u>acct.</u>; 14 Apr 1767; admx. Elisabeth Spalding (A 56.85)

Spalding, Thomas; Court House; <u>will</u>; 2 Jan 1768; 14 Mar 1769; wife Catharine; daus. Jane Power, Mary Ann, Ann Mahoney & her dau. Alusia; Susanna Abell, Mary Ann McGill & her son Thomas, Mary, Catharine, Ann Penny Spalding; sons Elexius & his sons Richard, Enoch Elias [Enoch & Elias], Thomas, Henry & his sons Richard, Augustus, Henry; tracts *Spalding's Adventure, Crackburns Purchase, St. Thomas's Hope, Improvements, Benham's March, The Exchange, Rich Neck* (MCW 14.91) [SMW TA1.581]; <u>inv.</u>; 14 Mar 1769; 10 Nov 1769; nok Henry & John B. Spalding, Jr.; admm./ex. Catharine Spalding (I 102.255); <u>acct.</u>; 17 Dec 1770; exs. Catharine & Thomas Spalding (A 66.74); <u>acct.</u>; 30 Jan 1772 (A 67.135)

Spalding, Edward; <u>will</u>; 28 Oct 1774; 5 Dec 1774; wife Ann; child. Winifred, Mary, Teresia, Ann (MCW 16.2) [SMW TA1.688]; <u>inv.</u>; 25 Dec 1775; 14 Apr 1775; nok Dorothy Thompson, Thomas Spalding; admx./extx. Ann Spalding (I 121.396)

Spalding, Cathrine; <u>will</u>; 19 Jul 1775; 21 Aug 1775; daus. Cathrine Mattingly, Mary Ann McGill, Mary, Jeane [Jane] Power, Ann Mahoney, Susanna Able [?dec'd], Ann Punny Ford; son Elesejus [Elexius]; [mentions son Thomas] (MCW 16.110) [SMW TA1.723]

Spalding, Thomas; <u>inv.</u>; 27 Feb 1777; 1 Jun 1777; nok Henrietta & Moses Clark Spalding; adm. Bennet Spalding (I 125.290)

SPINKE

Spink, Henry; *Linstead*; 100 ac.; sur. 2 Sep 1653; 1707 poss. Francis Spink; 1 Mar 1711 mentions Francis Spink & wife Eliz. and Dennis Mahauny & wife Mildred; 6 May 1712 Walter Davis & wife Ann; New Town Hundred (RR p. 30) (TLC p. 29)

Spink, Henry; wife Ellinor; 1663 (AM XLIX.37)

Spink, Thom; immigrated by 1667; carpenter; wife Margaret (SK 11.162)

Spinke, Henry; *Twittnam*; 300 ac.; sur. 18 Mar 1673; 1707 poss. Hen. Spink, Wm. Howard; New Town Hundred (RR p. 36) (TLC p. 35)

Spinke, Hen.; *Linsteads Addition*; 100 ac.; sur. 31 Mar 1682; 1707 poss. Francis Spink; New Town Hundred (RR p. 39) (TLC p. 38); 31 May 1682 cert./pat. (COL) *St. Williams Hermitage*; 200 ac.; sur. 29 Apr 1667; 1707 son Henry Spink; New Town Hundred (RR p. 34) (TLC p. 33); 170 ac.; 21 Apr 1684 cert./pat. (COL)

Spinke (Spink), Henry; [Sr.]; <u>will</u>; 9 Mar 1693; 22 Dec 1695; sons Edward, Francis, Henry, William (MCW 2.99) [SMW PC1.93]; <u>inv.</u>; 28 Oct 1695 (I&A 13b.69); <u>acct.</u>; 8 Sep 1696; exs. sons Henry and William Spink (I&A 14.6)

Spinke, William; <u>will</u>; 13 Feb 1697; 21 May 1698; wife Elizabeth; bro. Henry; dau. Ellinor; unborn child; 3 bros.; [father Henry Spinke]; tracts *Twitnam, St.*

William's Hermitage (MCW 2.145) [SMW PC1.105]; <u>inv.</u>; 20 Jun 1698 (I&A 16.195); <u>acct.</u>; 22 Apr 1710; extx. Elisabeth, w/o Charles Daft (I&A 31.129) (SMAA p. 161)

Spink, Henry; *Spink's Rest*; 100 ac.; sur. 1 Jun 1714 (TLC p. 70); 20 Apr 1715 cert./pat. (COL)
  Divided Hills; 51 ac.; sur. 20 Apr 1716 (TLC p. 75); 25 Apr 1717 cert./pat. (COL)
  Hickory Hollows; 119 ac.; sur. 20 Apr 1716 (TLC p. 75); 25 Apr 1717 cert./pat. (COL)
  The Branch; sur. 20 Apr 1716 (TLC p. 76) *Branch*; 50 ac.; 21 Oct 1718 cert./pat. (COL)

Spinke, Henry; planter; <u>will</u>; written 6 Jan 1718/9; sons Clement, Henry; daus. Leocresia, Henrieta, Monica; nieces Margarett, Mary; father Henry Spinke; bro. Francis; mentions Ann w/o Samll. Grasty; tracts *Gilmort's Fields; Spinkes Rest, The Adjoyner, Gilmort Hills, The Branch, Hickory Hollow, Dividing Hills* (MCW 4.198) [SMW PC1.244]

Spink, Francis; <u>will</u>; 30 Jan 1718/9; 4 Mar 1718; daus. Cathrine, Teclo [Tela]; wife Eliner; tracts *Farney Hill, Deviding Values* [*Valley*] (MCW 4.199) [SMW PC1.243]

Spinke (Spink, Spinkes), Edward; <u>will</u>; 18 Nov 1717; 1 Dec 1717; daus. Elizabeth, Margaret, Mary; son William; bros. Henry, Francis; tract *Hicors* [*Hickory*] *Hallows* (MCW 4.127) [SMW PC1.215); <u>acct.</u>; 8 Nov 1718; exs. Henry & Francis Spink (A 1.302) (SMAA p. 345); <u>acct.</u>; 15 Jun 1720; dau. Marrgrett Spinke, dec'd (A 3.98)

Spink (Spinke), Henry, Mr.; <u>inv.</u>; 19 May 1718; 3 Jun 1719 (I 2.46); <u>acct.</u>; 21 Mar 1720 (A 2.422)

Spinke, Francis; <u>inv.</u>; 7 Apr 1719; 3 Jun 1719; nok Francis Neaver, William Meadcefe; admx. Elisabeth Spinke (I 2.94); <u>acct.</u>; 27 May 1720; extx. Elisabeth, w/o William Bradburne (A 2.507) (SMAA p. 447)

Spink, Henry; <u>acct.</u>; 17 Sep 1724; ex. William Spink (A 6.130)

Spink, Henry; planter; <u>will</u>; 6 Feb 1733; 1 Mar 1733; bro. Clement; nephew Ignatius Jarboe [s/o sister ____ Jarboe]; sisters Henrietta Woodward, Lucretia Spink; b-i-l Peter Jarboe; mentions Anastatia w/o Thomas Howard, Frances d/o John Ford, Jr., William s/o William Spink; tracts *Spinks Rest, Gilmut's Hills, St. Williams Hermitage, Twittinham* (MCW 7.59) [SMW TA1.21]; <u>inv.</u>; 1 Mar 1733; 27 May 1734; nok Heneretta Woodward, bro. Clement Spink (I 18.128); <u>acct.</u>; 17 May 1735 (BB13.226)

Spink, William, Mr.; <u>inv.</u>; 4 May 1743; 9 Jun 1743; nok Francis & Clement Spink; adm./ex. Edward Spink (I 28.12); <u>acct.</u>; 10 May 1744; orphans Edward, Francis, Elinor, Mary (A 20.233)

Spinke (Spink), Francis; <u>will</u>; 26 Dec 1749; 8 Mar 1749; son Thomas; daus. Elizabeth, Anastatia; wife Mary; tract *Paupall* (?) [*Pawpaw*] (MCW 10.72) [SMW TA1.242]; <u>inv.</u>; Mar 1750; 4 Sep 1750; nok Clement & Edward Spink; admx.extx. Mary Spink (I 43.382); <u>acct.</u>; 2 Dec 1752; extx. Mary w/o John Norris (A 33.325)

Spink, Clement; <u>will</u>; 10 Apr 1752; 3 Jun 1752; child. Ellinor, Mary, Anastatia, Dorothy, Henrietta; wife Teresia; tracts *Gilmott Hills, All That's Left* (MCW 10.224) [SMW TA1.296]; <u>inv.</u>; 29 Nov 1752; nok Monico & Bennett Jarboe; admx./extx. Tertia Spink (I 52.81, 86); <u>acct.</u>; 5 Sep 1753; orphans Stacia [age 9], Dorothy [age 5], Hennoretta [age 1], Enenor & Mary [both d. since father]; extx. Teretia Spink (A 35.116); <u>dist.</u>; 5 Sep 1753; extx. Teresa Spink; child.Stasia [age 10 next May], Dorothy [age 5 next 17 Sep], Henrietta [age 2 next 1 Mar], Eleanor & Mary [d. after their father] (BB 1.89)

Spincks (Spink) [Spinks], Anastasia; <u>will</u>; 7 Sep 1762; 25 Oct 1762; sisters-i-l Henrietta and Dorothy Spincks; g-father Peter Ford; uncles Peter, Richard [Robert] and John Ford (MCW 12.159) [SMW TA1.425]; <u>inv.</u>; 7 Mar 1763; 19 May 1763; nok Peter, Sr. & John Ford; ex. Peter Ford, Jr. (I 81.235); <u>acct.</u>; 6 Sep 1763 (A 49.617)

Spink, Clement; *All That's Left*; 31¼ ac.; sur. 1744 (TLC p. 110); 31 ac.; 30 Jul 1744 cert./pat. (COL)

Spink, Edward and Monica; child. Joseph [b. 22 Apr 1759], Mary [b. 29 Jul 1762], Mary [b. 21 Dec 1765] (SA p. 9, 38, 43)

SPRY

Spry, Christopher; service by 1675 (SK 18.338; 12.473)

Sprye (Spry), Henry; <u>inv.</u>; 20 Sep 1678 (I&A 5.356); <u>acct.</u>; 24 Jul [filed with 1679] (I&A 6.208)

ST. CLAIR

St. Clair, Dorothy; <u>inv.</u>; 16 Mar 1765; 19 Mar 1765; mentions Susanna St. Clair; adm. Vernon St. Clair (I 87.6, 7)

St. Clare, Bernard; m. 24 Dec 1778 Dorcas King (BRU p. 536)

STANFIELD

Stanfield, John, Mr.; <u>inv.</u>; 10 Jun 1766; 20 Feb 1767; nok Caleb Stanfield, John Abell (youngest); adm. Richard Stanfield (I 91.324, 326); <u>acct.</u>; 9 Mar 1767 (A 56.66); <u>acct.</u>; 24 Apr 1770 (A 64.96); <u>dist.</u>; 24 Apr 1770 (BB 5.384)

Stanfield, Caleb; <u>will</u>; 9 Feb 1768; 1 Apr 1768; bro. Richard (MCW 14.32) [SMW TA1.556]

STEVENS

Stevens, Mary; servant; killed bastard child; 1671; St. Mary's Hundred (AM LXV.12)

Stevens, Benjamin; <u>will</u>; 2 Jan 1732/3; 28 May 1733; sons Benjamin, Daniel, Joseph; daus. Susana Lock, Elizabeth Stevens, Ann Blacksham [Blackiston]; wife Lettice (MCW 7.16) [SMW TA1.5]; <u>inv.</u>; 12 Jun 1733; 8 Aug 1733; nok Benjamin Stevens, William Lock; adm./ex. Lettice Stevens (I 17.330); <u>acct.</u>; 24 Aug 1734 (A 12.528)

Stevens, Benjamin; *Stevens' Chance*; 46 ac.; sur. 15 Feb 1728 (TLC p. 93); 17 Nov 1737 cert./pat. (COL)

Stephens, Benjamin; inv.; 26 Mar 1744; 3 Jul 1744; nok Lettice & Joseph Stevens; admx./extx. Elisabeth Stephens (I 29.249); acct.; 5 Jun 1745; orphans Joseph, Benjamin, Rebecca, Susanna; admx. Elisabeth, w/o Henry Fowler (A 21.358)

Stevens, Joseph; *Joseph's Venture*; 54 ac.; sur. 21 May 1750 (TLC p. 116); 21 May 1750 cert./pat. (COL)

Stephens, Mark; inv.; 22 Dec 1753; 12 Nov 1753; nok William & Elisabeth Stephens; admx./extx. Elisabeth Stephens (I 57.47); inv.; 10 Jul 1755; 14 Jul 1755; nok William & Elisabeth Stevens (I 59.1); acct.; 17 Aug 1756; orphans William [age 18], Elisabeth [at age], Mary [age 14], Mark [age 10], Sarah [age 8] (A 39.225); dist.; 25 Oct 1756; dist. to same (BB 2.33)

Stephins, Mary; inv.; [filed with 1755]; mentions Negroes Seazor [age 40], Jude [age 38], Dark [age 10], Peter [age 5], Clare [age 3] (A 38.136)

Stevens, John; will; 3 Nov 1759; 7 Feb 1763; dau. Mary, w/o Abraham Tennison; wife Elizabeth; d-i-l Ann Richardson; mentions John, s/o William Russell (MCW 12.176) [SMW TA1.436]; inv.; 9 Feb 1763; 2 Aug 1763 (I 81.256); acct.; 24 Nov 1767; admx. Ann Richardson, w/o William Taylor (A 57.331)

Stephens, Joseph; *Stevens' Luck*; 15 ac.; 7 Jun 1770 cert./pat. (COL)

Stephens, John, Rev.; *Charles's Lot*; 200 ac.; 29 Jun 1774 cert./pat. (COL)

Stephens (Stevens), Joseph; will; 9 Oct 1774; 18 Dec 1774; wife Sarah; sons Joseph, James, John, William, Hezekiah; daus. Sarah Glasscock, Lidia Green, Mary Alstan (MCW 16.89) [SMW TA1.739]; inv.; 13 Jan 1775; 10 Apr 1775; nok Ann Suit, Thomas Payne; admx./extx. Sarah Stevens (I 121.409)

STEWART

Steward, John; immigrated by 1669 (SK 12.345, 382)

Stuerd, William; 20 May 1707; 6 Dec 1710 (SMAA p. 212)

Steward, William; inv.; 7 Apr 1713 (I&A 34.174); acct.; 29 Jul 1713; admx. relict, w/o John Jones (I&A 35b.108) (SMAA p. 240)

Stewart, John; *Steuarts Hope*; 134 ac., 125 ac.; part of *Mills Marsh*; resur. 2 Oct 1736 (TLC p. 94); *Stewart's Hope*; 737 ac.; 26 Jan 1738 cert./pat. (COL)

Stuert, John, Mr.; inv.; 6 Mar 1738; 9 Nov 1744; admx./extx. Monica Stuert (I 30.215)

Stewart, Monica; inv.; 4 Mar 1752; nok Ann Knott, Henry Mattingly (I 48.292); acct.; 3 Apr 1753 (A 33.409)

Steuart (Stewart), John, Gent.; will; 27 Mar 1738; 6 Mar 1738/9; daus. Mary, Ann; wife unnamed (MCW 8.21) [SMW TA1.82]

STILES

Stiles, James; St. Inegoes Hundred; will; 21 Jan 1762; 1 Jun 1762; sons Sim, Solomon, Stephen; wife Winifred; daus. unnmaed; tracts *Elizabeth Mannor*,

Stiles' Chance, Wallace's [Whaller's] Chance, What Care I (MCW 12.134)
[SMW TA1.426]; inv.; 1 Jul 1762; 7 Sep 1762; nok John Stiles, Francis
Greenwell; extx. Wineford Stiles (I 79.246)

Stiles, John; will; 5 Dec 1766; 23 Feb 1767; daus. Elizabeth Jarboe, Mary Lee;
wife Catharine; sons Seph, John; g-child. Mary Magdalene Lee, John Baptist
Jarbo; dau. tracts *St. Inagoes Hundred, Cross Manor, Elizabeth Mannor,
Nevet St. Ann* (MCW 13.151) [SMW TA1.527]; inv.; 10 Mar 1767; 16 Jan 1768; nok
Frances Greenwell; admx. Catharine Stiles (I 97.95)

STONE
Stone, William; inv.; 11 Aug 1714 (I&A 36a.183)

Stone, William; acct.; admx. Mary; 19 Nov 1718 (SMAA p. 328)

Stone, Joseph, Sr.; will; 16 Nov 1751; 10 Feb 1752; child. John, Dority,
Elizabeth, Joseph, Edward (MCW 10.198) [SMW TA1.288]; inv.; 11 Feb 1752; 13
Nov 1752; nok Wilam & Joseph Stone; adm./ex. John Stone (I 51.65); acct.;
[field with 1753]; orphans John, Dorothy & Elisabeth [all of age], Joseph [age
10], Edward [age 8]; ex. John Stone (A 34.156, ?185); dist.; 22 May 1753; same
child. (BB 1.78)

Stone, Ignatius and Monica; sons Ignatius [b. 6 Feb 1762], Matthew [b. 8 Sep
1764] (SA p. 2)

Stone, William; will; 13 Aug 1765; 24 Jun 1766; sons William, Henry, Charles,
John, Joseph, Ignatius; daus. Anne Greenwell, Mary, Priscilla; tract *Graden*
(MCW 13.109) [SMW TA1.490]; inv.; 10 Jan 1767; [Sr.]; nok William & Henry
Stone; ex. Ignatius Stone (I 91.82); dist.; 22 Jun 1767; dau. Ann Grunwell, son
Henry Stone, g-son Joseph Stone (BB 5.55)

Stone, John; inv.; 9 Apr 1769; 2 Aug 1769; nok Joseph & Lydia Stone; admx.
Jane Stone (I 101.339); acct.; 10 Jun 1771 (A 66.177); dist.; 14 May 1771 (BB 6.90)

Stone, Joseph; m. 29 Dec 1772 Dorothy Spink (MM); son John [b. 13 Nov 1773]
(SA p. 24)

Stone, William; will; 2 Jul 1774; 1 Nov 1774; wife Drayden Anne; sons
William, George; daus. Susanna, Anne, Ellianor, Rebecca, Margaret, Mary;
tract *Grayden* (MCW 16.1) [SMW TA1.674]; inv.; 15 Jan 1775; nok Ignatius &
William Stone; admx./extx. Ann Draden (I 120.183)

Stone, Joseph and Winifred Hutchins (by license); m. 28 Nov 1780 (SA p. 58); son
Francis [bapt. 6 Aug 1781] (SA p. 30)

STRATFORD
Stratford, Joseph; inv.; 2 Feb 1687 (I&A 9.469); acct.; 8 Jan 1688 (I&A 10.187)

Stratford, Joseph; will; 1 Feb 1732/3; 16 Mar 1732/3; daus. Frances, Monica,
Ann, Mary, Elizabeth; sons Clement, Joseph (MCW 7.10) [SMW TA1.16]; inv.; 18
Apr 1733; 3 Jul 1733; nok Christopher & Giles Horrill; admx./extx. Mary
Stratfoord (I 171.174); acct.; 3 Sep 1734 (A 12.531)

Stratford, Clement; will; 19 Aug 1762; 17 Jul 1764; wife Ferronia [Teresa]
(MCW 13.43) [SMW TA1.480]; inv.; 16 Oct 1764; nok Ann Alvey, Joseph Walker;
extx. Teresis Stratford (I 86.65)

Stratford, Teresa; will; 3 Apr 1772; 10 Oct 1772; child. William Rapour, Ann
Diner Walker, w/o Joseph Walker (MCW 14.188) [SMW TA1.615]; inv.; 9 Oct
1771; 1 Mar 1772; nok Ann Walker, William Rapour; ex. Richard James
Rapour (I 110.93)

STYLES

Styles, Wm.; *Knevets St. Ann*; 100 ac. sur. 10 Nov 1647; 1707 poss. Thos.
Nottingham; New Town Hundred (RR p. 27) (TLC p. 26)
Raccoone Point; 100 ac.; sur. 3 Jun 1649; 1707 poss. James Gough; resur. into
Bacon Neck; New Town Hundred (RR p. 28) (TLC p. 26)

Styles, William d. by 6 Oct 1663 (AM XLIX.113)

Styles, John; *Styles Chance*; 200 ac.; sur. 12 Jun 1685; 1707 poss. John Wheatly,
Mich. Welman; New Town Hundred (RR p. 42) (TLC p. 41); *Styles' Chance*; 200
ac.; 12 Jun 1685 cert./pat. (COL)

SUITE

Sute (Suite), Thomas; will; 16 Oct 1765; 4 Nov 1771; child. Dent, Thomas, Ann
Noe; g-child. Dent s/o Thomas Sute, Sarah d/o Joseph Edwards; d-i-l Mary
Bright (MCW 14.188) [SMW TA1.616]

Suit, Walter; m. 26 Aug 1777 Susanna Davis of CH Co. (BRU p. 536)

SULLIVANT

Sulevant, Dennis; service by 1667; wife Ann, service by 1679 (SK WC2.14)

Swelovan (Swillivan, Sullivant) [Sullivan], Timothy; will; 28 Dec 1711; 21 Jan
1711/2; sister Ann Mackman; son Arthur; wife Ellen; [mentions Ann Briarly,
wife of Isaac] (MCW 3.219) [SMW PC1.178]; inv.; 21 Apr 1712; nok Elisabeth and
Daniell Swillevan and Anne Makmery (I&A 33a.214); acct.; 25 Apr 1715; extx.
Ann Briarly (I&A 36c.68) (SMAA p. 290); acct.; 21 Apr 1721 (A 3.426) (SMAA p. 459)

SUTTLE

Suttle, John; *Suttles Range*; 100 ac.; sur. 25 Nov 1673; 1707 poss. Widow
Tippett; St. Clements Hundred (RR p. 46) (TLC p. 44)
Suttles Range; 370 ac.; sur. 2 Apr 1680; 1707 poss. John Suttle; St. Clements
Hundred (RR p. 47) (TLC p. 45)
Beverly; 380 ac.; sur. 17 Nov 1674; 1707 poss. widow Jane Doyne; St.
Clements Hundred (RR p. 46) (TLC p. 44)

Suttle, John; inv.; 26 Jul 1680 (I&A 71.185); acct.; 7 Oct 1681; extx. Mary
Mattingly, wife of Thomas (I&A 7b.150)

Suttle, John; will; 19 Sep ___; 19 Nov 1751; son William & his sons William, John Baptist; daus. Eleoner, Mary Ann, Elizabeth Tippet and Mary Wathing [dec'd]; wife unnamed; tract *Suttle's Rest* (MCW 10.197) [SMW TA1.265]

SWALES

Swailes, Francis; inv.; 23 Jul 1698 (I&A 16.197) (I&A 20.24); acct.; 5 Aug 1700 (SMAA p. 105)

Swales, Thomas; inv.; 30 Jun 1717 (I&A 39a.30); acct.; 29 Nov 1718 (A 1.316) (SMAA p. 324)

Swale, William; Gent.; [Dr.]; will; 12 Aug 1728; 23 Sep 1728; sister Elizabeth Howson; wife Mary living in England (MCW 6. 78) [SMW PC1.319]; inv.; 24 Sep 1728; 8 Oct 1728 (I 13.200)

Sweales (Swals), Francis; inv.; 5 Feb 1728; 7 Apr 1729; nok John Attway, William Bullock (I 14.8); acct.; 3 Jun 1730 (A 10.306)

SWANN

Swann, Edw'd; *Hopewell*; 585 ac.; resur. 14 Nov 1669; 1707 no poss.; poss. Andrew Halton, Sam Swann; Choptico Hundred (RR p. 52) (TLC p. 50)

Swann, James; inv.; 19 Jun 1707; bro. Samuel Swann; sister Susannah Briscoe (I&A 27.145); acct.; 26 May 1708; [Capt.]; admx./extx. Judith Swann (I&A 28.217) (SMAA p. 169); acct.; 3 Apr 1710 (I&A 31.85) (SMAA p. 208)

Swann, Samuel; *Swanns Forrest*; 96 ac.; sur. 12 Apr 1727 (TLC p. 88)

Swann, James; *Swann's Adventure*;155½ ac.; originally named *Retirement*; resur. 10 Aug 1738 (TLC p. 95); 155 ac.; 12 Feb 1739 cert./pat. (COL)

Swann, James; inv.; 22 May 1746; 3 Jun 1746; nok John & James Swann; admx./extx. Mary Swann (I 33.42); acct.; 14 Nov 1747 (A 24.233)

Swann, Samuel; *Swann's Venture*; 140 ac.; 4 Dec 1754 cert./pat. (COL)

Swan, James; *Swan's Adventure*; 150 ac.; 29 Sep 1765 cert./pat. (COL)

Swan, Rebecca; inv.; 30 Nov 1771; 5 Apr 1774 (I 116.218); acct.; 20 Mar 1774 (A 69.377)

Swan, Henry; m. 29 Dec 1777 Ann Dyson (BRU p. 536)

SWEATMAN

Swotnam, William; service by 1675 (SK18.336)

Sweatnam (Sweatman), immigrated by 1677; wife Mary, son John (SK 15.425)

Sweetman (Sweatman), John; inv.; 3 Feb 1736; 9 Apr 1737 (I 22.21); acct.; 2 Apr 1739 (A 17.107)

SYKES

Sykes, Haning; extx. wife Ann; 10 Dec 1703 (SMAA p. 125)

Sykes, John; acct.; 20 Jul 1714; adms. Robert Hawkins & wife Anne (I&A 36b.43); acct.; 24 Jul 1714 (SMAA p. 268)

Sykes, Thomas; age ca 80; 9 May 1723 (CCR p. 56)

TALTON

Talton, Samuel; acct.; 25 Nov 1735 (A 14.203)

Talton, James; acct.; 7 Mar 1736; orphan Joshua Talton; adm. John Talton (A 15.298)

TANEY

Taney (Tanny, Tanney), John; gent.; will; 3 Aug 1720; 5 Nov 1720; wife Catherine; son John Michael Thomas Taney; dau. Margarett; d-i-l Catherine Willson; bro. Michael & his son Thomas; tract *Fenwick Mannor* (MCW 5.28) [SMW PC1.253]; inv.; 9 Jun 1720; 10 Feb 1720; nok Thomas Taney; extx. Katherine Taney (I 4.270); acct.; 13 Mar 1722; extx. Katherine, w/o Col. William Watts (A 4.159)

Taney, John Michael Thomas; will; 15 Jan 1754; 18 Mar 1754; child. John, Thomas, Michael, Mary, Margret, Elizabeth (MCW 11.18) [SMW TA1.317]; inv.; 25 Apr 1754; 24 Jun 1754; nok Philip Clarke, Jr., George McCal Clarke; adm./ex. John Taney (I 57.238); acct.; 12 May 1755; orphans John [at age], Michael [age 17], Mary [age 14], Elisabeth [age 7], Margaret [age 5] (A 37.163); dist.; 12 May 1755; child. John [of full age], Michael [age 18 nexrt Dec], Mary [age 15 next Dec], Eliza [age 8 next Sep], Margaret [age 5] (BB 1.131)

Taney, John and Eleanor; daus. Eleanor, b. 10 Mar 1756; Sarah, b. 26 Dec 1764 (SA p. 193)

Taney (Tany), Thomas; will; 1 Dec 1762; 1 Jun 1762; sons Michael Thomas, John Frances and Raphael Taney; dau. Mary Eleanor Combs; g-sons Charles Taney, Raphael Combs; mentions g-child. of Rachel and Mary Taney; [wife Mary]; tracts *Beaver Dam Manor, Cobneck* (MCW 12.133) [SMW TA1.428]; inv.; 21 Dec 1762; nok Thomas & Raphael Taney; exs. Mary & John Francis Taney (I 80.158); dist.; 30 Oct 1765 (BB 4.149)

Taney, Thomas, Jr.; inv.; 30 Oct 1765; nok Mary & T. Francis Taney; admn. Raphell Taney (I 87.315); acct.; 30 Oct 1765; Jr.; adm. Raphel Taney (A 54.6)

Taney, John; will; 22 Jan 1765; 12 Mar 1765; wife Ellen; 3 unnamed child.(MCW 13.73) [SMW TA1.469]; inv.; 26 Mar 1765; 13 Aug 1765; nok Bennet Combs, Benjamin Fenwick; extx. Ellen Taney (I 88.76); acct.; 5 Nov 1767; admx. Eleanor Medly, w/o Philip Medly (A 57.327); acct.; 29 Oct 1768; admx. Hellen, w/o Philip Medley (A 60.188)

Taney, Michael; m. 25 Jun 1771 Monica Brooke (MM)

Taney, John Francis; inv.; 16 Jul 1772; 28 Jul 1772; adm./ex. Elisabeth Taney (I 110.110)

TANNEHILL

Tannehill, William; age ca 49 in 1702 (MD p. 180)

Tannihill, William; inv.; [filed with 1709] (I&A 31.121)

Tunnihill, Sarah; acct.; 14 Feb 1711; adm. Robert Tunnihill (I&A 33a.155) (SMAA p. 224)

Tannyhill, Robert; *Black Creek* (moiety); 100 ac.; 20 Mar 1713 incl. in resur. of escheat of *Blake Creek* (TLC p. 69); sur. 2 Dec 1714 cert./pat. (COL)

Tannehill, John; s/o Robert, dec'd; *Blake Creek*; 240 ac.; escheat land; sur. 20 Dec 1717 for Robert Tannehill (TLC p. 93); 15 Sep 1737 cert./pat. (COL)

Tunhill (Turnhill), Robert; will; 15 Feb 1730/1; 25 Feb 1730; wife Elizabeth; child. John, William, 3 unnamed (MCW 6.184) [SMW PC1.356]; inv.; 8 Apr 1731; 18 May 1731; nok Ann Simmes, Ales Kegg; admx./extx. Elisabeth Tunhill (I 16.184); acct.; 19 Feb 1731; exs. Elisabeth & John Tunhill (A 11.335)

TANT

Taunt, John; service by 1672 (SK 17.612)

Tant, John; *Tants Mark*; 160 ac.; sur. 14 Dec 1683; 1707 poss. Widow Tant; New Town Hundred (RR p. 41) (TLC p. 40); *Taunt's Mark*; 160 ac.; 17 May 1684 cert./pat. (COL)
Taunton Dean; 40 ac.; sur. 14 Dec 1683; 1707 poss. Widow Tant; New Town Hundred (RR, p. 41) (TLC p. 40); 14 Dec 1683 cert./pat. (COL)

Taunt [Tant], John; will; 17 Oct 1702; 12 Nov 1702; sons James, Mark; daus. Mary, Ann, Jane, Elizabeth, Winifred, Margaret; wife Margaret tract *Dry Dockett* [*Dockill*] (MCW 2.251) [SMW PC1.130]; inv.; 9 Dec 1702; daus. Mary, Ann, Jane, Elisabeth, Winefred, Margarett; sons Mark, James (I&A 22.94)

Tant, James; Mr.; *Hills*; 100 ac.; 10 Sep 1716 cert./pat. (COL)

Tant [listed as Gant], James; Brittain's Bay; will; 10 May 1717; 4 Aug 1717; sons John, Mathew; daus. Anne, Elizabeth, Mary; wife Mary; tract *Drydocking* (MCW 4.123) [SMW PC1.216]; acct.; 5 Jun 1718; extx. Mary Tant (A 1.43); acct.; 11 May 1719; extx. Mary, w/o Robert Ford (A 1.443); acct.; 11 May 1719; mentions orphans John, Matthew, Ann and Mary Tant (SMAA p. 393)

Tant, James; inv.; 14 Oct 1717 (I&A 39a.30); acct.; 5 Jun 1718; extx. Mary (SMAA p. 333)

Tant, John; acct.; 1 Dec 1724; extx. Margarett or Mrs. Mary Tant (A 6.254)

Tant, Margarett; will; 24 Dec 1725; 1 Feb 1725/6; g-sons Marke Lampton, William and Henry Thompson, John Manning, Joseph and Vitus Harbert, Walter Pye; g-daus. Margaret Pye, Jean Thompson, Winefrid Harbert; s-i-l Richard Thompson (MCW 5.200) [SMW PC1.300]; inv.; 26 Apr 1726; 3 Aug 1726; nok. Winifred Harbert, A. Thompson; ex. Richard Thompson (I 11.497)

TARE

Tare (Tear), John; will; 4 Apr 1768; 6 Jun 1770; wife Mary; sons John, Ignatius, James (MCW 14.134) [SMW TA1.611]; inv.; 12 Sep 1770; nok William & John Aud; extx. Mary Tare (I 103.334)

Teare, Edward; inv.; 27 Oct 1771; 10 Jan 1772; nok William Tear, Ann
Mandley; admx. Elisabeth Teare (I 109.14)

TARLTON
Tarleton, James; acct.; 22 Jul 1703; admx. Cassandra Tarleton (widow) (I&A 24.9)
(SMAA p. 124)
Tarlton, Samuel; inv.; 16 May 1734; 27 May 1734 (I 18.130)
Tarlton, James; will; 19 Jan 1756; 20 Apr 1756; sons John, James, Jeremiah,
Stephen; wife & 3 daus. unnamed; tracts *Thompsons Hope, Tarlton's Good
Luck, Beverdam, Indian Bridge, Tarlton's Venture, Elizabeth* (MCW 11.128)
[SMW TA1.343]; acct.; 4 Apr 1757; exs. John Tarlton, Ann w/o Richard Forrest
(A 41.31); acct.; 16 Oct 1758; orphans John [of age], James [age 20], Stephen
[age 20], Susannah [age 12], Chloe [age 8], Jeremiah [age 5] (A 42.153)
Tarlton, William and Jane; son Jeremiah [b. 12 May 1761] (SA p. 6)
Tarlton, James and Mary Anne; son Igantius [b. 16 Jul 1762], Elijah [b. 20 Jan
1765], John [b. 23 Sep 1772] (SA p. 23, 40)
Tarlton, John; will; 4 Feb 1763; 14 Mar 1770; child. William, Thomas,
Casandria, Priscilla, John, James, Nancy, Jeremiah; wife Ann (MCW 14.134)
[SMW TA1.599]; inv.; 14 Mar 1770; 12 Sep 1770; nok Thomas & John Tarlton;
ex. Ann Tarlton (I 103.326)
Tarlton, William; inv. 15 Sep 1763; nok Margrey & John Tarlton; admx. Jane
Tarlton (I 81.238)
Tarlton, John; *Tarlton's Elizabeth*; 96 ac.; 22 May 1766 cert./pat. (COL)
Tarleton, Richard; m. 18 Jul 1772 Eliz. Tiford (MM)
Tarlton, John; will; 2 Apr 1772; 16 Jun 1772; son Frederick; dau. Elizabeth;
bros. James, Jeremiah; sisters Susannah, Ann; wife unnamed (MCW 14.238)
[SMW TA1.643]; inv.; 25 Jun 1772; 15 Sep 1772; nok Stephen & James Tarlton;
extx. Ann Tarlton (I 109.397); inv.; 18 Apr 1774 (I 118.227); acct.; 1 Jul 1774 (A
72.15); acct.; 3 Mar 1774; exs. Moses Fowler & wife Ann (A 70.16); dist.; 3 Mar
1774; sisters Susannah, Ann; bro. James; mentions Frederick, Elisabeth &
Jeremiah Tarlton (BB 6.330)
Tarlton, James; will; 30 Apr 1775; 15 Aug 1775; sons Ignatius, John; dau. Ann;
wife Mary Ann (MCW 16.111) [SMW TA1.713]; inv.; 8 Aug 1775; 6 Nov 1775;
nok Stephen & Jeremiah Tarlton; extx. Ann Tarlton (I 124.17)
Tarlton, Ignatius and Mary Adams (by publication); m. 9 Mar 1783 (SA p. 61)

TAYLOR
Taylor, Robert; servant; age ca 22; 6 Feb 1649 (AM X.11)
Taylor, Henry; service by 1667 (SK 11.108)
Taylor, Henry; *Kingston*; 50 ac.; sur. 7 Jun 1670; 1707 poss. John Wheatly &
John Fossey; New Town Hundred (RR p. 35) (TLC p. 34)

Hampton; 100 ac.; sur. 8 Oct 1672; 1707 poss. 50 ac. each John Fossey, John Wheatly; New Town Hundred (RR p. 36) (TLC p. 35)

Taylor, Robert; immigrated by 1673 (SK 17.575)

Tayloard, William; immigrated by 1680 (SK WC2.358)

Taylor, Rich'd; *St. Teretia*; 100 ac.; sur. 24 Jan 1682; 1707 poss. Vincent Taylor; St. Clements Hundred (RR); 24 Jan 1683 cert./pat. (COL)

Taylor, Francis; *Fortune*; 50 ac.; sur. 19 Oct 1684; 1707 poss. John Tant; New Town Hundred (RR p. 41) (TLC p. 40)

Taylor, Robert; inv.; 2 Sep 1696; 22 Sep 1696 (I&A 14.30)

Taylor, Henry, Sr.; will; 27 Mar 1698; 8 Mar 1700; son Henry, John, William, Thomas and James; dau. Grace Greenwell (MCW 2.214); inv.; 5 Jul 1701 (I&A 20.218)

Taylor, Walter; inv.; 16 May 1698 (I&A 16.194)

Tailor, Thomas; inv.; 24 Aug 1702 (I&A 1.676)

Taylor, Alice [Alce]; will; 19 Sep 1702; 3 Feb 1703; son Thomas Watts; dau. Elizabeth Watts; g-son Daniel Watts (MCW 3.2) [SMW PC1.139]; inv.; 22 Feb 1702 (I&A 23.7)

Taylor, Mary; inv.; 18 Feb 1708; nok none (I&A 29.329); acct.; admn. James Taylor; 27 Mar 1710 (SMAA p. 210) (I&A 31.39)

Taylorad (Tayler), William; Mr.; inv.; 14 May 1712 (I&A 33a.241); inv.; 2 Jun 1714 (I&A 36a.200)

Taylor, William; will; 1 Mar 1714; 5 Jun 1714; daus. Mary, Grace, Elizabeth, Ann; son Upgate [Upgett]; wife Ann (MCW 4.21) [SMW PC1.196]

Taylor, Thos.; will; 23 Jul 1717; 13 Nov 1717; son Ignacius; dau. Grace; wife Ann; bro. James Taylor (MCW 4.127) [SMW PC1.221]; inv.; nok John Jynson, James Taylor; [filed with 1717] (I&A 39a.27)

Taylor, Henry; New Town Hundred; will; 8 Nov 1718; 26 Nov 1718; sons John and James; daus. Rachel and Grace; s-i-l James Delicourt (MCW 4.188) [SMW PC1.240]; inv.; 24 Apr 1719; 14 Jun 1719 (I 2.96); acct.; 2 Jul 1720; [Sr.]; wife dec'd (A 3.95) (SMAA p. 413)

Tayler (Taylor), Thomas; acct.; 4 Feb 1719; extx. Ann Tayler (A 2.436) (SMAA p. 453)

Taylard [Taylord], Audry; will; 3 Aug 1721; 28 Aug 1721; son Richard Lewellin; g-child. John and Margaret Lewellin; mentions Ann w/o John Baker & mother of John Baker; Elinor w/o William Langley (MCW 5.66) [SMW PC1.262]; inv.; 23 Nov 1721; 1 Jan 1721 (I 6.220); acct.; 5 Mar 1723 (A 5.387)

Taylor, Anne; inv.; 30 May 1724; nok Richard Moy, Elisabeth Carter; adm. James Taylor (I 9.445); acct.; 19 Apr 1725; adm. James Taylor (A 6.310)

Taylor, Vinson (Vincent), inv.; 1 Apr 1729; 4 Jun 1729; nok Anne Taylor, Elias Barber; admx./extx. Julia Taylor (I 14.166); acct.; 2 Jun 1730; 3 orphans; admx. Juliana Taylor (A 10.338)

Taylor, Thomas; <u>inv.</u>; 20 Apr 1731; 12 Jul 1731; nok James & Margaret Taylor; adm./ex. Robert Taylor (I 16.211); <u>acct.</u>; 8 May 1732 (A 11.407)

Taylor, Joseph; blacksmith; <u>will</u>; 15 Feb 1732; 30 Apr 1732; wife Mary; child. William, Joseph, John, Anne; tract *The Lot* (MCW 7.15) [SMW TA1.3]; <u>inv.</u>; 18 Jun 1733; nok minors; admx./extx. Mary Taylor (I 17.166); <u>acct.</u>; 16 Sep 1734 (A 12.540); <u>acct</u>; 27 Mar 1738 (A 16.87)

Taylor, Robert; *Willingborough*; 70 ac.; escheat land; resur. 10 Sep 1723 (TLC p. 90); 10 Jun 1734 cert./pat. (COL)

Taylor, Robert; planter; <u>will</u>; 24 Sep 1736; 22 Nov 1736; wife Mary; dau. Frances; s-i-l John Grant; bro. James; tract *Willing Burrough* (MCW 7.200) [SMW TA1.50]; <u>inv.</u>; 7 Feb 1736; 21 Feb 1736; nok James & Mary Taylor; admx./extx. Mary Taylor (I 22.163); <u>acct.</u>; 27 Mar 1738 (A 16.86)

Taylor, Mary; <u>will</u>; 22 Jan 1739; 10 Mar 1739; daus. Francis & Mary w/o John Curlott; son John Grant [Graunt]; cous. Mary Taylor (MCW 8.78) [SMW TA1.94] [SMW TA1.94]; <u>inv.</u>; 20 Apr 1740; 12 Aug 1740; nok John Grant, Francis Taylor (I25.194); <u>acct.</u>; 22 May 1742 (A 19.35)

Taylor, John; <u>inv.</u>; 22 Sep 1741; nok John & James Taylor; admx./extx. Elisa Taylor (I 26.334)

Taylor, James; <u>will</u>; 27 Jan 1743/4; 20 Feb 1743; bros. John, Joseph; sister Elizabeth Pain, Mary Hudman [Hindman], Hannah (MCW 8.242) [SMW TA1.136]; <u>inv.</u>; 9 Apr 1744; 14 May 1744; nok John Tayler, Joseph Lawrence (I 29.135); <u>acct.</u>; 6 May 1745 (A 21.351)

Taylor, James, Mr.; <u>inv.</u>; 6 Aug 1755; 3 Mar 1756; nok Margaret Burkmore, James Taylor; admx./extx. Mary Taylor (I 60.371)

Taylor, Vincent, Mr.; <u>inv.</u>; 5 Mar 1758; nok Ann & Martistes Gresty; admx.extx. Margaret Taylor (I 65.148); <u>acct.</u>; 9 Mar 1758 (A 41.405)

Taylor, Ignatious; <u>will</u>; 4 Jan 1761; 7 Apr 1761; wife Ann; son Ignatius, Junifer; dau. Ann; tract *Governor's Gift* (MCW 12.37) [SMW TA1.410]; <u>inv.</u>; 4 Aug 1761; nok James & Owen Taylor; exs. Ann & Ignatius Taylor (I 77.70)

Taylor, Henry; *Taylor's Plains Addn.*; 106 ac.; 24 Aug 1761 cert./pat. (COL)

Taylor, Thomas; <u>will</u>; 13 Dec 1762; 15 Jan 1763; wife Mary; unnamed child.(MCW 12.175) [SMW TA1.433]; <u>inv.</u>; 19 Feb 1763; 7 Apr 1763; nok James & Elisabeth Taylor; admx./extx. Mary Taylor (I 80.153)

Taylor, Ignatius; *Governor's Gift Addn.*; 5 ac.; 12 Jan 1764 cert./pat. (COL)

Taylor, Ignatius and Elizabeth Spink; daus. Mary [b. 1 Oct 1764], Henrietta [b. 5 May 1768], Ann [b. 15 Dec 1770] (SA p. 1, 11, 22, 45, 55)

Taylor, John Bennet; <u>acct.</u>; 16 Jun 1770; 29 Oct 1771; wife Christian; son James; child. by present wife William, John, Joseph, Prudence; tract *Frogs Marsh* (MCW 14.188) [SMW TA1.618]; <u>inv.</u>; 20 Feb 1772; 24 Feb 1772; nok William & John Taylor (I 109.6); <u>acct.</u>; 26 Oct 1772; extx. Christian Taylor (A

67.141); <u>dist.</u>; 26 Oct 1771 (sic); mentions child. by "present widow"; extx. Mrs. Christian Taylor (BB 6.174)

Taylor, John; <u>inv.</u>; 26 Oct ___; 27 Oct 1772 (I 109.390); <u>inv.</u>; 26 Oct 1772; extx. Christian Taylor (I 110.246)

Taylor, Oliver; planter; <u>will</u>; 10 Mar 1776; 16 Nov 1776; sons John, Oliver; dau. Margiry Beaston (MCW 16.174)

Taylor, Ann; <u>will</u>; 31 Jan 1774; 2 Mar 1775; nephew Ignatius Biscoe; niece Ann Biscoe; bros. Ignatius, Jenifer; mother unnamed (MCW 16.93) [SMW TA1.738]

Taylor, Ignatius and Margaret Jordan; m. 13 May 1780 (SA p. 58)

Taylor, John and Elizabeth Tarlton (by license); m. 13 May 1783 (SA p. 61)

TEARING

Tearing, Robert; <u>inv.</u>; 9 Sep 1734; 5 Nov 1734; nok John & Sarah Miller; admx./extx. Mary Tearing (I 20.98); <u>acct.</u>; 13 Feb 1737; orphans George & Robert Terring; admx. Mary w/o William Quidly (Quedly) (A 16.37)

Tearing, George; <u>inv.</u>; 28 Apr 1750; 4 Sep 1750; admx./extx. Mary Tearin (I 43.387); <u>acct.</u>; 7 May 1751; orphan Susannah [age 3]; admx. Mary, w/o John Senor (A 30.92)

TENNISON

Tennison, John; <u>will</u>; 20 Dec 1682; 8 Feb 1682; sons John, Justinian, Absalom, Matthew; s-i-l William Cheshire [Chaishure] & his wife Mary (MCW 1.124-125) [SMW PC1.41]; <u>inv.</u>; 29 Mar 1683 (I&A 8.91)

Teneson (Tennison), Absalom; <u>inv.</u>; 26 Sep 1694 (I&A 13a.184); <u>acct.</u>; 26 Mar 1695; admx. Elisabeth, w/o Charles Watts (I&A 13a.251)

Tenneson, John; <u>acct.</u>; 8 Oct 1685; ex. Justinian Tennison (I&A 8.483)

Tennison, Absalom; *John's Fortune*; 61 ac.; sur. 11 Aug 1735 (TLC p. 92); 11 Oct 1736 cert./pat. (COL)
Gilbert's Folly; 36 ac.; sur. 1 Oct 1740 (TLC p. 98); 4 Nov 1742 cert./pat. (COL)
Enclosure; 62 ac.; sur. 27 May 1748 (TLC p. 113); 27 May 1748 cert./pat. (COL)

Tenneson, Abraham; <u>inv.</u>; 26 Jan 1737; 19 Jun 1938; nok Absolam & John Tenneson; admx./extx. Mary Tenneson (I 23.204)

Teneson, Abraham; <u>acct.</u>; 5 Feb 1738; orphans John, Absalom, Joseph, Joshua, Matthew, Ann & Susannah Tenison; admx. Mary Tennison (A 17.71)

Tenison, Samuel, Mr.; <u>inv.</u>; 7 Mar 1743; 5 Jun 1744; nok Ignatius & Matthew Tennison; admx./extx. Mary Tennison (I 29.219)

Tenneson, Samuel; <u>acct.</u>; 5 Jun 1745; orphans, Matthew, Absolom, Mary Molohorne, Elisabeth, Susanna; admx. Mary Tenneson (A 21.356)

Tennison, Absolom and Susanna; child. John [b. 10 Mar 1754], Jesse [b. 13 Oct 1765], Susanna [b. 10 Oct 1758], Eleanor [b. 10 Oct 1763], Ann [b. 26 May 1766], Margaret [b. 14 Sep 1768] (SA p. 4)

Tinnison [Tennison], John; will; 22 Oct 1759; 28 Jan 1760; bros. Absolom,
Joseph, Joshua; sisters Ann Millard, Mary; nephew John Tinnison; wife
Susanna; mentions John s/o Susana Perry (MCW 11.262) [SMW TA1.392]; inv.; 13
Feb 1760; 9 Jun 1760; nok Absalom Tenison, Mary Tinneson; admx./extx.
Susannah Tennison (I 69.115); acct.; 1 Sep 1761 (A 47.218); dist.; 1 Sep 1761 (BB
3.110)

Tennison, John; will; 4 Apr 1765; 27 Jun 1768; father Absolom, dec'd (MCW
14.52) [SMW TA1.513]; inv.; 23 Apr 1769; ex. Jesse Tennison (I 101.23, 333); acct.;
25 Oct 1769; mentions Joanna Tennison (A 62.165); dist.; 25 Oct 1769; father
Abraham (BB 5.228)

Tennison, Absolem (Absalom); will; written 15 Dec 1767; wife Joana; daus.
Ann, Christian White, Sarah Doxsey, Peabe Cowar (?) [Seabe Corsar]; sons
Jestinian, Thomas, John, Jesse, [son Abraham]; d-i-l Elizabeth Tennison; g-
son Absolem s/o John (MCW 14.36) [SMW TA1.510]; inv.; 1767; 25 Apr 1769; ex.
Jesse Tennison (I 101.64); inv.; 21 Sep 1768; 25 Apr 1769; nok Sarah Duxey,
Ann Tennison (I 100.92); inv.; 23 Apr 1769 (I 101.24); inv.; 16 Nov 1769 (I
101.332, 333); acct.; 16 Nov 1769 (A 62.167); dist.; 16 Nov 1769; dau. Christian,
Sarah Doxey, Sebo Corror, Thomas Tennison, dau. Ann, Elisabeth Tennison,
Absalom Tennison (BB 5.353)

Tenneson (Tennison), John; inv.; 21 Sep 1768; 25 Apr 1769; nok Sarah Doxey,
Ann Tennison; ex. John Tennison (I 98.354, 355)

Tennison, Joanna [Susanna]; will; 23 Feb 1769; 4 Apr 1769; dau. Sary Dorcy
[Doxey]; child. Jesse, Abraham and Ann Tennison, Christian White, Sabra
Corsar [Coxey]; mentions dau. Sary and son Thomas (MCW 14.92) [SMW
TA1.584]

Tennison, Elizabeth; will; 28 Sep 1771; 10 Dec 1771; dau. Eleanor Stephens;
son Absalom Tennison (MCW 14.188) [SMW TA1.614]

Tenneson, Thomas; inv.; 16 Feb 1773; adm. Jesse Tenneson (I 112.405); acct.; 19
Apr 1774; adm. Justinian Tennison (A 70.137)

Tennison, Absalom; will; probate 10 Jun 1775; dau Ann; wife Susanna; sons-i-l
George Mills, Jeremiah Edwards (MCW 16.90) [SMW TA1.731]

TETTERSHALL

Tettersall, William; *St. Lawrances*; 300 ac.; sur. 27 Oct 1665; 1707 poss. Henry
Jarbo in right of orphans of John Jarbo; TLC poss. James Tant, devisee of
Lawrance Tettersell; not found; New Town Hundred (RR p. 33) (TLC p. 32)

Tettershall, William; Brittain's Bay; will; 30 May 1670; 25 Jun 1670; wife Ann;
dau. Mary; eld. son Lawrence; bro. John Tettershall of Wiltshire, Eng.; tracts
St. John's, Tettershall's Gift in CH Co.; bro. Lt. Col. John Jarboe (MCW 1.54)

Fetershull (Tetershall), William; acct.; 12 Jun 1674; mentions accountant
Lawrence ____ & his unnamed son & dau. Mary Fetershull (I&A 1.19)

Tetershall, William; New Towne; <u>acct.</u>; 12 Jun 1674; relict and extx. Anne Neal; mentions son Lawrence, dau. Mary (SMAA p. 39)

Tettersell (Totersell, Tevershall), Lawrence; <u>will</u>; 10 Feb 1701; 16 Mar 1701; b-i-l James Taut (MCW 2.234); <u>inv.</u>; 28 Apr 1702 (I&A 21.268); <u>acct.</u>; 13 Mar 1703 (I&A 9b.19); <u>inv.</u>; [filed with 1704] (I&A 3.360)

THOMAS

Thomas, Thomas; *Batchellors Rest*; 500 ac.; sur. 21 Jun 1657; 1707 poss. Wm. Arthur, Edw'd Field; St. Clements Hundred (RR p. 44) (TLC p. 42)

Thomas, John; service by 1676 (SK 15.371)

Thomas, John; <u>inv.</u>; 26 Mar 1677 (I&A 4.10)

Thomas, Philip; immigrated by 1678; transported wife Mary; sons Nicholas, John; dau. Susan (SK 15.446)

Thomas, Ellis; service by 1679 (SK WC2.67)

Thomas, Robert; Poplar Hill; <u>will</u>; 18 Feb 1684; 26 Apr 1686; wife Abigail; child. Honnorfadare [Hannah Fadare], Robert, Herbert, Hannah (MCW 2.1) [SMW PC1.59]; <u>inv.</u>; 22 Feb 1686; son Henery; extx. Abigall, w/o Henry Lewis (I&A 9.217); <u>acct.</u>; 8 Jul 1686 (I&A 9.31) (SMAA p. 86); <u>acct.</u>; 27 Mar 1695 (I&A 13a.257)

Thomas, William; <u>will</u>; 2 Jan 1684; 26 Mar 1685; wife Eliza:; son Thomas; dau. Sarah; unborn child; sister Grace Brewer[mentions Mary Dorrill d/o wife by her 1st husband John Dorill]; tracts *Newinton, Bachelor's Rest* (MCW 1.146-7) [SMW PC1.57]; <u>acct.</u>; 23 Feb 1685 (I&A 9.14)

Thomas, William, Sr., Maj.; [b. ca 1714]; d. 15 Aug 1808; age 94 (HGM)

Thomas, William; <u>inv.</u>; 19 Feb 1715 (I&A 36c.213); <u>acct.</u>; 17 Jan 1717; admx. Catherine, w/o Owen Evans (I&A 39c.121) (SMAA p. 313)

Thomas, Robert; <u>will</u>; 29 Aug 1720; 20 May 1721; sons James, Luke, Henry; dau. Mary Cooke; wife Mary; tracts *Brown Wood House, Pennancy* [*Pennamy*] (MCW 5.55) [SMW PC1.263]; <u>inv.</u>; 23 May 1721; 18 Aug 1721; nok James, Herbert & Margaret Thomas; extx. Mary Thomas (I 6.43); <u>acct.</u>; 8 Jan 1721; extx. Mary, w/o John Milliman (A 4.54); <u>acct.</u>; 11 Jan 1723 (A 5.315)

Thomas, William; age ca 37; 27 Oct 1721; tract *Watt's Lodge* (CCR p. 46)

Thomas, William; <u>inv.</u>; 19 Aug 1730; 19 Oct 1730; nok John Wheratt, Alice Jenkins; admx./extx. Rebecca Thomas (I 16.10)

Thomas, Luke; *Luke's Hardship*; 7 ac.; sur. 13 Mar 1734 (TLC p. 93); 28 Nov 1737 cert./pat. (COL)

Thomas, Luke; <u>will</u>; 6 Feb 1739; 5 Mar 1739; child. Thomas, James, Robert, Mary and Luke; wife Winifred; tracts *Brown's Woodhouse, Luxus Hardships, Ponancey* (MCW 8.78) [SMW TA1.87]; <u>inv.</u>; 3 Mar 1739; 9 Aug 1740; nok Harkall Thomas; adms./exs. Mark Thomas & wife Winifred (I 25.188, 190)

Thomas, Thomas; <u>will</u>; 10 Feb 1740/1; 31 Mar 1741; daus. Elizabeth Biggs, Mary Madgalen Elliss; g-child. Sarah Biggs, Thomas Ellis; wife Elianor; [tract *Well Cloaid*] (MCW 8.129) [SMW TA1.130]; <u>inv.</u>; 12 Jun 1741; 6 Aug 1741; nok Elisa Biggs, Mary Ellis; admx./extx. Elener Thomas (I 26.329); <u>acct.</u>; 3 Mar 1742 (A 19.372)

Thomas, Harbert (Herbis); <u>inv.</u>; 15 Jul 1741; 4 Aug 1741; nok Mark & John Thomas; admx./extx. Ruth Thomas (I 26.328); <u>acct.</u>; 2 Mar 1742; orphans John, Mars. (A 19.371)

Thomas, Luke; <u>acct.</u>; 24 Aug 1741; exs. John & Benjamin Burroughes (A 18.379)

Thomas, Mark; *Mark's Adventure*; 36 ac.; sur. 13 May 1734 (TLC p. 99); 5 Aug 1742 cert./pat. (COL)

Thomas, Mark; <u>inv.</u>; 26 Nov 1745; 6 Mar 1745; nok Thomas Huland, John Thomas; admx./extx. Winefret Thomas age 32.85); <u>acct.</u>; 26 Jun 1747; orphans Mark, Winefred, Nancy (A 24.23)

Thomas, Robert; <u>inv.</u>; 25 Jun 1748; 26 Jul 1748; nok James Thomas, Prudence Tayler (I 36.113)

Thomas, John; <u>inv.</u>; 4 May 1750; 18 Mar 1750; nok Prudence Slatery, James Thomas (I 45.80)

Thomas, William; <u>inv.</u>; 9 Jun 1752; 24 Aug 1752; nok J. Thomas, Will Jones; admx./extx. Elisabeth Thomas (I 49.108); <u>acct.</u>; 22 Oct 175 (A 36.17); <u>acct.</u>; 4 Nov 1754; orphans Jonathon, William, Mary, John & Elisha [all of age], Elisabeth [age 13], Levin [age 11], Leah [age 6], William [age 3] (A 36.517); <u>dist.</u>; 4 Nov 1754; admx. Elizabeth; child.Johnathan, William, Mary, John & Elisha [of age], Elijah [age 13], Levin [age 11], Leah [age 8], Mary [age 6], William [age 3] (BB 1.123)

Thomas, Joseph; <u>dist.</u>; 19 Sep 1755; adm./ex. Dorcas Thomas (BB 2.2)

Thomas, Mary; child. Stanhope Rule [b. 24 Dec 1755] Sarah [b. 15 Jan 1765] (SA p. 6)

Thomas, James and Elizabeth; child. Robert [b. 25 Jul 1756], Jemima [b. 4 Mar 1761] (SA p. 14, 48, 49)

Thomas, John; <u>acct.</u>; 21 Sep 1758; orphans John, Herbert, William, Susannah (A 43.20); <u>dist.</u>; 21 Sep 1758; orphans John, Herbet, William, Susanna (BB 2.107)

Thomas, James; <u>will</u>; 1 Jan 1761; 7 Apr 1761; son Robert, dau. Jemima; b-i-l John Edwards; tracts *Prinamsey, Brown's Wood House, Luke's Hardship* (MCW 12.35) [SMW TA1.418]

Thomas, James; <u>inv.</u>; 16 Apr 1761; 14 Dec 1761; nok Luke Thomas (I 76.307)

Thomas, Jonathon; <u>inv.</u>; 20 Feb 1762; 26 Oct 1763; nok John & Elisha Thomas; admx. Alice, w/o Richard Taylor (I 82.204); <u>acct.</u>; 26 Oct 1763 (A 50.178)

Thomas, Abell and Sarah; child. Luke, b. 24 Nov 1763], Elizabeth [b. 2 Mar 1769] (SA p. 3, 5)

Thomas, John and Dorothy; child. Ann [b. 16 Dec 1764], John [b. 1 Nov 1766] (SA p. 7)

Thomas, John; St. Inegoes Hundred; will; 29 Mar 1768; 11 or 24 Apr 1770; sons Philip, John, William; dau. Ann Milburn, Sarah, Elizabeth, Mary; wife Sarah; s-i-l Stephen Milburn; tracts *The Cross, Elizabeth Manner* (MCW 14.133) [SMW TA1.601]; inv.; 1 Jun 1770; 17 Jul 1770; nok Moses White, Leavin Thomas; ex. Sarah Thomas (I 103.324); acct.; 17 Jul 1771 (A 66.176); dist.; 17 Jul 1771; legatees Phillip, William, Mary, Sarah and Elisabeth Thomas & Ann Milburne; exs. Sarah Thomas, Stephen Millburn (BB 6.91)

Thomas, James, Mr.; inv.; 23 Nov 1768; 19 Sep 1771; nok James Mils; admx. Katharine Wilson Thomas (I 106.385); acct.; 1 Jun 1772; mentions John Allen Thomas (A 66.273); dist.; 1 Jan 1772 (BB 6.108)

Thomas, Mark and wife Elizabeth; son Mark [b. 10 Apr 1769] (SA p. 1)

Thomas, Sarah; widow; will; 19 Apr 1774; 2 Aug 1774; sons William, Philip; daus. Sarah, Elizabeth; [son John] (MCW 16.19) [SMW TA1.686]; inv.; 1 Jun 1775; nok Ann Williams, John Biscoe; ex. Philip Thomas (I 121.411)

Thomas, Mark; acct.; 6 Nov 1775; Elisabeth, w/o Thomas Fenwick (A 73.244)

Thomas, William and Henrietta Biscoe; m. 14 Apr 1779 (SA p. 57)

Thomas, Tyler and Rachael Thomas; m. 9 May 1779 (SA p. 57)

Thomas, William and Anne Allen; m. 2 May 1780 (SA p. 58)

Thomas, Thomas and Jane Abell (by license); m. 27 Apr 1781 (SA p. 59)

Thomas, Thomas and Jane; child. Edward [b. 13 Mar 1782], Mary [b. 31 Mar 1784], James [b. 16 Oct 1786] (SA p. 31)

Thomas, William; acct.; unnamed child; 23 Feb 1785 (SMAA p. 81)

THOMPSON

Thompson, Wm.; unnamed; 500 ac.; sur. 27 Jun 1646; incl. in *Resurvey of Medley*; 1707 no. poss.; New Town Hundred (RR p. 27) (TLC p. 25)

Thompson, Wm.; *Indian Quarter*; 250 ac.; sur. 8 Jan 1648; 23 Mar 1680 incl. in *Resurvey of Hopton Park*; New Town Hundred (RR p. 28) (TLC p. 26)

Thomson, William; New Towne; will; 8 Jan 1649; 11 Jan 1649; wife Anne, extx. (MCW 1.4)

Thompson, William; *Thompsons Purchase*; 100 ac.; sur. 12 Jan 1657; 1707 poss. John Cole; New Town Hundred (RR p. 30) (TLC p. 29)
Koaxes; 200 ac.; sur. 28 Jun 1658; resur. into *Hopton Park*; claimed Rob't Brooks as s/o the d/o sd. Thompson; New Town Hundred (RR p. 31) (TLC p. 30)

Thompson, Ja.; *Parnassus*; 200 ac.; sur. 16 Jul 1664; entered for 75 ac.; poss. Resurrection Hundred (RR p. 59) (TLC p. 56, 62)

Thomson, Arthur; *Finchley*; 300 ac.; sur. 29 Nov 1670; 1707 poss. James Gray; belongs to Rich'd Hughes of VA; St. Clements Hundred (RR p. 45) (TLC p. 43)

Hounslow; 100 ac.; sur. 5 Sep 1673; 1707 poss. Wm. Farthing; New Town
Hundred (RR p. 36) (TLC p. 35)
Highgate; 150 ac.; sur. 5 May 1681; sold to Geor. Hall; 1707 no poss.; St.
Clements Hundred (RR p. 47) (TLC p. 46)
Tompson, Michael; immigrated by 1676 (SK 15.385)
Thompson, George; gent.; unnamed; 350 ac.; [19 Nov 1680] cert./pat. (COL)
Eyre; 328 ac.; sur. 30 Nov 1680; 1707 poss. George Thompson; St. Mary's
Hundred (RR p. 8) (TLC p. 9); 30 Nov 1680 cert./pat. (COL)
Square Adventure; 100 ac.; 10 Apr 1682 cert./pat. (COL)
Chelsey; 100 ac.; sur. 25 Apr 1685; 1707 poss. same Thompson; St. Mary's
Hundred (RR p. 11) (TLC p. 12); 25 Apr 1682 cert./pat. (COL)
Wellingborough; 70 ac.; sur. 2 May 1684; 1707 poss. Cecill Butler; St. Mary's
Hundred (RR p. 11) (TLC p. 12); 2 May 1684 cert./pat. (COL)
Farnham; 80 ac.; sur. 28 Feb 1684; 1707 poss. Geo. Thompson; St. Mary's
Hundred (RR p. 10) (TLC p. 11); 28 Feb 1685 cert./pat. (COL)
Trophy; 100 ac.; sur. 28 Feb 1684; 1707 poss. Tho. Batson; St. Mary's
Hundred (RR p. 11) (TLC p. 12); 28 Feb 1685 cert./pat. (COL)
Massom; 1,300 ac.; resur. undated; containing *Skretton, Hawks Nest &
Addition*; 1707 poss. same Thompson; St. Mary's Hundred (RR p. 10) (TLC p. 11)
Saturday's Work; 100 ac.; 20 Jul 1704 cert./pat. (COL)
Thompson, Arthur; *Highgate*; 150 ac.; 12 May 1681 cert./pat. (COL)
Hampstead; 200 ac.; sur. 26 Jan 1682; 1707 poss. John Bayly; TLC says 100
ac. each Oswald Thompson & Tho. Payne; resur. into *Baptists Hope*; New
Town Hundred (RR p. 40) (TLC p. 39); 26 Jan 1683 cert./pat. (COL)
St. Oswald (Osward) ; 200 ac.; sur. 7 May 1683; 1707 poss. John Bayly; New
Town Hundred (RR p. 39) (TLC p. 39); 7 May 1683 cert./pat. (COL)
Thompson, John; inv.; 27 Jun 1682 (I&A 7c.167)
Thompson, Michaell; acct.; 9 Aug 1686; admx. Anastatia, w/o Richard Newman
(I&A 9.148)
Thomson, John; inv.; 10 Sep 1694 (I&A 13a.259)
Thompson, Robert; *Hard Fortune*; 100 ac.; sur. 6 Jul 1695; 1707 poss. James
Thompson; New Town Hundred (RR p. 40) (TLC p. 39); 5 Oct 1695 cert./pat.
(COL);
Thompson, Robert; watchmaker; inv.; 1 Nov 1697 (I&A 15.215)
Tomson, Jesse; acct.; 5 Aug 1700 (I&A 20.53)
Tomoson, Justinian, Jr.; m. Elizabeth; she m/2 Giles Hill; 29 Nov 1700 (CCR p.
13)
Thompson, Arthur; St. Clement's Bay; will; written 15 Dec 1701; child.
Sebastian, John, Oswald, Mildred Shirtcliff [Thompson] and Tecia [Toda (?)]
Thompson; wife Susanna (MCW 2.247) [SMW PC1.125]; acct.; 21 Jun 1704; extx.
Susanna Thompson (I&A 3.431)

Thompson, George, Capt.; age ca 65 in 1702 (MD p. 184)

Thompson, Geo.; *Saturdays Work*; 100 ac.; sur. 8 Jan 1703; 1707 poss. same
Thompson; St. Mary's Hundred (RR p. 10) (TLC p. 11)

Thompson, Robert; inv.; 28 Feb 1703 (I&A 3.170); acct.; 27 Sep 1707; adm.
James Thompson (I&A 27.150) (SMAA p.142)

Thompson, Oswald; *Thompson's [Tomson] Addition*; 85 ac.; sur. 18 Dec 1707
(TLC p. 64); 10 Oct 1707 cert./pat. (COL)

Thompson, George; Capt.; gent.; inv.; 17 Mar 1712; 12 Oct 1713; nok Mr.
Tuberfeld (I&A 35a.13); acct.; 27 Nov 1714 (I&A 36b.73) (SMAA p. 262)

Thompson, George; *Doe Park*; 146 ac. sur. 3 Apr 1711 for Geo. Thomson and
Jno. Brown (TLC p. 67); 146 ac.; 2 Sep 1713; 50 ac.; 21 Jul 1720 cert./pat. (COL)

Thompson, William; Britain's Bay; will; 10 Feb 1716; 7 Mar 1716; son
Michael; wife Barbara; f-i-l William Langham; tract *Hatfield Hills* (MCW 4.72)
[SMW PC1.226]; acct.; 27 May 1718; admx. Barbery, w/o John Thompson (A
1.45) (SMAA p. 370); acct.; 2 Oct 1722 (A 4.242)

Thompson, James; will; 10 Feb 1720; 21 Apr 1721; sons John, James; daus.
Elizabeth, w/o John Griggs & Sarah (MCW 5.47) [SMW PC1.264]; inv.; 22 Jun
___; 25 Sep 1721; nok John Thompson, Elisabeth Griggs; ex. James
Thompson, Jr. (I 6.134); acct.; 27 Apr 1722; Sr. (A 4.156)

Thomson (Thompson), John; inv.; 22 Feb 1723; 10 Mar 1723; nok James
Thompson, Elisabeth Grigges; extx. Jane Thompson (I 9.325); acct.; 16 Nov
1725 (A 7.206); acct.; 1 Aug 1726; extx. Jane, w/o William Feilder (A 7.507)

Tomson (Thompson], John; planter; will; 9 Aug 1723; 26 Nov 1723; wife Jane;
2 unnamed sons; tract *Tomson's [Thompson's] Chance* (MCW 5.151) [SMW
PC1.274]

Thomson, Joseph George, Mr.; inv.; 4 Apr 1729; 18 Nov 1729; nok Margaret
Caugragh, William Caneough (I 15.276)

Tompson (Thompson), James; inv.; 14 Aug 1732; nok John & James Tomson (I
16.557); acct.; 22 Sep 1732 (A 11.480)

Thompson, Richard; planter; will; 24 Oct 1733; 6 Nov 1733; wife Susana (MCW
7.47) [SMW TA1.13]; inv. 3 Jul 1734; admx./extx. Susannah Thompson (I 18.339);
acct.; 1 Jul 1735; mentions John, orphan of John Manning (A 13.233)

Thompson, Jonathon; inv.; 3 May 1735; 4 Jun 1735 (I 20.469); acct.; 18 Aug 1739
(A 17.242)

Thompson, William; will; 10 Jan 1736/7; 20 June 1740; son Thomas & his son
Thomas; g-sons Henry, Joseph, Richard Mathias (s/o Mathias), Richard s/o
Thomas; kinsman William Compton; wife Ann; mentions Ann and Mary
Baker, daus. of John Baker (MCW 8.100) [SMW TA1.103]; inv.; 5 Sep 1740; 6 Oct
1740; nok Thomas Thompson, Elisabeth Angel (I 25.199); acct.; 13 Jan 1740 (A
18.110)

Thompson, James; *Small Hopes*; 96 ac.; resur. 5 May 1735 (TLC p. 94); 4 Jul 1737
cert./pat. (COL)

Small Hope with Addition; 278 ac.; resur. 3 Oct 1743 James Thompson, Jr.; 2 tracts *Newington & Small Hope* (TLC p. 109); *Small Hopes*; 278 ac.; 1 Jul 1746 cert./pat. (COL)

Thompson, Joseph George; acct.; 12 Jan 1740 (A 18.113)

Thompson, Peter; inv.; 13 May 1742; 30 Oct 1741; nok one minor; admx./extx. Ann Thompson (I 27.158); acct.; 11 Aug 1744; admx. Ann, w/o Paul Grugun (A 20.428)

Thompson, Sebastian; will; 18 Oct 1742; 3 Mar 1742; child. Arthur, John, Sebastian, Monica, Charity Wheeler, Appolina, Mary Brown; wife Charity (MCW 8.206) [SMW TA1.142]; inv.; 3 Mar 1742; 9 Jun 1743; nok Oswal & Sabastian Thompson; admx./extx. Charity Thompson (I 28.11)

Thomason (Thompson), Sebastian; *Thomas' Expense*; 208 ac.; sur. 2 Apr 1742; his part of *Yeilding Resurveyed* (TLC p. 98); 28 Oct 1742 cert./pat. (COL)

Thompson, Robert and Elizabeth; child. Susanna [b. 7 Jul 1747], Athanasius [b. 6 Sep 1749], Elisabeth [b. 9 Apr 1752], Mary [b. 10 Feb 1755], Eleanor [b. 7 Aug 1757], Charles James [b. 14 Jul 1760], Bennett [b. 3 Jun 1763], Mary [b. 22 Nov 1765], James [b. 13 Dec 1767] (SA p. 8, 36, 43)

Thompson, James and Ann; dau. Eleanor, b. 16 Oct 1748 (CSM)

Thompson, James; Jr.; will; 10 Aug 1749; codicil 14 Dec; 18 Sep 1750; son Raphel Francis, James Charles; dau. Mary Elinore; wife Ann; bro. Francis; unnamed father [living]; tracts *Addition to Fortune, Small Hope, Natfields [Hatfields] Hills, Ferns [Fancy] Hills, Whitaker, [Prattlewell]* (MCW 10.111) [SMW TA1.248]; inv.; 9 Oct 1750; 22 Jul 1751; nok Francis Thompson, Mary Roach; adm./ex. James Thompson (I 27.127); inv.; 17 Sep 1755; 3 Mar 1756; nok Francis Thompson, Mary Roach; admx./ext. Ann Thompson (I 60.371); acct.; 18 Jul 1757; orphans Raphael Francis [age 13], James Charles [age 10], Mary Elisabeth [age 8] (A 41.78); dist.; 18 Jul 1757; mentions Francis Thompson (BB 2.69)

Thompson, George; will; 5 Nov 1749; 6 Feb 1749; sons William, George; wife Grace (MCW 10.71) [SMW TA1.233]; inv.; 6 Feb 1749; 16 Jul 1750; nok James, Jr., George & Thomas Thompson; admx./extx. Grace Thompson (I 43.295); acct.; 20 May 1751; child. Thomas, John, George, Robert, James, Sabasten, Elisabeth w/o James Hayden, Mary, William [age 20] (A 30.181)

Thompson, James and Elizabeth; child. Johnson [b. 9 Dec 1761], Elizabeth [b. 14 May 1764], James [b. 6 May 1766] Janet [b. 5 Nov 1768], Mary [b. 11 Jun 1771], Elijah [b. 12 Feb 1774] (SA p. 2, 29)

Thompson, Francis (Frances); inv.; 6 Jun 1767; 22 Sep 1768; nok Cuthbert & Eleanor Thompson (I 98.110); acct.; 22 Sep 1768 (A 60.194); inv.; 1 Mar 1769; 20 Jun 1769; nok William & James Roach; admx. Anne Thompson (I 101.322); acct.; 30 Jun 1773; admx. Anne, w/o Nicholas Manger (A 68.199); dist.; 30 Jun 1773 (BB 6.227)

Thompson, Charles; b. 11 Sep 1746; d. 6 Apr 1795 Bristol, England; ?s/o James
Thompson and Anne Neale (JM p. 321)

Thompson, William; <u>acct.</u>; 28 Apr 1750; g-son Richard Mathews Thompson;
admx. w/o John Dossey (A 28.64)

Thompson, John Medley; <u>inv.</u>; 6 Jun 1750; 3 Jul 1750; nok Thomas & Robert
Thompson; admx./exs. John Bradburn & wife Elenor (I 43.290); <u>acct.</u>; 4 Aug
1752; mentions Mary Ann, orphan of John Bold (A 32.416)

Thompson, James; <u>acct.</u>; 9 Mar 1752; ex. James Thompson (A 32.108); <u>dist.</u>; 9
Mar 1752 (BB 1.29)

Thomson, John, Mr.; <u>inv.</u>; 27 Sep 1752; 5 Sep 1753; nok Charles King, William
Aisquith (I 52.89); <u>acct.</u>; 23 Jul 1753 (A 35.127)

Thompson, Mark and Margaret; child. John Gerard, b. 16 Apr 1753; Mary Ann,
b. 17 Feb 1757], Ignatius [b. 29 Oct 1761], Mary [b. 12 Aug 1767] (SA p. 9, 22,
38, 44)

Thompson, John; Mr.; <u>inv.</u>; 14 Jun 1754; 7 Aug 1754; nok John Thompson, Ann
Edwards; admx./extx. Margarett Thompson (I 57.334); <u>acct.</u>; 6 May 1755;
mentions James & James Thompson, Sr.; admx. Ruth Thompson (A 37.160);
<u>dist.</u>; 6 May 1755; admx. Margaret; child. James, Eliz'a & Susannah [of full
age], Margaret [age 14 next Oct], John Baptist [age 10 next Feb], Mary Ann
[age 5 next 15 Mar] (BB 1.131)

Thompson, James; <u>inv.</u>; 3 Sep 1754; nok ___ Thompson, Mary Sissell;
admx./extx. Ruth Thompson (I 57.331); <u>inv.</u>; Apr 1755; 6 May 1755; nok Mary
Chesell, Ignatius Thompson (I 60.214)

Thompson, Thomas and Ann; child. Mary [b. 27 Sep 1754], John Barton [b. 12
Jun 1757], Thomas Alexius [b. 3 Nov 1761], Eleanor [b. 26 Mar 1763],
Joseph Edward [b. 16 May 1766], Joseph & Zachariah [b. 7 Feb 1769], Mary
Ann [b. 1 Apr 1773] (SA p. 3, 9, 10, 24, 38, 44)

Thompson, James; <u>will</u>; 11 Mar 1755 [1752]; 16 May 1755; son Francis; g-son
Charles; d-i-l Ann, widow of James; tracts *Hard Fortune, Small Hope,
[Landing] Neck* (MCW 11.83) [SMW TA1.338]

Thompson, John and Rebecca; son Samuel [b. 28 Mar 1755] (SA p. 190)

Thompson, Robert and Ann; child. James [b. 14 Nov 1757], Mary Ann [b. 28
Feb 1760] (SA p. 10, 44)

Thompson, James; <u>inv.</u>; 23 Feb 1759; 7 Mar 1759; nok Thomas & Robert
Thompson; admx./extx. Grace Thompson (I 66.238); <u>acct.</u>; 3 Apr 1759;
mentions ex. James Thompson, dec'd; extx. Ann Thompson (A 43.151); <u>acct.</u>; 5
Sep 1759; admx. Grace Thompson (A 43.301)

Thompson, Grace; <u>will</u>; 6 Sep 1759; 8 Aug 1760; daus. Susannah and Elizabeth
Thompson; sons Mathew Herbert, Mathew Thompson (MCW 12.1) [SMW
TA1.393]; <u>inv.</u>; 30 Aug 1760; 15 Oct 1761; nok Mathew Herbert, William
Hayden (I 76.317, 318); <u>acct.</u>; 13 Sep 1763 (A 49.611)

Thompson, John; *Thompson's Lot*; 665 ac.; 29 Sep 1763 cert./pat. (COL)

Thompson, Raphael and Susanna; child. Joseph [b. 9 Dec 1764], Mary [b. 9 Mar 1767], James Aloisus [b. 27 Jan 1769], Charles [b. 1 Oct 177], William [b. 24 Sep 1774] (SA p. 25)

Thompson, Margaret; inv.; 21 Nov 1764; 15 Jan 1765; nok Vincent Inge, Ignatius Thompson; adm. John Medcalf (I 87.4)

Thompson, Robert; inv.; 27 Feb 1767; 5 Mar 1767; nok Joseph & William Thompson; admx. Ann Thompson (I 93.290); acct.; 24 Nov 1767; shoemaker; admx. Anne Payne, w/o Richard Payne (A 57.342)

Thompson, William and Susanna; son George Matthews [b. 11 Dec 1767] (SA p. 8, 42)

Thompson, Thomas; m. 25 Feb 1772 Henrietta Abel (MM)

Thompson, Raphael and Anastatia; son John Barton [b. 24 Apr 1773] (SA p. 24)

Thompson, John Baptist and Susanna; dau. Sarah [b. 18 Feb 1774] (SA p. 25)

Thompson, Wilford; m. 11 Oct 1774 Ann Shircliff (MM)

Thompson, John, Jr.; *Good Luck*; 19 ac.; 8 Oct 1782 cert./pat. (COL)

TIPPET

Tippitt, Philip; inv.; 13 Jun 1706 (I&A 25.344)

Tippett, Philip; age ca 35;30 Apr 1717; tract *Bashfode Mannor* (CCR p. 39)

Tippitt, Dennis; *Suttle's Range*; 273 ac.; sur. 20 Jun 1719 (TLC p. 79); 28 Oct 1726 cert./pat. (COL)

Tippett (Tipet), William; inv.; 12 Mar 1729; 22 Apr 1730; nok Dennes & Phillis Tippett; admx./extx. Temperance Tippett (I 15.422); acct.; 2 Mar 1730; 4 child.; admx. Temperance, w/o Andrew Mills (A 11.61)

Tippit, Philip; inv.; 18 May 1735; 6 Aug 1735; nok John & Dennis Tippit; admx./extx. Mary Tippitt (I 21.97); acct.; 29 Mar 1736; orphans Philip, John & Sarah Tipett; adms. John Fanning (Faney) & wife Mary (A 14.293)

Tippitt, John; *Tippitt's Purchase*; 46 ac.; sur. 5 Feb 1744 (TLC p. 112); 18 Mar 1747 cert./pat. (COL)

Tippett, John; inv.; 17 Feb 1748; 7 Mar 1748; nok Danas & Thomas Tippett; adms./exs. Mathew Gibson & wife Elisabeth (I 38.63); acct.; 9 Sep 1749; child. Mary [of age], Edward Maddox [age 2], John [g-son, age 2] (A 27.115); acct.; 7 Oct 1751 (A 31.97); dist.; 7 Oct 1751 (BB 1.6)

Tippitt (Tippett), Henry; inv.; 7 Oct 1767; 10 Nov 1767; nok Philip Tippett; adm. Jonathon Tippet (I 94.206)

Tippett (Tipet), Dennis; will; 13 Feb 1773; 15 Oct 1773; daus. Elizabeth Taylor, Sarah Cartwright; sons John, Notley, Joseph & his wife Eleanor & dau. Mary Magdalene, James, Dennis; mentions Butler Tippett (MCW 15.90) [SMW TA1.651]

Tippett (Tippet), Dennis; inv.; 21 Oct 1773; 14 Dec 1773; nok Butler & James
Tippet; adms./exs. Notley & Joseph Tippet (I 116.202); acct.; 2 Apr 1775 (A
72.154); dist.; 2 Apr 1775 (BB 7.33)

Tippett, Dennis; inv.; 20 Sep 1774; nok Notley Tippett, James Mills; admx.
Elisabeth Tippett (I 119.149); acct.; 20 Apr 1775 (A 72.152); dist.; 20 Apr 1775
(BB 7.27)

TOLLE

Tolly, Margarett; widow; admx. of husband Edward; son Edward; dau. Mary; 3
Feb 1675 (AM LXVI.134)

Towle, Roger; rights by 1680 (SK WC2.213)

Towle, Roger; *Towles [Toll's] Last Shift*; 100 ac.; sur. 1 Apr 1681; 1707 poss.
same Towle; 25 Aug 1743 from Roger Towle to Stephen Mackay; St. Mary's
Hundred (RR p. 9) (TLC p. 10); 1 Apr 1682 cert./pat. (COL)

Tole, Thomas; inv.; [filed with 1698] (I&A 16.194); acct.; 8 Mar 1698 (SMAA p.
100)

Tolle (Toll), Roger; planter; will; 8 Nov 1708; 22 Jan 1709; sons Thomas,
Tobias & his son Roger, John, Timothy; daus. Mary, Usly [Usley], Tamar
[Jamair], Elizabeth; [dau. Frances]; tracts *Last Shift, The Chancellor's Old
Orchard* (MCW 3.166) [SMW PC1.157]; inv.; 27 Jan 1709 (I&A 31.19); acct.; 11 Jun
1711; nok Thomas Seager (I&A 32c.29); acct.; 31 Jul 1712; legatees Thomas,
John, Mary & Usley Tolle; ex. Timothy Tolle (I&A 33b.137); acct.; 31 Jul 1712;
ex. Timothy; mentions legacy to Thomas, Tobias, John, Mary & Usley Tolle
(SMAA p. 224) (SMAA p. 226)

Tolle, Ursuly (Ursula); inv.; 17 Jun 1723; 18 Jun 1723; nok John & Ceyas Tolle,
Robert Taylor; adm./ex. Timothy Tolley (I 8.232); acct.; 21 Mar 1723 (A 5.391)

Tole, Tobias; inv.; 9 Jul 1729; 13 Jul 1729; nok John Tolle, Robert Taller;
admx./extx. Rebecca Tolle (I 15.98); acct.; 7 Dec 1730; admx. Rebecca, w/o
John Williams (A 10.629)

Towles, Sibill; inv.; 11 Jan 1730; 16 Nov 1731; nok Rebekah Johns, Mary
Sothoron (I 16.315)

Tolly (Tolley), Thomas, Mr.; inv.; 5 Sep 1735; nok minors; admx./extx. Mary
Tolly (I 21.208); acct.; 3 Mar 1736 (A 15.297)

Toule (Tole), Timothy; inv.; 29 Jul 1745; nok Ann Toule, Joseph Bennet;
adm./ex. George Tole (I 31.143); inv.; 4 Aug 1746; nok Sarah Toule, Joseph
Bennet (I 33.59); acct.; 18 Aug 1747; mentions Sarah Tole (A 24.176)

Tole, John; inv.; 4 Jan 1746; 8 Apr 1746; nok Ann Tole, John Morris; adm.ex.
Roger Tole (I 34.214)

TOMPKINS

Tompkins, John; m. 21 Jan 1768 Mary Brewer (MM)

Tomkins, John and Mary; daus. Mary Attaway [b. 17 Sep 1771], Aletha [b. 31 May 1775] (SA p. 22, 26)

TONGE
Tonge, John; St. Clement's Manor; will; 16 Aug 1686; 1 Sep 1688; mentions Penelope [Thomuson], d/o Francis Hayden; tract *Bodell [Bedell]* (MCW 2.31) [SMW PC1.75]
Tong, John; inv.; 25 Sep 1688 (I&A 10.131)
Tongue, ___; unnamed; 200 ac.; sur. 1 Mar 1652; in *Fenwick Mannor*; Resurrection Hundred (RR)

TRACY
Tracy, Timothy; service by 1673 (SK 17.595)
Treacy, Thomas; inv.; 8 Feb 1697 (I&A 15.317)

TRUMAN
Trueman (Truman), Thomas; *Trent Neck*; 600 ac.; sur. 25 May 1657; 1707 poss. Tho. Truman Greenfield; resur. 10 Jul 1705; Resurrection Hundred (RR p. 58) (TLC p. 55)
Prevention; 50 ac.; sur. 22 Mar 1663; 1700 poss. John Green; not found; Resurrection Hundred (RR p. 58) (TLC p. 57)
Indian Creek with Addition; 750 ac.; sur. 10 Jun 1664; in 1704 not in 1707; Resurrection Hundred (TLC p. 57)
Refuse; 140 ac.; sur. 20 Dec 1665; 1707 poss. Tho. Trueman Greenfield; Resurrection Hundred (RR p. 60) (TLC p. 57)
Forkes; 60 ac.; sur. 20 Dec 1665; 1707 poss. Wm. Brample; Resurrection Hundred (RR p. 60) (TLC p. 60)
Punk Neck; 100 ac.; sur. 20 Sep 1666; 1707 poss. Geo. Akeeth; Resurrection Hundred (RR p. 60) (TLC p. 57)
Trumans Lott or *Charles Lot*; 40 ac.; sur. 5 Mar 1670; 1707 poss. John Southorn; Resurrection Hundred (RR p. 63) (TLC p. 58)
Cannough Neck; 100 ac.; sur. 3 May 1670; 1707 poss. Peter Harris; Resurrection Hundred (RR p. 60) (TLC p. 58)
Trumans Lot; 40 ac.; sur. 5 May 1670; in 1704 not in 1707; poss. Tho. Truman Greenfield; Resurrection Hundred (TLC p. 58)
Back Land; 185 ac.; sur. 14 Jun 1675; 1707 Tho. Trueman Greenfield; Resurrection Hundred (RR p. 61) (TLC p. 58)
Long Looked for Come at Last; 225 ac.; sur 1 Aug 1679; 1707 poss. Julian Whitter & Cha. Smith; Resurrection Hundred (RR p. 62) (TLC p. 59)
Snenton; 100 ac.; sur. 10 Aug 1679; 1707 poss. Thos. Trueman Greenfield; in *Resurvey of Trent Neck*; Resurrection Hundred (RR p. 62) (TLC p. 59)

Skigby; 165 ac.; sur. 20 Sep 1679; 19 Dec 1713 mentions Charles Green & wife Elizabeth; 10 Oct 1714 resur. into *Indian Creek*; Resurrection Hundred (RR p. 61) (TLC p. 61)

The Wedge; 75 ac.; sur. 19 Aug 1679; 1707 poss. Thos. Trueman Greenfield; 10 Jul 1705 resur. into *Trent Neck*; Resurrection Hundred (RR p. 62) (TLC p. 60)

Inclosure; 110 ac.; sur. 19 Sep 1679; 1707 poss. Thos. Trueman Greenfield; 10 Jul 1705 into *Trent Neck*; Resurrection Hundred (RR p. 62) (TLC p. 60)

Truman, Nathaniel; *Trueman's Hunting Quarter*; 200 ac.; sur. 5 May 1670; 1707 poss. John Davie; Resurrection Hundred (RR p. 60) (TLC p. 58)

Trumans Chance; 95 ac.; sur. 28 Apr 1676; poss. Tho. Trueman Greenfield; resur. into *Indian Creek with Addition;* Resurrection Hundred (TLC p. 59)

Trumans Hope; 127 ac.; sur. 29 Apr 1676; poss. Thos. Truman Greenfield; 10 Jul 1705 resur. into *Indian Creek*; Resurrection Hundred (TLC p. 60)

Trumans Lodge; 200 ac.; sur. Apr 1676; 1707 poss. Sarah Hulse; Resurrection Hundred (RR p. 62) (TLC p. 59)

Truman, Nathaniel; d. 4 Mar 1678 (HGM)

Truman, Thomas, Esq.; d. 6 Dec 1685; age 60 (HGM)

Truman, Mary; w/o Thomas; d. 6 Jul 1686; age 52 (HGM)

TURBEVILLE

Tuberville, Gilbert; immigrated by 1675 and assigns rights (SK 18.130)

Turbevile, George; gent.; age ca 45-46 in 1693 (MD p. 188)

Turbaville (Turberville) [Turbovile], Pain (Paine); will; 4 May 1698; 10 Jan 1711; wife Ann, widow of Robert Taylor; mentions sisters Mary and Bona (MCW 3.223) [SMW PC1.180]; inv.; 20 Feb 1711; nok Gilbert Turbervile (I&A 33a.233); acct.; 31 Jul 1713; extx. Ann w/o George Mason (I&A 35b.62) (SMAA p. 250)

Turbervile (Terbevile, Turbifield), Gilbert; will; 1 Dec 1718; 15 Jun 1719; g-child. Margaret and William Cavinaugh (MCW 4.205); inv.; 16 Jun 1719; 29 Aug 1719 (I 2.199); acct.; 20 Sep 1720 (A 3.225) (SMAA p. 443); acct.; 15 Mar 1721 (A 4.168); acct.; 16 Sep 1724 (A 6.132)

TURNER

Turner, Thomas; *St. Dorothye's*; 300 ac.; sur. 14 Sep 1661; 1707 poss. for Turner's orphans; 1707 poss. for Turner's orphans; New Town Hundred (RR p. 32) (TLC p. 31)

St. Winifred's; 2 Oct 1662; 21 Jan 1662; wife Emma and "our" 3 child. Thomas and Mary Turner and Eliza Johnson; kinsman Wm. Bretton (MCW 1.23)

Turner, Emma; *St. Thomases*; 550 ac.; sur. 9 Jul 1663; 1707 poss. for Turner's orphans; New Town Hundred (RR p. 32) (TLC p. 31)

Little St. Thomas; 200 ac.; sur. 23 Jul 1664; pat. 10 Oct 1668 for Wm. Rosewell; 1707 poss. for Turner's orphan; Choptico Hundred (RR p. 50) (TLC p. 48)

St. Barbaras; 500 ac.; sur. 26 Jul 1663; 1707 poss. Nicho. Poore; St. Clements Hundred (RR p. 44) (TLC p. 42)

Turner, Edward; will; 28 Dec 1693; 27 Jul 1709; sons Thomas, Samuel; dau. Elizabeth; her mother Elizabeth; wife Mary; g-daus. Mary and Eliza. Sly, daus. of Clement Sly [g-daus. Elizabeth and Mary Hely, daus. of Clement Hely]; mentions 2 former wives; (MCW 3.148) [SMW PC1.80]; inv.; 3 Aug 1709; 5 Aug 1709 (I&A 30.5); acct.; 25 Aug 1710; widow m. George Whitter; ex. Samuel Turner (I&A 31.335)

Turner, Thomas; will; 31 Oct 1696; 15 Feb 1696; sons Thomas, Joshua; dau. Monica; wife Eliza.; tracts *St. Thomas's, Audley End, St. Dorothy's* (MCW 2.123)

Turner, Edward; ex. Samuel; widow unnamed; 21 Aug 1710 (SMAA p. 210)

Turner, Joshua; inv.; 4 May 1718 (I 2.157); acct.; admn. Thomas Turner of CH Co.; 2 Nov 1720 (SMAA p. 427)

Turner, Joseph [Joshua?–Ed.]; acct.; adm. Thomas Turner of CH Co.; (A 3.234)

Turner, Thomas; of CH Co.; unnamed; 19 ac.; [1719]; sur. 8 Jan 1717; same land as *Small Addition* (TLC p.)

Turner, Edward; planter; will; 14 Jan 1772; 1 May 1773; sons Samuel, William, Randolph, Charles, Joshua, Joseph; daus. Betsey, Sally, Nelly, 3 others unnamed; sister Myshall; wife unnamed; tracts *Watsons Choice, Hingston, Partner's Purchase, Turners Forrest, Saint Vincent* (MCW 15.69) [SMW TA1.668]

TWISDEN

Twisdon, Levina; age ca 71; came to MD ca 1677; 8 Oct 1721 (CCR p. 50)

Twisden (Twisdell), William; will; 14 Jul 1705; 31 Jan 1709; Owen Smithson [?g-son]; tract *Hills* (MCW 3.164) [SMW PC1.136]; inv.; 29 Apr 1710 (I&A 31.119); acct.; 11 Jul 1712; ex. Levina Twisden (I&A 33b. 136)

Twisden (Twesden), William; Levina Twisden one of the accoutants; 11 Jul 1712 (SMAA p. 230)

UNDERWOOD

Underwood, Anthony; age ca 25 in 1684 (MD p. 189)

Underwood, Anthony; *Underwoods Choyce*; 200 ac.; sur. 28 Apr 1684; 1707 poss. John Brisco in right of his wife, d/o Thos. Jackson; St. Mary's Hundred (RR p. 11) (TLC p. 12)

St. Peter's; 10 ac.; 8 Mar 1687 cert./pat. (COL)

Underwood, Anthony; inv.; 23 Aug 1692 (I&A 10lc.1)

Underwood, Thomas, Sr.; will; 31 Oct 1747; 30 Jul 1753; wife Mary; son
Anthoney; tract *Ellmore* (MCW 10.278) [SMW TA1.302]; acct.; 14 Aug 1753; 30
Oct 1753; nok Anthony & Thomas Underwood; admx./extx. Mary
Underwood (I 57.42); acct.; 16 Sep 1754 (A 36.413); dist.; 16 Sep 1754 (BB 1.115)
Underwood, Mary; inv.; Mar 1758; 14 Aug 1758; nok William Sissel, Charles
Walwood (I 64.432); inv.; 3 Apr 1758; nok Charles Attwood, William Chessel (I
65.140); acct.; 1 Jan 1759 (A 43.26); acct.; 4 Sep 1759 (A 43.259); dist.; 8 Jan 1759
(BB 2.107)

URQUHART
Urquhart, Peter; *Poverty Hills*; 83 ac.; 27 Mar 1762 cert./pat. (COL)
Urquhart, John, Rev.; papers relating to will; 9 Jul 1764; mentions Urquhart
relatives in Scotland [SMW TA1.539-536]
Urquhart, John, Rev. Mr.; inv.; 16 Nov 1765; 22 Nov 1770; nok Peter Urquhart;
adm. Alexander Urquhart (I 104.156)
Urquhart, John, Rev.; inv.; 2 May 1771; admx. Ann Urquhart (I 108.11)

VANSWERINGEN
Vansweringen, Garrt.; *Vansweringen's Point*; 50 ac.; sur. 18 Aug 1667; 1707
poss. Wm. Goldsmith; St. Mary's Hundred (RR)
Vansweringen, Garrett; ante nuptial settlement on Mary Smith, spinster, 5 Oct
1676 (SK 19.381)
Vansweringen, Garret, gent.; age 48 in 1684; age 57 in 1693 (MD p. 190)
Vansweringen, Garrett; City of St. Mary's; will; 25 Oct 1698; 4 Feb 1698; sons
Joseph, Charles; mentions present wife; tracts *Council Rooms, Coffee House*
(MCW 2.167) [SMW PC1.111]; inv.; 19 Aug 1699; 11 Jan 1700 (I&A 20.94); acct.; 2
May 1702; adms./exs. Joseph and Mary Vansweringen (I&A 21.346)
Vanswearingen, Mary; *Charles Bounty*; 1,000 ac.; 1706 cert./pat. (COL)
Vanswearingen, Mary; widow; age 48; 12 Feb 1708/9 (CCR p. 16)
Vanswearingen, Zachariah; will; 13 Mar 1711; 22 Apr 1712; son Joseph; daus.
Ellinor, Jane; wife Martha; tracts *Lucases, The Oldfield* [SMW PC1.183]; inv.; 20
May 1712 (I&A 33b.16, 209)
Vansweringen, Martha; widow of Zachariah Vansweringen; will; 18 Jan 1712;
26 Jan 1712; dau. Jane (MCW 3.236) [SMW PC1.188]; inv.; 27 Jan 1712; nok Mary
Kirk (I&A 33b.219); acct.; 23 Oct 1714 (I&A 36a.181) (SMAA p. 349)
Vansweringen, Mary; widow; will; 17 Feb 1712/3; 6 Sep 1713; daus. ____
Bladen, Elinor Carroll, Dorithy, Tereshea; s-i-l William Bladen; son Joseph
[Joshua]; tract *The Point* (MCW 3.246) [SMW PC1.190]; inv.; 10 Apr 1714 (I&A
35a.131)
Vansweringen, Joseph; age ca 35; 29 Aug 1717 (CCR p. 39)
Van Sweringen, Mary; widow; age ca 39; 1-8 May 1721 (CCR p. 51)

Vanswearingen, Joseph, Mr.; <u>inv.</u>; 26 Sep 1721; admx. Mary Vanswearingen (I 6.133); <u>acct.</u>; 11 Oct 1722 (A 4.244); <u>acct.</u>; 13 Jun 1723; admx. Mary, w/o William Deacon (A 5.142) ; <u>acct.</u>; 4 Nov 1736 (A 15.228); <u>acct.</u>; 19 Oct 1738 (A 16.324)

Vansweringen, Mary; <u>acct.</u>; 11 Oct 1721; admx. Mrs. Mary Vansweringen, widow & extx. of Joseph Vansweringen who was ex. of dec'd (A 4.22)

Vansweringen, Dorothy, Mrs.; <u>inv.</u>; 10 Mar 1728; nok Stephen Higgins, Benjamin Tasker (I 13.435)

Vansweringen, Joseph; <u>inv.</u>; 4 May 1737; 18 Jul 1737; nok Elinor Pearce, Marake Rodes; admx./extx. Martha Vansweringen (I 22.323); <u>acct.</u>; 6 Oct 1739; orphans Thomas, Joseph & Jane Vansweringen; admx. Martha, w/o James Chissam (A 17.301)

Vanswearinggen, Garret; <u>inv.</u>; 1 Oct 1752; nok James Vanswearinggen, Elenor Pierce; adm./ex. Thomas Vansearinggen (I 51.71); <u>acct.</u>; 3 Sep 1753; admn. Thomas Vanswearingen (A 35.111); <u>dist.</u>; 3 Sep 1753; nephews Thomas & Joseph Vansweringer [of full age]; niece Jane Vansweringer (BB 1.88)

Vanswearingtin, Joseph; <u>acct.</u>; 28 Jun 1755mentions bro. Ger. Vanswearingin; Mary Neals & Susan Craycroft, daus. of Sarah Sly; Thomas Vanswearingen; admx. Mary, w/o William Deacon, Esq. (A 38.20)

VAUGHAN

Vaughan, Ruth; service by 1675; wife of Thomas (SK 15.344, 395)

Vaughan, Thomas; <u>inv.</u>; [filed with 1681] (I&A 7b.184); <u>acct.</u>; 15 Sep 1682; admx. Ruth Martindale (relict) (I&A 7c328)

Vaughon (Vaughen), Thomas; <u>acct.</u>; 7 Aug 1719 (A 2.221) (SMAA p. 385)

VADERY

Vadry (Vadery), Philemon; <u>inv.</u>; 6 Dec 1739; 6 Feb 1739; nok George Vadry, William Bond (I 24.531, 532); <u>acct.</u>; 7 Aug 1745 (A 21.443)

Vawdry, George; <u>inv.</u>; 15 Mar 1749; 1 May 1750; nok Sarah & Jane Vawdray (I 42.200); <u>acct.</u>; 12 Feb 1750; orphans Sarah [age 14], Jane [age 10]; adm. Lydia Vawdry (A 29.203)

Vandrie, George, Mr.; <u>inv.</u>; 15 Aug 1772; 25 Aug ___ (I 109.354)

VOWLES

Vowles, (Voules), Richard; *Vowles' Purchase*; 610 ac.; resur. 22 May 1714; formerly 4 tracts: *Red Bud Thickett, Bennetts Purchase, Thompsons Purchase & Manly* (TLC p. 71); 10 Apr 1715 cert./pat. (COL)

Vowles' Addition; 80 ac.; sur. 3 Aug 1720 (TLC p. 81); 25 Jul 1723 cert./pat. (COL)

Vowles' Purchase; 622 ac.; resur. 20 Dec 1720 (TLC p. 81); 25 Jul 1723 cert./pat. (COL)

Vowles, James, Mr.; inv.; 22 Mar 1724; 3 Jul 1725; nok Margaret Bullock for 2
sons of John Bullock; adm. John Vowles (I 10.418); acct.; 7 Jul 1726 (A 7.408);
acct.; 16 Dec 1729 (A 10.179)

Vowles, Richard; will; 4 Apr 1724; 22 Apr 1724; sons Richard, James,
Matthew, John; dau. Mary w/o John Chunn, Jr.; wife Mary; tracts *Rocky
Point, The Fox, Vowles' Purchase, Vowles' Addition, Hattfield's Hills* (MCW
5.165) [SMW PC1.279]; inv.; 4 May 1724; 4 Aug 1724; Sr.; nok Mary & John
Vowles; exs. Richard & James Vowles (I 10.15); acct.; 2 Jun 1725; legatees
James, John & Matthew Vowles; relict Mary; ex. Richard Vowles (A 6.432)

Vowles, Richard; acct.; 8 Aug 1726; legatees Mary, Mathew & John Vowles;
ex. Richard Vowles (A 7.513)

Vowles, John, Mr.; inv.; 6 Mar 1733; 7 Aug 1734; nok Margaret Griffin,
Richard Vowles; admx./extx. Elisabeth Vowles (I 19.52); acct.; 5 Jul 1736
orphans Richard, Mary (?Margaret), Elisabeth, Mary, Ann & Elenor Vowles
(A 15.86)

Vowles, Matthew; inv.; 16 Jun 1734; 19 Sep 1734; nok Richard Vowles, Mary
Chunn; admx./extx. Ann Vowles (I 19.138); acct.; 2 Dec 1746; orphan Cyrus;
admx. Ann, w/o Peter Mugg (A 23.128)

Vowles, Richard, Mr.; inv.; 22 Apr ___; 15 Jun 1736; nok Margret Griffin,
Margret Vowles; admx./extx. Ann Vowles (I 21.511); acct.; 5 Jul 1737; orphans
Thomas, Richard, James, Matthew, Garrat & Rebecca Vowles (A 14.299)

Vowles, Thomas and Susanna Chunn; m. 27 Dec 1747 (SA p. 57)

Vowles, Thomas and Susanna; child [b. 25 Mar 1749]; Henry [b. 25 Sep 1752];
Ann [b. 10 Oct 1754] (SA p. 36)

Vowles, Richard; inv.; 19 May 1750; 4 Sep 1750; nok Margaret Cissell, Thomas
Vowles; admx./extx. Mary Vowles (I 43.491); acct.; 6 Aug 1751; admx. Mary,
w/o James Taylor (A 31.55)

Vowles, Cyrus and Victoria; child. Jane [b. 25 Dec 1754] (SA p. 36); John [b. 1
Feb 1758]; Matthew [b. 27 May 1762]; Ann [b. 11 Feb 1765] (SA p. 41);
Thomas [b. 26 Jan 1767] (SA p. 42); Sarah [b. 3 Feb 1770] (SA p. 191); Mary [b.
20 Nov 1772] (SA p. 23); Elizabeth [b. 9 Jun 1777] (SA p. 29)

Vowels, Jac.; m. 19 Sep 1771 Priscilla Payn (MM)

Vowles, d/o James and Priscilla his wife; child. Susanna [b. 7 Jun 1772] (SA p.
21); Richard [b. 6 Mar 1774] (SA p. 25)

Vowles, Matthew and Ann his wife; son Henry [b. 6 Jun 1787] (SA p. 31)

WALKER

Walker, John; *Waughops Walker*; 100 ac.; sur. 23 Apr 1661; 1707 poss.
Marshall Low; Poplar Hill Hundred (RR p. 23) (TLC p. 18)

Waker (Walker), George; St. Jerome's; will; _ Jul 1674; 10 Mar 1675; mentions Isaac, s/o Jane Paine, widow (MCW 1.87) [SMW PC1.12]; inv.; [filed with 1675] (I&A 1.339); inv.; 19 Nov 1675 (I&A 1.467)

Walker, Rich'd; *Berry*; 65 ac.; sur. 4 Nov 1682; 1707 poss. Wm. & Rich'd Walkers; New Town Hundred (RR p. 39) (TLC p. 38); 4 Nov 1682 cert./pat. (COL)

Walker, Richard; will; 11 May 1698; 6 Jun 1698; sons Thomas, Richard, William; wife Ann; tract *Walker's Hollow, Berry, Walker's Delight* (MCW 2.139) [SMW PC1.82]; inv.; 20 Jul 1698 (I&A 16.193)

Walker, William; inv.; 20 Mar 1714; nok bros. Thomas and Richard (I&A 361a.103)

Walker, Richard; planter; will; 10 Oct 1717; 7 Nov 1717; son James; dau. Mary; nephews Thomas, s/o Thomas Walker, & Richard Walker; wife Ann; tract *Berry* (MCW 4.173) [SMW PC1.223]; inv.; 7 Nov 1717; 11 Jan 1717; nok Thomas Walker, Martin Yates (I&A 39c.186); acct.; 19 Nov 1718; extx. relict Ann, w/o Peter Peak (A 1.326) (SMAA p. 343); acct.; 7 Aug 1719 (A 2.188) (SMAA p. 394)

Walker, Thomas; will; 10 Jun 1727; 2 Aug 1727; sons Thomas, Joseph; dau. Susanna; dau. Heneretter Clark, w/o James Clark; wife Mary (MCW 6.37) [SMW PC1.324]; inv.; 7 Aug 1727; 7 Nov 1727; nok Henri Clark; extx. Mary Walker (I 12.404); acct.; 24 Nov 1729; extx. Mary, w/o Edward Welsh (A 10.106); acct.; 31 Aug 1731; child. James Clarke and Thomas, Joseph & Susanna Walker (A 11.228)

Walker, William, Mr.; inv.; 18 Mar 1736; nok John & James Winkinson; adm./ex. John Walker (I 22.204); acct.; 2 Mar 1740; orphans William, Eleanor, Dorcus (A 18.166)

Walker, Thomas; inv.; 1 Dec 1750; 1 Jan 1750; nok Robert & John Hendly; adm./ex. Joseph Walker (I 44.238); acct.; 13 May 1751; orphan Joseph [age 10] (A 30.93)

Walker, James; inv.; 20 Sep 1752; 8 Nov 1752; nok Edward & Electinos Knott; admx./extx. Monica Walker (I 51.59); acct.; 4 Dec 1754; orphans Ann [age 7], James [age 3] (A 36.519); dist.; 4 Dec 1754; admx. Monica; child. Ann [age 7], James [age 4 next 20 Apr] (BB 1.123)

Walker, Joseph; inv.; 10 Nov 1752; 8 Mar 1753; nok Joseph Clark, Clement Stratford; admx./extx Monica Walker (I 53.36); acct.; 5 Sep 1753; orphans James [age 9], Henry [age 5], Mary [age 4], Jane [age 1] (A 35.113); dist.; 5 Sep 1753; admx. Minica Walker; child. James [9 next 8 Sep], Henry [6 next 13 Feb], Mary [age 5 next 20 Oct], Jane [age 2 next 8 Jan] (BB 1.88)

Walker, Jon. (John); will; 6 Dec 1757; 6 Feb 1758; son Richard, child of former marriage; sons John, James, Roger; wife Jane [Jean] (MCW 11.191) [SMW TA1.404]; inv.; 9 Feb 1758; 14 Aug 1758; nok Margett & Richard Walker; admx./extx. Jane Walker (I 64.248); acct.; 30 Apr 1759; orphans Margarett [at age], Richard [age 19], John [age 15], James [age 14], Roger [age 10] (A 43.151)

Walker, Bowen and Elizabeth his wife; son Nathaniel, b. 31 Jan 1763 (SA p. 40)
Walker, William; <u>inv.</u>; 11 Feb 1765; 2 Mar 1765; nok William, Jr. & John
    Walker (I 87.5)
Walker, John and Mary his wife; dau. Mary, b. 16 May 1765 (SA p. 41)
Walker, James; <u>inv.</u>; 12 Sep 1773; 21 Mar 1774; nok Henry & Mary Walker;
    admx./extx. Susanna Walker (I 116.193); <u>acct.</u>; 10 Nov 1774 (A 71.317); <u>dist.</u>; 10
    Nov 1774 (BB 6.344); <u>inv.</u>; 20 Nov 1774 (I 118.226, 227); <u>inv.</u>; 20 May 1774; 31
    Aug 1774 (I 119.158)
Walker, Roger and Elizabeth his wife; dau. Margaret, b. 7 Dec 1776 (SA p. 28)

WALTERLIN

Walterling (Walterlin), Walter; 30 Aug 1672; 14 Sep 1672; dau. Mary
    Waterling; son John Barnes; g-daus. Grace and Eliza: Barnes (MCW 1.69);
    <u>acct.</u>; 21 Nov 1674; legatees g-child. Grace and Elisabeth Barnes; Mary
    Walterlin; ex. John Barnes (I&A 1.131)

WALTERS

Walters, John; carpenter; <u>inv.</u>; 15 Aug 1693 (I&A 10.266)
Walter (Wolter), John; <u>will</u>; 27 Sep 1760; 10 Nov 1760; sons William,
    Lawrence, Richard, James; dau. Rebecca; tract *Chaptico Forest* (MCW 12.21)
    [SMW TA1.401]; <u>inv.</u> 12 Nov 1760; adms./exs. ___ & Robert Walter (I 71.155)

WALTON

Walton, James, Rev.; d. 19 Feb 1803; age 33 (HGM)
Walton, Stephen; 22 Feb 1697; [no date of probate]; d-i-l Mary Brewer, s-i-l
    James Brewer; son William (MCW 2.132) [SMW PC.101]; <u>inv.</u>; 4 Mar 1698; 31
    Mar 1698 (I&A 19.20); <u>acct.</u>; 15 Apr 1699; 3 child. (I&A 19.16)

WARD

Ward, William; *Quainton*; 100 ac.; sur. 6 Nov 1668; lies in CH Co.; 1707 poss.
    Wm. Ward; Choptico Hundred (RR)
    Ward's Addition; 36 ac.; sur. 16 Feb 1713 (TLC p. 116); 10 Dec 1714 cert./pat.
    (COL)
Ward, Andrew; *St. Margrets*; 266 ac.; sur. 23 Apr 1672; 1707 poss. Wm. Ward;
    Choptico Hundred (RR p. 33) (TLC p. 32)
Warde, Thomas; service 1674 (SK 18.316)
Ward, Mary; ex. Matthew Ward; 1678 (AM LXVIII.85, 175)
Ward, Edward; <u>inv.</u>; 23 Nov 1685 (I&A 8.485)
Ward, Edward; (given with acct for James Watkins); <u>acct.</u>; 18 Oct 1697 (I&A
    15.258)

Ward, Benja.; *Ward's Defence*; 100 ac.; sur. 30 Sep 1714; 8 Aug 1743 from
George Ward 100 ac. to Abraham Brookbank (TLC p. 116)

Ward, Thomas; age ca 26; 9 Feb 1721 (CCRp. 44)

Ward, Benjamin; inv.; 28 Jul 1743; 4 Oct 1743; nok John Ward, Ann Brady;
admx. Lear Ward (I 28.198); acct.; 1 Jul 1744; orphans James, Benjamin,
Elisabeth, Judeth, Margaret, Holibame (A 20.419)

Ward, William; will; 13 Sep 1761; 19 Mar 1763; daus. Elizabeth Harrison, Mary
Gardener, Ann Ward; tracts *Quainton, Swann's Venture* (MCW 12.176) [SMW
TA1.437]; inv.; 7 Aug 1763; nok Mary Garner (I 81.226); acct.; 17 Aug 1763;
extx. Ann Ward (A 49.637)

WARDNER

Wardner [Warner], Andrew; 5 Oct 1660; 27 Mar 1662; wife Mary; son George;
dau. Isabel (MCW 1.21)

Wardner, Thomas; immigrated 1667; transported wife Sarah (SK 11.237)

Wardner, Thos.; *Wardners Rest*; 200 ac.; sur. 10 Jun 1666; 1707 no poss.;
Choptico Hundred (RR p. 50) (TLC p. 48)

WARE

Ware, Agnes; extx. and widow of Richard of St. Clements Manor; 15 Apr 1658
(AM XLI.53, 121)

Ware, Reggell; inv.; 3 Jan 1756; nok Thomas & Elisabeth Reggell; admx./extx.
Mary Regelle (I 60.362)

WARREN

Warren, Notley; of Charles Co.; *Rippon*; 350 ac.; 15 Aug 1683 cert./pat. (COL)

Warren, Augustine; acct.; 9 Jul 1686; adm. Ignatius Warren (I&A 9.48)

Warren, William; inv.; 20 Jul 1694 (I&A 13a.143)

Warren, John; acct.; 1 May 1695; adm. Ignatius Warren (I&A 13a.295)

Warren, William; acct.; 18 Aug 1696; admx. Elisabeth Warren (I&A 14.9)

Warren, Thomas; Newtowne; will; 30 Mar 1698; 6 Jun 1698; son John; dau.
Rebecca; mentions Sarah, d/o Robert Cole (MCW 2.139) [SMW PC1.105]; inv.; 25
Jun 1698 (I&A 16.198); acct; 7 Sep 1699 (I&A 19½b.116)

Warren, Thomas; acct.; 22 Apr 1710 (SMAA p. 208)

Warren, Thomas; age ca 40; 20 Sep 1718; tract *St. Lawrence* (CCRp. 41)

Warren, Thomas; will; 13 Mar 1744/5; 4 Jun 1744/5; child. Mary Kitting
[Ketting], Susanna Strong, Monica Hill, George; unnamed child. of dau.
Elizabeth Mattingly, dec'd (MCW 9.38) [SMW TA1.152]

Warren, Thomas; *Warren's Lot*; 148 ac.; sur. 22 Aug 1745 (TLC p. 114) ; 18 Mar
1747 cert./pat. (COL)

Worren (Warren) [Warrin], John; 28 May 1750; 25 Jun 1750; wife Briget; daus.
Ann Reader, Mary, Monica; son Thomas (MCW 10.96) [SMW TA1.257]; inv.; 28
Aug 1750; 5 Nov 1750; nok Ann Reader, Thomas Warren; adms./exs. Bridgit
& Thomas Warran (I 44.43); acct.; 9 Sep 1751; child. Thomas, Ann, w/o John
Reeder; Mary, w/o McKeteri Norris; Monica, w/o William Jackson (A 31.71)
Warren, Bridget; inv.; 1755; 6 Oct 1755; nok John Reader, Eluie Norriss;
admx./extx. Thomas Warran (I 59.201); acct.; 6 Oct 1755 (A 38.175)
Warren, Edward and Elizabeth his wife; child. William [b. 25 May 1755]; Mary
[b. 20 Nov 1759]; Britanina [b. 9 Mar 1762] (SA p. 6)

WATERS
Waters, Thomas; immigrated by 1666; drummer (SK 10.179-180)
Waters, John; of CH Co.; *Bristol*; 100 ac.; 27 Sep 1680 cert./pat. (COL)
Waters, John; will; written 26 Feb 1692; sons James, Joseph, Lewis, Thomas,
William, John; wife Penelope; mentions 7 child.; tracts *Bristol, James Gift*
(MCW 2.60)
Waters, Lewis; acct.; 4 Nov 1718; admx. Elisabeth Water (A 1.316); acct.; 4 Nov
1718 (SMAA p. 328)
Waters (Wayters), Thomas; 12 Mar 1744/5; 28 May 1745; child. Mary Waller
(?), Penelope, Sewell, Thomas, Elijah, Joseph [John] (MCW 9.44) [SMW
TA1.168]; inv.; 23 Jan 1745 (I 35.111); inv.; 14 Nov 1745; 23 Dec 1745; nok
William Naybors, Isaac Wheeler; admx./extx. Elisabeth Watters (I 31.429);
acct.; 18 Sep 1749; child. Elijah [of age], Joseph [age 18], Thomas [age 15],
Suel [age 12], Mary & Penelope [both of age]; ex. Elijah Waters (A 27.103)
Water, Thomas; inv.; 20 Feb 1774; 20 May 1774; nok Joseph Waters, Elisabeth
Waller; admx. Mary Waters (I 117.341)

WATHEN
Wathan, Richard; m. 28 Sep 1773 Eleanor Mattingly (MM)
Wathen, H. Hudson; 22 Apr 1774; 14 Jun 1774; will; sons Francis [Hudson],
Henry [Hudson], John Baptist; daus. Mary Ann, Ann; sister Elizabeth
Monnack; wife Ann; bro. Bennet (MCW 16.20) [SMW TA1.675]
Walthen, Henry Hudson; inv.; 26 Jul 1774; 20 Jan 1775; nok Richard Walthen,
Elisabeth Monneh; admx./extx. Ann Walthen (I 121.389)
Wathen, Henry Hudson and Ann his wife; child. Francis Hudson, b. 3 Nov
1764; Henry Hudson, b. 11 May 1766 (SA p. 17, 52)
Wathen, Henry Hudson; acct.; 10 Dec 1775; extx. Ann Wathen (A 72.289)
Wathen, Richard; *Ingsbeth*; 393 ac.; 29 Sep 1766 cert./pat. (COL)

WATKINS
Watkins, James; [and Edward Ward]; acct.; 18 Oct 1697 (I&A 15.258)

Watkins, Samuell, Mr.; <u>inv.</u>; 4 Nov 1700 (I&A 124); <u>acct.</u>; 25 Jul 1701; [gent.];
   extx. Ann Smith alias Watkins; mentions Susanna, extx. of Robert Mason
   (SMAA p. 109) (I&A 23.46); <u>acct.</u>; 19 Jan 1702 (I&A 23.47)
Watkins, Walter; <u>acct.</u>; 29 Jul 1709; admx. Mary, w/o Nicholas Burd (I&A 30.20)
   (SMAA p. 174)

WATKINSON

Watkinson, Cornelius; *Addition*; 78 ac.; sur. 28 Feb 1675; poss. Wm. Brample;
   in 1704 not in 1707; Resurrection Hundred (RR p. 62) (TLC p. 59)
   Best Land; 50 ac.; sur. 16 Jun 1675; 1707 pos. John Gillam; Resurrection
   Hundred (RR p. 61) (TLC p. 59)
Watkins (Watkinson, Walkinson) [Matteson], Cornelius; <u>will</u>; 15 Apr 1697; 9
   Apr 1698; wife Eliza.; mentions James, s/o Geo. Keeth and Cornelius, s/o
   Peter Watkinson (MCW 2.136) [SMW PC1.103]; <u>inv.</u>; 22 Apr 1698; 26 Jun 1698
   (I&A 16.42); <u>acct.</u>; 1 Mar 1698; extx. Elisabeth Walkinson (I&A 181.16)

WATSON

Watson, John; wife Jane, admx. William Williams; 1683 (AM LXX.340)
Watson, William; *Freestone Point*; 324 ac.; sur. for Watson & Thomas Love 5
   Mar 1687 (TLC p. 116); 5 Mar 1688 cert./pat. (COL)
Watson, William & Thomas Love; *Partnership*; 260 ac.; sur. 25 Jul 1694; 1707
   poss. Margret Watson 130 ac.; Choptico Hundred (RR p. 54) (TLC p. 52); 260 ac.;
   5 Oct 1695 cert./pat. (COL)
Watson (Wattson), John; [St. Inigoes Hundred]; <u>will</u>; 21 Jun 1696; 15 Apr 1699;
   b-i-l Thomas Mittford [of St. George's Hundred] & his son Thomas;
   mentions Robert, s/o Robert Graham; John & Thomas, sons of Capt. Edward
   Greenhalgh; wife Jane; tract *New Bottle* (MCW 2.191) [SMW PC1.121]; <u>inv.</u>; 10
   May 1701 (I&A 20.199); <u>acct.</u>; 20 Jul 1703 (I&A 24.20) (SMAA p. 123)
Watson, David; <u>acct.</u>; 29 Dec 1712; admx. Jane, w/o Thomas Manhee (Mankee)
   (I&A 33b.157) (SMAA p. 230)
Watson, David; <u>inv.</u>; 6 Feb 1730; 15 May 1731 (I 16.135); <u>acct.</u>; 4 Nov 1732;
   admx. Ann, w/o John Baker (A 11.518)
Watson (Wattson), John; <u>inv.</u>; 4 Feb 1736; Feb 1736; nok monirs; admx./extx.
   Esther Watson (I 22.162); <u>acct.</u>; 2 Mar 1738; extx. Esther, w/o Luke Bally (A
   16.85)
Watson, Joseph; *Hedge Barron*; 79 ac.; sur. 12 Mar 1741 (TLC p. 99); 28 Jul 1742
   cert./pat. (COL)
Watson (Wattson), Joseph; <u>will</u>; 3 Nov 1742; 1 Feb 1742; sons James, Joseph,
   John; wife Sarah; tracts *Hodge Barren, Partnership* (MCW 8.195) [SMW TA1.122];
   <u>inv.</u>; 3 Mar 1742; nok Elisabeth Harden, James Watson; admx./extx. Sarah
   Watson (I 27.365); <u>inv.</u>; 4 Oct 1743; nok Joseph & Sarah Watson; admx./ex.

James Watson (I 28.199); <u>acct.</u>; 15 May 1744; mentions James, Joseph, Edward, Samuel and Judith Watson; adm. James & Sarah Wattson (A 20.310)

Watson, William; <u>will</u>; 30 Apr 1750; 7 May 1750; son Edward; dau. Elizabeth (MCW 10.82) [SMW TAl.264]; <u>inv.</u>; 12 May 1750; 27 Aug 1750; nok Edward & Elisabeth Watson (I 43.378); <u>acct.</u> 24 Jun 1751; mentions Matthew & Mary, child. of Robert Hawkins (A 30.196)

Watson, Benjamin and Susanna his wife; son William, b. 29 Aug 1756 (SA p. 38); daus. Catherine and Sarah, b. 18 Jul 1759 (SA p. 39)

Watson, John and Elinor; dau. Elizabeth, b. 27 Mar 1757 (SA p. 37)

Watson, John; *Partnership Addition*; 60 ac.; 4 Feb 1762 cert./pat. (COL)

Watson, James; *Gore*; 20 ac.; 16 Oct 1776 cert./pat. (COL)

Watson, Hezekiah; m. 11 Feb 1778 Susannah Pratt (BRU p. 535)

Watson, Edward and Anne Sanner; m. 26 Nov 1779 (SA p. 58)

WATTS

Watts, Wm.; *Watts Lodge*; 250 ac.; sur. 18 Dec 1665; 1707 poss. Will'm Wherret, Tho's Watts; Poplar Hill Hundred (RR p. 24) (TLC p. 22)

Watts, William; <u>will</u>; 8 Mar 1677/8; 19 Apr 1678; sons Charles [age 8], William [age 6], Edmond (age 4) (MCW 1.202)

Watts, Peter; <u>will</u>; _ _ 1692; 23 Jul 1692; sons Thomas, William, John, Peter; wife and "her child"; tract *Nitopsen* (MCW 2.54); <u>inv.</u>; 5 Aug 1692 (I&A 10.258)

Watts, William; <u>acct.</u>; 30 Dec 1708 (I&A 29.188) (SMAA p. 171)

Watts, James; <u>inv.</u>; 2 Mar 1712; nok Thomas & Stephen Watts (I&A 36a.102); <u>acct.</u>; admx. Francis, wife of William Kirby; (calls dec'd Francis Watts); 17 Nov 1718 (SMAA p. 342); <u>acct.</u>; 17 Nov 1718 (A 1.322)

Watts, William; *Timber Swamp*; 100 ac.; sur. 14 Jul 1714; pat. 16 Dec 1714 (TLC p. 69); 2 Sep 1714 cert./pat. (COL)
Timber Swamp Addition; 60 ac.; sur. 6 Jul 1716 (TLC p. 76); 21 Oct 1718 cert./pat. (COL)

Watts, William, Jr.; <u>inv.</u>; 6 Jun 1715 (I&A 36c.131)

Watts, Peter; age ca 47 in 1716 (MD p. 196)

Watts, Thomas; <u>inv.</u>; 18 Mar 1716; nok Stephen Watts (I&A 37b.8); <u>acct.</u>; 28 Apr 1718; admx. Elisabeth Watts (I&A 39a.17) (SMAA p. 340)

Watts, Thomas; age ca 38; 2 Aug 1717 (CCR p. 39)

Watts, Peter; Gent.; <u>will</u>; 12 Mar 1718; 27 Jul 1719; g-son Thomas, s/o Thomas Waughap; mentions James, s/o James Watts; g-daus. Elizabeth Waughop, Hannah Clarke; dau. Mary w/o Thomas Waughop; s-i-l George Clarke; bro. Stephen Watts; tracts *Bennets Delight, Jenifer's Gift* (MCW 4.208) [SMW PC1.249]; <u>inv.</u>; 14 Aug 1719; 26 Sep 1719; nok Thomas Waughop, George Clarke; extx. Mrs. Elisabeth Watts (I 3.44); <u>acct.</u>; 21 Jun 1720 (SMAA p. 436)

Watts, William; <u>acct.</u>; 24 Jul 1718; admx. Elisabeth, admx. of Thomas Watts (A 1.199) (SMAA p. 352)

Watts, Thomas; <u>will</u>; 12 Oct 1721; 20 Nov 1723; sons Daniel, William, Thomas, Joshua; wife Elizabeth; tract *Watts Lodge* (MCW 5.151) [SMW PC1.280]; <u>inv.</u>; 22 Nov 1723; 18 Jan 1723; admx. Elisabeth Watts (I 9.264); <u>acct.</u>; 16 Nov 1724 (A 6.254)

Watts, William; age ca 61; 27 Oct 1721; tract *Watt's Lodge* (CCRp. 46)

Watts, Thomas; sister m. William Wherrell; 27 Oct 1721 (CCRp. 46)

Watts, William; <u>will</u>; 14 Jan 1723/4; 22 Jan 1723/4; s-i-l John Michael Thomas Taney; d-i-l [dau.] Margaret Taney; cousins William, Daniel, Thomas, Joshua Watts; s-i-l William Canady and his son John; tracts *Bushell's Rest, Timber Swamp, Addition to Timber Swamp* (MCW 5.155) [SMW PC1.280]; <u>inv.</u>; 13 Apr 1724; Col.; nok Daniel Watts, Peter Rule (I 9.322); <u>acct.</u>; 14 Apr 1725 (A 6.309)

Watts, Elisabeth, Mrs.; <u>inv.</u>; 12 Feb 1723; 2 May 1724; nok Patrick & William Forest; admx. Christian Forest, admx of Richard Forest (I 9.383); <u>acct.</u>; 14 Apr 1725 (A 6.307)

Watts, James; <u>inv.</u>; 12 Feb 1742; 25 Apr 1743; nok John & Peter Milburn; admx./extx. Mary Watts (I 27.374); <u>acct.</u>; 26 Apr 1744 (A 10.142)

Watts, William; <u>will</u>; 23 Dec 1744; 5 Mar 1745; wife Jane; child. William, Thomas, George, Daniel, Elizabeth (MCW 9.16) [SMW TA1.152]; <u>inv.</u>; 5 Mar 1744; 5 Jun 1744; nok Thomas & Daniel Watts; admx./extx. Jane Watts (I 31.145); <u>acct.</u>; 6 Oct 1746 (A 23.9)

Watt, Thomas; <u>inv.</u>; 15 Jul 1746; 29 Jul 1746; nok Thomas Breedon, Ea. Smith; admx./extx. Mary Watt (I 33.52); <u>acct.</u>; 22 Jan 1747 (A 24.13)

Watts (Watt), Stephen; <u>will</u>; 19 Feb 1750; 25 Mar 1751; wife Jean; son John; mentions John and Elizabeth, child. of Rogger Hendley & Mary, widow of Joseph Welman; cousins Ann Watts, Ann Morgin, Sarah Harbird; cousins John, Peter, [Joseph] and William Milbourn; cous. James Watts (MCW 10.143) [SMW TA1.278]; <u>inv.</u>; 1 Jul 1751; 15 Jul 1751; nok Robert & John Hendly; admx./extx. Jane Watts (I 47.124); <u>acct.</u>; 25 May 1752; mentions Ann Watts; orphan John Watts [age 17]; admx. Jean, w/o John Roads (A 32.345); <u>dist.</u>; 15 May 1752 (BB 1.45)

Watts, Thomas, Jr.; <u>will</u>; 19 Sep 1752; 11 Jul 1752; bros. William, George; mother unnamed (MCW 10.236) [SMW TA1.284]; <u>inv.</u>; 18 Apr 1753; nok Joan Gardiner, George Watts; adm./ex. William Watts (I 54.47a); <u>acct.</u>; 18 Apr 1753 (A 34.175); <u>dist.</u>; 18 Apr 1753; heirs George & William Watts, Jane Gardner (BB 1.79)

Watts, James; <u>will</u>; 3 Mar 1756; 19 Apr 1756; son John, Jr.; wife Ann; tract *Pauper Field* (MCW 11.128) [SMW TA1.343]

Watts, Thomas; *Watts' Hazard*; 65 ac.; 21 Sep 1756 cert./pat. (COL)

Watts, Ann; will; 21 Oct 1756; 1 Nov 1756; mentions Elizabeth and Mary, daus.
of John and Mary Morriss; sister Sarah Jole [Tole]; mentions George Jole;
tract *Poppanfields*; (listed in MCW as will of Robert Gouldsberry) (MCW
11.149) [SMW TA1.347]; inv.; 3 Nov 1756; 28 Feb 1757; nok Elisabeth Griffis,
Roger Tolle (I 62.252); acct.; 20 Feb 1758 (A 41.348); dist.; 20 Feb 1758 (BB 2.73)

Watts, John; will; 5 Feb 1759; 4 Jun 1768; mentions John Rhodes and wife Jane
(MCW 14.54) [SMW TA1.560]

Watts, Daniel; inv.; 18 Feb 1760; 25 Aug 1760; nok Thomas & Joshua Watts;
admx./ex. William Watts (I 70.55)

Watt, Mary; will; 13 Nov 1764; 3 Mar 1775; sons James, Mark, Matthew &
Abraham Breden [Breeden], Thomas Watt; daus. Elizabeth Warren, Rebeca
Watts & her child. Thomas Dillon and Daniel, Elisabeth & James Watts, Mary
Smith, Ann Hilton; g-dau. Clarano Breden; tract *Roads Rest* (MCW 16.94) [SMW
TA1.739]

Watts, Thomas; will; 5 May 1768; 8 Feb 1769; sons Joshua, Kenelm Bolt,
Thomas (MCW 14.93) [SMW TA1.585]; inv.; 1 Jun 1769; 1 Aug 1769; ex. Joshua
Watts (I 102.250); acct.; 20 Dec 1772 (A 66.275); dist.; 20 Dec 1771; sons Joshua,
Kenelm Bolt, Thomas (BB 6.115)

Watts, William; *Watts' Discovery*; 25 ac.; 28 Nov 1769 cert./pat. (COL)

Watts, Richard; will; 2 Dec 1771; 24 Feb 1772; child. Richard and Susannah;
bros. William, Robert; sisters Francis Harrison, Jane Fawcet; tract *Plum Point*
(MCW 14.213) [SMW TA1.635]

Watts, Willoughby and Jemima his wife; dau. Ann [b. 5 Jun 1773]; William [b.
26 Jun 1775] (SA p. 26)

Watts, Richard; inv.; 9 Mar 1774; 18 Apr 1774; exs. Sarah & Robert Watts (I
118.138); acct.; 18 Apr 1774; exs. Robert & Sarah Watts (A 70.148)

Watts, Joshua; inv.; 3 Aug 1774; nok Kenelm B. & William Watts; admx.
Hannah Watts (I 119.174)

Watts, Henry and Susannah Watts (by license); m. 7 Apr 1785 (SA p. 63)

WAUGHOP

Waughop [Waughoss], John; Piney Point; will; _ __ 1677; 18 Mar 1677/8; wife
Anne [Jane]; son Thomas; dau. Rebecca; g-son Thomas Hatton (MCW 1.200/1)
[SMW PC1.36]

Waughop, Thomas, Capt.; inv.; 9 Jun 1701 (I&A 1.692)

Wahop, Thomas; admx. Catharine; mention Mrs. Cohame, g-mother of
Katharine Waughop, orphan of Thomas; 9 Jul 1703 (SMAA p. 116) (I&A 24.7)

Waughop, Thomas; *Waughop's Chance*; 138 ac.; sur. 30 Mar 1724 for Tho.
Wanghop; Poplar Hill Hundred (TLC p. 83); 10 Dec 1725 cert./pat. (COL)

Waughop, Thomas, Jr.; inv.; 12 Jun 1733; 25 Jun 1733; nok Thomas & James
Waughop; admx./extx. Elisabeth Waughop (I 17.169); acct.; 16 Sep 1734;
orphan John Waughop; adms. Thomas Wherrett & wife Elisabeth (A 12.534)

Waughop, Thomas; Gent.; <u>will</u>; 11 Apr 1735; 17 Apr 1735; daus. Johanna,
Anne, Katherine and Elizabeth Waughop; dau. Mary Guyther; wife Katherine;
g-son John Waughop; bros. John, James; tract *Piney Point* (MCW 7.137) [SMW
TA1.39]; <u>inv.</u>; 30 Jul 1735; 29 Aug 1735; nok Ann Chesley, Mary Gaither;
admx./exs. Catherine & James Waughop (I 21.99); <u>acct.</u>; 25 Nov 1736 (A
15.234); <u>acct.</u>; 26 Sep 1737 (A 14.429)

Waughop, James; *Itchcomb's Freehold*; 344 ac.; 10 Sep 1744 cert./pat. (COL)

Waughop, James, Mr.; <u>inv.</u>; 18 Jul 1750; 25 Jul 1750; nok Thomas Pal &
William Coutanceau Waughop; admx./extx. Mary Waughop (I 43.300); <u>acct.</u>; 4
Jun 1751 (A 30.186); <u>acct.</u>; 16 Oct 1752 (A 33.200); <u>dist.</u>; 16 Oct 1752 (BB 1.71)

WEATHERINTON

Weatherinton, James; <u>acct.</u>; 31 May 1736; orphans John, Joseph, James,
William, Thomas, Eleanor & Mary Weatherinton; admx. William Dunbarr &
wife Elisabeth (A 15.79)

Weathernton (Weathington), James; <u>inv.</u>; 12 Mar 1759; 9 Mar 1759; nok
William Whearton, Thomas Weatherington; admx./extx. Hannah
Weatherington (I 66.241)

Weatherington, John; <u>will</u>; 2 Jan 1777; 15 Feb 1777; mentions James and
Thomas, sons of James Weatherinton; Joseph, s/o Joseph Weatherinton (MCW
16.173)

WELLMAN

Wellman, Michall; <u>will</u>; 2 Feb 1714; wife Martha; child. Michael, Thomas,
Alice, Jane, Joseph; tract *Stile's Chance* [SMW PC1.198]

Wellman (Welman), Michael; planter; <u>will</u>; 18 Apr 1715; 19 Apr 1718; son
Joseph; wife Martha; 5 child.; exs. Thomas and Joseph; tract *Siles Chance*
(MCW 4.129) [SMW PC1.236]; <u>inv.</u>; 25 Apr 1718; nok Jane Tanson (I 1.299); <u>acct.</u>;
14 Jun 1719; child. [all of age] (A 2.110) (SMAA p. 395); <u>acct.</u>; 9 May 1720; ex.
Joseph Welman (A 3.14) (SMAA p. 420); <u>acct.</u>; 24 Jul 1733 (A 11.718)

Wellman, Jos.; *Wellmans Chance*; 51 ac.; sur. 19 Aug 1719; land not found (TLC
p. 79); in BA Co. cert./pat. (COL)

Welman, Tho's & Joseph; *Brothers Dread*; 134 ac.; sur. 4 Jun 1723 (TLC p. 85)

Willman (Wellman), Thomas; *What Care I*; 28½ ac. sur. 21 Apr 1740 (TLC p. 96);
28 ac.; 18 Dec 1740 cert./pat. (COL)

Wellman, Joseph; planter; <u>will</u>; 13 Nov 1733; 16 Mar 1740/1; sons Michael,
Joseph, William; bro. Thomas; daus. Susannah, Ann; wife Ann; tracts
Wellmans Chance, Brothers Dread, Sisters to Have and Hold (MCW 8.122)
[SMW TA1.111]; <u>inv.</u>; 12 Jun 1741; 25 Jul 1741; nok Jane Gellder, Michael
Wellman; adm./ex. Thomas Wellman (I 26.129); <u>acct.</u>; 28 Jun 1742 (A 19.73);
<u>acct.</u>; 27 Feb 1745; orphans Michael, Joseph, Susanna, Ann (A 22.114)

Willman, Mary; acct.; 31 Jan 1742 (A 19.367)

Wellman, Josiah; inv.; 16 Feb 1750; 26 Apr 1751; nok Michael & Thomas Wellman; admx.extx. Mary Wellman (I 48.20); dist.; 17 Jan 1753 (BB 1.61)

Wellman, Thomas; will; probate 8 May 1751; sons Josiah, Thomas, John; wife Catharine; tracts *Brothers Dread, Wellmans Good Fortune* (MCW 10.154) [SMW TA1.270]; inv.; 29 Jul 1751; nok Michael Wellman, Jean Fealder; admx./extx. Catharine Wellman (I 47.133); inv.; 2 Oct 1752; nok Jane Feelder, Mary Wellman; adms./exs. Thomas & Joseph Wellman (I 51.75); acct.; 26 Feb 1754 (A 36.160)

Wellman, Joseph; acct.; 17 Jan 1753; orphan Jemima [age 3]; admx. Mary Willman (A 33.321)

Wellman, Michael and Elizabeth his wife; child. Joshua [b. 9 Oct 1753]; Jared [b. 13 Sep 1755] (SA p. 37); Rhoda (m) [b. 28 Nov 1758]; Jemima [b. 3 Mar 1762]; Elijah [b. 28 Oct 1764] (SA p. 40); James [b. 19 Jul 1767] (SA p. 42)

Wellman, Michael, d. 18 Oct 1773 (SA p. 64)

Wellman, Michael; planter; will; 2 Apr 1771; 21 Sep 1773; wife Elizabeth; son John Vowles Wellman, others unnamed (MCW 15.70) [SMW TA1.670]; inv.; 23 Oct 1773; 14 Dec 1773; nok Susanna Peacock; ex. Elisabeth Wellman (I 116.186)

WELLS

Wells, Pearce; acct.; 6 Aug 1685 (I&A 8.445)

Wells, Henry; inv.; 13 Dec 1751; 5 Mar 1752; nok minors; admx./extx. Mary Wells (I 48.293); acct.; 21 Jan 1755 (A 37.77)

WELSH

Welch, Thomas; will; 22 Jan 1716; 29 Mar 1717; daus. Elinor, Katherine, Ann; son John; [son Thomas] (MCW 4.73) [SMW PC1.213]; inv.; 25 Apr 1717; 12 Jul 1717 (I&A 37b.131); acct.; 2 Dec 1717 (SMAA p. 310)

Welsh [Welch], John; inv.; 29 Jan 1717; 30 May 1718; nok unnamed child. (I 1.57); acct.; 24 Dec 1719; planter; admx. Joane (Jane), w/o Joseph Hardyne (A 2.438); acct.; 24 Dec 1719 (SMAA p. 451); acct.; 5 Nov 1720 (A 3.223) (SMAA p. 426)

Welch (Welsh), Thomas; planter; will; 25 Mar 1724; 4 Apr 1724; sons William, Thomas; dau. Mary (MCW 5.161) [SMW PC1.285]; acct.; 3 May 1725 (A 6.329); acct.; 9 May 1726 (A 7.368)

Welch, John, Jr.; inv.; 28 Mar 1759; 16 Apr 1759; nok Lewis & Elisabeth Oliver; adm./ex. John Welch (I 67.92)

Welsh, Jonathon; inv.; 3 Mar 1761 (I 71.143)

Welsh, Edward; *Osfield Addition*; 8 ac.; 14 Oct 1761 cert./pat. (COL)

Welsh, John; inv.; 16 Mar 1764; 5 May 1765; nok William & Elisabeth Waters; admn. Edward Welsh (I 87.12)

Welsh (Welch), Edward; will; Sep 1766; 8 Jul 1767; daus. Sarah, Elizabeth Waters, Elizabeth; g-child. John and Mary Welsh, Susan & Edward Waters; wife Mary; tracts *Ossfield, Ossfield's Addition* (MCW 14.2) [SMW TA1.521]; inv.; 3 Aug 1767; 4 Aug 1768; nok infants; extx. Mary Welsh (I 97.286); acct.; 14 Feb 1769 (A 61.110); dist.; 14 Feb 1769; legatees dau. Sarah, Elisabeth Waters, g-son John Welsh (under 21), g-dau. Mary Welsh (under 16), Birgin Mitchel (under 21), wife Mary (BB 5.173)

Welsh, Mary; dist.; 26 Sep 1774 (BB 7.7)

WEST

West, Phillip; *Frogg Marsh*; 200 ac.; sur. 30 Jul 1640; 1707 poss. Thos. Mudd by marrying Jno. Low's widow & Thos. Medford; St. Georges Hundred (RR)

West, William; immigrated by 1670; transported son William (SK 12.618)

West, William, Rev. and Mrs. Susanna his spouse; son George William [b. 22 Jan 1770] (SA p. 21)

West, William; inv.; 12 Jan 1744; 7 Mar 1744; admx./extx. Jane West (I 30.308); acct.; 2 Dec 1746 (A 23.131)

WHARTON

Wharton, Henry; gent.; *Notley Hall*; 400 ac.; sur. 1 Jul 1708; part of St. Clements Manor (TLC p. 65); 13 Jun 1708 cert./pat. (COL)
   Neighbourhood; 146 ac.; resur. 16 Oct 1710; St. Clements Manor (TLC p. 68); 10 Dec 1713 cert./pat. (COL)
   Wolf Holes; 262 ac.; 1724 cert./pat. (COL)
   Westfields; 252 ac.; 10 Nov 1726 cert./pat. (COL)

Wharton, Eleanor; b. 1723; d. 6 Jan 1793 Lierre; d/o Henry Wharton and Jane Doyne (JM p. 321)

Wharton, Jane; age ca 50 in 1738 (MD p. 198)

Wharton, Henry; will; 26 Nov 1745; 4 Feb 1745/6; child. Ann, Eleanor, Henry, Francis, Jesse, Elizabeth Pile, Mary, Jane; bro. William; bro. [neph.] Edward Diggs; sons-i-l Joseph Pile, John Parrkam [Barnham]; [sis. ___ Darnall; g-son Joseph Pile]; [tracts *Exeter, Notley Hill*] (MCW 9.54) [SMW TA1.182]; inv.; 5 Mar 1745; nok __sd & Ann Wharton (I 32.86); acct.; 19 May 1747 (A 23.315)

Wharton, Charles Henry; b. 25 May 1748; d. 23 Jul 1833 Burlington, NJ; s/o Jesse Wharton and Anne Bradford (JM p. 321)

Wharton, Francis; b. 9 Nov 1729; d. 31 Mar 1753 Liege; s/o Henry Wharton and Jane Doyne (JM p. 321)

Wharton, Jesse; inv. 12 Nov 1753; 2 Apr 1754; nok Jane Parnham, Elisabeth Pile; admx./extx. Ann Wharton (I 57.128); acct.; 4 Dec 1754 (A 36.523); inv.; 3

Dec 1754; 25 Oct 1757; adms./exs. Edward Diggs & wife Ann (I 64.6a]; acct.;
25 Oct 1757; (A 41.253); acct.; 20 Nov 1758; orphans Charles Henry [age 11],
Jesse [age 5] (A 42.211); dist.; 20 Nov 1758; child. Charles Henry & Jesey
Wharton (BB 2.99)

WHEATLEY

Wheatly, Will'm; *Sherwell*; 100 ac.; sur. & pat. 18 Jul 1646; 1707 poss. Widow
Mason; Poplar Hill Hundred (RR p. 21) (TLC p. 20)

Wheatly, John; *Wheatly*; 50 ac.; sur. 26 Jan 1648; sold by Andrew, s/o John
Wheatly; St. Georges Hundred (RR p. 18) (TLC p. 18)

Wheatly, John; *Wheatlys Chance*; 272 ac.; sur. 3 Dec 1680; St. Mary's Hundred
(RR p. 7) (TLC p. 8); 8 Dec 1680 cert./pat. (COL)
Wheatlys Content; 297 ac.; sur. 29 Nov 1681; 1707 poss. John Norris & John
Wheatly; incl. in *Wheatleys Content with Addition*; New Town Hundred (RR p.
38) (TLC p. 37); 24 Nov 1681 cert./pat. (COL)

Wheatly, John; *Batchelors Comfort*; 190 ac.; sur. 27 Apr 1682; 1707 poss. John
Wheatly; New Town Hundred (RR p. 39) (TLC p. 38)
Wheatley Meadow; 110 ac.; resur. 27 Apr 1682; 1707 no poss.; New Town
Hundred (RR p. 39) (TLC p. 38)

Wheatly, Andrew; *Wheatlys Hill*; 28 ac.; sur. 13 Mar 1683; 1707 poss. Jno.
Wheatley for Andrew Wheatly's orphan; New Town Hundred (RR p. 41) (TLC p.
41); 13 Mar 1684 cert./pat. (COL)
Nintoquight; 116 ac.; sur. 16 Mar 1683; 1707 poss. John Wheatly; New Town
Hundred (RR p. 41) (TLC p. 41); *Nintoquint*; 116 ac.; 13 Mar 1684 cert./pat. (COL)

Wheatley, John; *Maiden's Lot*; 100 ac.; 10 Aug 1685; granted to wife Winifred
Horne in 1681 cert./pat. (COL)

Wheatly, Andrew; will; 28 Nov 1693; 2 Feb 1693; mentions Mary Wheatly
[dau.], cousins James and John Wheatly and Winifrede; bro. John (MCW 2.50)
[SMW PC1.79]; acct.; 25 Jul 1695; adm./ex. John Wheatley (I&A 13a.378)

Wheatley, John; of PG Co.; *Wheatley's Contentment*; 150 ac.; sur. 28 Mar 1707
(TLC p. 90); 1708 cert./pat. (COL)

Wheatley, John; *Hiccory Thickett*; 48 ac.; sur. 30 Mar 1707 SM Co. (TLC p. 65);
10 Oct 1708; PG Co. cert./pat. (COL)

Wheatly, Joseph; *Wheatly's Addition*; 100 ac.; sur. 21 Feb 1715 (TLC p. 75); 25
Apr 1717 cert./pat. (COL)

Wheatley, John; will; 25 Apr 1717; 8 Aug 1717; sons James, John, Joseph,
Thomas Francis; daus. Winifride, Anne, Elizabeth, Susannah, Mary; wife
Elizabeth; tracts *Wheatley's Meadows, Hiccory Plaines, Umtiguint* (MCW
4.109) [SMW PC1.219]; inv.; 10 Oct 1717; Sr. (I&A 39c.185); acct.; 3 Jul 1718;
extx. Elisabeth Wheatley (A 1.36) (SMAA p. 334)

Wheatly (Wheetly), James; <u>inv.</u>; 16 Nov 1720; 15 Dec 1720; nok Joseph & Winifurt Wheatly, Thomas Cooper; adm. John Wheatly (I 4.195); <u>acct.</u>; 2 Feb 1721 (A 4.76)

Wheatl(e)y, Thomas; *Buckland Plains*; 260 ac.; sur. 25 Sep 1732 (TLC p. 89); 10 Jun 1734 cert./pat. (COL)

Wheatley, Joseph; <u>will</u>; 15 Oct 1739; 21 Jan 1739; sons James, Joseph; wife Martha; tracts *Intequent [Intiquint], Wheatley's Addition* (MCW 8.66) [SMW TA1.90]; <u>inv.</u>; 17 Mar 1739; 19 Apr 1740; nok John Wheatly, Winifred Reson; admx./extx. Martha Wheatly (I 24.545); <u>acct.</u>; 16 Jul 1744; mentions Thomas Talton m. orphan of John Wheatly (A 20.421)

Wheatley, John, Jr.; *Wheatly's Meadows*; 276 ac.; resur. 26 Sep 1745 (TLC p. 113); 29 Sep 1747 cert./pat. (COL)

Wheatley, Thomas; *Wheatleys Content with Addition*; 380½ ac. resur. 2 Jan 1747 (TLC p. 116); *Wheatly's Content*; 380 ac.; 13 Sep 1750 cert./pat. (COL)

Wheatley, George and Elizabeth his wife; child. Henry [b. 10 Jan 1755]; Ann [b. 12 Aug 1756]; William [b. 18 Sep 1762]; Ignatius [b. 25 Feb 1765]; Bernard [b. 29 May 1768] (SA p. 193)

Wheatley, James and Henrietta his wife; child. Rebecca [b. 18 Sep 1755]; James [b. 23 Sep 1758]; Joseph [b. 27 May 1761]; Edward (Edmund) [b. 23 Dec 1765] (SA p. 12, 46, 47)

Wheatley, Mary; dau. Ann [b. 17 Oct 1758] (SA p. 195)

Wheatley, James and Eleanor his wife; sons William [b. 8 Jan 1763]; Benedict [b. 3 Nov 1766] (SA p. 13, 14, 48)

Wheatley, Ignatius and Henrietta; daus. Anastatia [b. 20 Feb 1765]; Eleanor [b. 9 Apr 1768] (SA p. 189)

Wheatly, James; <u>will</u>; 19 Dec 1767; 21 Apr 1768; sons William, Bennett; wife [Eleanor]; s-i-l Joshua Greenwell (MCW 14.33) [SMW TA1.566]; <u>inv.</u>; 28 May 1768; 18 Jun 1768; nok Winefred Dossey, Joseph Wheatley (I 95.249)

Wheatly, John; planter; <u>will</u>; 15 Aug 1768; 14 Nov 1770; wife Elizabeth; child. William, John, Thomas, Richard, Francis, Elias; mentions William Bowie & wife Margaret; tracts *Addition Enlarged, Manor Land, St. Clair* in CH Co., *Wantwood Forest Enlarged, Swamp Land* (MCW 14.149) [SMW TA1.590]; <u>inv.</u>; 13 Feb 1771; 10 Jan 1772; nok Richard Estep, Mary Wheatly; extx. Elisabeth Wheatly (I 109.2); <u>acct.</u>; 21 Oct 1772 (A 67.147); <u>acct.</u>; 1 Jan 1774 (A 70.17); <u>inv.</u>; 1 Jan 1774 (I 116.189)

Wheatley, James; <u>inv.</u>; 13 Jun 1769; 1 Sep 1769; nok _chibastiz (sic) Greenwell, Richard Clarke (I 101.330)

Wheatly, Francis, Sr.; wheelwright; <u>will</u>; 8 Jan 1773; 20 Jul 1774; sons Ignatius, Francis; daus. Ann Peek, Winifred Dillihay; tracts *Buxkland Plain, Wheatly's Content with Addition, Bobs Discovery* (MCW 16.23) [SMW TA1.684]

Wheatley, Sylvester; m. 7 Sep 1773 Eliz. Fraiser (MM)

Wheatly, Ignatius; inv.; 14 Feb 1775; 16 Jun 1775; nok Ann Peek, Francis Wheatly; admx./extx. Henrietta Wheatly (I 121.408)

WHEELER
Wheller, Samuell; inv.; 9 Jul 1703 (I&A 1.690)

Wheeler, Luke; 30 Nov 1741; 3 Mar 1741; sons Ignatius, William, Clement, Raphell, Bennet; wife Protheser [Crothe (?)]; tracts *Maiden's Bower, Planter's Delight* (MCW 8.161) [SMW TA1.125]; inv.; 10 May 1741; 3 Aug 1742; nok Ignatius & Susannah Wheeler; admx./extx. Pretheser Wheeler (I 27.56); acct.; 6 Sep 1743 (A 19.537)

Wheeler, Bennett; inv.; 4 May 1773; 10 Oct 1773; nok Ignatius Wheeler, Susannah Shardith (?); admx. Jane Wheeler (I 114.15)

Wheeler, Francis; m. 19 Dec 1775 Anna Birchmore (MM)

Wheeler, Francis and Ann his wife; son William, b. 18 Sep 1776 (SA p. 27)

Wheeler, Moses and Henrietta Redman; m. 28 Nov 1778 (SA p. 57)

WHERITT
Wherrett, William; inv.; 27 Feb 1716 (I&A 37b.10); acct.; 15 Dec 1718 (A 2.253); acct.; 15 Dec 1718 (SMAA p. 347)

Wherritt, John; 4 Aug 1764; nok Nicholas & Thomas Wherritt; admx. Joan Wherritt (I 84.277)

WHITE
White, Nicholas; will; St. Inigoes; 22 May 1659; 15 Nov 1659; wife Mary, extx., dau. Ellinor (MCW 1.10)

White, Mary; will; probate 15 Nov 1659; widow of Nicholas; child. Ellinor and Mary (MCW 1.11)

White, Jerome, Esq.; *Brick Hill*; 200 ac.; sur. 9 May 1665; 1707 poss. by Wm. Price; incl. in resur. of *Vineyard*; St. Mary's Hundred (RR p. 3) (TLC p. 4)
Vineyard; 100 ac.; sur. 9 May 1665; 1707 poss. by Tho. Price and/or Fran. Price; St. Mary's Hundred (RR p. 3) (TLC p. 4)

White, Thomas; service by 1674 (SK 18.158)

White, Kuzia; acct.; 6 Jan 1679 (I&A 6.601)

White, Nicholas; 5 Jan 1688; 26 Jan 1688; mentions cousins Robert Jordan and Frances Bouye (MCW 2.42) [SMW PC1.78]; acct.; [filed with 1692-3] (I&A 10.328)

White, David; inv.; [filed with 1715-6] (I&A 36c.282)

White, William; inv.; 28 Jun 1723; 27 Jul 1723; nok William & Ann Whitt; admx. w/o David Roach, Jr. (I 9.214); acct.; 11 Mar 1723 (A 5.386)

White, William; planter; will; 3 Apr 1732; 17 Apr 1732; b-i-l George Beverlye (MCW 6.219) [SMW PC1.351]; inv.; 15 May 1732; 6 Jun 1732; nok w/o George Barnerly (I 16.472); acct.; 25 Jun 1733 (A 11.715)

White, James; Sr.; <u>will</u>; 27 May 1732; 24 Jun1732; wife Sarah; sons James, William (MCW 6.231) [SMW PC1.353]; <u>inv.</u>; 25 Jul 1732; 25 Sep 1732; nok James & William White; admx./extx. Sarah White (I 16.612); <u>acct.</u>; 7 Dec 1733 (A 12.137)

White, John; <u>will</u>; 10 Apr 1734; 17 Jun 1734; sons Joseph, John, Moses; wife Martha (MCW 7.94) [SMW TA1.29]; <u>inv.</u>; 20 Jul 1734; 9 Sep 1734; nok John Ploumer, Joseph Bennett; admx./extx. Martha White (I 19.53); <u>acct.</u>; 27 Oct 1735 (A 14.107)

White, William; <u>acct.</u>; 17 Jun 1734 (A 12.351)

White, James; age ca 56; mentions William, s/o Solomon Jones; 21 Apr 1737 (CCRp. 81)

White, Joseph; <u>will</u>; 8 Mar 1755; 30 Jun 1755; son James; wife Ann; daus. Elizabeth, Darkey, Peggy; tract *Courses* (MCW 11.94) [SMW TA1.325]; <u>inv.</u>; 7 Jul 1755; 8 Sep 1755; nok Moses White, Mary King; admx./extx. Ann White (I 59.197); <u>acct.</u>; 1 Jan 1756 (A 39.65)

White, James; <u>will</u>; 24 Jan 1756; kinsman Joseph Bennett (MCW 12.35) [SMW TA1.406]

White, James; <u>inv.</u>; 4 Aug 1761; nok John & Maye Fletcher (I 74.270)

White, William and Veache; son Jesse, bapt. 18 Jun 1780 (SA p. 30)

WHITTLE

Whittle, William; New Towne; m. Susanna, widow of Thomas Williams; by 25 Oct 1659 (AM XLIX.54)

Whittle, William; *Hunters Hill*; 150 ac.; sur. 22 Oct 1667; 1707 poss. Robert Thomas; Poplar Hill Hundred (RR)

Whittle, William; 4 Mar 1673; 13 Mar 1673; wife Katherine; unnamed child. (MCW 1.79)

WILDMAN

Wildman, Cornelius; *Tradesman's Lot*; 200 ac.; 10 Oct 1707 cert./pat. (COL); sur. 18 Jun 1704 (TLC)

Wildman, Cornelius; <u>inv.</u>; 25 Jun 1718; mentions Mary Wildman (I 1.313); <u>acct.</u>; 9 Jun 1719; adm. James Wildman (A 2.16) (SMAA p. 392); 20 Apr 1719 (SMAA p. 399); <u>acct.</u>; 2 Aug 1721 (A 3.499)

Wildman, James; <u>will</u>; 5 Jan 1724/5; 1 Mar 1724/5; sister Mary Moony; uncle John Wildman; m-i-l Martha Wildman; b-i-l Thomas Mooney; tracts *Saint Edwards, Linstead, Tradesmans Lott* (MCW 5.185) [SMW PC1.294]; <u>inv.</u>; 20 Apr 1725; 2 Jun 1725 (I 10.414); <u>acct.</u>; 1 Aug 1726 (A 7.504); <u>acct.</u>; 12 Jun 1727 (A 8.272)

Wildman, Cornelius; *Wildman's Venture*; 54 ac.; sur. 22 Nov 1742 (TLC p. 97); 56 ac.; 29 Nov 1742 cert./pat. (COL)

Golden Grove; 153 ac.; sur. 12 May 1743 (TLC p. 101); 20 Jul 1743 cert./pat.
(COL)
Wildman's Levels; 168 ac.; sur. 26 Feb 1745 (TLC p. 110); 26 Feb 1746 cert./pat.
(COL)
Wildman, Cornelius; <u>will</u>; 10 Oct 1763; 2 Nov 1763; sons John, Cornelius; wife
Ann; daus. Mary Anne Snowden, Susannah, Monica; tracts *Brooks Chance,
Wildman's Venture, Tavern, The Golden Grove, Dillon's Dissapointment,*
(MCW 12.217); <u>inv.</u>; 1 May 1764; nok Susanah Wildman, John Reeder, Jr.; exs.
Cornelius & Ann Wildman (I 84.278); <u>acct.</u>; 28 Jul 1765; adms. Cornelius
Wildman, Henry Hudson Watkins and his wife Ann Watkins (A 53.84); <u>dist.</u>; 28
Jul 1765; mentions widow; child. John, Cornelius, Mary Ann Snowden,
Susanna, Monica; exs. Cornelius Wildman, Henry Hudson Wathin and wife
Ann (BB 4.131)

WILKINSON

Wilkeson, William; <u>will</u>; 16 Aug 1738; 18 Dec 1738; wife Rebecca; sons John,
James, William; daus. Elizabeth, Mary, Jane, Catherine, Sarah; ch./o son
William: William, Benet Dawkins, Mary (MCW 8.7) [SMW TA1.59]; <u>inv.</u>; 10 Feb
1738; 19 Apr 1739; nok James Wilkinson, Daniel Gore; adms./exs. Katharine
& William Wiellkison (I 24.53)
Wilkison (Wilkinson), William; <u>inv.</u>; 24 Apr 1742 (I 26.543); <u>acct.</u>; 28 Apr 1742;
exs. Rebecca & John Wilkinson (A 19.33)
Wilkinson, William and Nancy; child. Mark Thomas [b. 12 Jul 1765]; Winifred
[b. 24 Oct 1762]; James [b. 18 Feb 1769]; Mary [b. 23 Jun 1771] (SA p. 2, 41)
Wilkinson, William; immigrated by 1667 (SK 11.263)
Wilkinson, John; <u>inv.</u>; 29 Mar 1774; 10 Jul 1774; nok William & James
Wilkinson (I 119.113)

WILLAN

Willan, Richard; age ca 30; 11 Mar 1651 (AM X.147)
Willan, Richard; gifts to daus. Elizabeth and Grace; 1659 (AM XLI.304)
Willan, Elizabeth; relict of Richard; 1663 (AM XLIX.35, 51)

WILLES

Willis (Willes), William;; <u>inv.</u>; 25 Sep 1727; nok Samuel & Abigal Willis;
admx. Elisabeth Willis (I 12.266); <u>acct.</u>; 18 Jun 1728 (A 9.33); <u>acct.</u>; 3 Jun 1729
(A 9.380)
Willis, Elisabeth; <u>inv.</u>; 29 Aug 1734; 5 Jun 1735; nok Thomas & Ryall Reeves;
adm./ex. James Mills (I 20.473)

WILLIAMS

William, John; wife Mary; 25 Mar 1663 (AM XLIX.2); Mary of St. John's accused of theft; 1658 (AM XLI.207)

William, John; service by 1672 (SK 17.399)

Williams, William; <u>inv.</u>; 10 Feb 1678 (I&A 5.348); <u>acct.</u>; [filed with 1678] (I&A 5.362)

Williams, Rice; <u>will</u>; 6 Feb 1684; 25 Mar 1685; b-i-l Henry Franckham (MCW 1.157)

Williams, Michael; *Good Fortune*; 99 ac.; 10 Nov 1695 cert./pat. (COL)

Williams, John; <u>inv.</u>; 11 Feb 1708 (I&A 29.54); <u>acct.</u>; 30 Aug 1710; admx. Margarett, w/o John Carmichael (I&A 31.366) (SMAA p. 201)

Williams, Edward; <u>will</u>; 15 Mar 1709; 10 Mar 1710; son Henry; wife Margaret (MCW 3.166) [SMW PC1.169]; <u>inv.</u>; 20 May 1710 (I&A 31.348)

Williams, David; <u>inv.</u>; 20 Dec 1714; 20 Dec 1714 (I&A 36c.131); <u>acct.</u>; 7 May 1715 (I&A 36c.57) (SMAA p. 291)

Williams, Jacob; age ca 39; 11 May 1720 (CCR p. 47)

Williams, Jacob; <u>will</u>; planter; 6 Dec 1725; 1 Jan 1725; wife Elizabeth; sons William and Benjamin (MCW 5.209) [SMW PC1.300]; <u>inv.</u>; 8 Mar 1725; 25 Jun 1726; nok Anthony & Mary Evans; extx. Elisabeth Williams (I 11.483, 486); <u>acct.</u>; 31 May 1727 (A 8.226); <u>acct.</u>; 22 Mar 1728 (A 9.377)

Williams, Hugh; <u>inv.</u>; 20 Jun 1733; 4 Sep 1733; nok minor; admx./extx. Isabell Williams (I 17.340); <u>acct.</u>; 29 Apr 1734 (A 12.279)

Williams, Benjamin; *Neglect*; 53 ac.; sur. 25 Sep 1732 (TLC p. 92); 23 Aug 1736 cert./pat. (COL)

    Squires' Purchase; 37 ac.; sur. 9 Jan 1724 for John Squire (TLC p. 96) ; 16 Nov 1740 cert./pat. (COL)

    William's Fortune; 182 ac.; sur. 15 Aug 1745;originally *Bamfields Woods*; pat. 18 Mar 1746 to John Briscoe (TLC)

    Park; 68½ ac.; sur.; 28 Sep 1745; pat. vacated 5 Dec 1749 (TLC p. 106); 68 ac.; 29 Sep 1745 cert./pat. (COL)

    Walnut Point; 55 ac.; sur. 15 Jan 1748 (TLC p. 113); 15 Jan 1748 cert./pat. (COL)

    Fox Den; 89 ac.; sur. 1 May 1749 (TLC p. 114); 1 May 1749 cert./pat. (COL)

    Williams' Addition; 22 ac.; sur. 4 Oct 1748 (TLC p. 116); 4 Oct 1748 cert./pat. (COL)

    Muggs' Adventure Addition; 186 ac.; 21 Nov 1768 cert./pat. (COL)

Williams, Elizabeth; <u>will</u>; 23 Sep 1736; 6 Dec 1736; sons Philip and Anthony Evans; sons William and Benjamin; dau. Mary Pearce (MCW 7.200) [SMW TA1.51]; <u>inv.</u>; 1 Mar 1736; 4 Mar 1736; nok Philip Evans, William Williams; adm./ex. Benjamin Williams (I 22.212); <u>acct.</u>; 17 Nov 1740 (A 18.110)

Williams, William; <u>inv.</u>; 14 Feb 1744; 4 Jun 1745; nok William & George Brown; admx./extx. Rebecca Williams (I 31.154); <u>acct.</u>; 21. Jan 1745 (A 22.89)

Williams, William; *Mugg's Adventure*; 252 ac.; resur. for William Harrison 30 May 1738; orig. *Balla Keyting* (TLC p. 106); 29 Mar 1745 cert./pat. (COL)

Williams, Benjamin, Capt.; b. ca 1748; d. 15 Jul 1821; age 73 (HGM)

Williams, John; will; 16 Mar 1749; 5 Jun 1750; sons Jeremiah, John; daus. Susanna, Mary, [Eliza]; wife Eliza (MCW 10.96) [SMW TA1.255]; inv.; 25 Aug 1750; 3 Sep 1750; nok Jeremiah & Susannah Williams; adms./exs. Elisabeth & John Williams (I 43.384); acct.; 18 Jul 1751; mentions John & Susannah [both at age], Jeremiah [age 15], Mary [age 12], Sarah [age 11] (A 30.202)

Williams, Elizabeth; will; 20 Jan 1763; 29 Jun 1763; daus. Mary and Susanna (MCW 12.205) [SMW TA1.444]; inv.; 2 Nov 1763; nok Mary Williams, Susannah Welsh; extx. Susannah Williams (I 82.205a); acct.; 31 Oct 1765 (A 54.7); dist.; 31 Oct 1765; daus Mary, Susanna (BB 4.152)

Williams, William; inv.; 2 May 1770; 9 May 1770; admx. Ann Williams (I 104.285); acct.; 30 May 1771; Jr. (A 66.167)

Williams, Joseph; m. 5 Feb 1771 Ann Heard; d/o Jac. (MM)

Williams, Benjamin; will; probate 8 Dec 1771; wife Ann; child. Elizabeth Benit [Bennett], Henrieta Henly, Ann, Benjamin, Jacob; tract *Punchneys* [*Pamunkey's*] (MCW 14.194) [SMW TA1.628]

Williams, Hugo; m. 21 Mar 1773 Lydia Stone (MM)

Williams, Benjamin; inv.; 1 Jul 1773; ex. Benjamin Williams (I 112.418); acct.; 1 Jul 1773 (A 68.208)

Williams, William; will; 21 Nov 1775; 12 Mar 1776; wife Frances; sons James, Joseph; daus. Nancey James, Monica; g-dau. Nancy Williams; tract *Robert's Neck* (MCW 16.117)

Williams, Mary; consort of Benjamin; d. 3 Aug 1814; age 56 (HGM)

WILLIAMSON

Williamson, Christopher; service by 1680 (SK WC2.281)

Williamson, Samuel; *Tanyard*; 210 ac.; sur. 22 Dec 1706; Choptico Manor; "let fall" (TLC p. 66); 1710 cert./pat. (COL)
Nicholl's Hope; 185 ac.; 15 Oct 1713 cert./pat. (COL)
Williamson's Chance; 210 ac.; sur. 5 Jan 1713; resur. into *Cawoods Expense* (TLC p. 70); 10 Apr 1714 cert./pat. (COL)

Williamson, Samll.; age ca 55; 26 Feb 1714; tract *Westham* (CCRp. 32); age 71 in 1729 (MD p. 203)

Williamson, Samuel, Mr.; inv.; 30 Oct 1729; 24 Nov 1729; admx./extx. Mrs. Judith Williamson (I 15.357); acct.; 13 Oct 1730 (A 10.469); acct.; 4 Nov 1731 (A 11.256)

Williamson, Samuel; gent.; will; written 19 Jun 1713; articles of agreement with Judith Swann, widow prior to marriage (MCW 6.142) [SMW PC1.338]

WILSON

Wilson, William; immigrated from VA 1670 (SK 12.582)

Wilson, Alexander; service by 1671 (SK 16.405)

Wilson, Giles; service by 1673 (SK 17.516)

Wilson, John; inv.; 6 May 1706 (I&A 26.3); acct.; 17 May 1707; admx. Katherine, w/o John Taney (I&A 26.319) (SMAA p. 159); acct.; 12 Jul 1709 (I&A 29.393) (SMAA p. 178); acct.; 7 Mar 1712 (I&A 33b.232) (SMAA p. 236)

Wolson (Wilson), John; inv.; 14 Dec 1722; admx. Barbery Wilson (I 9.18); acct.; 21 Nov 1723 (A 5.290)

Willson, Barbary; inv.; 19 Mar 1724; 12 May 1724 (I 9.381); acct.; 26 Apr 1725 (A 6.328)

Wilson (Willson), William; inv.; 18 Jun 1734; 15 Nov 1734; nok Mary Shanks, Sarah Willson; admx./extx. Susanna Wilson (I 20.108); acct.; 15 Sep 1735; orphans Mary Ann & Sarah Wilson (A 13.322)

Wilson, Susannah; will; 26 Jan 1739; 16 Apr 1740; sons John and Abraham Langly; dau. Susannah Wildman; g-dau. Mary Ann Wildman (MCW 8.79) [SMW TA1.114]

WIMSATT

Wimsett, Richard; planter; inv.; 28 Oct 1725; 4 Nov 1725; nok Richard & John Wimsett; admx. Sarah Wimsett (I 11.139)

Wimsett (Wimsatt), John; inv.; 18 Jun 1734; 19 Sep 1734; nok Richard & Thomas Wimsett; admx./extx. Ann Wimsett (I 19.137); acct.; 3 Nov 1736; orphans Ignatius, John, Monica & Priscilla Wimast (A 15.225)

Winsett, Thomas; acct.; 3 Jul 1750; admx. Tomason Winsett (A 28.229)

Wimsett, Richard; will; 19 Feb 1752; 26 Feb 1752; sons Richard, Robert and Henry (2nd sons), Ignatious; daus. Mary, Monica, Dorothy, Susanna; wife Teresa; tracts *Willia. Indeavor*[*Williams Endeavor*], *Wimsetts Frolick* (MCW 10.200) [SMW TA1.200]

Wimsatt (Wimsett), Richard; inv.; 26 Feb 1752; 8 Jun 1752; nok Henry & Robert Wimsatt; adms./exs. Teresia, Richard & Robert Wimsatt (I 49.25); acct.; 15 Apr [filed 1753]; orphans Richard & Robert [both of age], Henry [age 18], Ignatious [age 13], Mary & Monica [both of age], Dorothy [age 11], Susannah [age 8]; exs. Tereitia, Richard & Robert Wimsatt (A 34.148); dist.; 15 Apr 1753; exs. Teresa, Richard & Robert Wimsett; child. Mary, Monica, Richard & Robert [of full age], Henry [age 19 next Dec], Ignatius [age 14 next Apr], Dorothy [age 12 next Aug], Susannah [age 9 next Oct] (BB 1.78)

Wimsatt, John and Henrietta his wife; child. Ralph [b. 1 Oct 1754]; William [b. 16 May 1757]; Elizabeth [b. 14 Nov 1759]; Robert Henry [b. 9 May 1762]; Ann [b. 27 Dec 1764] (SA p. 11, 45)

Winsett, Robert; *Hard Times*; 150 ac.; 18 Oct 1760 cert./pat. (COL)

Bob's Discovery; 150 ac.; 29 Sep 1762 cert./pat. (COL)

Wimsatt, Henry; inv.; 15 Jun 1762; 12 Mar 1762; nok Robert & James Wimsatt; admx. Frances Wimsatt (I 80.144); acct.; 20 May 1763 (A 49.618)

Wimsatt, Richard; inv.; 4 Jun 1767; 12 Jan 1767; nok Tereasa & Ignatius Wimsatt; admx. Eleanor Wimsatt (I 94.198); inv.; 22 Oct 1770 (I 105.1); acct.; 30 Oct 1770 (A 64.233); acct.; 25 Jun 1771 (A 66.175)

Winsatt, John and Henrietta his wife; dau. Priscilla, b. 5 Apr 1769 (SA p. 4)

Wimsatt, Stephen; m. 25 Aug 1770 Mary Low (MM)

Wimsatt, Ignatius; m. 31 Dec 1772 Mary Medley (MM)

Wimsatt, Stephen and Mary his wife; child. Joseph Zachariah [b. 24 May 1773]; Frances [b. 5 Mar 1774] (SA p. 26)

WINSTED

Winsted, Richard; oral; will; 2 Aug 1725; 3 Aug 1725 (MCW 5.198) [SMW PC1.298]; acct.; 18 Jul 1726; admx. Sarah Winsted (Winsett) (A 7.503)

Winsted, Thomas; inv.; 2 Apr 1750; 1 May 1750; nok William, Jr. & Thomas Winstead; admx./extx. Tomason Winsett (I 42.224)

WISE

Wise, Richard; will; 10 Mar 1728/9; 16 Jan 1732; sons William, Adam, Mathew; s-i-l John Newton (MCW 7.10) [SMW TA1.15]; inv.; 13 Jun 1733; nok Adam & Mathew Wise; adm./extx. William Wise (I 17.160); acct.; 25 Jul 1734; mentions Matthew and William Wise (A 12.456)

Wise, Richard and Mary; child. Caleb [b. 6 Nov 1752]; Jane [b. 6 Feb 1755]; Dorothy [b. 18 Sep 1760]; Margaret [b. 25 Nov 1763] (SA p. 3)

Wise, John and Margaret his wife; child. Clarke [b. 7 Jan 1753];Eleanor [b. 27 Dec 1754]; Rhode [b. 15 Mar 1756]; John [b. 10 Feb 1758]; James Manning [b. 17 Apr 1762] (SA p. 4)

Wise, Joseph and Sarah his wife; daus. Nancy [b. 7 Nov 1755]; Henrietta [31 Aug 1762] (SA p. 41)

Wise, Jemima; child. Dorcas [b. 3 Jun 1763]; Edward Swann [b. 10 Apr 1768] (SA p. 6)

Wise, Thomas and Mary his wife; sons Jeremiah [b. 15 Apr 1764] (SA p. 40); Ransean [b. 29 Jan 1766] (SA p. 42)

Wise, John; wife Margaret; son Cuthbert [b. 9 Apr 1765] (SA p. 1)

Wise, Adam and Frances his wife; son James [b. 17 Mar 1767] (SA p. 3); John [b. 28 Jan 1770] (SA p. 191); George [bapt. 16 Jul 1780] (SA p. 30)

Wise, William and Elizabeth Clocker; m. 19 Nov 1778 (SA p. 57)

Wise, Adam and Susannah Bryan; m. 2 Nov 1779 (SA p. 57)

Wise, Caleb and Catharine Wise (by license); m. 13 Nov 1783 (SA p. 61)

Wise, James and Allethea: child William Cornelius Francis [b. 25 May 1799; bapt. 11 Oct 1799] (SA p. 31)

WISEMAN

Wiseman, Robert; will; probate 16 Apr 1650; son John (MCW 1.4)

Wiseman, John; *Batchelors Hopewell*; 200 ac.; sur. 20 Jul 1665; 1707 poss. John Wiseman's widow, w/o Rich'd Shirly; resur. *Batchellors Hopewell Rectified*; Harvey Hundred (RR p. 56) (TLC p. 53)

Wiseman, John; *Wisemans Chance*; 100 ac.; sur. 6 Apr 1682; 1707 poss. Cornelius Manning; Harvey Hundred (RR p. 57) (TLC p. 54); 6 Apr 1682 cert./pat. (COL);

Wiseman, John; will; 6 Dec 1703; 13 Jul 1704; sons John, Robert; dau. Mary. w/o Cornelius Manning; wife Catherine (MCW 3.38) [SMW PC1.133]; inv.; 12 Aug 1704 (I&A 3.589); acct.; 20 Sep 1705; extx. Katherine, w/o Richard Shirley (I&A 25.52) (SMAA p. 130); acct.; 4 Jun 1708 (SMAA p. 165); acct.; 20 Jul 1720; child. John, Robertt & Katherine, w/o Mr. John Greenwell (A 3.71) (SMAA p. 433)

Wiseman, John; will; 26 Jan 1716; 18 Apr 1716/7; father Richard Shirley; mother Katherine Shirley; bros. Robert Wiseman, Richard Shirley, sister Catherine Greenwell; cousin Francis Miles (MCW 4.73) [SMW PC1.204]; inv.; 9 Jul 1716; nok Robert Wiseman, Katherine Grenwell (I&A 37a.164); acct.; 23 Jul 1717 (I&A 37b.133, 134) (SMAA p. 316)

Wiseman, Robert; inv.; 15 Aug 1737; 30 Aug 1737; nok Richard Shirly, John Wiseman; admx./extx. Elisabeth Wiseman (I 22.407); inv.; 29 Dec 1737 (I 23.24); acct.; 21 Aug 1738; orphans John, Edward, William, Richard, Mary, Ann & Elisabeth Wiseman (A 16.295)

Wiseman, John; *Bachelor's Hopewell Resurveyed* or *Rectified*; 374 ac.; orig. *Battchellors Hopewell*; resur. 3 Aug 1744 (TLC p. 112); 5 Apr 1748 cert./pat. (COL)

Wiseman, Elizabeth; will; 25 Oct 1762; 20 Feb 1763; sons John, Richard & his son Robert; dau. Ann Vanrishrick & her child. Monica, Wilford; dau. Mary Leigh & her dau. Peggy; dau. Elizabeth Downie (MCW 12.175) [SMW TA1.435]; inv.; 26 Jan 1763; 25 Oct 1763; nok John Wiseman, David Downie; ex. Richard Wiseman (I 82.201); acct.; 30 Oct 1765; ex. Richard Wiseman (A 53.229); dist.; 30 Oct 1765; child. John, Richard, Mary Leigh, Ann Vanrishwick, Elisabeth Downie; g-child. Monica & Milford Vanrishwick, Robert Wiseman, Peggy Leigh (BB 4.147)

Wiseman, Robert and Eleanor King (by license); m. 5 Feb 1792 (SA p. 60)

WITHERINGTON

Witherington, James; inv.; 20 Jan 1733; 8 Apr 1734; nok Henry Attwood, minors; admx./extx. Elisabeth Witherington (I 17.718)

Witherington, James; acct.; 28 Jul 1760; admx. Johannah, w/o Thomas Clark (A 46.16)

WOOD

Wood, Wm.; *Green Hill*; 250 ac.; sur. 19 Apr 1662; 1707 poss. John Ryley; New Town Hundred (RR p. 32) (TLC p. 31)

Woods, Mathias; service by 1675 (SK 18.319)

Wood, James; *Woods Addition*; 12 ac.; sur. 30 Sep 1714 partly in SM Co. (TLC p. 117)

Wood, Joseph; *WoodLand*; 150 ac.; sur. 21 Dec 1726; resur. into *Wood Inclosure* (TLC p. 91)
   Brotherhood; 150 ac.; 10 Nov 1735 cert./pat. (COL)
   Wood's Enclosure; 344 ac.; sur. 6 Jan 1742; orig. called *Brotherhood* (TLC p. 104); 6 Jan 1744 cert./pat. (COL)

Wood, Samuel; *Wood's Wilderness*; 100 ac.; 10 Jun 1727 cert./pat. (COL)

Wood, James; inv.; 4 May 1729; 5 Nov 1729; nok James & Benjamin Wood; admx. Rachell Wood (I 15.144); acct.; 4 Aug 1730 (A 10.420)

Wood, Abraham; *Woods Pleasure*; 210 ac.; sur. 26 Jun 1731 CH & SM Cos. (TLC p. 90); pat. CH Co. 13 Jun 1734 cert./pat. (COL)

Wood, James, Jr.; gent.; *Arabia*; 76 ac.; sur. 21 Nov 1724 (TLC p. 96); 13 Aug 1740 cert./pat. (COL)

Wood, David; inv.; 2 Oct 1743; 16 Jan 1743; nok 1 minor; admx./extx. Elisabeth Wood (I 28.445); acct.; [filed with 1744] (A 20.145)

Wood, Samuel; planter; will; 22 Feb 1758; 4 Jul 1758; daus. Ann Briscoe, Susanna Suit, Elizabeth Banner; sons Jonathan, Samuel; other unnamed child.; g-son Jeared [Leonard] Briscoe (MCW 11.207) [SMW TA1.365]; inv.; 3 Oct 1758; 8 Nov 1758; nok Samuel Wood, Lydia Lyon; adm.ex. Jonathon Wood (I 65.424); acct.; 24 Oct 1759 (A 43.354)

Wood, Nathan; bann published 23 Feb 1783 Elizab. Wm. (BRU, p. 536)

WOODWARD

Woodward, John; 24 Aug 1700; 19 Sep 1720 (I 4.232)

Woodworth, John; inv.; 23 Feb 1703 (I&A 1.689)

Woodward, Robert; inv.; 29 Oct 1706 (I&A 26.161); acct.; 8 Feb 1709; mentions William, s/o James Bland (I&A 31.37); acct. 8 Feb 1709 (SMAA p. 186)

Woodward, Thomas; Poplar Hill Hundred; will; written 27 Apr 1718; daus. Johanna, Mary; wife Rachel (MCW 4.164) [SMW PC1.231]; inv.; 25 Jul 1718; nok young child. (I 1.410); acct.; 12 Dec 1719; extx. Rachell Woodward (A 2.413) (SMAA p. 365)

Woodward, John; will; 2 Feb 1719/20; 28 Feb 1719/20; daus. Margaret, Anne; sons John, James (MCW 5.2) [SMW PC1.256]

Woodward, John; acct.; 19 Nov 1726; orphans (A 8.77); acct.; 11 Mar 1728 (A 9.290)

Woodward, John; will; 15 Mar 1757; 20 Jun 1757; wife unnamed; son William (MCW II.170) [SMW TA1.359]; inv.; 23 Jun 1757 17 Oct 1757; nok Ann Lee, Joseph Shurmindine; admx./exs. Charles Warlorum & wife Ann (I 64.2); acct.; 20 Nov 1758 (A 42.220); acct.; 10 Nov 1760; orphan William [age 17] (A 46.159); dist.; 10 Nov 1760 (BB 3.50)

WOOTTON

Wootton, Thomas and Susanna his wife; child. Susanna [b. 7 Mar 1759]; Isaac [b. 9 Jun 1761]; Bennet [b. 10 Jul 1762]; Frances [b. 9 May 1765] (SA p. 18, 53)

Wootton, Joseph and wife Mary; child. John [b. 5 Nov 1759]; Thomas [b. 5 Feb 1762]; Elizabeth [b. 19 Mar 1764]; Joseph [b. 30 Sep 1766] (SA p. 2, 3)

Wootton, Thomas and Elizabeth; son Thomas [b. 27 Apr 1769] (SA p. 191)

Wootton, Thomas and Nancy Bentley (by publication); m. 5 Jun 1781 (SA p. 59)

WRIGHT

Wright, Arthur; *Wright*; 150 ac.; sur. 14 Aug 1642; 1707 Widow King; Harvey Hundred (RR)

Wright, William; will; 3 Jun 1660; 23 Apr 1662; wife Mary; 3 unnamed child.; son William (MCW 1.20)

Wright, Robert; *Wrights Gift*; 150 ac.; sur. 25 Feb 1666; 1707 no poss.; Harvey Hundred (RR p. 56) (TLC p. 53)

Wright, Ismael; *Ismaels Right*; 300 ac.; sur. 5 Oct 1666; 1707 poss. John Evans of PG Co. Harvey Hundred (RR p. 56) (TLC p. 53)

Wright, Thomas; St. Jerome's; will; 2 Aug 1673; 3 Sep 1673; mentions John and Thomas, sons of Joseph Hackney; wife unnamed (MCW 1.75); inv. and acct.; 20 Nov 1674; relict Jane Ryder; (/s/ Jane Wright) (I&A 1.125, 127)

Wright, William; s/o William of *Poplar Hill*, dec'd; 1673 (AM LXV.95)

Wright, George; St. Inigoes; will; 25 Aug 1679; 22 Apr 1680; mentions James and Shuny, child. of John Thompson (MCW 1.91)

Wright, William; acct.; 9 Jul 1686 (I&A 9.47)

Wright, Thomas; acct.; 18 Jul 1687 (I&A 9.326); acct.; 5 Apr 1688 (I&A 9.489)

Wright, William; acct.; 14 Oct 1721; admx. Rachel Wright (A 4.21); acct.; 2 Jun 1724 (A 6.37)

Wright, James; inv.; 6 Mar 1739; nok Thomas Edward (I 24.534)

Wright, John; inv.; 2 Apr 1740; 31 Mar 1741; nok Thomas & Dennis Tippett; admx./extx. Ann Wright (I 25.440)

Write, Samuel; inv.; 21 Mar 1770; 17 May 1772; nok Kezia & James Davis;
admx. Susannah Wright (I 109.349); acct.; [filed with 1774]; admx. Susan, w/o
Richard Pickering (A 70.141)

WYNNE
Wynne, Thomas; m. Elizabeth, relict of Richard Willaine; 16 Oct 1665 (AM
LVII.6)
Wynne, Tho.; *Denby*; 250 ac.; sur. 2 May 1666; 1707 poss. Edward Digges; St.
Mary's Hundred (RR p. 5) (TLC p. 5)
Rithing; 100 ac.; sur. 2 May 1666; 1707 poss. John Brisco; 4 May 1686
mentions Hen. Taylor & wife Margt. Wynne; St. Mary's Hundred (RR p. 5)
(TLC p. 5)
Wynne, John; service by 1670 (SK 16.96)
Wynne, John, Dr.; Poplar Hill; will; 22 Jan 1683; 10 Mar 1684; wife Anne; son
John; others unnamed; tract *Governor's Gift, Bennett's Delight* (MCW 1.136)
[SMW PC1.50]; inv.; 10 Mar 1684 (I&A 8.385); acct.; 10 Aug 1686; admx. Ann
(relict), w/o James Berry (I&A 9.132)
Wynne, Thomas; inv.; [filed with 1685] (I&A 8.393)
Wynn, John; *Hog Neck Addition*; 16 ac.; 6 Mar 1756 cert./pat. (COL)
Wynne, Thomas; inv.; [filed with 1685] (I&A 8.393)

YATES
Yates, John; service by 1673 (SK 17.575)
Yates, Isaiah; inv.; 18 Jan 1710; 17 Mar 1710 (I&A 32c.45)
Yates, Martin; age ca 49; Jun 1715; tract *Fenwick Manor* (CCR p. 33)
Yeates, Martin; innholder; will; 28 Sep 1722; 23 Apr 1724; sons William,
Martin, Thomas, John, Elextious; wife Elizabeth (MCW 5.166) [SMW PC1.283]
Yates, Thomas; elder; planter; will; 19 Aug 1763; 15 Feb 1771; wife Mary;
child. Ignatius, John, Thomas, Ann, Mary (MCW 14.181) [SMW TA1.626]
Yates, Thomas; inv.; 10 Oct 1770; nok John & Ignatius Yates; admx. Mary
Yates (I 103.340)
Yates, Martin; 9 Jul 1770; 28 Aug 1775; sons John, Edward, Martin; wife Ann;
mentions unnamed child. (MCW 16.110) [SMW TA1.722]

YOUNG
Young, William; wife Sarah; ack. right to Thomas Bennett of 50 a. of *Poplar
Neck* in Brettons Bay; 14 Oct 1663 (AM XLIX.572)
Young, Sarah; age ca 27 in 1665 (MD p. 209)
Young, Nicholas; will; 11 Jan 1669; 29 Jan 1669; wife Elizabeth; s-i-l Edward
Parker, dec'd; tract *Fresh Pond Neck* (MCW 1.50) [SMW PC1.7]

Young, Elizabeth; relict of Edward Parker; son Edward Parker; mentions *Fresh Pond Neck*; mentions Sarah, w/o William Clawe & Margaret Jolly, widow of Edward, m/2 John Stevens; 17 Sep 1679 (CCR p. 4)

Young, Elisabeth; inv.; [filed with 1696] (I&A 14.38)

Young, John Abell and Ann his wife; sons James, b. 26 Jun 1766; John Standfill, b. 16 Jan 1768 (SA p. 17)

Young, John; inv.; 23 May 1731; 20 Dec 1732; nok Samuell & Samuell Young, Jr.; adm./ex. Mary Young (I 17.16)

Young, John, Mr.; acct.; 14 Jan 1737; orphans Mary & Elisabeth Young (A 16.31)

Abbott, Samuel; service by 1676 (SK 15.377)

Adkinson, Joshua and Susanna; dau. Mary Brent [b. 25 Aug 1759]; gd/o Brent
  Nutthall s/o Mary Brent who was sister to William Brent, Esq. (SA p. 39)

Aftin, John; inv.; 25 Sep 1733; 5 Nov 1733; adm./ex. Eleanor Aftin (I 17.538)

Alcock, Isaac; service by 1669 (SK 12.247)

Alexander, Charles; age ca 22; 1663 (MD p. 2)

Allamond, John Baptist; inv.; 14 Aug 1767; 30 Apr 1768 (I 95.252)

Allerton, Isaack; wife Elizabeth, admx. of Symon Overzee (AM XLIX.466; XLI..389)

Allford, Elizabeth; transported by 1667 by Walter Hall, gent. (SK 11.230)

Allman, Thomas; m. legatee of John Tongue; 26 Jun 1719 (CCR p. 41)

Ames, John; inv.; 1761; admx. Susanna, w/o Stephen Lucas (I 76.315)

Amos, Michael; service by 1675 (SK 18.305; 15.310)

Aram, Thomas; service by 1674 (SK18.83)

Arnold, Thomas; planter; service prior to 1667 (SK11.5)

Ashbrook, Tho.; *Yeildingsbury*; 100 ac.; sur. 8 Apr 1653; 1707 poss. John
  Bayly; New Town Hundred (RR p. 30) (TLC p. 28)

Ashby, James (Middlehurst); priest; 23 Sep 1767; age 52 (HGM); will; 15 Jun
  1761; 19 Nov 1767 (MCW 14.18) [SMW TA1.516]

Ashman, Richard; *Ashmans Freehold*; 150 ac.; sur. 13 Jun 1666; 1707 poss.
  John Dent, Sr.; New Town Hundred (RR p. 33) (TLC p. 33)

Aston, Elenor [listed as will of Mary Jones]; will; 17 ?Mar 1738/9; 14 Apr 1746;
  child. John and Sarah Smoot; g-child. Thomas, William Neale, Sarabella and
  Winifred Rigg, William Harrison, Asten Sanford Smoot, Sarah Rice,
  Elizabeth & John Dorsey, John Thomas (MCW 9.69) [SMW TA1.210]; inv.; 18
  Apr 1746; 18 Aug 1746; nok Thomas Doxey, William Harrison (I 33.312);
  acct.; 2 Nov 1747 (A 24.241)

Atkinson, Vincent; age ca 20; servant; 1650 (MD p. 5)

Atte, George; service by 1668 (SK11.543)

Aude, Thomas; acct.; 1 Sep 1694 (I&A 13a.206)

Avery, William; service by 1672 (SK 15.332)

Backworth, Ann; acct.; 24 Jun 1734 (A 12.352)

Bactson [Bartson], Thomas; planter; will; 29 Nov 1708; 24 Feb 1708; sons John,
  Thomas; s-i-l Henry Bayly; wife Penelope (MCW 3.123) [SMW PC1.154]

Bager, Thomas; acct.; 30 Mar 1715 (I&A 36c.62)

Ball, Benjamin; of CA Co.; 3 Jul 1712 (SMAA p. 232)

Balsell, Thomas; inv.; 8 Apr 1755; 14 Apr 1755; nok minors; adms./extx. Lutner
  Middleton & wife Elisabeth (I 60.219)

Banbridge, Christopher; inv.; 24 Dec 1709 (I&A 30.298)

Bancroft, Thomas; service by 1674 (SK 18.144)

Barberry, Christian; cooper; acct.; 8 Mar 1717 (I&A 39a.15)

Barecroft (Bearcroft, Bercraft), John; will; 4 Jul 1693; 20 Jul 1693; mentions John, s/o Col. Nehemiah Blackiston; William Gouldsmith, s-i-l of Richard Clouds; William, s/o Samuel Cookseley; Jane, w/o Thomas Williams; Mary Taylor, d/o Mary Price; Madam Susan, w/o Col. Nehemiah Blackiston; Sarah, w/o Michael Curtis; Eliza. & John, ch/o John and Rebecca Newman; bro. Stephen; tracts *Worchester, Burresses Gift* in CA Co. (MCW 2.63); inv.; 27 Oct 1693; 1 Jun 1694 (I&A 13a.1); acct.; 1 Oct 1696; extx. Rebeckah, w/o John Newman (I&A 14.60)

Barker, Thomas; mariner; inv.; 25 Apr 1698 (I&A 16.201); acct.; 5 Jul 1699; mentions 2nd inv. (I&A 19.59)

Barrow, Paul; service by 1673 (SK 17.495)

Bartlet, Katherine; w/o George; service by 1667 (SK 11.122)

Barton, William, Sr.; age ca 52 in 1657 (MD p. 9)

Bassen, Thomas; acct.; 29 Jul 1682; Margarett, w/o Thomas Fishwick (I&A 7c.197)

Basett, John; inv.; 21 May 1733; 16 Jul 1733; nok Richard Griffin, Parthena Miller; adm./ex. William Basset (I 17.321); acct.; 7 Jan 1733; orphan John Basset (A 12.162)

Batsill, Thomas; acct.; 20 Jun 1757; orphan John [age 8]; admx. Elisabeth, w/o Lutener Middleton (A 41.76); dist.; 20 Jun 1757; to widow and John Batsill (BB 2.63)

Bayne, Walter; of PG Co.; *Indian Giants Sepulchre*; 203 ac.; sur. 16 Sep 1714 (TLC. p. 68); *Indian Giants*; 14 Dec 1714 cert./pat. (COL) *Rippon*; 300 ac.; 15 Mar 1714 cert./pat. (COL)

Bazley, Ralph; acct.; 26 Aug 1731; orphan Samuel Bazley (A 11.217)

Beadle, Tho.; *Parish Beadle*; 200 ac.; sur. 4 May 1665; 1707 poss. Edw'd Morgan; Poplar Hill Hundred (RR p. 23) (TLC p. 22)

Beadnall, James; priest; 9 Apr 1772; age 54 (HGM)

Beame, John; acct.; 9 Dec 1719 (A 2.416)

Beck, Elizabeth, Margaret and Mary, infants; 11 Feb 1679 (CCR p. 10)

Beckwith, Charles; *Beckwith's Lodge*; 600 ac.; sur. 8 Oct 1704; (TLC p. 65); 10 Oct 1707 cert./pat. (COL)

Bedon, Dorothy; inv.; 16 Apr 1689 (I&A 10.211)

Benbridge, Christopher; acct.; 16 Jan 1710 (I&A 32c.96) (SMAA p. 192)

Berger, Thomas; acct.; 30 Mar 1715 (SMAA p. 292)

Berriman (Berryman), James; acct.; 10 Jan 1763; child Rebecca; admx. Ann Berriman; (A 49.99); dist.; 10 Jan 1763 (BB 3.179)

Besseck, John; age ca 22 in 1663 (MD p. 13)

Beveridge, George; inv.; 10 May 1721; 10 May 1721 (I 6.131)

Binks, John; will; 22 Aug 1747; 31 Aug 1747; mentions Misery [Ulisey], s/o George Griggs, Sr., and William, s/o William Harrison; child. of my late wife:

John Dorsey, Bridget Roads, Hannah Dorsey (MCW 9.122) [SMW TA1.195]; <u>inv.</u>;
3 Sep 1747; 30 Nov 1747 (I 35.466); <u>acct.</u>; 2 May 1748 (A 25.63)

Birckhead, Richard; 1673; immig. by 1666 with Margaret, his wife (SK 17.478)

Blackborne, John; immigrated from VA by 1672 (SK 17.38)

Bladen, William; <u>inv.</u>; 15 Dec 1718; nok Joseph Vansweringen (I 2.177)

Blake, Henry; immig. from VA by 1675; sons Henry & Robert, wife Katherine (SK 15.331)

Bland, Thomas; wife Damoras, relict of Nicholas Wyatt of AA Co.; 14 Oct 1679 (CCR p. 10)

Blankenstein, William; 17 Nov 1682; naturalized (CMN N15); *Elbert Field*; 500 ac.; 10 Jul 1684 cert./pat. (COL)

Bloff, William; dec'd; 1651 (?) (AM X.162)

Bohanan, George and Eliz'th; son Jonathan [b. 20 Jul 1767] (SA p. 5)

Boney, Thomas; m. 20 Oct 1771 Jean Davidson (MM & CSM); m. 20 Oct 1780 (SA p. 58)

Bonyman, James; <u>inv.</u>; 24 Nov 1760; nok Abraham Farrol, Ca. Swillaben; admx./extx. Ann Boniman (I 72.25)

Booker, Joseph; m. 3 Jan 1778 Eleanor Plummer (BRU 2.535)

Boomer, John; age ca 56; 2 Aug 1717; tracts *Westbury Mannor, Bean's Creek* (CCR p. 39)

Bord, Nicholas; <u>inv.</u>; 7 Sep 1749; 29 Nov 1749 (I 41.461)

Brumer, John; <u>inv.</u>;18 Feb 1720; 30 May 1721; nok Jean Boomer; admx. Mary Broomer (I 5.71); <u>acct.</u>; 4 Jan 1722; admx. Mary, w/o John Sledgmore (A 5.48)

Burke (Bourke), William; service by 1674 (SK 18.14); <u>will</u>; 8 Jan 1675; 25 Jan 1675 (MCW 1.115) [SMW PC1.13]; ; <u>inv.</u>; 30 Mar 1676 (I&A2.133); <u>acct.</u>; 4 Oct 1677 (I&A 4.305)

Boswell, William; <u>inv.</u>; 18 Feb 1697 (I&A 16.60); <u>acct.</u>; 8 Mar 1699 (I&A 18.125)

Boteler, Charles; *Dansbury Hill*; 100 ac.; sur.; 20 May 1667; 1707 poss. Peter Smith; New Town Hundred (RR p. 35) (TLC p. 34)

Boucher (Bouger), Anne; St. Michael's Hundred; <u>will</u>; 20 Jan 1712; 7 Feb 1712; sons Thomas, Randolph, James and George Egerton; dau. Mary Underwood (MCW 3.236) [SMW PC1.172]; <u>inv.</u>; 11 Feb [filed with 1713] (I&A 35b.97)

Bourne, James; <u>acct.</u>; 1 Mar 1687 (I&A 9.468)

Bovey [Beney], Francis; mariner; St. Maries, Cornwell, Kingdom of England; <u>will</u>; 6 Sep 1751; 23 Sep 1751; wife unnamed (MCW 10.177) [SMW TA1.279]

Bowes, Timothy and Mary; children Mary [b. 3 Mar 1763], Eleanor [b. 9 Jun 1766], Joseph [b. 23 Feb 1769] (SA p. 1, 12, 47)

Brackenbury, William; <u>inv.</u>; 7 May 1759; 7 Jun 1759; nok Joseph Burnam, William Brackenbury; admx./extx. Elisabeth Brackenbury (I 67.188, 191)

Bracklehurst, Anthony; <u>inv.</u>; 13 May 1735; 24 May 1736; admx./extx. Martha Brockelhouse (I 21.417)

Bradford, William; and Susannah his wife; service by 1674 (SK 18.144)

Bradshaw, Uriah; *Roundabout*; 130 ac.; 26 Nov 1759 cert./pat. (COL)

Brafeild, Edward; immigrated from Virginia by 1669 (SK12.388)

Bragg, William; inv.; 28 Feb 1742; 21 Apr 1743; nok J. Walter, Elisabeth Cowling; adm./ex. Thomas Bragg (I 27.374); acct.; 27 Apr 1744 (A 20.144)

Branan, John; inv.; 3 Jun 1746; 29 Jul 1746 (I 33.50); acct.; 8 Apr 1747 (A 23.195)

Branden, Richard; inv.; [filed with 1710-11] (I&A 32c.46)

Brannon, Cornelius; [planter]; will; 19 Mar 1702; 14 Apr 1703 (MCW 3.1) [SMW PC1.131]; inv.; 14 Apr 1703 (I&A 24.83, 96)

Brassey (Bressey), John, Esq.; inv.; 15 Jan 1721; 19 Feb 1721 (I 7.28); acct.; 24 Jan 1723 (A 5.347); 18 Jul 1724 (A 6.25)

Brenson, Thomas; transported by 1672 (SK17.56)

Briarly, Isaac; inv.; [filed with 1712]; nok Elisabeth Swillovan, Ann Mackman (I&A 331.230)

Brice, John and Elizabeth Harding; m. 25 Apr 1779 (SA p. 57)

Bridger, John; inv.; 19 Jun 1725; 8 Jul 1725; nok Elisabeth Bridger; admx. Mary Bridger (I 10.422); acct.; 28 May 1726; admx. Mary, w/o Painfull Sutton (A 7.371)

Bridges, Thomas; inv.; 31 May 1711 (I&A 32b.149)

Bridgin, Robert; inv.; 7 Aug 1685 (I&A 8.407); inv. & acct.; 14 Sep 1686; admx./extx. Mary Shanks (I&A 9.88)

Brin, John; inv.; 8 Feb 1721 (I 7.27)

Brinham, John; age ca 17 in 1752 (MD p. 21)

Brite, John, the elder; inv.; 17 Oct 1710; 27 Feb 1710; mentions James and William Bright (I&A 32b.1)

Britt, Benjamin; inv.; 12 Jun 1714 (I&A 36b.22)

Brittain, William; *Brittains Outlet*; 100 ac.; sur. 24 Oct 1649; 1707 poss. Mr. Wm. Hunter; New Town Hundred (RR p. 28) (TLC p. 26)

Brocklehouse, Anthony; acct.; 1 Feb 1738; admx. Martha Brocklehouse (A 17.66)

Broden, Daniel; inv.; 26 Feb 1736; 4 Apr 1737; nok Charles Flower; admx./extx. Sarah Broughton (I 22.208)

Bromhall, Thomas; immigrated by 1673 (SK 17.614)

Brower, George; acct.; 3 Jun 1735; mentions John, George, Susannah & Mary Brower and Ann Blackman; admx. Christian Brower (A 13.161)

Bruff (Bruffe), Joseph; inv.; 15 Sep 1674 (I&A 1.72); acct.; [filed with 1675/6] (I&A 2.91)

Bruse, William; inv.; 3 Jan 1776; 12 Mar 1776; nok Sarah Lock, Susanna Bruce; admx. Elisabeth Bruce (I 123.305)

Buckland, Walter; will; 4 May 1760; 1 Jul 1760; bro. John; sister Elizabeth (MCW 12.227) [SMW TA1.384]

Burkley (Buckley), Patrick; inv.; 5 Apr 1711 (I&A 32b.201); acct.; 14 Oct 1712; admx. Susannah Smith (I&A 33b.158) (SMAA p. 227)

Buckman, John Baptist; *Hayden's Discovery*; 295 ac.; 27 May 1756 cert./pat. (COL)

Buly, Patrick; <u>acct.</u>; 29 Jul 1734; orphans William & Ann Buly; admx. Ann
   Buly (A 12.356)
Bunnam, Martin; <u>acct.</u>; 12 Nov 1753; admx. Ann, w/o James Beary (A 36.21)
Burbara, Christopher; <u>inv.</u>; 24 Oct 1717 (I&A 39a.29)
Burdett, John; immigrated by 1678 (SK 15.523)
Burkett, Patience; 12 Aug 1698; 17 Sep 1698 (MCW 2.170) [SMW PC1.113]; <u>inv.</u>; 14
   Feb 1698 (I&A 18.137); 14 Feb 1698 (SMAA p. 105)
Burridge, John; service by 1672 (SK 17.44)
Bussey (Busey), Hezekiah; <u>will</u>; 30 Jun 1745; 26 Jun 1745; wife Rachel; [tract
   Taylor's Wash] (MCW 9.44) [SMW TA1.169]; <u>inv.</u>; 31 Oct 1745; 6 Feb 1745; nok
   Alexander Magruder, Barbary Wise; admx./extx. Rachel Bussey (I 32.1)
Bustle, Martha; immigrated from VA by 1681 (SK WC2.410)
Butcher, Andrew; *Andrew's Wood*; 124 ac.; 13 Jun 1734 cert./pat. (COL)
Byrn, Dennis; planter; <u>will</u>; 31 Aug 1771; 28 Feb 1777; dau. Ann; son
   Frederick; wife Mary; bro. Nicholas (MCW 16.173)

Cadloe (Cadle), Joseph; *Cadloe (Cadle)*; 200 ac.; sur. 4 Nov 1650; 1707 poss.
   James & William Cecill, ea. 100 ac.; New Town Hundred (RR p. 29) (TLC p. 27)
Cahill (Caghill), Roger; <u>inv.</u>; 4 Sep 1769 (I 102.254); <u>acct.</u>; 27 Feb 1770 (A 64.101)
Caldwell, Samuel; <u>inv.</u>; 11 Aug 1762; 4 Nov 1762; nok John & James Smith;
   admx. Martha Caldwell (I 79.255); <u>acct.</u>; 24 Mar 1772; adms. Robert Armstrong
   & wife Martha (A 66.278); <u>dist.</u>; 24 Mar 1772 (BB 6.109)
Callais, Richard; <u>acct.</u>; 10 May 1775; admx. Elisabeth, w/o Benjamin Cheshere
   (A 72.151); <u>acct.</u>; 14 Jul 1776; admx. Elisabeth Calliss (A 74.13); <u>dist.</u>; 14 Jul
   1776 (BB 7.68)
Calloway, Moses; <u>will</u>; 10 Nov 1758; 21 Mar 1759; wife Ann; child. Moses,
   Clammond, Aaron (MCW 11.233)
Calten, Rebecca; <u>inv.</u>; 23 Apr 1744; nok John Warren, Luke Russell (I 28.514)
Capshaw (Capstan), Francis; *Gilded Morton*; 150 ac.; sur. 24 May 1682 by
   assgn. from John Copes; 1707 escheat; Harvey Hundred (RR p. 57) (TLC p. 54);
   24 May 1682 cert./pat. (COL)
Carew, Henry; immigrated by 1674 (SK 18.141); age ca 36 in 1678 (MD p. 28)
Cary, Henry; <u>inv.</u>; 2 Feb 1775 (I 121.404)
Cate, Wm.; *Crokenfield*; 100 ac.; sur. 6 Jun 1667; 1707 poss. widow Mary
   Courtney; St. Mary's Hundred (RR p. 5) (TLC p. 6)
Causeen, Nicho.; *Causeen*; 50 ac.; sur. 27 Oct 1640; 1707 poss. Rich'd Brauden;
   St. Georges Hundred (RR p. 16) (TLC p. 16)
Cawsie, John; 19 Jan 1682; 7 Nov 1698 (MCW 2.161)
Caviner, Hugh; immigrated by 1671 (SK 1.171)
Ceely, Thomas; of Cornwall, Eng. and St. Mary's Co.; <u>will</u>; 1 Jul 1676; 20 Jul
   1676; bros. William and Peter Ceely; sisters Jane [Gregor], Honor [Henrietta],
   Katherine and Anne Ceely; sister Honor Pridaux, Judith w/o kinsman Robert

Quarme [Quarus]; aunt Jane Prade; mentions Judith and Honor Quarme (MCW 1.173) [SMW PC1.27]; <u>inv.</u>; 24 Jul 1676 (I&A 2.287)

Champ, William; 8 Oct 1667; 13 Dec 1667; <u>will</u>; mentions Elizabeth, eld. d/o Patrick Forrest (MCW 1.42) [SMW PC1.6]

Chancey, Alexander; service by 1675 (SK 15.303)

Chantry, Joseph; <u>inv.</u>; 20 Feb 1701 (I&A 21.378); <u>acct.</u>; 30 Jan 1702 (I&A 23.43)

Chaplear, Isaac; <u>inv.</u>; 24 Mar 1741; 6 Jul 1741; nok minors; adms./exs. Edward Brisco & wife Rachel (I 27.54); <u>acct.</u>; 11 Jul 1743; orphans Elias Arnold & James (A 19.441)

Chapman, Richard; <u>inv.</u>; 6 Mar 1674; 7 May 1675 (I&A 1.315); <u>acct.</u>; 29 Dec 1677; Gilbert Turbervile m. Lidia, widow of Thomas Pearce (I&A 4.577) (SMAA p. 74)

Chappell, Andrew; mariner; <u>inv.</u>; 28 Feb 1639 (AM IV.57)

Charmes, Manders (Maunders); <u>inv.</u>; 25 Oct 1716; nok Edward Morgan, Mary Charmes, Nicholas Richardson (I&A 38b.68); <u>acct.</u>; 12 Aug 1717; admx. Bridgett Charmes (I&A 37b.1) (SMAA p. 317); 28 Nov 1717 (I&A 39c.11) (SMAA p. 311)

Charnell, John; <u>acct.</u>; 9 Jul 1744; mentions John Sr. & Jr., Hannah Cheirnell (A 20.289)

Chester, Edward; immig. by 1680 with wife Ellinor, dau. and s-i-l (SK WC2.277)

Cheverlin, Jesse and Catharine Gruther; m. 12 Feb 1780 (SA p. 58)

Chinn, John; *Chinn's Purchase*; 50 ac.; 10 Jun 1683 cert./pat. (COL) *Muriel's Choice*; 50 ac.; 9 Feb 1687 cert./pat. (COL)

Chishollne, James; planter; service by 1667 (SK11.107)

Chrisman, Luke and Elisabeth; son John [b. 13 Apr 1766] (SA p. 7)

Christian, Adam; age ca 28; 1658 (AM XLI.240)

Chuner, Catharine; <u>inv.</u>; 30 Jan 1775; 14 Jan 1775; adm./ex. Edward Gardiner (I 121.416); <u>acct.</u>; 1775; [Chunn] (A 73.243); <u>dist.</u>; 1775 (BB 7.33)

Chunn, Joseph, Mr.; <u>inv.</u>; 7 May 1765; 4 Jun 1765; nok Rebecca Barber, Mary Morris; adm. Catharine Chunn (I 88.84); <u>dist.</u>; 2 Jul 1765 (BB 4.130)

Clapham (Clapom), Thomas; <u>inv.</u>; 18 Mar 1723; 22 Apr 1724; admx. Elisabeth Clapham (I 9.380); <u>acct.</u>; 7 Jun 1725; admx. Elisabeth, w/o William Innis (A 6.435)

Claw, William; 1 Oct 1675; 16 Nov 1675; wife Sarah; tract *Daily Desire* on Sassafras River (MCW 1.111); <u>inv.</u>; 14 Feb 1675; 14 Feb 1675 (I&A 1.534)

Clelen (Cleland, Clelelend), Alexander; <u>will</u>; 29 Jul 1726; 21 Sep 1726; sons Thomas, Alexander; daus. Martha, Esther, Elizabeth, Mary; wife Grace (MCW 5.231) [SMW PC1.309]; <u>inv.</u>; 4 Nov 1726; nok none of age; extx. Grace Clelon (I 11.711); <u>acct.</u>; 19 Apr 1727 (A 8.186)

Clow, James and Mary; sons John [b. 6 Sep 1761], James [b. 17 Oct 1763] (SA p. 39); daus. Catherine [b. 19 Feb 1767], Susanna [b 23 Sep 1759] (CSM)

Clure, Peter; <u>inv.</u>; 8 Feb 1675 (I&A 4.526)

Cocker, Thomas; service by 1666 (SK 18.161)

Cockshott, Jane; widow of John;1642 (MD p. 36); age ca 17 in 1658 (MD p. 36)

Coghill, William; acct.; 9 Apr 1703; extx. Christian, w/o Thomas Stonestreet (I&A 23.16); extx. Eloan, w/o Thomas Stonestreet (SMAA p. 121)

Colbey, Henry; inv.; 26 Jan 1732; 19 Mar 1732 (I 17.95); acct.; 22 Jul 1734; mentions John, Henry, Thomas, William, Mary & Elisabeth Colbey (A 12.452)

Coleman, Charles; inv.; 20 Apr 1722 (I 8.163); acct.; 31 May 1725; admx. Mary Bridger (A 6.431)

Collars, Richard; dist.; 10 May 1775; admx. Elisabeth, w/o Mr. Benjamin Cheshire (BB 7.26)

Collins, George; m. 21 Dec 1770 Ann Lucas (MM)

Collis (Colliss), Richard, Mr.; inv.; 23 Jun 1773; 10 Feb 1774; nok Yonell Attwell; admx. Elisabeth Colliss (I 116.212)

Colter, Rebecca; 18 Oct 1740; 28 Nov 1740; mentions 4 children; names only Mary (MCW 8.122) [SMW TA1.111]; acct.; 7 Jul [filed with 1746] (A 22.253)

Comberford, Garret; will; 5 Dec 1696; 10 Jul 1697 (MCW 2.125); inv.; 16 Sep 1697 (I&A 15.346)

Cooney, John; acct.; [filed with 1698] (I&A 18.131)

Copley, Lyonell; will; 7 Sep 1693; 23 Sep 1693; sons Lyonell & John; dau. Ann (MCW 2.65)

Coram, Henry; inv.; 8 Jan 1735; 16 Mar 1735; nok one minor; admx./extx. Elisabeth Coram (I 21.295)

Corbett, Hutton; *Corbet*; 100 ac.; sur. 22 Oct 1640; poss. Thos. Hobb; esch. 1707; in St. George's Hundred 1704; St. Mary's Hundred (RR p. 2) (TLC p. 2)

Corbisley, Samuel; merchant in Liverpool; acct.; 24 Nov 1720 (A 3.173)

Cornish, John; 1 Aug 1651; 5 Dec 1651; bro.-in-law Cepaphreditus Lawson; bro. William Pierce; sister Susanna (MCW 1.6)

Cornor, Job; service by 1667 (SK 18.161)

Corsair, John; inv.; 27 Apr 1770; 14 Oct 1770; admx. Sabra Corsair (I 103.339); acct.; 20 May 1772; admx. Sabra Corsair (A 67.139) (BB 6.152)

Corwyn, William; immigrated by 1671 (SK 16.121)

Cosden, Thomas, Gent.; immigrated by 1668 (SK11.469)

Cotten, Edward; Newtowne; will; 4 Apr 1653; 22 Apr 1653 (MCW 1.7)

Couant, Thomas; acct.; 15 Jan 1674 (I&A 1.164)

Coulter, Rebecca; inv.; 10 Apr 1741; 6 Jul 1741; nok John Warren, Luke Russell (I 26.127)

Courrey, John; [filed with 1698] (SMAA p. 102)

Coursey, Wm.; *The Craft*; 120 ac. sur. 3 Mar 1658; assgn. Mark Phepoe; 1707 poss. William Guither; 1707 poss. Owen Guither; resur. included in *The Crofts*; St. Michael's Hundred (RR p. 13) (TLC p. 14)

Coverdale, Thomas; service by 1680; immigrated by 1669 (SK WC2.159)

Cowley, John; planter; inv.; 3 Oct 1730; 6 Nov 1730 (I 16.45); acct.; 26 Nov 1730 (A 10.627)

Crackborn, Rich'd; *Crackbourn*; 350 ac.; sur. 2 Jul 1649; 1707 poss. Peter
    Harris; Resurrection Hundred (RR p. 59) (TLC p. 56)
Crafts, George; carpenter; inv.; 18 Mar 1725; 3 Aug 1726; nok Elisabeth Crafts;
    admx. Elisabeth Crafts (I 11.500); acct.; 27 Feb 1727 (A 8.538)
Craxson, James; gent.; *Craxson's Rest*; 51 ac.; 6 Feb 1729 cert./pat. (COL)
Creston (Chesteson), Robert; planter; will; written 29 Sep 1722; wife Elizabeth;
    daus. Dorothy Duell [Duall], Mary, Judith; son John (MCW 5.122) [SMW
    PC1.269]; inv.; 8 May 1722; admx./extx. Elisabeth Creston (I 8.30); acct.; 12 Jul
    1725; extx. Elisabeth, w/o Jeremiah Gridley (A 7.95)
Crew, Jonas; service by 1677 (SK 15.434)
Crioens, Philip; age 50 in 1723 (MD p. 44)
Croft, Robert; acct.; 9 Aug 1686; unnamed child dead; admx. An (relict), w/o
    John Skelton (I&A 9.145]
Cropper, Gilbert; *Eaglestone*; 100 ac.; sur. 6 Nov 1668; 1707 poss. Rich'd
    Highfeild; Choptico Hundred (RR p. 52) (TLC p. 50)
Crosman, Robert; commander of *The Vine*; mentions Robert Graham & wife
    Ann (MD p. 45)
Cullen, James; age ca 30 in 1684 (MD p. 45)
Cully, John; transported prior to 1666; planter (SK 10.266)
Cuningham, John; acct.; 25 May 1680 (I&A 7a.100)
Curlet, John; will; May 1775; 10 Nov 1776; wife Mary; mentions McKeliva ,
    s/o John Hammett, Sr.]; tracts *Saturdays Work, Curlets Force Put, Snow Hill
    Mannor* (MCW 16.174)
Cushman, William and Eleanor; child. John [b. 6 Apr 1760], James [b. 6 Mar
    1761], Mary [b. 23 Nov 1763], Ann [b. 5 Sep 1767], Eleanor [b. 10 Feb 1769]
    (SA p. 189)
Cutbertt, Robertt; of Barbadoes; inv. & acct.; 17 Dec 1675 (I&A 1.483, 494)
Cutterson, Francis; immigrated by 1678 (SK15.523)
Cuttler, William; inv.; 22 Apr 1746; 28 Apr 1746; nok Margaret Russell, Joseph
    Cutler; admx./extx. Ann Cutler (I 32.222); acct.; 23 Jun 1747 (A 24.11)

Dainbry (Daintry, Dantery), Richard; will; 30 Mar 1748; 28 Apr 1748 (MCW
    9.144) [SMW TA1.213]; inv.; 4 May 1748; 21 Jul 1748 (I 36.111); acct.; 17 Jun
    1749 (A27.17)
Dakins, John (Thomas?); service by 1679 (SK WC2.53)
Dalton, Richard; age ca 25 in 1678; mentions John Deery [d. 2/3 Dec 1677], his
    sister Ellenor Deery, bro. Owen Quigley, cousin Capt. John Quigley (MD p. 46)
Dar, Oswald, Jr.; age ca 36; s/o relict of John McCarty; 26 Jun 1719 (CCR p. 41)
Darwell, John; acct.; 20 Nov 1679; admx. Elisabeth Darwell (I&A 6.535)
Dawson, Richard; immigrated from VA by 1670 (SK 16.11)
Deacon, William; [Esq.]; will; 19 Jun 1758; 7 Jan 1760; nephew William
    Deacon of Portsmouth; sister Mary Deacon (MCW 11.261) [SMW TA1.389]

inv.; 14 Feb 1760; 28 Jul 1760 (I 70.72, 81); acct.; 6 Feb 1769; mentions
William Deacon in England (A 61.115)

Deakins, Elinor; inv.; 2 Mar 1713 (I&A 35a.328)

Deason, William, Esq.; acct.; 2 Sep 1761 (A 47.227)

Demar, Thomas; inv.; 12 Aug 1717 (I&A 37b.126)

Dennis, Robert; age ca 35; thief; 23 Dec 1665 (AM XLIX.541)

Derrick (Dereck), John; will; 21 Mar 1774; 3 Nov 1774; wife Frances (MCW
16.20) [SMW TA1.695]; inv.; 10 Oct 1775; nok Charles Smith; ex. Francis Derrick
(I 122.183)

Derry, John; innholder; St. Mary's City; will; written 2 Dec 1677; sister Ellinor
Derry; bro. Owen Quigley; cousin John Quigley (MCW 5.236); acct.; 30 Oct
1679 (I&A 6.512)

Diamond, George; *Diamond's Adventure*; sur. 29 Jul 1695; poss. Joseph
Edwards; Choptico Hundred (TLC p. 52); Resurrection Hundred (RR p. 64); 110
ac.; 14 May 1695 cert./pat. (COL)

Dick, David; will; approx. 1765; age 40 [SMW TA1.539-556]

Dilicoate, James; inv.; 30 May 1721; 8 Jun 1721; nok John Dillicoate; admx.
Elisabeth Dillicoate (I 5.55); acct.; 8 Jan 1721 (A 4.52)

Diniard, Thomas; will; 1 Nov 1659; 28 Dec 1659; Henry, s/o Robert Thomas;
John, s/o Benjamin Hamon; Furfer, w/o John Hocker; Thomas, s/o Stephen
Salmon; Mary, w/o Richard Shipps (MCW 1.11); d. 5 Nov 1659 (CCR p. 6)

Dobson, Samuel; age ca 63 in 1681 (MD p. 52)

Donn, Obediah; will; 24 Jan 1685/6; 15 Mar 1685/6; wife Elizabeth; son
Dennis; daus. Mary and Margaret (MCW 2.2) [SMW PC1.59]

Doolan, Robert; service by 1674 (SK 18.179)

Dor, William; *Bissingham*; 100 ac.; sur. 6 Mar 1681; Dor left province; no
claimant; 1707 no poss.; Chaptico Hundred (RR p. 53) (TLC p. 51)

Doran, George; (oral); will; 8 May 1761; s-i-l George Smith (MCW 12.76) [SMW
TA1.417]; inv.; 14 Aug 1761; 8 Nov 1761 (I 706.308)

Dordine, Peter; service by 1674 (SK 18.158)

Dosen, Obedyah; inv.; [filed with 1685-6] (I&A 8.451)

Dovenish, Charles, Capt.; mentions ship; 1 Apr 1709 (SMAA p. 177)

Dover, Assilla; acct.; 5 Aug 1751; Thomas, orphan of Thomas Little (A 31.53)

Dowagans (Dowgin), John; acct.; 8 Aug 1719; widow dec'd (A 2.150) acct.; 7
Aug 1719 (SMAA p. 393); inv.; 5 Mar 1718; 5 Jun 1718 (I 2.61)

Doyal (Doyall), Edmond; inv.; 9 Sep 1718; 3 Sep 1720; nok John Pile,
Benjamin Boarman; extx. Mary Boarman (I 4.235); acct.; 10 Sep 1720 (A 3.220)
(SMAA p. 424)

Drake, Thomas; service by 1680 (SK WC2.378-379)

Driver, David; immigrated by 1672 (SK 16.513); inv.; 29 Jul 1680 (I&A 7a.347);
acct.; 12 Sep 1682; admx. Agnes Driver (widow) (I&A 7c.314)

Drudge, Jos.; m. 12 Jul 1774 Ann Howard (MM)

Duart, Emmanuel; planter; age ca 31 in 1659 (MD p. 56)

Dubler, Joseph; acct.; 27 Mar 1712; admx. Elinor Harwood (I&A 33b.158) (SMAA p. 228)

Dugins (Duggens), Daniel; inv.; 15 Feb 1744; nok Mary Duggens, William Jones (I 30.299); acct.; 9 Jan 1745 (A 22.71)

Durden, John; inv.; 23 May 1733; 19 Jun 1733; admx./extx. Mary Durden (I 17.167); acct.; 16 Sep 1734; orphan Thomas Durdin (A 12.537)

Dyatt, John; St. Clements Bay; found dead 14 Oct 1665 (AM XLIX.510)

Dyer, Thomas; acct.; 4 Oct 1722 (A 4.242)

Dynard, Thomas; *Dynard*; 500 ac.; sur. 22 Nov 1654; 1707 poss. James Martin, Oswald Ash, Joshua Gaibert; esch. 20 Oct 1682; resur. granted widow Ann Martin; St. Clements Hundred (RR p. 43) (TLC p. 42)

Early, Michael; inv.; 18 Feb 1725; 4 Jul 1726; admx. Francis Earley (I 11.376); acct.; 4 Jul 1726; admn. Francis Early (A 7.402)

East, Simon (Symon); immigrated by 1668; boatwright (SK 11.294); *Stamps Neglect*; 50 ac.; sur. 2 Aug 1679; 1707 poss. Widow Mason; Poplar Hill Hundred (RR p. 25) (TLC p. 23)

Edis, Wm.; unnamed; 50 ac.; sur. 10 Nov 1647; no cert. or pat. on record; Poplar Hill Hundred (RR p. 22) (TLC p. 21)

Edwin, Will'm; *St. Williams*; 50 ac.; sur 1648; 114 ac. resur. 12 Sep 1695 Daniel Bell; 1707 poss. Francis Hopewell; St. Georges Hundred (RR p. 17) (TLC p. 18)

Elivin, John; immigrated from VA by 1670 (SK 12.566)

Emory, Thomas and Elizabeth Hopewell; m. 23 Sep 1779 (SA p. 57)

England, Thomas; inv.; 30 Mar 1717 (I&A 37b.1); acct.; 13 Feb 1717 (I&A 39c.27) (SMAA p. 348)

English (Engelich), Alexander; 30 Jan 1716; 5 Feb 1716 (MCW 4.90) [SMW PC1.202]

Enloes, Edward; will; 21 Apr 1711; 14 Jun 1711; niece Henrietta Mariah Noble and nephew John Noble, ch/o bro. John Noble and sister Jane; tracts *Susquehannah Point, The Addition, Enloes Hope, Enloes Lott* [DO Co.] (MCW 3.195) [SMW PC1.180]

Evelin, George, Capt.; bro. Lt. Robert Evelin; recorded 30 May 1638 (AM IV.34)

Ewebank, Richard; 13 Apr 1718; 26 Apr 1718; son Richard; father Thomas Ewebank (MCW 4.174)

Ewens, Philip; service by 1667 (SK 11.139)

Fairbrother, Isaac; inv.; 29 Jul 1772; 15 Nov 1772 (I 109.388); acct.; 22 Mar 1774 (A 69.379)

Faney, Thomas; inv.; 21 Dec 1762; 7 Mar 1764; nok Benjamin Fenwick, Elisabeth Combs; adm. John Faney (I 83.87)

Fangley, John; dist.; 20 Feb 1759; mentions John [at full age], Josiah [age 13 next Nov], John [dec'd]; admx. Jane Fangley (BB 2.107)

Farrar, Robert; will; 24 Aug 1675; 6 Nov 1675; wife Joanna (MCW 1.110)

Feeling, Ignatius; acct.; 15 Feb 1710 (I&A 32c.65)

Fendall, John; age ca 39 in 1713 (MD p. 63)

Fersess, Richard; age 46 in 1718 (MD p. 63)

Files, Thomas and Sarah; children Ann [b. 18 Dec 1756], William [b. 13 Feb 1760], Thomas [b. 1 Feb 1758], Sarah [b. 7 Feb 176], John [b. 24 Dec 1765] (SA p. 7)

Filiale, William; immigrated by 1670 (SK 12.552)

Finnacy, Stephen and Ann; children Mary Ann [b. 13 Oct 1760], John Archibald [b. 1 May 1765], Joseph Normand Mack [b. 1 Feb 1768], Rosanna [b. 12 Dec 1771] (SA p. 12, 28, 46)

Fitsgarald, Cornelius; inv.; 5 Apr 1711 (I&A 32b.266) ; acct.; 31 Oct 1712; admx. Jane, w/o John Thompson (I&A 33b.164) (SMAA p. 236)

Fleetwood, Edward; immigrated by 1675 (SK 15.316)

Fletchall, Thomas; inv.; 15 May 1719; 10 Dec 1725 (I 11.157)

Flintiffe, Elizabeth; age ca 30 in 1721 (MD p. 64)

Forger, Mazaler; inv.; 27 May 1757; 12 Sep 1757; nok John & Elisabeth Noble; admx.extx. Ann Furger (I 63.608)

Fox, Henry; Newtowne; 31 Mar 1656; 26 Jan 1657 (MCW 1.10)

Foy, Andrew; will;4 Mar 1775; 15 Aug 1775; wife Barbara (MCW 16.111) [SMW TA1.720]

France, John; service by 1677 (SK 15.409)

Francis, Jacob.; acct.; 27 Apr 1744 (A 20.143)

Freene, Mary; service by 1670; wife of Thomas (SK16.40)

Frees, William, Mr. inv.; 4 Jan 1733; 21 May 1734; nok Ann & Elizabeth Bayly (I 18.127)

Friend, Daniel; m. 8 Aug 1775 Cloe Sayr (MM)

Fulford, Humphry; servant; transported by 1640 (SK 3.18)

Fuller, Thomas; service by 1680 (SK WC2.278, 279)

Gaanwell, John; acct.; 1 Feb 1742; extx. Catherine, w/o John Manley (A 19.368)

Gadd, Thomas; service by 1668 (SK 11.543)

Gale, Benjamin; joiner; 16 Jul 1743; 22 Jul 1743; bro. Thomas; sisters Jemima [Teeme], Anne [Teeme] (MCW 8.217); inv.; 27 Jul 1743; 2 May 1744; nok Benjamin Gale (I 28.510, 514); acct.; 16 Jul 1745 (A 21.370)

Gam, John; acct.; 17 May 1718 (A 1.42) (SMAA p. 332)

Garner, Bullet; *Garner's Lot*; 129 ac.; 29 Apr 1768 cert./pat. (COL)

Gary, Richard; *Hardshift*; 50 ac.; sur. 13 May 1685; 1707 poss. Rich'd Gary; New Town Hundred (RR p. 40) (TLC p. 39); 13 May 1684 cert./pat. (COL)

Gatten, Jeremy; m. 14 Feb 1773 Eliz. Drury (MM)

Gayskill, Nicholas; age ca 36 in 1684)

George, Benjamin; acct.; 9 Aug 1686; adm. Thomas George (I&A 9.145)

Gerling, Simon; age ca 50; Jun 1715 (CCR p. 33)

Gill, John; service 1676 (SK 15.408); inv.; 18 Nov 1682 (I&A 8.251)

Gillaspie, George; acct.; 16 Nov 1724; admx. Catherine Palmer (A 6.252); 3 Nov 1725 (A 7.189)

Gittins, John; *Fosbury [Tosbury] Plain*; 430 ac.; sur. 19 Aug 1664; 1707 poss. Frances Rhodes; St. Mary's Hundred (RR p. 5) (TLC p. 5)

Gillam, John; will; 13 Dec 1711; 16 Sep 1712; daus. Rachel Wood, Mary Thorne; g-dau. Mary Thorne; wife Mary; tract *The Desert* (MCW 3.231) [SMW PC1.170]; inv.; 21 Oct 1712; s-i-l James Wood & William Thorn (I&A 33b.163)

Godfrey, John; inv.; 15 Mar 1732; 29 Jul 1733; nok And. Pilisha (?), Mary Graves (I 17.318); acct.; 10 Mar 1734 (A 13.8)

Goff, Benjamin; *Goff's Expense*; 7 ac.; 25 Mar 1767 cert./pat. (COL)
  Goff's Swamp; 3 ac.; 27 Mar 1767 cert./pat. (COL)

Gold, John; immigrated by 1671 (SK 16.122)

Goodman, Ann; widow; inv.; 23 Apr 1717 (I&A 37b.123); acct.; 6 Jun 1717 (SMAA p. 370); 6 Jun 1718 (A 1.29)

Goodrick, Frances (Francis); CH Co.; will; 14 Oct 1766; 10 May 1768; sisters Ann Vialette Sewell, Mary Stone, Ann Middleton; bro. George, nephew Richard [SMW TA1.562]; inv.; 12 May 1768; 18 Jun 1768; nok Ignatius Middleton, William Stone (I 96.168)

Goodson, Christopher; Poplar Hill; will; 8 Oct 1688; 8 Nov 1688; wife Frances; mentions Eliza. [d/o John Noble] (MCW 2.37) [SMW PC1.72]; inv.; 13 Dec 1688 (I&A 10.153)

Goodwin, George; 7 Jan 1672; 22 Jan 1672 (MCW 1.71); carpenter [PC1.10]

Gothrie, William; inv.; 13 Aug 1718; 9 May 1721 (I 5.57)

Goul, Eleanor; b. 10 __ 1763; d. 2 Jan 1800 (HGM)

Golthrop (Goulthorpe), William, Mr.; inv.; 22 Dec 1708 (I&A 29.239); acct.; 23 Jun 1715; admx. Grace, w/o John Watkins (I&A 36c.67) (SMAA p. 289)

Gover (Gower), Daniel; will; 23 May 1674; 9 Jun 1674; bro. Emanuel Ratcliffe (MCW 1.82); acct.; 14 May 1675 (I&A 1.273)

Graile (Grayle), Francis; 6 Feb 1675; 15 Mar 1675; mentions Edward, Thomas and John, sons of Thomas Pearce; [tract *Dowles*] (MCW 1.120) [SMW PC1-14]

Grant, John; inv.; 12 May 1718; nok Tobias & Timothy Tolle (I 1.50); acct.; 18 Aug 1718; extx. Mary Grant (A 1.319); 29 Oct 1718 (SMAA p. 329)

Graslay, Samuel; age ca 41 in 1705 (MD p. 74)

Grasty, Benjamin; will; 30 Dec 1775; 14 Feb 1775; wife Ann; sons Richard Waid [Ward], Clement; daus. Marthilus Head, Julaner [Juleann] Suttle; unmarried children unnamed (MCW 16.91) [SMW TA1.734]

Grayham, Francis; *Partnership*; sur. 10 Sep 1706 for Graham & James Somerhill (TLC p. 64); 200 ac.; 10 Oct 1707 cert./pat. (COL)

Grayson, Francis; mariner; acct.; 9 Oct 1677 (I&A 4.320)

Greas_, John; age ca 53; 26 Jun 1718 (CCR p. 41)

Greeneway, John; age ca 25 in 1649 mentions William Branthwaite m. Helenor Stephenson (MD p. 76); age ca 25; Michaelmas last past (1649/50) (AM X.34)

Greenhalgh (Greenhaugh), Edward, Capt.; inv.; 28 May 1699 (I&A 19.122); inv.; 10 May 1701 (I&A 20.199); acct.; 20 Jul 1703; son John; dau. Jane (I&A 24.22)

Greenhill, Stephen; *Colebrook's Levels*; 129 ac.; sur. 23 May 1720 for Wm. Bannistrer; pat. to Stephen Greenwell (TLC p. 80); 10 Jun 1734 cert./pat. (COL)

Greentree, Ezebell; inv.; 12 Dec 1748; nok Luke Russell, Rebecca Kilberry; adm./ex. Thomas Russell (I 37.381); acct.; 29 Sep 1749 (A 27.109)

Grimsditch, John; unnamed; 100 ac.; sur. 14 Jul 1647; New Town Hundred (RR p. 26) (TLC p. 25)

Guest, Walter; unnamed; 150 ac.; sur. 10 Nov 1652; 1707 no poss.; within sur. of *Resurvey of Hopton Park*; New Town Hundred (RR p. 29); *Guests Neck* (TLC p. 28)

Guida, John; m. 19 Jan 1768 Jane Brooks (MM)

Gulick [Goulick], Nicholas, Rev. Mr.; age ca 70; 3 Aug 1717 (CCR p. 39); will; 9 Apr 1718; 27 May 1718 (MCW 4.165) [SMW PC1.231]

Gutrick, Francis; acct.; 12 Mar 1771 (A 66.50)

Gwinn (Guin), Christopher; inv.; 4 Jun 1698 (I&A 16.201); acct.; 12 Sep 1700 (I&A 11b.44)

Hackings, Robert; 2 Jun 1735; mentions Robert, Mary & Martha Hackins; admx. Jane, w/o William Watson (A 13.128)

Haddock, John; inv.; 8 Feb 1728; nok minors; admx. Elisabeth Haddock (I 14.84); acct.; 4 Mar 1729; admx. Elisabeth, w/o Jeremiah Pickering (A 10.206)

Hagoe, Thomas; *St. Jansen*; 200 ac.; 27 Sep 1680 cert./pat. (COL)
 Good Intent; 650 ac.; 11 May 1695 cert./pat. (COL)

Haills, Thomas; age ca 39 in 1650 (MD p. 80)

Haines, William; inv.; 10 Mar 1706 (I&A 26.226)

Haines, John; admx. Jone; 3 Aug 1720 (SMAA p. 433)

Halbert, Elisabeth; inv.; 27 Apr 1739; 3 Jul 1739 (I 24.138)

Hallson, John; acct.; 20 Apr 1741 (A 18.171)

Halse, James; *Enclosure*; 14 ac.; *Inclosure* sur. 20 Jul 1714 (TLC p. 60); 10 Dec 1714 cert./pat. (COL)

Hands, Lawrence; inv.; 1 Sep 1733; 31 Oct 1733 (I 17.536); acct.; 13 Dec 1740; [Hand] (A 18.112)

Handy, William; cooper; inv.; 2 Aug 1726; 27 Jan 1726; nok Walter Watkins, minors; admx. Ann Wooldridge (I 11.723)

Haniford, Joseph; inv.; 1694 (I&A 13a.105)

Hanning, Caleb and Susannah Kelly; m. 22 Jun 1780 (SA p. 58)

Hanson, Randall; *Ferny Branch*; 50 ac.; sur. 15 Apr 1667; 1707 poss. Thos. Cecill; Poplar Hill Hundred (RR p. 24) (TLC p. 23)

Hardy, William; planter; will; 18 Nov 1737; 8 Jun 1738; tract *Collenwood* [*Cottonwood*] (MCW 7.251) [SMW TA1.61]; inv.; 4 Jul 1738; 2 Aug 1738 (I 23.352); acct.; 28 Sep 1738 (A 16.322)

Harkis, John; inv.; 12 Jun 1718 (I 1.525)

Harling, Richard; <u>inv.</u>; 21 Feb 1713 (I&A 35a.325)

Harney, Phillip; <u>inv.</u>; 30 Jan 1717 (I&A 39c.177); <u>acct.</u>; 28 May 1718 (A 1.28) 29 May 1718 (SMAA p. 335); 4 Aug 1719 (A 2.214) (SMAA p.397)

Harnung, ____; <u>acct.</u>; 10 Dec 1703; extx. widow Ann Sykes (I&A 9b.19)

Harpin, Thos.; *Stratford*; 100 ac.; sur. 2 May 1666; 1707 poss. Mark Cordea, Esq.; St. Mary's Hundred (RR p. 4) (TLC p. 5)

Harrard, William; <u>inv.</u>; 17 Mar 1720; 17 Mar 1720; nok Wany Harrard; admx. Phebby Harrard (I .219); <u>acct.</u>; 23 Aug 1720 (A 3.72) (SMAA p. 434)

Harrill, Christopher; <u>acct.</u>; 13 May 1736; orphans Clement, Christopher, Henry & John Horrel; admx./extx. Margret Horrill (A 14.234)

Harrington, John; <u>acct.</u>; 14 Sep 1677; mentions Morgan Jones, his wife, their dau. Elisabeth Davis now w/o Owen Guyther (I&A 4.243)

Harturpp, Richard; *Hickory Hill*; 1 100 ac.; 5 Oct 1682 cert./pat. (COL)

Harvey, Nicho.; *St. Josephs Mannour*; 1,000 ac.; sur. 2 Dec 1642; 1707 poss. Geo. Plater; resur. 12 Jun 1706; Harvey Hundred (RR p. 55) (TLC p. 52)

Harwar, William; service by 1675 (SK 15.330)

Hatch, Joseph; service by 1672 (SK 14.438)

Hawood [Haywood], Raphael; <u>will</u>; 22 Jul 1713; 5 Aug 1713 (MCW 3.254) [SMW PC1.189]

Haynie (Haney), James; *Londonderry*; 17 ac.; 8 Sep 1760 cert./pat. (COL)

Hazel, Elizabeth; <u>will</u>; 10 Oct 1750; 21 Jan 1750; sons John, William, Richard, Philip and Henry Hazel; daus. Barbary Edwards, Mary Joy, Elizabeth Saunders, Elizabeth Hazel, Ann Hening (MCW 10.125) [SMW TA1.247]; <u>inv.</u>; 28 Jan 1750; 7 Oct 1751; nok John Hazel, Elisabeth Sanders; adm../ex. William Hazell (I 48.101)

Hazeldine, Charles; <u>acct.</u>; 10 Oct 1771; adms. Thomas Fowler & wife Elisabeth (A 66.80); 19 May 1772 (A 67.137)

Heardman (Hardman, Herdman), James; <u>inv.</u>; 18 Dec 1719; 3 Feb 1719; nok Sarah & Thomas Bencraft; admx. Elliner Herdman (I 3.222); <u>acct.</u>; 9 Mar 1721; 3 child.; admx. Elinor, w/o Thomas Thomas (A 4.74); <u>acct.</u>; 4 Jun 1724 (A 6.39)

Heathman (Hathman), Allexander (Elixander); <u>will</u>; 4 Feb 1717/8; 25 Feb 1717/8; wife Frances; child. Mary, Thomas, Margaret, Anne, John (MCW 4. 133); <u>inv.</u>; 25 Feb 1717; 13 Mar 1717; nok unnamed children (I 1.104); <u>acct.</u>; 5 Aug 1719; ex. Mr. Francis Heathman (A 2.290); 15 Aug 1719 (SMAA p. 371)

Heartly, Joshua; <u>acct.</u>; 19 Nov 1739; orphans Joseph & Ann Heartly; admx. Mary Heartly (A 17.349)

Heath, Thomas and Kitty; dau. Ann Elizabeth [b. 15 Feb 1813; bapt. 23 May 1813] (SA p. 32)

Heather, William, Mr.; <u>inv.</u>; 22 Feb 1692 (I&A 12.89); <u>acct.</u>; 29 Apr 1695 (I&A 13a.288)

Hedger, Robert; *Itchcombs Freehold*; 400 ac.; sur. 1 Jun 1647; 1707 poss. Parson Jennings (Glebe land); St. Georges Hundred (RR p. 17) (TLC p. 17)

Hely, Clement; *Hely's Lot*; 104 ac.; 4 Nov 1687 cert./pat. (COL); inv.; 22 Apr 1695 (I&A 13a.268)

Hellen, David and Susannah; children George Aisquith [b. 18 Sep 1759], Ann Parran [b. 19 Jan 1762], Jane [b. 10 Nov 1763], Thomas [b. 10 Oct 1765], Susanna Aisquith [b. 25 May 1766] (SA p. 1)

Hemmett, Robert; *Hicory Hatt*; 67½ ac.; sur. 4 Jan 1744 (TLC p. 105)

Hepworth, John; immigrated 1673 (SK 17.570)

Henrick, Benjamin and Mary Smith; m. 3 Dec 1779 (CSM)

Henry, Martin and Mary; sons James [b. 17 Jun 1774], Philip [b. Feb 1776] (SA p. 25, 29)

Herrill, Christopher; inv.; 10 Apr 1735; 23 Apr 1735; nok Gilbert Herrill, Thomas Graners; admx./extx. Margrett Herill (I 20.398)

Heshtine, Charles; inv.; 3 Sep 1769; 10 Oct 1771; admx. Elisabeth w/o Thomas Fowler (I 107.191)

Heunton, William; inv.; 25 Jun 1698 (I&A 16.204)

Hewett (Hewitt, Hewet), John; will; 28 Jan 1675; 4 Feb 1675 (MCW 1.114) [SMW PC1.16]; inv.; 2 Mar 1675 (I&A 2.66); acct.; 13 Dec 1676 (I&A 3.1) (SMAA p. 43)

Hickman, Nathll.; will; 4 May 1758; 23 Nov 1759; wife Mary; sons Narth [Nathaniel], Henry; dau. Rebeco [Rebecca] (MCW 11.253) [SMW TA1.376]; inv.; 1 Sep 1761; nok Elisabeth & John Hickman; extx. Mary Hickman (I 76.319)

Higgens (Higgans), George; will; 22 Jan 1709; 25 Feb 1709 (MCW 3.164) [SMW PC1.164]; inv.; 4 Mar 1709 (I&A 21.120); acct. 25 May 1711; extx. Mary, w/o John Grant (I&A 32c.97) (SMAA p. 214)

Hillyard (Hillard, Halayrd), Edward; will; written 28 Oct 1716; dau. Frances, w/o Thomas Hebb, Jr.; their dau. Jeane Hebb; mentions Jane Hillyard, ex. (MCW 4.90); inv.; 25 Feb 1716; nok Thomas Hebb, Jr. (I&A 39b.65); acct.; 7 Jan 1717; extx. Jane, w/o Daniell Ray (I&A 39c.115) (SMAA p. 311)

Hilson, John; service by 1671 (SK 16.358)

Hinds, John; acct.; 6 Aug 1763; sons John & William [of age]; adms. Stephen Lucas & wife Susanna (A 49.527)

Hitchins, William; inv.; 3 Jan 1723; 3 Jul 1725; admx. Sarah Hutchins (I 10421)

Hlintifso, Elizabeth; spinster; age 30; 9 Feb 1721 (CCR p. 44)

Hodgis (Hogis), John; will; [prev. will probated 1655]; wife Mary; son John [age 11 mos.]; b-i-l William Stevens (MCW 1.9)

Hodgson {Hudgson], William; [planter]; will; 9 May 1698; 10 Jun 1698; son William; father Christopher; wife's dau. Ann Brookband, w/o Abraham; wife Mary (MCW 2.152) [SMW PC1.116]; inv.; 29 Oct 1698 (I&A 178.26)

Holloway, (Haliewell, Holliwell,), William; will; 2 Feb 1729; 13 Feb 1729; bros. Lawrence, John and Richard Holloway; William Ward, Thomas Asmuth [Aswith] and George Ashworth; mentions Jane d/o Phillip Tippet, Butler s/o Dannis Tippet, John and Alexander sons of Robert Cook (dec'd) (MCW 6.143) [SMW PC1.337]; inv.; 16 Feb 1723 (sic); 3 Mar 1729 (I 15.421); acct.; 25 Feb 1730 (A 10.636)

Holmes, Thomas; immigrated by 1674 (SK 18.127; 15.307)

Hooton, Matthew; immigrated by 1670 (SK 16.82)

Hotchkeys, Richard; *Cross Manor*; 15 Oct 1659; 22 Oct 1659 (MCW 1.15)

Houldcraft, George, Dr.; will; 21 Sep 1662; 2 Dec 1665; wife Susannah; bros. Michael and Valentine Houldcraft of England (MCW 1.32)

Houls, Luke Barber; inv.; 10 Jan 1763; 7 Jun 1763; nok Rebeccah Moran, Elisabeth Hulls (I 81.227)

Houlton, William; acct.; 18 Jul 1737; admx. Anne, dec'd, w/o Dennis Burn (Burne) (A 14.303)

How, Henry; *How's Advance*; 42 ac.; 10 Aug 1753 cert./pat. (COL)
    How's Fortune; 19 ac.; 10 Aug 1753 cert./pat. (COL)

Howes, Henry; *Forest*; 325 ac.; 25 Apr 1774 cert./pat. (COL)

Howknett (Hawknett), John; inv.; 28 Apr 1685 (I&A 8.336); acct.; 4 Mar 1685 (I&A 9.10) (SMAA p. 82)

Howley, Jasper; immigrated 1678 (SK 15.598)

Howstreet, Edward; age ca 1723 (MD p. 98)

Huddlestone, William; inv.; 19 Mar 1723; 17 Jun 1724; admx./extx. Elisabeth Huddlestone (I 10.8); acct.; 1 Feb 1724 (A 6.287); 11 Jul 1726 (A 7.502)

Humphreys, Thomas; *Marie's Choice*; 200 ac.; 1 Dec 1704 cert./pat. (COL)

Hunter, Andrew and Ann Poole (by license); m. 2 Feb 1783 (SA p. 60)

Hunton, Benjamin; 21 Apr 1675; 11 May 1675 (MCW 1.89)

Hurley, Dennis; inv.; 20 Aug 1686 (I&A 9.79); acct.; 18 Jul 1687 (I&A 9.324)

Husbands, William; service by 1673 (SK 17.589)

Hutchinson, Robertt; planter; inv.; 21 Apr 1674 (I&A 1.25)

Hutton, Charles; *Workington*; 350 ac.; sur. 11 Jul 1719; resur. into *Workington Park* (TLC p. 117); *Worsington*; [1722] cert./pat. (COL)
    Middle Ground; 102 ac.; sur. 10 Feb 1742 (TLC p. 81)

Hyakis, Peter; inv.; 6 Nov 1683 (I&A 8.117)

Ingalls, Thomas; oral; will; 12 Feb 1752; unnamed wife and 2 children in England; mentions James Dent, age 36, and John Bainham, age 17 (MCW 10.213) [SMW TA1.298]; inv.; 5 May 1752; 20 Jul 1752; nok Mark Shadrick, Sarah Caston (I 51.67); 27 Nov 1752 (I 54.48); acct.; 22 May 1753 (A 34.159); 3 Dec 1757 (A 41.323)

Inman, Benjamin; inv.; 21 Jun 1701 (I&A 21.165); acct.; 15 Jul 1704; admx. Elisabeth Inman (I&A 3.362)

Irgoe, Richard; age ca 47 in 1714 (MD p. 103)

Ives, James; wife Martha (AM LXVII.455)

Jacobs, Francis; inv.; 8 Jul 1742; 3 Mar 1742; nok Eliza Pilbrough (I 27.364)

Janner, John; *Salisbury Plain*; 100 ac.; 29 Nov 1680 cert./pat. (COL)

Jarves, Charles; inv.; 16 Jul 1739; 12 Feb 1739 (I 24.419); acct.; 14 Sep 1741 (A 18.381)

Jenkinson, Nathaniel; *Married Man's Hope*; 32 ac.; 21 Aug 1694 cert./pat. (COL)

Jennings, Henry; clerk; Rector of William & Mary's Parish; will; 13 Mar 1715/6; 27 Oct 1716; son Thomas; wife Elizabeth; b-i-l John Beale (MCW 4.89) [SMW PC1.209]; inv.; 22 Nov 1716 (I&A 38b.107)

Jersey, James; immigrated by 1667 (SK 11.170; 16.41)

Johns, John; inv.; 6 Jul 1752; 21 Apr 1753 (I 53.34)

Jolly, Edward; immigrated by 1662 (SK 17.332)

Jubb, James; acct.; 6 Jun 1720 (A 2.507)

Judge, Richard; service by 1674 (SK 18.72)

Junis, George; inv.; 25 May 1751; 1 Jun 1751; nok John Junia, Jane Jackson (I 47.104)

Keete, William; *Keete's Purchase*; 50 ac.; 6 Feb 1683 cert./pat. (COL)

Keirkly, Thomas; inv.; 26 Mar 1698 (I&A 16.188)

Kelshew, James and Elizabeth; dau. Mary Ann [b. 25 Sep 1773] (SA p. 24)

Kemp, Ann; immigrated by 1668 (SK 11.555)

Kendeloe (Kendalee), Thomas; will; 18 May 1719; 2 Jun 1719 (MCW 4.206) [SMW PC1.248]

Kenner (Kinner), William; *White Haven*; Cumberland Co., VA; mariner; will; written 11 Dec 1758; cousin Richard of Northumberland Co., VA; sister-i-l Elizabeth Hall & her bro. William Hicks of MD, merchant; son John William Hicks Kenner; ch/o bros. & sisters, Matthew and Francis Kenner, Elizabeth and Nancy (MCW 12.201) [SMW TA1.441); inv.; 15 Oct 1763; 30 Nov 1763; admx. Francis Kenner (I 82.203); inv.; 20 May 1763; 8 Jun 1763 (I 81.233); acct.; 10 May 1769 (A 60.358); acct.; 1 Jul 1770 (A 64.106)

Keough, Fargus; will; 13 Dec 1757; 11 Sep 1759; sons James, William; tracts *Wills [Mills] Swamp, Wheatly Addition, [Ferbuson's Folly]* (MCW 11.245) [SMW TA1.379]; inv.; 21 Sep 1759; 4 May 1760; admx./extx. Mary Keough (I 69.129); acct.; 10 Nov 1760; orphans James [age 17], Elisabeth [age 10], Mary [age 8] (A 46.151); dist.; 10 Nov 1760; children James, William, Elisabeth, Mary; extx. Mary Keough (BB 3.50)

Kerse, Arthur; planter; acct.; 11 Sep 1700 (I&A 20.45)

Kersey, James; service by 1674 (SK 18.72)

Kilgour, William; *Bon Accord*; 115 ac.; 25 Mar 1763 cert./pat. (COL)
   Aberdeen; 128 ac.; 29 Sep 1763 cert./pat. (COL)
   Bon Accord Addn.; 45 ac.; 7 Feb 1764 cert./pat. (COL)

Kinch (Kinck), John; cordwainer; inv.; 15 Apr 1732; 1 Aug 1732 (I 16.552); acct.; 7 Aug 1733 (A 12.39)

Kirkley (Kurtley), Thomas; inv.; 5 Mar 1754; 4 Jun 1754; nok Marmaduke Jackson, Luke Russell (I 58.190)

Knight, William; will; 5 May 1698; 17 Jun 1698; son Clement (MCW 2.138) [SMW PC1.102]; inv.; [filed with 1699] (I&A 19½a.156); inv.; 8 Aug 1698 (I&A 16.189);

inv.; 30 May 1699 (I&A 19.53); inv.; 14 Jun 1699 (I&A 19.53); acct.; 16 Jun 1699; unnamed wife and 2 sons, one age 6 (I&A 19.56)

Ky, John; immigrated by 1670 (SK 12.551)

Lampton, Mark; planter; 25 Oct 1733; 6 Nov 1733; cousin James Pye; aunt Susan Thompson (MCW 7.47) [SMW TA1.12]

Lander, Francis, Rev.; age ca 33 in 1764; age ca 35 in 1765 (MD p. 113) [SMW TA1.539-556]

Laney, James; inv.; 2 Jul 1764; 7 Oct 1764 (I 86.56)

Lang, John; m. 14 Feb 1778 Dorothy Williams (BRU 2.535)

Langford, Vincent; acct.; 11 Sep 1719 (SMAA p. 376); 19 Apr 1720 (A 3.29) (SMAA p. 419)

Langham, William; Brittain's Bay; will; 2 Oct 1717; _ Nov 1717; bros.-i-l Anthony Browne & his son William, Richard Walker and Nicholas Miles; wife Annastatia (MCW 4.170) [SMW PC1.226]; inv.; 4 Jan 1717 (I&A 39c.75); acct.; extx. Anastatia; 18 Nov 1718 (A 1.313) (SMAA p. 325)

Lant, Lawrence; Deputy Surveyor for SM Co.; *Ossfield*; 72 ac.; sur. 25 Aug 1725 (TLC p. 89); 10 Jun 1734 cert./pat. (COL)

Lark, Daniel; inv.; 26 Apr 1722; 13 Mar 1722 (I 8.56)

Lake (Lahee), William; inv.; 5 Dec 1716 (I&A 38b.70); acct.; 29 Oct 1717 (I&A 39c.119) (SMAA p. 314)

Lawson, John; gent.; acct.; 14 May 1675; mentions Jean and Dorcus Lawson (I&A 1.275)

Leaner, Henry; inv.; 26 Mar 1733; 24 Apr 1733 (I 17.101)

Leatherland, Wm. and Elizabeth Kirby (by license); m. 16 Jan 1781 (SA p. 59)

LeDuke, Joseph; immigrated by 1671 (SK 16.115)

Lefer, Remy; inv.; 18 Feb 1687 (I&A 10.10)

Legatt, Tho.; *Parnassus*; 75 ac.; resur. 31 Dec 1680; 1707 poss. John Whittor; Resurrection Hundred (RR p. 59) (TLC p. 56)

Legg, William; inv.; 11 Feb 1712 (I&A 34.136); acct.; 8 Oct 1714; admx. Elisabeth Gardiner (I&A 36a.209) (SMAA p. 260)

Lemarre, Tho.; *Fishing Place*; 50 ac.; sur. 30 Apr 1676; 1707 poss. Peter Harris; Resurrection Hundred (RR p. 63) (TLC p. 60); inv.; 25 Feb 1681 (I&A 7b.179)

Leonardson, Leonard; St. Leonard's; 24 Mar 1640; mother Alice Cales (MCW 1.1)

Lesuire, John; service by 1668 (SK 11.517)

Limbrey (Lumbrey), Humphrey; immigrated by 1668 (SK 16.331)

Lindsey, James; wife Mary; ack. 450 a. moiety of *Snow Hill* to be right of Philip Calvert; 10 Jul 1663 (AM XLIX.32)

Lippet, Notley & Ann Wood; banns published 2 Dec 1783 (BRU 2.536)

Livers, Arnold; 19 Mar 1761; 19 Nov 1767 (MCW 14.18) [SMW TA1.518]

Longhlin, Anthony; immigrated by 1672 (SK 17.77); will; 20 Nov 1684; 23 Feb 1684; wife Margaret; son Anthony; dau. Mary (MCW 1.148-149); called planter [SMW PC1.48]

Looton, Jacob; 13 May 1682; naturalized (CMN N14)

Lothian, Alexander; 2 Dec 1768; 14 Feb 1769; mentions relation Alexander
  Ferguson (MCW 14.92) [SMW TA1.572]; inv.; 12 Apr 1769; 20 Aug 1775 (I 122.193)
Ludwell, Mary; oral; 4 Feb 1755; dau. Ann Waters Davis Hilton (MCW 11.95)
  [SMW TA1.334]
Lukey, Alexander; inv.; [filed with 1722]; nok Francis Hopewell, John Cole (I
  7.223)
Lums, Michael; St. Jerome's; probate 4 Jan 1639 (MCW 1.2)
Lynes (Lynds), George; will; 4 May 1733; 22 Aug 1733 (MCW 7.31) [SMW TA1.9];
  inv.; 24 Jan 1733; 17 Jun 1734 (I 18.334)

Mack, Daniell; inv.; 9 Feb 1712 (I&A 34.118)
Mackentosh, John; inv.; 7 Mar 1725; 21 Mar 1725; nok Jehu & Mary Cambell;
  admx. Mary Mackentosh (I 11.230); acct.; 12 Dec 1726 (A 8.149)
Mackhart, John; 11 Jan 1675; 17 Apr 1676; wife Elizabeth; dau. Agnes;
  mentions Elizabeth, d/o John Bullock (MCW I.174) [SMW PC1.26]; inv.; 17 Apr
  1676 (I&A 2.142); acct.; 12 Nov 1677; dau. Agnes (under 16); extx. Elisabeth
  Dash (relict) (I&A 4.529)
Mackling, Robert; wife Margarite; 1664; conveyed 100 acres to John Tully (AM
  XLIX.335)
Mackmillian, Daniel; acct.; 19 Mar 1713 (I&A 35a.379) (SMAA p. 255)
Maides, John; immigrated by 1667 (SK 11.190)
Malbury, Francis; age ca 50 in 1713 (MD p. 123)
Maneaster, John; immigrated by 1657 (SK 19.41)
Manfeld, Waters; inv.; 30 Dec 1730; 8 Mar 1730 (I 16.187)
Mannaring, George; immigrated by 1670 (SK 12.548)
Manners, George; will; 17 Jul 1651; 6 Nov 1651; son Edward; dau. Barbara
  Manners, 100 ac. *St. Ellinor's*; son William, residue; wife Rebecca (MCW 1.5)
Markes, Amy; of Poplar Hill; spinster; charged with having bastard child 31 Jan
  last (AM LXV.27)
Marler, Jna.; *Retirement*; 200 ac.; sur. 27 Nov 1667; 1707 poss. widow Jane
  Swan; Choptico Hundred (RR p. 51) (TLC p. 49)
Marley, Cornelius; age ca 53; 13 Apr 1715; tract *Revill* (CCR p. 33)
Marsh, Paul; *Marshes Hope*; 150 ac.; sur. 10 Apr 1665; 1707 poss. Henry Jarbo
  for John Jarbo's orphans & John Heard; New Town Hundred (RR p. 33) (TLC p.
  32)
Martindale, Elizabeth; service by 1676 (SK 15.374, 412)
Massey, Leigh, Rev.; inv.; 24 Feb 1732; 22 May 1733; nok Thomas & James
  Waughop; admx./extx. Ann Massey (I 17.151); acct.; 12 Sep 1734; orphans
  Austin Leigh, Peter Leigh & Anna Marie Massey; admx. Ann Massey (A
  12.537)
May, Daniel; s/o Richard, dec'd; *Vineyard*; 343 ac.; 6 Jun 1681; assigned by
  George White of England; bro. of Jerome White, dec'd cert./pat. (COL)

McCartney, Edward and Mary; daus. Fanny [b. 9 Jun 1779], Sarah [b. 9 Apr 1781], Ann [b. 10 Mar 1784], Susanna [b. 26 Aug 1787] (SA p. 30, 31)

McFarlane, Alexander; will; 13 Apr 1762; 17 Aug 1766; wife Eleanor (MCW 13.152) [SMW TA1.500]; inv.; 18 Nov 1766; 4 Feb 1767; ex. Elleanor McFarlane (I 91.106, 109); acct.; 6 Sep 1771; exs. William Bayard & wife Eleanor (A 66.49)

McFederick (Federick), Archibald; inv.; 7 Dec 1727; 4 Mar 1727; admx. Mary Federick (I 13.9); acct.; 17 Oct 1728 (A 9.114)

McGeornehan (Macgeonnehom), Roger; inv.; 4 Feb 1739; 10 Mar 1739 (I 24.539); acct.; 22 Oct 1740 (A 18.96)

McPhearson, John (Johnson); inv.; 19 May 1770; 1 Jun 1771; nok James Brown, Mary McPhearson; admx. Rachel McPhearson (I 106.378); inv.; 20 Jul 1773 (I 112.412); acct.; 20 Jul 1773 (A 68.206); dist.; 20 Jul 1773 (BB 6.222)

McWherter, Andrew and Mary; dau. Elizabeth, bapt. 2 Apr 1780 (SA p. 29)

Meckin, Augustine; inv.; 1 Jun 1768; adm. Margaret Meckin (I 97.269)

Mee, George; probate 6 Aug 1662; wife unnamed (MCW 1.21)

Meech, Thomas; inv.; 1 Sep 1696 (I&A 14.7); acct.; 15 Mar 1697 (I&A16.72)

Mellethorpe, Thomas; service by 1671 (SK 16.446)

Merrydeth, Lewis; service by 1679 (SK WC2.67)

Merty, Stephen; immigrated by 1672 (SK 17.9)

Messar, Thomas; service by 1680 (SK WC2.315, 341)

Messenger, Joseph, Rev. and Mary; dau. Mary [b. 14 Jan 1776; bapt. 7 Apr 1776], William and John Feron, twin brothers [b. 25 Nov 1777; bapt. 26 Nov 1777] (SA p. 30)

Mickin, William; mentions orphans; undated [1695] (SMAA p. 92)

Minckin, Richard; inv.; 29 Apr 1699 (I&A 19.94)

Mirralls, Mary; age ca 40; 1679/80 (AM LXIX.122)

Monark (Monack, Monocock), Monica; 4 Feb 1743/4; 7 Feb 1743; daus. Mary, Margaret; son John, Joseph, Thomas; bros. Edward Price, John Temple (MCW 8.254) [SMW TA1.132]; inv.; 8 Mar 1743; 6 Jun 1744; nok Thomas & James Price; adm./ex. Edward Price (I 29.235); acct.; 20 Jun 1745; orphans John, Thomas, Mary, Monica (A 21.363)

Monteague, James; acct.; [filed with 1700] (I&A 20.59)

Montgomery, Katherine; inv.; 12 Nov 1724; 14 Jul 1725; nok William and Shusannah Williams (I 11.17)

Moody, Edward; inv.; 22 Sep 1730; 24 Nov 1730 (I 16.80); acct.; 8 Jun 1732 (A 11.429)

Moorecroft (Morecraft), John; gent.; inv.; 15 Dec 1673 (I&A 1.29); acct.; [Dr.]; 3 Mar 1675 (I&A 1.557)

Moreton, Joseph; m. 3 Jan 1778 Cath. Billingsley (BRU p. 536)

Mort, Jos. and Eleanor; children John [b. 20 Jan 1774], James [b. 2 Oct 1776] (AFP 2.350)

Mouett, John, Mr.; inv.; 22 Jun 1717; nok John & Ales Gibson (I&A 37b.127); acct.; extx. Francis Marrett; 13 Mar 1717/8 (SMAA p. 331)

Moundeford, Francis; <u>inv.</u> [filed with 1677] (I&A 4.406)

Mourice, Jacob; <u>acct.</u>; 8 Oct 1738; orphans Jasse, James, Ann & Elisabeth Morris; admx. Elinor, w/o Edward Onel (A 16.322)

Mullen, Mary; <u>inv.</u>; 29 Apr 1736; 11 Apr 1737 (I 22.214); <u>acct.</u>; 11 Apr 1737 (A 15.301)

Munday, Tho. & Edward Hudson; unnamed; 300 ac.; sur. 10 Nov 1647; incl. in *Resurvey of Medley*; 1707 no. poss.; New Town Hundred (RR p. 27) (TLC p. 25)

Muschamp, George; <u>will</u>; 2 Nov 1709; 12 Nov 1709 (MCW 3.157) [SMW PC1.163]; <u>inv.</u>; 12 May 1710 (I&A 31.354)

Musgrove, Charles; <u>inv.</u>; 4 May 1757; 25 Jul 1757; admx./extx. Sarah Farmon Musgrove (I 63.404); <u>acct.</u>; 5 Dec 1758; orphans Mary [age 10], Ann [age 8], Catharine [age 6], Sarah [age 2] admx. Sarah Truman Musgrove (A 43.22)

Nengfinger, William; 19 Apr 1671; Dutch; naturalized (CMN N4)

Nesham, Benjamin; service by 1679 (SK WC2.39, 140, 141)

Netherton, Rob.; *Nethertons Beginning*; 50 ac.; sur. 10 Nov 1673; listed in 1704 but not in 1707; St. Mary's Hundred (TLC p. 8)

Neuten [Newton], Frances; 9 Dec 1765; 6 Jun 1770; bro. Mathew Wise (MCW 14.134) [SMW TA1. 586]

Neverson (Never, Nevers), David; <u>will</u>; undated; [10 Dec 1750]; mentions Jane, d/o Stephen Taylor (MCW 10.124) [SMW TA1.245]; <u>inv.</u>; 10 Feb 1750; 10 Jun 1751 (I 47.121); <u>acct.</u>; 23 Dec 1751 (A 32.72)

Newbolt, George; <u>inv.</u>.; 2 Jun 1774; 29 Nov 1774; admx. Sarah Newbolt (I 118.225)

Noakes (Noaks), George; <u>inv.</u>; 14 Jan 1737; 19 Apr 1738; admx. extx. Mary Noakes (I 23.79); <u>acct.</u>; 7 Nov 1739; admx. Mary, w/o William Carrel (Carrall)] (A 17.348)

Nodding (Noding), George; <u>inv.</u>; 29 Dec 1726; 1 Jun 1727; nok minors; admx. Sarah Nodding (I 12.251); <u>acct.</u>; 27 May 1729; admx. Sarah, w/o John Bennet of CA Co. (A 9.378)

Nooke, William; <u>acct.</u>; 26 Jan 1735; extx. Susanah, w/o John Stanfill (A 14.182)

Northen (Norton), Andrew; *Fairfield*; sur. 29 Sep 1713 for Andrew Northen (TLC p. 68); Andrew of KE Co.; *Fearfield*; 50 ac.; 10 Dec 1713 cert./pat. (COL)

Novett, John; planter; age ca 70; s/o Richard Novett; 28 Sep 1711 (CCR p. 20)

Nuncy (Nuney, Nuny), Michael; tailor; <u>will</u>; 3 Nov 1740; 12 Mar 1740/1; daus. Judith, Sarah, Mary, Ann; wife Elizabeth; [tract *Draper's Neck*] (MCW 8.122) [SMW TA1.109]; <u>inv.</u>; 20 Jul 1741; nok minors; adms./exs. John Baker & wife Elisabeth (I 26.325, 326); <u>acct.</u>; 15 Aug 1744 (A 20.436)

Nuport, William; immigrated by 1670 (SK 16.11)

Nuthead (Nuthed), William; printer of St. Mary's City; age ca 39 in 1693 (MD p. 140); <u>inv.</u>; 2 Apr 1695 (I&A 13a.263)

Oard, William; <u>inv.</u>; 4 Nov 1773; 5 Apr 1774; nok Thomas & Jesse Oard; admx./rextx. Eleanor Oard (I 116.210)

Obert, Bartho. & Dominick; *Obert*; 200 ac.; sur. 4 Feb 1649; 1707 poss. Philip Lynes of CH Co.; tenant Wm. Bright; New Town Hundred (RR p. 28); called *Shepheards Fields* (TLC p. 27)

Oden, Vincent; *Oden's Fortune*; 16 ac.; 12 Jun 1770 cert./pat. (COL)

Ogilby (Oglesbie) [Agilby], Thomas; planter; <u>will</u>; 13 Jan 1733/4; 5 Jun 1734; dau. Mary (MCW 7.94) [SMW TA1.99]; <u>inv.</u>; 20 Jun 1734; 2 Dec 1734; nok minors, William Coks (I 20.111); <u>acct.</u>; 15 Sep 1740 (A 18.63)

Ogilvie, George; <u>inv.</u>; 2 Mar 1726; 2 Nov 1726 (I 11.605); <u>acct.</u>; 2 Nov 1726 (A 8.62)

Oney, Nathaniel and Mary Smith (by license); m. 18 Jul 1785 (SA p. 63)

Opey, Linsy (Lindsey), Mr.; <u>inv.</u>; 15 Apr 1748 (I 35.524); <u>acct.</u>; 17 Jun 1754 (A 36.309)

Orame, John; <u>inv.</u>; 20 Apr 1705 (I&A 25.25)

Ord, William; oral; <u>will</u>; 25 Oct 1773; 30 Oct 1773; wife Eleanor; bros. Thomas, Justinian (MCW 15.91) [SMW TA1.661]

Orton, Henry; St. Leonard's Creek; Patuxent River; <u>will</u>; 1 Oct 1696; 19 Jan 1696; son Henry; dau. Eliza.; sons-i-1 Thomas and William Davis; d-i-1 Mary Davis (MCW 2.117)

Otley, James and Elizabeth Richardson; m. 24 Jan 1780 (SA p. 58)

Overton, Thomas; immigrated by 1668 with wife Mary and daus. Mary, Jr. and Sarah (SK 16.222)

Ozey, James; probate 29 Dec 1665 (MCW 1.33)

Packer, Edw'd & Wm. Nanfin; *Gardiners Purchase*; 100 ac.; 23 Oct 1640; 1707 poss. John Miller; St. Georges Hundred (RR p. 16) (TLC p. 16)

Page, Rob't; *Desert*; 250 ac.; sur. 24 Sep 1668; 1707 poss. James Wood; Choptico Hundred (RR p. 51) (TLC p. 49)

Pannett, James; <u>acct.</u>; 1 Sep 1741; <u>dist.</u> to Isaac, John & Joseph Panett; admx. Elisabeth Panett (A 18.380)

Pantree, William; <u>inv.</u>; 13 May 1774; 27 May 1774; admx. Mary Pantree (I 118.134)

Pargrave, James; <u>acct.</u>; 2 Jun 1699; 1 orphan; admx. Margrett (widow), w/o Robert Farguson (I&A 19.172)

Patchal, John; <u>inv.</u>; 9 Dec 1735; 3 Mar 1735; one minor; admx./extx. Sarah Patchall (I 21.236); <u>acct.</u>; 3 Mar 1737; admx. Sarah, w/o William Daves of CH Co. (A 16.84)

Peaggrafe, James; <u>inv.</u>; 16 Mar 1684; 24 Mar 1684 (I&A 8.434)

Pean, James; <u>inv.</u>; 19 May 1679 (I&A 6.166)

Pears, John; service by 1667 (SK 11.246)

Pelers, Abraham; age ca 77 in 1711 (MD p. 146)

Pell, William; <u>will</u>; 20 Mar 1654; 2 Sep 1659 (MCW 1.14)

Pembrooke, John; inv.; 15 Aug 1745; 30 Sep 1745; nok Isabell Cook, John
Arters; admx./extx. Agnus Pembrooke (I 31.302); acct.; 26 Oct 1746; orphans
George, Izabella, Dryden Ann; admx. Agness, w/o William Doxsey (A 23.14)

Pennington, Francis; priest; age ca 36 in 1678 (MD p. 146); d. 1699; age ?22 (HGM)

Penniwell, Robert; service by 1670 (SK 12.552)

Penon, Thomas; inv.; Apr 1752; 1 Oct 1753; nok Thomas & John Reeder (I 57.34)

Perin (Perrin), Thomas; will; probate 4 Apr 1752; son Benet; mentions Anne,
d/o Col. George Clarke, and Anne, d/o Capt. James Biscoe (MCW 10.201) [SMW
TA1.287]; acct.; 24 Jul 1758; orphan Bennet [age 13] (A 41.481); dist.; 24 Jul
1758 (BB 2.90)

Peteate, Thomas; will; 19 Jan 1650; 18 Mar 1657; wife Anne (MCW 1.10)

Peters, Joseph; acct.; 5 Mar 1722; admx. Susanah, w/o Edward Stonestreet (A
5.33)

Pettit, Thomas; *Pettit's Addition*; 27 ac.; sur. 16 Dec 1742 (TLC p. 102); 8 Sep
1743 cert./pat. (COL)

Peweck, Ellenor; acct.; 29 Jun 1714 (SMAA p. 271)

Phelps, John; inv.; 9 Feb 1718; nok William Holland (I 1.197)

Philpott, Edward; age ca 49 in 1650 (MD p. 149)

Phipps, John; inv.; 24 Nov 1709 (I&A 31.18); acct.; 27 Feb 1710 (I&A 32c.95)
(SMAA p. 191)

Pickerl (Pickrel) [Pickeral], Jeremiah; will; 28 Apr 1745; 6 May 1745 (MCW 9.28)
[SMW TA1.172]; inv.; 6 May 1745; 4 Oct 1745 (I 31.289)

Piggott, Bartholomew; acct.; 22 Feb 1686 (I&A 9.218)

Pilbery, Robert; acct.; 4 Mar 1742; orphans John Thomas, Ephram, Robert;
admx. Elisabeth Philbory (Polborgh) (A 19.374)

Pilbinton, Hugh; inv.; 13 Sep 1743; 4 Nov 1743; nok John Penbe, James
Wolber; admx./extx. Mary Pilbinton (I 28.360)

Pilcher, Emmanuell; inv.; 1 May 1694; 14 Jun 1694 (I&A 13a.123)

Pinner, Richard; age ca 26 in 1679 (MD p. 149)

Piper, John; *Barford Manor*; will; 22 Oct 1673; 11 Apr 1674; wife Mary;
kinsman John Piper of VA (MCW 1.80); inv.; 4 May 1674 (I&A 1.45)

Pitcher, Emanuel; will; 24 Apr 1694; 22 May 1694; wife Jane; dau. Amye (MCW
2.68); acct.; [filed with 1696]; extx. Mary, w/o Thomas Rose (I&A 15.139) (SMAA
p. 95)

Poily, Richard; m. 7 Feb 1771 Susan Hayden (MM)

Pomroy, John, Jr.; inv.; 5 Jul 1735; 14 Aug 1735; nok Benjamin & John Pomroy
(I 21.98); acct.; 3 Nov 1736 (A 15.224)

Poole, Peter; *Buck Neck*; 53 ac.; 6 Sep 1757 cert./pat. (COL)

Poston, Judith; w/o Rev. Hatch Dent; b. 10 Jan 1758; d. 3 Mar 1814 (HGM)

Pountney, Henry; *Pountney Marsh*; 200 ac.; sur. 17 Sep 1651; 1707 poss. Ann
Bougher, relict of Charles Egerton, dec'd; St. Mary's Hundred (RR p. 2) (TLC p.
3)

Priest, Charles; planter; inv.; 16 Jan 1684 (I&A 8.363); acct.; 9 Jul 1686; admx. Sarah, w/o James Biscoe (I&A 9.45)

Proddy, Nicholas, Mr.; inv.; 13 Aug 1679 (I&A 6.239); acct.; 31 Jul 1679 (I&A 6.239)

Proove, Edward; inv.; 21 Jul 1703 (I&A 24.222)

Puny, Robert; acct.; 23 May 1726; extx. Mary, w/o Thomas Taylor (A 7.375)

Purdy, Nathaniel; immigrated by 1671 from VA (SK 16.358)

Purtle, Robert; inv.; 23 Sep 1750 1 Oct 1750; nok Robert Purtle, Mary Farthing; admx./extx Elisabeth Purtle (I 44.33); acct.; 1 Oct 1750 (A 29.48)

Pynn, Edward; immigrated by 1679 (SK WC2.391.392)

Quaide (Quaid), Morrice; inv.; 20 May 1729; 25 Aug 1729; nok minors; admx./extx. Sarah Quaide (I 15.100); acct.; 2 Mar 1729; admx. Sarah, w/o Francis Garry (A 10.205)

Racey, Thomas; inv.; 5 Apr 1717; nok Wettison Racey (I&A 37b.6); acct.; 4 Jun 1719; admx. Dorothy Racey (A 2.212)

Radford, Thomas; inv.; 24 May 1769; 17 Mar 1770 (I 103.227); acct.; 7 Mar 1770 (A 64.101)

Ragon (Rogan), Phillip; inv.; 2 Dec 1718; 23 Feb 1718 (I 1.478); acct.; 12 Nov 1719 (A 3.412) (SMAA p. 366)

Raleigh, Henry; inv.; 3 May 1754; 1 Jul 1754; nok John & J. Raley; admx./extx. Margaret Reed (I 58.186)

Rasin (Rasyn), Thomas; will; 18 Apr 1687; 23 Apr 1688; unnamed wife and 5 child. (MCW 2.25) [SMW PC1.67]; inv.; 6 Apr 1688; 18 Jul 1688 (I&A 10.35)

Raylons, William; acct.; 26 Mar 1695; admx. Sarah Raylons (I&A 13a.251)

Rayner, Richard; immigrated by 1670 (SK 12.599)

Readish, Daniell; inv.; 11 May 1721; 30 Jun 1721; admx. Mary Readish (I 5.149)

Reagan, Philip; will; 14 Feb 1718; 15 Nov 1718 (MCW 4.188) [SMW PC1.242]

Reall, Edward; inv.; 1 May 1764; extx. Jean Reall (I 84.274)

Rease, Gregory; inv.; [filed with 1679] (I&A 6.643)

Redley, Thomas; service by 1677 (SK 15.425)

Reman, John; Poplar Hill Hundred; will; 15 Apr 1699; 4 Mar 1700; dau. Ann; son John; tracts *Outlet, Redman's Adventure, Meeting Forever* (MCW 2.213)

Revell, Randall; *St. Georges Point*; 100 ac.; sur. 17 Oct 1640; 1707 no poss.; St. Georges Hundred (RR p. 16) (TLC p. 16)
Revell; 300 ac.; sur. 14 Dec 1641; 1707 poss. Luke Barber, Widow Tant, James Tant; New Town Hundred (RR p. 26) (TLC p. 24)

Riall, Edward; will; 29 Dec 1762; 6 Dec 1763; dau. Mary Price; g-sons John and Edward Price; wife Jane; tracts *Riall's Purchase, Riall's Venture* (MCW 12.217) [SMW TA1.441]

Rian (Rion), Ellenor; will; 12 Apr 1735; 20 May 1735 (MCW 7.134) [SMW TA1.39]

Rice, John; inv.; 20 Dec 1750; 21 Jan 1750; nok William Harris, Thomas Rigg (I 44.252); acct.; 21 Jan 1753; orphans: w/o accountant, Mary [age 13], Elisabeth [age 9]; admn. Anthony Smith (A 33.314); dist.; 21 Jan 1753; daus. Mary [age 15], Elizabeth [age 9], unnamed dau., w/o Anthony Smith (BB 1.61, 72)

Riddle, Archbold; inv.; 7 Jun 1759; 24 Jul 1759 (I 67.323)

Right, James; acct.; 15 Jul 1741 (A 18.274)

Rigg, James; inv.; 3 Mar 1759; 2 Jul 1759; nok Roger Tolle, Richard Taylor; adms./exs. James Richardson & wife Ann (I 67.193, 195); acct.; 16 Jun 1760; orphans John [age 8], James [age 5] (A 44.275); dist.; 10 Jun 1760 (BB 3.27)

Rinefinger, William; inv.; 18 Oct 1688 (I&A 10.126)

Ringe, Richard; acct.; [filed with 1680] (I&A 7a.168)

Riouston [Rioustone], Joseph; will; 12 Nov 1703; 27 Oct 1703; dau Margaret (MCW 3.94) [SMW PC1.148]

Ritchison, Timothy; planter; inv.; 29 Dec 1685 (I&A 9.455)

Robson, Winfred; acct.; 14 Aug 1766 (A 55.320)

Rodway, John; immigrated by 1670 (SK 12.551)

Rogers, George; will; 20 Mar 1739/40; 17 Nov 1740; daus Darcus, Dorothy; son George; wife Elizabeth (MCW 8.112) [SMW TA1.101]; inv.; 14 May 1741; nok minors; adms./exs. George Aisquith & wife Elisabeth (I 25.528); acct.; 11 Jan 1743 (A 20.58)

Rolle, Solomon; acct.; 1 Mar 1700; extx. Ann, w/o Henry Newell (I&A21.188)

Rolley, Thomas; *Addition to John Days Work*; 21 ac.; sur. 1 Jun 1738; (TLC p. 95)

Roode, John; service by 1675 (SK 18.339)

Rooker, Edward; immigrated by 1672 (SK 17.77)

Rosen (Rowsen), Winefred, Mrs.; inv.; 1 Oct 1765; 14 Aug 1766 (I 91.91)

Roules, Walter; immigrated by 1670 (SK 12.551)

Rouse, Gregory; will; 27 Oct 1679; 18 Nov 1679 (MCW 1.218); acct.; 3 Sep 1680 (I&A 7a.226)

Rubling, Thomas; acct.; 2 Oct 1753; orphan Ruth [age 5] (A 36.15)

Rudd, James; inv.; 18 Jan 1756; nok Elener Cowood, Dorothy Cartwright (I 60.375)

Runnells, Richard; St. Michael's Hundred; acct.; 13 Dec 1674; ex. Sarah Vaughan (SMAA p.38)

Rupers, Richard; inv.; 2 Jun 1752; 5 Sep 1753; nok Richard Ruptur, James Balye; adms./exts. Clement Startford & wife Teretia (I 55.19)

Rutte (Rottee), Solomon; inv.; 18 Jun 1698 (I&A 16.186); acct.; 24 Jul 1699; 1 orphan; extx. Ann , w/o Henry Nowell (I&A 19½a.153) (SMAA p. 94)

Rwightstone, Joseph; inv.; 29 Oct 1703 (I&A 24.247)

Ryland, William; service by 1679 (SK WC2.52); inv.; 7 May 1694 (I&A 13a.13)

Sacheverall, Theopolus; inv.; 9 Jan 1716 (I&A 38a.6)

Salley, Benjamin; will; 6 May 1749; 17 __ 1749; mentions Ann, sis.of Thomas
Aisquith & Monarkey, d/o John Forde (MCW 10.36) [SMW TA1.227]; acct.; 20 Jul
1754 (A 36.315)

Sandy, William; acct.; 4 Jul 1727; admx. Ann, w/o John Woolbridge (A 8.276)

Sanford, Alice; servant; killed 29 Feb 1663 at St. Winifred's (CCR p. 2)

Sanson, John and Mary; sons William [b. 3 Oct 1767], John [b. 5 Jul 1771] (SA p.
14, 48, 192)

Sarah; negro; will; children William, Mary, Elizabeth (MCW 7.63) [SMW TA1.23]

Satt, Robert; clerk; age 55; 27 May 1723 (CCR p. 52)

Sawell, John; inv.; 10 Mar 1698 (I&A 16.47); acct.; 8 Mar 1708; admx. unnamed
relict, w/o Adam Head (I&A 29.102) (SMAA p. 170)

Saxe, Henry and Rennis Denton (by license); m. 10 Jan 1783 (SA p. 60)

Saxon, John; *Fowle's Discovery*; 100 ac.; 16 Oct 1680 cert./pat. (COL)

Schurlooke (Schurlock), Richard; inv.; 25 Nov 1719; admx./extx. Kathrin
Schurlooke (I 3.219); acct.; 15 Aug 1720 (A 3.228) (SMAA p. 440)

Scrogan (Scrogin), James; inv.; 10 Feb __; 13 Dec 1763; nok John Scrogin,
Sarah Ockley; admx. Elisabeth Scrogin (I 82.197)

Seager, John, Dr.; *Folly*; 100 ac.; sur. 20 Jul 1714; in bounds of *Indian Creek*
(TLC p. 74); 25 Apr 1717 cert./pat. (COL)

Seaward, Josias; immigrated by 1668 (SK 11.579)

Seffort (Cyffert), Stephen; tailor; 26 Nov 1766; 21 Jan 1767; wife Elizabeth;
daus. Ann, Mary (MCW 13.151) [SMW TA1.525]

Sellman, Anne; acct.; 3 Aug 1751; son Scarbrough Sellman; mentions Kensey
Sparrow & son Jonathon; Ann, d/o Samuel & Anne Battee, Elisabeth d/o John
Sellman; Thomas, Charles & John Sellman (A 30.176)

Selo, Francis; Newtowne; will; 7 Jan 1674; 20 Jan 1674; unnamed son in VA
(MCW 1.86)

Setle, John; immigrated by 1674 (SK 18.72)

Sey (Saye), Susan; spinster; dec'd; 27 Mar 1637 (AM IV.24, 44)

Seycroft, Edward; immigrated by 1673 (SK 17.479)

Seymour, John; Hon., Esq.; inv. & acct.; 1 Oct 1710 (I&A 33b.26)

Shantry, Joseph; acct.; 30 Jan 1702 (SMAA p. 111)

Sharlin, Roger; service by 1673 (SK 17.551)

Shaw, John; service by 1681 (SK WC2.410)

Sheehee (Shehee), Roger; planter; inv.; 1 Jul 1674 (I&A 1.36); acct.; 19 Apr 1675
(I&A 1.222)

Shelley, Edward; will; probate 13 Oct 1653 (MCW 1.8)

Shells, Bridgett; age ca 35; former husband John Greenhill; 1661 (AM XLI.563)

Shener, Christopher; acct.; 4 Oct 1743; orphans John, Christopher, Joseph,
Anne, Mary; admx. Mary Shener (A 19.540)

Shermandine (Shurmandine), John; <u>inv.</u>; 21 Jan 1750; 21 Jan 1750; nok Joseph
& Elisabeth Shermandine (I 44.254); <u>acct.</u>; 14 Sep 1751; orphans Joseph [age
16], Elisabeth [age 13], James [age 12], Abintine [age 9], Jeremiah [age 8],
Ann [age 5], Hezekiah [age 3] (A 31.221); <u>dist.</u>; 14 Sep 1751 (BB 1.16)

Shewbottam (Shoobottom, Sherbottom), Richard; <u>inv.</u> 17 Aug 1708 (I&A 28.308);
<u>acct.</u> 23 Jul 1709; admx. Barbary, w/o Richard Mosely (I&A 30.21); 25 Jul 1709
(SMAA p. 174)

Shewer, Christopher; <u>inv.</u>; 19 Aug 1742; 5 Oct 1742; nok Nicholas & William
Moore; admx./extx. Mary Shewer (I 27.158)

Shippard, Catherine (Katherine); <u>acct.</u>; 24 May 1715 (SMAA p. 290); 15 May 1716
(I&A 37c.157) (SMAA p. 306)

Shippey, Rich'd; *Sheppyes Rest*; 100 ac.; sur. 9 Mar 1681; poss. James Murphy
for Rob. Solomon's orphan; in 1704 RR; not found in 1707; New Town
Hundred (RR); *Shippie's Rest*; 100 ac.; 9 May 1681 cert./pat. (COL)

Shorte, Ames; 3 Aug 1670; 7 Sep 1670 (MCW 1.55)

Shohon (Shuconshe, Sheanionshee), Darby; <u>inv.</u>; 20 Jan 1721; 30 Jan 1721;
admx. Elisabeth Sheanionshee (I 7.26); <u>acct.</u>; 14 Aug 1725 (A 7.99)

Sifertt (Siffert), Stephen; <u>inv.</u>; 8 May 1767; nok Mary Reynolds, John Bright;
extx. Elisabeth Siffert (I 91.330, 331)

Simeon, George; <u>acct.</u>; 17 Jun 1719; Cornelius Manning, ex. of Mary Manning,
ex. of dec'd (A 2.43) (SMAA p. 403); <u>acct.</u>; 23 Sep 1720 (A 3.177)

Sissary, Edward; <u>inv.</u>; 9 Apr 1697 (I&A 17.106)

Size, Edward; <u>acct.</u>; 10 Jul 1686; mentions Rebeccah Simons, w/o Bryan Daily
(I&A 9.53)

Skidmore, William; <u>acct.</u>; 17 Jul 1714; admx. Mary, w/o Henry Calvey (I&A
36b.38)

Skipper, John; <u>acct.</u>; 26 Mar 1694; admx. Jane Skipper (I&A 13a.253); <u>acct.</u>; [filed
with 1696] (I&A 14.7)

Slowers, Richard; <u>dist.</u>; [filed with 1769] (BB 5.138)

Smallpiece, John; immig. by 1671 (SK 16.117); <u>inv.</u>; 9 Jun 1675; mentions
Norland [BA Co.] (I&A 1.352)

Smart, William and wife Frances; dau. Susanna [b. 9 Nov 1769] (SA p. 2)

Smiles, John; *The Hope*; 110 ac.; sur. 17 Nov 1675; 1707 poss. Timothy
Mahoney; Resurrection Hundred (RR)

Snordin, George; <u>inv.</u>; 16 Jul 1711 (I&A 32c.110)

Snowden, John; <u>acct.</u>; [filed with 1687] (I&A 9.429)

Snuggs, John; age ca 42 in 1702 (MD p. 173)

Solby, George; service by 1669 (SK 12.382)

Souryton (Sourton), Francis, Gent.; immigrated by 1675 (SK 15.337); <u>inv.</u>; 23 Oct
1679 (I&A 6.562)

Sparkes, Richard; service by 1673 (SK 17.477)

Speak, Thomas; <u>will</u>; probate 6 Aug 1681; wife Eliza; son John; b-i-l James
    Bouring (MCW 1.101); <u>inv.</u>; 15 Aug 1681 (I&A 8.256); <u>acct.</u>; 12 Oct [filed with
    1682] (I&A 8.274)

Speed, John; <u>will</u>; probate 6 Oct 1639 (MCW 1.1)

Spong, Francis and Elizabeth; son James [b. 8 Sep 1760] (SA p. 39)

Spragg, William; service by 1678 (SK 15.523)

Sprigg, Tho.; unnamed; 500 ac.; sur. 29 Aug 1661; in *Beaverdam Manor*; 1707
    no poss.; New Town Hundred (RR)

Squires, John; age ca 44; 11 May 1720 (CCR p. 46); *Fridays Work*; 30 ac. sur. 29
    Jan 1724 (TLC); 21 Sep 1739 cert./pat. (COL)

Stanley, John; service by 1676 (SK 15.377)

Stannyon, Charles, Mr.; <u>inv.</u>; 4 Aug 1701 (I&A 21.75)

Stanton, Mary; age ca 35; 19 Sep 1722 (CCR p. 51)

Stanworth, Thomas; <u>inv.</u>; 2 Apr 1771; 1 Jun 1771; admx. Mary Stanworth (I
    106.381)

Stapelton (Stapleton), John; <u>will</u>; 6 Mar 1728/9; 17 Mar 1728/9; sons Henry,
    John; wife Margaret; tract *Bacon Point* (MCW 6.99) [SMW PC1.321]; <u>inv.</u>; 17 Apr
    1729; 25 May 1729; nok minors; admx./extx. Margaret Stapleton (I 14.86);
    <u>acct.</u>; 8 Jun 1730; extx. Margrat, w/o John Connally (A 10.341); <u>acct.</u>; 9 Jul
    1733; mentions Henry & John Stapleton (A 12.34)

Starkey, Lawrence; <u>will</u>; 29 Jan 1656; 19 Nov 1659 (MCW 1.10)

Startford (Standford), Mary; oral; <u>will</u>; 5 Feb 1749 [date of death]; children
    Clement, Elizabeth, Ann & others unnamed (MCW 10.71) [SMW TA1.233]

Stedmon, William; admx. Mary, wife of Henry Calvery; 17 Jul 1715 (SMAA p.
    273)

Steptoe (Suptoe), Kingsmale; immigrated by 1679; wife Penelope; service by
    1679 (SK 15.548.597)

Sticklin, Josias and Joanna; son Jeremiah [b. 11 May 1767] (SA p. 6)

Stockden, George; <u>acct.</u>; 26 Apr 1715; admx. Jane Stockden (I&A 36c.60); 26 Apr
    1715 (SMAA p. 291)

Stockes, John; 4 Mar 1671; 12 Apr 1672; wife Eliza: (MCW 1.67)

Stocking (Stocken), Ralph; <u>inv.</u>; 11 Aug 1755; nok John & Ann Hendly;
    admx./extx. Cathrine Stockin (I 59.209); <u>acct.</u>; 11 Aug 1755; orphans Mary [age
    4], Ann [age 2 mos.], Ralph [d. since his father]; admx. Katherine Stocken (A
    38.1818); <u>dist.</u>; 30 Jan 1756; orphans Mary, Ann, Ralph [dec'd] (BB 2.9)

Stooke, John; service by 1667 (SK 11.246)

Stourton [Stourter], Robert; <u>will</u>; 4 Dec 1714; 15 Mar 1714/5; wife Margery;
    tracts *St. Thomas, The Parting Path, Hopewell, [The Gardening Spot]* (MCW
    4.29) [SMW PC1.200]; <u>inv.</u>; 13 Apr 1715 (I&A 36c.52); <u>acct.</u>; 28 Apr 1716; extx.
    Margery Storton (SMAA p. 297)

Stowares, Richard; <u>inv.</u>; 25 Feb 1768; 2 Mar 1768 (I 97.91); <u>inv.</u>; 2 Mar 1768 (I 97,
    98); <u>acct.</u>; 28 Mar 1769; mentions Frances Stowers (A 61.112)

Stubbings, John; inv.; 8 Mar 1756; nok Mary Thomas, Thomas Pearce; admx./extx. Lydia Stubbings (I 60.372); acct.; 13 Dec 1756; orphans Sarah [of age], Mary [age 13], Hopa [age 8] Milla [age 6], William, age 2; admx. Lydia Stubbins (A 40.256); dist.; 3 Mar 1757 (BB 2.46)

Stunnard [Stanard], Abell; will; 23 Sep 1714; 30 Nov 1714 (MCW 4.24) [SMW PC1.194]

Subtill, John; will; 14 Apr 1680; 29 May 1680; sons John, William; daus. Jane, Mary; wife Mary; tracts *Beaverly, Subtill's Rest, Thomas, Subtill's Reins* (MCW 1.92-93) [SMW PC1.37]

Sully, Benjamin; surgeon; inv.; 22 Jun 1749; 31 Aug 1749 (I 40.349)

Summers (Sommers), Thomas; *Itchcomb's Freehold*; 344 ac.; 10 Sep 1744 cert./pat. (COL)

Sutton, Percifull (Perceful); inv.; 20 Jul 1741; nok John & William Sutton; admx./extx. Mary Sutton (I 26 128); acct.; 25 Oct 1742 (A 19.198)

Sword, James; dist.; 25 Apr 1776; admx. Mrs. Elisabeth Sword (BB 7.51)

Syse, Edmond; immigrated by 1671 (SK 16.119)

Tabbs, Moses; *Tabbs' Purchase*; 208 ac.; 25 Nov 1769 cert./pat. (COL)

Talbor, Mary; service by 1675 (SK 18.310)

Talbot, George, Col.; *Cold Wells*; 331 ac.; 21 Jul 1680 cert./pat. (COL)

Tanner, Henry; age ca 58; 20 Nov 1714; tract *Tattershall's Gift* (CCR p. 31)

Tapper, Lewis; service by 1672 (SK 17.9); *Mount Pleasant*; 100 ac.; sur. 9 Oct 1672; 1707 poss. Lewis Tapper; St. Clements Hundred (RR)

Tarleton, James; inv.; 25 Apr 1735; nok James Tarleton, Cassandra Lee; adm./ex. John Tarleton (I 20.399)

Tearon, William; inv.; 10 Jul 1733; 7 Nov 1733; nok Robert Tearon, Sary Miller; admx./extx. Ann Tearon (I 17.539)

Telling, Ignatius; will; 1 Oct 17; inv.; 10 Nov 1709 (I&A 31.187); acct.; 15 Feb 1710 (SMAA p. 192)

Tenley (Tennely), Philip, Jr.; inv.; 11 Sep 1773; 24 Nov 1773; nok William & John Tennally; admx. Hannah Tennelly (I 117.340)

Teppet, John; will; 25 May 1748; 5 Jul 1748; dau. Mary Dunbar & her son John; son Edward Maddox Teppet; wife Elizabeth (MCW 9.156) [SMW TA1.221]

Tewall, John; acct.; 1 Sep 1773 (A 68.205)

Thimbelby, John & Wm. Brown; *Honest Toms Inheritance*; 1707 poss. Pravis Burrell; New Town Hundred (RR)

Thornhill, Jos.; m. 22 Dec 1772 Monica Brown (MM)

Thorp, Thomas; inv.; 29 Sep 1762; 29 Dec 1762; nok Thomas Peace; mentions Elisabeth Tharp; admx. Ann Thorp (I 80.151); acct.; admx. Ann, w/o Thomas Villanaugh (A 49.598] (A 49.598)

Throne, William; inv.; 21 Apr 1740; 6 Aug 1740; nok Jonathon Throne, John Lorton; admx./extx. Jane Throne (I 25.191); acct.; 6 Nov 1741; nok Jonathon John Losson & William Nedlam (A 18.457)

Throughton, Mary; immigrated by 1638; widow (SK12.561)

Thynn, Walter; service by 1669 (SK 12.344)

Ticklin, Jeremiah and Mary Raily (by license); m. 6 Nov 1781 (SA p. 59)

Tierce, Andrew and Catharine; dau. Eleanor [b. 7 Mar 1772] (SA p. 22)

Timson, John; of Charles Co.; *St. John's*; 115 ac.; 10 Dec 1694 cert./pat. (COL)

Toate, Robert; inv.; 28 Jun 1688 (I&A 10.22)

Tottelson (Totershell), Lawrence; acct.; 22 Mar [filed with 1702-3] (I&A 23.28); 13 Mar 1703 (SMAA p. 127)

Trasque, James; acct.; 13 Feb 1676 (I&A 3.78)

Tredwell, William; service by 1673 (SK 17.615)

Trees, William; acct.; 1 Mar 1735; orphan Sarah Trees (A 14.184)

Trippy, William; acct.; 14 May 1713; admx. Mary, w/o John Tyler (Taylor) (I&A 34.222) (SMAA p. 254)

Troughton, Mary; *St.Barbaras*; 50 ac.; sur. 29 Mary 1640 (then in St. Mary's Hundred); 1707 poss. His Lordship; Poplar Hill Hundred (RR)

Tual, John; inv.; 17 Apr 1772; 26 Jul 1772; nok Mary & Elisabeth Torvall (I 109.351)

Tubb, James; acct.; 6 Jun 1720 (SMAA p. 448)

Tubman, Henry; age ca 29 in 1764; age ca 30 in 1765 (MD p. 187) [SMW TA1.539-556]

Tunck (Tuncks), William; service by 1668 (SK 11.548); age ca 30; 24 Dec 1665 (AM XLIX.541)

Tunnell, Will'm; *Marking Place*; 100 ac.; sur. 10 Apr 1666; 1707 poss. Luke Russel; Poplar Hill Hundred (RR p. 24) (TLC p. 23)

Turling, John; acct; [filed with ?1692]; adm. John Turling (I&A 10.340); [filed with ?1698] (SMAA p. 100)

Turnbull, James and Margaret; son John [b. 2 Mar 1764] (SA p. 40)

Turtle (Tuttle), Peter, Mr.; inv.; 18 Apr 1733; 6 Jun 1733; nok John Turtle; admx./extx. Mary Turtle (I 17.155); acct.; 3 Sep 1734; orphans Thomas & Mary Tuttle; admx. Mary, w/o James Brown (A 12.530)

Tuttey, Robert; New Towne; will; 15 Jun 1647; 21 Jun 1647 (MCW 1.2)

Tybills, James Theobold and Mary Griffin m. 13 Jan 1783 (by license) (SA p. 60)

Tyrling, John; immigrated by 1681 (SK WC2.412)

Upgate, Richard; St. Clement's Manor; will; 9 Nov 1671; 2 Aug 1672; son John; dau. Mary, w/o Thomas Reeves; wife Ann; tract *Bluff Point* (MCW 1.70)

Vandevear, Jacob; inv.; 21 Feb 1734; 24 Feb 1734; nok Elenor Asten, Dorathy Neale; admx./extx. Nicholas Green & wife Susanna (I 20.295); acct.; 22 Nov 1736; orphans John, William, Elisabeth & Ann Vandever (A 15.232)

Vaulx, James; *Vaulx's Venture*; 100 ac.; 21 Sep 1728 cert./pat. (COL)
Veale, William; will; 4 Jan 1737; 30 Jan 1737; wife Margaret; mentions
William, s/o William Harrison, and William Veale, s/o James Rigg (MCW
7.235) [SMW TA1.38]; inv.; 11 Feb 1737; 19 Jun 1738; nok Elenor Astin,
Elisabeth Vandean; adms./exs. Richard King & wife Margaret (I 23.197)
Venn, John; immigrated by 1674 (SK 17.633)
Vessels, Elijah and Ann Choram (by license); m. 5 Jan 1784 (SA p. 61)
Vickers, John; inv.; 23 Aug 1731 (I 16.290)
Viller, Nathaniell; inv.; 4 May 1702 (I&A 22.28)
Vincent, Francis, gent.; transported by 1671 (SK 16.357)

Wade, John; surgeon; *Bloomsbury*; 100 ac.; sur. 9 Sep 1652; 1707 poss. Widow
Mason; Poplar Hill Hundred (RR)
Wain (Waine, Wayne), Charles; will; 19 Feb 1722/3; 18 Mar 1722/3; mentions
Rebecca, w/o Benjamin Chum (MCW 5.137) [SMW PC1.276]; inv.; 7 Aug 1723 (I
8.315); acct.; 9 Nov 1724 (A 6.251)
Wainwright, Richard; planter; will; 3 Mar 1773; 20 Mar 1774; g-ch. Elizabeth,
Susanna, Richard; d-i-l Tamer, w/o son William, dec'd; tracts *Green Chase,
Comptons Poor Bargin* (MCW 15.151) [SMW TA1.696]; inv.; 14 Apr 1774; 25 Sep
1774; nok Susannah & James Wainright; adm./ex. Elisabeth Wainright (I
119.171); dist.; 6 May 1776; g-child.Elisabeth, Susanna, Richard (BB 7.61)
Wakefield, Benjamin; will; 7 Aug 1772; 7 Jan 1773; dau. Elinor (MCW 15.31)
[SMW TA1.667]; inv.; 30 Apr 1774; nok Ann Simpson (I 117.351); acct.; 10 May
1774 (A 71.365); dist.; 10 May 1774 (BB 7.8)
Walkers, John; *Crane* or *Waughops Walker*; 100 ac.; sur. 23 Apr 1661; pat.
Robert Crane; 1707 poss. Marshall Low; St. Georges Hundred (RR p. 18) (TLC p.
18)
Walkinson, Cornelius; acct.; 1 Mar 1698; extx. Elisabeth Walkinson (I&A 181.16)
Wallace, George; acct.; 16 Feb 1746 (A 23.191)
Walldrom, Charles; acct.; 18 Jul 1733; mentions Henry, Mary, Francis, Ann,
Eleanor & unborn child; admx. Mary Waldrom (A 12.37); inv.; 9 Jun 1733; 18
Jul 1733; nok Richard & Matthew Wise (I 17.322)
Waller, Isaac; will; 7 Apr 1747; 27 Jul 1747; wife Mary; son Edmund; dau.
Margaret; children's g-father Thomas Edmunds (MCW 9.113) [SMW TA1.198];
inv.; 14 Sep 1747; 20 Oct 1747; nok minors; adm./ex. George Waller (I 35.372)
Wallis, George; 8 Mar 1744; mentions Mary Curtis, age 28 [SMW TA1.149]; acct.;
8 Sep 1747; mentions Sarah, d/o Thomas Nicholls (A 24.72); inv.; 1 Apr 1745;
5 Jun 1745 (I 31.150)
Walls (Wall), Pearce; 18 May 1685; 26 Aug 1685; tracts *New Castle, Morrisses
Mount [Morris His Mount]* (MCW 1.157) [SMW PC1.56]; inv. 3 Aug 1685 (I&A
8.384)
Walraven, Mathia, G. V. A.; immigrated by 1673 (SK 17.573)
Walsh (Wealsh), Thomas; inv.; 8 Apr 1724; 23 Sep 1724 (I 10.162)

Walstore, William; immigrated by 1667 (SK 11.264)

Warden, James; dist.; 1 Oct 1771; admx. Susanna Warden (BB 6.85)

Warring, Thomas; service by 1667 (SK 11.228)

Wassell, William; planter; inv.; 11 Apr 1640 (PRPC)

Weaklin (Wheatly), Richard; inv.; 17 Sep 1772; 1 May 1773 (I 112.412)

Wedin (Weedon), James; inv.; 1 Oct 1770; nok John Dunbar, George Carpenter; admx. Susannah Wedin (I 103.337); acct.; 1 Oct 1771 (A 66.69)

Weston, Thomas; *WestburyMannour*; 1,200 ac.; sur. 10 Jan 1642; St. Georges Hundred (RR p.) (TLC p. 16)

Whaley, James, Mr.; inv.; 6 Feb 1749; 3 Apr 1750; nok Hugh Whaley, Sarah Craig; adm./ex. Jesse Craig (I 42.9); acct. 28 May 1751 (A 30.100)

Whillaux, John; acct.; 18 Oct 1736 (A 15.191)

Whisler (Whislor, Whisley), Thomas; will; 23 Nov 1729; 8 Dec 1729 (MCW 6.137) [SMW PC1.331]; inv.; 12 Dec 1729; 5 Mar 1729 (I 15.374); inv.; 25 Aug 1730 (I 16.83); acct.; 6 Mar 1731 (A 11.333); acct.; 31 May 1731 (A 11.71)

Whitehead, Mary; license to m. William Edwin; 26 Mar 1637 (AM IV 4.24)

Whitenhall (Whetenhall, Whittinhall), John; will; 24 Dec 1750; 6 Mar 1750; nephew Henry Rozer; mentions Elizabeth, w/o Ignatious Wheeler, her son Ignatius and dau. Monica; niece Elizabeth Rozer, w/o George Sly; kinsman Henery Jerregham (Jernegan) (MCW 10.142) [SMW TA1.274]; inv.; 12 Nov 1751; 4 Mar 1752; [Dr.]; nok H. Roger, Henry Jernegan; adms./exs. George Sly & wife Elisabeth (I 42.289, 290); acct.; 1 Apr 1773 (A 68.198); dist.; 1 Apr 1773 (BB 6.260)

Whitman, Robert; oral; will; probate 28 Jan 1764 (MCW 13.42) [SMW TA1.480] inv.; 15 Feb 1764; 8 Aug 1764 (I 84.284); acct.; 3 Mar 1767 (A 55.318); dist.; 8 May 1767 (BB 5.11)

Whitton, Thomas; service by 1672 and wife (SK 17.348)

Wicklif, David; *Wickliff*; 50 ac.; sur. 30 Nov 1649; ? esch.; 1707 poss. John Noble; St. Georges Hundred (RR)

Wilcox, John; immigrated by 1675 (SK 18.339)

Wildblood, Joseph; service by 1681 (SK WC2.410)

Wildey, William and Sarah Aderton (by license); m. 3 May 1785 (SA p. 63)

Wildgos, Robert; immigrated from VA 1679 (SK WC2.341-342)

Wilkes, William; m. Eliz., widow of Jno. Tayler of *Poplar Hill* by 1655 (SK ABH.427)

Wilkins, James; service by 1680 (SK WC2.276)

Winard, Thomas; inv.; 14 Jul 1742; 4 Jan 1742 (I 27.261); acct.; 21 May 1744 (A 20.235)

Windsor (Winsor), Alexander; service by 1675 (SK 18.387); inv.; 30 Nov 1676 (I&A 3.6); inv.; 30 May 1678; admx. Jane Jones (I&A 5.117)

Winers, Nathaniel; acct.; 17 Jul 1703 (SMAA p. 121)

Wintour, Robert, Capt.; inv.; 4 Sep 1638 (AM IV.85, 105)

Witter (Whittews), George; <u>will</u>; 13 Nov 1743; 12 Mar 1743/4; wife Margaret;
g-dau. Sarah Estep; dau. Mary, w/o Joseph Estep (MCW 8.255) [SMW TA1.157];
<u>inv.</u>; 15 Mar 1743; 8 Aug 1744; nok minors; admx./extx. Mary, w/o Mathias
Nottingham (I 29.415); <u>acct.</u>; 24 May 1745 (A 21.242)
Wolfe, Thomas; <u>acct.</u>; 2 Dec 1717 (I&A39c.3)
Wolstenholme, Daniel, Esq. and Deborah Beck (by license); m. 25 Aug 1783 (SA p.
61)
Woodburn, William; <u>inv.</u>; 6 Feb 1765; 6 Mar 1765; nok Briom Woodburn,
Sarah Virmier; admn. Daniel Woodburn (I 87.16)
Woodcocke, William; oral; <u>will</u>; 27 Apr 1683; 14 Sep 1683 (MCW 1.126) [SMW
PC1.42]
Woolingham, John and Appolonia his wife; child. John Baptist, b. 1 Nov 1758;
Ann, b. 1 Mar 1763 (SA p. 11, 45)
Woolman, Richard; planter; unknown; 50 ac.; 10 Jan 1696 cert./pat. (COL)
Word, Innocent; <u>will</u>; 18 Oct 1756; 12 Nov 1756; child. Jonathan, Prissilla and
Mary Whit Word; tract *Possem* (?) (MCW 11.150)
Worth, Charles; service by 1667 (SK 11.236)
Worthington, John; <u>dist.</u>; 28 Jul 1760; orphans John, James, Thomas; admx.
Johanna, w/o Thomas Clark (BB 3.39)
Wortley, John; *Wortley*; 100 ac.; sur. 22 Oct 1640; esch.; St. Georges Hundred
(RR)
Woughcone, Thomas; <u>inv.</u>; 22 Jul 1717; 27 Mar 1719 (I 2.87)
Wyndham, George; m. 11 Dec 1783 Mary Cord (BRU, p. 536)

Yeale, William; <u>acct.</u>; [filed with 1742]; extx. Margrett, w/o Richard King (A
19.37)
Yeedon, George; <u>will</u>; 1 Sep 1685; 19 Jan 1685; bro. Thomas in Galway,
Ireland; mentions Mrs. Eliza: Shanks and son John (MCW 1.158) [SMW PC1.56]
Yore, James; <u>inv.</u>; 3 Oct 1691; 1 Sep 1692 (I&A 10lc.2)

Mary Piercy, 4
Mary, 4
Sm., 4
Susan, 4
Susannah, 4, 169
Thomas, 4, 21, 57,
148, 223, 340
William, 4, 135,
150, 176, 223,
281
Akeeth, Geo., 284
see Keith
Alanson, Sarah, 23
see Allison
Albert, Elizabeth, 5
William, 5
Alcock, Isaac, 315
Alexander, Anne, 145
Charles, 315
Robert, 145
*All That's Left, 1, 164,
263*
Allamond, John
Baptist, 315
Allaway, Elizabeth, 27
Allen, Anne, 277
Henry, 5
Joseph, 11
Mary 5
Owen, 39
Philip, 5
Robert, 5
Thomas, 5
William, 5
Allerton, Elizabeth,
315
Isaac, 315
Allford, Elizabeth,
315
Allison, Ann, 5
Elizabeth, 5
George, 5
Henry, 5
Jacob, 5
James, 5
John, 5
Joseph, 5

Mary, 5, 184
Penelope, 5
Sarah, 5, 23, 125
Self, 5
Thomas, 5
Allman, Thomas, 315
Allstone, Drayden, 12
Thomas, 12, 134
Allvoy, Elizabeth, 39
Alroy, Mary, 57
Alstan, Mary, 264
Alvey, Ann, 5, 6, 132,
266
Arthur, 6
Eleanor, 6
Elizabeth, 5, 6
Jeste, 6
John, 6, 39
Joseph, 5, 6
Leonard, 6
Margaret, 6
Mary, 6
Pope, 5, 6, 132, 217
Thomas, 6
Winifred, 6
*Ambersly, 56, 145,
187, 188*
*America Felix
Secundus, 17*
*America Felix
Secundus, Resurvey,
260*
*America Felix, 118,
119*
Ames, John, 315
Amos, Michael, 315
Anctill, Barnaby, 6
Elisabeth, 6
Francis, 6
Anderson, Alexander,
116, 162
Aloysisus, 7
Benjamin, 7
Catharine, 7, 260
Chloe, 7
Elizabeth, 7
Gilbert, 7

Henrietta, 7, 116,
162
James, 7
Jane, 7
John Baptist, 7
John, 7
Joseph, 20
Margaret, 7
Mary Ann, 111
Mary, 7
Sarah, 192
Tabitha, 7
Thomas, 7
William, 6, 7
Anderton, Roger, 90
Sarah, 90
*Andrew's Wood, 209,
319*
Andrews, Anthony, 7
Helen, 7
Susanna, 7
Angell, Elisabeth, 279
Angelor, 217
Ann, 7, 217
Barnaby, 7, 142
James, 7, 217
John, 7, 217
Mary, 7
Winifred, 7
Anketill, see Anctill
Anstruther, 76, 200
Anthers, John, 222
Arabia, 311
Aram, Thomas, 315
Arcadia, 118, 119
Archie's Hills, 214
Ark (ship), 68
Armstrong, Dinah, 7
George, 7
Hellen, 7
James, 7
John, 7
Martha, 89, 319
Robert, 7, 89
William, 7
Armsworthy, John, 8
Aaron, 8

Edward, 19
Eleanor, 19, 23, 251
Elisabeth, 19
Francis, 19
George, 19
Jane, 251
John, 19
Katharine, 19
Margaret, 19
Pennelephe, 19
Richard, 19, 23
Sus__, 19
Thomas, 19
William, 19
Bay Side, 200
Bayard, ____, 25
Eleanor, 334
William, 334
Bayley, Bayly, see
Bailey
Bayly's Purchase, 12
Baylys Rest, 12
Bayne, Ann, 110
John, 110
Walter, 316
Bazley, Ralph, 316
Samuel, 316
Beach, Anna, 19
Anne, 19
Elias, 19, 59
Francis, 186
Frances, 196
Mary, 19
Rebecca, 19
Sarah, 59
Thomas, 19, 228
Beadle, Tho., 316
Beadnall, James, 316
Beale, Basil, 20
Daniel, 19
Eliza., 20
Jane, 20, 124
John, 19, 20, 175,
331
Josias, 20
Mary, 20, 124, 125
Moses, 20

Nathaniel, 20
Ninian, 19
Roger, 20
Thomas, 19, 20,
124, 175
Beall, see Beale, Bell
Beam Point, 181
Beame, John, 316
Bean, Alexander, 20
Barton, 20
Benjamin, 20, 74
Bennet, 20
Elizabeth, 20, 175
Faith, 20
Frances, 20
Francis, 140
George, 20
Jeseaway, 20
John, 20
Joshua, 20
Margaret, 20
Mary, 20
Philip, 20
Ralph, 20
Robert, 20, 158
Thomas, 20
Bean's Creek, 317
*Bean's Thoroughfare,
20*
Beane, see Bean
Beans Point, 159
Beans Thurofare, 20
Beard, Christopher, 20
John, 21
Muriall, 21
Richard, 66
Robert, 20, 21
Beard's Choice, 20
Beary, see Berry
*Beaver Dam Manor,
34, 38, 45, 95, 97,
113, 122, 342*
Beaver Dam Neck, 124
*Beaver Dam, 4, 123,
129, 255*
Beaverly, 343
Beavin, Hugh, 21

Bebergham, 165
Beck, Deborah, 347
Elizabeth, 316
Margaret, 316
Mary, 316
Becker, Peter, 219
Beckwith, Ann, 66
Charles, 316
George, 14
*Beckwith's Lodge, 40,
316*
Bedford, 229
Bedon, Dorothy, 316
Bell, Adam, 21, 132
Ann, 21
Daniel, 21, 324
Ellinor, 21
Jane, 21
John, 21
Mary, 21
Thomas, 21
William, 21
Belleon, 237
Bellwood, Ann, 21
Elezabeth, 212
Frances, 21
Henry, 21
Samuel, 21
William, 21
Bellwood's Grove, 21
Belt, John, 182
Benbridge,
Christopher, 316
Bencraft, Bennet, 17
Sarah, 328
Thomas, 328
Benden, see Bending
Bendex Neck, 58
Bending, Elizabeth, 21
Gilbert, 21
Jane, 21
Jean, 21
John, 21
Monica, 21
Beney, Francis, 317
Benham, Ann, 22
George, 22

Richard, 36, 108,
249
Robert, 35, 36, 95,
226, 277
Sarah, 36
Susannah, 36
Thomas, 9, 35, 36,
107
Brooks Chance, 305
Broome, Rebecca, 120
Broomer, Mary, 317
Matthew, 252
*Brother's Agreement,
Resurvey of, 81*
*Brother's Joint
Interest, 179*
Brotherhood, 259, 311
*Brothers Dread, 298,
299*
Brothers, Elizabeth,
189
*Brothers' Joint
Interest, 80*
*Brough, 36, 58, 65,
239, 242*
Brough, James, 36
Sarah, 36
William, 36
Broughey Neck, 92
Broughton, Arbella,
37
Daniel, 37
Richard, 37
Sarah, 37, 318
Brower, Christian,
318
George, 318
John, 318
Mary, 318
Susannah, 318
Brown, see Browne
*Brown Woodhouse, 37,
275, 276*
Browne, Anastatia,
219, 220
Anthony, 229, 332
Anton, 38

Cecilia, 27
Christopher, 37
Derrick, 37
Dorcas, 38
Dorothy, 37
Dryden, 38
Eleanor, 38
Elizabeth, 37, 38,
64, 235
Ellen, 37
Frances, 37, 38
George, 306
Gerrard, 37
Henrietta, 38, 58
Ignatius, 38
James, 37, 38, 92,
334, 344
Jereboam, 38
Joel, 37
John Baptist, 38
John, 37, 235, 279
Leander, 38
Leonard, 38
Lucy, 38
Margaret, 130
Martin, 38
Mary Ann, 38, 58
Mary, 37, 38, 280,
344
Michaell, 37
Monica, 37, 38, 343
Nicholas, 37, 38
Peter, 37, 38
Raphael, 38
Rebecca, 37, 38,
120
Richard, 37, 38, 55
Robert, 37, 38
Samuel, 37
Sarah, 37, 92
Susanna, 37, 38
Thomas, 38
Walter, 37
Widow, 229
William, 37, 306,
332, 343
Winifred, 38

Bruce, Elisabeth, 234,
318
Henrietta, 260
Norman, 168
Susanna Gardiner,
168
Susanna, 318
William, 318
Bruce's Neglect, 260
Bruden, Mary, 145
Bruff, Joseph, 318
Sarah, 244
Wm., 244
Brumer, John, 317
Brushey Neck, 92, 159
Bryan, 38
Bryan, Bryan, 38
Eleanor, 38, 39, 249
Elener, 34
Elisabeth, 34, 145
Francis, 6
Henerita, 34
Henry, 34, 38
Ignatius, 34, 38, 39
James, 38
John, 33, 34, 38, 39
Margaret, 6
Mary, 34
Mathias, 38
Philip, 39
Susannah, 38, 309
Thomas, 39
William, 34, 38

Buchanan, Aaron, 39
Elizabeth, 39
George, 39
Jane, 39
John, 39
Margaret, 39
Moses, 39
Rebecca, 39
William Thompson,
39
Buck Hills, 229
Buck Neck, 337
Buck Park, 88

Rachel, 319
Bustle, Martha, 319
Butcher, Andrew, 319
Butler, Cecill, 42, 52,
79, 154, 278
Cecilus, 42
Frances, 42
George, 42
Johannah, 42
John, 42
Margaret, 42
Mary, 42
Thomas, 42
Butson, Thomas, 99
Butterworth, James,
43
Jane, 43
Michael, 43
Byrn, see Burne

Cadger, Thomas, 43
Cadloe, 319
Cadloe, Joseph, 319
Cage, Anne, 129
John, 129
Cager, Dorothy, 155
Robert, 43, 155
Thomas, 43
Cahill, Roger, 319
Cain, Elizabeth, 43
John, 43
Martha, 43
Richard, 43
William, 43
Caldwell, Martha, 319
Nancy, 88
Samuel, 319
Cales, Alice, 332
Callacome, 118
Callais, Richard, 319
Elisabeth, 319
Calloway, Aaron, 319
Ann, 319
Clammond, 319
Moses, 319
Calten, Rebecca, 319
Calvert, Ann, 44

Barbary, 44, 170
Benedict Leonard,
44
Charles, 44
Elizabeth, 44, 84, 89
John, 44, 84
Leonard, 43, 44
Nelson, 115
Philip, 44, 332
Richard, 44, 258
William, 44
Calvert's Hope, 30
Calverton Manor, 255
Calverton, 55
Calvey, Henry, 341,
342
Mary, 341, 342
William, 175
Cambell, Catherine,
45
Dorothy, 45
Elizabeth, 147
James, 45
Jehu, 333
John, 44, 45, 147
Joshua, 45
Mary, 45, 333
Richard, 45
Thomas, 44, 45,
118, 225
William, 45
Cambell's Farm, 45
Cambridge, 27, 168
Campbell, Jean, 45
Dinah, 170
Joshua, 66
Mary, 66
Richard, 170
Canaday, Ann, 45
Cornelius, 45
James, 45
John, 45, 296
Margaret, 45
Mathew, 45
Monica, 45
Palmer, 45
Richard, 45

William, 45, 296
Cane, William, 46
Caneough, William,
279
Canes Rest, 46
Cannon Hill, 159
Cannon Neck, 108
Cannough Neck, 284
Canoe Neck, 51
Cantancean, John,
215
Peter, 215
William, 215
Calloway, Moses, 319
Capshaw, Fran., 319
Capstan, Francis, 319
Carberry, Eleanor, 46
Elisabeth, 46, 126,
244
John Baptist, 46,
244
Joseph, 46
Peter, 46
Thomas, 46
*Carberry's Discovery,
46*
Carew, Henry, 319
Carmichael, Ann, 7,
46, 196
Elisabeth, 46, 92
John, 46, 196, 306
Joseph, 46
Margarett, 306
Mary, 46
Priscilla, 46
Carnell, Christopher,
46
Eliza., 46
Carnelowe's, 6
Carpenter, Charles,
46
Elisabeth, 46, 186
George, 46, 78, 93,
222, 346
John, 39, 46
Mary, 93
Rebecca, 46

William, 46
Carr, Elisabeth, 47
John, 47
William, 46, 47
Carrell, Mary, 335
William, 335
Carres Rest, 46
Carroll, Charles, 47,
90, 93
Daniel, 76
Elinor, 287
Hariot, 47
Henry, 47
Ignatius, 47
James, 47
Julian, 47
Juliana, 47
Margaret, 47
Mary, 246
Carrollton, 47
Carter Jane, 145
Carter, Darby, 47
Elisabeth, 47, 229,
271
Grace, 47
Henry, 47
James, 100
Mary, 47
Matt'w, 71
Richard Moye, 47
Richard, 47
Sarah, 41, 47, 48
Taylar, 47
Cartwright,
Catharine, 48, 119
Dorothy, 48, 339
Elizabeth, 48, 119
Johanah, 47
John, 9, 31, 41, 47,
48, 119, 183, 240
Judith, 48
Margaret, 9, 41, 47,
48
Mary, 47, 48
Matthew, 47, 48, 94,
240
Peter, 47, 94

Sarah, 47, 48, 210,
282
Susanna, 31, 47, 183
Teresia, 48
Thomas, 47
William, 48, 166
Cartwright's Pasture,
47, 48
Caruolour, 7
Carvile, Robert, 27,
48, 52, 79, 154
Thomas, 48
Carwardine, John, 48
Peter, 48
Thomas, 48
Cary, Henry, 319
Casheans Manor, 235
Cassell, Thomas, 54
Caster, Edward, 233
Sarah, 233
Caston, Sarah, 330
Cate, Wm., 319
Caterpillar Spite, 247
Catler's Rest, 6
Caugragh, Margaret,
279
Causeen, 319
Causeen, Nicho., 319
Cavenaugh, William,
6, 48, 285
Margaret, 6, 285
Caviner, Hugh, 319
Cawood, Anne, 49
Benjamin, 49
Dorothy, 49
Eleanor, 49
Elizabeth, 49
Esther, 49
Martha, 49
Stephen, 28, 49
Thomas, 49
Cawood's Expense,
49, 307
Cawood's Experience,
49
Cawsie, John, 319

Caywood's Discovery,
49
Caywood's
Inheritance, 49
Cecill, Adam, 176
James, 54, 319
John, 20, 85, 133,
176
Thomas, 36, 133,
176, 327
William, 3, 176,
133, 319
Cedar Point, 90, 216
Ceely, Anne, 319
Henrietta, 319
Honor, 319
Katherine, 319
Peter, 319
Thomas, 319
William, 319
Cela Brooke, 36
Celby, Henry, 62
Mary, 62
Cerneabdy Manor,
212
Cessill, see Cecill
Chamberlin, Ann, 49
Catherine, 39
Charles, 49
Elisabeth, 49
Ignatius, 62, 77
John, 49
Mary, 126
Thomas, 39, 49
Chambers, George,
49
Robert, 49
Thomas, 49
Champ, William, 251,
320
Chance, 85, 118, 221,
245
Chancellor's Old
Orchard, The, 283
Chancellor's Point,
47, 101

368   *Colonial Settlers of St. Mary's County, Maryland*

Dianna, 65
Eleanor, 65
Elizabeth, 65
Henry, 65
Isabell, 337
Jane, 66
Johanna, 65, 66, 228
John, 65, 110, 329
Magdalin, 82
Margaret, 65
Mary Magdalene, 82
Mary, 65, 66
Rachel, 66
Richard, 65
Richard Donaldson, 82
Robert, 65, 66, 329
Sarah, 65
Susannah, 66, 126, 235
Thomas, 36, 65, 66, 126, 205, 229
William, 65
Cooke's Folly, 188
Cooks Race, 242
Cooksey, Samuel, 316
Susannah, 183
William, 316
Coombs, Elizabeth, 184
Margaret, 185
Mary, 184, 185
Philip, 185
William, 184
Cooney, John, 321
Cooper, Anne, 66, 67, 123, 124
Basil, 67
Bridgett, 66
Catherine, 67
Christina Barbara, 66
Clement, 67
Dorothy, 66
Eleanor, 67
Elizabeth, 66, 67

Henrietta, 66, 67
Henry, 66, 67
Jonathan, 66
Katharine, 66
Mark, 67
Martha, 67
Mary Ann, 67
Mary, 34, 67
Matthew, 67
Nathan, 66, 67
Nathaniel, 66, 67
Richard, 66, 67
Robert, 66
Sampson, 66
Samuel, 66
Susan, 66
Susannah, 63
Teresa, 66, 67
Thomas, 34, 66, 67, 251, 253, 302
Timothy, 253
Walter, 66
Cooper's Addition, 66, 67
Copes, John, 319
Copley, Ann, 321
John, 321
Lyonell, 321
Copsey, Betty, 113
Martha, 113
Roger, 113
Copt Hall, 239
Coram, Elisabeth, 321
Henry, 321
Corbet, 321
Corbett, Hutton, 321
Corbin, Elisabeth, 237
George, 67
Henry, 67
Sarah, 237
Sary, 67
William, 67, 237
Corbisley, Samuel, 321
Cord, Mary, 347
Cordea, Hester, 68
Marke, 68, 328

Cordea's Hope, 68
Cornabes His Swamp, 128
Cornelius Swamp, 184, 222
Cornelius, 6, 7, 198
Cornish, John, 321
Susanna, 321
Cornor, Job, 321
Cornwallis Cross, 68
Cornwallis, Penelope, 68
Thomas, 68
Cornwell, John, 258
Corsair, John, 321
Sabra, 321
Corum, Barbara, 68
Henry, 68
Isaac, 68
James, 68
Corwyn, William, 321
Coston, Thomas, 321
Coston, 235
Cotton, Edward, 321
Cottonwood, 327
Couant, Thomas, 321
Coulter, Rebecca, 321
Council Rooms, 287
Courrey, John, 321
Courses, 304
Coursey Point, 130
Coursey, William, 136, 321
Courtney, Ellinor, 239
James, 59
Mary, 68, 69, 220, 319
Sarah, 68
Thomas, 26, 59, 68, 69
Courtney's Fancy, 7, 69, 221
Courtney's Neck, 40, 69
Courts Freehold, 225
Courts, John, 166, 225

Susannah, 100
William, 100
Flintiffe, Elizabeth,
325
Flower of the Forest,
27, 168
Flower, Charles Holt,
100
Charles, 318
Elizabeth, 100
Joseph, 100
Thomas, 100
William, 100
Floyd, Jesse, 100
Folley, 119, 127, 340
Forbes, Charles
Samuel, 100
Clarrissa, 164
Dryden, 100, 131,
164
George, 50, 100,
192
James, 100, 131,
164
Jane, 100
John, 50, 100, 164
Margaret, 100
Margory, 100
Mary, 50
Robert, 100
Thomas, 100
Force Putt, 147
Ford, Amon T.
Teresia, 101
Anastatia, 101
Ann Punny, 261
Anne, 102, 229
Athanathus, 101,
102, 122, 185
Bennett, 101, 102
Charles, 102
Clare, 102
Dorothy, 102
Eleanor, 102
Francis, 262
George, 102
Henrietta, 102, 208

Ignatius, 101, 102
Jesse, 102
John Francis, 101
John Jannat, 102
John Jarrat, 102
John Javett, 102
John, 101, 102, 219,
237, 238, 245,
262, 263, 340
Joseph, 102
Margaret, 13, 101,
102
Mary, 101, 102,
199, 269
Monica, 101, 123,
340
Peter, 101, 102, 134,
199, 238, 263
Philip, 102
Priscilla, 102
Rachel, 151
Raphael, 102
Richard, 102, 229,
263
Robert, 55, 100,
101, 102, 245,
255, 263, 269
Susanna, 101
Teresia, 101
Ford's Discovery, 102
Ford's Enclosure, 101,
102
Ford's Hopewell, 101
Forest Denn, 182, 224
Forest Lodge, 103
Forest of Dean,45, 63,
200, 223
Forest of Harvey, 87,
157
Forest Ordain, 223
Forest, 45,103, 330
Forgee, see Fergoe,
210
Forger, Ann, 325
Mazalar, 325
Forges, George, 191

Forguson, Alexnader,
232
Rebecca, 232
Forks, The, 119, 284
Formby, 248
Forrest, Ann, 88, 103,
270
Catherine, 45, 103
Christian, 103, 296
Elisabeth, 89, 103,
320
Ellinor, 103
Frances, 103
Francis, 149
Helena, 103
Henratia, 103
John, 103
Margaret, 103, 135
Nancy, 103
Patrick, 89, 103,
135, 296, 320
Richard, 45, 103,
270, 296
Sarah, 103
Thomas, 238
Uriah, 103
William Canady, 45
William, 103, 296
Zachariah, 88, 103
Fortune, 7, 18, 184,
271
Fortune, Addition to,
176, 280
Fortune's Outlet, 7
Fosbury Plain, 326
Fossey, John, 103,
213, 270, 271
Treacha, 103
Foster, Elenor, 104
Elizabeth, 104, 117
George, 104
James, 104
John, 104
Ralph, 104, 117,
196, 225
Richard, 104
Robert, 104

William, 327
Halbert, Elisabeth, 5,
327
Half Pone, 30
Halfehead, Elizabeth,
4
John, 4, 90, 129
*Halfeheads Folly, 4,
129, 150*
Halfes, 69
Halford's Folly, 198
Hall, Abraham, 130
Ann Mary, 130
Ann, 56, 130, 191,
225
Aquilla, 130
Arthur, 130
Benjamin, 130
Bennet, 130
Catherine, 130
Daniel, 130
Dorothy, 130, 180
Edward, 130
Elizabeth, 130, 331
Esther, 37
Frances, 130
George, 130, 278
Henry, 130
James, 130
Jestenuall, 225
John Basil, 130
John, 26, 52, 129,
130, 191, 225
Joseph, 130
Margaret, 130
Mary, 130
Priscilla, 130
Rebecca, 130
Thomas, 129, 130
Walter, 129, 217,
315
William, 129
Hallbridge Town, 118
Halles, James, 105
Mary, 105
Halley's Grant, 61
Halley's Manner, 175

Hallson, John, 327
Halse, James, 327
Halton, Andrew, 267
Haly, Clement, 130,
178
Elizabeth, 130, 178
Mary, 130, 178
Haly's Lot, 130
Hambleton, see
Hamilton
Hame, Richard, 107
Hamilton, Arthur, 131
George, 131
Hugh, 131
Jane, 130
John, 130, 131
Jonathan, 131
Mary, 203
Philemon, 131
William, 13, 131,
203
Hammer, 238
Hammersley, Francis,
131
William, 131
Hammett, Ann, 131,
132
Bennet, 132
Cartwright, 131
Catharine, 131, 132
Chris., 173
Dolly, 131
Dorothy, 48
Elisabeth, 48, 131
Frances, 131, 132
Henrietta, 131, 175
Henry, 131
J., 175
James, 131
Jeremiah, 131
John, 131, 132, 322
Margaret, 131
Margery, 132
Mary, 121, 131
McKelvie, 103, 131,
132, 322
Rebecca, 131

Richard, 131
Robert, 48, 121,
131, 132, 329
Sarah, 48, 131
William, 131
*Hammett's Beginning,
131*
*Hammett's Chance,
131*
*Hammett's Discovery,
132*
*Hammett's Swamp,
131*
Hammitt, see
Hammett
Hammond, Anne, 132
Barbary, 132
Daniel, 132, 217
Elisabeth, 132
John, 5, 66, 132,
217
Margaret, 132
Mary, 132
Maudlin, 132
Monneca, 132
Mordecay, 132
Rachel, 132
Sarah, 132
Susanna, 132
Uel, 132
Hamon, Benjamin,
323
John, 323
Hampam, Hannah, 20
*Hampstead, 70, 132,
278*
*Hampstead, Scotch-
Mans Wonder, 21*
Hampstead, William,
132
*Hampton Iron Works.
81*
Hampton, 271
Hand, John, 99
Mary, 99
Sarah, 99
Handel, Ann, 84

David, 329
George Aisquith,
329
Jane, 329
Mary, 20
Susanna Aisquith,
329
Susannah, 223, 329
Thomas, 329
Hely, Clement, 286,
328
Elizabeth, 286
Mary, 286
Hely's Lot, 328
Henderson, George,
141
Sarah, 141
Hendley, see Henley
Hendrick, see
Kendrick
Henikin, Ann, 110
Henley, Ann, 141, 342
Daniel, 141, 150
Elizabeth, 141, 235
Henrietta, 240, 307
James, 141, 240
Jane, 141
Jean, 141
Jeremiah, 141
Johannah, 141
John Waughop, 141
John, 141, 235, 290,
296, 342
Joseph, 141
Mary, 141, 257
Robert, 13, 141, 290
Rose, 150
Roger, 141, 296
Sarah, 141
William, 141
Henley's Addition, 141
Henner, Mary, 144
William, 144
Henning, Ann, 20,
142, 328
Caleb, 142
Gilbert, 142

Jeremiah, 142
John, 142
Nathan, 142
Sarah, 142
Thomas Arnold, 142
Hennington,
Elisabeth, 64
Henrick, Benjamin,
329
Henry, James, 329
Martin, 329
Mary, 329
Philip, 329
Henwood, Mary, 28
*Hepburne's Choice,
181*
Hepworth, 112
Hepworth, John, 329
Herbert, Ann, 143
Barbara, 143
Bennet, 143
Cuthbert, 143
Elender, 143
Elizabeth, 137, 142,
143
Frances, 143
Francis, 85, 137,
142, 143
Grace, 136, 142
Henrietta, 143
James, 143
John, 32, 142, 143
Joseph, 142
Luke, 142
Mark, 142
Mary, 143
Mathew, 142, 143,
281
Michael, 142, 143
Priscilla, 143
Sarah, 143, 197
Vitus, 142, 143
William, 68, 142,
143, 217
Winifred, 142
also see Harbert

Herbert's Greef, 142
*Herbert's Invention,
142*
Herbert's Swamp, 142
Herbut, Elizabeth, 47
Herd's Hardship, 138
Herdman, Elinor, 328
James, 328
Hermintine, Anne, 70
Hernson, Priscilla,
184
Herrill, Christopher,
329
Gilbert, 329
Margrett, 329
Heshtine, Charles, 329
Hesletin, Charles, 28
Joh , 28
Heunton, William,
329
Hewett, John, 329
Hews, Monica, 245
Hey, Hannah, 57
Heyley, Mary, 64
Heyton, Nell, 74
Thomas, 74
Hiccory Thickett, 301
Hickery Flatt, 131
Hickman, Elisabeth,
329
Henry, 329
John, 329
Mary, 110, 329
Nathll., 329
Rebecca, 329
Hickory Bottom, 128
Hickory Hall, 131
Hickory Hallows, 262
*Hickory Hills, 4, 120,
328*
Hicks, George, 144
John, 44, 89, 144
Priscilla, 140
William, 144, 331
Hicory Hatt, 329
Higden, Millicent, 30
Higgins, George, 329

Jackson, Ann, 154
  Barnaby, 154
  George, 154, 155
  Hannah, 252
  Jane, 155, 331
  John, 155
  Margaret, 4, 154
  Marmaduke, 331
  Martha, 154
  Mary, 8
  Monica, 293
  Robert, 8
  Theodorah, 155
  Thomas, 154, 286
  William, 155, 293
Jacobs, Francis, 330
Jacobson,
  Christopher, 155
  Jane, 155
  John, 155
James Addition, 94
James Gift, 293
James Land, 155
James, Abell, 155
  Champion, 155
  Charles, 155
  Chloe, 155
  Diana, 155
  George, 155
  Hannah, 155
  Jane, 155
  John, 155
  Margaret, 155
  Mary, 155
  Nancey, 307
  Owen, 155
  Thomas, 155, 156
Jameson, Anne, 155
  Benjamin, 230
  Francis, 42
  John, 155
  Joseph, 156
  Margaret, 155, 156
  Mary, 85, 156, 252
  Susanna, 155

  Thomas, 42, 155,
    156
  William, 155, 156
Janes, Ann, 156, 182
  Henrietta, 156
  John, 156
  Sarah, 156
  Thomas, 156
  William, 156
Janey, Raphael, 128
Janner, John, 330
Jarboe, 113, 156
Jarboe, ___, 262
  Abner, 157
  Ann, 11, 156, 157,
    180
  Bennett,157, 263
  Charles, 149, 156,
    157, 215
  Clement, 157
  Col., 68
  Eleanor, 157
  Elisabeth, 68, 125,
    141, 156, 157,
    265
  Frances, 157
  Garard, 157
  Henry Barton, 157
  Henry, 90, 122, 156,
    215, 274, 333
  Ignatius, 156, 157,
    215, 262
  James, 156, 157
  Jean, 157
  John Baptist, 265
  John, 91, 156, 274,
    333
  Joshua, 157
  Mark, 90
  Mary, 68, 122, 156,
    157, 215, 252
  Monica, 156, 157,
    215, 263
  Nancy, 157
  Peter, 156, 157, 215
  Philip, 157
  Robert, 157

  Rod, 157
  Stephen, 156, 157
  Thomas, 157, 180
*Jarboe's Discovery,
  157*
Jarboe's Ramble, 157
Jarves, Charles, 330
Jarvis, 206
Jay, Temperance, 33
Jeamson, Sarah, 229
Jeamston, Mary, 15
  William, 15
Jeanes, see Jeans,
  Janes
Jeans, Ann, 182
  John, 182
  Thomas, 182
  William, 182
Jefery, Charles, 100
  Whiton, 100
Jenan, Mary, 34
Jenegan, Henry, 346
Jenifer, Ann, 157,
  158, 257
  Daniel of St.
    Thomas, 148,
    157, 158
  Daniel, 78, 157,
    231, 257
  Darkey, 89
  Elisha, 257
  Elizabeth, 9, 157,
    158, 257
  Ellen, 158
  Jacob, 157
  John Read, 158, 231
  Margaret, 257
  Mary Ann, 89
  Mary, 157, 158
  Michael Parker,
    157, 257
  Michael Tasker, 257
  Michael, 89, 157
  Parker, 89
  Samuel, 157, 158
  Thomas, 157

Jenkin, 161
John, 91, 161, 162,
  163, 242, 264
Johnson, 163
Joseph, 162
Katharine, 161
Margaret, 125, 162
Mary,77, 162, 163,
  315
Matthias, 163
Monica, 162
Mordicai, 163
Morgan, 77, 328
Morrice, 161
Rebecca, 161
Robert, 91, 161
Ruth, 162
Sarah, 161, 163
Solomon, 40, 161,
  162, 163, 304
Susanna, 162, 163,
  257
Thomas, 161, 162,
  163, 218
Uel, 163
Walter, 162
Widow, 186
William, 161, 162,
  163, 276, 304,
  324
Jones' Woods,
  Addition to, 61
Jones's Conveniency,
  162
Jones's Fortune, 162
Jones's Lane, 162
Jones's Wood, 161
Jordain, Jordaine,
  see Jordan
Jordan, Abigal, 189
  Charles, 163
  Elisabeth, 73, 112,
    149, 163, 201,
    202
  Frances, 73
  Gerrard, 43

James, 163, 164,
  202
Jane, 163
Jean, 163
Jeremiah, 163
John Skipper, 163
John, 91, 163, 164,
  202, 248
Justinian, 59, 65,
  164, 202
Lucretia, 135, 164
Margaret, 163, 273
Mary, 65, 163, 247
Mathew Holts, 164
Mildred, 164
Notley, 149
Rebecca, 43, 163
Robert, 164, 303
Samuel, 163, 164
Sarah, 163
Susannah, 163
Theodorus, 163, 201
Thomas, 43, 73,
  112, 163, 245,
  247
William, 163, 164
Joseph Hopewell's
  Defense, 148
Joseph, Ann, 260
  Clement, 164
  Elisabeth, 106, 107
  James, 132
  John, 164
  Joseph, 164
  Mary, 164
  William, 96, 106,
    164
Joseph's Venture, 264
Joshua's Plain, 116
Jourdaine, see Jordan
Jove, Jerry, 56
Jowles, Dryden, 50,
  164
  Dryden, 50
  Henry Greenfield,
    164

Henry Peregrine, 50,
  164
Henry, 164
Kenelm Greenfield,
  164
Kenelm, 164
Mary, 164
Peregrine, 118
Rebecca, 100, 164
Sybill, 164
Jowles' Calf Pasture,
  164
Joy, Athanasius, 165
  Barbray, 170
  Charles, 112, 165
  Eleanor, 165
  Elisabeth, 165
  Enoch, 165
  Henrietta, 165
  Ignatius, 165
  John Baptist, 165
  John, 165
  Mary, 165, 328
  Peter, 156, 165
  Sarah, 165
  Tekla, 165
  Thomas Tarlton,
    165
  William, 165
  Winifred, 165
Joyner, Katharine,
  165
  Mary, 165
  Robert, 165
Jubb, James, 331
Judge, Richard, 331
Junis, George, 331
  John, 331
Jurefin, Elizabeth, 32
Jynson, John, 271

Kannady, see
  Canaday
Keachen, James, 28
  John, 28
Keave, Elinor, 127
Keech, Charles, 165

John, 205, 283, 297
Mary, 30, 53, 57,
205, 297, 320
Robert, 205
Thomas, 57, 205,
228
Morriss, see Morris
Mort, Eleanor, 334
James, 334
John, 334
Jos., 334
Moryson, Jane, 95
Robert, 95
Moseley, 27
Mosley, Barbary, 341
Elizabeth, 205
Margaret, 205
Patience, 205
Richard, 341
Robert, 205
Thomas, 205
Mossell Wells, 160
Mothon, Mary, 249
Mouett, John, 334
Mount Misery, 189
Mount Olivet, 118, 119
Mount Paradise, 49
Mount Pleasant, 343
Mount Sinai, 155
Mourice, see Morris
Moy, Daniel, 206
Elizabeth, 205, 206
Richard, 205, 206,
271
Roger, 205
Mudd, Rebecca, 179
Thomas, 179, 206,
300
Mudd's Rest, 206
Mugg, Ann, 183, 206,
289
Elizabeth, 206
John, 206
Notley, 206
Peter, 206, 289
Priscilla, 206
Thomas, 206

Walter, 206
*Mugg's Adventure,
169, 307*
*Muggs' Adventure
Addition, 306*
Mulahone, see
Malohane
Mullen, Mary, 335
Munday, Thos., 335
Muriel's Choice, 320
Murly, Marthat, 82
Murphey, see Murphy
Murphy, Daniell, 206
David, 206
Elinor, 76
Hezekiah, 207
James, 207, 341
John, 76, 207
Margret, 207
Michael, 207
Thomas Truman, 76
Zekhaniah, 207
Murray, Susanna, 56,
244
Murtagh, see Murphy
Murty, Anthony, 207
Elizabeth, 207
John, 207
Stephen, 207
Muschamp, George,
335
Musgrove, Ann, 335
Anney, 112
Catharine, 335
Charles, 335
Mary, 335
Sarah Farmon, 113,
335
Sarah Truman, 112,
113, 335
Sarah, 335
My Lord's Manor, 1
My Quarter, 9
Myles, Margarett, 136

Nabbs, Mary, 33
Thomas, 33

Nalle, Jane, 153
John, 153
Nanfin, Wm., 336
Napler, Mary, 164
Narrow Chance, 178
Narrows, 88, 256
Naybors, William,
293
Neale, Ann, 61, 168,
207, 208, 253, 275,
281
Anthony, 224, 241
Arthur, 207
Bennett, 25, 207,
208
Benone, 208
Bozwell, 207
Charles, 53, 208
Daniel, 208
Dorathy, 344
Edward, 139, 180
Elinor, 207, 208
Elizabeth, 25, 54,
207
Henry, 101, 207,
208, 253
James, 25, 89, 101,
207, 208, 241
Jeremiah, 207, 208
John, 207
Lamar, 207
Mary, 50, 81, 89,
101, 179, 180,
207, 208, 253,
288
Mildred, 62
Ozwell, 207
Peter, 207
Raphael, 25, 36, 81,
207, 208
Rebecca, 207
Roswell, 25, 207,
223, 241
Samuel, 207
Sarah, 208
Thomas, 241
Wilfred, 81, 208

Jane, 238
John Bazil, 238
Mary Ann, 212
Mary, 124, 212, 347
Mathias, 124, 212, 347
Philip, 212
Raphael Ignatius, 212
Stephen, 212
Thomas, 212, 266
Novett, John, 335
Richard, 335
Nowell, Ann, 339
Edward, 213
Elisabeth, 129, 213
Henry, 129, 213, 339
Lydia, 213, 243
Nowland, Mary, 22
Nowlen, Mary, 22
Nugen's Folly, 213
Nugen's Venture, 213
Nugent, Ann, 213
Edmond, 213
Elizabeth, 213
Robert, 93, 213
Susannah, 180, 213
William, 213
Willibar, 213
Nun's Cake, 142
Nun's Oeck, 103
Nuncy, Ann, 335
Elizabeth, 335
Judith, 335
Mary, 335
Michael, 335
Sarah, 335
Nunn, John, 213
Nunns Oak, 213
Nuport, William, 335
Nuthall, ____, 169
Ann, 33, 213
Ariminta, 213
Barbara, 213
Brent, 213, 315
Elinor, 213

Elizabeth, 169, 213
John, 68, 213
Mary Brent, 213
Nuthead, William, 335
Nutons Rest with Addition, 209
Nutthall, 68

O'Bryan, see Bryan
O'Daly see Daly
O'Neale, see Neale
Oakely, Ann, 214
Elizabeth, 214
Lyonell, 214
Mary, 214
Thomas, 214
Oard, Eleanor, 336
Jesse, 336
Thomas, 336
William, 336
Oare, Mary, 52
William, 52
Obert, Batho., 336
Dominick, 336
Ockley, Sarah, 340
Oden, Vincent, 336
Oden's Fortune, 336
Offley, 138
Ogilby, Mary, 336
Thomas, 336
Oglivie, George, 336
Okaine, see Cain
Old Branford, 5
Old Crafts, 128
Oldfield, The, 287
Oliver, Blanch, 214
Clement, 214
Elisabeth, 299
John, 214
Lewis, 214, 299
Mary, 7, 214
Roger, 214
William, 214
Olnewy, Mary, 56
Oneall, see Neale, Neall

Onel, Edward, 335
Oney, Nathaniel, 336
Onion, see Orion
Opey, Lindsey, 336
Orame, John, 336
Orchard Neck, 231
Ord, Eleanor, 336
Justinian, 336
Thomas, 336
William, 336
Orion, Ann, 214
Edward, 214
Elizabeth, 214
Malligo, 214
Thomas, 214
William, 214
Orphan's Gift, 164
Orton, Eliza, 336
Henry, 336
Osbaldston, William, 206
Winifred, 206
Osbeston, see Asbeston
Osbestons Oak, 8
Osborn, Caleb, 250
Catharine, 214
Henry, 214
John, 214
Richard, 214
Osfield Addition, 299, 300
Ossfield, 300, 332
Ossly, 138
Otley, James, 336
Outlet, 45, 338
Oversight, 1
Overton, Mary, 336
Sarah, 336
Thomas, 336
Overzee, Symon, 315
Owens, James, 214
John, 214
Joseph, 174, 214
Patrick, 214
Sarah, 214

Oxford, 90
Oyster Shell Neck, 45
Ozey, James, 336

Pace, Ann, 215
John, 215
Jonathan, 215
Mildred, 215
Stephen, 215
Thomas, 214
Packer, Edw'd, 336
Paden, Timothy, 49
Page, Rob't, 336
Paine, see Payne
Paine's Lott, 217
Paines Range, 217
Pake, 215
Pake, Mary, 215
Walter, 215
Palmer, Katherine,
197, 215, 326
Tho., 20
Pamunkey's Marsh, 89
Pamunkey's, 307
Panett, Elisabeth, 336
Isaac, 336
James, 336
John, 336
Joseph, 336
Pantree, Mary, 336
William, 336
*Paradise Regained,
168*
Paradise, 21, 188
Pargrave, James, 336
Paris, 79
*Parish Beadle, 234,
316*
Parish, 204
Park, 87, 306
Park, Rally & Cole,
216
Parkee's Addition, 169
Parker, Edward, 215,
216, 313, 314
Eliza, 216
Elizabeth, 216

George, 43, 44, 216
Judea, 216
Judith, 55, 189
Margaret, 216
Richard, 216
Robert, 55, 216
Samuel, 216
Sarah, 216
Parker's Delight, 116
*Parker's Land, 215,
216*
Parks Addition, 169
Parks, William
Thomas, 216
Parnassus, 277, 332
Parnham, Jane, 300
Parran, Charle
Someresett, 216
Thomas, 216
Parrott, Elizabeth,
256
Gabriel, 44
Parsons, Anna, 216
Camas, 257
Censure, 216
Charles, 216
Clement, 216
Cosine, 216
Cosmas, 78, 157,
216
David, 191
Edward, 216, 217
Elizabeth, 216, 217
James, 216
John, 216
Joseph, 216
Mary, 216
Phillis, 216
Robert, 216
Part of Scotland, 66
Parting Path, 26, 342
*Partner's Purchase,
286*
*Partnership Addition,
295*

*Partnership, 62, 87,
179, 245, 258, 294,
326*
Pascotowagh, 89
*Pasture Ground, 140,
155*
Patchal, John, 336
Sarah, 336
Paten, Gerrard, 110
Pattison, Elizabeth,
142
James, 142, 144,
157, 217
Margaret, 217
Paty, John, 15
Paul's Marsh, 156
Paupall, 262
Pauper Field, 296
Pavatt, Elisabeth, 217
Isaac, 24, 217
James, 217
John, 217
Joseph, 217
Margaret, 24, 217
Susanna, 217
Pawpaw, 262
Payne, Allelusia, 219
Anastatia, 151, 219
Ann, 10, 54, 111,
212, , 218, 219,
282
Baptist, 219
Benjamin, 219
Bernard, 219
Catharine, 218
Charles, 10, 55, 217,
218, 219
Diana, 218
Eleanor, 218, 219
Elizabeth, 30, 217,
218, 219, 272
Ezekiel, 10, 218
Frances, 219
Francis, 10
Francis Exlinerus,
218
Hannah, 217, 218

Joseph, 224, 227
Mary, 224
Sarah, 224
Piles Discovery, 183, 224
Piles Woodland, 121
Piles Woodlane, 120, 123, 224
Pilisha, And., 326
Pilkinton, Hugh, 224
Margaret, 224
Richard, 224
Susanna, 224
Pilkinton's Venture, 224
Pimlico, 78
Piney Land,133, 255
Piney Neck, 89
Piney Point, 20, 55, 57, 98, 116, 181, 298
Pinner, 229
Pinner, Richard, 337
Piper Hill, 253
Piper, John, 337
Mary, 337
Pissimore Point, 64
Pitcher, Amye, 337
Emanuel, 337
Jane, 337
Plaines of Jericho, 87
Plaines, The, 86, 160
Plains of Jericho Addition, 88
Planter's Delight, 303
Plater, Ann, 224
Elizabeth, 224
George, 30, 224, 328
Rebecca, 30
Pleasant Levels, 157
Pleasant Spring, 24, 154, 156
Plimouth, 152
Ploumer, John, 304
Plowden, Dominica, 102

Dorothy, 225
Edmond, 95, 96, 225, 253
Edward, 253
Francis Jarret, 225
George, 18, 68, 213, 222, 225
Henrietta, 225, 253
Jean, 260
Winifred, 225
Plowden's Discovery, 225
Plum Point, 117, 297
Plummer, Eleanor, 317
Eliza., 77
John, 225
Margaret, 225
Thomas, 77, 225
Pococomoco Point, 193
Poeverty, 242
Poily, Richard, 337
Point Lookout, 256
Point Patience, 9
Point, The, 287
Pomfreit Field, 200
Pomroy, Benjamin, 337
John, 337
Ponds, The, 56
Poole, 138, 242
Poole, Ann, 330
Peter, 337
Susannah, 209, 211
Poor Wales, 61
Poore, James, 227
John, 226
Mary, 227
Nicho., 226, 286
Patience, 226
Sarah, 226
Pope, Francis, 225
Nathaniel, 225
Pope's Freehold, 254

Pope's Hogpen, 127
Poplar Hill, 14, 22, 45, 91, 92, 140, 159, 160, 161, 162, 311, 346
Poplar Neck, 22, 36, 53, 76, 201, 313
Poplar Point, 18
Poppanfields, 297
Poppleton, 109
Porkhall Neck, 184
Portwood, John, 225, 226
Possem, 347
Poston, Judith, 337
Potter, Ann, 226
Audry, 226
Elenor, 226
Elisabeth, 226
Henry, 226
Jane, 226
Jean, 226
Jonas, 226
Minder, 226
Robert, 226
Susanna, 226
Poulter, Fernando, 226
Henry, 226
Mary, 226
Poulton, Henry, 226
John, 226
Poultshelly, 240
Pountney Marsh, 89, 337
Pountney, Henry, 337
Pountneys Oversight, 163, 256
Poverty Hills, 287
Poverty Level, 220
Poverty, 162
Powell, Cosmus, 226
George, 226
John, 226
Joseph, 226
Powers, Ann, 227
Clement, 227

Susanna, 247
William, 247
Shanke, John, 25
Sarah, 230
Thomas, 230
Shanks Adventure, 247
Shanks Risque, 136, 247
Shanks, 247
Shanks, Abigall, 247
Alexander, 248
Ann, 247
Diana, 248
Eliza., 347
Emma, 160
Heneritta, 247
Henry, 83
John, 83, 160, 247, 248, 347
Joseph, 248
Judith, 112
Lettice, 248
Margaret, 151, 247
Mary Ann, 248
Mary, 12, 83, 247, 308, 318
Robert, 248
Sarah, 248
Susanna, 12, 189, 248
Thomas, 247, 248
Shantry, Joseph, 340
Sharedons Reserve, 236
Sharith, Susannah, 303
Sharlin, Roger, 340
Sharp, 256
Sharp, Jonathon, 217
Shaw, John, 340
Mary, 221
William, 118
Shaws, 229
Sheads, 158
Sheanionshee, Elisabeth, 341
Sheehee, Roger, 340

Sheircliff, see Shercliffe
Shelley, Edward, 340
Shells, Bridgett, 340
Shelly, Elizabeth, 75
William, 75
Shemwell, see Shamwell
Shenboton, John, 205
Shener, Anne, 340
Christopher, 340
John, 340
Joseph, 340
Mary, 340
Shepey, Richard, 248
Shepheards Fields, 336
Sheppard, Catherine, 248
John, 248
Mary, 248
Richard, 248
Sheppyes Rest, 341
Shercliff, 249
Shercliffe, Ann, 55, 80, 199, 249, 282
Anna, 249
Elizabeth, 249
Henry, 118, 249
John, 55, 199, 249
Joseph, 249
Mary, 151, 239, 249
Monica, 38, 249
Peter, 249
Richard, 249
Thomas, 38, 249
Ticia, 249
William, 55, 151, 248, 249
Sherlly, Monica, 101
Shermandine, Abintine, 341
Ann, 341
Elisabeth, 341
Hezekiah, 341
James, 341
Jeremiah, 341

John, 341
Joseph, 312, 341
Mary, 137
Sherwell, 301
Shewbottom, Richard, 341
Shewer, Christopher, 341
Shipard, Catherine, 341
Shippey, Rich'd, 341
Shipps, Mary, 323
Richard, 323
Shirborn, Clare, 249
Nicholas, 36, 249, 250
Richard, 36, 249
Shircliff, see Shercliffe
Shirley, ___, 184
George, 250
Grace, 250
Ignatius, 250
John, 250
Katherine, 310
Richard, 147, 200, 250, 310
Robert, 250
Sarah, 250
William, 250
Shirley's Point, 21
Shoare, Thomas, 250
Shocks Park, 103, 142
Shohon, Darby, 341
Shonburt, Alice, 252
Richard, 252
Shore, Katheren, 176
Mary, 152
Richard, 152
Shores Delight, 250
Shorte, Ames, 341
Shrubby Thicket, 1
Siffert, Elisabeth, 341
Stephen, 341
Sikes, Ann, 205
John, 204, 250
Joseph, 251

Thomas, 321
Stoney Hills, 254
Stooke, John, 342
Stourton, Margery, 342
Robert, 342
Stowers, Frances, 342
Richard, 342
Strand Addition, 102, 251
Strand, The, 100, 101, 102
Strap, 171
Stratford Addition, 251
Stratford, 328
Stratford, Ann, 265
Clement, 265, 266, 290
Elizabeth, 150, 265
Ferronia, 266
Frances, 265
Joseph, 150, 265
Mary, 265
Monica, 265
Teresa, 266
Strautran, John, 252
Strife Addition, 201
Strife, 18, 27, 79, 81, 200, 201, 281
Strong, Ann, 69
George, 80
Mary Ann, 80
Mary, 2
Susanna, 292
Strutton, Robert, 26, 107, 196, 248
Stuart, see Stewart
Stubbings, Hopa, 343
John, 343
Lydia, 343
Mary, 343
Milla, 343
Sarah, 343
William, 343
Stunnard, Abell, 343
Styles Chance, 266
Styles, John, 266

William, 215, 266
Subtill, Jane, 343
John, 343
Mary, 343
William, 343
Subtill's Rest, 343
Sugar Rains, 211
Suger Land, 225
Suite, Ann, 264
Dent, 266
Susanna, 311
Thomas, 266
Walter, 266
Sullivant, Ann, 266
Arthur, 266
Daniell, 98, 266
Dennis, 266
Elisabeth, 266
Ellen, 266
Sully, Benjamin, 343
Sumersett, 36
Summer Seat,35, 234
Summerfield, 198
Summers, Thomas, 343
Sun is Down, 79
Susanna, 234
Susquehannah Point, 87, 241, 254, 324
Suttle, Eleoner, 267
John Baptist, 267
John, 266, 267
Julaner, 326
Mary Ann, 267
William, 267
Suttles Range, 266, 282
Suttles Rest, 267
Sutton, John, 343
Mary, 318, 343
Painfull, 318, 343
William, 343
Swales, Elizabeth,100, 112
Francis, 267
Margaret, 112
Mary, 267

Thomas, 267
William, 267
Swamp Island, 97
Swamp Land, 302
Swamp, 29, 229
Swan, 225
Swan's Harbour, 3
Swann, Constantia, 62
Edward, 267
Henry, 267
James, 11, 49, 267
Jane, 333
Jermiah, 146
John, 267
Jonathan, 34
Judith, 49, 267, 307
Mary , 34, 267
Rebecca, 267
Samuel, 267
Swann's Adventure, 267
Swann's Venture, 267, 292
Swanns Forrest, 16, 267
Sweatman, John, 267
Mary, 267
William, 267
Sweeney, ____, 197
Ann, 154
Major, 154
Swift, Anna, 172
Swillaben, Ca., 317
Swillenham, 154
Swillovan, Elisabeth, 318
Swipe His Land, 101
Sword, Elisabeth, 343
James, 343
Jane, 155, 231
William, 252
Sykes, Ann, 328
Catherine, 65
Haning, 267
John, 20, 267
Thomas, 267
Walter, 65

Yates, Ann, 85, 313
　Edward, 313
　Elextious, 313
　Elizabeth, 313
　Ignatius, 313
　Isaiah, 313
　John, 313
　Martin, 55, 290, 313
　Mary, 31, 105, 313
　Thomas, 313
　William, 31, 313
Yeale, William, 347
Yeedon, George, 347
　Thomas, 347
Yeilding Resurveyed,
　280
Yeilding, 210
Yeildingsbury, 315
Yets, Susan, 220
Yoakly Chance, 106
Yore, James, 59, 347
　Patience, 59
Young Man's Venture,
　98
Young, Ann, 314
　Claire, 246
　Elizabeth, 313, 314
　James, 314
　John Abelle, 314
　Mary, 314
　Nicholas, 215, 216,
　　313
　Samuell, 314
　Sarah, 313
　William, 313
Young's Alliant, 34

Zoak, *106*

Heritage Books by Elise Greenup Jourdan:

The Greenup Family

Abstracts of Charles County, Maryland Court and Land Records:
Volume 1: 1658–1666
Volume 2: 1665–1695
Volume 3: 1694–1722

Colonial Records of Southern Maryland:
Trinity Parish and Court Records, Charles County;
Christ Church Parish and Marriage Records, Calvert County;
St. Andrew's and All Faith's Parishes, St. Mary's County

Colonial Settlers of Prince George's County, Maryland

Early Families of Southern Maryland:
Volume 1 (Revised) and Volumes 2-10

Early Settlers of Tidewater Virginia:
Volumes 1-4

Settlers of Colonial Calvert County, Maryland

Settlers of Colonial St. Mary's County, Maryland

The Land Records of Prince George's County, Maryland:
1702–1709
1710–1717
1717–1726
1726–1733
1733–1739
1739–1743

with Francis W. McIntosh

1840 to 1850 Federal Census: Tazewell County, Virginia

1860 Federal Census: Tazewell County, Virginia

1870 Federal Census: Tazewell County, Virginia